The Art of Family

GENEALOGICAL

ARTIFACTS IN NEW ENGLAND

The Art of Family

GENEALOGICAL ARTIFACTS IN NEW ENGLAND

D. Brenton Simons and Peter Benes

with an introduction by John Demos

**Jeremy Dupertuis Bangs • Georgia Brady Barnhill • Abbott Lowell Cummings
Laurel K. Gabel • Wendell Garrett • Lauren B. Hewes • Arthur B. and Sybil B. Kern
Jane Cayford Nylander • Betty Ring • Elle Shushan • Maureen A. Taylor
Laurel Thatcher Ulrich • Barbara McLean and Gerald W. R. Ward**

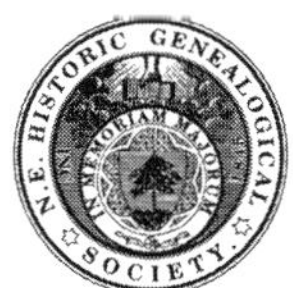

New England Historic Genealogical Society   Boston, Massachusetts   2002

Distributed by Northeastern University Press

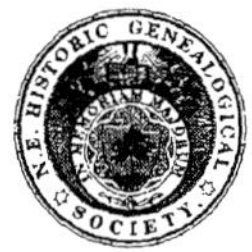

Cover design by Carolyn Sheppard Oakley

First Edition
Third Printing

International Standard Book Number: 0-88082-132-9
Library of Congress Control Number: 2001094555

Library of Congress Cataloging-in-Publication Data

The art of family : genealogical artifacts in New England / D. Brenton Simons ... [et al.].
p. ; cm.
Includes bibliographical references and index.
ISBN 0-88082-132-9 (alk. paper)
1. Decorative arts—New England. 2. New England—Genealogy—Archival resources. I. Simons, D. Brenton. II. New England Historic Genealogical Society.
NK810 .A78 2002
704.9'499292'0973—dc21
2001094555

Published by
New England Historic Genealogical Society
101 Newbury Street
Boston, Massachusetts 02116-3007

Printed by Sheridan Books Inc., Ann Arbor, Michigan.

Contents

Acknowledgments

The Art of Family would never have come to fruition without the tireless efforts of Peter Benes. I have long admired Peter's work with the Dublin Seminar for New England Folklife and I knew from the earliest brainstorming sessions on this volume that his editorial assistance and expertise in the study of material culture would be essential to its success. Peter, along with his wife, Jane Montague Benes, took great pains to review each chapter thoroughly, make suggestions, offer advice or direction, and input adjustments or corrections. Peter was patient and encouraging throughout what at times was an excruciatingly slow process. I cannot thank Peter and Jane enough for their invaluable participation in *The Art of Family*.

Each of the authors deserves special praise and warm thanks for their insightful contributions to this volume—Jeremy Dupertuis Bangs, Peter Benes, Georgia Brady Barnhill, Abbott Lowell Cummings, John Demos, Laurel K. Gabel, Wendell Garrett, Lauren B. Hewes, Arthur B. Kern, Sybil B. Kern, Jane Cayford Nylander, Betty Ring, Elle Shushan, Maureen A. Taylor, Laurel Thatcher Ulrich, Barbara McLean Ward, and Gerald W. R. Ward.

Four organizations have been extremely generous in allowing the use of images from their collections or publications: the Society for the Preservation of New England Antiquities, the Dublin Seminar for New England Folklife, the American Antiquarian Society, and the New England Historic Genealogical Society. Many other organizations have been most helpful in granting permissions or in providing other assistance, including: Abby Aldrich Rockefeller Folk Art Museum, Cape Ann Historical Society, Connecticut Historical Society, Cincinnati Public Library, Connecticut State Library, Haverhill Public Library, Historic Deerfield, Lexington Historical Society, Library of Congress, Metropolitan Museum of Art, Nantucket Historical Associations, National Archives, New Hampshire Historical Society, New York Genealogical and Biographical Society, New-York Historical Society, New York State Historical Association, National Museum of American History, National Society of the Daughters of the American Revolution, Old Sturbridge Village, Rhode Island Historical Society, Peterborough Historical Society, Sandy Bay Historical Society, Shelburne Museum, Smithsonian Institution, Stratford Historical Society, Vermont Historical Society, and Winterthur Museum.

For generously contributing to the costs of printing and production of this book, I would like to thank several individuals who wish to remain anonymous. Special thanks also to Selina F. Little for making a gift to this book in memory of her parents, Bertram K. Little and Nina Fletcher Little, as well as to M. David Sherrill and the Society of Colonial Wars in the State of New York. I also acknowledge Jane S. Huntington, who graciously sponsored our initial *Art of Family* luncheon meeting in Boston.

I especially want to thank Ralph J. Crandall, Executive Director of the New England Historic Genealogical Society, for encouraging this publication, assisting me in fundraising for it, and providing much support to me throughout my career at NEHGS. Gabrielle S. Stone deserves special acknowledgment for picking up the production reins late in the project and seeing the book to completion. Several other individuals contributed to this publication, including Carolyn Sheppard Oakley, who designed the dust jacket, scanned scores of photographs, and created promotional materials for the book; Linda Rupnow McGuire, who handled a multitude of image permissions; Julie Helen Otto, who checked bibliographic citations and made text corrections; David Allen Lambert, who conducted genealogical research on several individuals treated herein; Timothy Salls and Christopher Hartman, who provided image research; and Lynn Betlock and Erin Nikitchyuk, who provided marketing assistance. Several former colleagues—Thomas D. Kozachek, Jayna Stafford, and Linda Skinner Austin—also participated at various stages of the project. David Ford designed the book layout and Paula Martin served as compositor. Thanks also to Natalie Greenberg who proofread the book and Ann-Marie Lindstrom, who indexed it. I would also like to thank the following colleagues who helped or participated along the way—Jerome E. Anderson, Robert Charles Anderson, Jonathan L. Fairbanks, Jane Fletcher Fiske, Marsha Hoffman Rising, and Gary Boyd Roberts. John Weingartner, of Northeastern University Press, offered much advice and enthusiasm over several years.

Peter Benes would like to thank Gregory H. Laing, of the Haverhill Public Library, for his valuable assistance.

On a personal note, I would like to acknowledge members of my family, including my mother, Mary Hoyt Fitch, in whose memory I find joy and inspiration, as well as my sister, Katherine Bailey Egan, and my aunt, Margaret R. Cuddeback. Finally, I wish to dedicate my efforts on *The Art of Family* to my uncle, Herbert D. Simons.

D. Brenton Simons
Boston, Massachusetts

Notes on Contributors

Jeremy Dupertuis Bangs is founder and director of the Leiden American Pilgrim Museum, The Netherlands. He is the author of *Cornelis Engebrechtsz's Leiden: Studies in Cultural History* (1979), *Church Art and Architecture in the Low Countries before 1566* (1997), *Seventeenth-Century Town Records of Scituate, Massachusetts* (1997–2001), and *Indian Deeds, Land in Plymouth Colony, 1620–1691* (forthcoming).

Georgia Brady Barnhill is Andrew W. Mellon Curator of Graphic Arts at the American Antiquarian Society and editor of *Prints of New England* (1991) and author of "The Catalogue of American Engravings" (2000).

Peter Benes is co-founder and Director of The Dublin Seminar for New England Folklife. He is author of *The Masks of Orthodoxy: Folk Gravestone Carvings in Plymouth County, Massachusetts, 1689–1805* (1979), *Old-Town and the Waterside* (1986), and *Charles Delin: Port Painter of Maastricht and Amsterdam* (1987).

Abbott Lowell Cummings, an antiquarian, architectural historian, and genealogist, is Charles F. Montgomery Professor Emeritus of American Decorative Arts, Yale University. He is author of *The Framed Houses of Massachusetts Bay, 1625–1725* (1979).

John Demos is Samuel Knight Professor of American History at Yale University. His books include *A Little Commonwealth: Family Life in Plymouth Colony* (1970), *Entertaining Satan: Witchcraft and the Culture of Early New England* (1982), and *The Unredeemed Captive: A Family Story from Early America* (1994).

Laurel K. Gabel is author of numerous studies of eighteenth- and nineteenth-century gravestone art in New England including *Gravestone Chronicles I* (1990) and *Gravestone Chronicles II* (1997), both co-authored with Theodore Chase.

Wendell Garrett is the editor-at-large of *The Magazine Antiques*, Senior Vice-President of Sotheby's, and author of numerous books on art and architecture of eighteenth- and nineteenth-century America.

Lauren B. Hewes is Project Bibliographer for the Print Council of America and a former Associate Curator at Shelburne Museum. She is author of a forthcoming publication on the portrait collection of the American Antiquarian Society, Worcester, Massachusetts.

Arthur B. and **Sybil B. Kern** are researchers, writers, and lecturers on American folk art. Their work has been published extensively in *The Clarion*, *Folk Art*, and *The Magazine Antiques*.

Jane Cayford Nylander is President of the Society for the Preservation of New England Antiquities. She is author of *Fabrics for Historic Buildings* (1990), *Our Own Snug Fireside: Images of the New England Home, 1760–1860* (1993) and *Windows on the Past: Four Centuries of New England Homes* (2000).

Betty Ring is the author of *Let Virtue Be a Guide to Thee: Needlework in the Education of Rhode Island Women, 1730–1830* (1983), *American Needlework Treasures: Samplers and Silk Embroideries from the Collection of Betty Ring* (1987), and *Girlhood Embroidery: American Samplers and Pictorial Needlework, 1650–1850* (1993).

Elle Shushan is a specialist dealer in portrait miniatures. She actively lectures and writes on the subject; her most recent articles were published in *Connaissance des Arts* and *The Catalogue of Antiques and Fine Arts.*

D. Brenton Simons is Assistant Executive Director of the New England Historic Genealogical Society, Executive Editor of *New England Ancestors*, author of *The Langhornes of Langhorne Park* (1997), and is the originator and co-editor of *The Art of Family: Genealogical Artifacts in New England.*

Maureen A. Taylor is the author of several books including *Preserving Your Family Photographs* and a contributing editor of *Family Tree Magazine.* She was formerly a librarian at the New England Historic Genealogical Society and the Rhode Island Historical Society.

Laurel Thatcher Ulrich is the James Duncan Phillips Professor of Early American History at Harvard University; she is author of *Good Wives: Image and Reality in the Lives of Women in Northern New England, 1650–1750* (1982), *A Midwife's Tale: The Life of Martha Ballard, Based on Her Diary, 1785–1812* (1990), and *The Age of Homespun: Objects and Stories in the Creation of An American Myth* (2001).

Barbara McLean Ward is Director/Curator of the Moffatt-Ladd House and Garden, Portsmouth, New Hampshire, and former research associate at the Strawbery Banke Museum. She is co-editor of *Silver in American Life* (1979), and a major contributor to *Colonial Massachusetts Silversmiths and Jewelers: A Biographical Dictionary* (1988).

Gerald W. R. Ward is Katharine Lane Weems Senior Curator of Decorative Arts and Sculpture, Art of the Americas, Museum of Fine Arts, Boston. He is the co-editor of *Silver in American Life* (1979) and *Silver and Silversmithing in New England, 1620–1815* (2001).

Introduction

John Demos

What's in an object? . . . In a sampler? A mourning ring? A portrait? A gravestone?

What indeed! The present volume is, quite literally, an object-*lesson* for all who have sought to grasp the history of family life through written words. Conversely, others whose primary focus has always been objects will find here a different kind of lesson—an impulse, or even a compelling reason, to connect their doings with the framing "surround" of cultural circumstance.

If we could somehow step back to about the year 1950, we would find that the subfield of family history had not blossomed. At that point, the attention of professional historians was fixed almost entirely on large public matters: large events, large ideas, large institutions (especially political ones). Genealogists, for their part, were busily engaged in family research—but with goals limited mostly to details of kinship. Meanwhile, too, scholars of the decorative arts were pursuing their own separate track, in terms of (what has come to be called) connoisseurship. Now, four decades later, *The Art of Family* brings professionals from all these fields together, asks them to talk to each other (in at least a figurative sense), and serves to promote an authentic exchange.

But why has this sort of result has been so slow to develop? When historians first broached the family as a legitimate target of study (in the 1960s and 1970s), their concerns ran strongly to intangibles. Questions of "structure" and "function" loomed especially large. How was authority defined, and distributed, within the family group? What range of roles and responsibilities attached to different family members? Where, and to what extent, did family experience intersect the interests of the wider community? A different, though related, set of issues embraced the emotional life of families. Scholars divided quite sharply, for example, about the premodern situation—with a good many, perhaps the majority, arguing an utter absence of the sentimental, affectionate style that we regard as the norm today. Yet another focus involved numbers: in short, the demographic contours of domestic life. What was the membership of families in one or another historical era? How many children were born to the average parental pair? At what age did individuals most often marry? And what was the usual size of a household? None of these matters, be it noted, directly engaged the material side of family life. And all could be developed from written documents alone: personal correspondence and diaries, account books, legal records (including wills and "last testaments"), newspapers, religious and devotional literature (including sermons), and the archives of local communities. Again: words and numbers ruled supreme, with nary an object in sight.

To be sure, the branch of scholarship known today as "material culture history" was taking an increasingly well-defined shape. Allied in many cases to museum programs, this endeavor had—as early as the 1970s—brought newly sophisticated standards to the study of "object" remains. But historians at large were disinclined to notice. Differences of language, of technique, of conceptualization—and, for that matter, differences of sensibility and taste—kept the various groups mostly at arm's length.

Fortunately, in recent years the gap has begun to close. Few word-based historians would any longer doubt that "documents" about the past come in material as well as verbal forms. And "object" scholars (so to speak) seem more and more concerned to set their work against the backdrop of broadly operative cultural trends. In this respect *The Art of Family* is timely—is exemplary—is necessary.

What's in an object?

Taken as a whole, the essays included here provide a remarkably comprehensive answer. Starting in virtually every case from a particular form (or type), the scholars involved have canvassed a broad array of questions. What, first of all, is the nature of the form: its physical properties, its durability, its visual and emotional texture? And, related to this, how was it produced—and by whom? And, also related, what costs (monetary and otherwise) were entailed in its making? Second, who—that is, what sorts of people—were likely to have owned and used it? (In some cases, very specific conclusions are possible; in others, one must rely on informed guesswork.) Third, where—that is, in what particular places and spaces—was it most likely to have been found? Fourth, when was it made, owned, and used? (Did it have a kind of life-history? A birth date? A period of peak impact and importance? And then, finally, a moment of disappearance?) Fifth, how was it owned and used? (In what ways? On what occasions? For what specific purposes?) Sixth, and last, why was it significant—and meaningful—to its owner-user(s)?

Though every part of this agenda deserves (and here receives) careful attention, the final two seem especially important. Were the volume defined primarily as a study of material culture, the contributors would presumably have focused on the matter of production. But where "family" considerations are set up front (as in the title), questions of use and meaning necessarily take pride of place.

In one sense the "use" of these objects begins from the simple fact of possession. But there is also an active dimension here—which, in turn, leads directly to the element of meaning. Thus, many family-significant objects were intended for visual display: on walls, shelves, tables, chests, and other prominent surfaces. Indeed, with some this intention was primary—for example, silver tableware from our colonial era (see Barbara McLean Ward and Gerald W. R. Ward, pp. 177–190). Another category of use embraced various acts of giving (and receiving), most especially those of bequeathing (across time and between generations). "Heirlooms" often assumed a special significance; and sometimes their history became, in itself, a powerful family datum (Abbott Lowell Cummings, pp. 191–199). Nor should we overlook use of a much simpler, more pragmatic sort: that is, how these objects performed the day-to-day, even minute-to-minute, work of domestic life (Jane Cayford Nylander, pp. 201–221).

But behind display, and giving, and practical "performance" lies a host of inner connections to the experience of owners. Why were these objects so valued—not to say, treasured? (The word does not seem too strong.) Why, for that matter, were they so needed—and thus created—in the first place? Several important possibilities readily suggest themselves. Some object-types expressed a clear motive of status assertion. Again, colonial silver makes an obvious case in point—and, so too, does some of the portraiture, especially where it presents family groups (Lauren B. Hewes, pp. 114–126). *Look! Here we are: confident, established, upstanding, important.* Other imagery declared deeply held values: for instance, portraits of children holding books and Bibles or of a man reading a newspaper (Arthur B. and Sybil B. Kern, pp. 245–273). *Yes, we are committed—most definitely—to learning and piety.* Yet another purpose here was straightforward record keeping—witness the astonishing plethora of family registers analyzed in several of the chapters to follow (Peter Benes, pp. 13–59; Georgia Brady Barnhill, pp. 60–74; Maureen A. Taylor, pp. 75–89; D. Brenton Simons, pp. 91–113). *We must, and we will, keep account of vital facts in our lives—above all, those involving the great passages of birth, marriage, and death.* From record keeping it is but a short step to remembrance, and then to full-blown commemoration. Individuals could be remembered—for instance, with a miniature portrait hung from a chain and worn around the neck (Elle Shushan, pp. 127–143). Events could be remembered, too—most commonly, the end of a life made into the subject of a mourning picture or, for that matter, of a gravestone (Betty Ring, pp. 145–149; Laurel K. Gabel, pp. 150–175). And history itself could be honored, in memorials like Plymouth Rock (Jeremy Dupertuis Bangs, pp. 222–244). *We will never, ever forget you, and all you have meant to us!* Finally—after record keeping and beneath remembrance—lies a deeper, more emotional layer and the motive, in particular, of linkage. In the registers, most of all, was this quite literally inscribed—with whole generations subsumed in a richly evocative iconography of hearts, flowers, chains, and elaborately branching trees. *We are forever, and unbreakably, joined; we belong to each other; we are one.*

In so many ways, then, these various object categories bespeak the fundamental theme of family unity. And they thus engage one of the most encompassing elements in the modern history of the West: the rise of (what might be called) intensive family life. For "intensive" the family everywhere became; also, affectively charged—and highly self-conscious—and carefully walled off from other forms and venues of social experience. It is not that premodern families were shaped exclusively by instrumental concerns, and not that they lacked their own emotional side, and not that domestic life (before, say, 1800) had been in any sense discounted. But there *was* a major realignment as "modernization" took hold, with its linked "revolutions" of politics, and industrial growth. Public and private experience became, in direct consequence, increasingly separate and distinct. Moreover, the "public" (including many forms of productive work, now cut loose from the home environment) presented a special, sometimes menacing, aspect. In this context—as another historian has put it—the family assumed the role of "a haven in a heartless world." Protection (not self-assertion), sentiment (rather than agency), fellow-feeling (as opposed to competitive striving): these came, for many in the nineteenth century and thereafter, virtually to *define* family.

Put simply: the family was rendered important as never before. And "unity" became its central attribute. These trends have been evident to historians for some time, yet the usual written sources reflect them only in rather abstract and idealized ways. So here, finally, is the thrust and power of *The Art of Family:* to make the same themes—*not* abstract, *not* idealized—but visible, tangible, and profoundly real.

List of abbreviations used in notes and checklists

AARFAC	Abby Aldrich Rockefeller Folk Art Center
AAS	American Antiquarian Society
CAHS	Cape Ann Historical Society, Gloucester, Mass.
CHS	Connecticut Historical Society
CPL	Cincinnati Public Library
CSL	Connecticut State Library
HPL	Haverhill Public Library, Haverhill, Mass.
HD	Historic Deerfield, Deerfield, Mass.
LHS	Lexington Historical Society, Lexington, Mass.
LC	Library of Congress, Prints and Photographs Division
MMA	Metropolitan Musum of Art
MCNY	Museum of the City of New York
NHA	Nantucket Historical Association
NA	National Archives, Washington, D.C.
NEHGS	New England Historic Genealogical Society
NHHS	New Hampshire Historical Society
NYGBS	New York Genealogical and Biographical Society
NYHS	New-York Historical Society
NYSHA	New York State Historical Association
NMAH	National Museum of American History, Smithonian Institution
NSDAR	National Society of the Daughters of the American Revolution
OSV	Old Sturbridge Village
RIHS	Rhode Island Historical Society
SBHS	Sandy Bay Historical Society, Rockport, Mass.
SM	Shelburne Museum, Shelburne, Vt.
SI	Smithsonian Institution
SPNEA	Society for the Preservation of New England Antiquities
VHS	Vermont Historical Society
WM	Winterthur Museum

SECTION I

Two Historians' Views on Family History and Genealogy

Families and the Decorative Arts

Wendell Garrett

THE HISTORY OF the family, long the private reserve of antiquarians and sociologists, has in recent times enjoyed an extraordinary growth and is now considered a subject appropriate for serious study by decorative-arts historians. Sometime between 1700 and 1850 in northwestern Europe and North America, the extended family became the nuclear family: marriages arranged by parents for economic reasons gave way to marriages arranged by spouses themselves based on sexual attraction and romantic love; family life, previously lived largely in public, became a private affair in a single-family dwelling; and the treatment of children as adults in embryo was replaced by the recognition that childhood is a distinct phase of human development. These massive changes, first perceived by social historians and demographers, can no longer be ignored by genealogists and historians of material culture, as the constellation of formidably researched and beautifully written pieces in this volume attest. We can no longer neglect the abundant artifactual evidence of this transition to modern forms of family life.

Controversy rages over the ways in which families and households of the past differed from and resembled those of today. For example, needlework family registers, family Bibles, and tombstones long fostered the belief that "mothers, over a period of twenty-five years, brought into the world between fifteen and twenty-four children," as the French sociologist Frédéric Le Play put it in the nineteenth century. It now appears that this is far from accurate. Statistics compiled by a group of demographic historians led by Peter Laslett at Cambridge University indicate that the average household in England between the late sixteenth and early nineteenth centuries numbered 4.75 persons. Even though American fertility levels were higher in the eighteenth and early nineteenth centuries than those of western Europe, Maris A. Vinovskis claims that "a sustained decline in birth rates began in some parts of the United States before the nineteenth century—well before a comparable decline in most European countries."

In addition to these fertility demographics, Philippe Ariès, in his *L'Enfant et la vie familiale sous l'Ancien Régime*, contends that privacy was unknown among families when in both palaces and hovels everyone—wives, children, domestic servants, and visitors—lived publicly "in state." And Edward Shorter claims in his *Making of the Modern Family* that because of the tragic reductions among offspring by infant mortality, the absence of affection within the families was normal before the nineteenth century.

Questions have also been raised about the alleged prevalence of the extended family in the past. It now appears that long before industrialization in England and America the nuclear family was the rule. Peter Laslett has termed the extended family a rarity in England, and Rosalind Mitchison has called it a "sociological myth" in America. Edward Shorter documents the evidence of rising illegitimacy and premarital pregnancy between 1750 and 1790. He finds that this was the assertion of a new "sense of self" among women caught up in a modernized economy and amounted to a change so great as to be a "sexual revolution."

In writing an affectionate sketch of his adopted country, Michel-Guillaume-Jean de Crèvecoeur (1735–1813), a well-to-do French *émigré* and farmer who settled in the Hudson River valley, asked his famous question, "What then is the American, this new man?" His answer was that Americans were not transplanted Englishmen, but a mixture of many European peoples, a nation of immigrants "melted into a new race of men." According to this view the widely respected American character derives some of its distinctiveness from the process of amalgamation. "We are the Romans of the modern world," boasted the senior Oliver Wendell Holmes in 1858, "the great assimilating people."

The common people, the plain folk, the American family have recently been placed at the center of the American experience by the new historians of diversity and pluralism. The historical net has been widened to include the powerless as well as the powerful, followers as well as leaders, low culture as well as high culture. It is in fine art and household artifacts that we hear more directly the voices of the plain folk. The objects allow us to see these people not as inarticulate, impotent, irrelevant ciphers existing on the periphery, but rather as actors in their own right, who, to a larger extent than we had previously imagined, were able to build a culture. This culture defined their values and aspirations, gave them a religious and social ethic, molded their family patterns and social relationships, and provided them with standards of conduct and measures for assessing themselves and other people. Alternately disparaged, patronized, and ignored, these common people have never received what every group is entitled to—a sympathetic look into their history and culture that seeks to understand them on their own terms, rescuing them, in E. P. Thompson's phrase, from the "enormous condescension of history."

The modern emphasis on family history rather than the bare bones of genealogy represents a break with past interests. The ancient tradition of compiling family trees was to legitimize power and bolster authority by purporting to trace royal descents from gods and heroes. At Hatfield House, where the famous Rainbow portrait of Queen Elizabeth I shows her dress embroidered with eyes and ears that signify her ability to see and hear everything that was going on in her realm, a pedigree on view in the Long Gallery depicts innumerable coats of arms and heraldic devices, painted in color on a parchment roll, purporting to trace the queen's ancestry all the way back to Adam. The majority of English people are, in fact, unlikely to be able to trace a continuous line beyond the sixteenth century. In these earlier centuries the establishment of pedigrees of families below the level of the aristocracy was made, not as a matter of family pride, but for individual legal purposes, when a challenge at a court of law might deprive a family of its inheritance.

Genealogy became a sophisticated interest during the next couple of centuries, when it was pursued by heralds and county antiquarians. From that time onwards, a large number of pedigrees of rural gentry and wealthy urban tradesmen appeared in print. Sufficient evidence survives to show that some poorer families were equally interested in their origins and connections. When Robert Furse, a Devon yeoman, wrote an account of his family in 1593, he was able to record ten generations of it before his own. Richard Gough's *History of Myddle* (1700–1702) shows that Shropshire farmers, craftsmen, and laborers were fascinated by their ancestors and by the family histories of their neighbors. Such accounts were not normally written down but were passed on orally. Thomas Bewick, the eighteenth-century artist and wood engraver, spoke of this interest in family history amongst the old inhabitants of the cottages scattered around the edges of the common on the south bank of the Tyne in the 1750s and 1760s: "After I left the country, I always felt much pleasure in revisiting them, and over a tankard of ale to listen to their discourse. It was chiefly upon local biography, in which they sometimes traced the pedigree of their neighbours a long way back." Thomas Hardy drew extensively on the stories that he had heard from grandparents, parents, uncles, aunts, and cousins scattered around the Dorset countryside. In 1879, when he was working on *The Trumpet Major*, Hardy walked over to Puddletown and talked with his cousin James Sparks about their great-great-great grandfather, who had lived in Puddletown in the seventeenth century and had built the cottage which had remained in the family ever since.

In the broad context of Western civilization, scholars have discovered that the family as we understand it did not come into being until about the sixteenth century. Before then, at the head of each household stood the master-father-husband who owned his wife, his children, his slaves, his animals, and his land. Life was polymorphous, promiscuous, and collective: family, relatives, servants, and friends lived together in these *extended* households, in which the family unit guaranteed the transmission of life, property, and names, but, in the words of Philippe Ariès, "did not penetrate very far into human sensibility." Children were not very important as long as there were enough of them, and they were frequently apprentices or sent to live with other families for training at an early age.

Sometime in the late sixteenth or early seventeenth century the modern family began to emerge when it was established that the family's primary obligation was to train and nurture children. At that time the *nuclear* household came to be marked by the modern characteristics of comfort, privacy, isolation, and domesticity. During the Enlightenment the moralistic certainty of children's depravity began to give way to the assumption of their essential innocence. John Locke and Jean Jacques Rousseau were preeminent in demanding new respect for children and a new approach to their education. The American family was shaped by a confluence of complicated factors, among them Lockean politics, the Protestant religion, Enlightenment ideas, and a common culture learned in the academies and maintained by the common reading of a widely literate public. The shift in sentiment in the modern family—the rise of romantic life, the growth of mother-child bonding, and the increasingly intense interaction between members of the relatively isolated nuclear family—also was influenced by wealth, leisure, and mobility of those Americans who were "born free."

Studies of eighteenth-century New England towns and nineteenth-century immigrant groups have demonstrated the persistence of extended families long after the nuclear family was commonly thought to prevail in America. It has been found that in a presumably democratic society, where the Victorian woman was treated with reverence and respect as an equal, domesticity in fact made her inferior. Severe strains were introduced into family life in the nineteenth century as the predominant pattern of romantic love and the free choice of a mate led to early marriages, bad choices, inadequate preparation, and eventually divorce. As the family itself became more democraticized and parents more open and permissive with their children, the home became "loose"—the opposite of the warm, cozy, orderly shelter from the impersonality and competitiveness of society. And with permissiveness at home, the emergent public school system became the major source of discipline. American critics launched their wide attack on the corruptions of the home: the child was wrongly nursed, wretchedly fed, overdressed, and too closely supervised while playing. By the middle of the nineteenth century British travelers thought children in the United States were nothing short of pampered brats and recorded that they were "precocious, saucy, self-reliant, wild, spontaneous, immodest, independent, demanding, irreverent." The disorder of the American home was attacked in the 1850s by the Swedish novelist and traveler Fredrika Bremer, who claimed that the American woman—"the center and law-giver in the home of the New World"—showed her love for her children "by spoiling them."

Quite early in the nineteenth century the American family was already rather different from its Western European counterpart as egalitarian democracy penetrated not only the government economy and church but the family as well. There existed here less hostile and repressive attitudes toward the child's will and more loving and tender methods of child rearing. A steady flow of travelers from abroad sensed deep differences between American and European parents and fully agreed that the American child was a new creature: American children were more independent, individualistic, and socially precocious than European children. They were also less deferential to adults, appalling some European travelers but charming others. In political life as much as in family life authoritarian codes and traditions were not so much right or wrong as they were useless. "In America," as Alexis de Tocqueville observed, "the family, in the Roman and aristocratic signification of the word, does not exist." The hierarchical family of a traditionalist society, with the father at its apex, was undermined by the force of democratic principles. The loosening of family authority and ties to tradition gave rise in the 1830s and 1840s to a feeling that what the self-reliant American could achieve was boundless. Everyone felt both a push and pull at the hearth, contrasting tendencies that were intoxicating for some while terrifying to others as they yearned for roots, continuity, control, and order in the family.

Conscious in our own day of the respective rights and duties of husband and wife, their authority over their children, and the role of the family in the upbringing of children, how can we fail to be interested in the family lives of our forefathers? The time has come to focus the flickering spotlight of historical concern on the murky chaos of the domestic life of the masses in the past. After all, as Oscar Wilde sensibly said, "The one duty we owe to history is to rewrite it."

Creating Lineages

Laurel Thatcher Ulrich

THE THESIS OF this essay is simple: genealogists are not in the business of tracking lineages so much as creating them.[1] In saying this I am not accusing genealogists of inventing the lines they trace, nor am I in any way casting aspersions on the work they do. I have done enough of it myself to know that real genealogical research is in many respects the most difficult kind of research because it focuses on individuals. You can always find 100 people typical of a category, but try to document just one person, a particular person—that is tough. I have immense respect for the standards of scholarship exemplified by the New England Historic Genealogical Society, but sometimes I think that genealogists are too modest about what they attempt. Even the simplest genealogy is not an exercise in finding out what is there, an enterprise in fact gathering. It is about making meaning.

In saying that genealogists create lineages, I do not mean that they imagine connections that did not exist. I am simply saying that genealogists, like historians, select and give form to evidence that is on the one hand always incomplete and on the other hand overwhelmingly complex and full. Constructing lineages is an act of creativity, and I would argue that it has a lot more to do with culture and with personal choice than with DNA. The concepts of self and family that we bring to our research, whether we are historians or genealogists, are shaped not just by biological facts but by law and custom, historical accident, and personal choice.

Perhaps I can illustrate those three points by talking about the name tag I was given at the Sesquicentennial Conference held by this Society in 1995. It read, "Ms. Laurel Thatcher Ulrich, Durham, New Hampshire." I was not in the building twenty minutes when someone came and asked me whether Ulrich was a German or a Swiss name. I answered, "It's my husband's name. Actually I'm English. My maiden name was Thatcher." I remember how proud I was of the name Thatcher when I went with my father as a young girl to the Hezekiah Thatcher family reunion. I remember standing up, as I had been instructed, and saying with confidence, "I'm Laurel, daughter of Kenneth who is the son of Nathan who was the son of Hezekiah." I looked around the park and tried to see the Thatcher nose, or whatever other evidence of family connection was there. I was happy to bear my father's name and pleased to be able to trace my lineage through him to Hezekiah.

But as I thought about that experience recently, the more artificial and strange it seemed. I am not just a daughter of Kenneth Thatcher, but a daughter of Alice Siddoway, who was the daughter of Alice Harries who was the daughter of Mary Rees who was the daughter of Eleanor Thomas, and there was no way on this earth that I would be able to say that at a family reunion—unless it was a reunion celebrating me. If I went to the Siddoway family reunion, I would be Laurel Thatcher, the daughter of Alice Siddoway, the daughter of Frank. If I went to the Harries family reunion, I would be Laurel, the granddaughter of Alice Harries, the daughter of Henry, and so on. At each point, I would have to connect back to a father, grandfather, great-grandfather, and so on, in a patrilineal succession.

Patrilineal families survive because women drop out in each generation. My father's contribution to my DNA is no greater than my mother's, but because law and custom say that I am a Thatcher, I will always be a Thatcher (except, of course, when I am an Ulrich). Law and custom also dictated that I would take my husband's name when I married in 1958. I was happy to do that. There appears to be no escape. What genealogists call the "umbilical" line does not make a whole lot of sense on a name tag. Mine would have to say "Laurel Siddoway Clayton Jackson Ragg Harries Thomas Rees Anderson Ipson Folkman Wooley David Kitchen Thatcher." And even I had to go look up those names because I could not remember them all.

In scholarly usage as well as in common usage, we speak lightly of "the Thatcher family," "the Siddoway family," "the Adams family," "the Kennedy family," and so on. Biologically there is no such thing. One can speak of a particular family through time only by ignoring the fundamental basis of reproduction: that every child requires both a mother and a father. Barring sibling incest, half of the genes in each generation must come from outside the original group. It is thus not biology that makes me a Thatcher, but law, culture, and convenience. That is a source of mystery and wonder to me. I think it should be to everyone who presumes to trace a family history.

Families are shaped not only by law and custom. They are also created by accidents of history. Why was a family reunion held in a park in Logan, Utah, dedicated to the memory of Hezekiah Thatcher? Because Hezekiah Thatcher and his wife Alena made choices that affected generations. By breaking with his own past, Hezekiah became the Adam from whence all things Thatcher flowed. He left West Virginia, went on to Indiana, then Illinois where he joined up with the Latter-day Saints and moved on to Utah. Because he and Alena were the first of a long succession of Latter-day Saints, they are remembered. The folks behind Hezekiah were as important, but family organizations, like family identity, spring not from biology, but from history.

Succeeding generations also have an effect on how we define our lineages. Our families are not just "out there." We create them over and over again by what we choose to remember about the past. A Thatcher family story tells us that Alena (Kitchen) Thatcher, who was in most ways a pillar of the Latter-day Saints, a charitable woman, a hardworking pioneer mother, never gave up smoking her West Virginia clay pipe. That little bit of whimsy preserved by some early family historian helped me remember her name. That name was given a new meaning when my daughter Melinda and her husband Henry named their newborn daughter Alena Min-Yiu Chiou. My tiny granddaughter, born in Connecticut, inherited the name of a maternal ancestor who migrated from West Virginia to the Rocky Mountains in the 1840s and of a paternal ancestor who left northern China at about the same time to settle in a country we now know as Taiwan. The coming together of those two names exemplifies one of the central patterns in American history—the creation of new lineages out of old.

Alena Min-Yiu's name illustrates all three of the themes I have introduced here. It reminds us that lineages come from mothers as well as fathers. It reminds us that historical events, like religious conversion or migration, change the way we define our families. Finally, it teaches us that each generation creates lineages in the way it remembers and appropriates the past.

The kind of choices we make as historians and genealogists will have a profound impact on how future generations know and see their families. If we imagine a family as only a patriarch and his descendants, we close off possibilities that would be there if we saw things more broadly. Beginners often see lineage as a highway. A straight line is the shortest distance, and they do not want to get distracted by "collateral lines." But lineage is not a highway. Families are trees. They exfoliate, blossom, drop their leaves, bud out, and begin again. No matter how hard we work, we can never comprehend every leaf, but unless we want to pave over whole acres of the past, we need to make creative and purposeful choices about what we choose to study and remember.

To illustrate some of the possibilities for a more expansive kind of research, I would like to share three examples from my own current work. In the past few years I have been studying how artifacts were created and used by ordinary people in times past. Working to identify the origins of these objects and trace how they ended up in a particular museum or collection, I found myself doing a great deal of genealogical research. As I pursued various trails, I realized that the enterprise material-culture folks call "establishing provenance" is just loaded with social history. How people transmit objects over time and how they understand those objects in relation to their own family histories help us understand how they understood their families and what they thought of as "a family." The more I worked with this material, the more I realized that the patrilineal line has been a problem in every generation—a problem to be solved. Different generations have solved it in different ways. The complexity of biological connections demands some sort of solution, because you cannot hold on to every potential link. But solutions differ over time—and they differ in the same time, depending on where a person stands in any given group of kin.

My first example is a marvelous oak cupboard made in Hadley, Massachusetts, around 1715 (*Figure 1*). It is a very colorful and flamboyant cupboard, painted all over with pomegranates, hearts, fruits, vines, flowers, and with bold Roman letters that spell a woman's name—HANNAH BARNARD. When the cupboard was displayed at the Wadsworth Atheneum in Hartford, Connecticut, several years ago, a newspaper reporter decided it was a "feminist" cupboard. In a period when married women could not own property, he concluded that Hannah Barnard was asserting her independence. Another commentator came to the opposite conclusion. He decided that since men controlled property in this period, the cupboard had to have been a gift from Hannah's future husband. It was a love token between a man and a woman. Each of these persons used twentieth-century assumptions about what it meant to control property to define the meaning of an eighteenth-century artifact. To one a marriage was repressively patriarchal, to the other a romantic partnership.

Both were wrong. Marriage was many things in the eighteenth century, but it was fundamentally an economic unit, a system for distributing land and livelihood over time. The relationship of men and women to property was different. Real property—land and houses—typically moved from father to son. Personal property—what contemporaries called "movables"—formed the core inheritance of women. In some sense, women themselves were movables, shifting their name and allegiance from one male-headed household to another when they married. But they also had primary responsibility for providing and maintaining food, clothing, animals, and other movable goods. This became obvious when I found the will and probate inventory recorded in the Hampshire County probate court when Hannah Barnard's husband died in 1725. Hannah was already long dead. Married in 1717, she had died in childbirth a year later, leaving a daughter named Abigail. Her husband remarried and had several other children, but because he was still quite young when he died his daughters had not yet married. His will noted that each girl was to receive her portion out of the goods her own mother had brought to the marriage. His inventories clearly identified what had belonged to each of his three wives.

So hidden behind the patrilineal mechanisms of the law was another system of inheritance, one that did not get recorded very often in probate court. Abigail Marsh was Hannah Barnard's heir. Abigail married Waitstill Hastings and had a daughter whom they named not just Hannah Hastings, but Hannah Barnard Hastings, and she inherited the cupboard. I know of only one other woman in this period in Hadley who had a surname for a middle name. Hannah Barnard Hastings was named for her grandmother—and for her grandmother's cupboard. Then she married a Kellogg and had a daughter named Hannah Barnard Kellogg and a son who named his daughter Hannah Barnard Hastings Kellogg. The cupboard passed on through the family until they ran out of Hannah Barnards, when it ended up in the antiques market and eventually at the Henry Ford Museum. I would not have discovered any of this if I had not been willing to look beyond patrilineal lines. My researches took me to county courthouses and to marvelous nineteenth-century histories of the Barnards, the Hastings, and the Kelloggs.

The example of the brother who named his daughter for his sister is a reminder, however, that lineal descent from either mothers or fathers is only one of the ways people define themselves as families. I have found many examples of this sort of thing in my work, but an example from my own collection will serve to make the point. In a single drawer in my spare bedroom I have textiles that came from my maternal grandmother, my paternal grandmother, my father's sister, my mother-in-law, and my father's sister's husband's grandmother. What these artifacts teach us is the impoverished notion of family confined to direct-line patrilineal descent patterns, which are at best a convenience. We need to take these narrow definitions a whole lot less seriously.

Custom and law encouraged people to arrange their memories as well as their genealogical charts in patriarchal lines. But real people, interacting with real relatives, always pushed against that. Even in past times, there were multiple conceptions of what a family was.

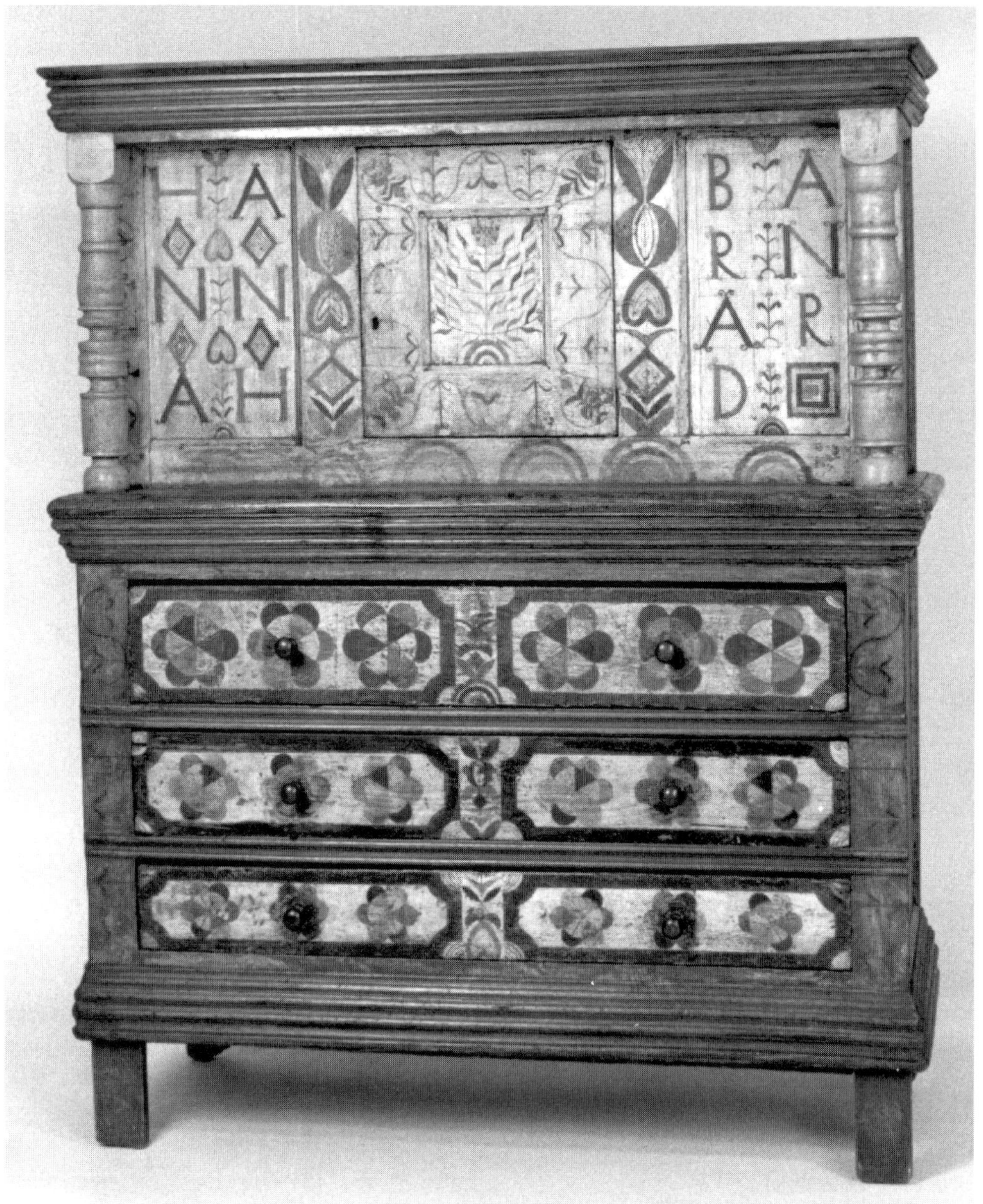

Figure 1 Oak cupboard. Inscribed "Hannah Barnard." Hadley, Massachusetts, circa 1715. From the collections of Henry Ford Museum and Greenfield Village.

Families are also created by history. Again the weight of tradition leans toward male progenitors, those who fought in wars or held town office. But stories passed on in the privacy of individual families often balance that bias. My second example shows how a good story perpetuated one woman's name and memory for many generations. The New Hampshire Historical Society, the Royal Ontario Museum, the Henniker (New Hampshire) Historical Society, and the Daughters of the American Revolution Museum in Washington, D.C., all hold textiles associated with one Mary Wilson Wallace. How did she get to be so important? Like Hezekiah Thatcher, she was a "first settler." But it was her birth that made her journey from Ireland to New Hampshire so interesting. Here is how the 1851 history of Londonderry tells the story:

> In 1720 a company of emigrants on their passage from Ireland to this country were taken by pirates and while in their hands, Mrs. Wilson was delivered of her first child, which so moved the pirate band and particularly the captain who had a wife and family that he permitted them to pursue their voyage, bestowing on Mrs. Wilson some valuable articles of apparel among which was a silk dress, pieces of which are still retained among her descendants as memorials of her peril and of her deliverance.

Those little pieces of silk still exist.

The silk dress is a stretch, but there was a pirate ship, and she probably was born on the crossing. It was not just historical accident, however, that turned this ordinary woman into a heroine but the transmission of a story from generation to generation. Mary could not possibly have remembered the journey from Ireland. Her father died shortly after their arrival, so she had to have learned the story of her birth from her mother, a woman remembered in the town as a storyteller. Horace Greeley said Mary's mother filled his own mother's head with "traditions, ballads and snatches of history." Though some of these accounts were distorted, "they served to awaken in me a thirst for knowledge and a lively interest in learning and history." The story of Mary Wilson Wallace's birth made it into the town history, and since then her descendants have been busy embellishing her memory. The New Hampshire Historical Society has a photograph of an affidavit made in 1889 attesting that the warp of a fragment of linen, now in the society's collections, was spun by "Ocean-Born Mary" (*Figures 2* and *3*). A house in Henniker, New Hampshire, built by her son or grandson is known not by his name—even though he was arguably an important man, a member of the legislature and holder of public office—but by hers. It is the "Ocean-Born Mary" house. Stories create families and their histories.

The final object I want to talk about is an embroidered sampler made in Boston by a girl named Sarah Silsbe (*Figure 4*). It is one of the "Adam and Eve" embroideries that Betty Ring describes in *American Samplers and Pictorial Needlework*. A picture like this was not an original expression so much as a ritual

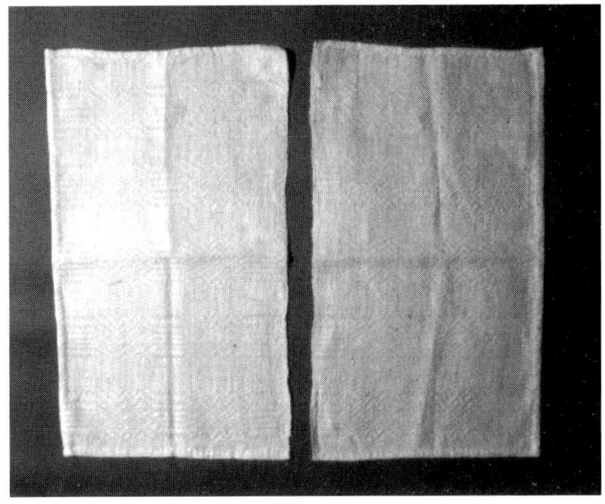

Figure 2 Linen towel whose warp was spun by Irish immigrant Mary Wilson Wallace, known as "Ocean-Born Mary." Henniker, New Hampshire, eighteenth century. New Hampshire Historical Society.

invocation of the values of a needlework teacher and the parents who spent money to send their daughters to school. What interests me is not the way these samplers taught traditional values, but how they taught young girls to value themselves. A girl who made a sampler like this was not being taught to be invisible. She might imagine growing up to be a movable, but not an invisible. The composition has a striped serpent, a romping rabbit, and butterflies as large as deer. Despite the presence of the serpent, it is a very cheerful rendition of the temptation in Eden. It is also surprisingly egalitarian. Adam and Eve both clutch the forbidden fruit. There is also a kind of partnership reflected in the presence of an alphabet. Textiles were among the most valuable possessions in early American households, more valuable than the cupboards and chests that contained them. When a young woman stitched her initials on linens, she claimed an identity as mistress of a household and joint partner in an economic enterprise.

There is another way in which the young girl is made to seem important in these embroideries. Fully 40 percent of the surface of Sarah Silsbe's sampler is covered by words. This is quite typical of New England embroidery. The embroiderer was learning more than marking. She was preparing to become a mistress of words. This departs from an earlier tradition in which girls were taught to read

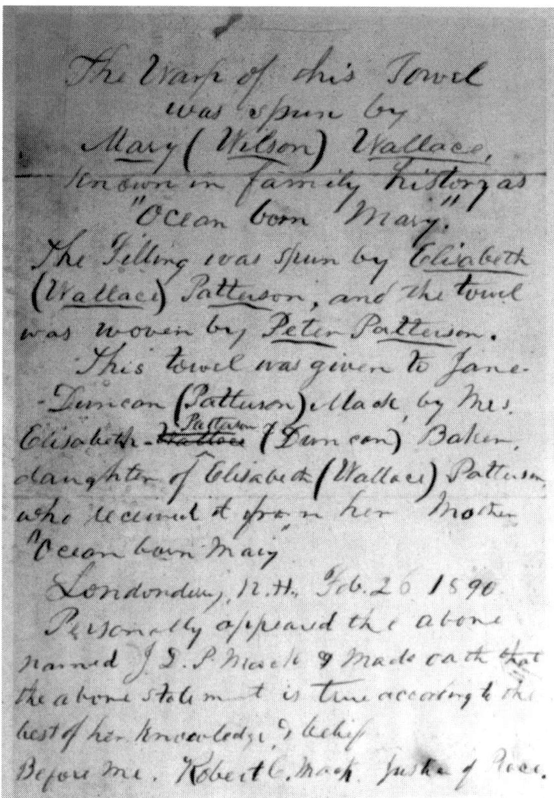
The Warp of this Towel
was spun by
Mary (Wilson) Wallace,
known in family history as
"Ocean born Mary."
The Filling was spun by Elizabeth
(Wallace) Patterson, and the towel
was woven by Peter Patterson.
This towel was given to Jane
Duncan (Patterson) Mack by Mrs.
Elisabeth ~~Wallace~~ Patterson (Duncan) Baker,
daughter of Elisabeth (Wallace) Patterson
who received it from her Mother
"Ocean born Mary"
Londonderry, N.H. Feb. 26 1890.
Personally appeared the above
named J. D. P. Mack & made oath that
the above statement is true according to the
best of her knowledge & belief
Before me. Robert C. Mack. Justice of Peace.

Figure 3 Affidavit attesting in 1889 that the warp of the linen fragment shown in the previous figure was spun by Mary Wilson Wallace, known in family history as "Ocean-Born Mary." New Hampshire Historical Society.

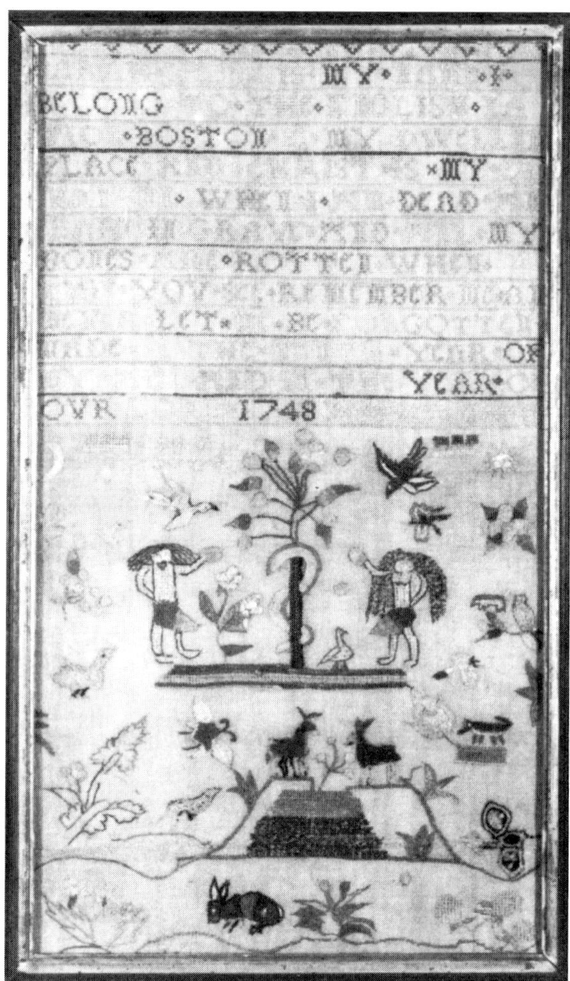

Figure 4 Sampler. Sarah Silsbe. Boston, Massachusetts, 1748. Photograph courtesy of Sotheby's, 31 January 1981. Theodore H. Kapnek Collection of American Samplers.

but not to write. Although she learned her letters with a needle rather than a pen, a girl was nevertheless expressing herself with words. The verses are not original. Sarah used two of the most conventional in New England. In the first she established her identity as a Silsbe, as a Christian, as a Bostonian, and as part of a larger English world:

> Sarah Silsbe is my name.
> I belong to the English nation.
> Boston is my dwelling place.
> And Christ is my salvation.

The second verse introduced a different theme:

> When I am dead and laid in grave,
> And all my bones are rotten.
> When this you see, remember me.
> And never let me be forgotten.

When I first read this grim little verse, I thought about dreary sermons in unheated churches, gaunt skulls on eighteenth-century gravestones, and Puritan repression.

Then something very interesting happened. My husband and I decided to remodel the upstairs of our house. Since our children were grown and gone, we felt free to rearrange several rooms. As part of the project, we tore out some pine paneling. Underneath we discovered several little notes that our children had dropped through knotholes in 1972. With a blue felt-tipped pen, our daughter Melinda—the one who grew up to become the mother of Alena Min-Yiu—had written, "I am nine years old, but when you find this early history, I'll probably be dead." Reading her note, I concluded that there was only one thing worse than being the child of a Puritan, and that was being the child of a historian. But as I thought more about it, I realized that Melinda, like Sarah Silsbe, was beginning to imagine time stretching out beyond her own lifetime, quite an intellectual leap for a child. One of the reasons she was able to do that is because she had already learned to think about what had come before her. She had a sense of the past. I think in order to have a sense of the future, you have to have a sense of the past. They come together.

Hannah Barnard, Ocean-Born Mary, and Sarah Silsbe all actively constructed a place for themselves in history. They show us how early Americans used personal possessions to bend legal notions that constricted women's right to own property, how family stories create narratives lost in conventional political narratives, and how writing—with a needle as well as with a pen—offered a way of extending one's identity beyond death. When we are dead and in the grave and all our bones are rotten, perhaps some of the things we create will remain. The chain of memory that links one generation to another is fragile. It is not about DNA. It is about culture, and it must be constantly attended.[2]

NOTES

[1] An earlier version of this paper was given at the sesquicentennial meeting of the New England Historic Genealogical Society in Boston, Massachusetts, 15 July 1995.

[2] Betty Ring, *Girlhood Embroidery: American Samplers and Pictorial Needlework, 1650–1850,* 2 vols. (New York: Knopf, 1993); Leander W. Cogswell, *History of the Town of Henniker, Merrimac County, New Hampshire* (Concord, N.H.: Republican Press, 1880); Edward L. Parker, *The History of Londonderry, comprising the Towns of Derry and Londonderry, New Hampshire* (Boston: Perkins and Whipple, 1851).

SECTION II

Family Representations and Remembrances

Decorated New England Family Registers, 1770 to 1850

Peter Benes

WHEN VERMONT portrait painter Thomas Ware began his picture of the eight-member Hutchinson family of Woodstock, Vermont, he started with a single piece of canvas about waist-high in height but which in width stretched out to more than ten feet (*Figure 1*).[1] On the left he painted Clarissa (Sage) Hutchinson and her fourteen-year-old daughter Clarissa. On the right, and facing the women, he placed forty-nine-year-old Titus Hutchinson, a Princeton-educated lawyer and United States Attorney for the Vermont District, and his five sons in descending order from Titus (aged about twenty-one) to Oramel, Henry, Edwin, and Alexander (aged about eight). Alexander, who is noticeable for his crossed eyes, seems the least prepared for this experience. Different background hues suggest that each subject was painted in a separate and individual pose, but we can assume all members of the family were present in Woodstock at some point in 1820 in what must have been a long painting process. They make an unusual statement. The children's increasing heights and sizes distinguish their years and their maturity; their placement by the mother or father indicates their gender. True to this painter's early-nineteenth-century style, all eight members of the family stand poised and erect as if at military attention. It looks like a review of the troops.[2]

A different approach to family portraiture was taken by a calligraphic or sketch artist named Reuben Barns when he "copied" (meaning delineated) the family of Jonathan Bennet of Poland, Maine, in 1804 (*Figure 2*). Jonathan Bennet and Miss Polly Hasker are shown holding hands with their ten children. The two older boys, aged thirty-three and thirty-two, stand next to the parents; seven younger girls are arranged immediately to their right and left. Isaac, the youngest child at age eight and still in pantaloons, is almost out of the picture. Like Alexander Hutchinson he is the least prepared for this experience. Although the overall pose is not likely to have been taken from nature (unless all twelve posed before him at one time), the gender, relative size, and maturity of each family member are clear from their place in the composition.[3] In this case, the genealogical information, which is included as part of a caption, significantly adds to the picture.[4]

Although the Hutchinson and Bennet family portraits are unique in early American art, the effort by the artists to portray families as complete units was a widely shared impulse in New England at this period and goes to the core of our subject. This essay covers a wide range of watercolor, manuscript, and embroidered family registers made in New England in the period from 1770 to 1850 that used art and symbolism to sustain the concept of genealogical identity. In the case of these two portrait painters, family unity was accomplished by extending canvas size or by having their subjects hold each other's hands. In the case of the family registers, artists used less direct means such as criss-crossed vines, fruited

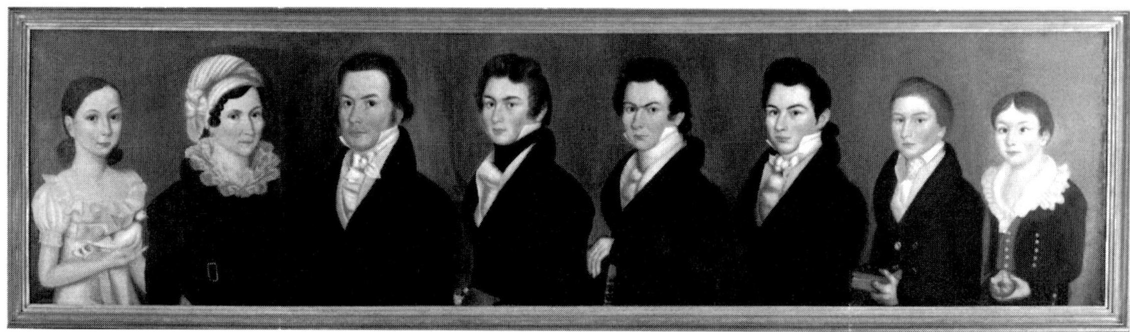

Figure 1 Family of Titus Hutchinson and Clarissa Sage. Attributed to Thomas Ware (1803–circa 1826). Woodstock, Vermont, 1820. Oil on canvas, 30 × 120 inches. Courtesy of The Woodstock Historical Society, Woodstock, Vermont.

trees, superimposed or touching hearts, or linked pieces of chain to emphasize or reproduce the various genealogical details of the progeny of married couples. Much of this art was accomplished by school pupils under the direct supervision of their teachers. These were part of a calligraphic or decorative arts curriculum—what the young student brought home to his or her parents after each year. Mrs. Gill's school in West Cambridge (see *checklist 39 through 42* on pp. 277–78) and B. H. Cheever's East School in Newbury (see *checklist 28 through 30* on p. 277) were two such schools in Massachusetts whose pupils produced these registers during the first several decades of the nineteenth century. But others were done by occasional or professional artists such as Edward D. Burke of Nantucket, Massachusetts (see *checklist 98 through 100* on p. 281). Still others were executed by school teachers or town clerks with a sure command of calligraphy such as William Saville of Gloucester, Massachusetts (see *checklist 65 through 70* on pp. 279–80), or Joseph Odiorne, of Pittsfield, New Hampshire (see *checklist 91 and 92* on p. 281).

Decorated family records came into New England's school and household art roughly at the time of the American Revolution.[5] This was already a relatively late period in the region's history and signaled a shift in expectations commensurate with a provincial society maturing into a new republic. Taste for genealogy had been working its way into the population at large, and families wanted a cheaper and more personal visual remembrance of their ancestry than the old decorated arms and family portraits that hung in the homes of wealthy Boston residents in the mid-eighteenth century.[6] No longer satisfied with the practice of inserting family names into their Bibles, consumers now looked to family registers created by calligraphers and decorators as well as those being sold by engravers such as Richard Brunton and Benjamin Blythe.[7] The older forms of genealogical taste were also still being produced, and watercolor coats of arms continued to surface in some quantity in the 1780s and 1790s. But it was a period of change. Arms and hatchments generally lost their function as funereal escutcheons in the celebration of death and simply became devices to treasure and hang on the wall.

The new printed and hand-worked registers were more naive and more genealogically specific than the old arms. Almost all began with a format such as "The Genealogy of . . ." or "The Family Register: Births, Marriages, Deaths." (A number of registers from Maine list "Offspring" and "Progeny" instead of "Births.") Their function, like old gravestones, was to encourage remembrance of the past. Richard Brunton, for example, titled his pieces as a reminder to "Keep Sacred the Memory of your Ancestors" or "Remember your Ancestors." Typically, family registers—especially school pieces done by children in their early teens on the subject of their own family or that of a close relative—looked back on a marriage that had taken place about fifteen to twenty years earlier and which had produced a number of children. But some, for example those by William Saville and Joseph Odiorne, seem to have been drawn up at the time of marriage. Blanks in the design were to be filled out as required as children were born.

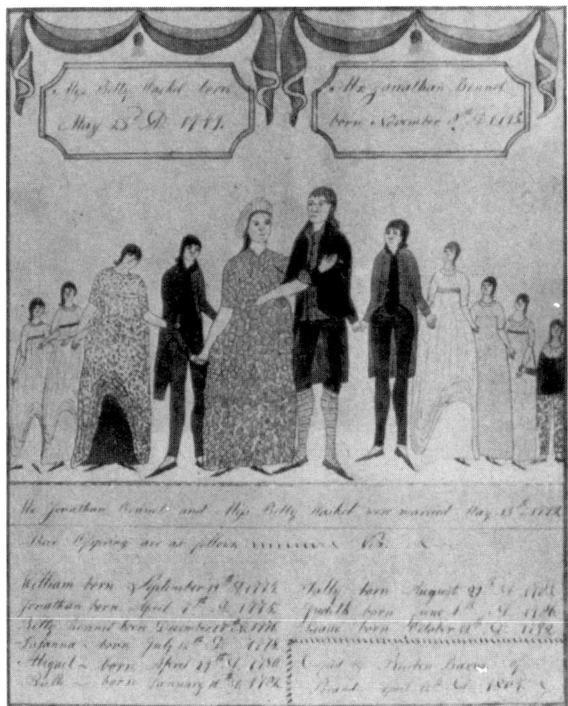

Figure 2 Family of Jonathan Bennet and Polly Hasker. Reuben Barns. Poland, Maine, 1804. Watercolor, 14 × 11 inches. Eleanor and Mabel Van Alstyne American Folk Art Collection, National Museum of History and Technology, Smithsonian Institution, Washington, D.C.

Regardless of whether they looked forward or backwards, naïve genealogical diagrams and artwork rapidly achieved a high value both in terms of how they were preserved in the family and by the public at large. One Connecticut family member remembered a genealogy that had been hanging in the house for years: "I have been accustomed to see it from my childhood."[8] Others genealogies ended up in early museums. When Boston entrepreneur Daniel Bowen lost his entire collection of wax-works and paintings (after his second disastrous museum fire in 1807), he made a practice of visiting in a "beggerly way" former patrons and friends in Essex County, Massachusetts, hoping to rebuild his collection. One of the items he acquired on these trips was "the tree of the Bowen family," drawn by watercolorist Ashley Bowen of Marblehead, later known for his extensive maritime diary and sketches.[9]

Two major iconographic ideas or subthemes accompany these documents. The first concerns the larger vocabulary of their symbols. A remarkable consistency runs throughout New England's genealogical art that also appears on its early gravemarkers, in its written anagrams and epitaphs, and in its religious hymns. (There are even a number of parallels to grave boards, tavern signs, and other commercial signage of the period.) The lines between language and symbol are so close that they form a populist or vernacular "genealogical poetry." The newer symbols were free of the formality and procedure of old English coats of arms, but like them they drew on everyday concepts and traditional motifs. Family unity was shown by interlocking chains, by adjacent circles, by standing architectural structures, and by planted grids or "fields" of names. Marriages were shown as a coming together of "pairs" of things—a pair of vines, a pair of hearts, or a pair of birds. Bloodlines were conveyed by trees or vines assuming the shape of trees.[10] Parentage was shown by heavy or Gothic typography. Death was conveyed by gravestone devices such as coffins, urns, and released souls (such as winged cherub heads); by missing or broken branches; by withered buds or flowers. The language was interchangeable among genealogical mediums. Family registers used images resembling or mimicking those on gravestones (paired columns, paired vines), or used gravestone concepts (coffins, urns, epitaphs), or depicted gravestones themselves.[11] Gravestones, in turn, depicted genealogical trees or genealogical "rows" in order to indicate schematically successive generations emanating from a single individual. In some instances, gravestones simply reproduced a coffin on the stone itself.[12] Gravestone makers also found a number of devices by which persons "gave up the ghost"—terminology that can be found in gravestone epitaphs and other sources.[13]

A second iconographic idea concerns the origin of specific design motifs. Schoolmade versions of family records, as well as those created by occasional or professional artists, sometimes went much further than printed versions and drew on innovative and highly complex design elements connected variously to classical art, to folk speech, and to traditional ideas or icons associated with family life. Their aim, as in the case of the Hutchinson and Bennet family portraits, was to communicate the chronological sequence and identity of family groups in a single image using representations or icons of love, reproduction, and unity. Hearts within hearts, fruited trees growing from a pair of hearts, or an architectural structure of two or three pillars were the register's "text" and served not only to distinguish the family's identity, but specifically identified lines within families which were derived from second or third marriages. Were any of these images or representations known by name? Was there a term for the very specific apple-bearing trees that were common in Gloucester's Fifth Parish? Or, equally possible, were any of these images taken from printed originals? Copying existing printed work may in fact have been common. Richard Brunton's printed family record was copied in watercolor at least twice in the 1790s or the early 1800s.[14] Other images, such as the embroidered heart-and-tree registers in eastern Middlesex County, Massachusetts, seem so similar they may have been copied from a printed original.

Related to this are certain geographical patterns in the use of emblems. Why, for example, did motifs like the heart-and-tree or heart-and-vine keep within the confines of specific places such as Nantucket Island and Martha's Vineyard and other areas of intensive genealogical concentration? Although the examples that have been found of this design represent only a small fraction of an unknown quantity of similar pieces that have been lost or destroyed, this degree of concentration in isolated New England locations is rare for any group of surviving decorative arts objects and bears directly not only on the identification of sources, but on the transmission and replication of the emblem within a given region. It also sheds new light on the highly complex and little understood relationships between cultural templates or patterns fixed by a literary and print medium and the much looser milieu of spoken and imitated "ideas." Did folk use of these emblems long precede their appearance in genealogical decorative art?

Some Early Genealogical Images

A number of early makers of family registers drew on symbols of progression and pairing already long established in the common vocabulary. One of the first artists to draw genealogical records in eastern New England was an unidentified watercolorist who in the 1770s and 1780s recorded families living in what were then coastal areas of eastern Massachusetts, later set off as Maine District (see *checklist 1 through 3* on p. 275). Two examples, one for the offspring of William Buckman and Ann Pote of Falmouth and a second for the children of George Walker and Elizabeth Snow of Kittery Point, can be dated between 1771 and 1773. A third example, made for the family of Samuel Knight and Mary Knight, was probably done after 1787 (*Figure 3*). Knight was a house carpenter from Falmouth. The artist's method is simple. In each piece he follows the names of the parents with a list of children beginning with the roman numeral "I" and proceeds on to "II," "III," and so on down to the youngest child. Flowers and vines fill in the remainder of what are highly ornamental calligraphic pieces. The unifying element in both pieces is the roman numerals which follow the order of birth. No evidence suggests these were executed by a family member. The artist may have been a writing clerk or calligrapher who had taught himself flower painting and other decorative arts, possibly a schoolteacher because of the precision and accuracy of the letters. It is also possible that the artist was a house carpenter like Samuel Knight who typically used roman numerals in assembling house frames.

Another common idea was the pairing of identical decorative or symbolic images which represent the married state. The names of the parents and their marriage date was followed with the names of children and their dates of birth (see *checklist 5 through 9* on pp. 275–76). A pair of facing birds (possibly two pigeons) decorates the watercolor record made by Thomas Hackett in 1829 for Stephen Sargent and Betsey Currier, a couple living in Warner, New Hampshire. Hackett used highly ornate if somewhat crude capital letters, each decorated with internal hatchings; only his signature is in script. A pair of kissing birds and two hearts form the centerpiece of the family record of the marriage between Asa Church and Juliaette Humphrey. Sixteen children were born between 1790 and 1816, each child growing in a squared field planted between two grape-entwined pedestals. Paired birds were a common gravestone concept which provided the released spirit a means of flight or an indication of grace. In eastern Essex County, Massachusetts, gravestone makers such as Jonathan

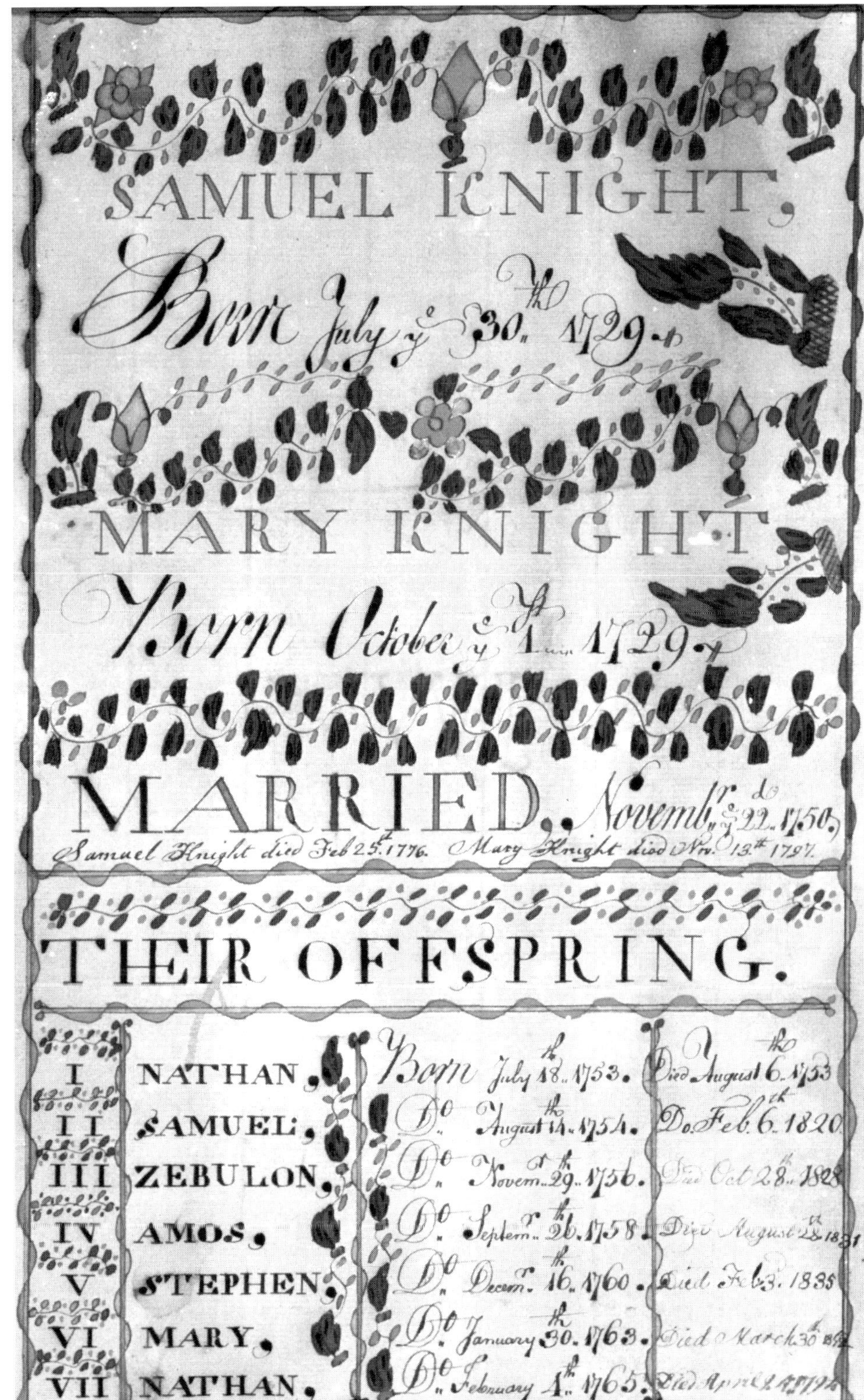

Figure 3 Family record. Samuel Knight and Mary Knight. Falmouth, Maine, circa 1780. Watercolor. Courtesy, Winterthur Museum.

Hartshorn carved a face carried between the beaks of two birds; others simply put two facing birds on the stone. In other marriage pieces, angels took the place of the usual birds. Two winged angels, two flowers, and a pair of winged heads symbolize the marriage of Moses Dudley and Nancy Glidden of Raymond, New Hampshire. This artist, too, filled his letters out with internal lines. A pair of trumpeting angels form the centerpiece of "The Family" of Loa Richardson and Salley Travis married in 1797. This cutwork paper register was probably made in 1810 and marked the births of eight children (*Figure 4*); a final child born in 1813 was added in another hand.

Pillars and Columns

A more abstract but equally focused set of symbols was provided by architectural motifs. In these, remembrance of the family was usually expressed by means of a standing or upright structure on which (or around which) was written the names of the parents and their issue. In a sense these were like tavern signage or other professional signs which were hung out ostentatiously between two large poles. An early version of this idea was the three pillars marking the marriage and offspring of William Stoughton and Eleanor Prior of East Windsor, Connecticut (*Figure 5*, see *checklist 10* on p. 276). In this watercolor design, completed in 1796, the unknown artist drew three columns side by side connected overhead by half-circle segments. Between the first pair, the artist inscribed the parents' names, birth dates, and marriage date; between the second pair, the four children's names and birth dates. All the names are executed in gothic script. The initials "W" and "S" decorate the outside columns as well as an inkstand and pen, suggesting it was the work of William Stoughton himself, possibly a Windsor schoolteacher. Although the design of the columns is naive, it is purposeful. The concept of unity or family is conveyed by the "standing" nature of the image. The family is remembered because the structure, like a commercial sign or advertisement, stands upright and can be read.

Later versions of the pilastered or columnar motif often incorporate the parents' names in the upper portion with the children shown below (see *checklists 11 through 15* on p. 276). A family register "Done by John Dodds April 1806" has the two parents under the arch with births of their children below a prominent line. Two highly decorated pillars support the structure. The same form was followed by a genealogical sampler embroidered by fourteen-year-old Nancy Batten of Salem, Massachusetts, in 1809; she left the most prominent space for her own name and listed her two brothers and five sisters below. Other versions of the design marked each of the columns as the parents, using the intervening space for an elaborate inscription. Triple standing columns and archways were common in Rhode Island where embroidered family records sewn at Mary Balch's school used three columns in their design, lining up the names of parents and their offspring between the columns on the left and their death dates on the right.[15]

At some point, possibly after 1810, a clockface appeared in the archway between the two columns (see

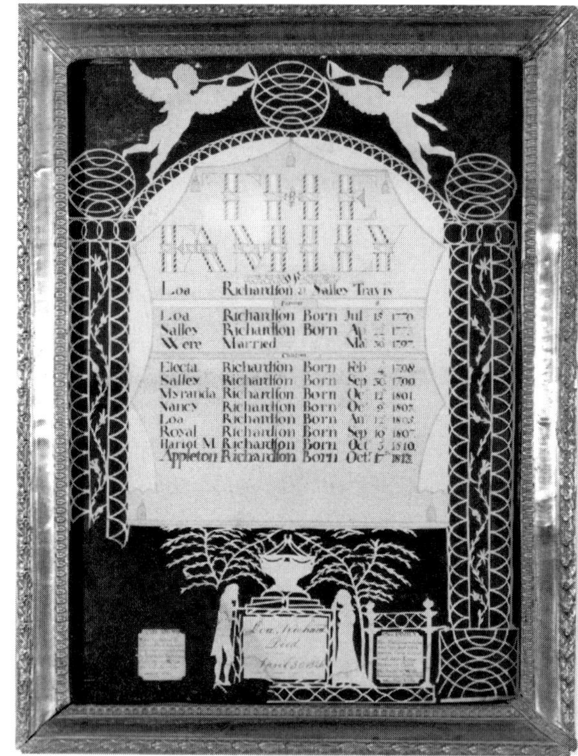

Figure 4 Family record. Loa Richardson and Salley Travis. New England [?]; circa 1810. Paper cutwork. Old Sturbridge Village, 20.21.23/B20769. *Photograph by Thomas Neill.*

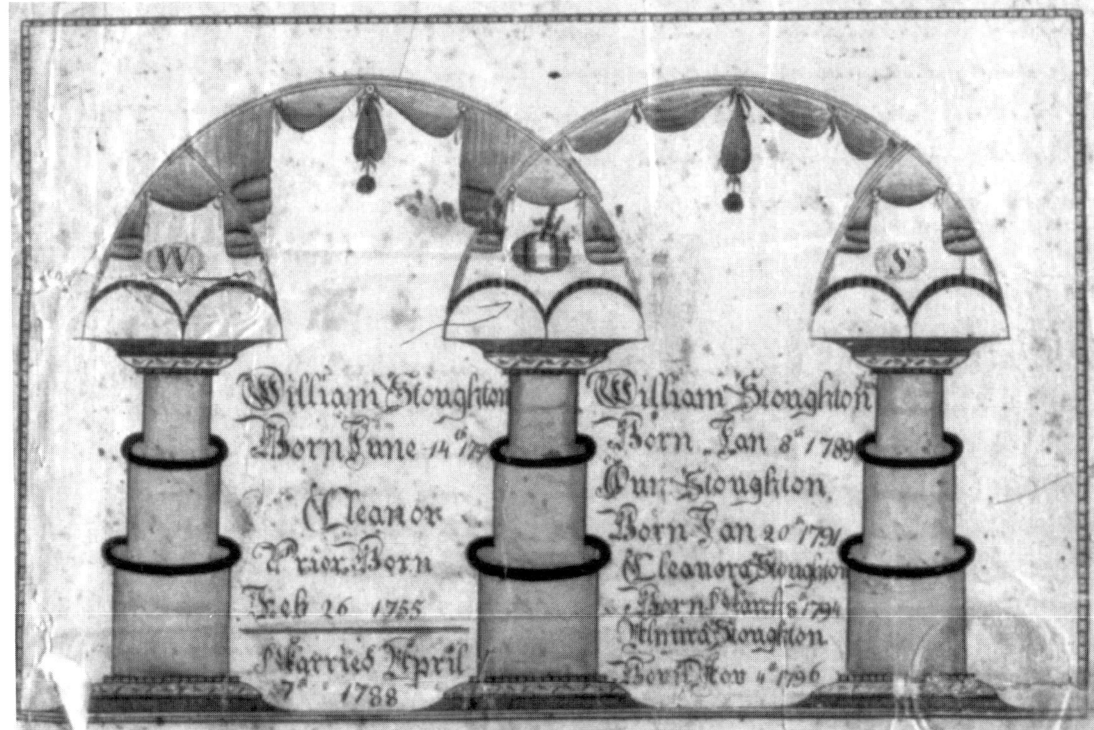

Figure 5 Family record. William Stoughton and Eleanor Prior. Signed: "W S." East Windsor, Connecticut, 1796. Watercolor. The National Archives and Records Administration.

checklists 16 through 18 on p. 276), perhaps influenced by the growing presence of tall clocks in New England or perhaps by an unknown print source. For example, an embroidered piece by twelve-year-old Hannah B. Loring (1800–1868), a pupil at Miss Perkins's Academy in Boston in 1812, involves "The Family" of Mathew Loring and his wives, Nancy Floyd, Sarah Blake, and Mercy Bates, who produced nine children born between 1787 and 1811. Hannah, Sarah Blake's only child, inscribed all their names in the space between two paired columns; below she added the death dates of her mother and several half-brothers and half-sisters. Above, joining the paired columns, was a clock showing 12:30. A related design using a clockface and a partial moon (the time shows 12:00) is found on a watercolor family register composed by Joseph Merriam Jr. in 1826, possibly as a writing exercise in an eastern Massachusetts school (*Figure 6*). This time the artist worked in a number of common posies, each dedicated to the duties of parents and children. Other genealogical artists used these same posies. Twin columns, linked by a clock pointing to 11:25, was used by a New Hampshire watercolor artist named J. Forbes who was responsible for "The Family of Mr. Chester and Mrs. Achsah Barrett" circa 1816 and a second watercolor register executed in 1824.[16]

Chain Designs

Another set of registers involves the use of circles, chains, or links that symbolized the unity of the family. Chain images had long been used in religious song texts. A verse from Isaac Watts's *Horae Lyricae* (1743) stipulates the unbroken nature of family unity even after death: "Yet never let our Hearts divide, / Nor Death dissolve the Chain: / For Love and Joy were once ally'd, / And must be joined again."[17] Chains were also present in political emblems and cartoons especially in regard to the united opposition against British rule. During the Federal period, Amos Doolittle's 1789 *Display of the United States of America*[18] arranged thirteen interlinked chain segments to symbolize the new country, each identified

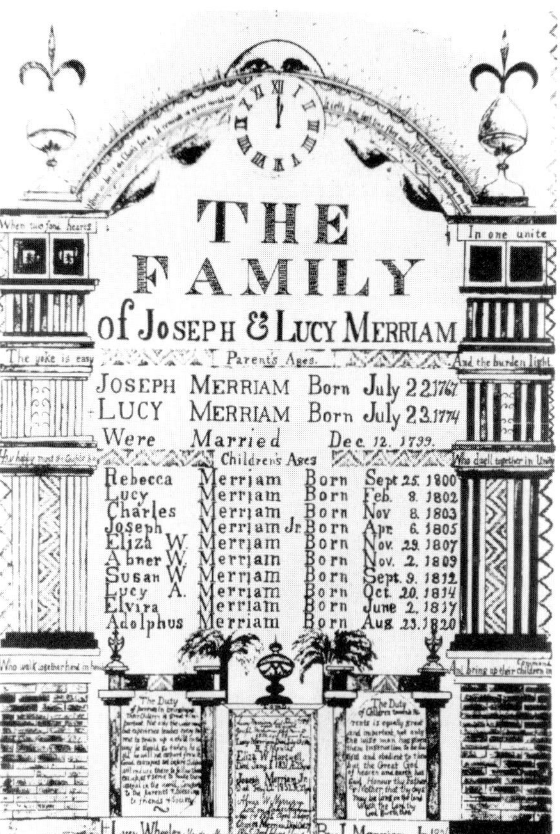

Figure 6 Family record. Joseph Merriam and Lucy Wheeler. Concord, Massachusetts. "By J. Merriam, Jr 1826." Watercolor. Location unknown. Courtesy of Concord Free Public Library.

with its coat of arms; within the circle was an engraving of George Washington. In a related 1791 ink and watercolor piece, Oliver Kendall, a schoolchild in Sterling, Massachusetts, drew a thirteen-linked chain of states that surrounds "Liberty" (an anthropomorphic sun) and a verse.[19]

In genealogical pieces tangent circles and chains represented the indissoluble links between family members. Sometimes variations in typography indicated differences in generations. The Root family record (*Figure 7*, see *checklist 19* on p. 276) documenting the 1788 marriage of Ezekiel Root and Cynthia Cole in Farmington, Connecticut, uses two tiers of touching circles. The first tier depicts the marriage of the father and mother; the second, their six children. Individual letters are decorated according to use. Flowers almost obscure the title "Genealogy." Gothic script and large circles are reserved for the parents. Plain uppercase letters and smaller circles are set aside for the children. The unity of the family is conveyed by a single line that touches all of the circles. The Root genealogy seems to have been a writing curriculum school exercise. But the oldest child, Horace, was eleven in 1798, and the use of several scripts again suggests the artist was a calligrapher or writing clerk.

More commonly, however, chains were usually represented in circles or ovals. In an embroidered family register made in 1807, twelve-year-old Sally Dwight Wells surrounded a central domestic scene with twelve members of her family in Hatfield, Massachusetts, each identified by his or her name inscribed in an enclosed circle (*Figure 8*, see *checklist 20* on p. 276). Her grandparents fill the top circles; her father, Moses Wells, on the right, and her mother, Abigail (Dwight) Wells, on the left, occupy the middle. On the bottom are inscribed circles to her three siblings and an aunt, Dorcas Dwight. Two additional circles surround her own name. Later chains (see *checklist 21 through 25* on p. 276) were more precise and reflected a shared sense that a link was unbound at death only temporarily, to be "reunited" in the afterlife. An embroidered family record signed by Polly Giles of Groton, Massachusetts, uses fourteen rings to connect the members of the family of Deacon John Giles, his first and second wives, and his nine children, four of whom were lost in an epidemic that just preceded her own birth in 1801. The names are positioned sequentially under an archway of two columns. A version of this design, common during the 1830s and 1840s, sometimes added an image of a church, school, or home in the space enclosed by the links. An 1846 watercolor by Emeline Newcombe (Quincy South School) has in the center a colonnaded porch and belltower of Quincy's First Parish church. The chain register for the Parker/Clark family, done at the Medfield School, Medfield, Massachusetts, by Frances D. Parker in 1854, interlocked the links between the husband at the top of the chain and the wife at the bottom (*Figure 9*). In the oval within is a finely executed house, possibly the school building or the Parker home.[20]

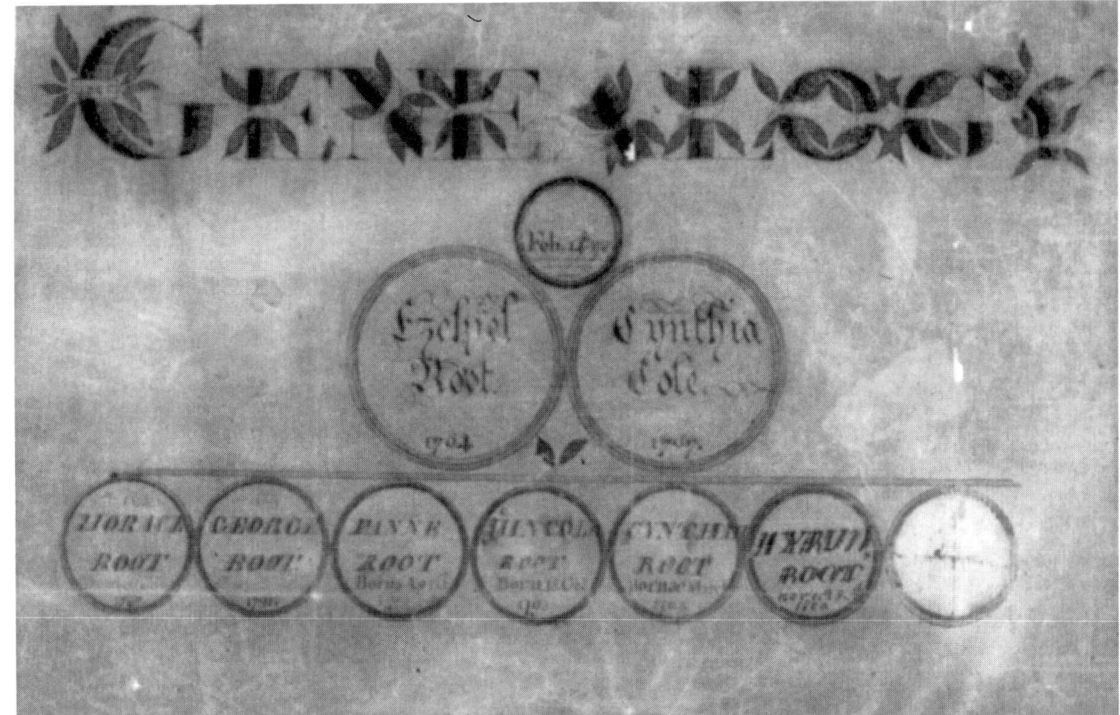

Figure 7 Family record. Ezekiel Root and Cynthia Cole. Farmington, Connecticut. Watercolor, 9 × 11 inches. The National Archives and Records Administration.

In some cases the chain imagery was worked around the special circumstances of marriage. John Howe prepared a family record in 1803 of the double marriage of the Howe and Richardson families of Boston[21] in which one pair of siblings married a second pair of siblings (see *checklist 26* on p. 276). An inner chain represented the joining of James Howe and Susan Richardson, on the one hand, and of Jane Howe and John Richardson, on the other. An outer chain represented the seventeen new members in the family made up of the combined offspring of both pairs of siblings. Those on the left were Howes; those on the right were Richardsons.

Heart Emblems

Two icons lay at the center of the genealogical emblemism in eighteenth- and early-nineteenth-century New England. Together, or in combination with other symbols, the heart and the tree were the most common devices used to express the art of family. The heart, especially a joining or superimposition of two or more hearts, is virtually as old and universal as Western civilization[22] and was intermingled with a conceit commonly used in love poetry of the period.[23] The symbol had only recently emerged from its medieval role as a devotional image of Christian life. Engravers and artists in Europe had previously been under a proscription not to use the image, but it was now being applied to newer roles in funereal and popular art. In New England the heart icon entered the repertory of Boston gravestone makers at the end of the seventeenth century. In Plymouth County, Massachusetts, heart-adorned spirits and heart-shaped spirits, often in the form of skulls with heart-shaped mouths, became an iconographic standard in the area after 1710. Some carvers in Plymouth County, such as Seth Tinkham, of Middleborough, added features to a heart-shaped image; others simply drew winged hearts instead of winged

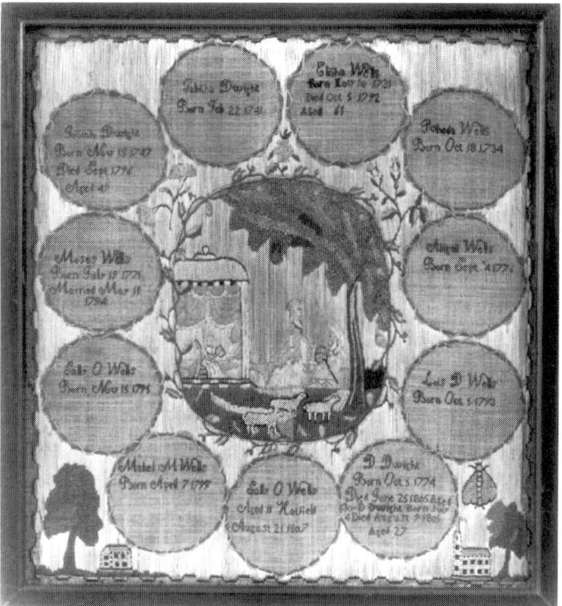

Figure 8 Family register. Moses Wells and Abigail Dwight. Sally D. Wells. Hatfield, Massachusetts, 1807. Embroidery. Courtesy of Historic Deerfield. *Photograph by Amanda Merullo.*

skulls.[24] Elsewhere carvers added hearts as borders, as wings, or they framed the released spirit between a pair of hearts. Hearts entered into the work of at least one unknown carver in Worcester County, Massachusetts, who engraved a pair of such hearts (side by side) on a stone in Rutland, Massachusetts (*Figure 10*).[25] In all these roles the heart icon acted as an image of religious "grace" or everlasting life.

By the time the heart icon had passed into New England's genealogical artwork in the last quarter of the eighteenth century, it had acquired the more specific vernacular or popular meaning of love—the "heart" pierced by Cupid's arrow. Here the image is often seen as two adjacent or touching hearts, or a heart placed within another heart. They represent a union of two persons bonded in marriage as well as the larger idea of love and family cohesion. Only a few examples are actually known of what may have been a common symbol. The idea was expressed in an old valentine attributed to engraver Richard Brunton in the late eighteenth century: "The farther I fly, The faster we tye."[26] Two birds hold either end of a lover's knot; above them, an arrow transfixes a pair of adjacent hearts. The idea is expressed in an old posy transcribed on a family register made in eastern Massachusetts: "When two fond hearts / In one unite / The yoke is easy / The burden light."[27] Other examples are found on marriage furniture, such as the decorations on the so-called Hadley chests in the Connecticut River Valley,[28] or on silverwork presumably given as love-tokens. A 1722 silver patch box at the Museum of Fine Arts, Boston, is engraved with a winged cupid releasing an arrow into a heart. A second patch box made about 1760 and bearing the touchmark of Boston silversmith Zachariah Brigden, has an engraved rebus on the bottom: "If u Love me as i Love you / then i and u will make [a pair of hearts] (*Figure 10A*)."[29] Years later early American stencil scholar Janet Waring recorded its use in western Massachusetts: "In another old house in the first settlement of Tyringham are two hearts cut in the upper panels of the parlor door, which are definitely recorded as having marked the coming of a bride."[30]

Some of the most spectacular heart compositions on family records occur in the late eighteenth century when these images were first introduced in school coloring and writing exercises. "The Records of Joseph Camps Family of Newington in Wethersfield Town," made in Connecticut in 1787, consists of a large heart with ten hearts arranged within it (*Figure 11*, see *checklist 27* on p. 276). The two principal inner hearts represent Joseph Camp and his wife Anna Camp; the remaining hearts identify their eight children born from 1772 to 1790, including the young artist Anna Camp who was then in her fourteenth year. The result looks like a family burial plot of hearts. The one deceased member (an earlier Anna Camp) is marked by means of a coffin. The unifying element here is the larger enclosing heart which also presents a legend or field in which the main inscription is written. The piece may have been a school composition, although no others like it are known. It is so unusual that it may simply represent the spontaneous affection a fourteen-year-old child felt for her family.

A clearer idea of a schoolmaster's role in these early heart pieces is seen in several examples in eastern Essex County, Massachusetts, where hearts and hearts-within-hearts were employed by young

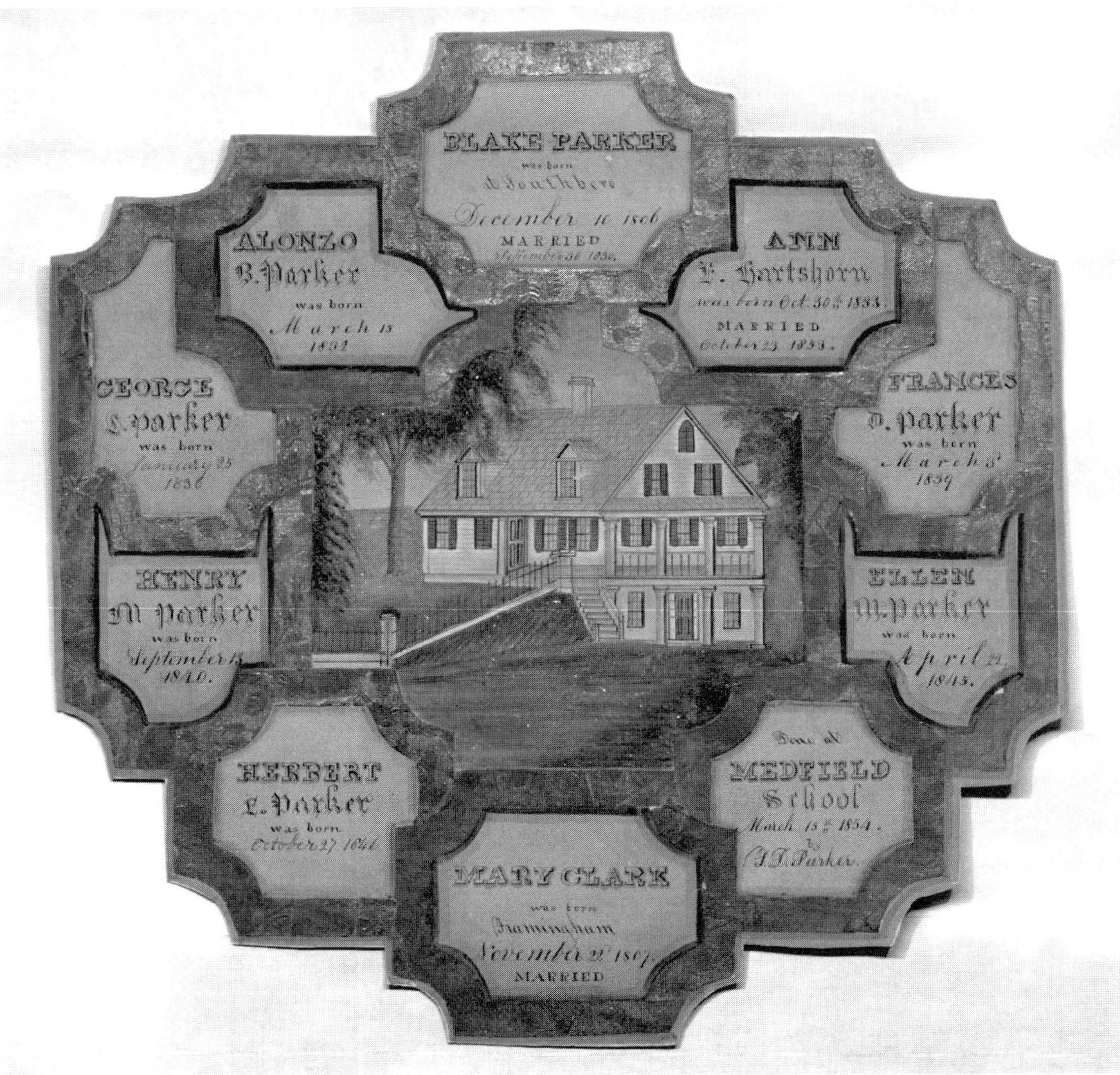

Figure 9 Family register. Blake Parker and Mary Clark. "Done at Medfield School March 15 1854 F. D. Parker." Watercolor. New England Historic Genealogical Society.

scholars who signed their work and in one case by a student who also identified his school and teacher (see *checklist 28 through 30* on p. 277). In 1809 fourteen-year-old Daniel Moody Lankester, of Newbury, Massachusetts, made and signed a watercolor register (*Figure 12*) he called "A Genealogical Family Piece." It traces the two marriages of Daniel Dodge (1745–1835) of Newbury, first to Martha Moody (1735–1798) and second to Mary (Kimball) Dudley (1746–1813). The first marriage produced five children of whom three survived; the second marriage produced none. A large encompassing heart was punctuated in the center by a red inner heart. The children's names are inscribed on evenly spaced half-circles appearing to stick up out of the ground. The effect again almost imitates gravestones. A line at the bottom of the piece identifies it as "Newbury East School, B. H. Cheever," presumably the name of the teacher. Unclear is Daniel Moody Lankester's relationship to the principal, Daniel Dodge; possibly he was a relative of Dodge's first wife, Martha Moody.

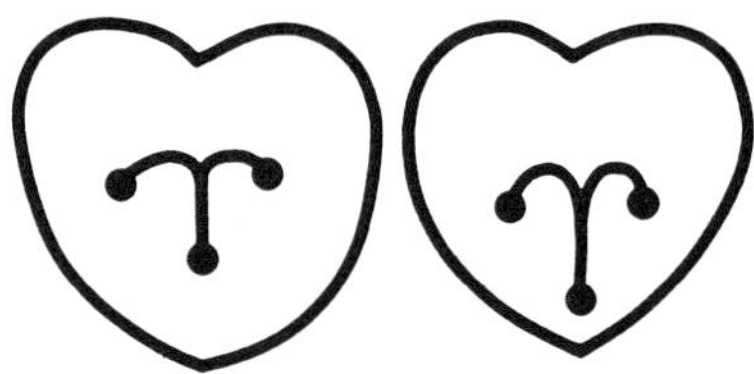

Figure 10 Gravestone with paired heart-faces. Carver unknown. Rutland, Massachusetts, 1749.

At least two other family registers dated 1814 and 1816 were probably done at the Newbury East School and probably under the same teacher. Both of these are signed by Atkinson Stanwood of Newbury. Both use the same half-circle markers for identifying family names; in cases of decease, a line below the name gives the year of death. The first, "Taken by Atkinson Stanwood Aet 13 Feby 25th 1814," lists the marriages of Joseph Stanwood (1764–1833), a Newburyport tallow chandler, to Eunice Marchant, Sarah Dodge, and Ruth Burnham (*Figure 13*). The piece indicates generations by color and by lines. Four gold-backed half-circles indicate the parents; nine blue-backed half-circles indicate the one child issued from the first marriage and eight children from the second, including the youngest, Atkinson (born 1801). Two large coffins near the bottom indicate the deaths of Atkinson's mother and stepmother; a smaller coffin identifies the death of two-year-old John Stanwood. A second register, this one again signed by "Atkinson Stanwood, Newburyport, June 7, 1816," represents the same family (*Figure 14*). The register provides the same information in a large heart similar but not identical to the one by Lankester.[31] Again, the regular placing of the half-circles suggests a genealogical or family plot with all members of the family occupying adjacent places positioned side by side in the order of their precedence.

The regimentation of all three registers from the East School in Newbury seems to follow a local formula or one initiated by schoolmaster B. H. Cheever. However, the lining up of progeny by age or rank, which is present in many manuscript family registers in New England, may have had a wider currency. All three Newbury pieces have much in common with the gravestone attributed to a member of the Pratt family[32] of Abington, Massachusetts, that was carved for Mrs. Sarah Pratt of nearby South Hingham, who died 22 October 1761 in the one hundred first year of her age and with ". . . a numerous posterity running to the 5th generation in numbers 187." Behind her own image are seventeen members of those of her posterity, half hidden in four evenly-spaced rows (*Figure 15*).[33]

Over time, touching and multiple heart images became an established graphic convention of professional family record artists working in watercolor in New England in the nineteenth century. About three unidentified artists (all are known for their use of pillared architectural motifs) typically used single hearts or multiples of hearts under the column headed "Marriages."[34] Two were active in Vermont and the third in Maine. Another in eastern New England, now called the "Heart and Hand"

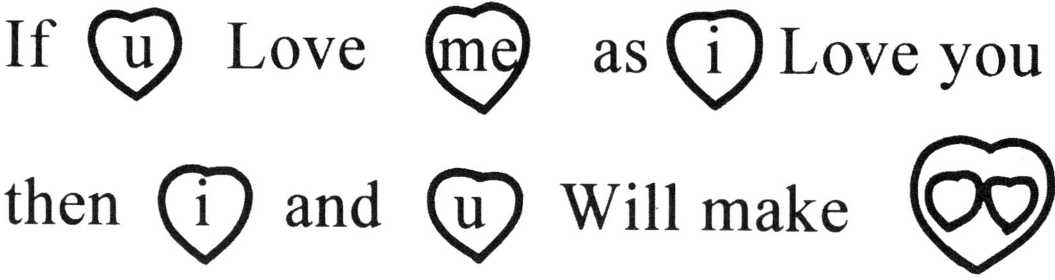

Figure 10A Rebus transcribed from the underside of a patch box. Zachariah Brigden. Boston, circa 1760. Location unknown.

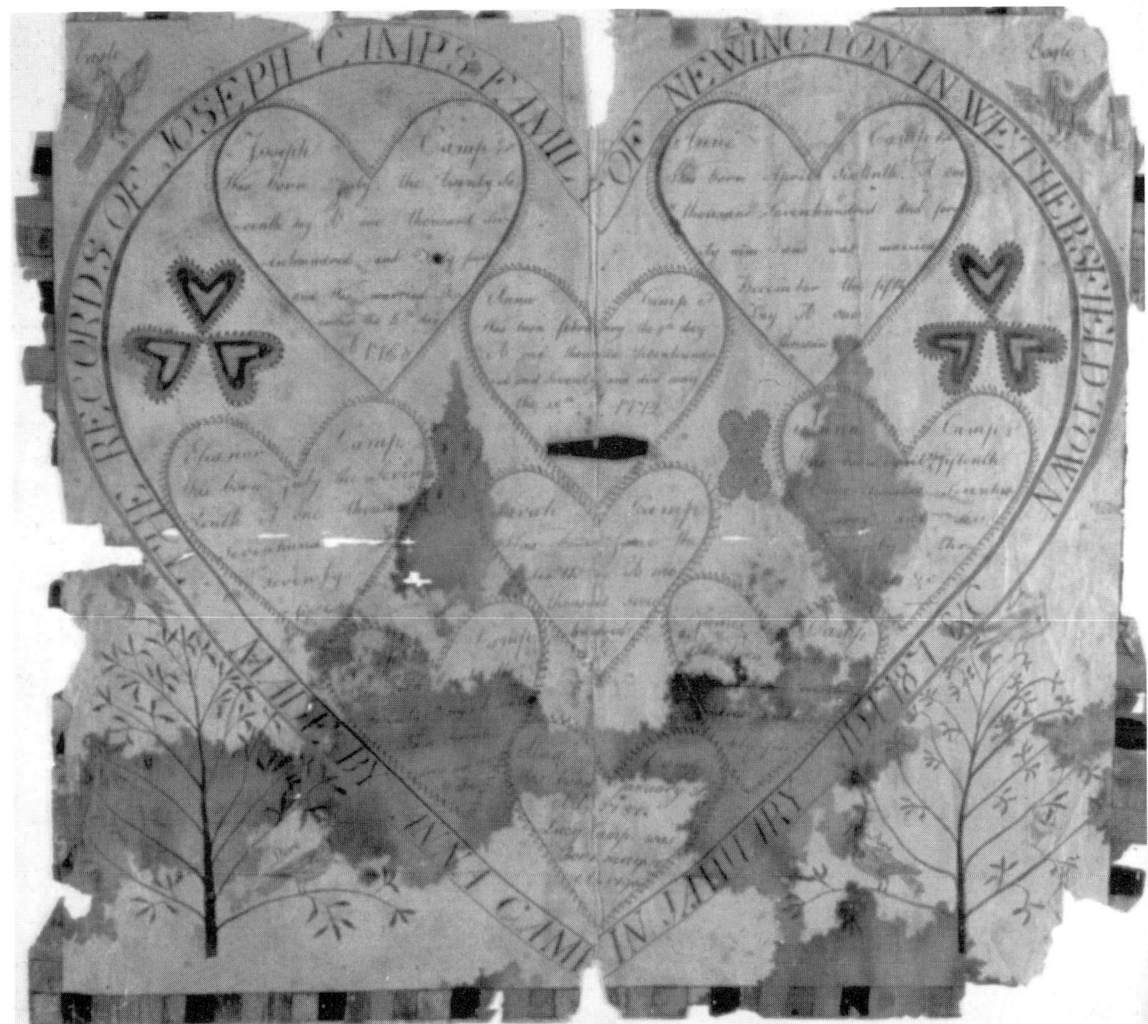

Figure 11 Family register. Joseph Camp and Anna Camp. "Made by Anna Camp in January AD 1787." Newington, Connecticut. Watercolor and ink, 13 × 14 inches. Courtesy of Newington Historical Society and Trust, Inc.

artist, frequently combined hearts and hands in the same images.[35]

Tree Emblems

A second core icon was the tree. Long associated with religious and genealogical meaning,[36] the family "tree" and its related "roots," "branches," and "fruits" have been synonymous for bloodlines in Western culture. First cited in English literature in the fourteenth century,[37] genealogical trees have remained in folk usage in the region's speech as well as in associated iconographic, literary, and decorative traditions that go back six centuries and perhaps earlier. As the "Tree of Life," or symbol of immortality, the term has an Old Testament origin.[38] In the verse of John Milton it appeared in the garden of Eden, "High, eminent [and] blooming ambrosial fruit."[39] Tree imagery repeatedly entered into the devotional verse of the Reverend Edward Taylor (1642–1729) of Westfield, Massachusetts. In his poetry the tree of life was hung with clusters "Of lovely fruits, and Flowers

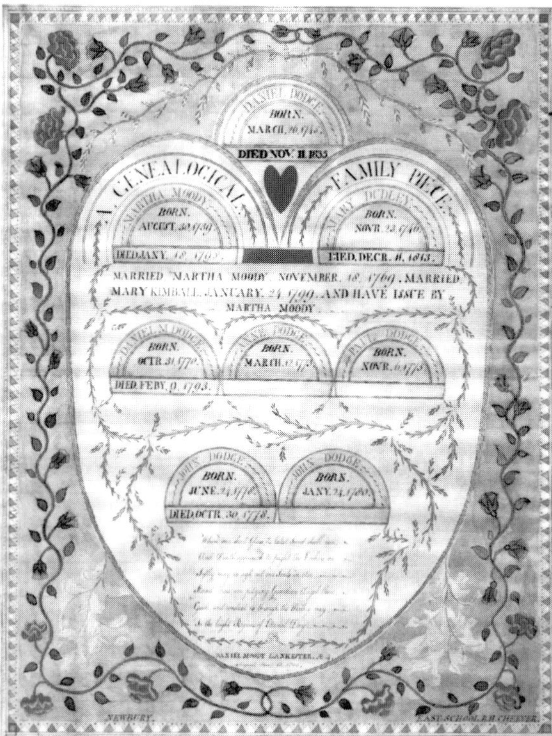

Figure 12 Family register. Daniel Dodge and Martha Moody. Daniel Dodge and Mary Kimball. "Daniel Moody Lankester, Newbury East School, B. H. Cheever." Newbury, Massachusetts, 1809. Watercolor. New England Historic Genealogical Society.

more sweet than spice / [which] Bend down to us and doe out shine the sun." Drawing on his experience with orchard cultivation, Taylor develops the tree metaphor with supporting images that in some instances parallel those found on family records. He asks, for example, to have "this Tree of Life" grafted within him so that he may bear "Living Fruits"; he compares himself to a "withred twig" that is "writh off by vice" and asks to be "grafft[ed]" back again to the stock.[40] Elsewhere, in a versed elegy commemorating the passing of Samuel Hooker of Farmington, Connecticut, Taylor says to his descendants:

> And as for you, his Buds, and Blossoms blown,
> Stems of his Root, his very Flesh and Bone.[41]

Entering into common written English as "the family tree" in the early part of the nineteenth century, even today it is part of our everyday language.[42]

Like hearts, tree images had widespread applications in early New England gravestone art, appearing in late-eighteenth- and early-nineteenth-century markers usually in the form of the spirit being separated from its supporting stem or roots. Images such as fallen flower blossoms, broken stems, and fallen trees served as emblems of mortality and were the visual equivalents of the period term "cut off," meaning to come to an untimely death.[43] As one contemporary epitaph writer observed, "Death . . . [is] a moving Flower / Cut down and withered in an hour."[44] On some gravestones, the hand of God (holding an axe) emerges from the clouds to lop off a tree,[45] leaving a nearby tree standing. On others, broken or lopped limbs serve to mark the arrival of death before its time. The four young sons of Appleton and Lydia (Goodrich) Holmes of East Glastonbury, Connecticut, who died literally within days of each other in February 1795, are portrayed on their stone by means of four broken branches connected to the tree.[46] Much more rarely, trees are added to the gravestone as a metaphor of descent. The most explicit (and brilliant) example of this is the thirteen-branched tree carved on the Park gravestone in Grafton, Vermont, depicting the thirteen children of Thomas and Rebecca Park (*Figure 16*). The head of each child is connected by an extended branch to a central trunk. The image was cut in 1803 by the stonecarver Moses Wright Jr. (1758–after 1807) of Rockingham, Vermont, who is known to have used at least some printed sources when composing his designs (such as a spread eagle).[47]

Unlike other genealogical symbols, tree designs reverse the positions of parents and their progeny. The trunk or roots at the bottom represent the original parents or family founders; the limbs and upper branches over them are the resulting offspring. A very early English expression of the idea is found in a 1590 heraldic family tree tracing the ancestry of John, Lord Lumley, which grows in a representative mound of earth. (It is similar to those on eighteenth-century Nantucket compositions.)[48] Here the various lines are composed by chains of twenty-five family crests which branch out from the original trunk. This format, with the tree rooted firmly in the ground, became a common genealogical document in early-nineteenth-century New England and the

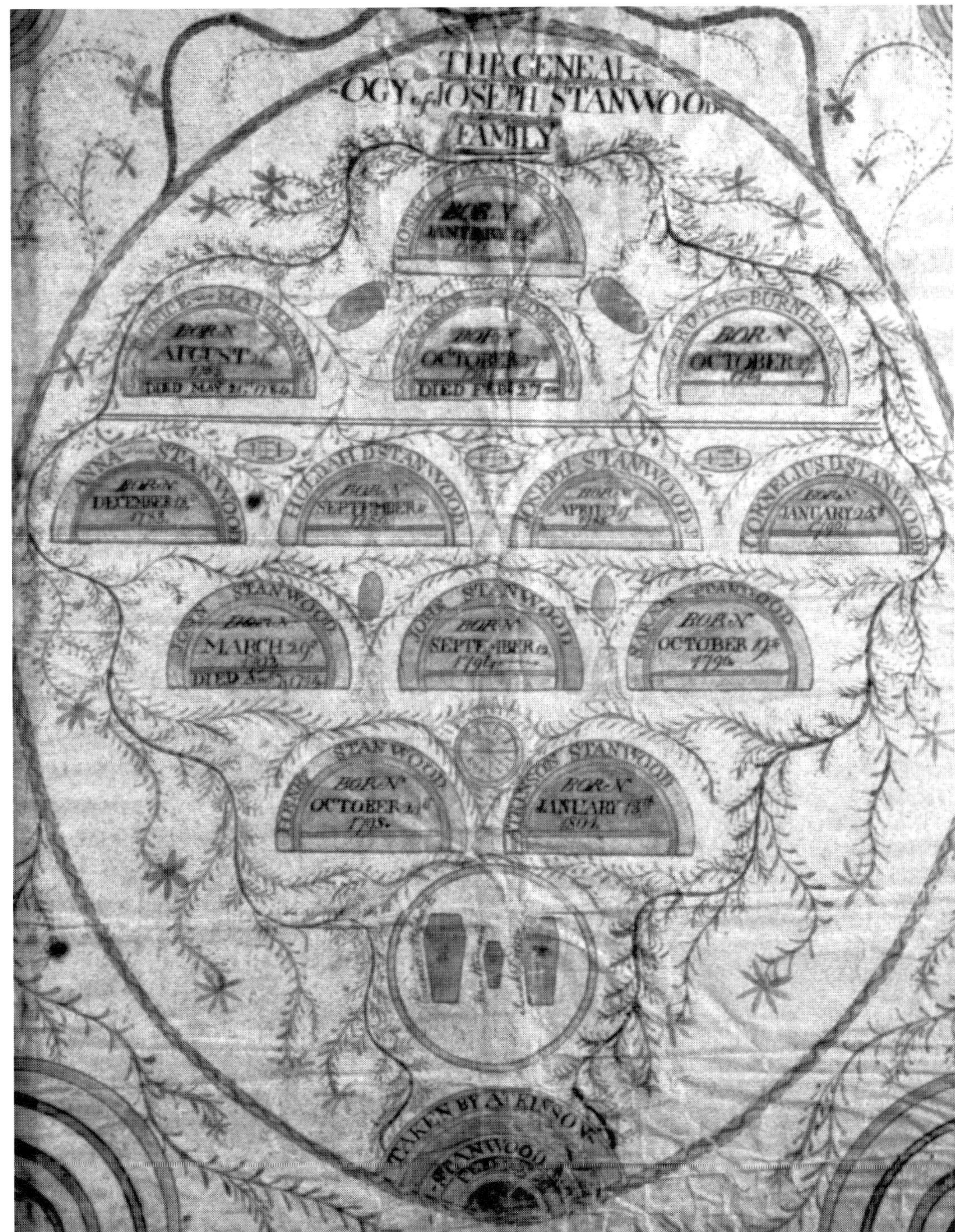

Figure 13 Family register. Joseph Stanwood and Eunice Marchant; Joseph Stanwood and Sarah Dodge; Joseph Stanwood and Ruth Burnham. "Taken by Atkinson Stanwood Aet 13 Feby 25th 1814." Newbury, Massachusetts. Watercolor, 15 × 12 inches. Historical Society of Old Newbury.

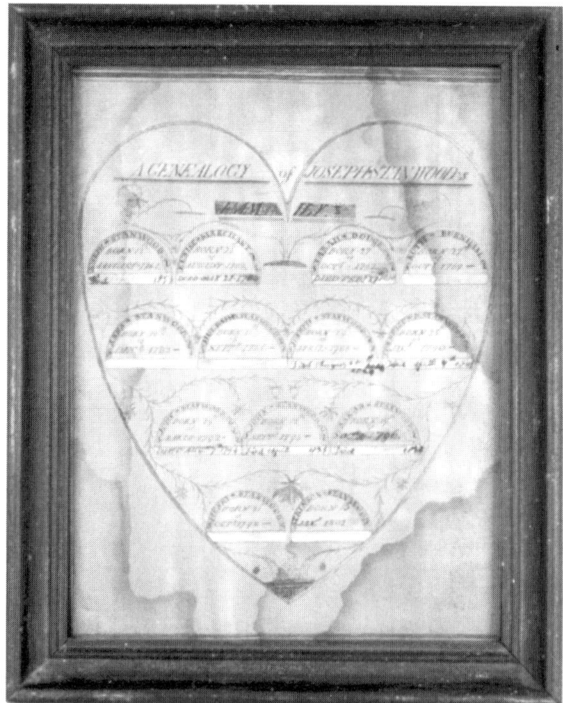

Figure 14 Family register. Joseph Stanwood and Eunice Marchant; Joseph Stanwood and Sarah Dodge; Joseph Stanwood and Ruth Burnham. "Atkinson Stanwood, Newburyport, June 7, 1816." Newbury, Massachusetts. Watercolor, 10 × 8 inches. Courtesy of the Society for the Preservation of New England Antiquities.

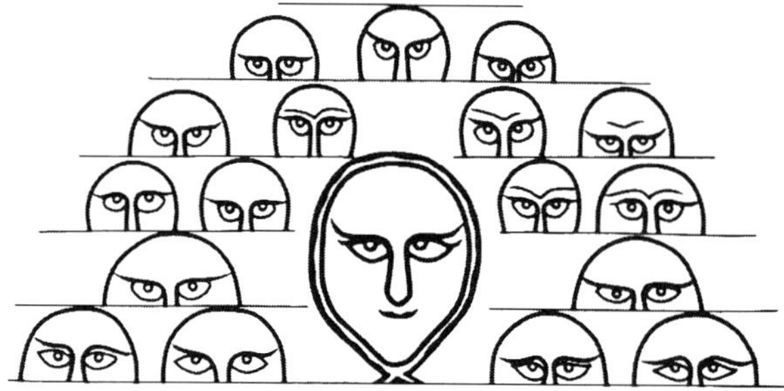

Figure 15 Gravestone. Attributed to Pratt family, Abington, Massachusetts. South Hingham, Massachusetts, 1761.

model for the numerous lithographed versions after 1850.[49] Joseph S. Russell, of New Bedford, Massachusetts, made up such a tree for the Russell/Shoemaker family in 1838 (see *checklist 35* on p. 277). Beginning with his ancestor Hugh Lowndes (born in England in 1650), through his son James Lowndes, his grandson Joseph Lowndes, his great-granddaughter Elizabeth Shoemaker, and great-great-granddaughter Sarah Russell, he traced five generations. Each generation was indicated by a new branch on the tree. Brown ink identified deceased members, whereas "branches painted green were then living."

At times this idea was carried to unprecedented and detailed lengths. One such document is the large (thirty-eight by twenty-eight inches) manuscript tree made out in the 1820s for the family of Moses Emery (1715–1789) and Lydia Emery (1717–1800) of Newbury, Massachusetts (*Figure 17*, see *checklist 36* on p. 277). The tree has ten main branches, one for each of their ten children, whose names (and spouses) are inscribed like ornaments on carefully made circles or fruits. Each of the ten branches in turn is set off by the marriages of about forty grandchildren and their spouses in their own circles. Still smaller branches name about 100 great-grandchildren and about six great-great-grandchildren. Altogether, 290 names appear on the document and about seventy-five marriage unions ranging over five generations between 1728 and about 1822. The genealogical grammar of the piece follows a distinctive pattern as well. The artist has blacked out the circles of deceased persons and has used red branches to indicate offspring without issue.

The Emery family tree uses fruit-like circles for every name inscribed on the document. The precise origin of using articulated trees to represent children as fruits or flowers, however, is as hard to pin down graphically as it is linguistically. Again the practice is found early. Trees as conveyors of virtue and vice were part of a sixteenth- and seventeenth-century visual tradition in France.[50] In New England the idea that "Trees of Life bear fruits of love" was common in the language of early-nineteenth-century epitaphs."[51] It may also have been common in everyday language that is now lost. And the idea was in visual currency in North America at the beginning of the last quarter of the eighteenth century. An embroidered tree dated 1775 by an "unknown girl" illustrates a number of religious concepts (selection, faith, security).[52] In New England the idea occurs twice in John Norman's 1794 *Hieroglyphic Bible*, a picture book with appropriate engravings to teach

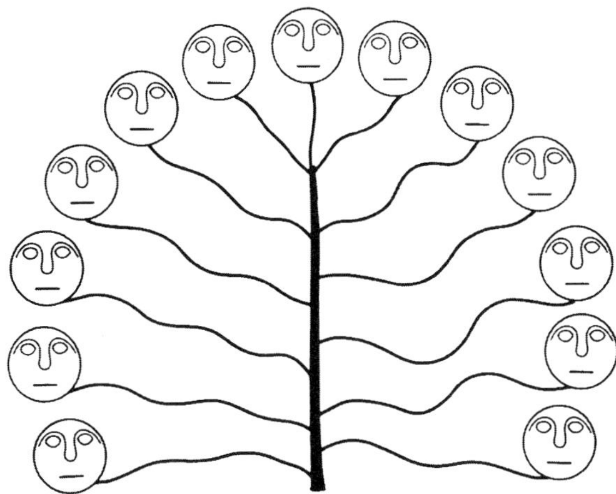

Figure 16 Gravestone. Moses Wright Jr., Rockingham, Vermont. Grafton, Vermont, 1803.

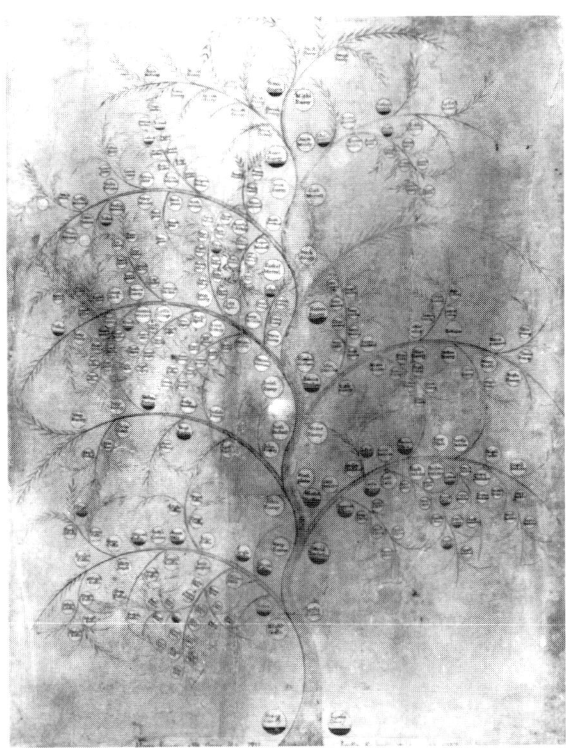

Figure 17 Family tree. Moses Emery and Lydia Emery. Maker unknown. Newbury, Massachusetts, circa 1820. Ink and watercolor, 23 × 17 inches. Courtesy of Gregory H. Laing.

biblical stories. First is an image of *Hieroglyphicks of a Christian*, which shows a tree bearing fruits labeled with concepts such as "Joy," "Peace," and "Humility" leading to "Grace" above the tree. A second illustration, titled *Hieroglyphics of the Natural Man*, shows an appropriately labeled leafless and barren tree leading up to "Wrath."[53] The printed record continued this concept well into the nineteenth century: an 1870 lithographed "Family Record" by G. F. Short had an articulated tree named with attributes (Piety, Economy, Order, Patience) with spaces below the tree to add photographic images.[54]

Regardless of its actual origins, the variety of tree types and tree formats suggests that makers of family registers were drawing on a common idea that circulated widely in New England and the American Northeast. Some variations even have a differing grammar or logic. For example, a tree (*Figure 18*, see *checklist 37* on p. 277) marking the circa 1811 union of Ephraim H. Gilson (b. 1787) and Lydia Barrett (b. 1790) has the two parents named on the lowest tier of apples; above them are their seven children born in Townsend, Massachusetts, between 1812 and 1833. This seems to have been a naive version of the idea; it may have been done in imitation of another family register. More commonly the parents are associated specifically with the roots. The family tree (see *checklist 38* on p. 277) marking the two marriages of Levi Butterfield to Jarusha (m. 1781) and then Isabela Comins (m. 1787) has a prominent legend near the base: "This tree is call'd a Tree of Life because it contains the fruites of the three [persons] mentioned at the roots of this tree." The Butterfield/Comins record dates to the mid-nineteenth century, probably composed by a former New England family after its arrival in Jefferson County, New York. This, too, may be a one-of-a-kind format expressing what was a widely held but nevertheless largely inarticulate idea.

A more formal or schooled version of a genealogical tree was taught at Mrs. Gill's Academy in West Cambridge, now the town of Arlington, Massachusetts. Four family records are known from this school, all done between 1809 and 1821 and all by young women in their early teens living in West Cambridge (see *checklist 39 through 42* on pp. 277–78). Three of these are watercolors, including a record of the family of Daniel Reed and Priscilla Wyman, a memorial by Sophronia Fessenden (*Figure 19*), and a register of the marriage of John Tufts and Rebecah Cutler. A fourth in this series is an embroidery by Lydia Russell. All

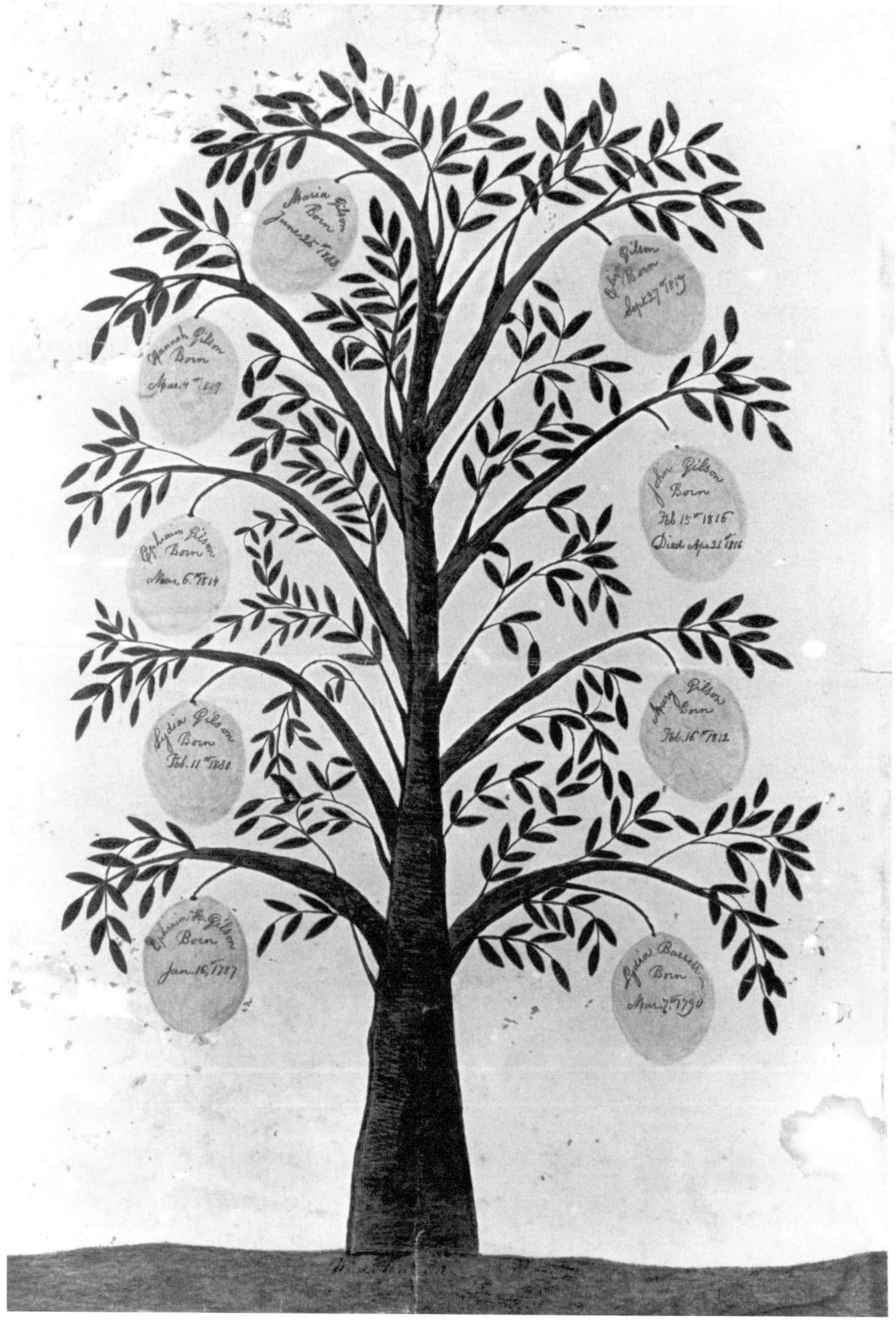

Figure 18 Family tree. Ephraim H. Gilson and Lydia Barrett. Townsend, Massachusetts, circa 1833. Watercolor. Courtesy of the Nantucket Historical Association.

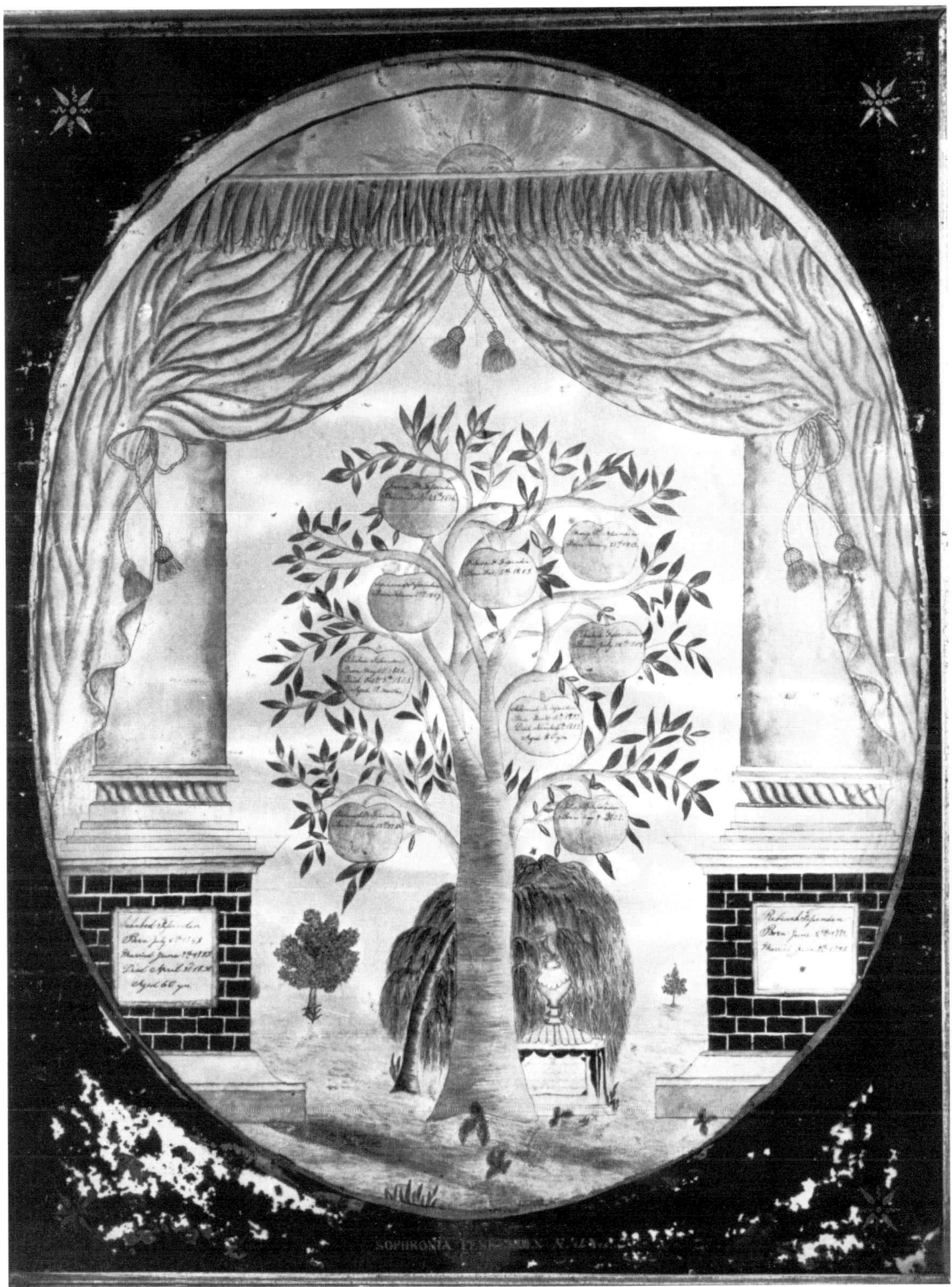

Figure 19 Family register. Ichabod Fessenden and Rebeccah Munroe. "Sophronia Fessenden AE 14 Yrs." West Cambridge, Massachusetts, 1821. Watercolor. Private collection.

have an identical fruit-bearing apple tree enclosed within an arcade or bower which is supported on pedestals and columns. The parents are named on the two flanking column bases; children are shown as named apples in the tree. Although some details are different, all of the watercolors seem to have been copied after the same original. Two of the watercolors (Reed/Wyman and Tufts/Cutler) are almost exactly alike. This may explain the "pin pricks" seen by the auction cataloguer of the Tufts example,[55] possibly evidence that it was used to pinpoint the design of another copy.

Trees and Paired Hearts

The family registers that speak most directly to the intertwining of schooled, professional, and folk origins are those that combine trees (or a pair of vines) growing from a pair of touching hearts. Seventy-one of these have been identified with known New England histories. Most originate in five areas of eastern and southeastern Massachusetts and interior New Hampshire (*Figure 19A*). First is an embroidered school-taught group originating in eastern Middlesex County. Second are unrelated embroidered and watercolor groups originating in northern and western Middlesex County and in adjacent towns in southern New Hampshire. A third group consists of watercolor pieces made in Gloucester's Fifth or Sandy Bay parish (now the town of Rockport, Massachusetts). A fourth group are watercolors in the Pittsfield and Gilmanton area in central New Hampshire. And a fifth group are watercolor registers made on Nantucket Island and Martha's Vineyard. These pieces intersect New England society at several social and occupational levels. Two of these are fishing or whaling communities; one is the location of an élite finishing school for rural eastern Massachusetts families; the remaining two are "receiver" communities in Massachusetts and New Hampshire in part settled by former residents from the first three.

The pieces most representative of refined or academic culture are fourteen almost identical genealogical samplers that record marriages in a group of contiguous towns in Middlesex County centering in Lexington, Waltham, and Watertown, Massachusetts (see *checklist 43 through 56* on pp. 278–79). The

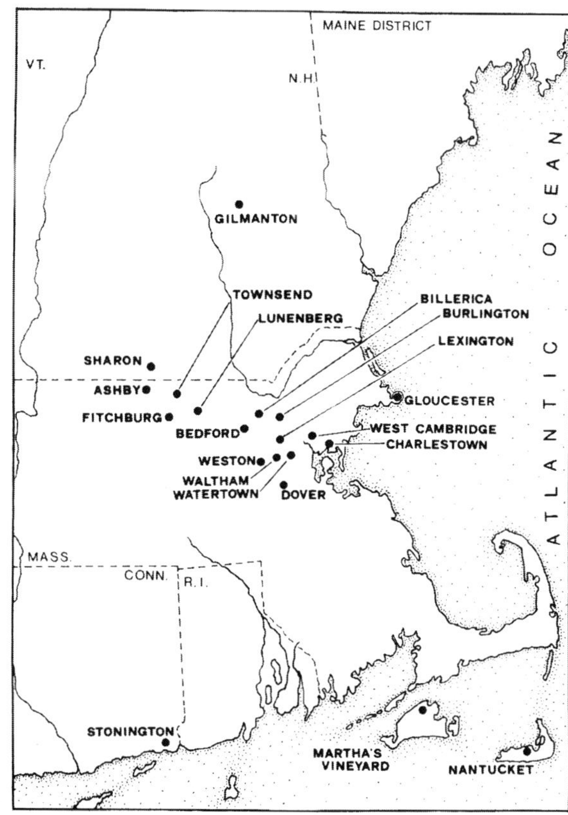

Figure 19A Location of seventy-one New England family records using heart-and-tree or hearts-and-vines compositions, circa 1790 to 1825. Map courtesy of the author.

compositions in these silk embroideries consist of shaded, fruit-bearing apple trees growing from a pair of overlapping hearts. An early example in this series is the unsigned record made for the 1773 marriage of David Townsend and Sarah Jenison, both of Watertown (*Figure 20*). If it is the work of the oldest daughter Sarah Townsend, born 1775, the piece may have been made as early as 1785 or 1790, but no evidence has yet been uncovered to confirm this date. Sparing in its use of decoration, the Townsend/Jenison embroidery is one of two in this group that have plain sawtooth borders; more important, it is the only one that has an earth/sky horizon line in the background. This may tie it more closely than the others to a hypothetical print source in which the paired hearts rise out of a representative mound of earth—the same representative earth that appears as a horizon line in some registers or as a symbolic mound

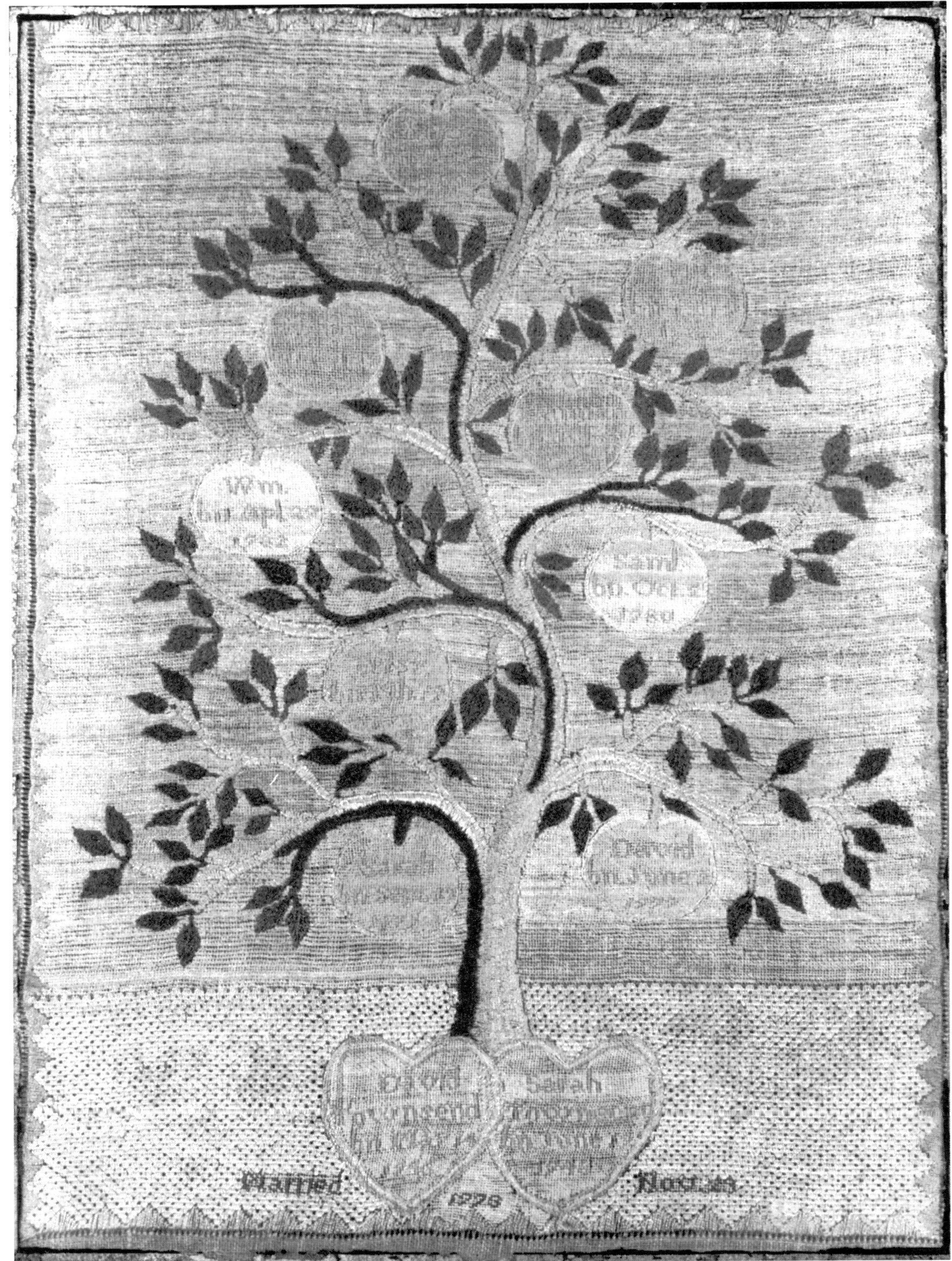

Figure 20 Family register. David Townsend and Sarah Jenison. Attributed to Sarah Townsend. Watertown, Massachusetts, circa 1790. Embroidery. Concord Museum. *Photograph courtesy of the Concord Museum, Concord, Massachusetts.*

in others. The remaining thirteen Middlesex County embroideries can be reliably dated to an eighteen-year period between 1807 and 1825 (*Figures 21 through 23*), with a maximum date span of twenty-nine years, 1800 to 1829. All are adorned with swags, vines, and other attenuated decorative work characteristic of needle embroidery in the Federal and early national periods; most are signed by children and grandchildren of prosperous landholding parents, some distinguished in the military and legal professions, who were married in the 1790s. Six of the fourteen marriages recorded in these embroideries took place in the town of Lexington; three, in Waltham; two, in Watertown; and one each, in nearby Bedford, Burlington, and Dover.

Because their known or presumed makers are school-aged girls, they are all believed to have been pupils of the same preceptress at one or perhaps several boarding schools or female academies located in Lexington, Watertown, Bedford, or Boston. This preceptress has not been identified. Because private academies frequently drew children from the same families, however, the transmission of the emblem was channeled through her along genealogical lines—in this instance principally among the Fiske, Stearns, Hagar, and Simonds families of Watertown and Lexington. For example, Martha Simonds and Elizabeth Simonds, who are the mothers cited in two of these genealogical pieces, were sisters; Grace Hagar and Susanna Hagar were also sisters and were also cousins and cousins by marriage to Sarah Stearns and Abraham Fiske. More important, as part of a formal curriculum of ornamental needlework that also included conventional alphabet samplers, mourning pictures, tableaux, and some heraldic devices, the embroideries represented a cultivated art form whose only real link to tradition was through the preceptress herself, either through her childhood memory or through a now-lost printed design source with which she was familiar.

Once framed and displayed in the parlors of their owners, academy-taught compositions may have inspired copies. A hearts-and-tree family record embroidered for the marriage of Oliver Whitney and Mercy Whitcomb of Lunenberg in central Middlesex County (*Figure 24*, see *checklist 57* on p. 279) is sufficiently different in style and execution from the fourteen Lexington-area embroideries to suggest it was sewn at home or at another school under the direction of a teacher who had a different model. More to the point, perhaps, is a circa 1815 to 1820 watercolor record of the 1800 marriage in Billerica of John Stearns and Mary Lane (*Figure 25*, see *checklist 58* on p. 279). In this instance there is a direct family connection to an embroidered piece. John Stearns was the brother of Sarah Stearns (1759–1807) whose marriage to Thaddeus Davis of Bedford in 1779 is the subject of a Lexington-type embroidery tentatively dated 1800. (Both were children of the Honorable Isaac Stearns of Billerica.)[56] If each record was made by children of the respective families, as was usually the case, the two pieces were made by cousins familiar with each other's households—the watercolor probably being derived from the embroidery. Reinforcing this link is the similarity of the branches or fronds surrounding the hearts of the Stearns/Lane watercolor to those on embroideries such as Wellington/Ball and Underwood/Munroe.[57]

At the same time, the discovery of unrelated hearts-and-tree emblems in northwestern Middlesex County and in adjoining towns of southern New Hampshire (see *checklist 59 through 64* on p. 279) suggests the existence of a collateral popular aesthetic. The watercolor composition recording the 1796 marriage in Fitchburg of Vashti Carter of Fitchburg and Asa Farwell of Harvard (*Figure 26*) is a fielded variant in which the paired hearts are fixed in a landscape that includes trees, flowers, and a house; ribbons binding the hearts identify the two marriage partners. Two other hearts-and-tree compositions in watercolor, both attributed to the same hand (*Figure 27*), record marriages that took place in or near Sharon, New Hampshire, among families who also owned farms and mills in neighboring New Ipswich—a town directly bordering Ashby and Townsend in northwestern Middlesex County. A fourth example is an embroidered recording of Hezekiah Morse of Sherborn and Sarah Bigelow of Weston. All four are naive compositions iconographically distinct from the academy-taught forms of the emblem. The Morse/Bigelow record lacks paired hearts and places succeeding generations on the same tree; the hearts in the Fitchburg record are fielded in a landscape; the trees in one of the

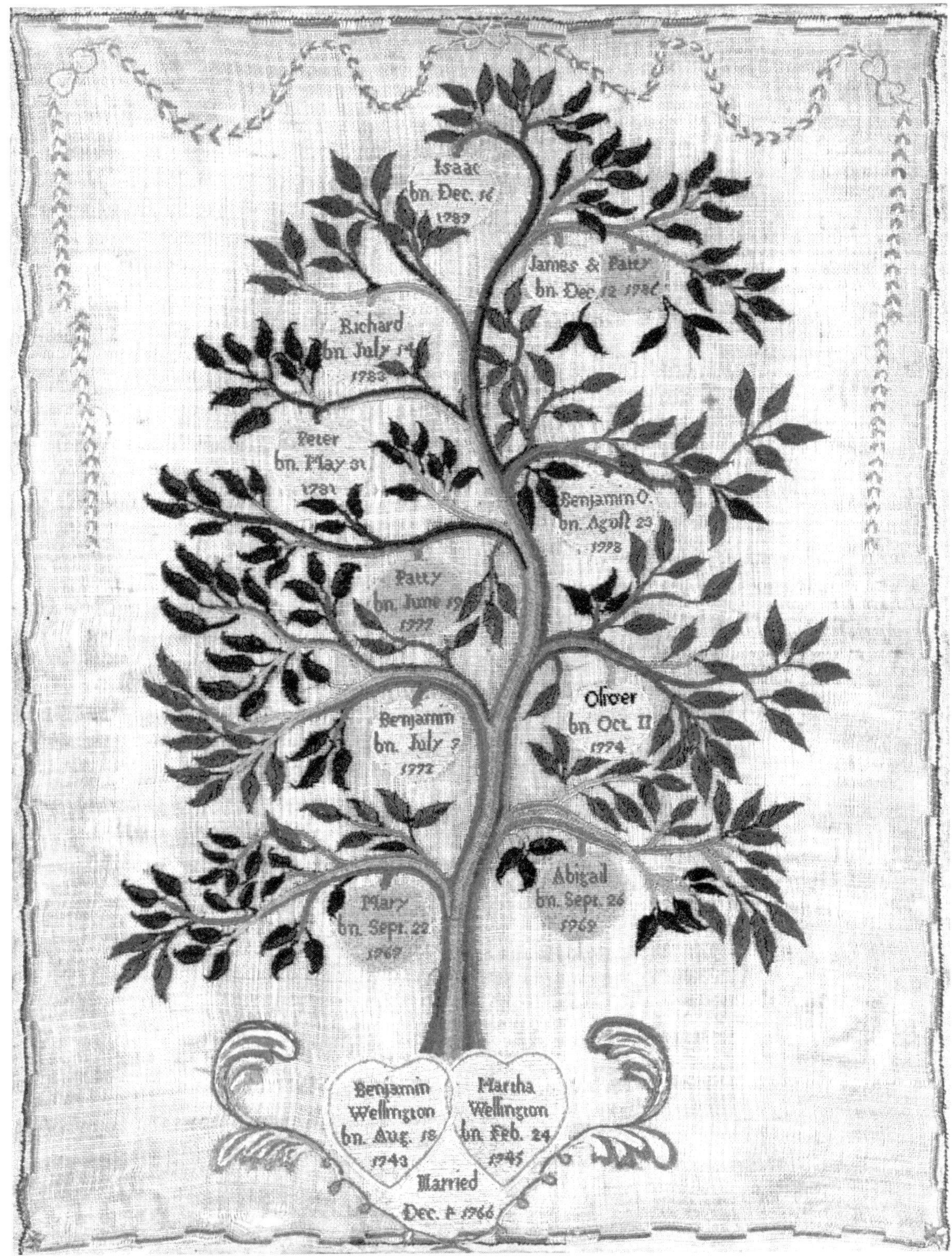

Figure 21 Family register. Benjamin Wellington and Martha Ball. Attributed to Patty Wellington. Lexington, Massachusetts, circa 1801. Embroidery. Private collection.

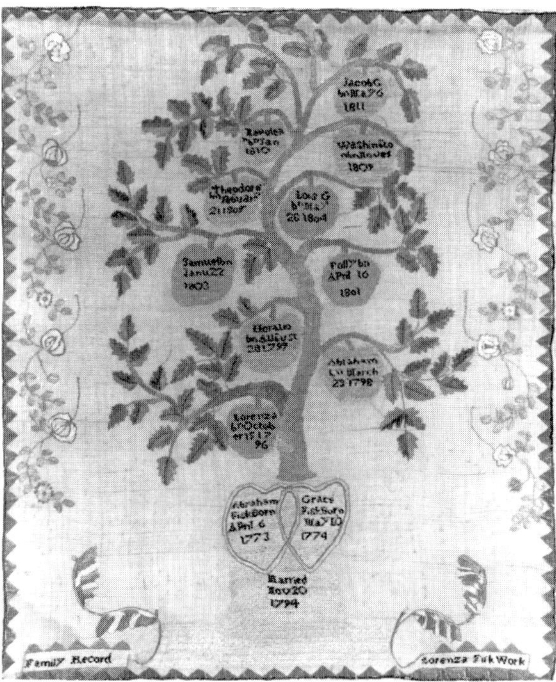

Figure 22 Family register. Abraham Fisk and Grace Hagar. "Lorenza Fisk Work." Waltham, Massachusetts, circa 1811. Embroidery. From the collections of the Lexington Historical Society.

Sharon records grows from a pot. Left unexplained is why an "idea" or taste was apparently transmitted along a small band of towns extending the length of Middlesex County to the southernmost tier of towns in adjoining New Hampshire to the apparent exclusion of other areas of New England and the American Northeast. No simple answer to this question is likely to be found, but any consideration of it must begin with kinship patterns in Lexington, Watertown, and Waltham as well as the gradual outward migration of families westward from Lexington and Watertown into central Middlesex County communities such as Townsend, Lunenberg, Fitchburg, and Ashby, and into south central New Hampshire.

William Saville of Gloucester, Massachusetts

The decorated family trees originating on Cape Ann in eastern Essex County (see *checklist 65 through 90* on pp. 279–81) are, by contrast, principally the work of three genealogical artists. William Saville (1770–1853) of Gloucester's Sandy Bay parish signed and dated ten known watercolor family records for Gloucester and Ipswich marriages in a twenty-year period from 1795 through 1815 (*Figures 28 through 30*). Saville was probably responsible for two additional unsigned watercolors, either as the artist or as instructor of the children who drew them; he also signed four pen and watercolor mourning pictures commemorating Cape Ann families. Joshua Pool Jr. (born 1787), of Gloucester, signed three watercolor records in 1805 (*Figure 31*), 1811, and 1820; and William Richardson, also probably of Gloucester, signed one in 1838. These three artists, and their imitators, are responsible for twenty-six documented family trees.

In a typical double composition signed by William Saville (Parsons/Lane, Parsons/Knights), the children of the first marriage are recorded in the fruits of the apple tree on the left, and those of the second marriage in those on the right (*Figure 32*). The trees are rooted in a landscape of dwelling houses, orchards, fences, and a harbor scene; a cluster of five upside-down hearts attached to the trunks of the tree identifies the marriage partners and records the date of each marriage. The signed watercolors of Joshua Pool Jr. depart from this formula only in minor ways. A watercolor record signed and dated by Pool in 1811 for the two marriages of Tammy Goss of Sandy Bay in Gloucester, whose first husband drowned in 1808, provides a scroll, rather than a third upside-down heart, in which to record the marriage date; a cut out tinfoil sun shines in the sky (*Figure 33*). William Richardson's signed but undated watercolor record for the 1817 marriage of Job Dennen and Lucy Gott of Sandy Bay, whose last child was born in 1838, has a similar scroll to record the date of the marriage. Richardson's drawing technique is also more attentive to detail: strap hinges appear on the barn windows; the house seems to be an actual structure rather than a generic type; and reef ties are visible on the sails of a fishing schooner in the harbor. An unsigned watercolor recording the marriage of Felix Doyle and Tamma Clark of Gloucester, married in 1816, has some but not all of these characteristics (*Figure 34*).

William Richardson has not been identified. Joshua Pool Jr. has been tentatively identified as a Gloucester resident, son of sea captain Mark Pool

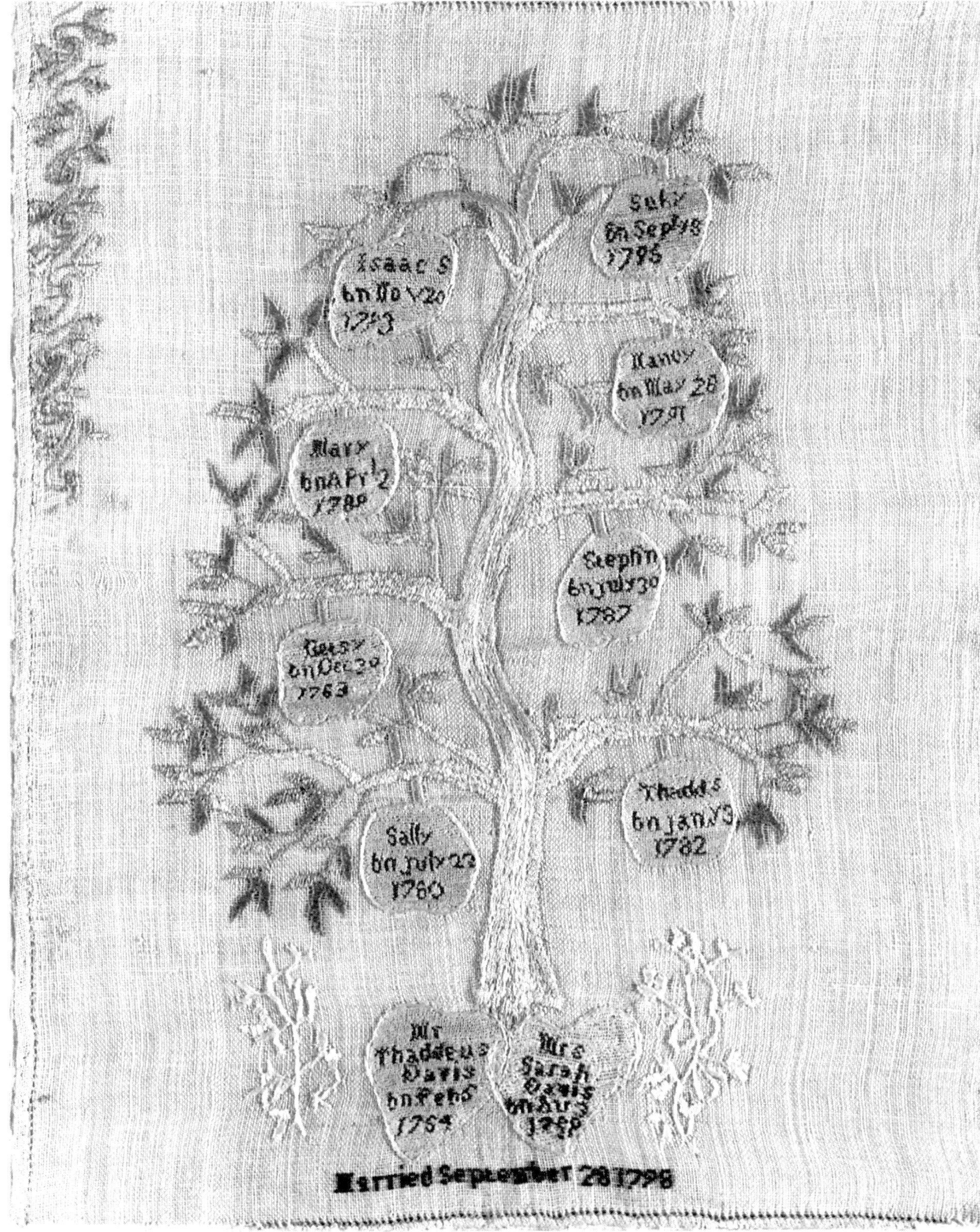

Figure 23 Family register. Thaddeus Davis and Sarah Stearns. Bedford, Massachusetts, circa 1800. Embroidery. Location unknown.

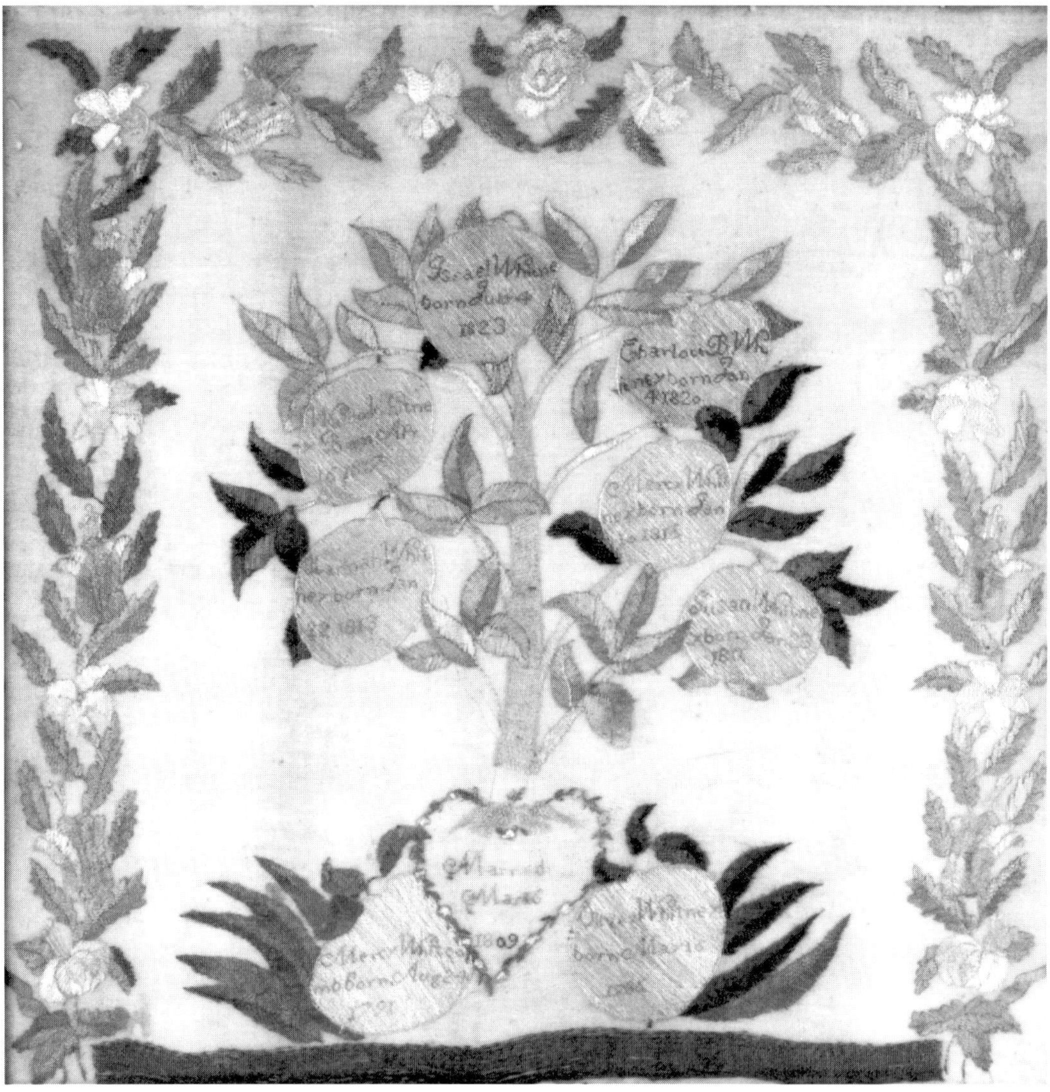

Figure 24 Family register. Oliver Whitney and Mercy Whitcomb. Lunenberg, Massachusetts, circa 1825. Embroidery. Private collection.

and Anna of Sandy Bay parish, who married Elisabeth Pool in 1808. Neither is known to have been related to the partners whose marriages they record. William Saville, however, was a local public figure. Son of Gloucester Custom House officer Jesse Saville (d. 1823), William Saville was the only one of six brothers who did not follow a maritime career. He was known for his skill in verse and served in 1808 as the chairman of the committee printing a new hymnbook for the Universalist Society in Gloucester; he is said to have written the final hymn in that volume. He also composed and circulated in 1828 a poem supporting a petition to save the meeting house of Gloucester First Parish from being destroyed—one of the earliest pleas for architectural preservation on record in New England. Saville was employed as town treasurer in Gloucester from 1809 through 1811; he surveyed and drew a map of the harbor at Sandy Bay in 1819; he served as town clerk in Gloucester from 1827 through 1849.

In the years from 1798 to 1803 Saville taught school in Gloucester's fifth or Sandy Bay parish. It was then that his watercolors—presumably drawn to supplement his tuition income—gained the attention of the

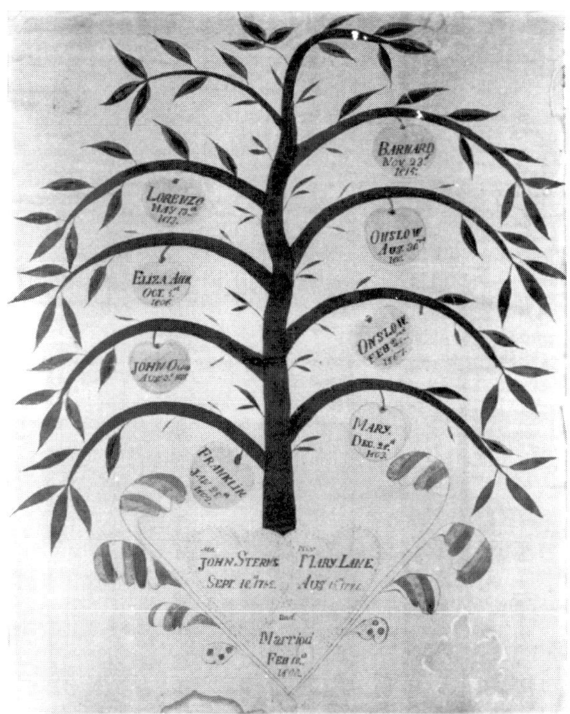

Figure 25 Family register. John Stearns and Mary Lane. Billerica, Massachusetts, circa 1815–1820. Watercolor. Location unknown.

Salem clergyman and diarist William Bentley who toured Cape Ann in a chaise in 1799. At the home of Rollins, a Sandy Bay trader and house carpenter, the Reverend Mr. Bentley found "infant specimens of taste, some monumental drawings in memory of some deceased Children, done by one Saville, a School master. . . ." The next day Bentley noted Saville had been hired to teach writing at a proposed academy in Gloucester but predicted that the school would fail.

That an "idea" rather than a printed source or pattern guided Saville is no more clear in Gloucester than it is in Middlesex County. Saville's use of upside-down hearts attached to the tree trunk and Pool's and Richardson's use of scrolls clearly distinguish the Cape Ann variants of the motif from the academy-taught embroideries. Additionally, the hearts are tacked down at the bottom of the tree in order to identify the "roots." (There may have been a local custom of attached cutaway hearts on the trees of young newly wedded couples.) At the same time, the Gloucester examples to some extent reflect local landscape and architectural features. Some of the dwellings illustrated in this group are, generically, the same half-houses described by William Bentley in his May 1799 tour of Sandy Bay whose "doors are commonly on the side so as to afford a good front room & back kitchen, with a bedroom back of the front entry."[58] Others were two-and-a-half-story Federal mansion houses, such as the one possibly lived in by James Dennison. Represented with some accuracy, however, was the home of Jabez Tarr, a half-house notable for its leanto roof and side chimney, still standing in Rockport on the south side of the road to East Gloucester,[59] and (probably) the home of Joseph Hicks whose damaged chimney was being repaired by a mason working with a level and an assistant on the ladder. One Gloucester record was even set in the appropriate season of the year: an unsigned watercolor of the 25 December 1816 marriage of Benjamin Colbey and Lois Tarr has as its background a winter landscape with leafless trees and a snow-blown road (*Figure 35*).

The concentration of Saville-type watercolors in Sandy Bay suggests that the practice of drawing family trees was introduced by William Saville in that parish in the 1790s. Joshua Pool and William Richardson may very well have been his pupils. This idea is supported by an unfilled (meaning the spaces are blank) hearts-and-trees exercise preserved in a local Tarr family "scrap book."[60] The book has other mathematical and drawing exercises indicative of a navigational school, and the drawing may have been a way of teaching pupils to use a compass and to apply watercolor paints. The further concentration among typical Sandy Bay surnames (principally Tarr, Dennison, Parsons, Lane, Clark, Robbins, and Pool) suggests the practice was transmitted, as it was in Middlesex County, along family lines. Patience Knights, for example, was the sister of Thomas Parsons Knights; Dorcas and Annis Robbins were sisters, both daughters of Thomas Robbins and Dorcas Thurston of Sandy Bay. At least one watercolor, presumably by Saville, records the family of the artist's older brother Thomas Saville.

Although the highly insular society of Cape Ann apparently prevented the spread of the practice of drawing family trees beyond a few dozen households, a secondary migration or networking seems to have

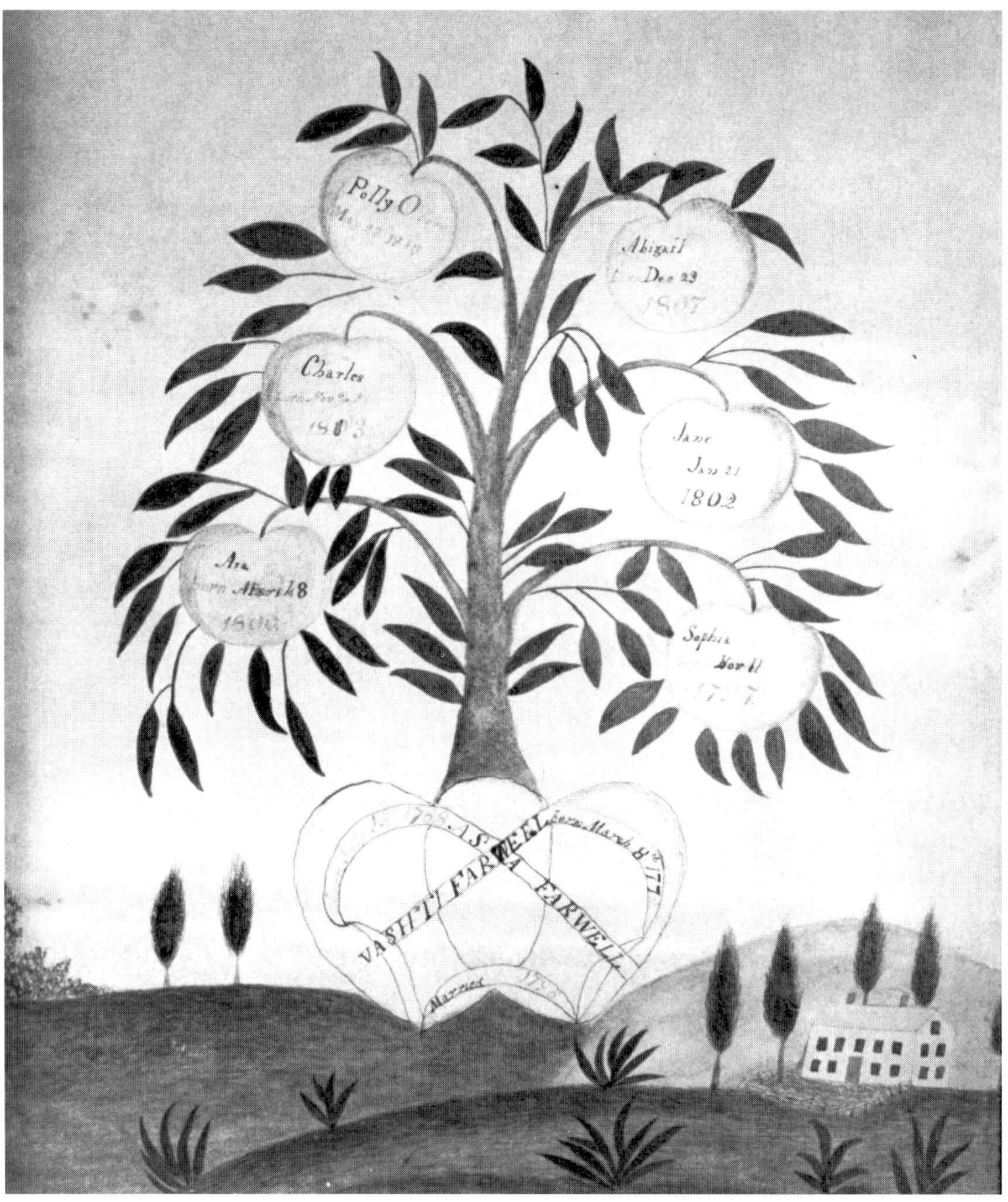

Figure 26 Family register. Asa Farwell and Vashti Carter. Fitchburg, Massachusetts, circa 1807. Watercolor. Courtesy of Pam Boynton.

taken place here as it did in Middlesex County. Except for one, all the marriage partners cited in the twenty-six Gloucester watercolors are known to have been native-born permanent residents of the immediate Cape Ann region. The exception was Andrew Bickford, who married Olive Clark of Gloucester in 1808. According to the family tree, "Done by J. Pool" about 1820 or 1825,[61] Bickford was born "in Gilmantown," a New Hampshire community located just north of Concord. It is possible that a Gloucester

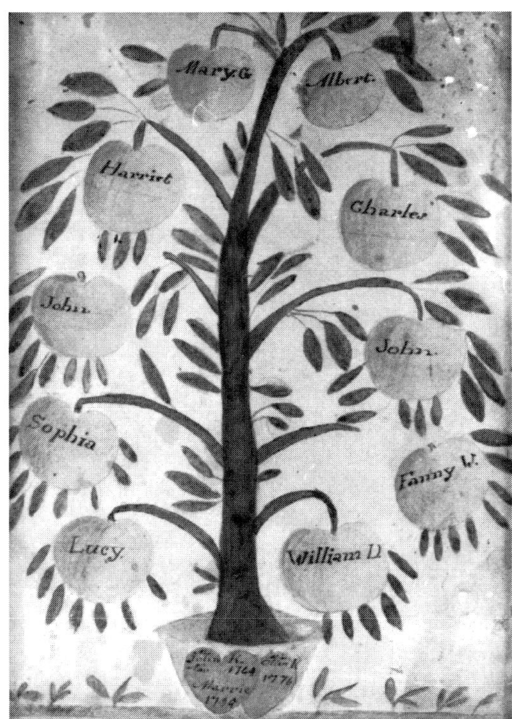

Figure 27 Family register. John K. and Olive K. Sharon, N.H.[?], circa 1816. Watercolor. Location unknown.

watercolor provided the inspiration, though certainly not the pattern, for a number of unusual genealogical trees painted in the area of Gilmanton and neighboring Pittsfield in the period following 1820 (see *checklist 91 and 92* on p. 281). These are attributed to Joseph Odiorne, a Pittsfield, New Hampshire, town clerk, who signed a decorated marriage intention in 1818 (*Figure 36*) entered between Mr. Enoch Blake Jr. and Miss Lydia Smith "both of Pittsfield."[62] He was also responsible for a watercolor family tree marking the births of this couple's children, Hannah E. and Charlotte M. Blake (in 1820 and 1823). The design of this piece is unusual (*Figure 37*). The tree springs from three joined hearts at the bottom (similar to William Saville's), but in the middle of the tree is the half-figure of an angel with a raised hand. A motto reads: "Peace be within thy walls & prosperity within thy palaces." Six of the eight apples are uninscribed, suggesting that he completed the record at the time of their marriage. Another record attributable to Odiorne marked a marriage between Asa K. and Sally Blake; this marriage may not have taken place, however, because the piece is incomplete. A copy (see *checklist 93* on p. 281) of a now-lost Odiorne piece was made for the 1806 marriage of Benjamin Sleeper and Miriam Clough and for the 1836 marriage of their daughter Amanda Sleeper (born 1816) of Gilmanton and Samuel Gilman Kelley (*Figure 38*).[63] The copyist, who was working in the 1860s, added two more generations among the remaining apples, including the death of twenty-year-old Edwin A. Kelley, who was killed in the battle of Chancellorsville in 1863. The copyist lacked Odiorne's skill: instead of a raised hand, the angel holds up a crude paper scroll.[64]

The Vine and Hearts Designs of Nantucket

The family trees most representative of a folk cultural process in New England are the watercolors recording eighteenth- and nineteenth-century marriages on Nantucket Island, Martha's Vineyard, and adjacent portions of Connecticut (see *checklist 95 through 110* on pp. 281–82). Sixteen are now known, all watercolors excepting one related embroidery, and all with a central motif of one or more entwined climbing roses or flowering vines that grow from a pair of fielded hearts. The design seems to be an emblematic variant related to the traditional symbol of entwined lovers' roses, but linguistic evidence comes short of offering a parallel. Epitaphs sometimes employ the term *vine*, such as the one added by Samuel Sewall to the gravestone of his father, Henry Sewall of Newbury, after the death of his mother, Mrs. Jane Dummer, in 1700: "His Fruitfull Vine Being Thus Disjoined, Fell To The Ground January 13 Following."[65] (In this case it is probably a grapevine.) There also may have been a maritime element to the design. A whalebone busk at the New Bedford Whaling Museum is engraved with a pair of hearts side-by-side, each pierced by an arrow, and from each grows a rose stem which intertwines and is stopped by a flower (*Figure 39*).[66]

One of the earliest of the Nantucket pieces is an entwined rose painted for the 1751 marriage of Ebenezer Gardiner Jr. and Ruth Beard (*Figure 40*). As in most Nantucket watercolors, the hearts are

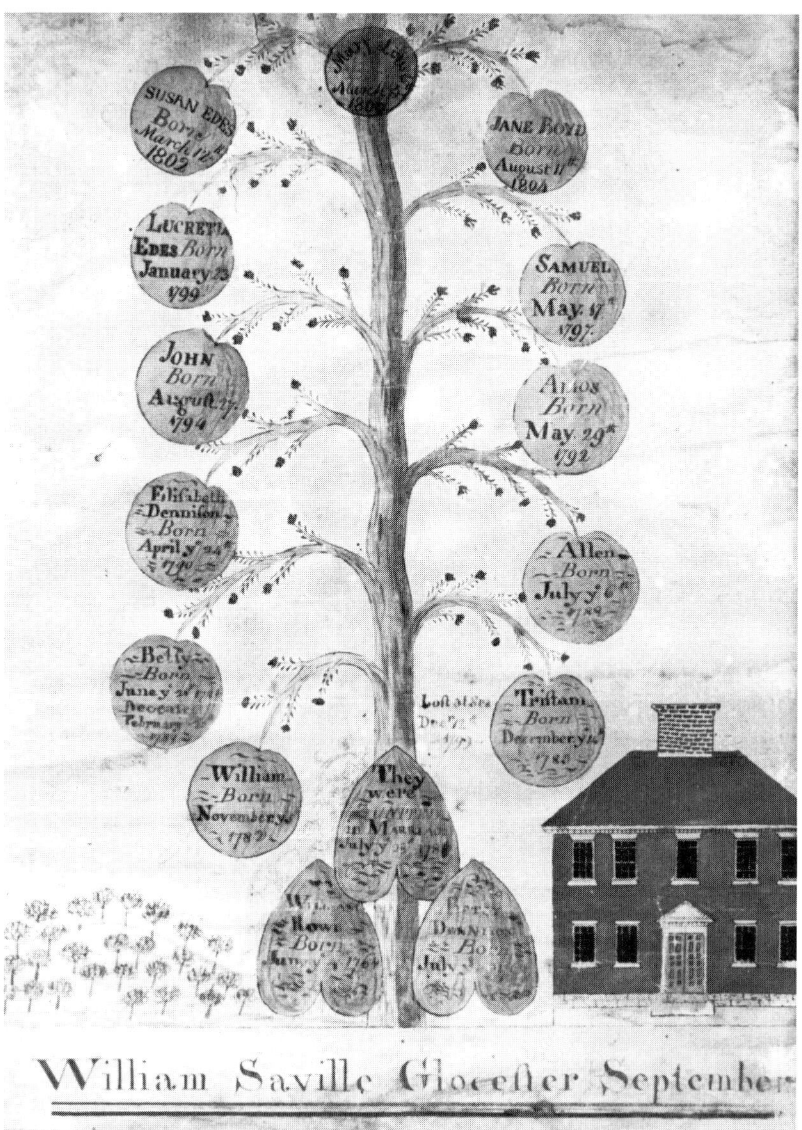

Figure 28 Family register. William Rowe and Betsy Dennison. "William Saville Glocester September 17 [ ]." Gloucester, Massachusetts, circa 1790. Watercolor. Sandy Bay Historical Society.

embedded in a representative circular mound of earth; a ribbon connecting the stems of the two roses marks the date of the marriage. Interspersed between the loops of the two rose stems are the names of ten children inscribed on unattached pods or plaques. The stem of Ebenezer's rose ends with a broken blossom labeled with the date of his death in 1778, indicating it was painted as a memorial piece. A second early watercolor, drawn by Phebe Folger of Nantucket, is also a memorial—in this instance for the family of Zaccheus Coffin who died in 1788 after two and a half years of captivity in Algiers (*Figure 41*). Two hearts set into a curved mound represent the married pair; two prominent roses are emblems of their children.

A number of Nantucket family records dated in the period from 1790 to 1800 have identical five-petal pink rose blossoms, dark-green serrated leaves, and a distinctive manner of placing birth inscriptions in an enlarged seed pod at the base of each flower. One

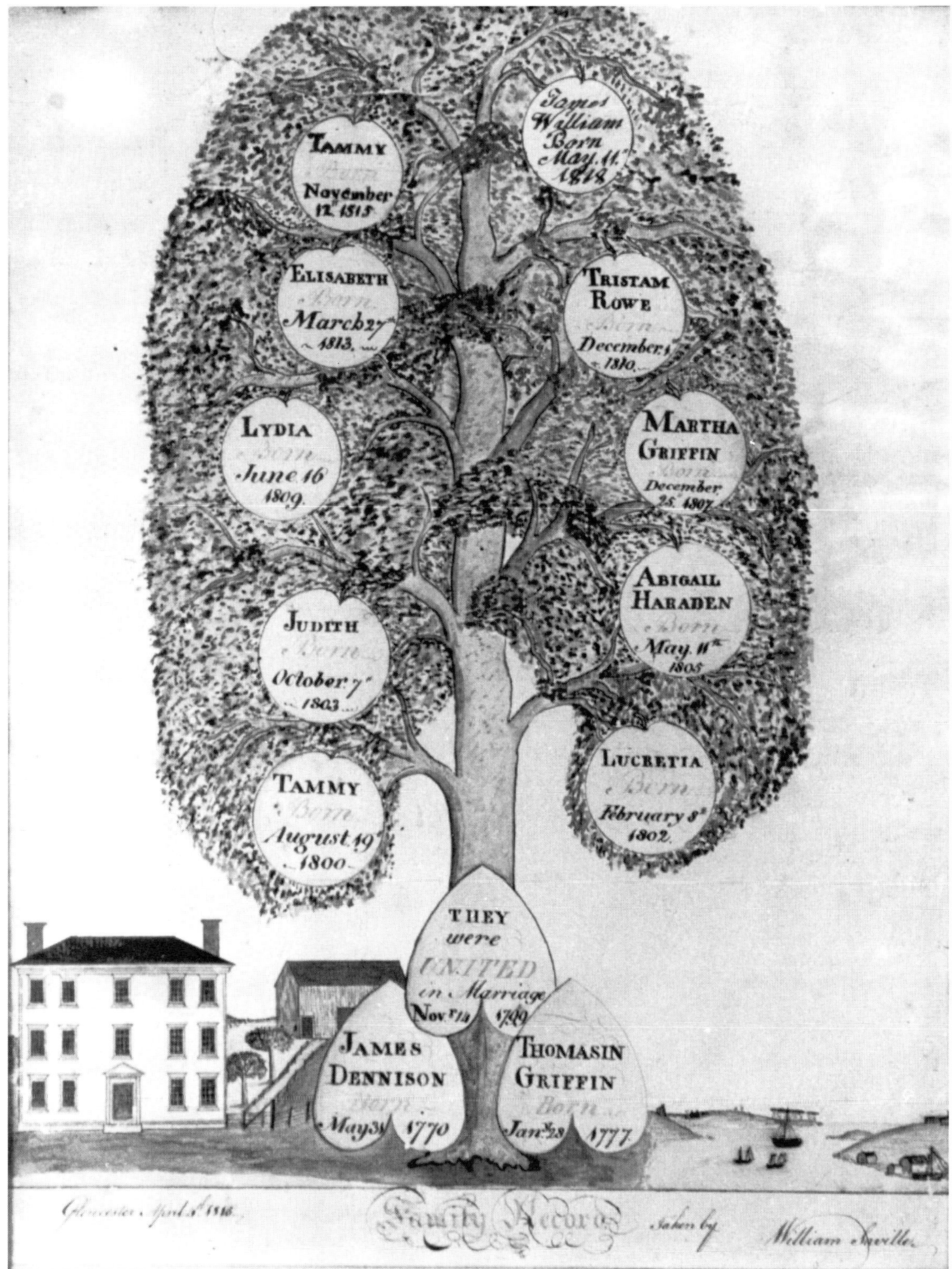

Figure 29 Family register. James Dennison and Thomasin Griffin. "Gloucester April 10th, 1815 / Taken by William Saville." Gloucester, Massachusetts. Watercolor. Cape Ann Historical Museum, Gloucester, Massachusetts.

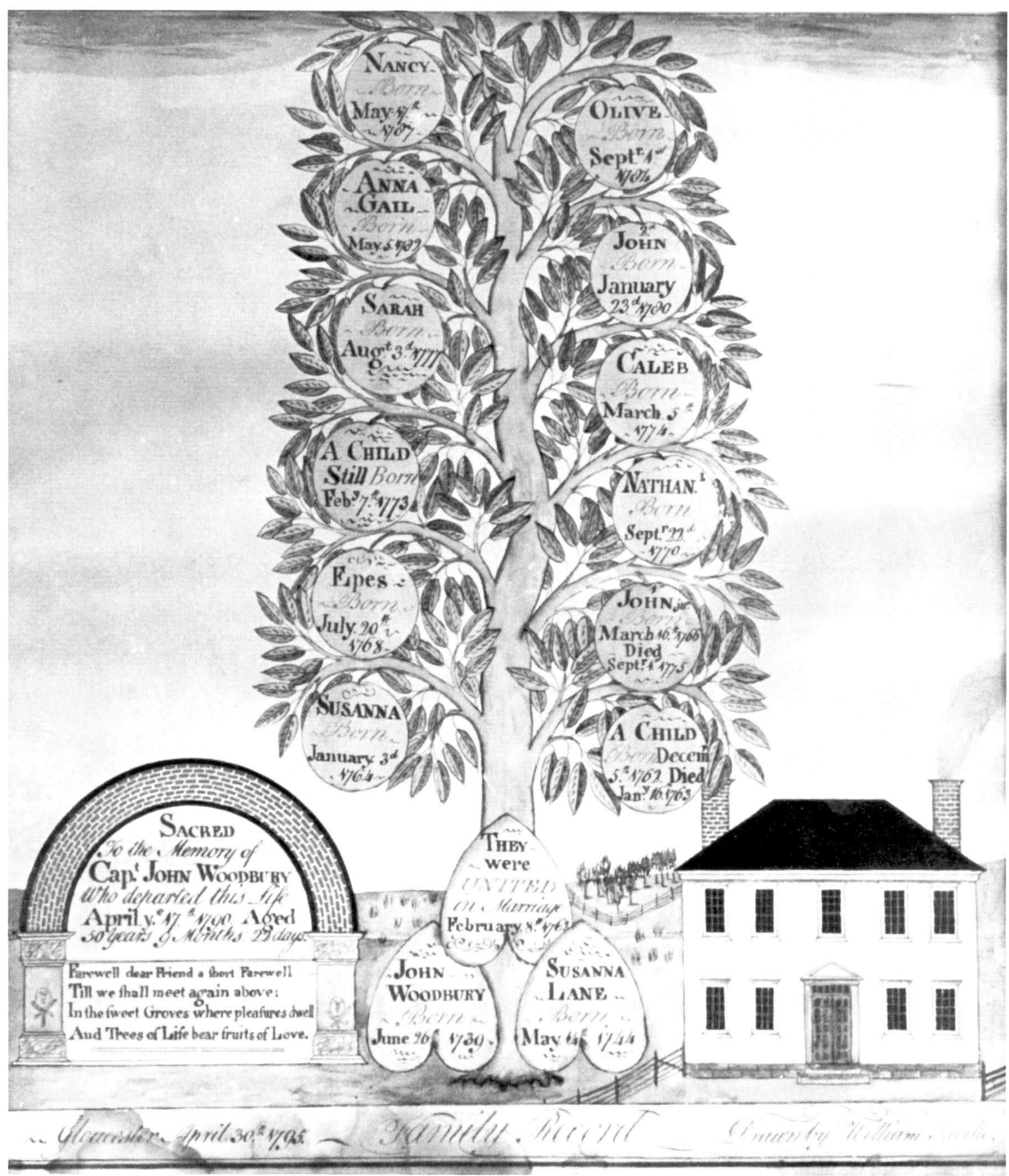

Figure 30 Family register. John Woodbury and Susanna Lane. "Gloucester April 30th 1795 / Drawn by William Saville." Gloucester, Massachusetts. Watercolor. Cape Ann Historical Museum, Gloucester, Massachusetts.

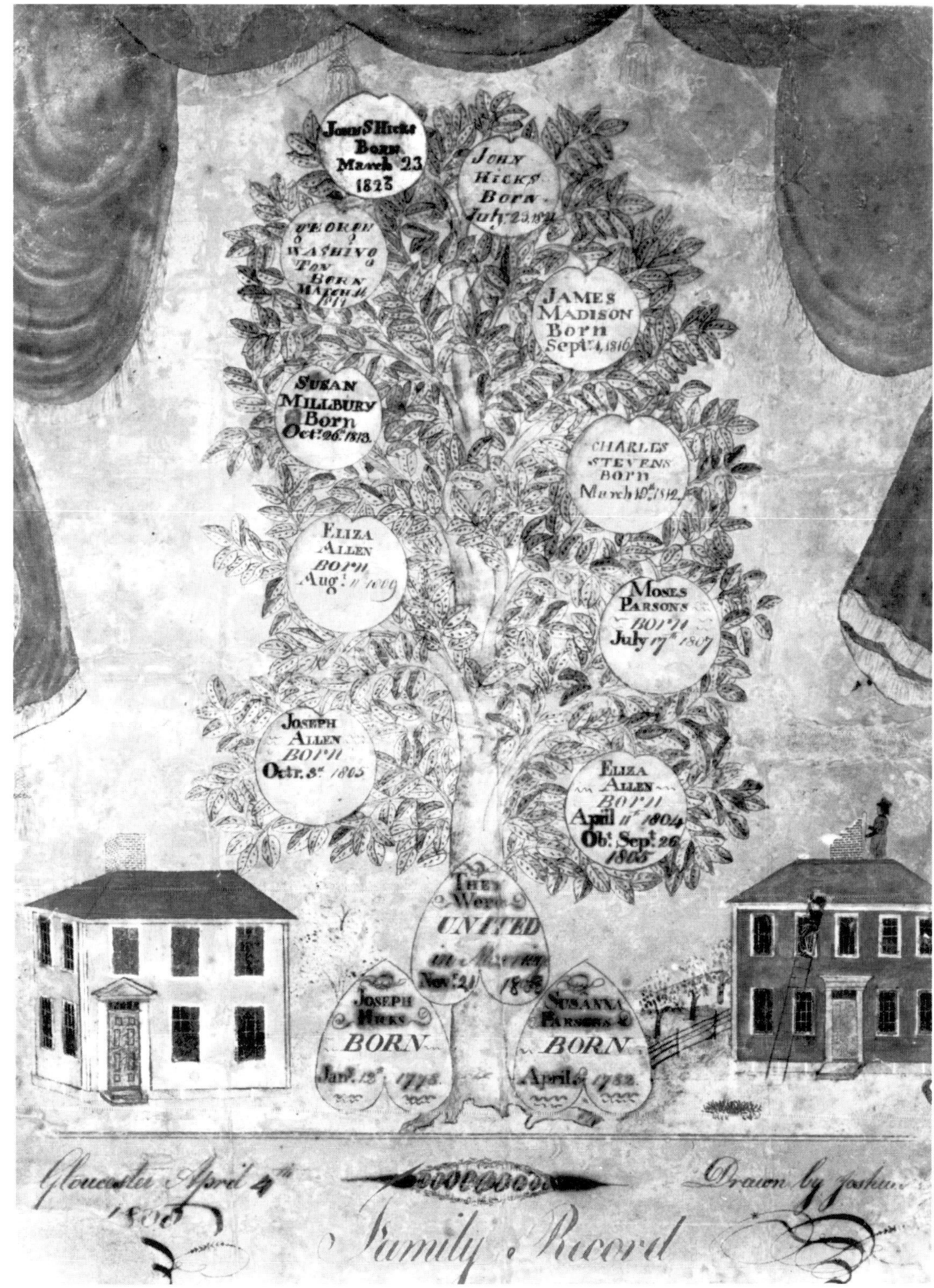

Figure 31 Family register. Joseph Hicks and Susanna Parsons. "Drawn by Joshua P[ ]." "Gloucester [Massachusetts] April 4th / 1805[?]." Watercolor. Location unknown. *Photograph courtesy of Kennedy Galleries.*

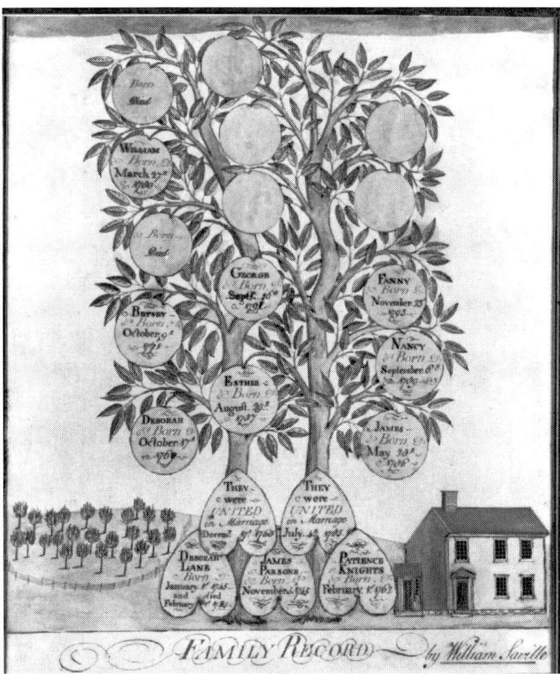

Figure 32 Family register. James Parsons and Deborah Lane; James Parsons and Patience Knights. "by William Saville." (1770–1853), Gloucester, Massachusetts, circa 1793. Watercolor. Courtesy of the Society for the Preservation of New England Antiquities, Beauport Collection. Gift of Constance Betts, Helena Guest, and Frasier McCann. *Photograph by J. David Bohl.*

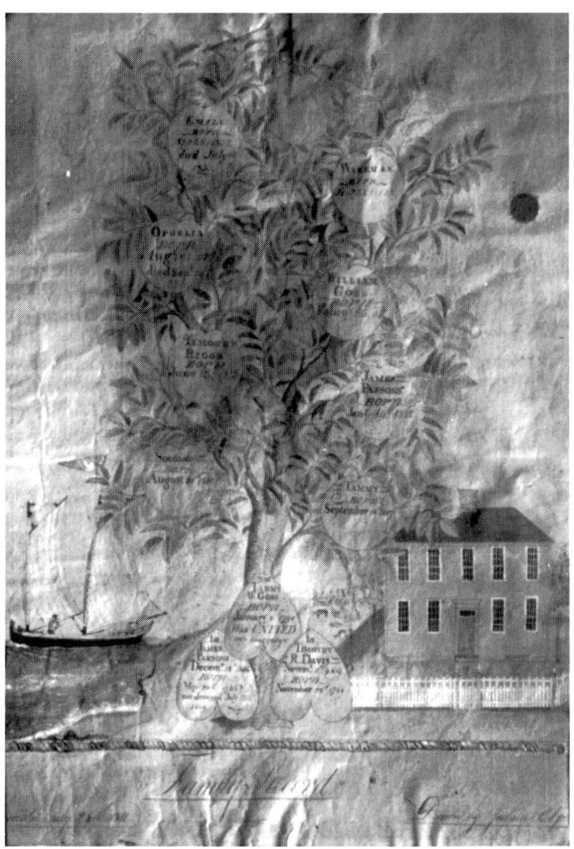

Figure 33 Family register. James Parsons and Tammy W. Goss; Timothy Riggs Davis and Tammy W. Goss. "Gloucester July 24th 1811 / Drawn by Joshua Pool Jr." Gloucester, Massachusetts. Watercolor. Location unknown.

of the best examples in this style is a watercolor signed by Edward D. Burke for the 1784 marriage of Nantucket sea captain Thomas Hiller and Elizabeth Smith, tentatively dated 1794–1796 by a change in the penmanship and ink characteristics of the inscription (*Figure 42*). Burke's composition is balanced; the flowers are arranged in three tiers with each flower set off in a cluster of leafage. The paired hearts and two flowering sprigs grow from a representative mound of earth. In the same style and coloring but less finely executed is a watercolor for the 1766 marriage of Crispus Gardner and Margaret Chase of Nantucket signed by Daniel Stanton. This piece is so similar to the several signed Burke compositions it may be a copy of one of them. A third example in the style—this one clearly not a copy—is the triple composition drawn by Eunice Gardner in 1796 recording the 1788 marriage of Benjamin Cartwright to Abigail Paddock, as well as the prior marriage and offspring of each partner (*Figure 43*). The names of nine surviving children from the three marriages are lettered in the pods of opened rose blossoms; the names of four deceased children, in those of collapsed and discolored blossoms. The characteristic downward hanging five-petal roses are colored in shades of dark and light pink.

Little is known of the artists. Edward D. Burke, who signed two other Nantucket watercolors similar to the Hiller/Smith record, may have been a schoolteacher or a professional genealogical artist. An entry made by Nantucket judge of probate Isaac Coffin, 6 October 1796, noting the drowning of Edward D. Burke's unnamed son (who was serving on board a Nantucket whaler) is unusual in view of the absence of any other references to Burke.[67] At the least it

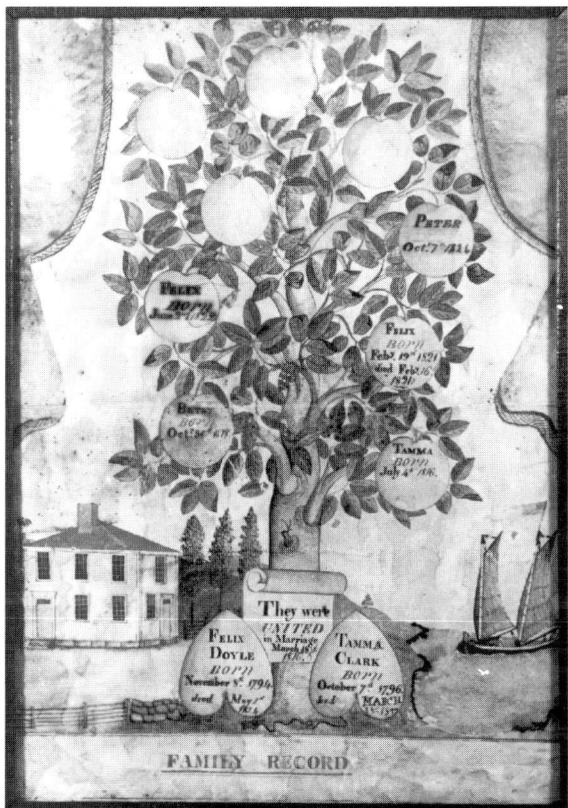

Figure 34 Family register. Felix Doyle and Tamma Clark. Gloucester, Massachusetts, circa 1821. Watercolor. Sandy Bay Historical Society.

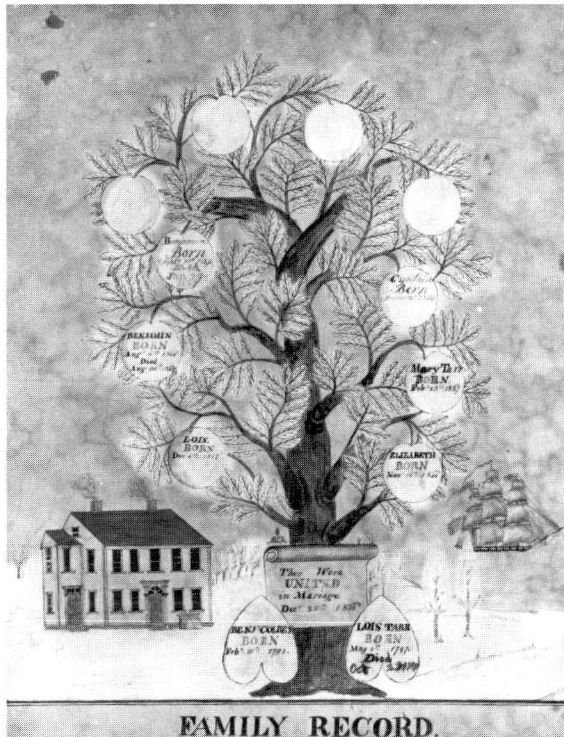

Figure 35 Family register. Benjamin Colbey and Lois Tarr. Gloucester, Massachusetts, circa 1824. Watercolor. Sandy Bay Historical Society.

suggests that the older Burke was a permanent resident of Nantucket in the 1790s and not an itinerant. Daniel Stanton has been tentatively identified as the son of Latham Stanton (b. 1776) and Huldah Butler of New Garden, North Carolina, and the grandson of William Stanton (d. 1811) and Phebe Macy (d. 1802) of Nantucket. William Stanton left Nantucket between 1771 and 1775 to help found a Quaker colony at New Garden; Daniel Stanton is not known to have been a resident of Nantucket but apparently visited the island about 1815 to 1820. The similarity of Stanton's piece to those of Burke suggests that Stanton attended a school taught by Burke on Nantucket or perhaps elsewhere. Eunice Gardner (b. 1776) of Nantucket, twenty at the time she drew the Cartwright/Paddock record, was the daughter of Barnabas Gardener and Abigail Cartwright, Benjamin Cartwright's sister. She was still young enough to have been attending school and may have received her inspiration from Burke or Stanton. Unlike Eunice Gardner, however, neither Burke nor Stanton is known to be related to any of the partners whose marriages they recorded.

A later Nantucket style, dated between 1790 and 1820, consists of fielded hearts and a pair of entwined vines flowering with bluebells, carnations, fuchsias, and berries. Two watercolors in this style record marriages in the Folger family of Nantucket and may be the work of Rebecca Folger (1778–1823), wife of Nantucket cooper Alexander Folger, who appears as the youngest child in the first (*Figure 44*) and as a marriage partner in the second (*Figure 45*). The main elements of this style are present in a hearts-and-vine record signed by John B. Copp (b. 1779) of Stonington, Connecticut, recording the marriage of his father, Deacon Samuel Copp (*Figure 46*). These elements are also present in a mid-nineteenth-century copy of the circa 1778 climbing rose Gardiner/Beard family

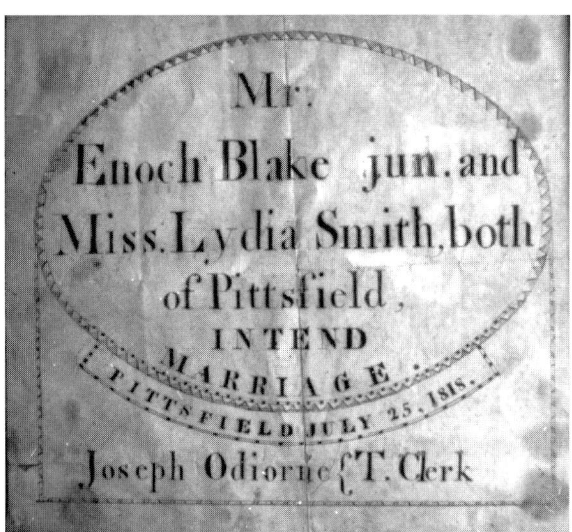

Mr.
Enoch Blake jun. and
Miss. Lydia Smith, both
of Pittsfield,
INTEND
MARRIAGE.
PITTSFIELD JULY 25, 1818.
Joseph Odiorne T. Clerk

Figure 36 Marriage intention. Enoch Blake Jr. and Lydia Smith. "Joseph Odiorne T. Clerk." Pittsfield, New Hampshire, 1818. Pen and ink. Don Randall.

record (*Figure 47*). (The original was discovered beneath the copy in the same frame when acquired by the Nantucket Historical Association.)

The two most recent Nantucket compositions, dated 1825 to 1830, record an 1815 marriage on Nantucket (Myrick/Mitchell) and an 1805 marriage on Martha's Vineyard (Pent/Ripley) (*Figure 48*). Clearly the work of the same unidentified artist, these compositions have white roses instead of the usual pink ones, and children who have died are represented by wilted blossoms hanging from broken stems and identified by a banner held in the beak of a dove. The white rose compositions represent a fully developed form of the earliest Nantucket design (Gardiner/Beard) in which the names of the children are interspersed between the loops in groups of four. The earth has evolved into a formal landscape with rolling hills, trees, shrubbery, and flowers. Rather than fielded, the hearts are literally "planted" pointed-end first into the ground.

Sources for the Nantucket variants of the emblem have not been located. However, much more so than the Middlesex County and Cape Ann examples—many of which were reproduced in an academy setting or offered in the repertory of an individual genealogical artist—the Nantucket variants of the emblem appear to represent a vernacular aesthetic sustained regionally in southeastern and coastal New England and one that in some regards may be closer to the centuries-old folk or popular images from which they all may have been derived. A pair of entwined climbing roses (or other entwined plants) is an old literary emblem that may still have been current in Nantucket speech at that time. The heart-shaped base in turn was a feature of dyed palampores imported from England and India. The central or curved mound of earth in which the paired hearts are grounded, a formula that appears on all the Nantucket pieces before 1820, is also a palampore concept.[68] The use of banners or swags between the rose stems to record the date of marriage in turn was a cartoonist's convention.

The supposition that this was a regional emblem is confirmed by several other factors. First of all is the clearly defined limits of the variant to Nantucket, Martha's Vineyard, and nearby coastal towns such as Stonington—a coastal and insular cultural zone sharing a common occupation in the fishing, seafaring, and whaling industries, bound together by five generations of intermarrying, and likely to bond together with local cultural forms. And it is suggested by the wide range of styles within the variant—five are now known—and the continuance of these styles beyond the lifespans of the individual artists who used them. Two of these styles significantly changed the format. One example, made about 1816 for the marriage of David Paddock and Mary Starbuck, adds an extra pair of hearts to the design; the children are shown in seven plaques distributed between the interwoven vines. A second example, possibly made as early as 1781, marks the three marriages of "Nathaniel Starbuck born 26 June 1746." This time only a single heart is shown, with Starbuck's name on a banner held between two horse posts. Three banners identify his marriages to Eunice Barnard (1765), Salley Fullenton (in 1777), and Patience Coffin (in 1778). Named flowers attached to each vine identify his eight children, five of whom died in infancy.

In addition there is at least one other register, associated with a town in the southern tier of Massachusetts communities near Nantucket, that seems to mix the Nantucket motifs with others. A register for the family in Raynham, Massachusetts, done in 1817, combines a pair of pillars and pair of fielded or

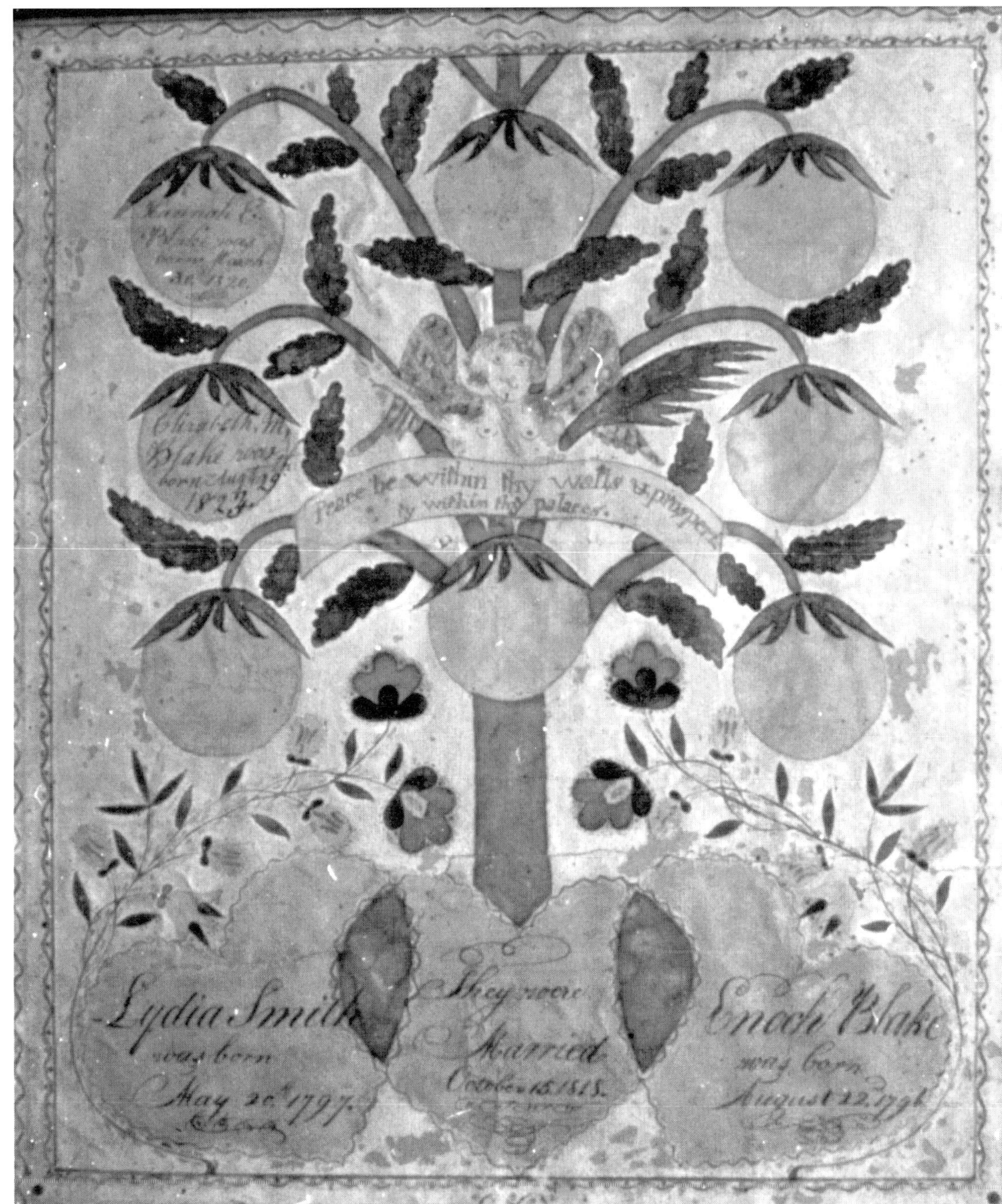

Figure 37 Family register. Enoch Blake Jr. and Lydia Smith. Attributed to Joseph Odiorne. Pittsfield, New Hampshire, 1820 or 1823. Watercolor. Don Randall.

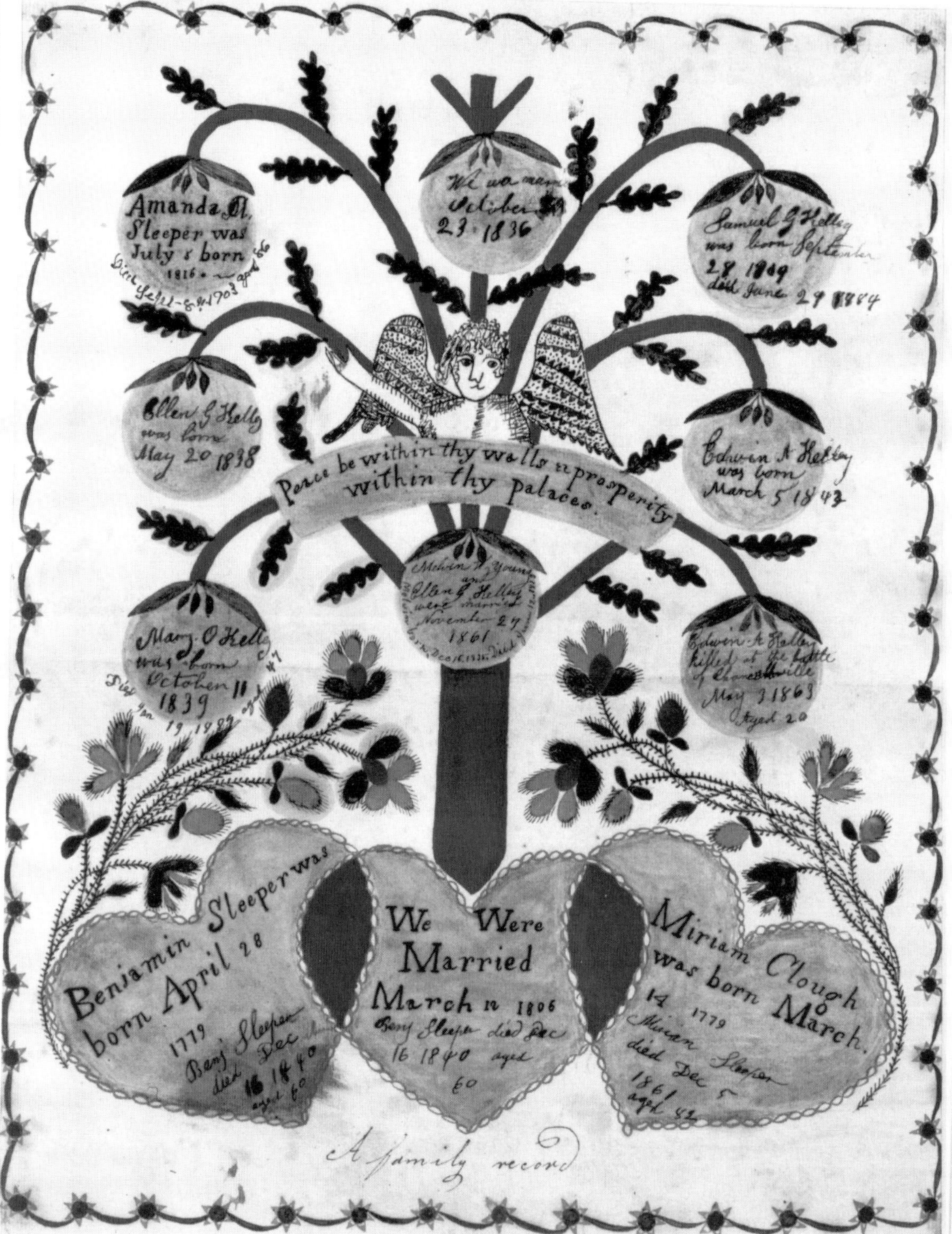

Figure 38 Family tree. Benjamin Sleeper and Miriam Clough. Gilmanton, New Hampshire, circa 1863. Watercolor, 13 × 10 inches. Courtesy of the Society for the Preservation of New England Antiquities, Beauport Collection. Gift of Constance Betts, Helena Guest, and Frasier McCann. *Photograph by J. David Bohl.*

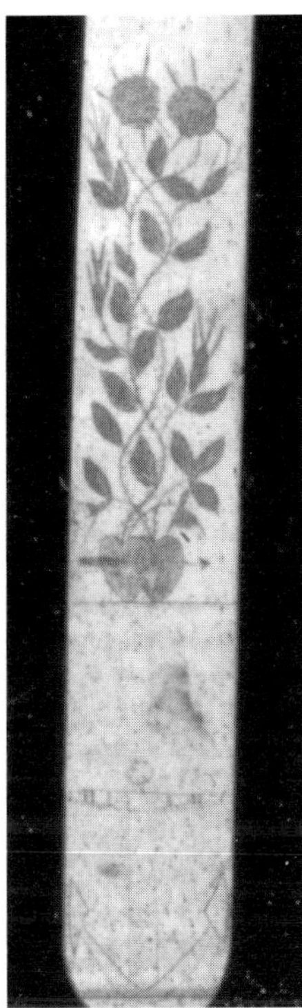

Figure 39 Busk (detail). New England or eastern North America, circa 1800–1850. New Bedford Whaling Museum.

overlapping hearts, two pairs of birds, and a pair of labeled vines rising from the hearts. It marks the two marriages of Obed Hall, first to Abigail Dean and second to Eliza Fox.[69]

Contributing to this aesthetic may have been the unique adaptability of the hearts-and-vine emblem to changing family alignments. Although marriages of widows and widowers with families were common throughout New England, the frequency of second and third unions was considerably higher among families constantly engaged in high-risk maritime occupations than among farming families. An emblem that could as easily record the union of families with already existing children as first-time marriages was likely to be more popular in New England's coastal towns than in its interior communities. This may, at least in part, explain the relatively high number of survivals of the emblem on family records from coastal southeastern New England, as well as on the Cape Ann peninsula. Also contributing to this aesthetic may have been the religious attitudes of Nantucket's Quaker population which reached a numerical peak on the island at the end of the eighteenth century. Because Quakers proscribed any form of gravestone art or ornamentation (Nantucket Quakers refused to erect gravestones altogether), members of this denomination on the island may have found in decorated family records the same creative outlet that off-island Congregational communities in New England found in stonecutting art.[70]

If this interpretation is correct, the family trees recording marriages in coastal southeastern Massachusetts may have been equivalent to relict expressions still in circulation in the everyday speech of isolated coastal Massachusetts communities but already extinguished among "off islanders" whose lives were not protected by an insular or peninsular geography. It was St. John Crèvecoeur who first noted (in 1782) the "secluded situation" and "simplicity of diction and manners" of the residents of Nantucket and Martha's Vineyard. The islands' speech characteristics were recorded systematically in 1848; as late as 1939 linguistic field workers noted the survival in Nantucket Sound of the terms *menhaden* (for the more common "quahog") and *kitchen closet* (for "pantry"). Even in the 1970s, it was still possible to measure the rate at which relict expressions such as *tempest* (for "storm") were receding toward a corner of Martha's Vineyard least exposed to off-island influences (Gay Head, populated by descendants of the island's Algonkian Indians). The family trees were equivalent, too, to the highly specialized style of rattan "lightship" baskets, woven on graduated-sized forms, that evolved uniquely on Nantucket in the absence of off-island artisans' influences.[71]

It is this, perhaps, that provides a clue to the identity of the pink roses found on the 1790s-period Nantucket compositions. These may be none other than the common salt spray rose (*Rosa rugosa*) that grows in low-lying clusters on the immediate high ground of the southeastern New England shoreline and whose name is derived from its resistance to wind-blown seawater. Typically dark pink in color, the small five-petal blossoms of this rose are still attached to their seed pods today as they were when drawn by Eunice Gardner, Daniel Stanton, and Edward D. Burke at the end of the eighteenth century. It is entirely appropriate that a family tree variant as closely identified with Nantucket should also bear this most regional emblem of coastal New England's wildlife.

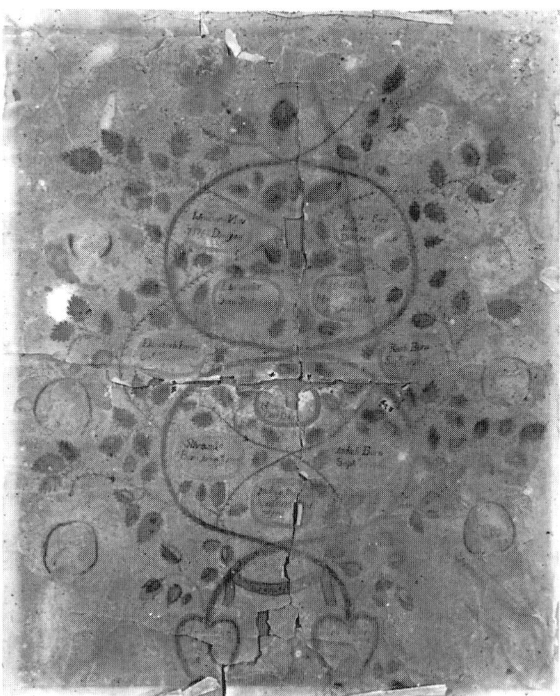

Figure 40 Family register and memorial. Ebenezer Gardiner Jr. and Ruth Beard Nantucket, circa 1778. Nantucket, Massachusetts. Watercolor. Courtesy of the Nantucket Historical Association.

NOTES

[1]This is an expanded version of an article by the author entitled "Decorated Family Records from Coastal Massachusetts, New Hampshire, and Connecticut," *Families and Children: 1985 Dublin Seminar for New England Folklife* (Boston: Boston University Scholarly Publications, 1987), pp. 91–146. It is based on new communications from Glee F. Krueger, Judith Lund, Don Randall, Victoria Taylor Hawkins, Selina Little, Betty Ring, Brian E. Hogg, Gregory H. Laing, and D. Brenton Simons. Especially helpful in this effort was the work of Gloria Seaman Allen, *Family Record: Genealogical Watercolors and Needlework* (Washington, D.C.: Daughters of the American Revolution Museum, 1989). Shirley Barnes and Abbott Lowell Cummings are also thanked for identifying the Levi Butterfield family tree.

[2]Titus Hutchinson (b. 1771) and Clarissa Sage, Woodstock, Vt., 1820. Oil on canvas, 30 × 120 in.; attributed to Thomas Ware. Woodstock Historical Society, Woodstock, Vt. Gift of the Ottauqueechee Chapter of the Daughters of the American Revolution and Dr. Frederick Kidder. See Arthur B. Kern and Sybil B. Kern, "Thomas Ware, Vermont Portrait Painter," *Clarion* (winter 1983/1984): 36–45.

[3]Bennet Family Record, Poland, Maine (Jonathan Bennet, b. 1745, and Polly Hasket, b. 1749). "Copied by Reuben Barns, of / Poland: April 12, A.D. 1804"; watercolor 14 × 11 in. Eleanor and Mabel Van Alstyne American Folk Art Collection, National Museum of History and Technology, Smithsonian Institution, Washington, D.C. Reproduced in Sandra Brant and Elissa Cullman, *Small Folk: A Celebration of Childhood in America* (New York: Museum of American Folk Art, 1980), plate 79.

[4]Later in the nineteenth century American portrait painters such as Erastus Salisbury Field experimented with photography and painting in the same way. When Field composed *Reuben Gilbert Puffer Family*, he painted on photographic images using in this case a child some time dead. See Diane E. Forsberg, "Erastus Salisbury Field: Mezzographs and Other Experiments with Photography in Portrait Painting," *Painting and Portrait Making: 1994 Proceedings of the Dublin Seminar for New England Folklife* (Boston: Boston University Scholarly Publications, 1995), pp. 235–46. For other examples of composite portraits, see the portrait of the family of the Reverend Ezra Stiles by St. John Honeywood who lined up cartoon portraits like different denominations of coins. They are identified through inscriptions. Reproduced in Edmund S. Morgan, *The Gentle Puritan* (New Haven: Yale University Press, 1962), opp. p. 434.

[5]Bolton and Coe dated the earliest New England genealogical sampler to 1774 (made for the Olmstead family of Connecticut). Ethel Stanwood Bolton and Eva Johnson Coe, *American Samplers* (Boston: Massachusetts Society of the Colonial Dames of America, 1921), pp. 18, 28.

[6]Arms were common in eighteenth-century Boston. Suffolk County, Mass., probate records reveal that twenty-one escutcheons, twenty-nine family arms, and three occupational arms (brasiers, peweters, lawyers) were inventoried in Boston in the years 1718 through 1770.

[7]See Georgia Brady Barnhill's essay on printed family registers in this volume.

[8]Quoted in Allen, *Family Record*, p. 12.

[9]William Bentley, *The Diary of William Bentley, D. D., Pastor of the East Church, Salem, Massachusetts* (1905–1914; reprint, 4 vols., Gloucester, Mass.: Peter Smith, 1962), 15 February 1809 (3:416). Ashley Bowen, *The Journals of Ashley Bowen of Marblehead*, 2 vols. (Boston: Colonial Society of Massachusetts, 1973).

[10]Mary Little Poor, Poor family register, 1813; MS collection, New England Historic Genealogical Society.

[11]Clarissa Squire, Fairfield, Conn., reproduced in Allen, *Family Record*, entry 48.

[12]For example, a stone by Alpheus Wright of Rockingham; see William Hosley, "The Rockingham Stonecarvers," *Puritan Gravestone Art II: 1978 Proceedings of the Dublin Seminar for New England Folklife* (Boston: Boston University Scholarly Publications, 1978), p. 77.

[13]For examples of gravestones that reflect the release of spirits during the Great Awakening religious revival, see Peter Benes, "'Distinguishing Signs of Truly Gracious and Holy Affections': Revival Motifs in Eighteenth-Century New England Gravestone Carvings," in *Mirror and Metaphor: Material and Social Constructions of Reality*, ed. Daniel W. Ingersoll Jr. and Gordon Bronitsky (Lanham, Md.: University

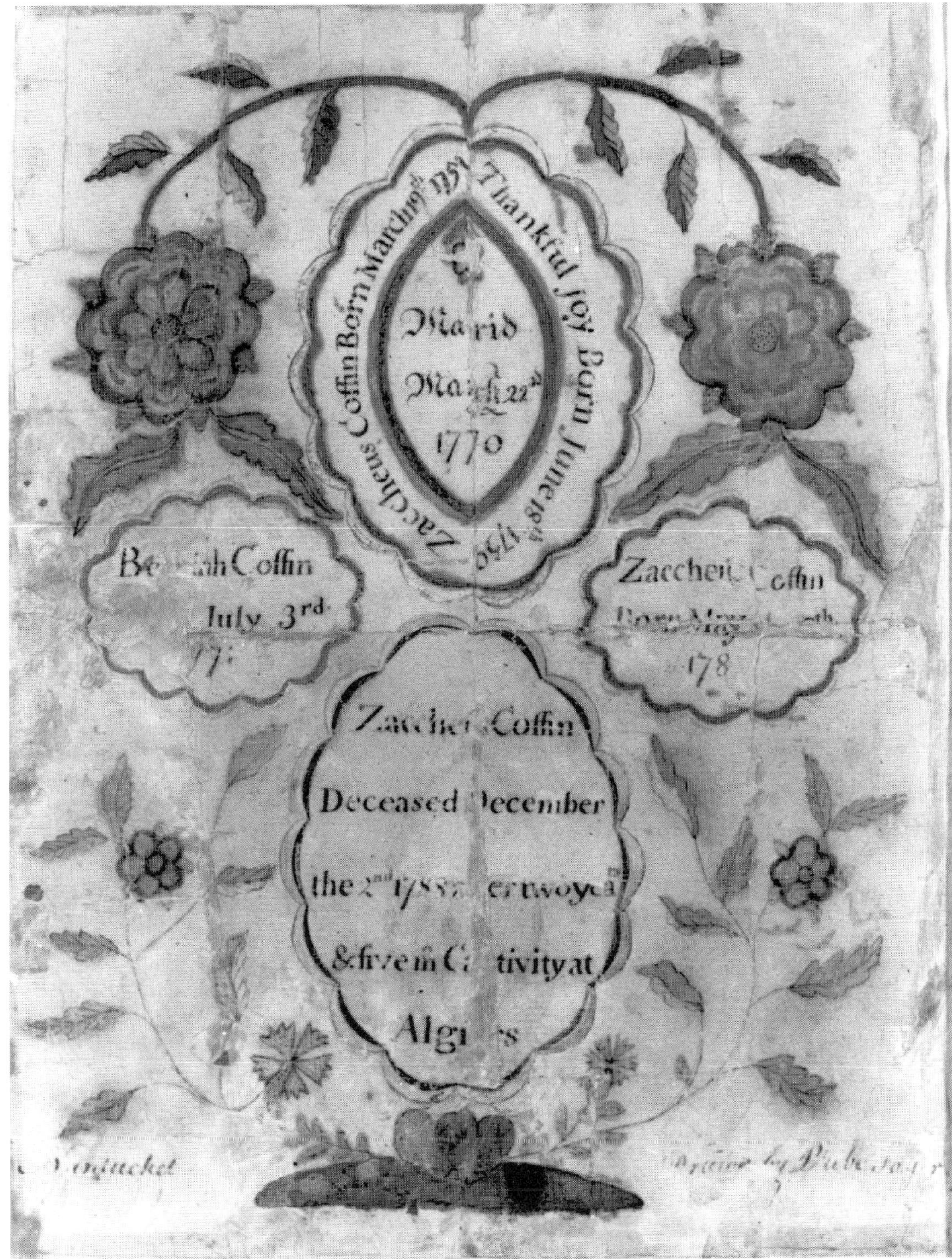

Figure 41 Family register and memorial. Zaccheus Coffin and Thankful Joy. "Drawn by Phebe Folger." Nantucket, Massachusetts, circa 1778. Watercolor. Courtesy of the Nantucket Historical Association.

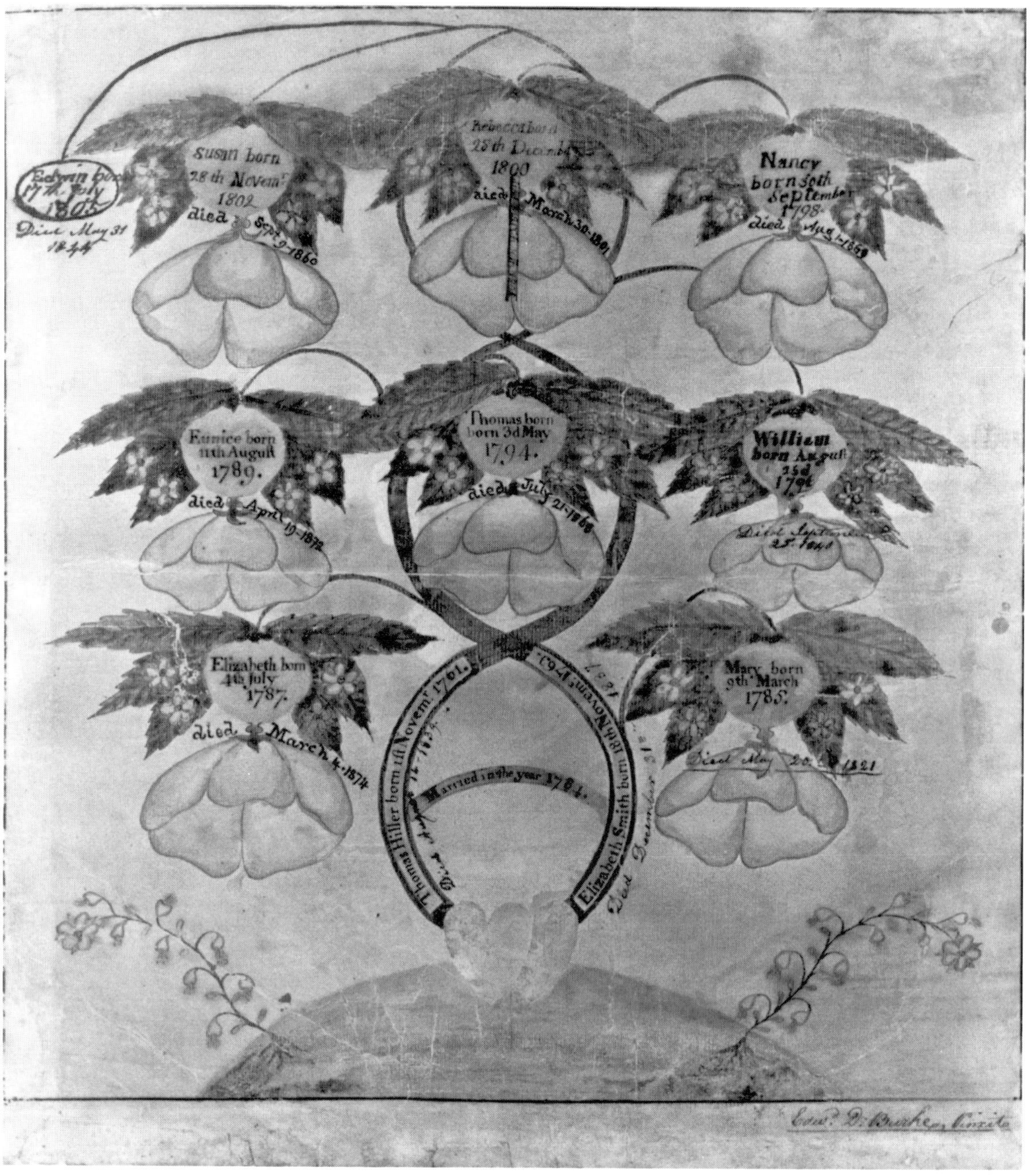

Figure 42 Family register. Thomas Hiller and Elizabeth Smith. "Edw.d D. Burke, Pinxit." Nantucket, Massachusetts, circa 1794–1796. Watercolor. Courtesy of the Nantucket Historical Association.

Press of America, 1987), pp. 137–60. In family registers see, for example, the winged cherub head on the Fanney Whitney sampler, Portland, Maine, 1822; in Allen, *Family Record*, entry 88.

[14]Barnhill checklist, in this volume, numbers 28 and 29.

[15]Betty Ring, *Let Virtue Be a Guide to Thee: Needlework in the Education of Rhode Island Women, 1730–1830* (Providence: Rhode Island Historical Society, 1983), plates 64 and 65. Allen, *Family Record*, entries 42 and 43.

[16]The clockfaced gravestone of Abigail Williams of Deerfield, Mass., dated 1754 but carved much later (1800 or after), was probably made during the same period.

[17]Allan I. Ludwig and David D. Hall, "Aspects of Music, Poetry, Stonecarving, and Death in Early New England,"

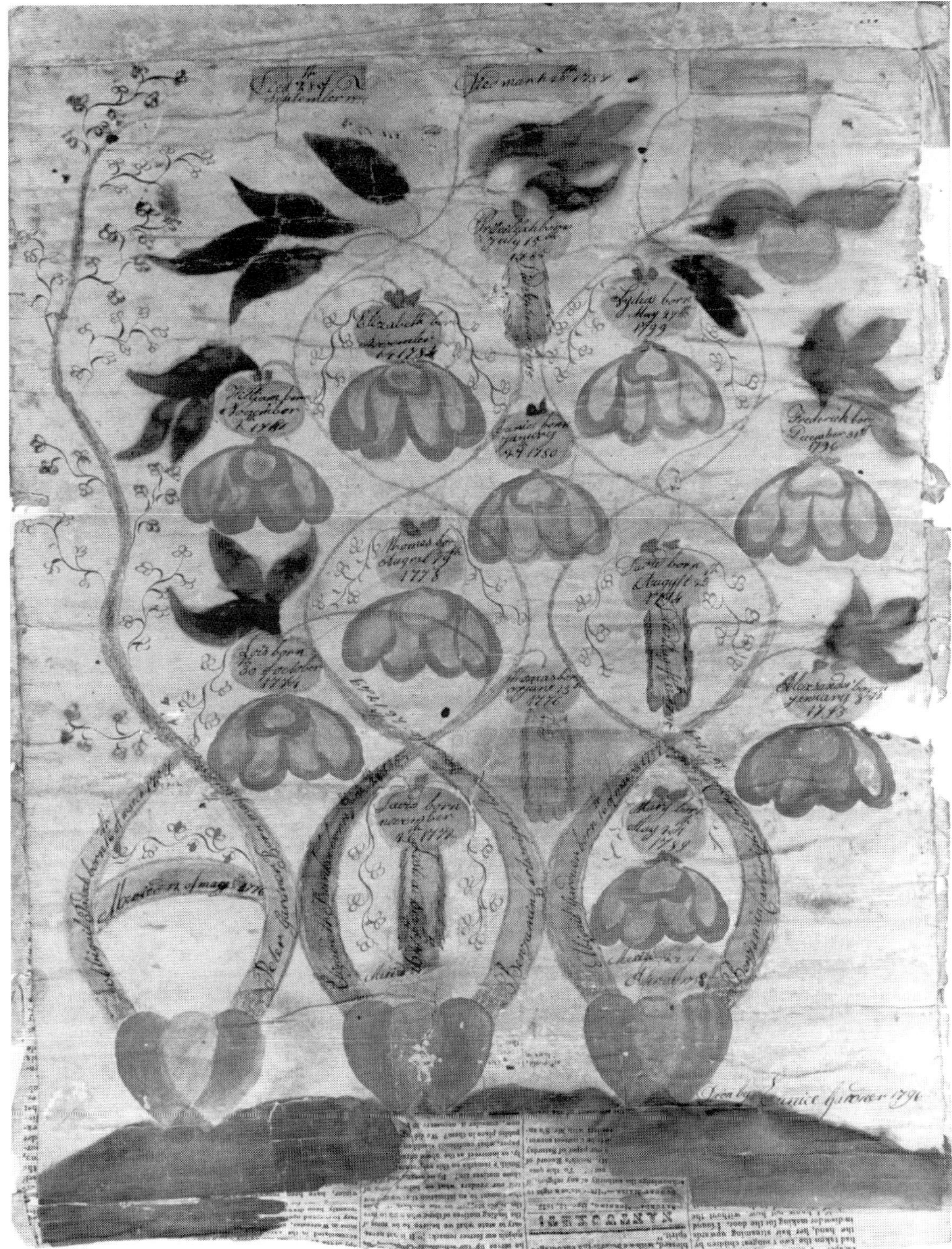

Figure 43 Family register. Peter Gardiner and Abigail Paddock; Benjamin Cartwright and Elisabeth Bunker; Benjamin Cartwright and Abigail Paddock. "Dron by Eunice Gardner 1796." Nantucket, Massachusetts. Watercolor. Courtesy of the Nantucket Historical Association.

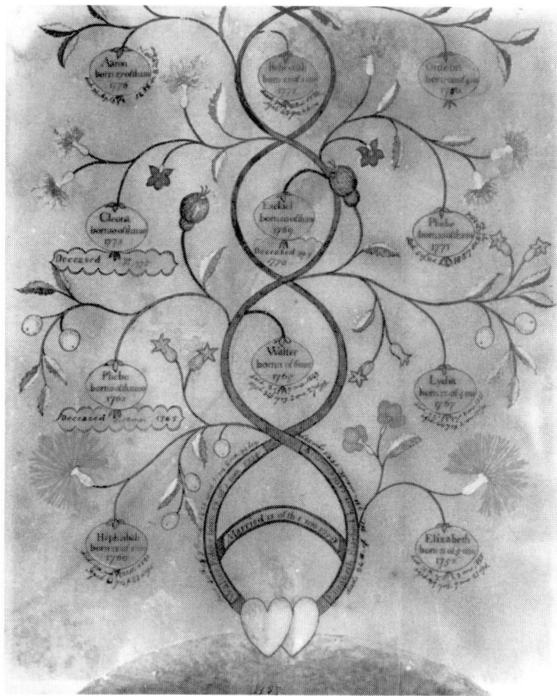

Figure 44 Family register. Walter Folger and Elizabeth Starbuck. Attributed to Rebecca Folger. Nantucket, Massachusetts, circa 1790–1800. Watercolor. Courtesy of the Nantucket Historical Association.

Puritan Gravestone Art II: 1978 Proceedings of the Dublin Seminar for New England Folklife (Boston: Boston University Scholarly Publications, 1978), p. 24.

[18] *A Display of the United States of America*, 1791 stipple and line engraving. Illustrated in *American Printmaking: The First 150 Years* (New York: Museum of Graphic Art, 1969), no. 79.

[19] "Fair liberty sits goddess of our states." Political cartoon "AD 1791" by Oliver Kendall, Sterling, Mass. Sterling Historical Society; the author is grateful to Ruth M. Hopfman, Curator. See also, *Witness to America's Past: Two Centuries of Collecting by the Massachusetts Historical Society* (Boston: Massachusetts Historical Society, 1991), entry 102, p. 132.

[20] Much later versions of the chain combined photographs. See "Planetary Photographic Record," Hartford Lithographers, 1869, entry no. 157 in Allen, *Family Record*.

[21] Nina F. Little, *Country Arts in Early American Homes* (New York: Dutton, 1975), fig. 73.

[22] Rudolf Arnheim, *The Valentine Heart: A Theme with Variations* (New York: Cooper Union Art School, 1957); Richard Lewinsohn, *Eine Weltgeschichte des Herzens* (Hamburg: Rowohlt Verlag, 1959), p. 13, and opp. pp. 29, 53; Anne Sauvy, *Le Miroir du coeur* (Paris: Cerf, 1989), p. 84.

[23] For example, Anne Bradstreet, "To my Dear and loving Husband." "If ever two were one, then surely we, / If ever man were lov'd by wife, then thee." Elsewhere she muses on her husband's absence: "Flesh of thy flesh, bone of thy bone, / I here, thou there, yet both but one." *The Works of Anne Bradstreet in Prose and Verse*, ed. John H. Ellis (Gloucester, Mass.: Peter Smith, 1962), pp. 338–39.

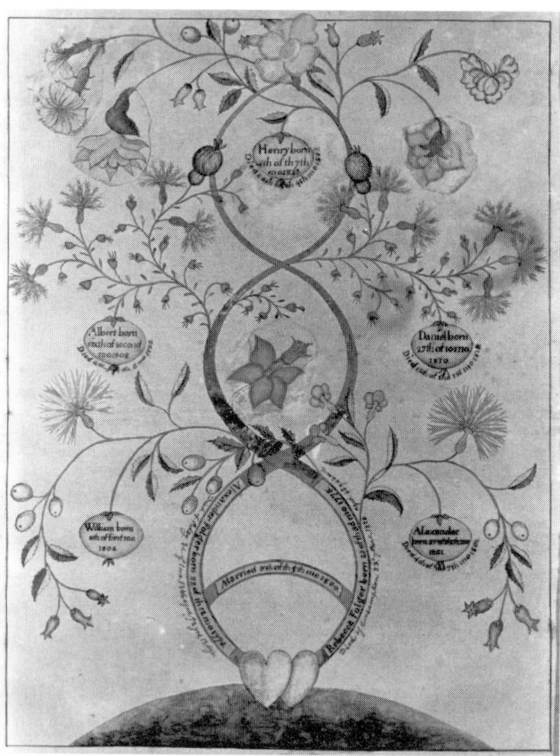

Figure 45 Family register. Alexander Folger and Rebecca Folger. Attributed to Rebecca Folger. Nantucket, Massachusetts, circa 1813. Watercolor. Courtesy of the Nantucket Historical Association.

[24] Peter Benes, *The Masks of Orthodoxy: Folk Gravestone Carving in Plymouth County, Massachusetts, 1689–1805* (Amherst: University of Massachusetts Press, 1977).

[25] Gravestone of Micah and Abigail Moore, Rutland, Mass., 1749.

[26] Alexandra Grave, *Three Centuries of Connecticut Folk Art* (New Haven, Conn.: Eastern Press, 1979), fig. 154.

[27] See "The Family of Joseph & Lucy Merriam," no. 17 in the checklist.

[28] More than half of the chests illustrated in a 1935 checklist of early-eighteenth-century Hadley chests were decorated with hearts, usually upside down, some as opposed pairs. See Clair F. Luther, *The Hadley Chest* (Hartford, Conn.: Case, Lockwood and Brainard, 1935).

[29] *Maine Antique Digest*, March 1988, p. 30-A.

[30] Janet Waring, *Early American Stencils: Their Origin, History, and Use* (New York: Scott, 1937), p. 39.

[31] "A Genealogy of Joseph Stanwood's Family." Watercolor, 10 × 8 inches. Society for the Preservation of New England Antiquities, gift of Nina F. Little.

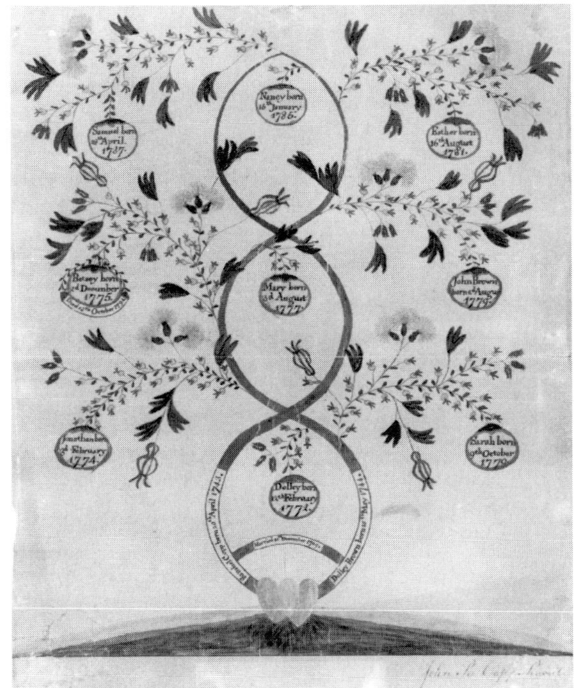

Figure 46 Family register. Samuel Copp and Dolley Brown. "John B. Copp Pinxit." Stonington, Connecticut, circa 1790. Watercolor. Courtesy of the Smithsonian Institution.

[32]Attributed to stonecutter Nathaniel Pratt of Abington, Mass., or possibly his sons Noah or Robert Pratt.

[33]Heart themes seldom appeared in genealogical embroideries. An exception is the three hearts that joined together to form a central motif in needlework samplers taught at a Charlestown, Mass., finishing school (*checklist 31 through 34*). There are four examples, dated 1824 to 1831. In the Hunt/Tuft/Snow family record, "wrought by Eliza Ann Hunt aged nine years 1824," the heart on the left identifies her father, and the one on the right her mother and stepmother; a tombstone to the right indicates the date each one died.

[34]Jane C. Beck, ed., *Always in Season: Folk Art and Traditional Culture in Vermont* (Montpelier: Vermont Council on the Arts, 1982), pp. 10, 91; *Maine Antique Digest*, November 1986, pp. 1B and 2B.

[35]*Maine Antique Digest*, November 1986, p. 2-B.

[36]James Hall, *Illustrated Dictionary of Symbols in Eastern and Western Art* (Cambridge, England: John Murray, 1994), pp. 58–60.

[37]*Oxford English Dictionary*, 12 vols. (Oxford, England: Clarendon Press, 1933); s.v. "tree" [6], p. 313.

[38]Genesis ii 9.

[39]John Milton, *Paradise Lost*, 4:218–19.

[40]See Meditations 19, 33, and 56 in Edward Taylor, *The Poems of Edward Taylor*, ed. Donald E. Stanford (New Haven: Yale University Press, 1960).

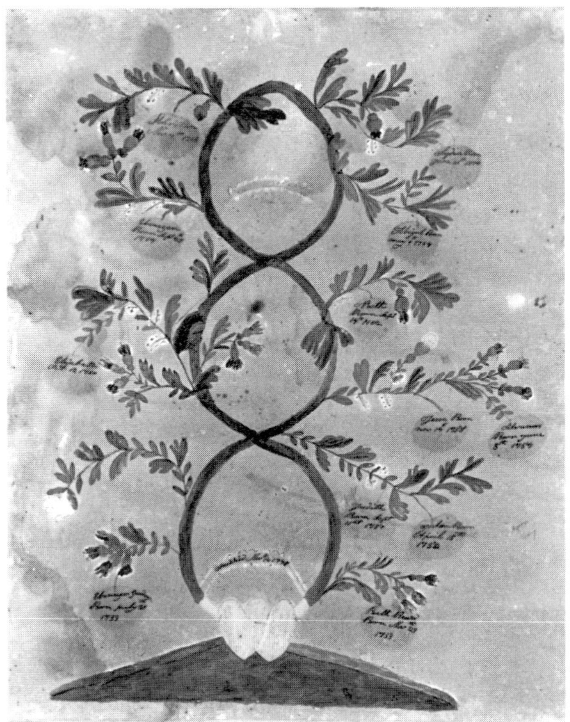

Figure 47 Family register. Ebenezer Gardiner and Ruth Beard. Nantucket, Massachusetts, mid to late nineteenth century. Watercolor. Courtesy of the Nantucket Historical Association.

[41]Edward Taylor, *Edward Taylor's Minor Poetry* (Boston: Twayne Publishers, 1981).

[42]*Oxford English Dictionary*, s.v. "family tree," 5:708. According to Gloria S. Allen, the term "Family Tree" appeared on American family registers at about the time of the American Civil War. See in *Family Record*, entry 152.

[43]The meaning of the term "cut off" was recorded in English literature in the fourteenth century and was still in use in 1880. *Oxford English Dictionary*, 2:1290.

[44]Allan I. Ludwig, *Graven Images: New England Stonecarving and Its Symbols, 1650–1815* (Middletown, Conn.: Wesleyan University Press, 1966), p. 88.

[45]Ibid., p. 123.

[46]Harriette M. Forbes, *Gravestones of Early New England* (Boston: Houghton Mifflin, 1972), opp. p. 106.

[47]Ludwig, *Graven Images*, plate 108.

[48]Illustrated in *The Treasure Houses of Britain*, ed. Gervase Jackson-Stops (New Haven: Yale University Press, 1985), p. 61.

[49]See Maureen Taylor's article in this collection.

[50]Natalie Zemon Davis, *Society and Culture in Early Modern France* (Stanford, Calif.: Stanford University Press, 1965), p. 199, reports that "the 1541 *Calendrier* [a French almanac book] has two literal trees with branches showing the Fruits of the Flesh and Fruits of the Spirit."

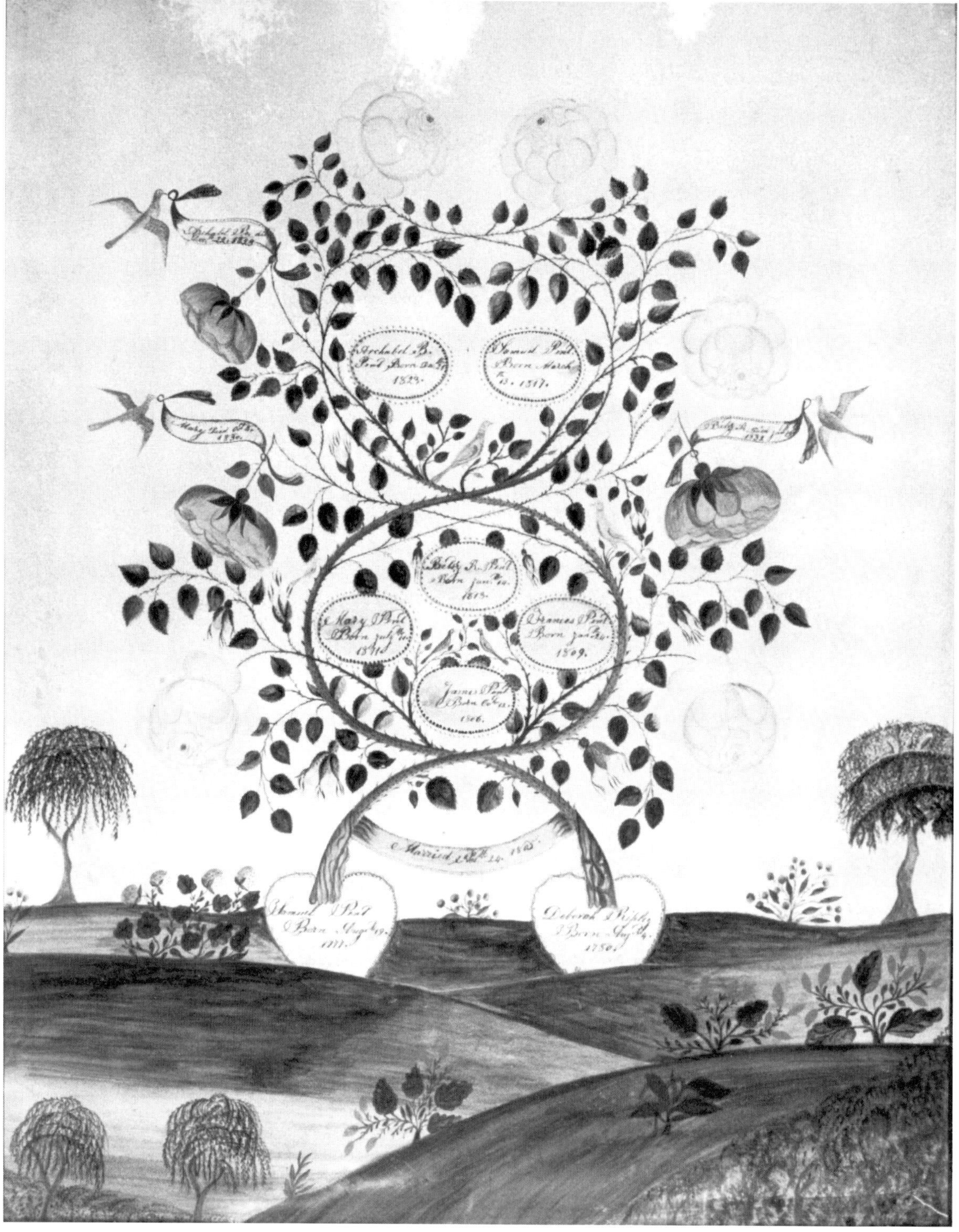

Figure 48 Family register. Samuel Pent and Deborah Ripley. Martha's Vineyard, Massachusetts, circa 1825–1830. Watercolor. Courtesy of Pam Boynton.

[51]"Farewell Bright Soul a short farewell / Till we shal meet again Above / In the Sweet groves where Pleasures dwell / And Trees of Life bear fruits of love." Quoted in Ludwig, *Graven Images*, p. 116.
[52]"Sampler by an Unknown Girl. 1775" illustrated in Bolton and Coe, *American Samplers*, plate 28.
[53]John Norman, *Hieroglyphic Bible* (Boston, 1794).
[54]Allen, *Family Record*, entry 158.
[55]Mrs. Gill advertised in Boston's *Columbian Centinel*, 23 March and 13 April 1811 (see Krueger, *New England Samplers*, p. 188); Glee Krueger kindly provided the name of Mrs. Gill's Academy from a piece she was researching for Arthur Liverant. See also *Kennedy Quarterly* 9, no. 3 (1969): 215.
[56]Avis Stearns Van Wagenen, *Genealogy and Memoirs of Isaac Stearns and His Descendants* (Syracuse, N.Y.: Courier, 1901), pp. 77–81.
[57]The connection leads to another possible identification of the teacher in charge of this type of needlework (see Benes, "Decorated Family Records," n. 21). In May 1806, Elijah Stearns, a well-known merchant, tithingman, and postmaster in Bedford, Massachusetts, and a cousin of the Honorable Isaac Stearns, advertised for a school for young ladies to commence near the meeting house in Bedford on 2 June. He announced it would include "Painting, Embroidery, all kinds of fine Needle Work" at a cost of $6 per quarter with boarding and washing at $2 per quarter. He identified the preceptress as "Miss Sprague." See *Columbian Centinel*, 24 May 1806. See also Van Wagenen, *Genealogy and Memoirs of Isaac Stearns*, pp. 46, 81, 189.
[58]Bentley, *Diary*, 14 May 1799.
[59]Marshall W. S. Swan, *Town on Sandy Bay: A History of Rockport, Massachusetts* (Rockport, Mass.: Town, 1980), pp. 82–83; the house is located at 133A Main Street, Rockport.
[60]Formerly in the collection of Sandy Bay Historical Society. Present location unknown. A copy of the blank tree was provided to the author by Gregory H. Laing, Haverhill Public Library, Haverhill, Mass.
[61]Cynthia V. A. Schaffner and Susan Klein, *Folk Hearts: A Celebration of the Heart Motif in American Folk Art* (New York: Alfred A. Knopf, 1984), p. 57.
[62]Information on Joseph Odiorne was supplied by Don Randall of Contoocock, N.H.; he also kindly provided the unfinished record by Odiorne from *Nineteenth-Century Folk Painting: Our Spirited National Heritage* (Storrs, Conn.: William Benton Museum of Art, 1973), no. 25 (Peter H. Tillou Collection).
[63]This piece is erroneously dated 1816 in both Benes, "Decorated Family Records," fig. 69, and in Allen, *Family Record*, plate 18.
[64]A much later local type of hearts-and-tree form is found in this area, among them the "Seavy family record" (*checklist 94*) which was described as being from the Drake house in Pittsfield, N.H. This register has a tree emerging from two horizontally aligned hearts. This one has few affinities with the Gloucester prototype, but both are tied to Pittsfield/Gilmanton families. *Maine Antique Digest*, September 1987, p. 22-A.
[65]Gravestone of Henry Sewall, 1699, First Parish burying ground, Newbury, Mass.
[66]The author is indebted to Judith Lund, curator of the Old Dartmouth Historical Society, New Bedford, Mass.
[67]Barbara P. Andrews, librarian, Nantucket Athenaeum, to the author, 9 February 1987; the text of Coffin's entry reads: "Edward D. Burke's son fell overboard and was drowned out of Ship Harlequin, Wm. Clark Master, at Woolwich Bay."
[68]Laurel T. Ulrich et al., "Four Perspectives on a Bed Rug," in *Textiles in New England: Four Centuries of Material Life: 1999 Annual Proceedings of the Dublin Seminar for New England Folklife* (Boston: Boston University Scholarly Publications, 2001). See Iona Lincoln's comment: "They [bed rug designs] were most often grounded in a pot or vessel or sometimes reminiscent of the Indian palampore; there would be a small mound of green indicating earth" (p. 24).
[69]Halpert Sale Catalogue, Sotheby Parke Bernet Sales 3572, November 1973, item 203. Kindly provided by Betty Ring. For Hall's location in Raynham, Mass., see *New England Historic Genealogical Register* 51 (1897): 290, and 54 (1900): 19.
[70]J. Hector St. John Crèvecoeur, *Letters from an American Farmer* (1782; reprint, Gloucester, Mass.: Peter Smith, 1986), p. 147.
[71]Ibid., p. 133; William Labov, "The Recent History of Some Dialect Markers on the Island of Martha's Vineyard, Mass.," in *Studies in Linguistics*, ed. L. M. Davis (University of Alabama Press, 1973), pp. 81–122.

“Keep Sacred the Memory of Your Ancestors”: Family Registers and Memorial Prints

Georgia Brady Barnhill

EARLY IN THE nation’s history, American families were, like their European counterparts, concerned about recording genealogical information and generally kept track of marriages, births, and deaths on pages in their family Bibles.[1] In the final decades of the eighteenth century, individuals began to produce ornamented family records in watercolor and ink and as samplers. In the years of the new Republic, schoolgirls produced many of these genealogical records as part of their education. These works exhibit a great deal of skill and charm, and some are closely related to printed forms used to record marriages, births, and deaths. As education reform caused the number of hand-painted works to decline in numbers in the 1830s, commercial print publishers began to issue a variety of blank forms in large editions that allowed individuals to record genealogical information and preserve the memory of family members.[2] Publishers and print sellers widely distributed such family registers and memorial prints in urban and rural areas. Examining these genres reveals a certain amount about the print trade, the use of extant iconography, and the popularity of maintaining information about family history.

By the end of the eighteenth century, publishers of Bibles such as Isaiah Thomas in Worcester, Massachusetts, included printed blank forms in Bibles. Thomas incorporated an unornamented one in his folio Bible published in 1791. Thirty years later, in 1821, Holbrook and Fessenden in Brattleboro, Vermont, included pages embellished with pictorial vignettes. The one for children’s marriages depicts Father Time with a seated child. The form for recording the names and birth and death dates of children is ornamented by a scene depicting a woman seated on the ground writing on a tablet, an infant on a blanket, and a woman dressed in mourning leaning against a monument surmounted by an urn and flanked by a weeping willow. Above is a cloud formation labeled “Marriage” with two birds on it.[3] In the late 1830s, the typefounder George Bruce included a memorial form in his book of type specimens. Rather than commission their own images, publishers could purchase stereotyped blocks from typefounders such as Bruce. Pictorial forms continued in use for decades. The Bible published by William W. Harding in Philadelphia in 1860 featured several pages of forms for marriages, births, and deaths.[4] Bibles were a part of almost every American household, and they were passed down from generation to generation with the genealogical records intact, the foundation for many genealogies today. It is important to note that forms in Bibles persisted in the nineteenth century even as separately published engraved and lithographed forms proliferated.

Family Registers

Between 1790 and 1810, three engravers capitalized on the vogue for ornamented forms and produced decorative pictorial engravings that supplemented the printed forms in Bibles and unique works by professional artists, students in female academies, and amateur artists.[5] The first generation of engraved family registers are few in number; only eighteen are recorded. The examples engraved by Richard Brunton (active 1790–1832), Benjamin Blythe (active 1769–1786), and Jervis Cutler (1768–1846)[6] share several aspects of their iconography. On these forms are allegorical female figures of Hope, Faith, Peace, and Charity, and other elements such as cornucopias, pelicans feeding their young, decorative floral ornamentation, children, beehives, and the allegorical figure of Fame. The space for family names and birth and death dates most often resembles a simple headstone. The combination of decorative ornaments and the naive style of the engravers produces a charming image (*Figure 1*). On one form, Brunton

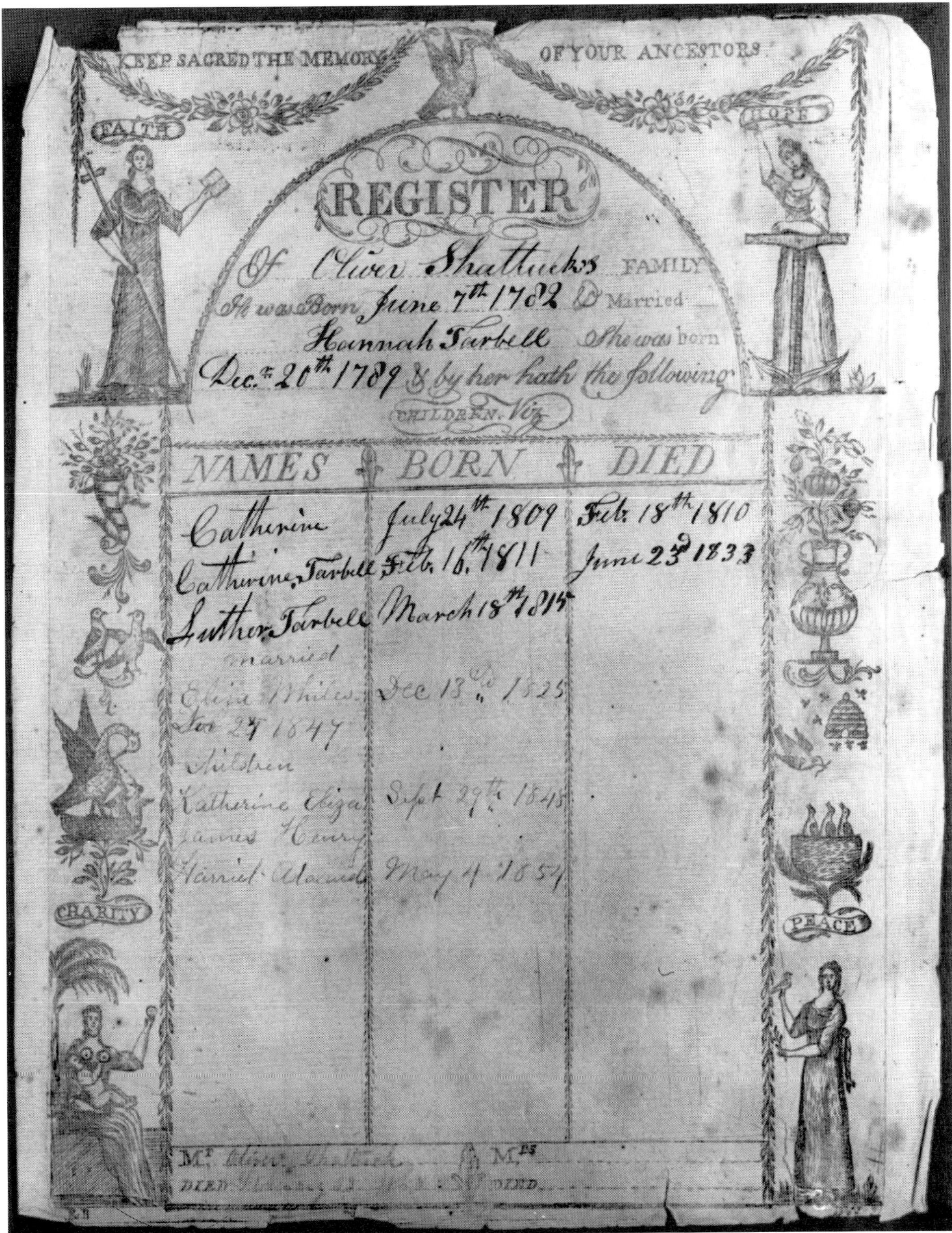

KEEP SACRED THE MEMORY OF YOUR ANCESTORS

FAITH

HOPE

REGISTER

Of Oliver Shattuck's FAMILY
He was Born June 7th 1782 & Married
Hannah Tarbell She was born
Dec.r 20th 1789 & by her hath the following
CHILDREN, Viz

NAMES	BORN	DIED
Catherine	July 24th 1809	Feb. 18th 1810
Catherine Tarbell	Feb. 16. 1811	June 23d 1833
Luther Tarbell	March 18th 1815	
married		
Eliza White	Dec 13d 1825	
Nov 2d 1847		
Children		
Katherine Eliza	Sept 29th 1848	
James Henry		
Harriet [illegible]	May 4 1854	

CHARITY

PEACE

M.r Oliver Shattuck M.rs
DIED [illegible] DIED

Figure 1 Family record. "Keep sacred the memory of your ancestors." Richard Brunton (d. 1832). Connecticut [?], 1805. Line engraving, 22.6 × 16.0 cm. The Connecticut Historical Society, Hartford, Connecticut. (1985.3.0).

used the iconography of the four seasons instead of allegorical figures. The progression of the seasons is similar to a progression in chronological age, from youth (spring) to old age (winter).

In the absence of account books and similar documents, we can only estimate the size of the editions of these forms. Brunton's lightly incised copperplates probably wore out after one hundred or so impressions were taken. The distribution of these early forms was, therefore, probably limited to the towns where the engravers worked and other nearby communities. Brunton engraved almost fifteen varying forms. Little is known about this engraver, described by William Dunlap as "an English engraver of no great merit," who was in New Milford, Connecticut, around 1790. He also worked in Suffield, Hartford, and Enfield. About 1810 he moved to Groton, Massachusetts, where he died in 1832.[7] We know his family registers were circulated because copies were made by several watercolorists including Eunice Pinney of Windsor, Connecticut, and Lucy King of Suffield, Connecticut.[8] Moreover, surviving impressions of the forms are filled with genealogical data; most show evidence of having been framed or remain in their original frames. What is not known is the source of his designs. Did Brunton create the compositions himself or was he working from printed sources? Elements such as cornucopias, birds, plants, and figures do appear in other works by Brunton. These works are so naïve in style that he probably was responsible for their design and did not copy from other sources. He also did a watercolor in 1815 as a memento mori for two children of Nathaniel Lawrence of Groton, Massachusetts.[9] Working at the same time as Brunton was Jervis Cutler, who probably engraved his two forms in Ohio where he resided between 1788 and 1809. Benjamin Blythe worked in Salem, Massachusetts, until 1782 when he moved to the South.[10] It is not known where he was working in 1805, the date that appears on the form he engraved. His composition is very similar to Brunton's although the number of decorative elements are fewer leading to a neater form. From the similarity of the compositions, it is likely that Blythe had seen Brunton's work.

Sometime between 1810 and 1820, Peter Maverick (1780–1831) of Newark, New Jersey, engraved a very handsome large "Family Register," designed by Henry Williams in a far more sophisticated style, using a different iconography and composition. The space for inscribing the names of the children born in the family is flanked by the allegorical figures of Hope and Charity standing on marble pedestals. Behind each figure are a pair of columns with an arch above connecting them. Betty Ring has determined that this print, or one derived from it, is the source for at least six stitched, paper, or reverse glass registers.[11] At the time of Maverick's death, 1,100 impressions of the form were sold for just $31.50.[12] Two watercolors derived from it are in the collection of Old Sturbridge Village. The one by Susannah Townsend is dated 1830.

About the same time as Maverick engraved his form, William B. Annin in Boston engraved a form based on the same design (*Figure 2*). There was no legal prohibition to prevent print publishers from copying each other's designs. Where did the figures of Hope and Charity come from? Beginning in the 1790s, other engravers had used the same allegorical figures and architectural features on membership certificates for Masonic lodges. Indeed, Annin and his partner George Girdler Smith engraved a membership certificate for the Massachusetts Grand Lodge with the figures of Charity, Hope, and Christianity between 1820 and 1825 that had been designed by John Ritto Penniman and Mills. The designers of this group of family registers incorporated several of the elements of the Masonic certificate into their compositions. Since Jervis Cutler, Peter Maverick, William B. Annin, George G. Smith, and John Ritto Penniman were Freemasons, their appropriation of Masonic imagery for this purpose is not surprising.[13] The new use bears out an assertion made by Alan Gowans that "Masonic imagery seems to permeate American culture almost as Christian symbolism permeated the art of the Middle Ages."[14] Another use of the same allegorical figures was T. W. Sumner's design for a meeting notice of the Massachusetts Charitable Society, engraved by Samuel Harris prior to his death in 1810, aged only twenty-seven. The iconography continued in use in the 1830s and 1840s with prints issued by Daniel W. Kellogg in Hartford and Nathaniel Currier in New York. But after a single generation of lithographed

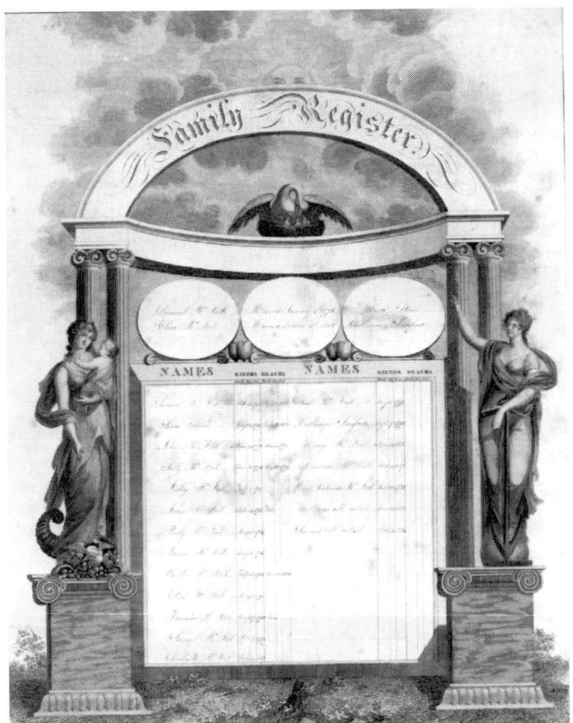

Figure 2 Family register. Henry Williams (1787–1830). Engraved by William B. Annin (1791?–1839). Boston, Mass., 1823. Line engraving, 39.9 × 30.4 cm. Old Sturbridge Village, 20.21.29/B254.31. *Photograph by Thomas Neill.*

derivatives, the use of Hope and Charity ceased as the fascination with classical motifs in the decorative arts waned.

Family registers became a popular staple for print publishers in New York and Hartford. As the genre evolved in the 1830s and 1840s, certain elements became standard. The forms consisted of four columns with lines for the names of family members, dates and places of births, marriages, and deaths. Each column was topped by an appropriate image of family life—parents with children, parents with infants, weddings, and scenes related to death. This format was not echoed by the works of students in female academies; schoolgirls turned to other types of images for their school art projects.

The earlier forms, particularly those published by Nathaniel Currier in the 1830s and 1840s, have relatively simple architectural and floral ornamentation, although one family register issued by Nathaniel Currier does feature more ornate Gothic architectural detail (*Figure 3*). Those issued by Currier and Ives in the 1860s feature far more intricate framing devices, reflecting a change in taste throughout the decorative arts. The vignettes of family life also demonstrate a parallel change. The weddings, for example, become more complex compositions featuring bridal attendants in addition to the minister, bride, and groom at the altar.

The Kellogg firms issued at least eight different family registers. The earliest example, by D. W. Kellogg, derives its ornamentation and vignettes from one issued by Nathaniel Currier. However, the allegorical figure of Hope next to a gravemarker replaces a mourning figure in a graveyard. On the tomb next to Hope is the phrase, "I Know my Redeemer Lives." Other forms by the Kellogg firms diverge from examples published in New York. On three Kellogg forms scenes of agricultural activity and views of buildings are added to the scenes of family life. One of the forms published by the Kelloggs mimics another of their compositions; the vignettes are similar, but the floral ornamentation is heavier and more ornate on one than on the other. The Kelloggs both derived their imagery from other publishers and created their own.

One example issued by James Baillie of New York is closely related to one by Nathaniel Currier (*Figure 4*). Both feature columns supporting the four vignettes that are identical in subject matter. One major difference is that the Currier form incorporates swans in the spaces for "Family Names," "Born When and Where," and so on across the form. In fact, Baillie derived many of his prints from Nathaniel Currier; this family register is no exception.

The use of lithography in the United States beginning in the 1820s enabled print publishers to issue large editions relatively inexpensively. A printer employed by Nathaniel Currier could print 1,000 impressions from a lithograph stone each day. At the same time, the audience for prints grew as the population increased and as travel and trade between the rural countryside and cities was facilitated by the improved network of roads, canals, and travel by railroads and steamboats. Indeed, the wide dispersal of forms printed in New York by Nathaniel Currier, Currier and Ives, and James Baillie to towns in New England is impressive and is one way to document

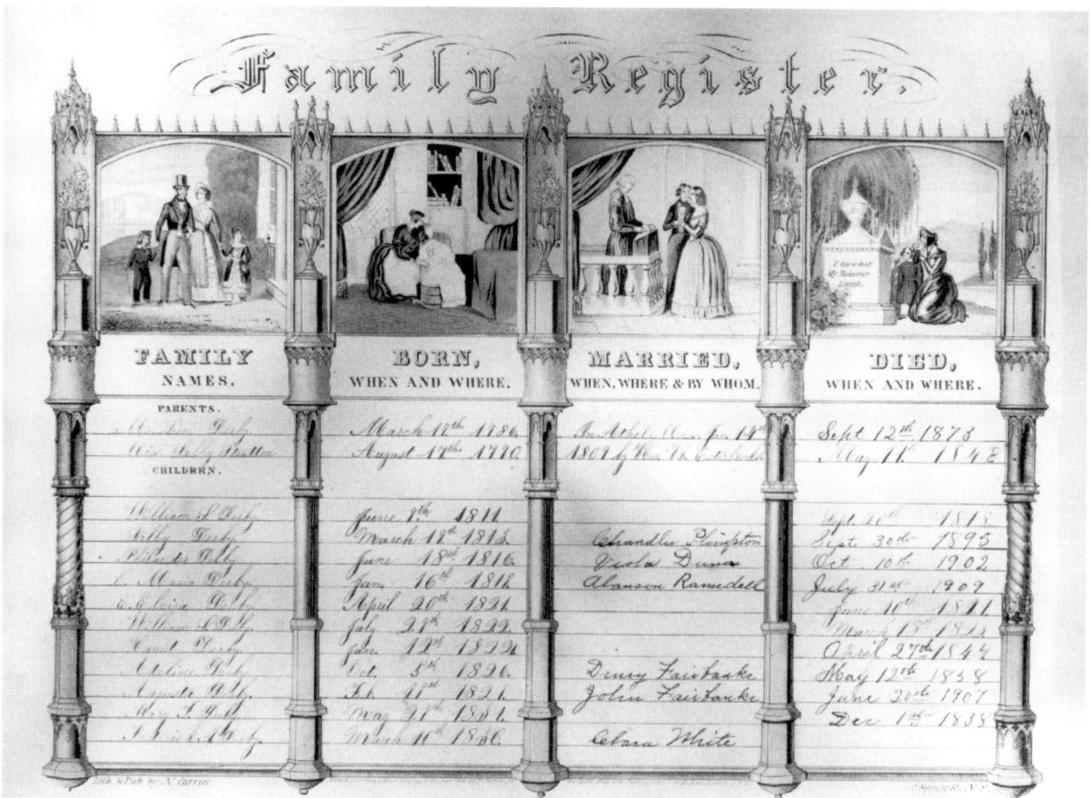

Figure 3 Family register. Nathaniel Currier (1813–1888). New York, 1835. Lithograph, 22.8 × 32.6 cm. Courtesy, American Antiquarian Society.

the circulation of nineteenth-century lithographs. The Kellogg firm of Hartford had offices in Buffalo and New York, aiding in the circulation of their prints to Ohio and cities of the Midwest (*Figure 5*). Also, print dealers in small New England towns sold the prints of other publishers. Such was the case of Lewis Robinson of Reading, Vermont.[15] Currier and Ives had an enormous mail-order business in addition to selling prints to customers in New York (*Figure 6*). The form with the largest single print run was undoubtedly the one issued in *Gleason's Pictorial Drawing-Room Companion* at a time when the circulation of this popular magazine was 110,000 copies each week.[16]

Beginning in the 1860s, spaces for carte-de-visite photographs were incorporated into family registers, usually replacing the earlier pictorial elements. C. F. Short in St. Louis published one form with spaces for ten photographs; Kurz and Allison of Chicago published a form with spaces for the photographs of the parents with the pages of an open book below to record births and deaths of children. Ten small circular vignettes of family life surround the central space flanked by two angels. Currier and Ives published a "Family Photograph Register" with spaces for fourteen likenesses and the traditional columns that appeared in the forms issued earlier by Nathaniel Currier. Beginning in the 1860s, a few publishers also issued marriage certificates with spaces for photographs of the bride and groom.

The publication of family registers by Currier and Ives and the Kelloggs, the two firms that were in existence from the 1830s through the 1880s and had dominated the production of this genre, declined in the 1860s. Perhaps because of a growing national preoccupation with genealogy and family history that spawned the founding of institutions such as the New England Historic Genealogical Society (in 1845) and later several hereditary societies,[17] commercial lithographers in many cities produced family

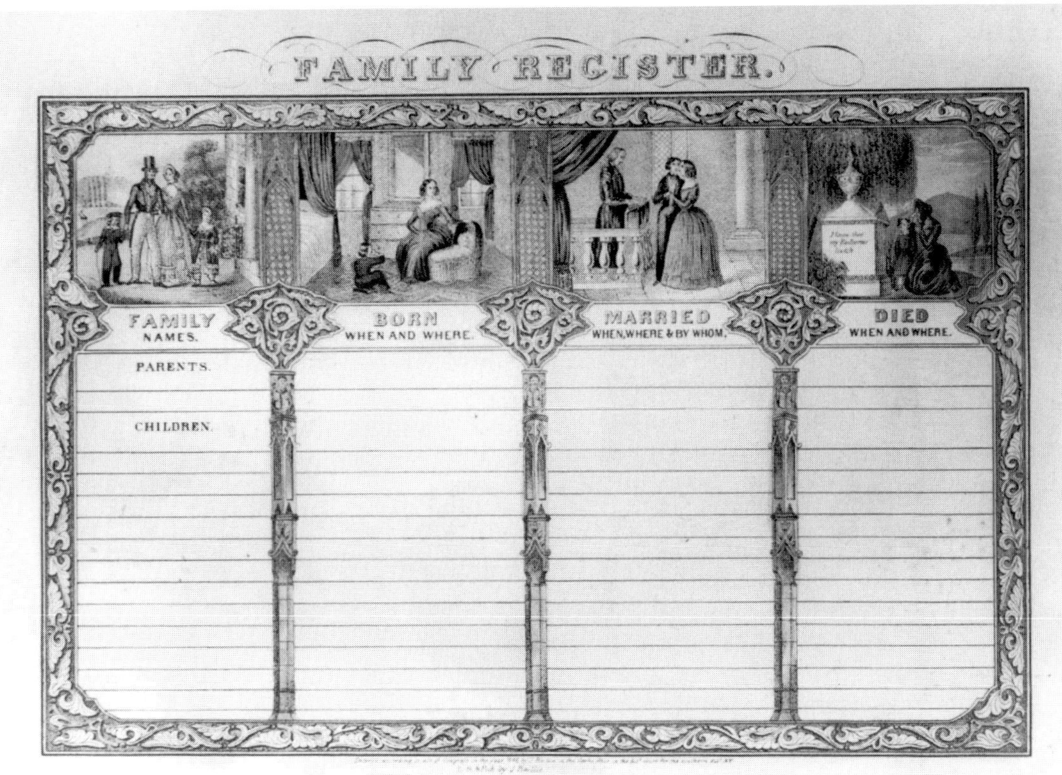

Figure 4 Family register. James S. Baillie. New York, 1846. Lithograph, 22.8 × 31.4 cm. Courtesy, American Antiquarian Society.

registers as their ambitions expanded beyond the general job work that generally preceded the publication of large framing prints. Production of these forms continued into the 1890s, and publishers conformed to the needs of their local communities. A. M. Bleichrode published his "Memory Table for dear departed ones" in New York in 1874 with the texts in Hebrew, German, and English. The Moline Plow Company published an "Allegorical Family Record" with agricultural scenes in 1881 in Buffalo, New York. Other lithographers in Chicago, Cincinnati, St. Louis, Terre Haute, and York, Pennsylvania, issued their own registers.

Memorial Prints

Instead of preserving genealogical information about a whole generation of a family, mourning pictures preserve information about just one, or less frequently, two or three individuals. Published prints providing a funerary monument with space for a commemorative inscription became a staple of the firms of Nathaniel Currier, Currier and Ives, and James Baillie in New York, and the Kelloggs in Hartford. Such mourning prints were important links between the living and the dead. In terms of burial practices, Gary Laderman documents the desire among the living to retain the corpse as long as possible.[18] He also notes that works of art were part of the "visual cues that reminded people of the prevalence of death in everyday life."[19] Posthumous portraiture and photography also comforted survivors and served a similar purpose as memorial prints.[20] Commercially published memorial prints supplanted the embroidered works of the students at female academies as the curriculum changed in the 1830s and 1840s.

The first successful publisher of lithographs in the United States was the firm founded by William and John Pendleton in Boston in 1825. Among their

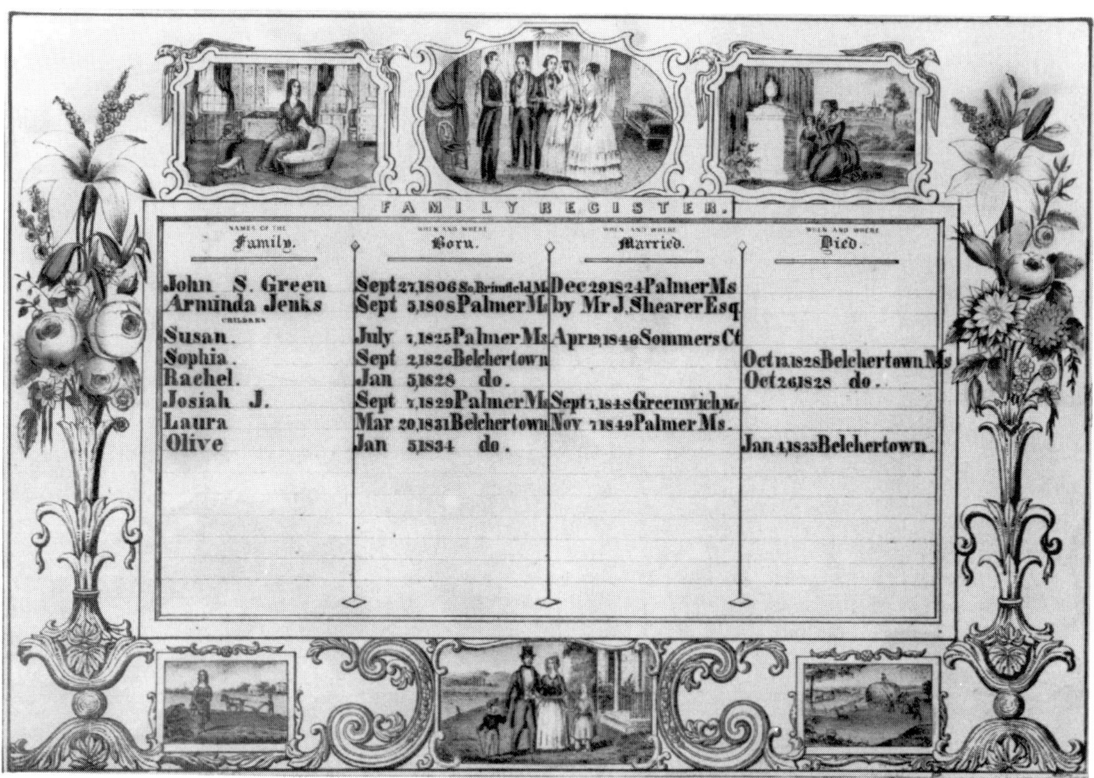

FAMILY REGISTER.

Family.	Born.	Married.	Died.
John S. Green	Sept 27,1806 So. Brimfield Ms	Dec 29 1824 Palmer Ms	
Arminda Jenks	Sept 5,1808 Palmer Ms	by Mr J. Shearer Esq	
Children			
Susan.	July 7,1825 Palmer Ms	Apr 19,1846 Sommers Ct	
Sophia.	Sept 2,1826 Belchertown		Oct 13,1828 Belchertown Ms
Rachel.	Jan 5,1828 do.		Oct 26,1828 do.
Josiah J.	Sept 7,1829 Palmer Ms	Sept 1,1848 Greenwich Ms	
Laura	Mar 20,1831 Belchertown	Nov 7 1849 Palmer Ms.	
Olive	Jan 5,1834 do.		Jan 4,1835 Belchertown.

Figure 5 Family register. Edmund Burke Kellogg (1809–1872) and Elijah Chapman Kellogg (1811–1881). Hartford and New York, 1858. Lithograph, 22.2 × 32.8 cm. The Connecticut Historical Society, Hartford, Connecticut (49738b).

earliest works was a memorial print by Mannevillette Elihu Dearing Brown (1810–1896).[21] This image, neoclassical in style, features a classically dressed female figure standing next to a large tomb upon which an inscription memorializing an individual could be written. A weeping willow hangs over the monument and a glimpse of distant landscape is given. Elements in this lithograph—a tomb or monument, a mourning figure, and a weeping willow—are all found in later prints. A second mourning print featuring a woman in classical costume was published by Thomas Moore, the successor to the Pendleton firm, in 1837. Benjamin Franklin Nutting (d. 1887),[22] a native of New Hampshire who went on to a career as a landscape painter and teacher, drew this image. Sources for the designs of the tombs in these two prints may be engravings of tombs in the Parisian cemetery, Père Lachaise, founded early in the nineteenth century.[23] A demand in Boston for visual information about the French cemetery existed because of the planning for Mount Auburn Cemetery founded in 1831. Both prints follow in the tradition of mourning pieces embroidered by schoolgirls in New England and elsewhere.[24] However, mourning figures in other lithographs are depicted in contemporary mourning dress.[25]

Pictorial sources for memorial prints include imported memorial kerchiefs issued in England and Scotland at the time of George Washington's death in 1800. Featuring tombs flanked by mourning allegorical figures, these items were widely circulated in major cities.[26] American memorial prints were also published in the United States at the time of Washington's death. Examples include one engraved by Thomas Clarke that is circular in composition with the mourning figures clothed in contemporary dress. A print engraved by Lewis Robinson in 1830 closely resembles Clarke's, suggesting that Clarke's print survived in some homes long after Washington's death. In 1804, at the time of

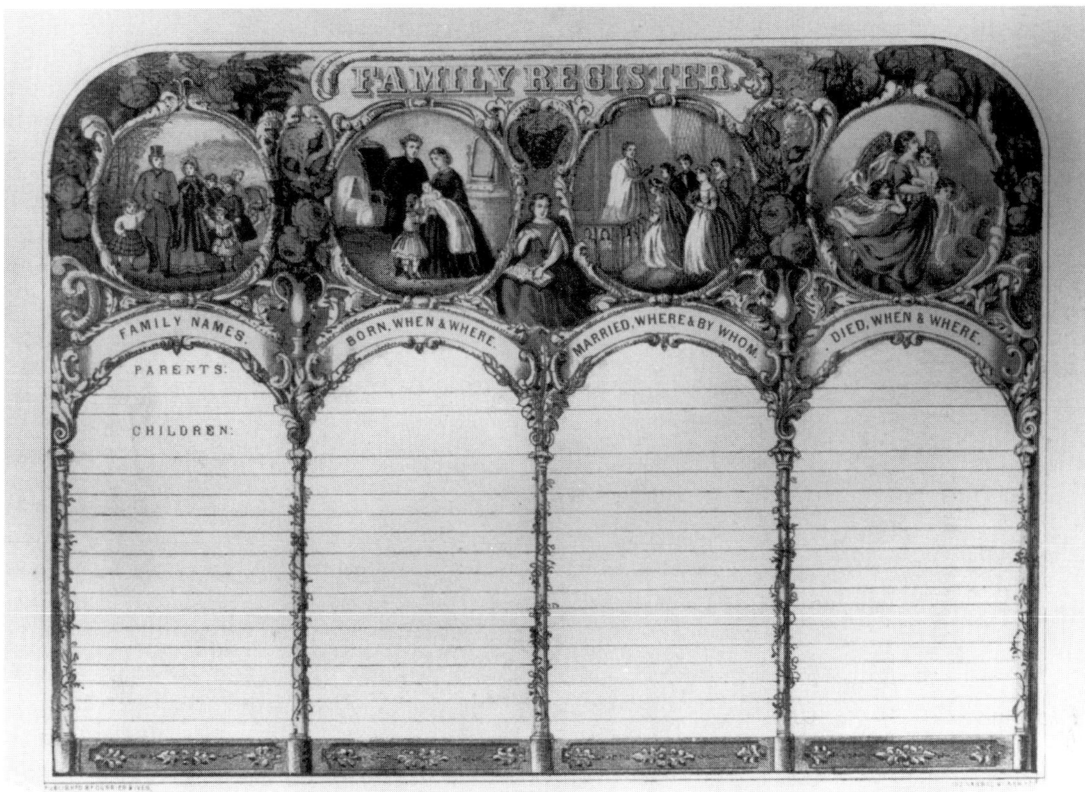

Figure 6 Family register. Currier and Ives. New York, circa 1850. Lithograph, 23.5 × 32.2 cm. Courtesy, American Antiquarian Society.

Alexander Hamilton's death, other kerchiefs were printed with similar imagery.

The prototype for many memorial prints was *A View of Cooke's Tomb In Saint Paul's Church Yard, N. York*, an aquatint by John Rubens Smith engraved and issued in New York in 1821 and published the next year in London (*Figure 7*). George Cooke, the popular British actor, died in New York in 1811. The print features a large monument surmounted with an egg-shaped urn topped by a finial with a view of the church to the side. Edmund Kean and John Wakefield Francis stand to the right of the monument. Nathaniel Currier published at least ten memorial prints derived from Smith's work (*Figure 8*). D. W. Kellogg published one of this type, as did Kelloggs and Comstock, and James Baillie (*Figure 9*). The same publishers occasionally reused the tomb in different settings. The popularity of Cooke's tomb on paper translated into three-dimensional tombs in cemeteries; the egg-shaped urn does appear on funeral monuments in New England graveyards.

Nathaniel Currier and Currier and Ives published over thirty memorial prints with titles such as "In Memory of," "Sacred to the Memory of," and "To the Memory of." The Kelloggs issued over twenty. Just as Nathaniel Currier copied Smith's aquatint, other publishers copied the prints issued by Currier. For example, one print issued by Nathaniel Currier depicts two children on the left side of an elaborate monument, with another child kneeling on the right. A print issued by E. B. and E. C. Kellogg reverses the composition and changes a few other details but is clearly derived from the Currier image.

In another instance, a figure group—an adult couple with a girl—was lifted from one composition and used in another. Nathaniel Currier published a print with the title "In Memory of" derived from John Rubens Smith. The three figures are on the right of the tomb. James Baillie lifted the figure

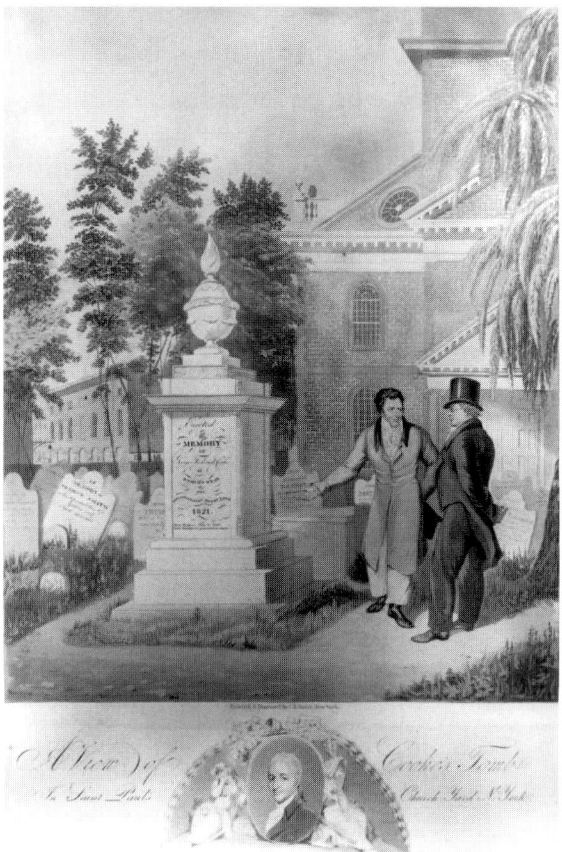

Figure 7 Memorial print. "A View of Cooke's Tomb In Saint Paul's Church Yard, N. York." John Rubens Smith (1775–1849). Courtesy, American Antiquarian Society.

group from that composition, placing it in a landscape, and changed the base of the monument. In addition, Nathaniel Currier reused the original composition, reversing it for another print and turning the man ninety degrees so that he is facing the monument with his spouse. The variations of these prints seem endless.

It is important to note that James Baillie and the Kelloggs frequently introduced their own imagery; not all of their prints were straight copies. Individual artists signed few of these prints; the exceptions are, therefore, notable. James G. Batterson signed two memorial prints issued by Kelloggs and Comstock (*Figure 10*). He was a sculptor in Hartford who specialized in mantle pieces, fountains, and monuments.[27] The prints that bear his signature may have served as advertisements for his funerary monuments. Henry Bucholzer initialed one print, an original composition, for James Baillie dated 1849.[28] Maria B. Cowles, one of the few women whose name appears in the annals of the commercial print trade, signed a family register issued by Kelloggs and Comstock in 1850.[28]

The imagery of memorial prints suggests that publishers were aware that differentiating the mourners in the prints by age and sex helped in marketing the prints. A print for a deceased husband might feature just a single woman, a woman with children, or even three generations—children, spouse, and parents. Many prints showed adult men and children standing before a monument bearing an inscription to a woman who probably died in childbirth. One very poignant print by the Kelloggs, explicitly titled "The Mother's Grave," shows a young child weeping under a willow tree next to the tomb. James Baillie also published a print titled "The Mother's Grave" with a boy and a girl next to a monument printed with text, leaving no space for an additional inscription by a family member. A few memorial prints lack human figures altogether. These were truly "generic" prints.

During the Civil War, memorials were issued specifically for men who were killed in battle. Typical is "The Soldier's Grave" by Currier and Ives showing a woman weeping by a gravestone with "In Memory of" at the rounded top above a relief sculpture on the stone of a military cap, flags, and weapons and text on the stone leaving space for the name of the soldier's company and the place of death (*Figure 11*). It closes with "A brave and gallant soldier, and a true patriot. His toils are past, his work is done, / And he is fully blest; / He fought the fight, the victory won, / And enters into rest." Versions of this print were published in 1862 and 1865; their "Soldier's Memorial" was issued in 1863. The firm of Caldwell and Company issued "The Soldier's Grave" in 1862, a large folio lithograph depicting a woman prostrate next to her husband's grave. Memorial prints such as these were particularly important to families since some soldiers killed in action failed to receive appropriate burials. Often bodies were covered with a minimal amount of soil; many casualties were never identified.[29] Although memorial prints could not replace the comfort of an appropriate funeral and proper monument, they provided an object to venerate.

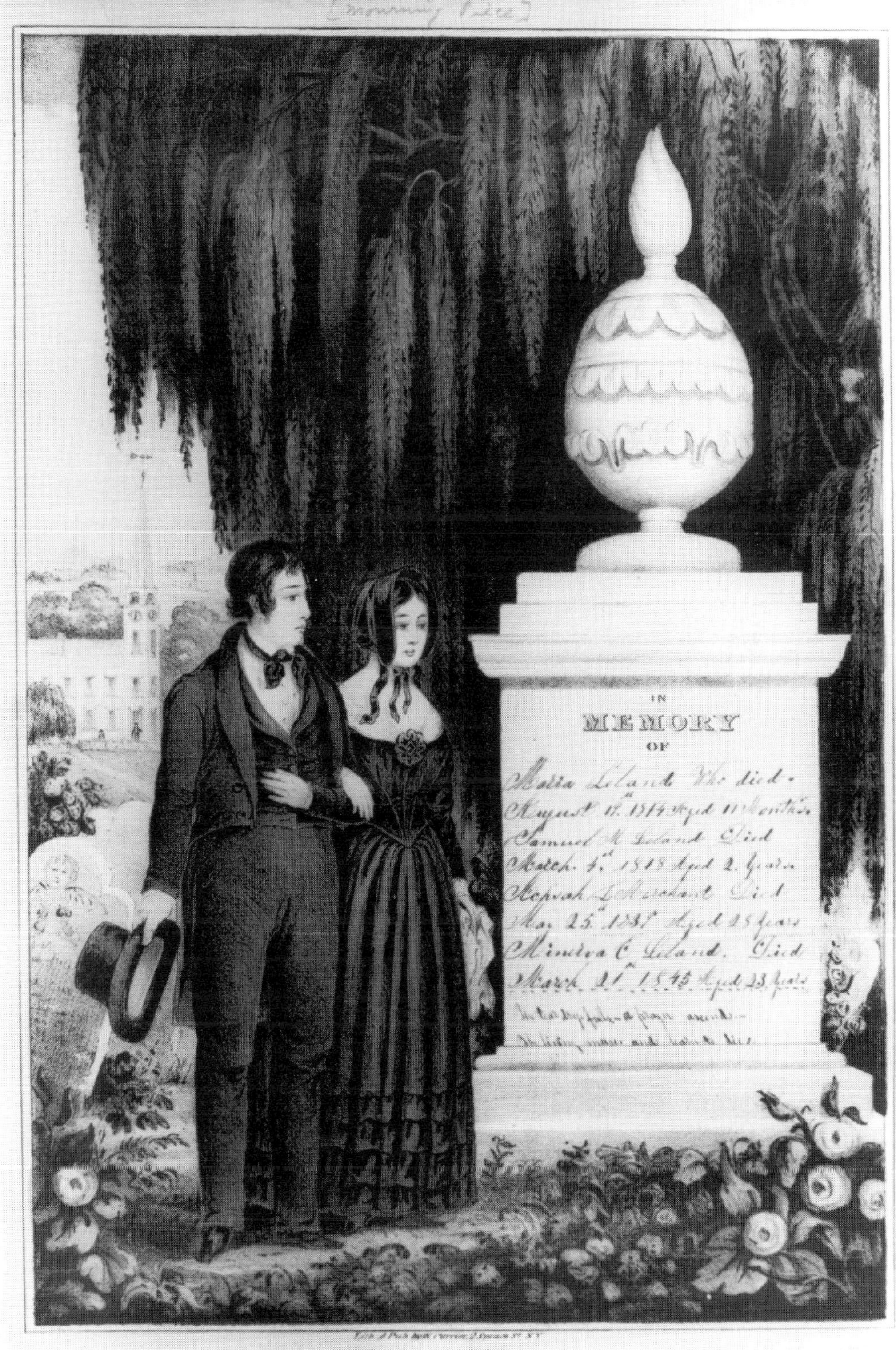

Figure 8 Memorial print. "In Memory of . . ." Nathaniel Currier (1813–1888). New York, 1845. Lithograph, 33 × 22.8 cm. Courtesy, American Antiquarian Society.

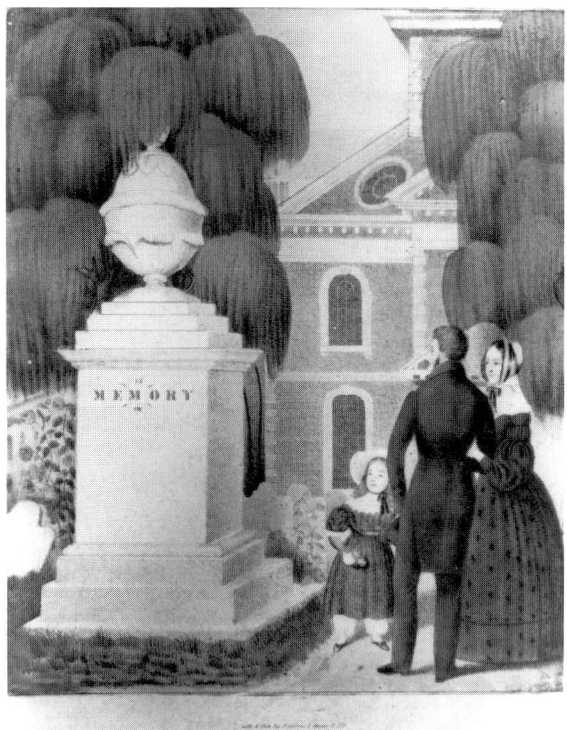

Figure 9 Memorial print. "In Memory of . . ." Nathaniel Currier (1813–1888). New York, 1845. Lithograph, 33 × 22.6 cm. Courtesy, American Antiquarian Society.

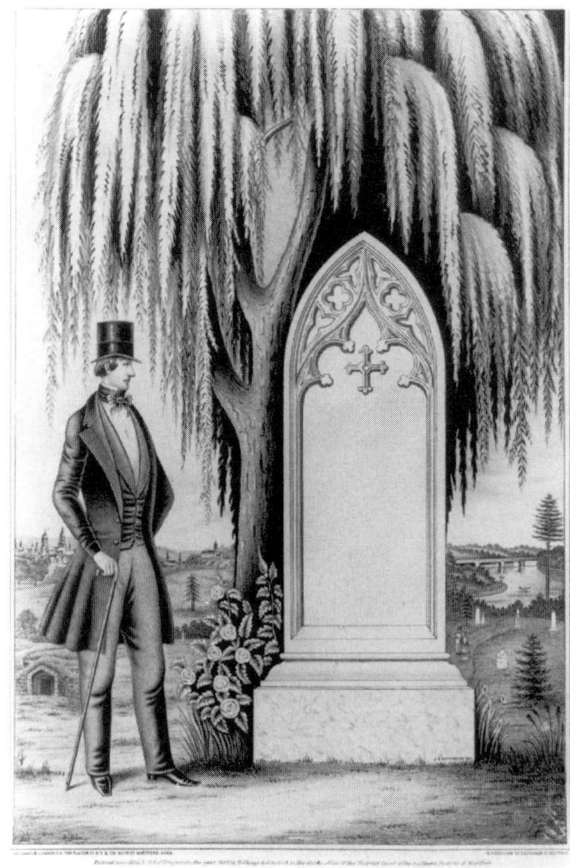

Figure 10 Memorial print. James G. Batterson (1823–1920). Hartford, New York, and Buffalo: Kelloggs and Comstock, 1848. Lithograph. The Connecticut Historical Society, Hartford, Connecticut (689).

Most memorial prints have pictorial elements in common: a funerary monument, suggestions of a church and graveyard, flowers and trees, a river, sometimes with a boat, and mourners. These pictorial elements had standard meanings to their nineteenth-century viewers. The monuments symbolized, of course, the deceased. The churchyards and churches reinforced the sacredness of the image. Laura Mills writes that the weeping willow tree was commonly incorporated into these compositions because the ability of the tree to regenerate itself after being cut suggested the resurrection of Christ. She also suggests that the presence of rivers and boats in these compositions "alludes to the soul's voyage to heaven."[30] Many of the settings suggest rural churchyards, with flowering plants in the foreground and old-fashioned headstones in the middle ground. A few incorporate a church into the composition, but not other gravestones or monuments. Later lithographs suggest the existence of rural cemeteries with larger vistas. One by Currier and Ives includes a decorative iron fence around the monument, a common feature of rural cemeteries.[31]

Memorial prints were copied by other artists in other media. In one private collection, several "sandpaper" drawings are derived from prints by Nathaniel Currier, D. W. Kellogg, and Thomas Moore. In at least one instance, it seems that two prints served as the source for one drawing. Lydia L. Gay of Peterborough, New Hampshire, painted a watercolor version of a Kellogg print while a student at the Hancock Literary and Scientific Institute in November 1842. It memorializes her father who died in 1839. The instructor of French, Italian, and "ornamental branches" was Miss M. C. Willard. A wood engraving is closely related to lithographs published by D. W. Kellogg and William S. Pendleton.

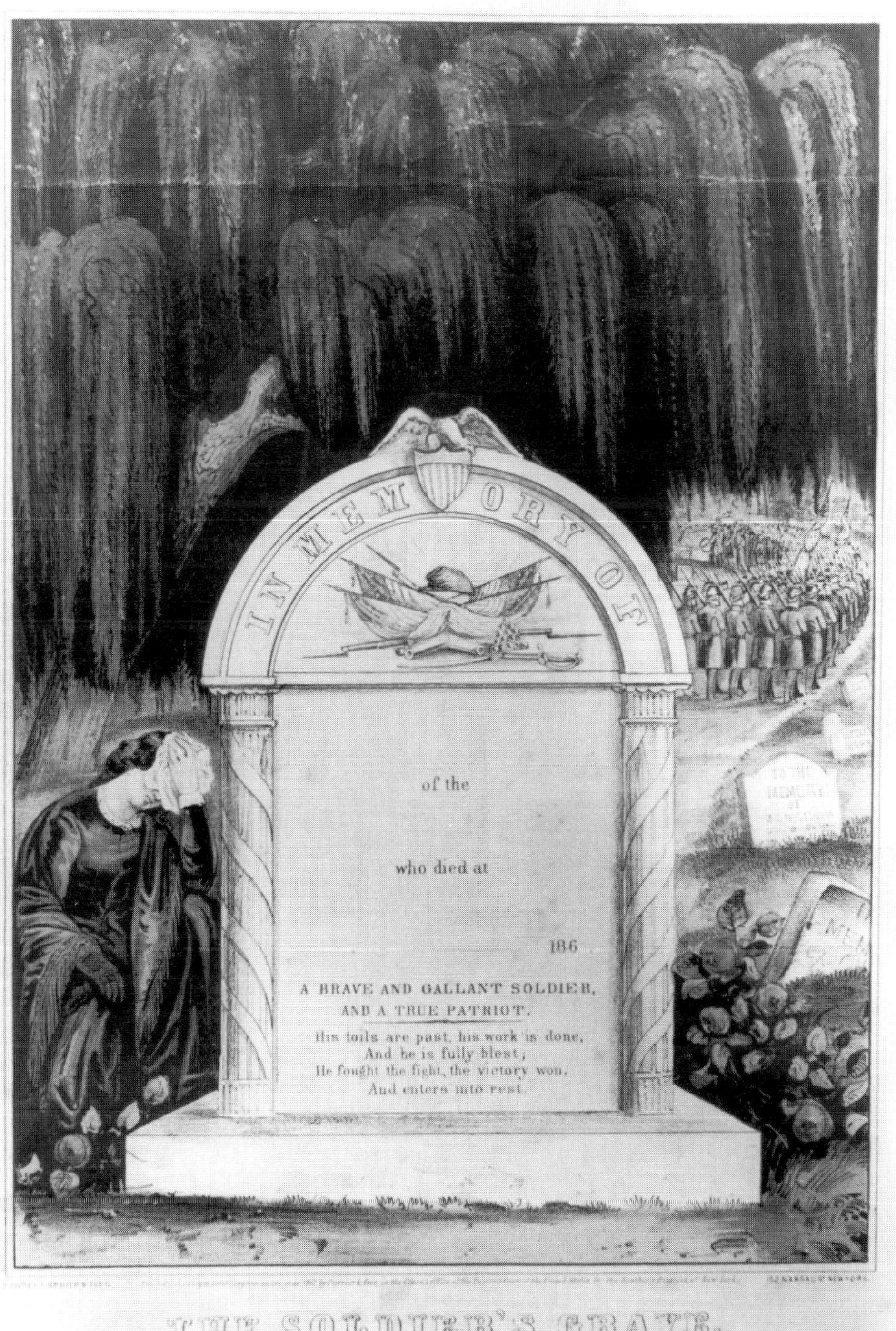

Figure 11 Memorial print. "The Soldier's Grave." Currier and Ives. New York, 1862. Lithograph, 32.6 × 21.6 cm. Courtesy, American Antiquarian Society.

The existence of memorial art has been noted in the literature on death in nineteenth-century America but without specific reference to these lithographed forms.[32] Stitched and painted memorials executed by dutiful daughters reinforce the role of devout women in the ceremonies surrounding death. The multiplicity of lithographed forms, each issued in editions of thousands of impressions, suggests that they became an integral part of the visual culture of the home, even after schoolgirls turned to academic subjects in their schools and academies.

Memorial prints were a means to connect the living with the dead, much in the same way that Spiritualists did in their seances in the second half of the nineteenth century.[33] Relating the large number of memorial prints published in the middle of the nineteenth century to the development of Spiritualism is tempting. The handwritten inscription on one memorial print is quite suggestive: "Our Father & Mother / William David / Who went in to the spirit world June 12, 1851 and of his wife Mary Fletcher who joined him the far off land Oct. 25 1860."[34] Gary Laderman asserts that "Spiritualists in the Gilded Age were attracted to domesticated heavenly scenes of individual and familial continuity, and practitioners made concerted efforts to provide strict scientific evidence that validated their claims about visitations during seances. For both Spiritualists and liberal-to-moderate Protestants, the spirits of the dead were present and could be accessible to the living."[35] This movement gave much comfort to its believers; others found it merely entertaining. Still others wrote books and articles exposing the trickery of Spiritualists.[36]

Spiritualism began in upstate New York in 1848 when mysterious rappings occurred in the presence of two girls, Kate and Margaret Fox, in their home in Hydesville, New York. A means for communication between the living and the dead was then said to be available for public observation through similar rappings during seances elsewhere. Within a very few years, Spiritualism had adherents throughout the United States, crossing class lines and geographic boundaries. In *Radical Spirits* Ann Braude emphasizes the domestic nature of Spiritualism. "The ritual of the seance perfectly suited the domestic environment. It required no participants beyond the family, no facilities beyond the home."[37] A print dedicated to the memory of the deceased with whom the family was trying to communicate seems an appropriate accompaniment to the scene of the family group seated around the parlor table, hands linked, and minds focused on the deceased. The growing interest in Spiritualism in the late 1840s and 1850s may explain the popularity of mourning prints. By 1857, for example, sixty-seven periodicals had been in circulation during the period. What weakens the argument is the absence of precise publication dates on many nineteenth-century prints. Some dates are deceiving; prints published by Currier and Ives after 1857 were actually first printed and copyrighted by Nathaniel Currier before 1857; yet the earlier copyright date is in the imprint. Many prints were kept in stock for several years after the copyright date on the print. This explains why so many forms were filled out several years after the print was first published. However, about half of the eighty-five memorial prints recorded in the checklist were published in the years just before and after 1848.[38] Nathaniel Currier was not unaware of the Fox sisters; he published a lithograph of the two girls and their older sister, Leah (Fox) Fish, in 1852.[39] If nothing else, Currier was able to gauge public interest and publish prints with great commercial potential. Unlike public interest in Spiritualism, which grew during the 1860s and claimed eleven million adherents at its height in 1870,[40] the publication and use of mourning prints declined precipitously after the Civil War.

It is clear from extant forms preserving genealogical data that families in New England acquired and used them. Although some collections include unused forms, most impressions bear inscriptions. Several engraved and lithographed forms at Old Sturbridge Village remain in their original frames; impressions in other institutions show evidence of having been framed at one time. Contemporary evidence such as a watercolor by Joseph H. Davis shows a framed memorial print or needlework on a wall above a parlor table.[41] A mourning picture appears on the parlor wall in Henry F. Darby's portrait *The Reverend John Atwood and His Family.*[42] A family record forms part of the background for a watercolor by Caroline Hill depicting the family of Job Hill.[43] Robert Peckham's *The Children of Oliver Adams* also features the family record of Oliver and Zilphia (Saywer) Adams on the wall.[44]

The publication of prints enabling families to record genealogical data was an important phenomenon in the nineteenth century attesting to the strong interest in collecting and preserving genealogical data, continuing practices that had existed for several generations in other media. The sheer number of different forms attests to the importance of these genres to commercial publishers and the attractiveness of them to their audience.

NOTES

[1]The author would like to thank Cathy Cherbosque of the Huntington Library and Peter Benes for their comments and suggestions on the essay. The author is grateful to Randall and Tanya Holton, Gail Schuster formerly at the Connecticut Historical Society, Donald R. Friary at Historic Deerfield, Elliot Davis at the Metropolitan Museum of Art, Cathleen Latendresse at the Henry Ford Museum, Harry Katz at the Library of Congress, Jacqueline Calder at the Vermont Historical Society, James Ganz at the Sterling and Francine Clark Art Institute, Lynne Z. Bassett formerly at Old Sturbridge Village and now at the Connecticut Historical Society, Laura Mills at the Worcester Art Museum, and Martha M. Strum and Sharon Greene at the Shelburne Museum, Wendy Shadwell at the New-York Historical Society, the reference department of the Museum of the City of New York, as well as Scott A. Bartley and D. Brenton Simons of the New England Historic Genealogical Society for assistance in the preparation of the checklist. Dealers Chris Lane of the Philadelphia Print Shop, Donald Heald, and Rona Schneider brought impressions of prints to my attention that the American Antiquarian Society purchased. The author is grateful to her own institution for the time to visit other collections in pursuit of these forms.

[2]The decline in numbers of genealogical watercolors and samplers is documented by Gloria Seaman Allen in *Family Record: Genealogical Watercolors and Needlework* (Washington, D.C.: Daughters of the American Revolution Museum, 1989). Page two charts the decline in watercolors beginning in 1810 and in samplers and embroideries beginning in 1820.

[3]These examples at the New England Historic Genealogical Society are in MSS C3767 and filled out for members of the York-Durgin family.

[4]These forms at New England Historic Genealogical Society are filled in for the Ebenezer Berry family, MSS A78.

[5]Peter Benes has documented a large body of genealogical art in "Decorated Family Records from Massachusetts, New Hampshire, and Connecticut" in *Families and Children: 1985 Annual Proceedings of the Dublin Seminar for New England Foklife* (Boston: Boston University Scholarly Publications, 1987) which has been revised and updated for the present volume. Likewise, Betty Ring reproduced many genealogical samplers from this period in *Girlhood Embroidery: American Samplers and Pictorial Needlework* (New York: Alfred A. Knopf, 1993).

[6]George C. Groce and David H. Wallace, *The New-York Historical Society's Dictionary of Artists in America* (New Haven and London: Yale University Press, 1957), pp. 160–61.

[7]For information on Brunton, see Albert C. Bates, *An Early Connecticut Engraver and His Work* (Hartford: Lockwood and Brainard Company, 1906) and two articles by William L. Warren, "Richard Brunton—Itinerant Craftsman," *Art in America* 39 (April 1951) and *Art in America* 41 (spring 1953). Dunlap's comment is quoted in the first article, p. 81. The death of Richard Brenton [*sic*] on 8 September 1832 is recorded in *Vital Records of Groton, Massachusetts to the end of the Year 1849*, 2 vols. (Salem: Essex Institute, 1927), 2:106.

[8]Reproduced in Warren's 1953 article, pp. 76–77. A third watercolor copy is at Old Sturbridge Village, filled in for the family of Prudence Healey and Parker Willard of Dudley, Massachusetts. (*Vital Records of Dudley, Massachusetts, to the End of the Year 1849* [Worcester: Franklin P. Rice, 1908], pp. 181, 239.) See also the *M. and M. Karolik Collection of American Water Colors and Drawings, 1800–1875*, 2 vols. (Boston: Museum of Fine Arts, Boston, 1962), 2:208–11.

[9]Described in Warren's article in *Art in America* (April 1951): 94, and reproduced (spring 1953): 74.

[10]Bettina Norton, "The Brothers Blyth: Salem in Its Heyday," in *Painting and Portrait Making in the American Northeast: 1994 Annual Proceedings of the Dublin Seminar for New England Folklife* (Boston: Boston University Scholarly Publications, 1995), p. 55.

[11]The form by Peter Maverick is owned by Betty Ring and is reproduced in Allen, *Family Record*, p. 101.

[12]Stephen D. Stephens, *The Mavericks, American Engravers* (New Brunswick, N.J.: Rutgers University Press, 1950), p. 126.

[13]John D. Hamilton, *Material Culture of the American Freemasons* (Lexington, Mass.: Museum of Our National Heritage, 1994) contains reproductions of many membership certificates as well as information on the engravers.

[14]Quoted by Barbara Franco, "Masonic Imagery" in *Aspects of American Printmaking, 1800–1950*, James F. O'Gorman, ed. (Syracuse, N.Y.: Syracuse University Press, 1988), p. 1.

[15]George R. Dalphin and Marcus A. McCorison, "Lewis Robinson—Entrepreneur" in *Vermont History* 30 (October 1962): 304.

[16]Many of the manuscript notations on the forms reveal the towns and states where the families who used the forms resided. This information is helpful in assessing the wide circulation of the lithographs published by commercial lithographers.

[17]Allen, *Family Record*, p. 3.

[18]Gary Laderman in *Sacred Remains: American Attitudes toward Death, 1799–1883* (New Haven: Yale University Press,

1996) documents this aspect of the rituals surrounding death in his chapter "Morbid Obsessions," pp. 73–85.

[19]Laderman, *Sacred Remains*, p. 26.

[20]A broadside advertisement issued by the portrait painter Charles L. Fenton in the collection of the American Antiquarian Society reads: "'Secure the shadow e're the substance fade.'... Would it not be a high and holy gratification, when that being has passed out of your natural sight into the spirit land, to have an image of the earthly appearance of the dear one?" Printed at New London, Conn., 1848.

[21]Sally Pierce and Catharina Slautterback, *Boston Lithography, 1825–1900: The Boston Athenaeum Collection* (Boston: Boston Athenaeum, 1991), p. 166; print is reproduced on p. 23.

[22]Reverend John Keep Nutting, *Nutting Genealogy: A Record of Some of the Descendants of John Nutting of Groton, Massachusetts* (Syracuse, N.Y.: C. W. Bardeen, 1908), p. 90.

[23]Several possible engravings are reproduced in Blanche Linden-Ward, *Landscapes of Memory and Boston's Mount Auburn Cemetery* (Columbus: Ohio State University, 1989), pp. 95–101.

[24]Many beautiful examples of embroidered mourning pictures are reproduced in Ring, *Girlhood Embroidery.*

[25]The clothing worn by the mourning figures in these prints is probably descriptive of actual practice and would be a good source for costume historians. Although most women, for example, were dressed in black, occasionally somber browns, deep blues, and reds were used in the dresses and cloaks. The changing styles of the children's clothes and other apparel such as hats are very interesting.

[26]Two of these kerchiefs are reproduced in Herbert Collins, *Threads of History* (Washington: D.C.: The Smithsonian Institution Press, 1979), p. 56. Both are in the collection of the American Antiquarian Society.

[27]George C. Groce and David H. Wallace, *The New-York Historical Society's Dictionary of Artists in America* (New Haven: Yale University Press, 1957), p. 36.

[28]D. Brenton Simons of the New England Historic Genealogical Society located a Maria B. Cowles in the *Genealogy of the Cowles Family in America* (New Haven: Tuttle, Morehouse and Taylor, 1929), 1:359. She was born in Amherst, Mass., married Lemuel Dewey in Hartford in 1856, and died in San Francisco in 1894. She probably is the same woman who drew the lithograph for the Kelloggs.

[29]For additional detail, see Laderman, *Sacred Remains*, part 2.

[30]Laura Mills, *American Allegorical Prints: Constructing an Identity* (New Haven: Yale University Art Gallery, 1996), p. 11.

[31]Stanley French, "The Cemetery as Cultural Institution: The Establishment of Mount Auburn and the 'Rural Cemetery' Movement," in *Death in America*, ed. David E. Stannard (Philadelphia: University of Pennsylvania Press, 1975), p. 80.

[32]See, for example, French, "The Cemetery as Cultural Institution," pp. 73–74.

[33]Ann Braude, *Radical Spirits: Spiritualism and Women's Rights in Nineteenth-Century America* (Boston: Beacon Press, 1989), thoroughly explores this important religious movement.

[34]Inscription on an impression of a Nathaniel Currier form, Museum of the City of New York 56.300.1296. Braude, *Radical Spirits*, p. 54, notes the use of terms such as "passed to the Spirit Land" or "awakened to the newness of life in the Spirit World" on gravestones.

[35]Laderman, *Sacred Remains*, p. 170.

[36]One example is the Reverend H. Mattison's *Spirit Rapping Unveiled! An Expose of the Origin, History, Theology and Philosophy of Certain Alleged Communications from the Spirit World* (New York: Mason Brothers, 1853).

[37]Braude, *Radical Spirits*, p. 24.

[38]Publication dates can be assigned by using the addresses found in city directories, and this has been done for many of the Kellogg, Currier, and Baillie prints.

[39]This print is reproduced in Braude, *Radical Spirits.*

[40]This statistic is quoted by Laderman from Sydney Ahlstrom's *A Religious History of the American People* (New Haven: Yale University Press, 1972), p. 490.

[41]The author is very grateful to Laura Mills for providing this reference. The watercolor is reproduced in *Magazine Antiques* 153, no. 1 (January 1998): 59.

[42]This painting, at the Museum of Fine Arts, Boston, is reproduced in Elizabeth Donaghy Garrett's *At Home: The American Family 1750–1870* (New York: Harry N. Abrams, 1990), p. 151.

[43]The watercolor is reproduced in Garrett, *At Home*, p. 222.

[44]Reproduced in Allen, *Family Record*, iv. This form does not correspond to any printed form seen by the present author.

Tall Oaks from Little Acorns Grow: The Family Tree Lithograph in America

Maureen A. Taylor

MID-NINETEENTH-CENTURY families in America used many different media to record their descent from earlier generations. Some chose to compile genealogy books or write journal articles, while others commissioned pictorial ancestry or descendancy charts using the family tree—a literal interpretation of an ancient botanical metaphor indicating blood lines. They often employed the most up-to-date printing method—the lithograph—to disseminate family information. Creation of such family icons was a collaborative effort. The family patriarch, his relatives, or their agents collected data; the artist produced a design; and the lithographer printed it. These trees were produced by printers and publishers throughout the United States.

Scholars have generally overlooked the tree as an icon in genealogical tabulation.[1] The absence of a body of scholarship on this subject may be attributed to the lack of a single descriptive term for family trees, which in the nineteenth century were variously called "decorated family records," "pedigrees," "genealogical charts," "genealogical arbors," or "tabular pedigrees." In fact they are a combination of all of those images because they use standard icons and genealogical information to create a family's history. Nevertheless, the lack of a single term to describe such charts makes them difficult to locate.[2]

English and American traditions of the tree as a symbol of life and family descend from Old Testament religious symbolism which in turn comes down, at least in part, from prehistoric beliefs. The vision of an ancestor as tree, explicit in the messianic vision of Isaiah 11 ("And there shall come forth a rod out of the stem of Jesse, and a branch shall grow out of his roots..."), was depicted in late medieval panel painting and church decoration and survives in several English hymns. Central to the world view of English and American Puritans was the tale of Adam and Eve in the Garden of Eden. Their beguilement by the Serpent beneath the spreading branches of the Tree of the Knowledge of Good and Evil—with their dreadful fall, in consequence—was known to every one of the eighteenth- and early-nineteenth-century schoolgirls who stitched trees and floral motifs along with genealogical data to create family records in samplers and other needlework. This symbolic tradition inspired moral and religious allegories such as the Tree of Temperance, the Tree of Grace, and the Tree of Life.[3] And typical of the nineteenth-century's optimism and faith in progress, the oldest impulses found expression using the latest printing technology. One of the earliest examples of a printed genealogical tree refers not to a single family in ordinary life, but to English royalty.[4]

Standard elements of printed family trees are the use of the trunk for the immigrant ancestor's name, branches for his children, and stumps to denote lines dying without issue. The root or ground bears the immigrant ancestor's name (showing the family's foundation in America and suggesting the "roots" of its future success), and the trunk represents his children, with each branch representing the third generation, and additional branching-off added as needed for later descendants. In a few cases, the artist used a tree's roots to outline the family's history prior to immigration. The size of the prints ranged from approximately six-by-nine inches (which could be inserted or bound into a family history) to wall-sized versions. Oversize prints could be prominently displayed in a frame or hung from a wooden bar.

Nevertheless, there is amazing variation in design of the trees and the presentation of data. Besides the central image of the tree, other elements of the design may include houses, background or foreground landscape scenes, portraits, or heraldic crests. Most trees appear without foliage, as in winter. In this stark, simplified depiction, branches correspond to each succeeding generation. There seems to be no special significance to the absence of leaves other than as an artistic device to allow more space for information.

Foliage, when present, may identify the species of tree. Oak, a symbol of integrity and stability since the medieval period, was a popular choice. In the 1852 Francis Peabody tree, (*Figure 1*) for example, oak leaves and branches support circles filled with family names and dates. Only two other identifiable species motifs were found: pine, chosen by the Skinner family of Mississippi (*Figure 2*), and beech, selected by the Lippincott family of Pennsylvania. The Skinner tree's branches bear genealogical data set into a background of pine needles. On the Lippincott tree, each leaf contains a family member's name. The John Cowell and Joseph Talbot trees, both nineteenth century (*Figures 3 and 4*) and the 1867 Isaac Collins tree also used a single leaf for each name, but these designs are simple compared to the quantity of persons represented on the Lippincott tree. Twentieth-century examples such as the Canfield tree use foliage as a background element for visual interest. Family data appear in empty spaces within a border of stylized greenery.

In several cases, branches represent male lines, while female lines are leaves. In the 1861 Anthony Morris tree, for example, women are clumps of foliage while in the Caspar Wistar tree, late nineteenth century (*Figure 5*) they are either a clump of foliage or a single leaf.

In the twentieth century, two trees reject the descendancy model and reverse the lineage to depict the ancestry on all lines of the chart's creator or the family's current generation. In the Sewall tree, for example, the children of the creator are the trunk, with their immigrant ancestors ranged at the end of the branches.

The use of stumps to depict lines that die out is universal in all the prints located. In some cases the branch is shown sawed off, while in others it has the appearance of being broken off the tree. According to Peter Benes, the term "cut off" was in popular usage until the 1880s and referred (in at least one definition) to dying before one's time.[5] In most families, a few members die young or do not marry and have children. In the Kennedy tree (*Figure 6*) representing descendants of William and Mary (Henderson) Kennedy from 1730 to 1881, the healthy branches (indicating lines that left descendants) are outnumbered by stumps representing early deaths or unmarried members. The 1895 William Hersey tree, however, contains a key to distinguish between two types of cut-off branches. The first refers to family members known to have died without issue, while the second symbolizes those for whom no record of descendants (if any) had reached the compiler. The focus of nineteenth-century genealogy was the agnate (male) line of the family, following the surname, and trees copied that form. Even in trees where female descendants are listed, most daughters' lines are not followed forward. Only male descendants of Isaac Cook appear on the Cook print (nineteenth century), while the John Lathrop family art included both men and women.

Color could be employed to highlight the chart, as in the Lippincott tree with its autumnal shades. A creative use of color appears in the Collins tree: gray denotes the dead, while green signifies living family members.

As a source of genealogical information, most trees lack space for dates and references, which provokes questions about the veracity of the presented data. Individuals claiming authorship occasionally mentioned that genealogists were consulted. In the 1903 John Houston tree, completed by Ann E. Elliott of Bloomington, Illinois, two genealogists (George Jones Kollock and Ann E. Elliott herself) are credited, while in the 1834 William Henry Jones chart, a separate sheet outlining the family history accompanied the printed tree. Averill B. Canfield offered a short statement regarding sources: "The authority for names and dates is drawn from records of town, county, court and state. Also family bibles and statements of living persons."[6] In a few cases family-tree designers were also genealogists. Peter Roome Warner (1804–1896), (*Figure 7*) for example, delineated the John Roome-Rachel DeGroot family tree in 1868; fifteen years later he published *Descendants of Peter Willemse Roome.*[7]

But in some instances, genealogists and family history writers chose not to use these charts. In 1859 Orrin Read of Providence, Rhode Island, decided not to include a tree to symbolize his family and offered an explanation:

> [The] Genealogical Arbor, or Tree of consanguinity signified a genealogy or lineage drawn out under the figure of a tree with its root, stock and branches, the

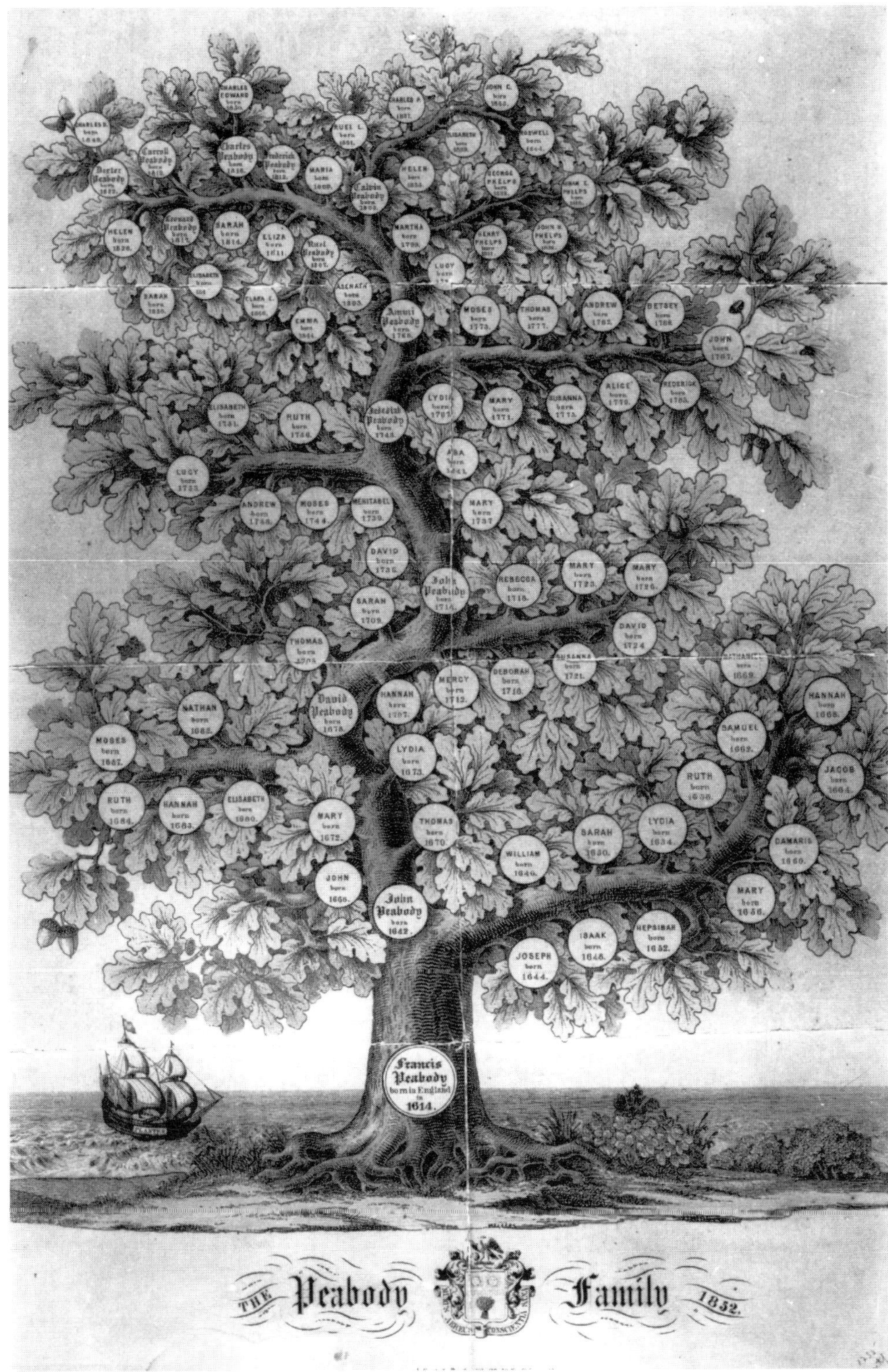

Figure 1 The Peabody Family. Descendants of Francis Peabody (b. 1644). L. Gast & Brother lithographers, 4th St., St. Louis, Missouri, 1852. Lithograph, 66 × 40.5 cm. New England Historic Genealogical Society.

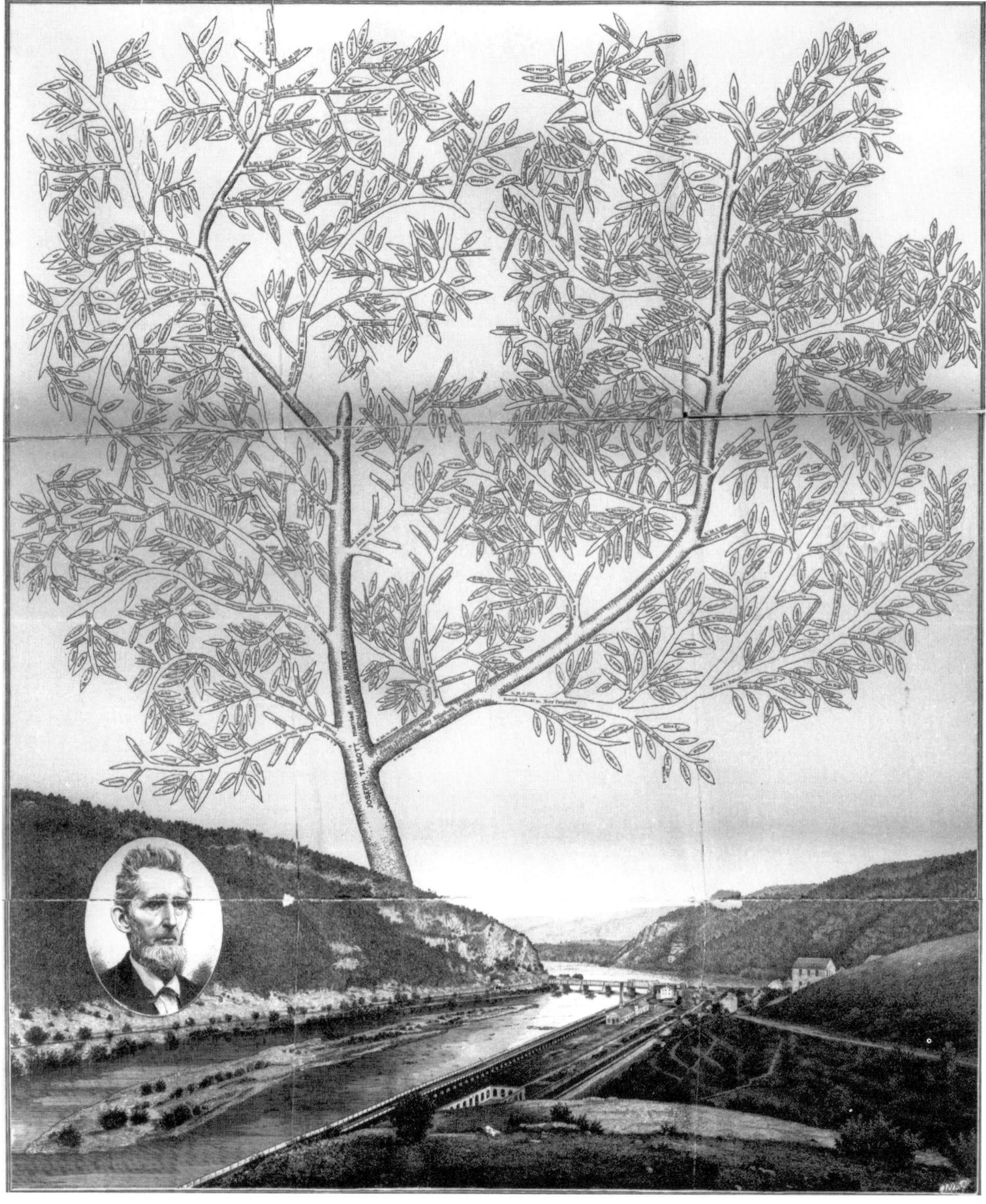

Figure 4 Joseph Talbot Tree. G. W. White. New York: Moss Engineering Company, nineteenth century. 62 × 54 cm. New England Historic Genealogical Society.

genealogical degree of which, are usually represented in circles, ranged over, under, and aside each other; but such fanciful schemes cannot be printed short of the expense of an engraved plate and even then, can never be rendered as perspicious as the nature of genealogy seems to demand.[8]

The complaint raised by Read about the imprecise nature of the genealogical information listed on a tree is accurate. Family-tree charts were intended to be a visually appealing representation of the family, not a detailed account of the individuals listed. It is often difficult even to decipher the number of generations shown. The majority of the prints list only names. There are few exceptions in twentieth-century charts. Both the Edward Hawes tree and that for the Randolphs of Virginia list at least some dates.

The commissioning of a printed family tree was expensive and primarily a male pursuit. Only a few women are known to have involved themselves in the process and not until the late nineteenth century. The tree prepared in 1874 in Boston for the descendants of Richard Sears was "compiled by Olive H. Sears Kelley." Women drew the 1912 Peter Foy tree, the 1914 Thomas Clarke tree, and the Thomas Bullard tree (late nineteenth century or early twentieth century).

Those unable to afford to have a chart commissioned and produced by professional artists could purchase blank trees. In 1845 Jarvis Griggs Kellogg and his partner Hanmer of Hartford, Connecticut, printed a design by Edwin Hubbard (*Figure 8*), a tree with open spaces where names could be added. It came complete with an explanation that the first space was for the "name commencing the record" and continuing for seven generations.[9] Another variation of the standard used family photographs instead of information. It was printed by Currier and Ives of New York City and contained fourteen oval spaces where photographs—probably a small card photograph such as a carte de visite—could be inserted.[10]

Families represented in these prints are not exclusively New England–based; in fact, there are many trees for Quaker families from the Philadelphia area. The only discernible difference between designs used by eastern families and those from the Midwest and South is the type of secondary symbolism. Families whose ancestors had immigrated from Europe might include a view of the ocean, a seacoast, and a ship, all of which signified the immigrant journey—as seen, for example, in the 1852 Francis Peabody tree. In families who had traveled inland from the ocean, a different background scene may appear. The Joseph Talbot tree (nineteenth century), for instance, depicts a river with two banks and a train.

These prints fall into distinct design categories in a chronological progression. The earliest use the form of a tree to carry the genealogical information in branches or foliage and often resemble the watercolors and needlework family records of the eighteenth century. The Francis Peabody tree, in which Francis Peabody's descendants appear as circles or fruit on a Tree of Life, is an example of that style. As the nineteenth century progressed and photomechanical reproductions came into use, the stylistic elements of the trees became abstract. By the early twentieth century, the trees achieved the designs familiar to genealogists today—the fan chart or drop-line chart. The William Eddy tree, for instance, compiled by Charles Eddy, consists of straight lines forming a diagram that closely resembles a tree bare of foliage.

Similarities among early prints may also be related to conditions in the contemporary lithographic industry. Itinerant artists traveled between lithographic printers looking for work. It is possible (though undocumented) that they brought their designs with them. The lithographers themselves usually apprenticed or worked for other firms before opening their own companies. Lithographers mentioned on these family trees could be among the most influential companies in their cities of operation.

An example of the interrelatedness of the printing business is reflected in the principal contributors to the 1861 Anthony Morris tree. The chart was drawn by L. Haugg, who had formerly drawn locomotive chromolithographs for another Philadelphia firm, Alphonze Brett, before moving on to Frederic F. Bourquin's company. Bourquin had worked for Peter S. Duval, a leading Philadelphia lithographer, before opening his company in 1856. Bourquin advertised that "Our facilities for executing work of the largest size are not surpassed by those of any other establishment in the country."[11] An entrepreneur looking to commission a large print of his family tree may well have been encouraged by such claims to give a company his business.

Thomas Sinclair, another prominent Philadelphia lithographer, printed the Isaac Collins family tree. Coincidentally, John Collins of Burlington, New Jersey, who designed and drew this document in 1867, had operated a lithographic press before selling the business to Sinclair. The Thomas Mayhew tree is also a product of Sinclair's.[12]

In two cases, the Peter Roome tree and the Francis Peabody tree, little is known about the lithographers' other work. The Peabody tree, by L. Gast and Brother of St. Louis, is one of two prints by that firm known to exist, the other being a view of Christian Staehlin's Phoenix Brewery in St. Louis.[13] The Roome tree is one of a small number of lithographs by Peter Maverick Jr., who took over his father's company in 1831.[14]

The first lithograph was printed in Philadelphia in 1818; by century's end, companies such as Forbes Company of Boston advertised that they had offices around the country. Another Boston firm, J. H. Bufford, specialized in large prints and marketed prints using catalogues and agents. His firm printed the 1859 Thomas Howes tree.[15]

Lithographers accepted commercial job work for clients such as advertisers and book publishers. They also issued series of prints similar to those by Currier and Ives. However, compilers of these trees did not produce these as a commercial product, but out of a sense of filiopietism and as a way of displaying their own accomplishments. Clement Acton Griscom, president of the International Navigation Company, selected the tree motif in 1876 to illustrate his descent from Andrew Griscom, an original proprietor of Philadelphia who built the first brick house there in 1683. A tree could be framed and displayed so individuals could see Clement's lineage without having to read through a printed genealogy. Many oversize prints can be found with the hanging mechanism in place.[16]

In 1868 William H. Whitmore, a noted genealogist, published a bibliography of genealogies, complete with an appendix of genealogical tables. The list of tables included a few family trees. Many of these items have been found in collections, but the vast majority of what was located date from after 1865. Since discovery of these trees is somewhat serendipitous, it is possible that many more still exist in private collections. Clues as to their existence appear on updated copies of the originals, such as the Robert Taft print which mentions an earlier version or the John Cowles tree that refers to an 1850 print which in 1895 was in the possession of William A. Cowles.[17]

It is difficult to determine how popular this genre of genealogical tabulation was in the nineteenth century or what proportion of the charts produced has survived. Most publications on lithography and exhibition catalogues of this medium are concerned with views, examples of advertising, and popular prints, quite overlooking (and thus undervaluing) the phenomenon of the family tree as a privately commissioned print.

Key to Checklist

Arranged by surname. Titles supplied by the author appear in brackets, while those handwritten on the print are within quotation marks. Other titles appear as printed. Call numbers are in parentheses.

TEMPLATES

Ancestral Tree. Artist: Edwin Hubbard. Printer: Kellogg and Hanmer, Hartford, Connecticut, 1845. CHS.

Family Photograph Register. Printer: Currier and Ives, New York, 1871. Lithograph, 32.7 × 21.5 cm. LC.[18]

FAMILY SPECIFIC

1. Arnold. Pedigree of Arnold. Artist: George Arnold, Jun. Printer: Forbes Co., Boston, 1896. Facsimile reproduction by Graphic Co. New York., n.d. Lithograph, 76.5 × 61 cm. RIHS.

2. Bartram. Genealogical Chart of the Bartram Family. Artist: Morgan Bunting, Darby, Pennsylvania, 1893. Photostat. New England Historic Genealogical Society (hereafter cited as NEHGS) (TP/BAR/9250). *Depicts the descendants of John Bartram (1699–1777).*

3. Bryant. [Bryant Family Tree] Compiled and arranged by Lester P. Bryant, Princeton, Illinois. July 1894. Reprint 1970. VHS. *Descendants of Dr. Peter Bryant (1767–1826) and his wife Sarah Snell (1768–1847).*

4. Bullard. Descendants of Thomas of Virginia and North Carolina. Original drawn by Miss M. C. Bagley, Jackson,

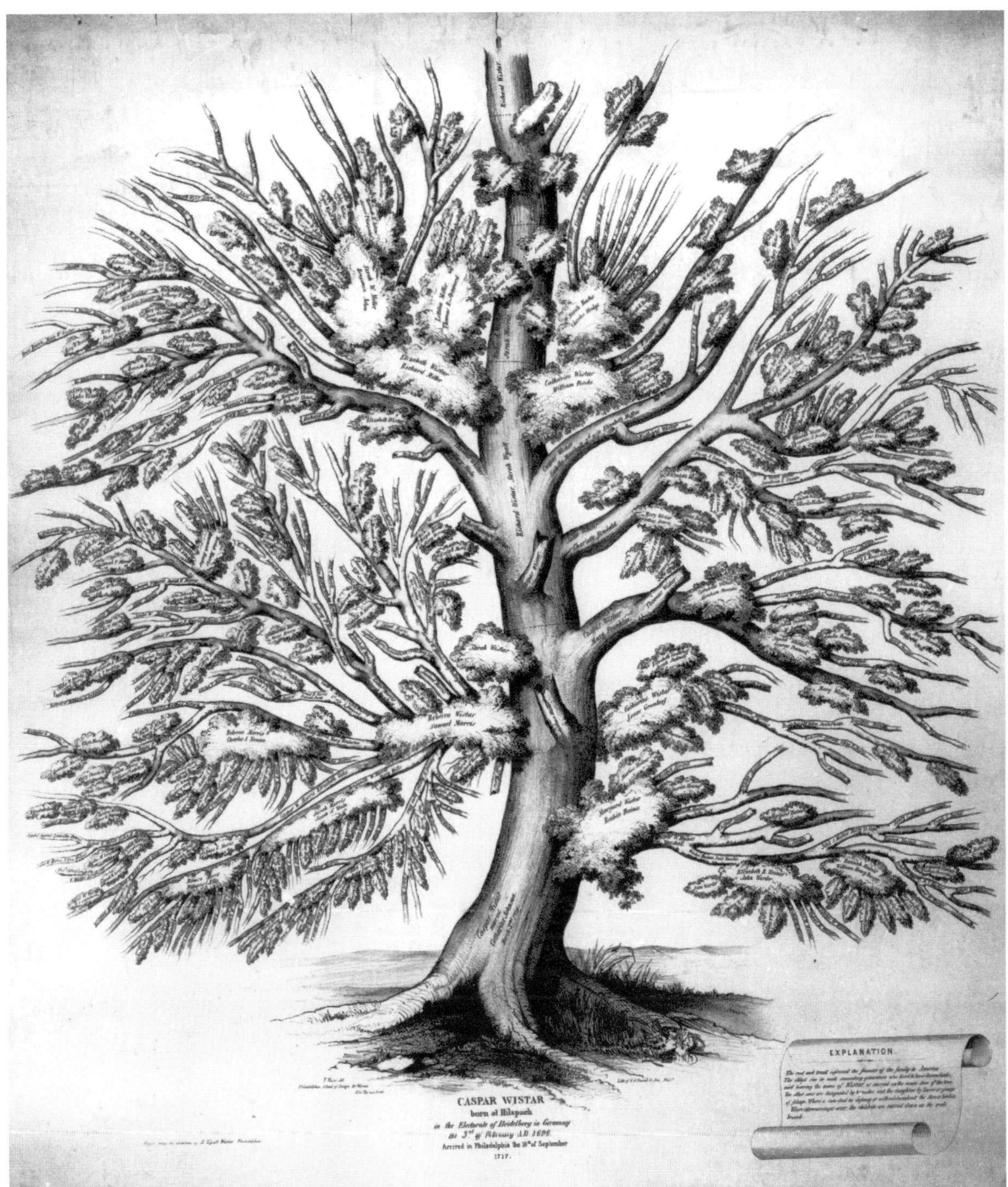

Figure 5 Detail from the Wistar Tree. Mary Ann (Wistar) Chase. Drawn by T. Harris, Philadelphia. "T. Hains Del. Philadelphia, School of Design for Women, 1334 Chestnut St., Lith. of P. S. Duval & son, Phila.," n.d. Lithograph, 124 × 99.3 cm. New England Historic Genealogical Society.

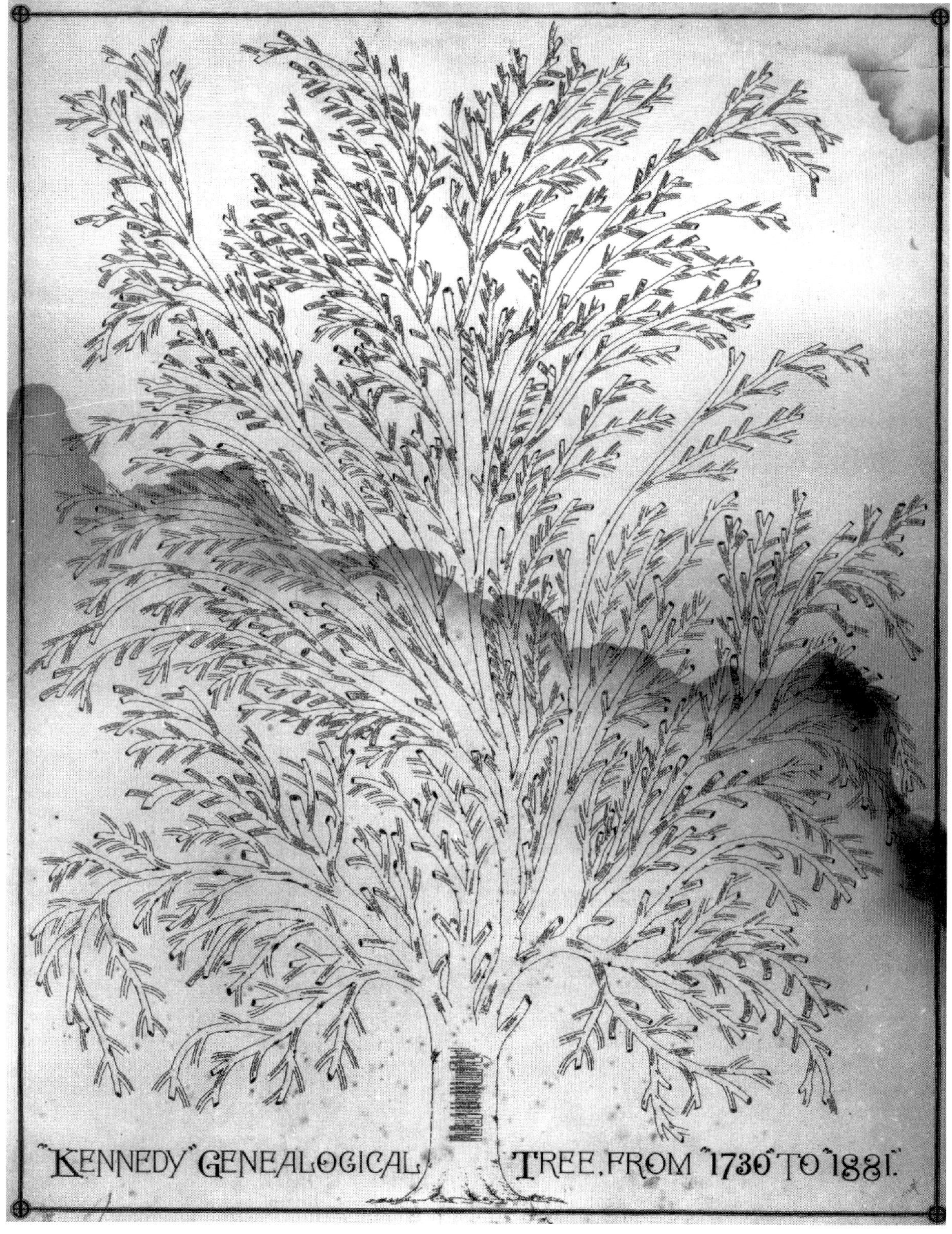

Figure 6 Kennedy Genealogical Tree from 1730 to 1881. Printed on cloth. 79 × 65 cm. New England Historic Genealogical Society.

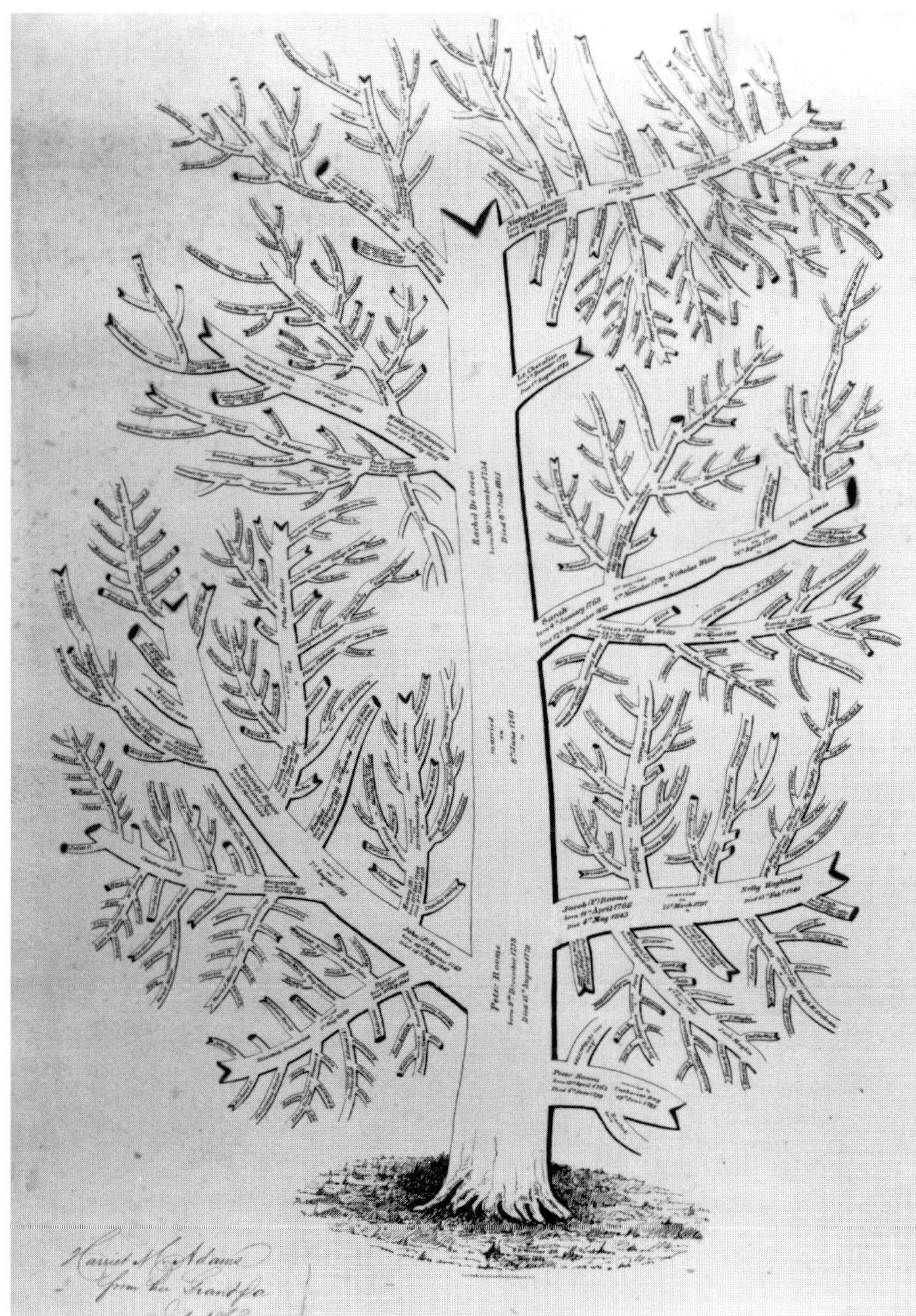

Figure 7 Roome Family Tree. Descendants of Peter Roome (1738–1778) and Rachel DeGroot (1734–1815) of New York City. Artist: Peter Roome Warner. Inscribed "P.R. Warner del. May 1968." Printer: Maverick, Stephan and Co., N.Y. Inscription: "Harriet M. Adams, from her Grandpa July 1868." Lithograph, 40 × 55 cm. Courtesy of D. Brenton Simons.

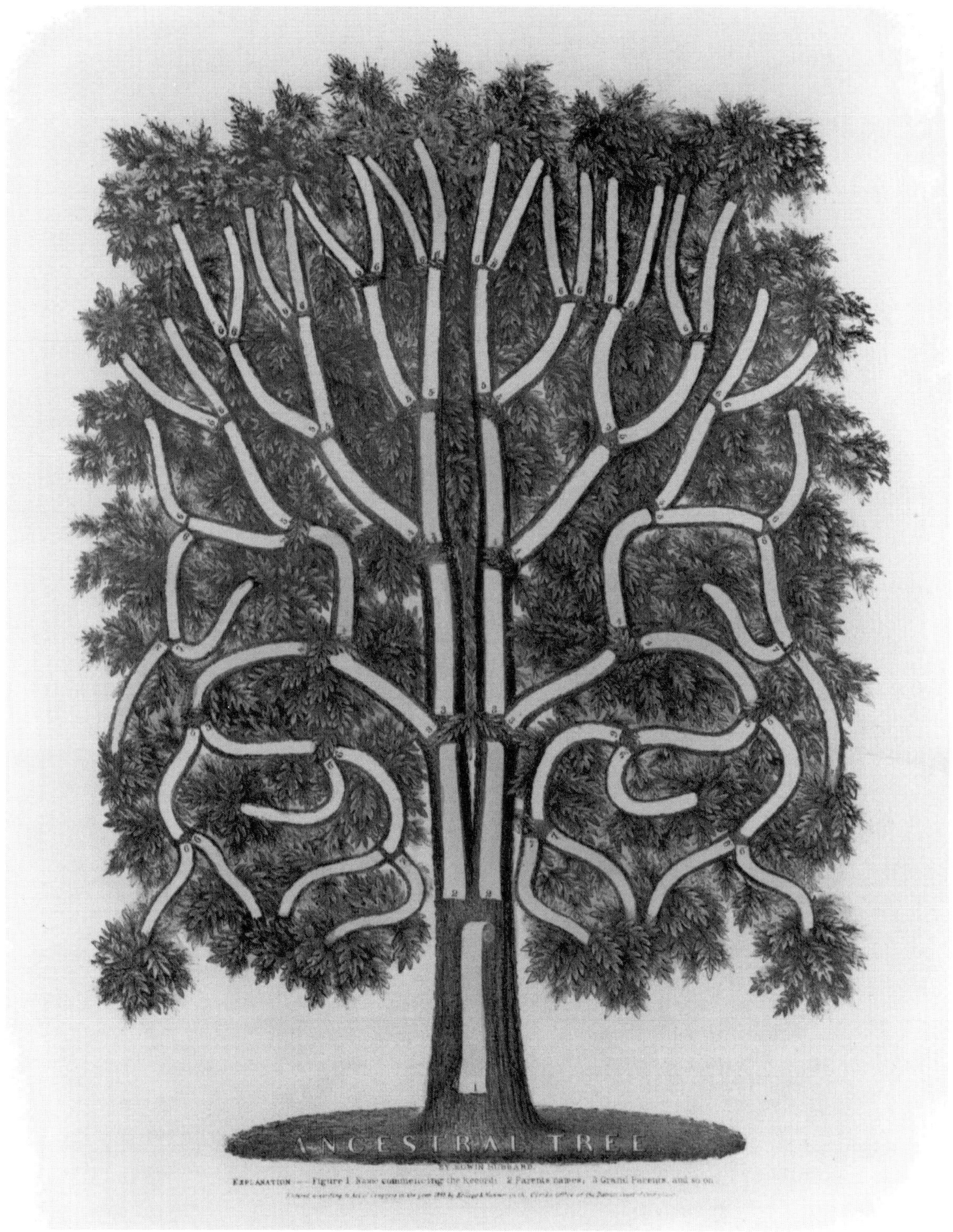

Figure 8 "Ancestral Tree." Edwin Hubbard. Printer: Kellogg and Hanmer, Hartford, Conn., 1845. The Connecticut Historical Society, Hartford, Connecticut.

North Carolina. Photomechanical reproduction, 15 × 23 cm. NEHGS (TP/BUL/205). *Depicts the descendants of Thomas Bullard (1759–1837).*

5. Bunting. Anthony and Ellen Bunting of Matlock, Derbyshire, Eng[land]. Printer: F. R. Bourquin, n.d. Lithograph, 172 × 113 cm. NEHGS (STP/BUN/10).

6. Bunting. Genealogical Chart of the Bunting Family. Drawn by Morgan Bunting, Darby [Pennsylvania], 1895. Photostat, 91.5 × 60.4 cm. NEHGS (TP/BUN/2350). *Depicts the descendants of Samuel Bunting (1692–1758).*

7. Burroughs. The Burroughs Family. Collected by Mac H. Burroughs of Brunswick, Georgia, 1949. Photomechanical reproduction, 47.4 × 59.2 cm. NEHGS (TP/BUR/11240). *Descendants of John of Salem, 1637. Developed from family data in James Riker,* The Annals of Newtown, in Queens County, New-York *(New York: D. Fanshaw, 1852).*

8. Canby. [Thomas Canby]. Printer: Worley and Bracher, Philadelphia; n.d. Lithograph, 76 × 86 cm. NEHGS (TP/CAN/825). *Descendants of Thomas Canby who came to America in 1683.*

9. Canfield. This chronological tree was designed and brought to its present state of perfection by Averill B. Canfield, B.A. of South Britain, Ct. . . . n.d. Photomechanical reproduction, 66 × 52.3 cm. VHS, NEHGS (STP/CAN/3754). *Descendants of Timothy, Thomas, and Matthew Canfield.*

10. Clarke. Clarke tree. Artist: Carrie L. Barnett. Washington, D.C.: Norris Peters Co., 1914. Photolithograph, 96.3 × 60.9 cm. NEHGS (TP/CLA/1807). *Descendants of Thomas Clarke and Martha Dunlap.*

11. Collins. Descendants of Isaac Collins. Designed and Drawn by John Collins of Burlington, New Jersey; Lithograph of T. Sinclair, Philadelphia, 1867. Chromolithograph, 77 × 102 cm. NEHGS (TP/COL/4278; listed in Whitmore).

12. Cook. Genealogical tree, exhibiting in lineal order, up to the year 1813, the descendants of Isaac Cook. First delineated by James Carrington; a copy of which was made by Luther Dutton Cook and his sister, Sibyl Beach Cook. Kellogg Lithographers, n.d. Lithograph, 76 × 51 cm. NEHGS (STP/COO).

13. Cooper. A Cooper Genealogical "Tree." Arranged (with additions) by Henry Byron Phillips from a compilation by Robert B. Hull, New York, 1882. San Francisco, California, 1917. Photomechanical reproduction, 53.5 × 46.5 cm. NEHGS (TP/COO/1384). *Descendants of William and Margaret Cooper, emigrants from England to Coopers Point, Gloucester County, New Jersey, 1679.*

14. Cooper. Descendants of Daniel Cooper and Grace Runyon of Long Hill, Morris County, New Jersey. 1695–1895. Collated by Arthur E. Cooper, ca. 1895. Photolithograph, 55.5 × 71.4 cm. NEHGS (TP COO 1384).

15. Cowell. Cowell tree. n.d. Lithograph, 36 × 27 cm. NEHGS. *Descendants of John Cowell and his son Joseph who settled in Wrentham, Massachusetts.*

16. Cowles. Cowles. 1895 copy of an original made about 1850. Photolithograph, 48.3 × 63 cm. NEHGS (TP/COW/2021). *Descendants of John Cowles (1599–1675).*

17. Dupuy. Bartholomew Dupuy and Susanna LaVillan, refugees from France. Mrs. M. J. Stovall. Printer: S. C. Touf and Co., Memphis, Tennessee, 1867. Lithograph, 28 × 63 cm. CPL.

18. Eddy. Eddy Family Tree. Compiled by Charles Eddy, M.D.; Photo-Litho Co., n.d. Photolithograph, 40.5 × 55 cm. NEHGS (TP/EDD/532). *Descendants of William Eddy, d. 1616.*

19. Foy. Foy tree. Carrie L. Barnett. Norris Peters Co., Washington, D.C., 1912. Photolithograph, 95 × 60 cm. NEHGS (TP/FOY/10). *Descendants of Peter Foy and Hamital Moore.*

20. Gilbert. The Abijah Gilbert Family; revised by Elizabeth Denny Gardiner, Katharine Gilbert Francke, Frances Beck, and Nanine Kimball Harrris (1937), 1947. Photomechanical reproduction, 53.5 × 43 cm. NEHGS (TP/GIL/156).

21. Grew. Grew Tree. Compiled and drawn by Theodore Alfred Bingham. 1886. Blueprint of original, 80 × 76.6 cm. NEHGS (STP/GRE/10). *Descendants of William Grew, d. 1616.*

22. Griscom. Griscom Family Tree. Made for Clement Acton Griscom by Anna Griscom of Reading, Pennsylvania, 1876. J. Joshua Fish, 1939. Tracing of the original, 92 × 69.5 cm. NEHGS (TP/GRI/1075). *Descendants of Andrew Griscom, died 1694.*

23. Haskell. A Genealogical Tree Showing the Descendants of William Haskell of Gloucester, Massachusetts. Data by William O. Haskell [Sr.]; designed and drawn by William O. Haskell Jr., 1880. Mason, New Hampshire, 45 × 58 cm. Private Collection.

24. Hawes. Edward Hawes of Dedham, Mass. Married 15 April 1648. Photomechanical reproduction, after 1920. 44.8 × 36.2 cm. NEHGS (TP/HAW/311).

25. Hersey. [Hersey Family Tree]. Compiled by Francis Hersey, 1895. Photolithograph, 68 × 67 cm. NEHGS (TP/HER/3006). *Descendants of William Hersey of Hingham, Mass., 1635.*

26. Higginson. Higginson Family. Henry F. Waters, twentieth-century Mylar copy, 124 × 163 cm. NEHGS.

27. Houston. Houston Family. Completed by Ann E. Elliott. Drawn by George Jones Kollock, 1903. Photomechanical reproduction, 42 × 57 cm. NEHGS (TP/HOU/1213). *Descendants of John Houston who settled in Pennsylvania.*

28. Howes. Thomas Howes and his wife Mary arrived in New-England Anno Domini 1637. Designed by W. M. Bassett. Perfected by J. S. Howes. Drawn by F. F. Myrick. Printer: J. H. Bufford's Lithography, Boston, 1859. Lithograph, 56.5 × 71 cm. NEHGS (STP/865A).

29. Jones. 1854. Cited in William H. Whitmore, *The American Genealogist.* No copies extant. *Descendants of William Henry Jones.*

30. Judson. Genealogy of the Judson Family. Collated by Jeremiah Judson, 1860. Lithograph, 30 × 42 cm. Private Collection. *Descendants of William Judson, who died 29 July 1662 at New Haven, Connecticut.*

31. Kennedy. Kennedy Genealogical Tree from 1730–1881. Printed on cloth. 79 × 65 cm NEHGS (STP/KEN/2). *Descendants of William Kennedy and Mary Henderson who settled in Bucks County, Pennsylvania in 1730.*

32. Lathrop. Lathrop Family Tree. Collected and Arranged by John Lathrop. n.d. Chromolithograph, 65 × 55.5 cm. NEHGS (STP/LAT/639). *Descendants of John Lathrop of Scituate, Massachusetts, 1634.*

33. Lippincott. Lippincott. 198 × 114 cm. CPL, NEHGS, RIHS.

34. Lord. Family Tree of Benjamin Lord. In Kenneth Lord, *Genealogy of the Descendants of Thomas Lord* (New York, 1946). Photomechanical Reproduction. HPL.

35. Mayhew. The Mayhew Family Tree. Drawn by Frederic Mayhew. Printer: Thomas Sinclair, 1855. Lithograph, 74 × 93 cm. NEHGS (TP/MAY/1260). *Descendants of Thomas Mayhew of Nantucket, Martha's Vineyard, and the Elizabeth Islands.*

36. Montague. Descendants of Richard Montague, b. 1614. Ed. W. Welcke and Bros. n.d. Photolithograph, 46 × 33 cm. NEHGS (TP/MON/2640).

37. Morris. Morris Tree. Compiled by Anthony Saunders Morris. Artist: Thomasine Harris. Lith. by L. Haugg. Printer: F. Bourquin and Co., 1861. Lithograph. NEHGS (STP/MOR, cited in Whitmore). *Descendants of Anthony Morris who married Elizabeth Senior; he was lost at sea leaving one child.*

38. Munger. [Descendants of Nicholas Munger.] Copy of an old family tree found in the attic of the Josiah Munger house at Madison, Connecticut. J. B. Munger, 1913. Photomechanical reproduction, 25.4 × 32.9 cm. NEHGS (TP/MUN/1495).

39. Otis. A Genealogical Tree of the Otis Family in America from the First to Eighth generations, 1905. Photomechanical reproduction, 30.5 × 24.5 cm. NEHGS (TP/OTI/146). *Descendants of John Otis.*

40. Peabody. The Peabody Family; L. Gast & Brother lith. 4th St., St. Louis, Missouri, 1852. Lithograph, 66 × 40.5 cm. NEHGS. *Descendants of Francis Peabody, born in England in 1614.*

41. Randall. Randall family, twentieth century, 114.3 × 67.4 cm. RIHS.

42. Rockefeller. Family Tree of Diell Rockefeller and his descendants who were born Rockefellers. Drawn and arranged by Henry O. Rockefeller, n.d. Photomechanical reproduction, 33 × 27 cm. NEHGS.

43. Roome. [Roome Family Tree]. Artist: Peter Roome Warner. Inscribed *P. R. Warner del. May 1868.* Printer: Maverick, Stephan and Co., N.Y. Inscription: "Harriet M. Adams, from her Grandpa July 1868." Lithograph, 40 × 55 cm. Private Collection. *Depicts descendants of Peter Roome (1738–1778) and Rachel DeGroot (1734–1815) of New York City.*

44. Sears. [Descendants of Richard Sears, b. 1590]. Compiled by Olive H. Sears Kelley. Drawn by George E. Jones, Boston. Printer: Am. Photo Lithographic Co., New York, 1874. Photolithograph, 76 × 60.5 cm. NEHGS (TP/SEA/2851).

45. Sewall. [Sewall Ascendency Tree], twentieth-century Photographic copy of a print, 46.2 × 56.3 cm. NEHGS (TP/SEW/1005).

46. Skinner. The Skinner Family Genealogical Tree. Designed by Alanson Skinner. Lith. of Harry E. Pease, Albany, N.Y., nineteenth-century lithograph, 47 × 61 cm. NEHGS (TP/SKI/1809). *Descendants of Timothy Skinner (1761–1843) and Ruth Warner (1770–1849).*

47. Taft. Robert Taft. Printer: Ehrgott, Forbriger and Co., Lith. Carlisle Black S.W. cor. of 4th and Walnut Str. Cincinnati, Ohio, n.d. 62 × 52 cm. NEHGS (STP/TAF/375).

48. Taft. Robert Taft. Copied and enlarged by C. O. Owen, 1910. Photomechanical reproduction, 52.5 × 42.7 cm. NEHGS (TP/TAF/365A).

49. Taft. The Descendants of Robert Taft Through His Second Son. Russell S. Taft, Russell W. Taft and Clara Owen, 1931. Print with blue ink, 88.6 × 54.3 cm. NEHGS (TP/TAF/416).

50. Talbott. Joseph Talbott married Mary Burkett. G. W. White. New York: Moss Engineering Co., nineteenth century, 62 × 54 cm. NEHGS (TP/TAL/575).

51. Washburn. Washburn Family, 1591–1895. 1895. Mimeograph, 41 × 55 cm. NEHGS (TP WAS 909). *Descendants of John Washburn (1591–by 1632).*

52. Waterman. The Waterman Genealogy direct line from Thomas Waterman (1636–1957), ca. 1957. Photomechanical reproduction, 57.4 × 35.6 cm. Private Collection.

53. Wistar. The Wistar Tree. Prepared by Mrs. Mary Ann (Wistar) Chase. Drawn by T. Harris, Philadelphia.

T. Hains Del. Philadelphia, School of Design for Women, 1334 Chestnut St., Lith. of P. S. Duval & Son, Philadelphia, n.d. Lithograph, 124 × 99.3 cm. NEHGS (STP/WIS/1940). *Descendants of Caspar Wistar, who married Catharine Johnson 2 March 1726.*

54. Young. Young Family Tree. Capt. Calvin Duvall Cowles, U.S. Army. Washington, D.C., 1895. Photolithograph, 48.5 × 63 cm. NEHGS (TP/YOU/416). *Descendants of Michael Cadet Young and Martha Sadler.*

NOTES

[1] An exception is Peter Benes, "Decorated Family Records from Coastal Massachusetts, New Hampshire, and Connecticut," in *Families and Children: 1985 Annual Proceedings of the Dublin Seminar for New England Folklife* (Boston: Boston University, Scholarly Publications, 1987), pp. 91–147, which has been revised and updated in the present volume.

[2] A large collection of family trees is located at the New England Historic Genealogical Society, Boston, Mass. (hereafter cited as NEHGS).

[3] *The Tree of Temperance* (Hartford, Conn.: —— and Comstock, n.d.), Collection of the Shelburne Museum; Tree of Grace found in the *Child's Hierographical Bible* (Boston: Samuel Wood and Son, 1815); *Tree of Life—The Christian* (New York: N. Currier, n.d.).

[4] *Chronologie d'Angleterre. Appliquée a la Généalogie des Rois Princes et Princesses qui ont eu des Prétentions sur Cette Couronne,* 1836, at NEHGS.

[5] Benes, "Decorated Family Records," p. 11.

[6] Averill B. Canfield, Canfield family tree, located at the Vermont Historical Society, Montpelier, Vt., and NEHGS.

[7] Peter Roome Warner, Roome family tree, private collection; Peter Roome Warner, *Descendants of Peter Willemse Roome* (New York: David M. Gildersleeve, 1883), pp. 187–88; Theodore Langdon Van Norden, *The Van Norden Family: Three Hundred Years in America, 1623–1923* (South Salem, N.Y.: Lancaster Press, 1923), p. 58.

[8] Orin A. Read, Read family chart, Providence, R.I., 1859. Located at the Rhode Island Historical Society Library, Providence, R.I.

[9] Edwin Hubbard, "Ancestral Tree" (Hartford, Conn.: Kellogg and Hanmer, 1845). Located at the Connecticut Historical Society, Hartford, Conn. (Also see Barnhill checklist no. 143 in this volume.)

[10] "Family Photograph Register" (New York: Currier and Ives, 1871), cited in *Currier and Ives: A Catalogue Raisonné,* vol. 1 (Detroit: Gale Research, 1984), no. 2002.

[11] Nicholas Wainwright, *Philadelphia in the Romantic Age of Lithography* (Philadelphia: Historical Society of Pennsylvania, 1958), p. 86.

[12] Ibid.

[13] Harry T. Peters, *America on Stone: The Other Printmakers to the American People* (New York: Doubleday, Doran, 1931; reprint, New York: Arno Press, 1976), p. 192.

[14] Ibid., pp. 273–75; Stephen DeWitt Stephens, *The Mavericks: American Engravers* (New Brunswick, N.J.: Rutgers University Press, 1950), p. 179. Peter Roome Warner, author of *The Roome Family Tree,* was related by marriage to Peter Maverick.

[15] Sally Pierce and Catharina Slautterback, *Boston Lithography, 1825–1880: The Boston Athenaeum Collection* (Boston: Boston Athenaeum, 1991), pp. 130, 136–37.

[16] *The Twentieth Century Biographical Dictionary of Notable Americans,* ed. Rossiter Johnson (Boston: Biographical Society, 1904), vol. 4; *Encyclopedia of American Biography* (New York: American Historical Society, 1934–).

[17] William H. Whitmore, *The American Genealogist, Being a Catalogue of Family Histories and Publications* (Albany, N.Y.: Joel Munsell, 1868).

S E C T I O N   I I I

Families and Portraiture

New England Family Record Broadsides and Portraiture, and the Letterpress Artist of Connecticut

D. Brenton Simons

SOMETIME PRIOR to 1820 a pair of records for two generations of a Chapman family of Groton, Connecticut, were composed and printed as broadsides in what was presumably a small batch for private distribution to members of the immediate family (*Figure 1*).[1] The author of these particular pieces may have been "Master" Rufus Chapman himself, a "splendid penman," according to one historian, as well as a schoolmaster and merchant in Center Groton.[2] The vital data for Rufus's family are recorded in one broadside, and a second presents the family of his father, Joseph Chapman Jr., a church deacon, tavern keeper, and member of the Connecticut General Assembly in 1803.[3] What might have inspired Rufus Chapman, this "splendid penman," his father, and countless other New Englanders to create or commission unique works of genealogical art—in particular family record broadsides and related forms in the period from 1800 to 1840—is a subject of study for those interested in the fields of material culture and genealogy. Yet, remarkably, almost none of the following family record examples have been used either as documentary sources or illustrative matter in compiled genealogies, even though many printed treatments exist for these families. Further, New England genealogical broadsides, as a genre, are almost completely unstudied.

In the late eighteenth and early nineteenth centuries, family documentation in New England often appeared in decorative forms such as needlework samplers, pen-and-ink or printed records, and watercolor family trees (followed later in the nineteenth century by lithographed family trees). Many pieces were self-identified with various interchangeable terms: "Family Record," "Family Register," "The Family of . . . ," and, occasionally, "The Genealogy of . . ." or, even more simply, "Genealogy." Each recorded births, marriages, deaths or burials, or a combination of these events. Some scholars see these artifacts as an outgrowth of earlier American forms of personal or family identification, such as the initials, names, or dates found on late-seventeenth- and early-eighteenth-century dower chests and other household possessions.[4]

An even more immediate precedent for creating family records, however, may be related to the widespread tradition of preserving family data in a written form within the household, specifically the custom of entering data in family Bibles (in which special sections have long been devoted to this purpose). The creation of unique works of genealogical art, however, went well beyond the simplicity of their ubiquitous "cousins"—family Bible forms—to specimens that conveyed not only family identity but also individual accomplishment or training: a fine calligraphic hand or a mastery of line, ornament, or symbolism. New and artistic family record forms were created in private homes or academies and increasingly purveyed by professional penmen.[5] As a result, in the early decades of the nineteenth century New England families had the opportunity to record

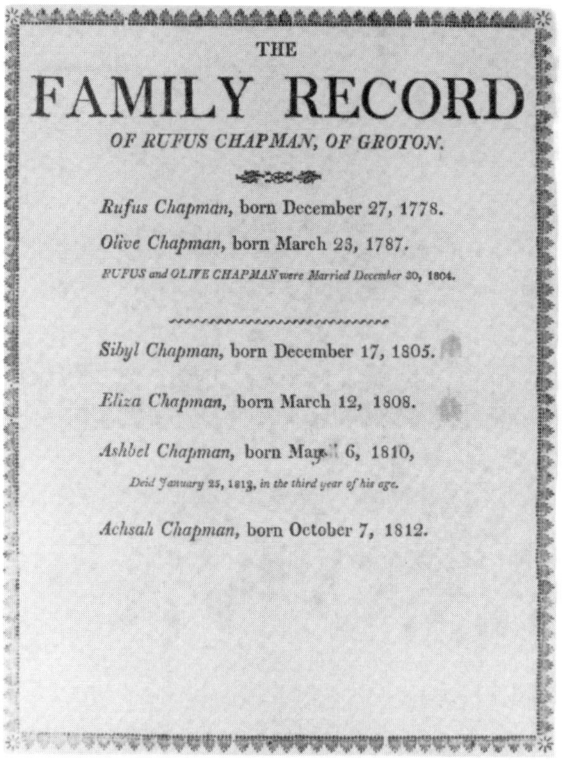

THE

FAMILY RECORD

OF RUFUS CHAPMAN, OF GROTON.

Rufus Chapman, born December 27, 1778.

Olive Chapman, born March 23, 1787.

RUFUS and OLIVE CHAPMAN were Married December 30, 1804.

Sibyl Chapman, born December 17, 1805.

Eliza Chapman, born March 12, 1808.

Ashbel Chapman, born May 6, 1810,

Died January 25, 1813, in the third year of his age.

Achsah Chapman, born October 7, 1812.

Figure 1 Family record. Rufus Chapman and Olive Chapman (married 1804). Groton, Connecticut, printed prior to 1820. Courtesy, American Antiquarian Society.

and display their vital data with great personalization. Handwritten or painted family records were framed and displayed in homes and, as such, represented a vernacular parallel to the more formal New England genealogical studies that commenced in the 1830s and 1840s.[6]

Family Records and Portraiture

A rare surviving depiction of the decorative family record in a domestic setting appears in the 1831 oil portrait by Massachusetts artist Robert Peckham (1785–1877)[7] of the children of merchant and hotel keeper Colonel Oliver Adams (1790–1839) and his wife, Zilpha Sawyer (d. 1852), of Westminster,[8] wherein a pen-and-ink family record listing the first six of the couple's nine children is prominently displayed on a wall in the background.[9] One child posthumously depicted in the portrait, Joseph Sawyer Adams, died at Westminster 18 January 1831; his death is noted in the family record portion of the painting.[10] The 1837 watercolor group portrait by Caroline Hill (1816–1854), aged twenty-one, of the family of Job Hill (1780–1858), a cooper, and Betsey Perry (1782–1879) of Peterborough, New Hampshire, depicts a large pen-and-ink family record prominently displayed on the wall. The portrait illustrates the Hills and their surviving children gathered at a table (*Figure 2*).[11] Like the aforementioned Adams portrait, the Hill family portrait features a record up-to-date in its listing of family mortalities.

Another example of the relationship between folk portraiture and family record art is the vibrant watercolor and ink portrait record prepared for the family of William Ingersell [*sic*] (1779–1858) and Susanna Shaw of Columbia, Maine. In what may be an unusual acknowledgment of family record art, the Ingersoll genealogy states "portraits of the six oldest children of the family were painted by Charles Dundas of England,"[12] but it is not certain this is a reference to the watercolor family record. The watercolor depicts the couple's eldest *seven* children (out of an eventual sixteen) and is dated 1818 but is, perhaps, a later work. Nine vignettes are featured—Mr. and Mrs. Ingersell at the center top with the baby, Peggy Mayheu [*sic*], between them. All the other children are posed beneath swags bearing their names. Birth information is boxed beneath each subject, and red, poppy-like flowers surround each member of the family (*Figure 3*).

In 1840 when thirteen-year-old Julia Maria Abbe of Enfield, Connecticut, painted a richly decorated double portrait "family register"[13] for her parents, hotel keeper Robert Morrison Abbe (1797–1883) and his wife, Maria Norcott (1800–1851) (*Figure 4*),[14] she borrowed from an oft-repeated vocabulary of family record symbolism: flower-filled urns atop double columns, a tiny arrow shot through paired hearts, and a nested bird offering nourishment to its hatchlings. However, the distinctive oval portraits presented as Julia's parents are misleading. They are, in fact, adaptations from an earlier printed source: a generic family record form printed by Hiram Ferry, of Northampton, Massachusetts, circa 1827–1828 (*Figure 5*).[15] The likeness of "Mrs. Abbe" has clearly been altered from its original source in details of coiffure and dress. A shawl in the original

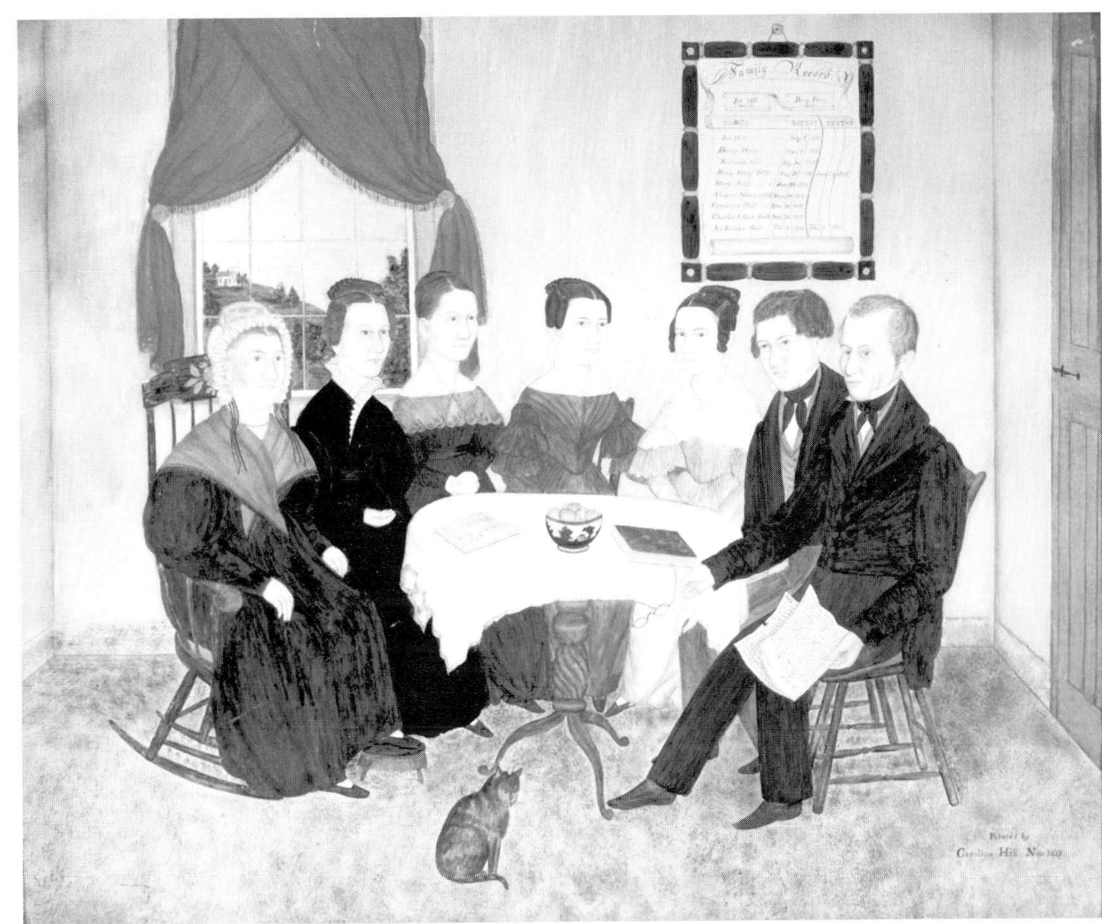

Figure 2 Family portrait. Job Hill and family by Caroline Hill, aged twenty-one. Peterborough, New Hampshire, 1837. Ink and watercolor on paper. Collection of the Peterborough Historical Society.

has been removed and a headband reduced to a small bunch of flowers in Julia Maria Abbe's 1840 copy, but a telltale ringlet of hair dangles identically on the shoulder of both ladies. "Mr. Abbe," while tilted awkwardly, remains substantially unchanged from the original Hiram Ferry image. The Ferry print, in turn, with its unusual double portrait and family register format, is also significant because it bears a strong thematic resemblance to the double profile and family record composition used shortly thereafter by the "Letterpress Artist" of Connecticut.

Handwritten Family Records

In this period prior to the mass availability of decorative fill-in-the-blank family records by lithographers like Nathaniel Currier (and later the firm of Currier and Ives) or the Kellogg brothers of Hartford, several distinctive record types appeared in the region, particularly in Connecticut and Massachusetts.[16] Many family records were made for agricultural families of the Connecticut River Valley and environs; others were representative of pioneer families on the move from southern New England into New York State. Hand-written and hand-painted family records, often based on or similar to Bible record forms, flourished; and professional penmen, such as the individual identified only as "C—" (the remainder of the name or initials being torn away in a signed example of his work), produced scores of family records. Two circa 1810–1820 pen-and-ink works by "C—" made for Massachusetts farmers are owned by the Connecticut Historical Society:[17] the "family record" of Gaius Taylor (1770–1834) and Flavia Root (1780–1840),

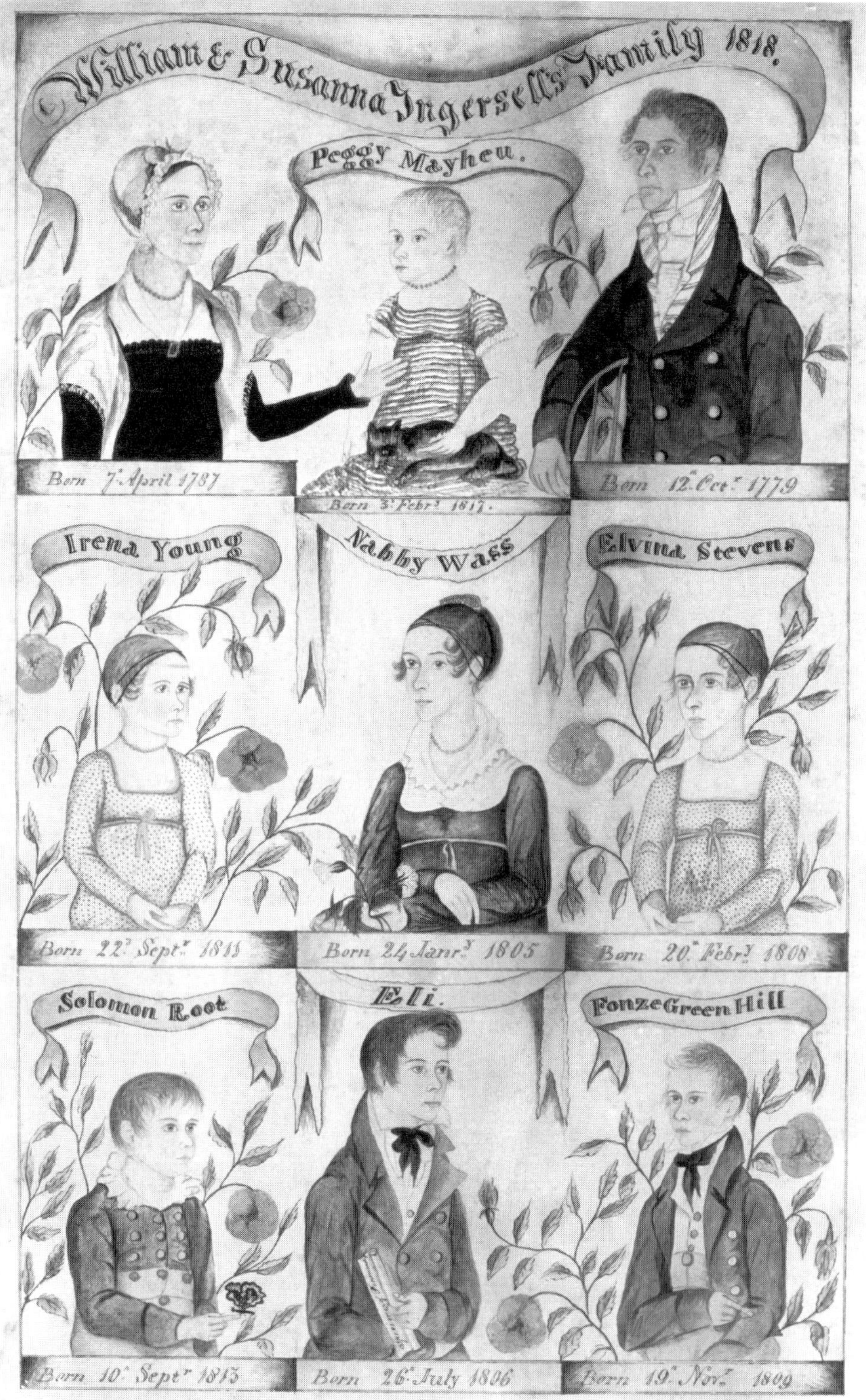

Figure 3 Family record. William Ingersell and family. Artist unknown. Columbia, Maine, 1818. Ink and watercolor on paper. Private Collection.

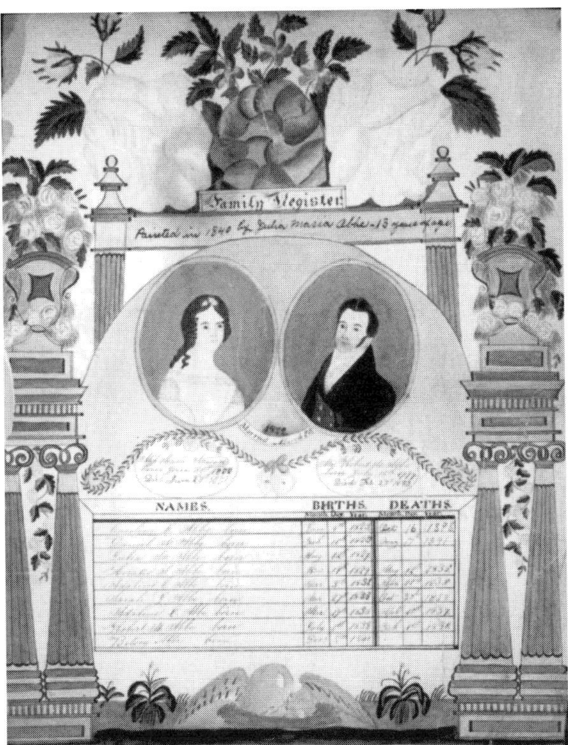

Figure 4 Family record. Robert Morrison Abbe and Maria Norcott. "Painted in 1840 by Julia Maria Abbe, 13 years of age." Enfield, Connecticut. Ink and watercolor on paper. Private Collection.

and their seven children, of South Hadley,[18] and the "family register" of Daniel Hannum (1762–1842) and Phebe Baggs (b. 1769), and their nine children, of Belchertown.[19] The Hannum record is identified by its author as "no. 387," a clue to the vast output of family record art by just a single penman.

Some professional and amateur pieces of this period resembled their Pennsylvania-German "cousins," fraktur—a relationship that has been studied by fraktur experts Russell and Corinne Earnest.[20] A birth record for Mary Fitch (b. 1778) features paired birds perched on bent twigs overlooking a potted plant while a divided heart floats in the upper left-hand corner (*Figure 6*).[21] An ornate pen-and-ink marriage record was created in the early nineteenth century in Massachusetts for the Bible of Asa Bugbee (1790–1831) and his wife, Jane Kelton Robinson (b. 1795), and is signed "John Howe pinx^{t}."(*Figure 7*).[22] The record features bold lettering and is banded by oak leaves and floral compotes. These pieces, and many others like them, represent the fluidity of regional family record art styles.

Family Record Broadsides

The family record broadside form in the period from 1800 to 1840 is most frequently associated with families in Connecticut and Massachusetts, but was preceded by at least one compiled genealogy published in the form of a monograph: *A Genealogy of the Family of Mr. Samuel Stebbins and Mrs. Hannah Stebbins, his Wife,* printed in 1771 by Ebenezer Watson of Hartford, Connecticut (*Figure 8*). This twenty-four-page "genealogical catalogue" traces descendants of Samuel Stebbins (b. 1683), and his wife, Hannah Hitchcock (b. 1684), of Springfield, Massachusetts, and is the earliest known American publication of its kind. It resembles broadside genealogies in terms of typography and general composition, and like broadsides was clearly intended for private distribution among the family.[23] In addition to southern New England, family record broadsides were also associated with Pennsylvania and the British Isles.

The Rudolph Bollinger family record owned by the New England Historic Genealogical Society was printed at Ephrata Cloister in Lancaster County, Pennsylvania, in 1763 and may be the first American broadside of its kind. (*Figure 9*).[24] An early Philadelphia example at the Historical Society of Pennsylvania is the ornamental family record broadside of printer Robert Aitken (b. 1735) and Janet Skeoch (b. 1738), married 1763, with four children born (two died young) in Paisley, Scotland, 1764–1769, and three born (one died young) in Philadelphia, 1772–1777. The Aitken record also states that "Robert Aitken, Printer, Bookseller, and Bookbinder, and his Spouse, Janet Skeoch, arrived in Philadelphia 10 May 1792, with two Children, Jane and Robert." Another Pennsylvania record features an ornate border entitled "John Townsend's Family" and was "taken 10th Mo. 1st. 1826" for the family of John Townsend (1716–1803) and his wife, Joanna England (1721–1786),[25] members of the Society of Friends. A more unusual family record broadside is self-identified simply as "Birth Days." In it are listed the dates of birth, and no other data, for thirteen

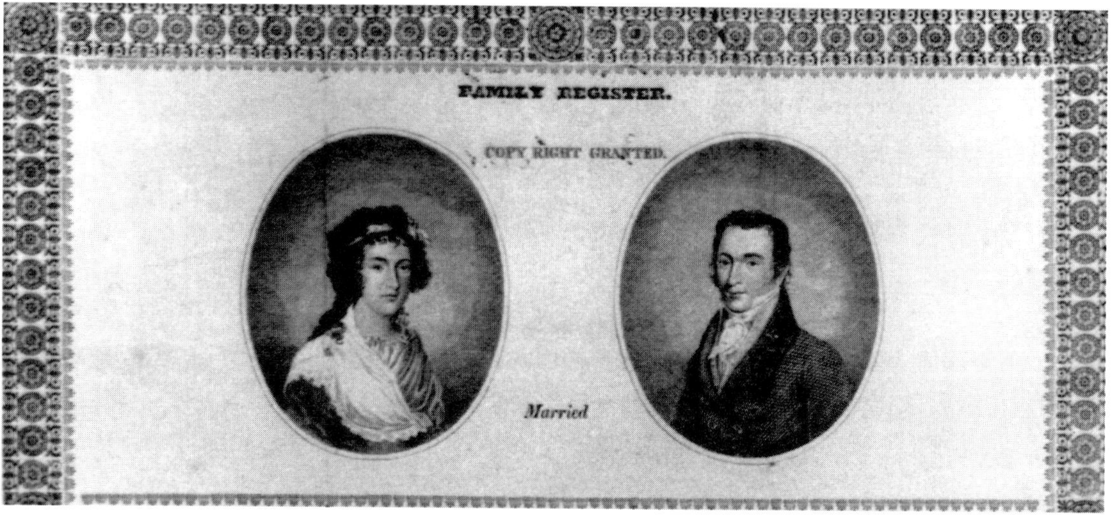

Figure 5 Family record (detail). Printed by Hiram Ferry, circa 1827–1828. Northampton, Massachusetts. New England Historic Genealogical Society.

children, born 1784–1805, of Jonathan Denny and Martha Cross of Coombs, Suffolk, England.[26]

New England broadside-type family records were, in contrast to their watercolor, ink, and needlework counterparts, relatively simple typeset compositions. Their basic purpose was identical to those in other genres with one important difference: broadsides composed with letterpress type could be readily reproduced for several members of a family. They were probably executed by small printing shops, itinerant printers, or, in several cases, by family members known to be in the printing trade.

Understandably, the typesetters who prepared these documents were fallible. In terms of typography, spelling, and, more importantly, the consistency, accuracy, and scope of data provided, family record broadsides vary. The Rufus Chapman family record, for instance, has three typographical errors in just a single entry—two were hand-corrected in ink (Ashbel Chapman's month of birth and year of death), but the word "deid" [*sic*] stands uncorrected.

The Baxter-Barnum family record broadside, owned by the Connecticut Historical Society, may date to 1809 and is one of the earliest in the genre. Thomas and Hannah (Barnum) Baxter, originally of Fairfield County, Connecticut, and later of North Salem, Westchester County, New York, were the parents of nine children—all recorded in the broadside. Vital data are set off by ornamental type elements—swags of vines and berries, tiny four-petalled flowers, geometric motifs, and dark conjoined arches. As is typical of similar pieces, the compositor of this piece was inconsistent in the categories of vital data provided. While several useful details were presented (such as the names of the fathers of Thomas and Hannah, births corrected to "new style" dates, and exact places of birth including county), space was omitted for similar detail in the following generation. This record also neglects dates of family marriages occurring prior to its composition (in or post-1809), although considerable space for such data was provided. For example, the marriage of Thomas and Hannah Baxter's daughter, Abigail, to Isaac Keeler on 17 December 1789 at Norwalk, Connecticut,[27] curiously was not included in the record. This blanket omission of sons- and daughters-in-law and marriage dates implies that the compositor was only given partial data and that individuals in the family were expected to fill in their own sections as events transpired.

The family record broadside for Enoch Badger Jr., of Coventry, Connecticut, is banded in a calligraphy-style typeset border and is prominently self-identified as "Badger's Family Register." It presents a different set of anomalies. Minor discrepancies quickly become apparent between data in the broadside, published vital records for Coventry, and a published genealogy

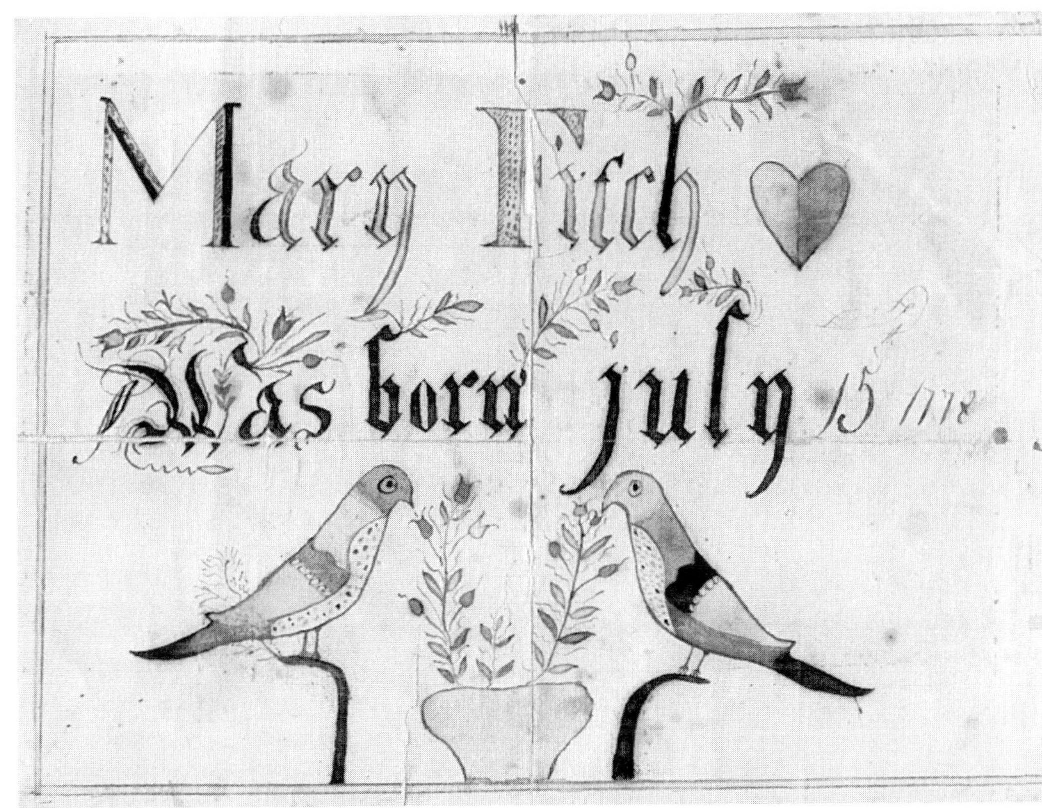

Figure 6 Birth record. "Mary Fitch was born July 15th 1778." Ink and watercolor on paper. Circa 1778. Courtesy of The New York Genealogical and Biographical Society.

of the family. For example, the birth date for Enoch Badger Jr., on the record is given as "12 July 1750," which differs from both other sources: "5 July 1750 " in the published vital records,[28] and "9 July 1750" in *Giles Badger and His Descendants*.[29] Another incongruence occurs in the date of birth of Enoch's eldest son and namesake, Enoch Badger, 3rd. In the family record, this date is given as "5 June 1774"; in the published vital records it is presented as "5 January 1774,"[30] and no date of birth is offered in the compiled genealogy. Like many other family records, the Badger-Lamphier-Tryon piece represents the combined progeny of two marriages.

A more ambitious effort is found in the three-generation Tallcott-Root-Huntington broadside (*Figure 10*). It was an attempt, however, that backfired with incorrect and missing information. This piece presents vital data for Gad Tallcott (or Talcott) and his wife, Abigail Root, of Hebron, Connecticut; seven of their children; and the family of their daughter Abigail Tallcott (1772–1815), who married Oliver Huntington (1771–1823) of Lebanon, Connecticut.[31] The problems begin with the birth dates of Gad and Abigail, presented therein as 1724 and 1726 ("old style"), respectively. These are more than twenty years off the correct years of 1745 and 1747.[32] The broadside is also missing other pertinent information. Gad Tallcott's year of death, 1830, has been left blank, and no mention is made of his second marriage, to widow Susannah Welles, in 1809.[33] Flawed though it may be, the broadside is unusual in that it traces one branch of a family through the line of a daughter, who with her husband removed from Connecticut to New York State shortly after the turn of the nineteenth century. It may be presumed that the Huntingtons, perhaps by this time out of touch with their Tallcott relations in Connecticut, were responsible for the creation of this family memorial.[34]

Printed or hand-illustrated family records were clearly not meant to replace more traditional forms,

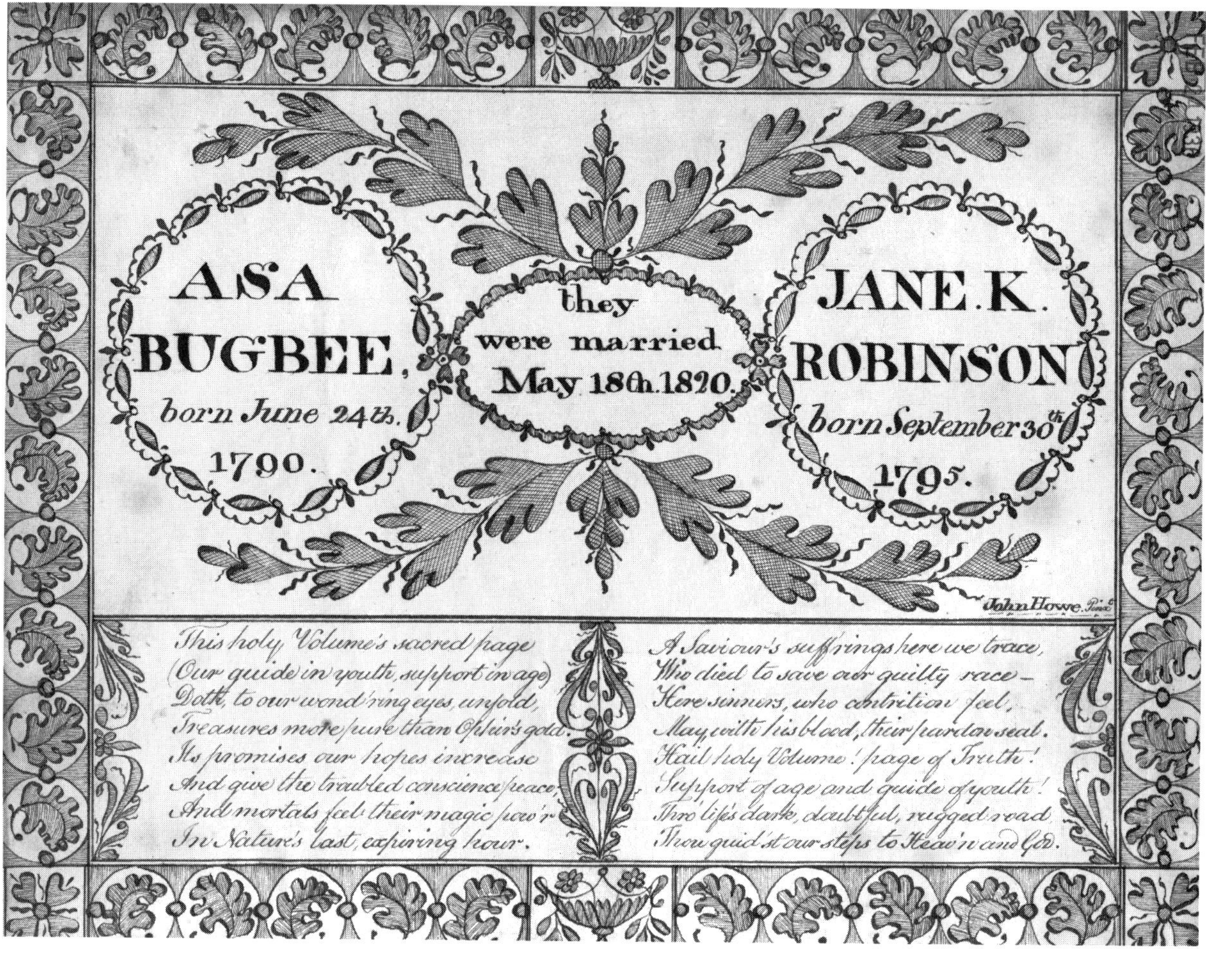

Figure 7 Marriage record. Asa Bugbee and Jane Kelton Robinson. Signed "John Howe, pinxt." Massachusetts, circa 1820. Ink on paper. New England Historic Genealogical Society.

such as Bible record entries, but to make the data more readily available to many individuals. Nowhere is this more evident than in the case of Joseph Hines (1770–1835) and his wife, Phebe Cooke (1770–1818), who kept detailed information in a Bible record (now owned by the New England Historic Genealogical Society) for sixteen children born between 1790 and 1813. Perhaps with only one family Bible to pass on to his offspring, Joseph had printed circa 1820–1828 a broadside "Register of . . . Births and Deaths" for his many children. Interestingly, two of his daughters-in-law and a grandson recorded in the Hines Bible were omitted from the broadside.[35]

Family record broadsides were sometimes created by family members in the printing trade. Robert F. Gibson III of the New York Genealogical and Biographical Society has studied two records for the Packard family in his ancestry. Isaac Packard (1737–1795) and his wife, Eunice Rawson (1744–1824), originally hailed from Massachusetts but eventually settled in Albany, New York. One Packard family record, printed circa 1800, outlined the births of ten children born to the couple between 1768 and 1784 in three localities: Milton, Dorchester, and Petersham, Massachusetts. The second family record, "collected and printed July 1831," was printed on four pages and outlined twelve family groups descended from the couple. Two of Isaac Packard's sons were known to have been printers in Albany: Robert Packard (Packard and Van Benthuysen) and Benjamin Packard (B. D. Packard and Co.).[36]

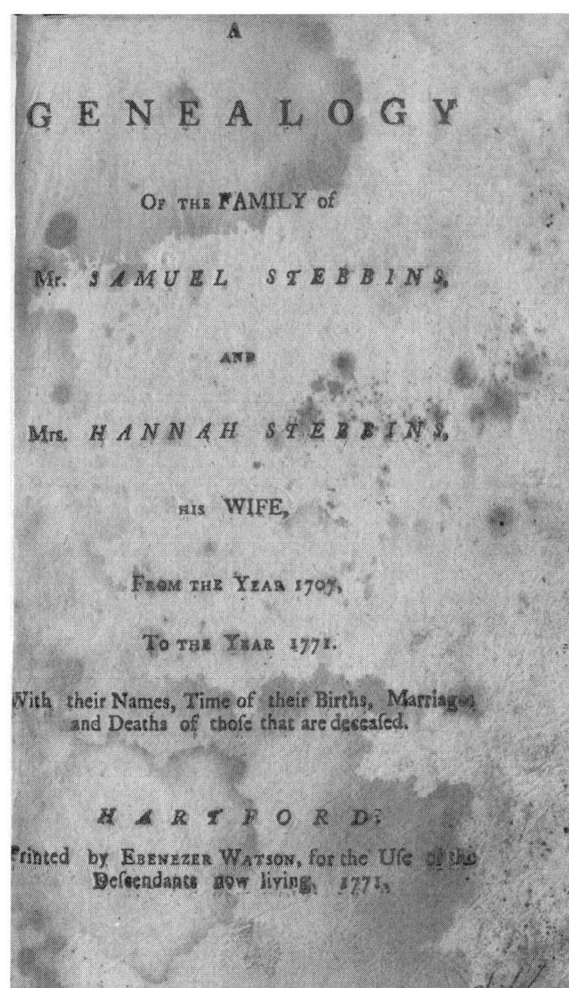

A

GENEALOGY

OF THE FAMILY of

Mr. SAMUEL STEBBINS,

AND

Mrs. HANNAH STEBBINS,

HIS WIFE,

FROM THE YEAR 1707,

TO THE YEAR 1771.

With their Names, Time of their Births, Marriages and Deaths of thoſe that are deceaſed.

HARTFORD:

Printed by EBENEZER WATSON, for the Uſe of the Deſcendants now living, 1771.

Figure 8 *A Genealogy of the Family of Mr. Samuel Stebbins and Mrs. Hannah Stebbins, his Wife.* Printed by Ebenezer Watson, Hartford, Connecticut, 1771. New England Historic Genealogical Society.

Occasionally broadsides were printed for families that had lost loved ones in tragic circumstances. The family record of John Pilsbury (1782–1824) and his wife, Abigail Elliot (1787–1829) (*Figure 11*), is remarkable for its frank treatment of their deaths. In it, we learn that "Mr. John Pilsbury, fell from the roof of a factory at Chelmsford [Massachusetts] and instantly expired, November 24, 1824."[37] This fatal mishap was not recorded in *The Pillsbury Family*,[38] but was elaborated in Chelmsford cemetery records: "[He] fell 75 feet from the gable end of one of the factories, into the wheel pit."[39] The family record also referenced Mrs. Pilsbury's final illness with a long passage that began with the information that "she had for some time been aware that her end was near. She looked forward to it with joyous hope." (Abigail [Elliot] Pilsbury died from phthisis in Lowell on 18 April 1829).[40] The Pilsbury broadside was almost certainly printed by the couple's son, John Gilman Pilsbury (1812–1858) who began a long printing and publishing career "when [as] quite a young man [he] removed to Lowell, entering a printing office."[41]

An even more unusual broadside-type family record was printed on satin-weave silk by or for Horace Dresser (b. 1803) (*Figure 12*).[42] Dresser, who was born in Pomfret, Connecticut, moved into New York State in the 1820s and in 1828 was hired in Chenango County as schoolmaster of the Guilford Center Academy at the rate of $75 a year. There he met (and on 24 March 1830 married) Lucy Knapp, the daughter of another Connecticut native, Dr. Colby Knapp.[43] The Dressers soon had three children, Vergilia Eliza (b. 1831), Horace Carroll (b. 1832), and Joseph Brown (b. 1834), but on 9 July 1833 their elder son died. The following year disaster struck: in a three-week period between 29 April and 17 May the remaining two children and their mother all died. To commemorate this tragic series of events a unique family record was printed on silk by or for the bereaved father:

Buried.
May 20, 1834.
In the burial ground,
At Guildford Centre, Chenango Co., N.Y.
The total family of Horace Dresser, Esq.
The remains of his Dear Little Children
were exhumed
At Bainbridge churchyard, which together
with those of
Their Dear Mother
Were followed by a large procession to
Guilford meeting house,
Where an appropriate and impressive
discourse from Eccl. Viii 12.
Was preached by the Rev. Geo. Spalding,
to a numerous and
Solemn audience, which seemed to
sympathize deeply with the
Mourning Friends*;*
After which they were all interred side by
side in
One Grave.[44]

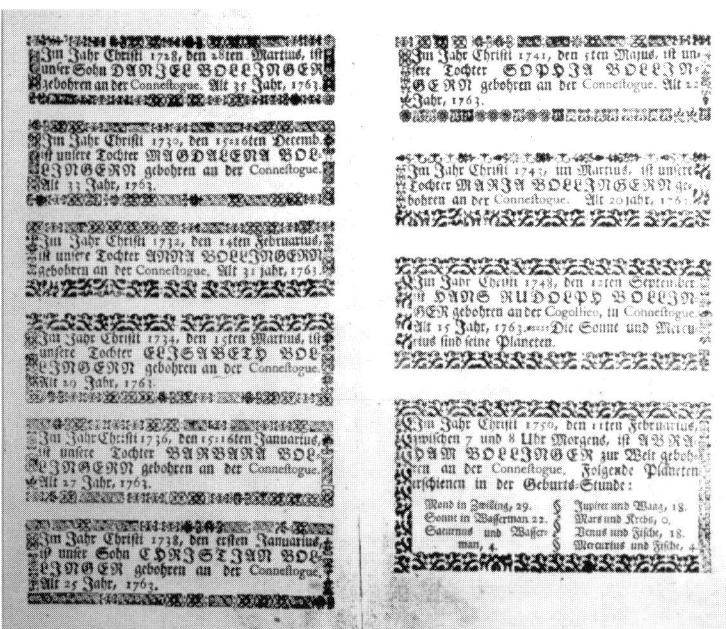

Im Jahr Christi 1728, den 28ten Martius, ist unser Sohn DANIEL BOLLINGER gebohren an der Connestogue. Alt 35 Jahr, 1763.

Im Jahr Christi 1730, den 15=16ten Decemb. ist unsere Tochter MAGDALENA BOLLINGERN gebohren an der Connestogue. Alt 33 Jahr, 1763.

Im Jahr Christi 1732, den 14ten Februarius, ist unsere Tochter ANNA BOLLINGERN gebohren an der Connestogue. Alt 31 jahr, 1763.

Im Jahr Christi 1734, den 15ten Martius, ist unsere Tochter ELISABETH BOLLINGERN gebohren an der Connestogue. Alt 29 Jahr, 1763.

Im Jahr Christi 1736, den 15=16ten Januarius, ist unsere Tochter BARBARA BOLLINGERN gebohren an der Connestogue. Alt 27 Jahr, 1763.

Im Jahr Christi 1738, den ersten Januarius, ist unser Sohn CHRISTIAN BOLLINGER gebohren an der Connestogue. Alt 25 Jahr, 1763.

Im Jahr Christi 1741, den 5ten Majus, ist unsere Tochter SOPHIA BOLLINGERN gebohren an der Connestogue. Alt 22 Jahr, 1763.

Im Jahr Christi 1743, im Martius, ist unsere Tochter MARIA BOLLINGERN gebohren an der Connestogue. Alt 20 jahr, 1763.

Im Jahr Christi 1748, den 12ten September, ist HANS RUDOLPH BOLLINGER gebohren an der Cogolico, in Connestogue. Alt 15 Jahr, 1763. Die Sonne und Mercurius sind seine Planeten.

Im Jahr Christi 1750, den 11ten Februarius, zwischen 7 und 8 Uhr Morgens, ist ABRAHAM BOLLINGER zur Welt gebohren an der Connestogue. Folgende Planeten erschienen in der Geburts-Stunde:

Mond in Zwilling, 29.	Jupiter und Waag, 18.
Sonne in Wasserman, 22.	Mars und Krebs, 0.
Saturnus und Wasserman, 4.	Venus und Fische, 18.
	Mercurius und Fische, 4.

Figure 9 Family record. Rudolph Bollinger family. Printed in 1763 at Ephrata Cloister, Lancaster County, Pennsylvania. New England Historic Genealogical Society.

Textile prints, such as the Dresser record, were generally produced during the first half of the nineteenth century and were frequently commemorative or instructional in nature. The relationship between broadsides on paper and those on fabric was a close one. According to Diane L. Fagan Affleck, "textile prints produced by paper printers usually combined text with images or other decorative elements to create a publication which, like a broadside, was self-contained and printed on a single sheet, in this case, fabric instead of paper."[45] The Dresser textile print features iconography traditionally associated with family records or mourning pieces: paired hearts, hourglasses, and a churchyard gravesite flanked by a weeping willow.

As the nineteenth century progressed, some family record broadsides evolved from small family groups to be multi-generational in presentation—a parallel to the then-growing national interest in genealogy. Some broadsides outlined descents from Great Migration period immigrants (1620–1640) or even more remote antecedents. Two such broadsides exist for a single family: a "Genealogical Record of the Thorndike Family, from 1470 to 1859," printed in 1859 for the family of Joseph Perry Thorndike (b. 1814) (*Figure 13*), of Portland, Maine, and his wife, Elizabeth T. Sweet (or Swett); and "A Genealogical Record of the Thorndike Family, from 1470 to 1859, Making Thirteen Generations," printed the same year for Captain William H. Thorndike, a livery stable keeper of Rockland, Maine. Both broadsides feature ornate typography, intricate border patterns, and along genealogical lines purport descents from William Thorndike (b. 1470) of Little Carlton, Lincolnshire. Joseph Perry Thorndike's record highlights the fact that the American immigrant, John[1] Thorndike (d. prior to 3 November 1668), returned to England and was buried in Westminster Abbey.[46]

While most multi-generational broadsides presented data in the male surname line only, a more unusual presentation was printed in or post-1877 by George E. Dunbar of Waterville, Maine, for Winslow Roberts (b. 1821). It traces Winslow Roberts's descent from John Hall, who settled in Dover, New Hampshire, "about 1650," through five generations and via two female lines.[47]

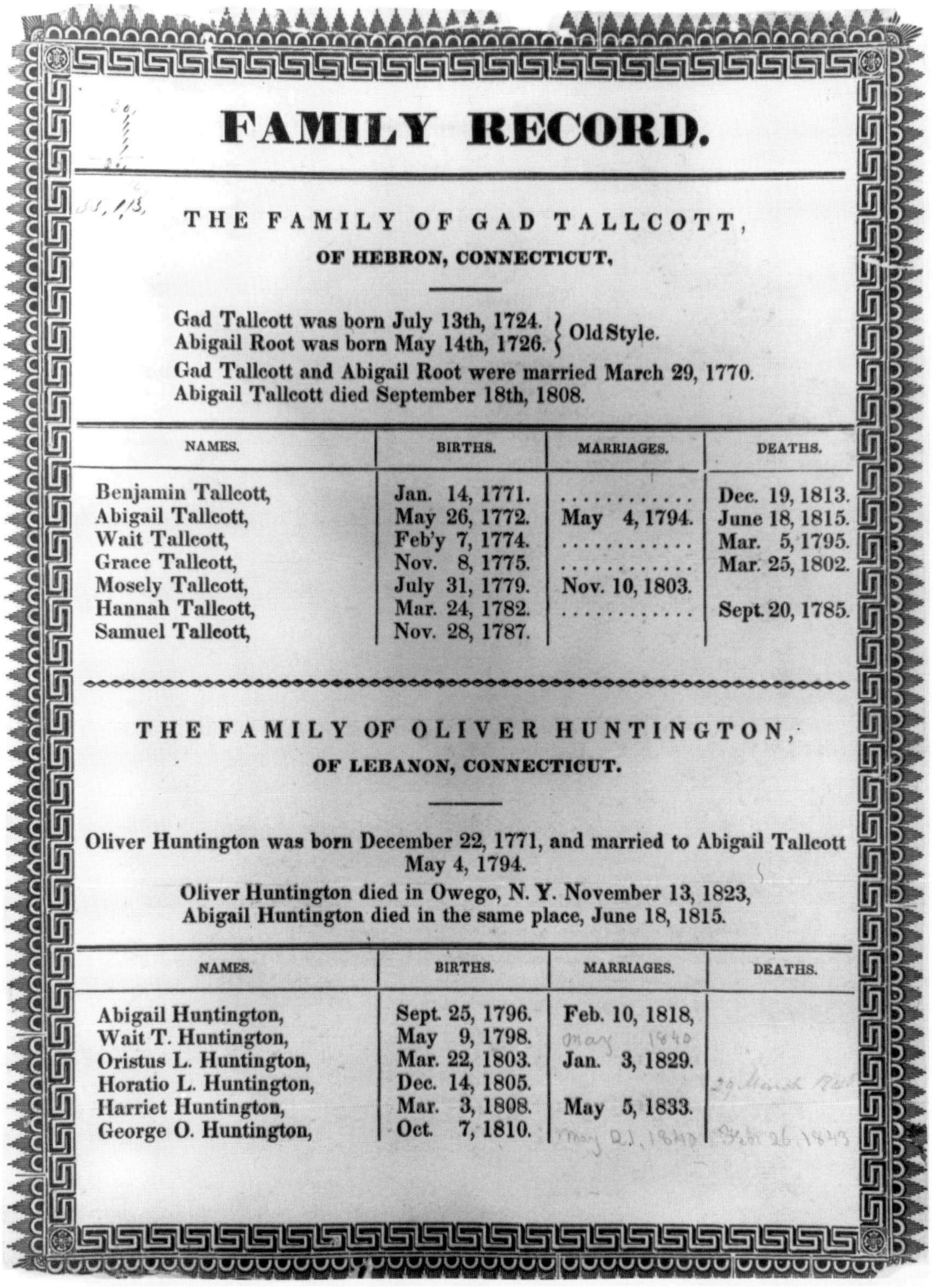

FAMILY RECORD.

THE FAMILY OF GAD TALLCOTT,

OF HEBRON, CONNECTICUT,

Gad Tallcott was born July 13th, 1724. } Old Style.
Abigail Root was born May 14th, 1726. }
Gad Tallcott and Abigail Root were married March 29, 1770.
Abigail Tallcott died September 18th, 1808.

NAMES.	BIRTHS.	MARRIAGES.	DEATHS.
Benjamin Tallcott,	Jan. 14, 1771.	....	Dec. 19, 1813.
Abigail Tallcott,	May 26, 1772.	May 4, 1794.	June 18, 1815.
Wait Tallcott,	Feb'y 7, 1774.	....	Mar. 5, 1795.
Grace Tallcott,	Nov. 8, 1775.	....	Mar. 25, 1802.
Mosely Tallcott,	July 31, 1779.	Nov. 10, 1803.	
Hannah Tallcott,	Mar. 24, 1782.	....	Sept. 20, 1785.
Samuel Tallcott,	Nov. 28, 1787.		

THE FAMILY OF OLIVER HUNTINGTON,

OF LEBANON, CONNECTICUT.

Oliver Huntington was born December 22, 1771, and married to Abigail Tallcott May 4, 1794.
Oliver Huntington died in Owego, N. Y. November 13, 1823,
Abigail Huntington died in the same place, June 18, 1815.

NAMES.	BIRTHS.	MARRIAGES.	DEATHS.
Abigail Huntington,	Sept. 25, 1796.	Feb. 10, 1818,	
Wait T. Huntington,	May 9, 1798.		
Oristus L. Huntington,	Mar. 22, 1803.	Jan. 3, 1829.	
Horatio L. Huntington,	Dec. 14, 1805.		
Harriet Huntington,	Mar. 3, 1808.	May 5, 1833.	
George O. Huntington,	Oct. 7, 1810.		

Figure 10 Family record. Gad Tallcott and Abigail Root (married 1770); Oliver Huntington and Abigail Tallcott (married 1794). Printer unknown. Connecticut, after 1833. The Connecticut Historical Society, Hartford, Connecticut.

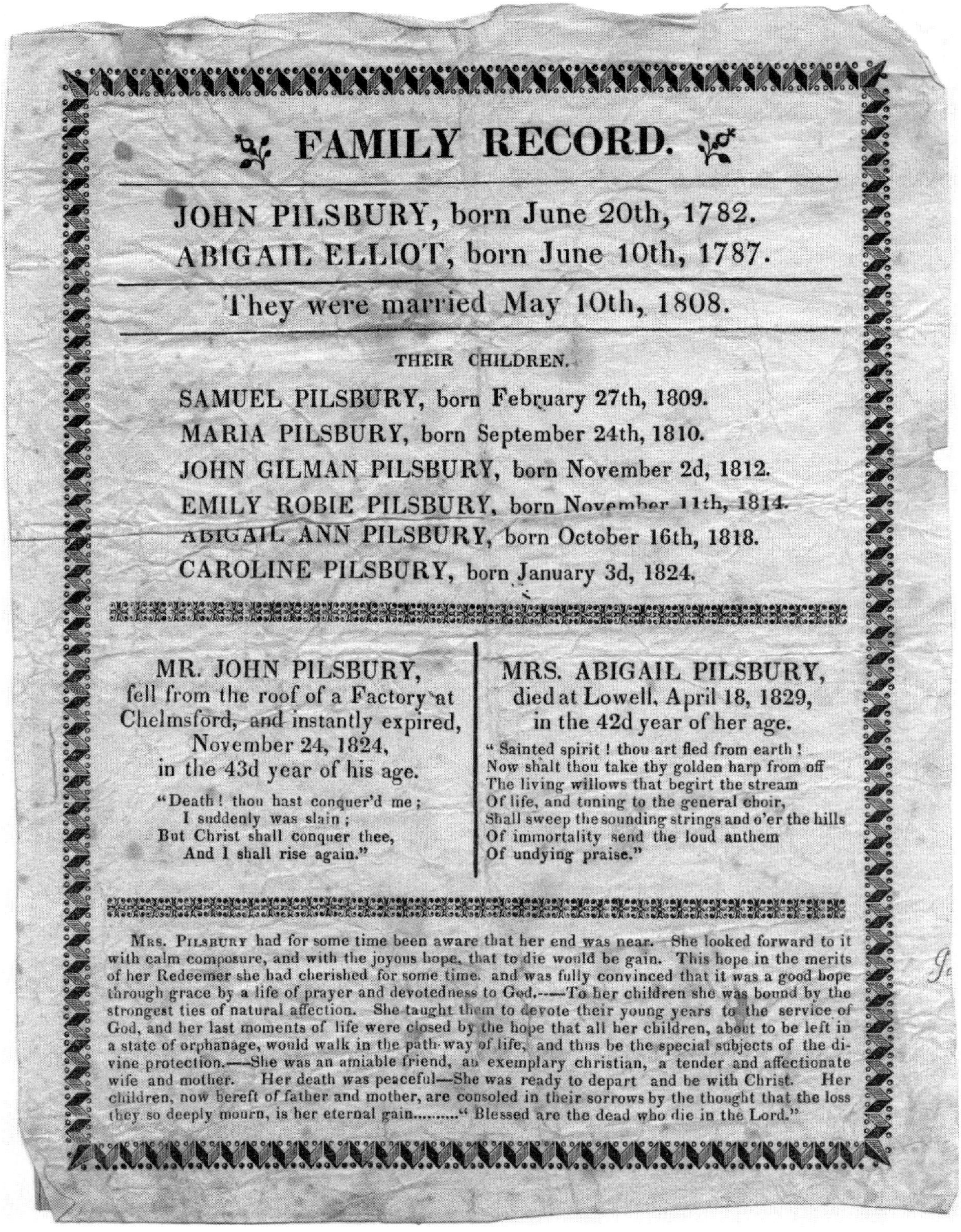

FAMILY RECORD.

JOHN PILSBURY, born June 20th, 1782.
ABIGAIL ELLIOT, born June 10th, 1787.

They were married May 10th, 1808.

THEIR CHILDREN.

SAMUEL PILSBURY, born February 27th, 1809.
MARIA PILSBURY, born September 24th, 1810.
JOHN GILMAN PILSBURY, born November 2d, 1812.
EMILY ROBIE PILSBURY, born November 11th, 1814.
ABIGAIL ANN PILSBURY, born October 16th, 1818.
CAROLINE PILSBURY, born January 3d, 1824.

MR. JOHN PILSBURY,
fell from the roof of a Factory at Chelmsford, and instantly expired, November 24, 1824, in the 43d year of his age.

"Death! thou hast conquer'd me;
I suddenly was slain;
But Christ shall conquer thee,
And I shall rise again."

MRS. ABIGAIL PILSBURY,
died at Lowell, April 18, 1829, in the 42d year of her age.

" Sainted spirit! thou art fled from earth!
Now shalt thou take thy golden harp from off
The living willows that begirt the stream
Of life, and tuning to the general choir,
Shall sweep the sounding strings and o'er the hills
Of immortality send the loud anthem
Of undying praise."

MRS. PILSBURY had for some time been aware that her end was near. She looked forward to it with calm composure, and with the joyous hope, that to die would be gain. This hope in the merits of her Redeemer she had cherished for some time, and was fully convinced that it was a good hope through grace by a life of prayer and devotedness to God.——To her children she was bound by the strongest ties of natural affection. She taught them to devote their young years to the service of God, and her last moments of life were closed by the hope that all her children, about to be left in a state of orphanage, would walk in the path way of life, and thus be the special subjects of the divine protection.——She was an amiable friend, an exemplary christian, a tender and affectionate wife and mother. Her death was peaceful—She was ready to depart and be with Christ. Her children, now bereft of father and mother, are consoled in their sorrows by the thought that the loss they so deeply mourn, is her eternal gain..........“ Blessed are the dead who die in the Lord.”

Figure 11 Family record. John Pilsbury and Abigail Elliot (married 1808). Probably printed by John Gilman Pilsbury, Lowell, Massachusetts, after 18 April 1829. New England Historic Genealogical Society.

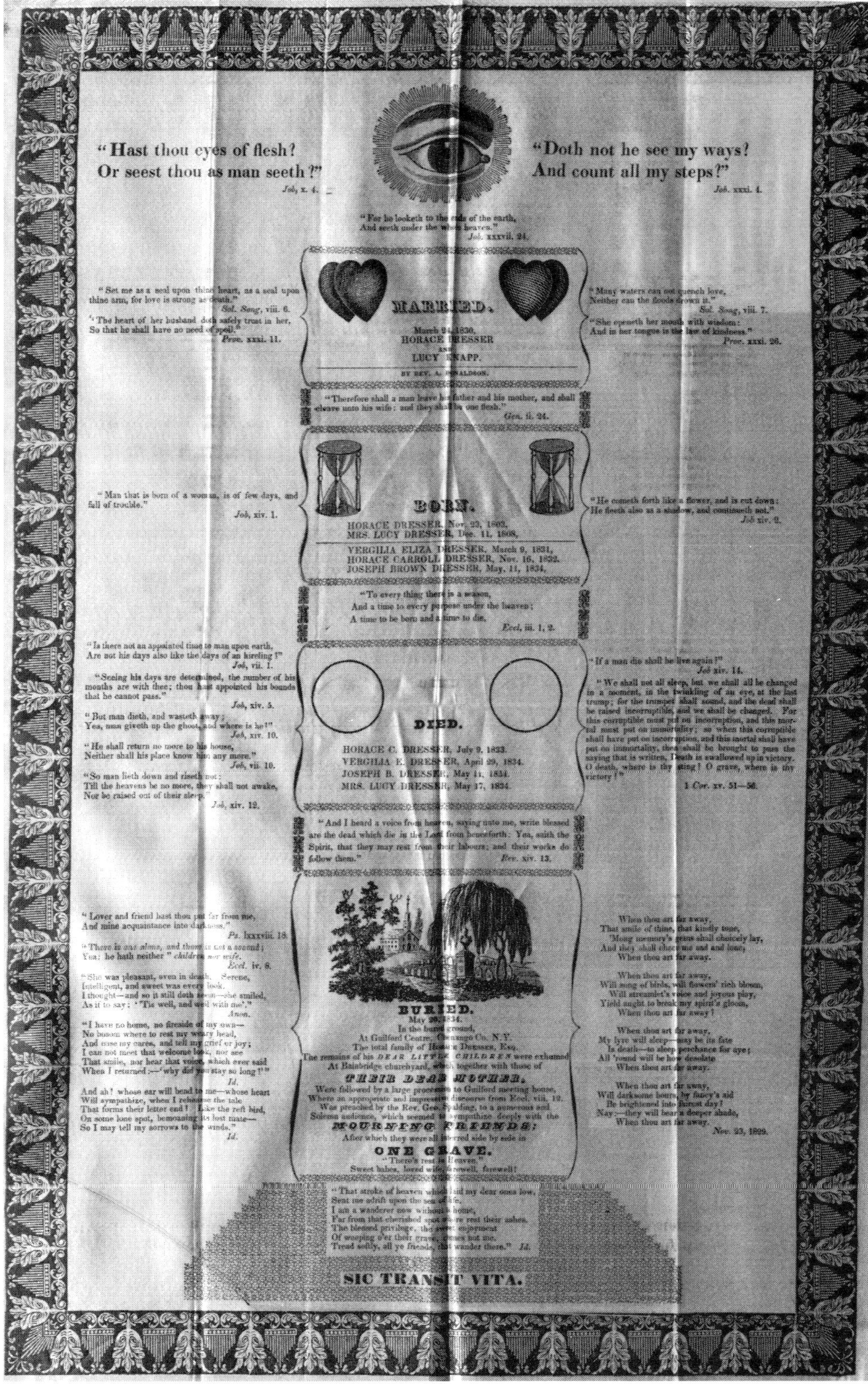

"Hast thou eyes of flesh?
Or seest thou as man seeth?"
Job, x. 4.

"Doth not he see my ways?
And count all my steps?"
Job. xxxi. 4.

"For he looketh to the ends of the earth,
And seeth under the whole heaven."
Job. xxxvii. 24.

"Set me as a seal upon thine heart, as a seal upon thine arm, for love is strong as death."
Sol. Song, viii. 6.

"The heart of her husband doth safely trust in her,
So that he shall have no need of spoil."
Prov. xxxi. 11.

MARRIED.

March 24, 1830,
HORACE DRESSER
AND
LUCY KNAPP.

BY REV. A. DONALDSON.

"Many waters can not quench love,
Neither can the floods drown it."
Sol. Song, viii. 7.

"She openeth her mouth with wisdom:
And in her tongue is the law of kindness."
Prov. xxxi. 26.

"Therefore shall a man leave his father and his mother, and shall cleave unto his wife: and they shall be one flesh."
Gen. ii. 24.

"Man that is born of a woman, is of few days, and full of trouble."
Job, xiv. 1.

BORN.

HORACE DRESSER, Nov. 23, 1803,
MRS. LUCY DRESSER, Dec. 11, 1808,

VERGILIA ELIZA DRESSER, March 9, 1831,
HORACE CARROLL DRESSER, Nov. 16, 1832,
JOSEPH BROWN DRESSER, May, 11, 1834,

"He cometh forth like a flower, and is cut down:
He fleeth also as a shadow, and continueth not."
Job xiv. 2.

"To every thing there is a season,
And a time to every purpose under the heaven;
A time to be born and a time to die.
Eccl, iii. 1, 2.

"Is there not an appointed time to man upon earth,
Are not his days also like the days of an hireling?"
Job, vii. 1.

"Seeing his days are determined, the number of his months are with thee; thou hast appointed his bounds that he cannot pass."
Job, xiv. 5.

"But man dieth, and wasteth away;
Yea, man giveth up the ghost, and where is he?"
Job, xiv. 10.

"He shall return no more to his house,
Neither shall his place know him any more."
Job, vii. 10.

"So man lieth down and riseth not:
Till the heavens be no more, they shall not awake,
Nor be raised out of their sleep."
Job, xiv. 12.

DIED.

HORACE C. DRESSER, July 9, 1833.
VERGILIA E. DRESSER, April 29, 1834.
JOSEPH B. DRESSER, May 11, 1834.
MRS. LUCY DRESSER, May 17, 1834.

"If a man die shall he live again?"
Job xiv. 14.

"We shall not all sleep, but we shall all be changed in a moment, in the twinkling of an eye, at the last trump; for the trumpet shall sound, and the dead shall be raised incorruptible, and we shall be changed. For this corruptible must put on incorruption, and this mortal must put on immortality; so when this corruptible shall have put on incorruption, and this mortal shall have put on immortality, then shall be brought to pass the saying that is written, Death is swallowed up in victory. O death, where is thy sting! O grave, where is thy victory!"
1 *Cor*. xv. 51—56.

"And I heard a voice from heaven, saying unto me, write blessed are the dead which die in the Lord from henceforth: Yea, saith the Spirit, that they may rest from their labours; and their works do follow them."
Rev. xiv. 13.

"Lover and friend hast thou put far from me,
And mine acquaintance into darkness."
Ps. lxxxviii. 18.

"There is one alone, and there is not a second;
Yea; he hath neither" *children nor wife*.
Eccl. iv. 8.

"She was pleasant, even in death. Serene,
Intelligent, and sweet was every look.
I thought—and so it still doth seem—she smiled,
As if to say; 'Tis well, and well with me'."
Anon.

"I have no home, no fireside of my own—
No bosom where to rest my weary head,
And ease my cares, and tell my grief or joy;
I can not meet that welcome look, nor see
That smile, nor hear that voice, which ever said
When I returned:—'why did you stay so long?'"
Id.

And ah! whose ear will bend to me—whose heart
Will sympathize, when I rehearse the tale
That forms their latter end! Like the reft bird,
On some lone spot, bemoaning its lost mate—
So I may tell my sorrows to the winds."
Id.

BURIED.
May 20, 1834.
In the burial ground,
At Guilford Centre, Chenango Co. N.Y.
The total family of Horace Dresser, Esq.
The remains of his *DEAR LITTLE CHILDREN* were exhumed
At Bainbridge churchyard, which together with those of
THEIR DEAR MOTHER,
Were followed by a large procession to Guilford meeting house,
Where an appropriate and impressive discourse from Eccl. viii. 12.
Was preached by the Rev. Geo. Spalding, to a numerous and
Solemn audience, which seemed to sympathize deeply with the
MOURNING FRIENDS;
After which they were all interred side by side in
ONE GRAVE.
"There's rest in Heaven."
Sweet babes, loved wife, farewell, farewell!

When thou art far away,
That smile of thine, that kindly tone,
'Mong memory's gems shall choicely lay,
And they shall cheer me sad and lone,
When thou art far away.

When thou art far away,
Will song of birds, will flowers' rich bloom,
Will streamlet's voice and joyous play,
Yield aught to break my spirit's gloom,
When thou art far away!

When thou art far away,
My lyre will sleep—may be its fate
Is death—to sleep perchance for aye;
All 'round will be how desolate
When thou art far away.

When thou art far away,
Will darksome hours, by fancy's aid
Be brightened into fairest day!
Nay;—they will bear a deeper shade,
When thou art far away.
Nov. 23, 1829.

"That stroke of heaven which laid my dear ones low,
Sent me adrift upon the sea of life,
I am a wanderer now without a home,
Far from that cherished spot where rest their ashes.
The blessed privilege, the sweet enjoyment
Of weeping o'er their grave, denies but me.
Tread softly, all ye friends, that wander there." *Id*.

SIC TRANSIT VITA.

Figure 12 Memorial. Horace Dresser, Esq., of Chenango County, New York. Printed on silk, circa 1834. New England Historic Genealogical Society.

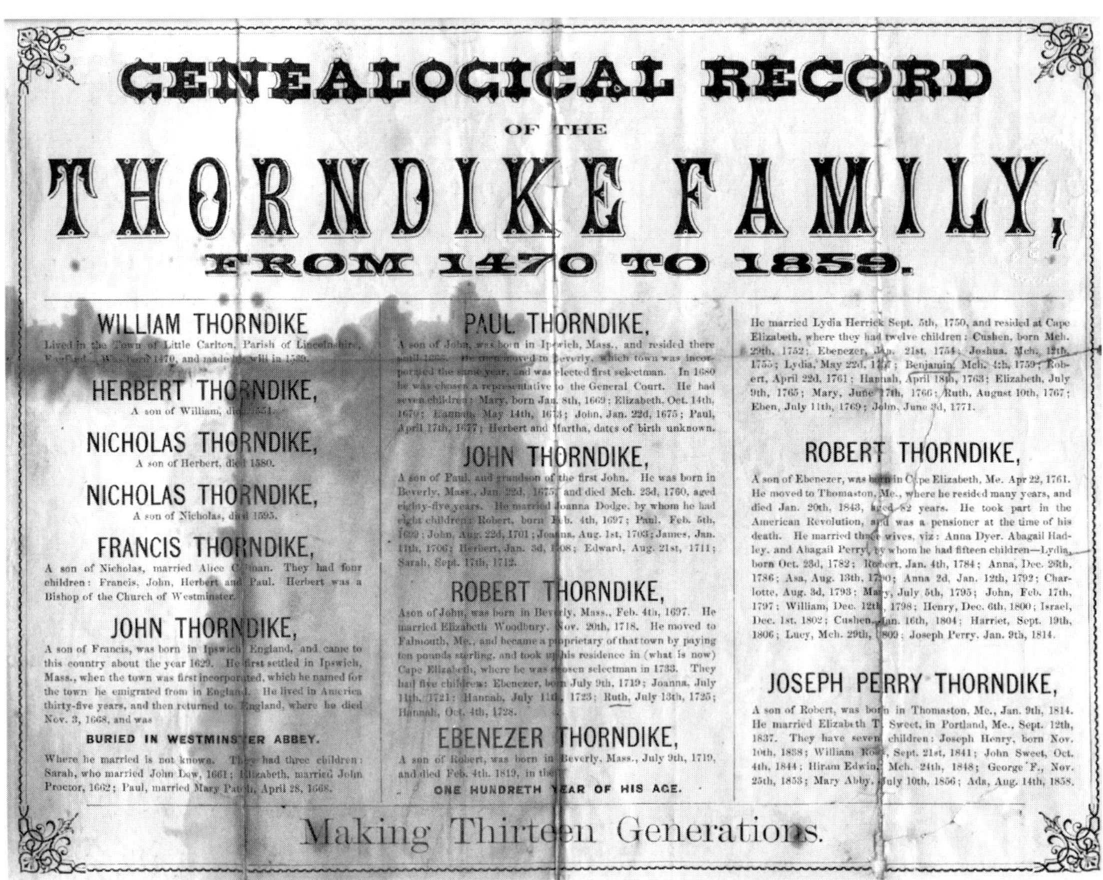

GENEALOGICAL RECORD
OF THE
THORNDIKE FAMILY,
FROM 1470 TO 1859.

WILLIAM THORNDIKE

Lived in the Town of Little Carlton, Parish of Lincolnshire, England. Was born 1470, and made his will in 1530.

HERBERT THORNDIKE,

A son of William, died 1551.

NICHOLAS THORNDIKE,

A son of Herbert, died 1580.

NICHOLAS THORNDIKE,

A son of Nicholas, died 1595.

FRANCIS THORNDIKE,

A son of Nicholas, married Alice C[illegible]man. They had four children: Francis, John, Herbert and Paul. Herbert was a Bishop of the Church of Westminster.

JOHN THORNDIKE,

A son of Francis, was born in Ipswich, England, and came to this country about the year 1629. He first settled in Ipswich, Mass., when the town was first incorporated, which he named for the town he emigrated from in England. He lived in America thirty-five years, and then returned to England, where he died Nov. 3, 1668, and was

BURIED IN WESTMINSTER ABBEY.

Where he married is not known. They had three children: Sarah, who married John Dow, 1661; Elizabeth, married John Proctor, 1662; Paul, married Mary Patch, April 28, 1668.

PAUL THORNDIKE,

A son of John, was born in Ipswich, Mass., and resided there until 1668. He then moved to Beverly, which town was incorporated the same year, and was elected first selectman. In 1680 he was chosen a representative to the General Court. He had seven children: Mary, born Jan. 8th, 1669; Elizabeth, Oct. 14th, 1670; Hannah, May 14th, 1673; John, Jan. 22d, 1675; Paul, April 17th, 1677; Herbert and Martha, dates of birth unknown.

JOHN THORNDIKE,

A son of Paul, and grandson of the first John. He was born in Beverly, Mass., Jan. 22d, 1675, and died Mch. 23d, 1760, aged eighty-five years. He married Joanna Dodge, by whom he had eight children: Robert, born Feb. 4th, 1697; Paul, Feb. 5th, 1699; John, Aug. 22d, 1701; Joanna, Aug. 1st, 1703; James, Jan. 11th, 1706; Herbert, Jan. 3d, 1708; Edward, Aug. 21st, 1711; Sarah, Sept. 17th, 1712.

ROBERT THORNDIKE,

A son of John, was born in Beverly, Mass., Feb. 4th, 1697. He married Elizabeth Woodbury, Nov. 20th, 1718. He moved to Falmouth, Me., and became a proprietary of that town by paying ten pounds sterling, and took up his residence in (what is now) Cape Elizabeth, where he was chosen selectman in 1733. They had five children: Ebenezer, born July 9th, 1719; Joanna, July 11th, 1721; Hannah, July 11th, 1723; Ruth, July 13th, 1725; Hannah, Oct. 4th, 1728.

EBENEZER THORNDIKE,

A son of Robert, was born in Beverly, Mass., July 9th, 1719, and died Feb. 4th, 1819, in the

ONE HUNDRETH YEAR OF HIS AGE.

He married Lydia Herrick Sept. 5th, 1750, and resided at Cape Elizabeth, where they had twelve children: Cushen, born Mch. 29th, 1752; Ebenezer, Jan. 21st, 1754; Joshua, Mch. 12th, 1755; Lydia, May 22d, 1757; Benjamin, Mch. 4th, 1759; Robert, April 22d, 1761; Hannah, April 18th, 1763; Elizabeth, July 9th, 1765; Mary, June 17th, 1766; Ruth, August 10th, 1767; Eben, July 11th, 1769; John, June 3d, 1771.

ROBERT THORNDIKE,

A son of Ebenezer, was born in Cape Elizabeth, Me. Apr 22, 1761. He moved to Thomaston, Me., where he resided many years, and died Jan. 20th, 1843, aged 82 years. He took part in the American Revolution, and was a pensioner at the time of his death. He married three wives, viz: Anna Dyer, Abagail Hadley, and Abagail Perry, by whom he had fifteen children—Lydia, born Oct. 23d, 1782; Robert, Jan. 4th, 1784; Anna, Dec. 28th, 1786; Asa, Aug. 13th, 1790; Anna 2d, Jan. 12th, 1792; Charlotte, Aug. 3d, 1793; Mary, July 5th, 1795; John, Feb. 17th, 1797; William, Dec. 12th, 1798; Henry, Dec. 6th, 1800; Israel, Dec. 1st, 1802; Cushen, Jan. 16th, 1804; Harriet, Sept. 19th, 1806; Lucy, Mch. 29th, 1809; Joseph Perry, Jan. 9th, 1814.

JOSEPH PERRY THORNDIKE,

A son of Robert, was born in Thomaston, Me., Jan. 9th, 1814. He married Elizabeth T. Sweet, in Portland, Me., Sept. 12th, 1837. They have seven children: Joseph Henry, born Nov. 10th, 1838; William Ross, Sept. 21st, 1841; John Sweet, Oct. 4th, 1844; Hiram Edwin, Mch. 24th, 1848; George F., Nov. 25th, 1853; Mary Abby, July 10th, 1856; Ada, Aug. 14th, 1858.

Making Thirteen Generations.

Figure 13 "Genealogical record of the Thorndike Family, from 1470 to 1859." Printed for Joseph Perry Thorndike, of Portland, Maine, circa 1859. New England Historic Genealogical Society.

Profiles and the Letterpress Artist Compositions[48]

From the late eighteenth century and especially in the decades preceding the advent of daguerreotypy and photography, profiles were inexpensively produced and achieved great popularity in New England and elsewhere; in combination with family record forms they proved an appealing keepsake. Commercially produced profiles were frequently cut two or more at a time and like broadside-type family records—or even the more unusual engraved profile portraits by Charles Balthazar Julien Févret de Saint-Mémin (1770–1852)[49]—were presumably distributed to family members. These simple likenesses often portrayed many members of a single family, and sometimes, albeit rarely, were cut for extended members of a family, including servants. Such is the case of "Flora's profile" (*Figure 14*). Flora Benjamin, an African-American woman purchased by Asa Benjamin (1763–1833)[50] of Stratford, Connecticut, from Margaret Dwight in 1796 for £25.[51] In the 1800 Census of Fairfield County, Asa Benjamin is listed as having one servant in his household.[52]

One of the most curious family record forms in New England appeared at the end of the 1820s and lasted for only a few years. A combination of folk portraiture and family data record-keeping, these pieces present a striking composition: handset letterpress type on printed forms placed below paired hollow-cut profiles (more commonly called "silhouettes" post-1840s) in separate panels of a mahogany or rosewood veneer frame (*Figures 15–18*).[53] The profiles were almost invariably of a man and wife facing each other and were often, but not always, divided by a green silk ribbon.

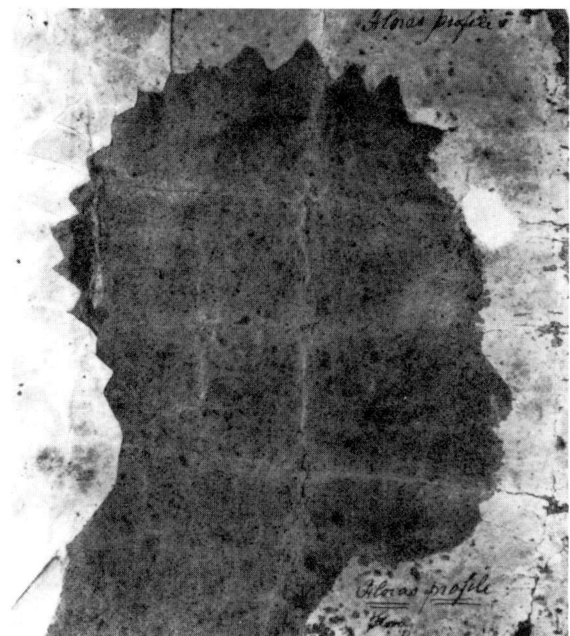

Figure 14 Profile. Flora Benjamin, servant to Asa Benjamin, of Stratford, Connecticut, 1796. Stratford Historical Society.

For the purpose of discussion, the unidentified artist examined here will be called the "Letterpress Artist" in recognition of the typographic medium used to record family record data.[54] (It remains possible, however, that two or three people, such as itinerant profilists and a printer, worked together to create these novel forms.)[55] Surprisingly, the authors of existing literature on American profiles have not identified the artist responsible for these compositions, perhaps not recognizing them as the collective labor of one or two individuals. Nor has the geographic range of this craftsperson's work been previously narrowed to a particular state—Connecticut.[56] Subjects resided in such towns as Berlin, Bolton, Durham, East Windsor, Enfield, Hamden, Harwinton, Middletown, Simsbury, Somers, Stafford, and Suffield (*Figure 19*). Unlike several itinerant profilists in New England, including Samuel Bradburn Banton (1795–1864),[57] Moses Chapman (1783–1821),[58] and Rufus Porter (1792–1884),[59] for whom printed handbills exist (and a much greater number who advertised in newspapers), the Letterpress Artist has not been identified by way of a surviving handbill, broadside, or newspaper announcement. Nor has the examination of contemporary diaries, estate files, and local sources established his identity. One possible identification, based presumably on stylistic similarities, can now be eliminated: profilist William Chamberlain (1790–1860), of Loudon, New Hampshire, who was otherwise (and elsewhere) engaged during the pertinent period in Connecticut, circa 1828 to 1834.[60]

Unlike other contemporaneous unidentified New England profilists, who have become known by distinguishing motifs in their work—for example, the "Puffy Sleeve Artist" or the "Red Book Artist"[61]—the compositions examined herein have been treated by scholars as intriguing anomalies without further analysis. Stylistically, the Letterpress Artist pieces are derived from more elaborate family record types. Like many fill-in-the-blank family registers, such as the boldly stylized William Putnam and Submit Fisk family register owned by the New England Historic Genealogical Society[62] (*Figure 20*), a pair of pilasters or columns frame each family's vital statistics. Decorative elements in the surround are formed by groupings of six-petalled flowers, tiny suns or star bursts, stylized buds or leaves, and a woven pattern base—perhaps simulating an ornate tile floor upon which the family temple or arcade rests. Such printers' ornaments were readily available for purchase in the 1820s from type foundries in Boston and New York.[63] Subtle variations in the family record prints (upon which vital records were later printed, stamped, or handwritten) indicate that they were printed at separate times. In terms of cutting method, the profiles are similar in quality to those cut with the aid of mechanical devices, such as the physiognotrace, which flourished in the earlier decades of the century and at the end of the previous one. Like the physiognotrace artists, the Letterpress Artist added minor details of coiffure and dress to the profiles in pencil and ink. Peter Benes has estimated that between 1790 and 1810 more than thirty profile artists used mechanical imaging devices throughout New England and New York,[64] but this activity had apparently waned by the late 1820s.

It is also possible that in addition to itinerating, the Letterpress Artist worked from a fixed location in Connecticut. One prospective location for such profile-cutting activity is the Hartford Museum, an establishment founded there in 1797 by artist (and

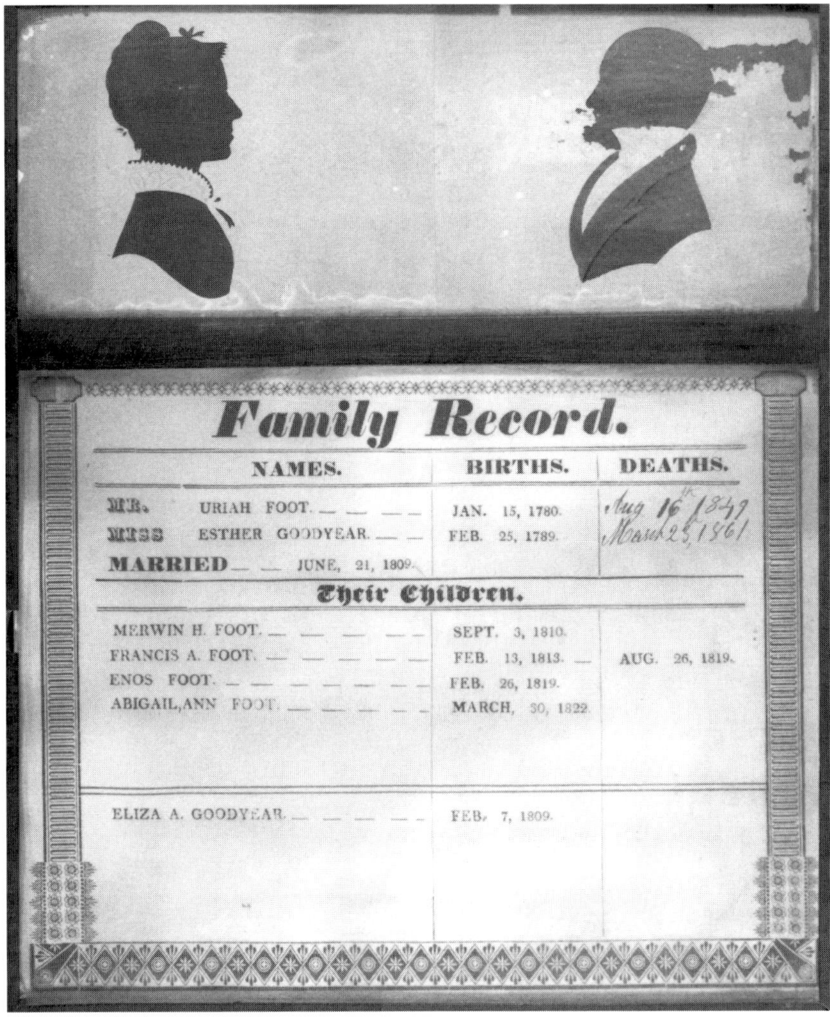

Family Record.

NAMES.	BIRTHS.	DEATHS.
MR. URIAH FOOT.	JAN. 15, 1780.	Aug 16th 1849
MISS ESTHER GOODYEAR.	FEB. 25, 1789.	March 25, 1861
MARRIED — JUNE, 21, 1809.		
Their Children.		
MERWIN H. FOOT.	SEPT. 3, 1810.	
FRANCIS A. FOOT.	FEB. 13, 1813.	AUG. 26, 1819.
ENOS FOOT.	FEB. 26, 1819.	
ABIGAIL,ANN FOOT.	MARCH, 30, 1822.	
ELIZA A. GOODYEAR.	FEB. 7, 1809.	

Figure 15 Profiles and family record. Uriah Foot and Esther Goodyear. Attributed to the Letterpress Artist. Connecticut, circa 1829–1830. Private Collection.

former minister) Joseph Steward (1753–1822).[65] Not only were profiles commonly cut at museums (such as at Charles Willson Peale's museum in Philadelphia), but the Hartford Museum featured several attractions frequently associated with the profile arts: electrical treatments, wax works, and elaborate organs and other unusual musical instruments.[66]

The museum advertised itself frequently in the *Connecticut Courant* and *Connecticut Mirror*;[67] citing such enticements as the "Solar Microscope," a German device used to magnify objects to enormous proportions—making "mites in cheese appear like hedge-hogs" and "various fluids. . . magnificent beyond description."[68] At least some printing processes were also available at the museum, including "Lithographic Printing, form [*sic*] Paris." Joseph Steward died in 1822, and the museum was by 1825 under the management of Charles Dickerson. It is almost certain that profile-cutting had taken place at the museum at an earlier time; in Steward's will his daughter, Sarah M., was to receive a machine for cutting profiles. The museum had further management changes and appears to have subsided in or about 1838.[69] Further research may reveal what affiliation, if any, the Letterpress Artist had with the Hartford Museum and, perhaps, in time, the personal identity of this family record artisan.

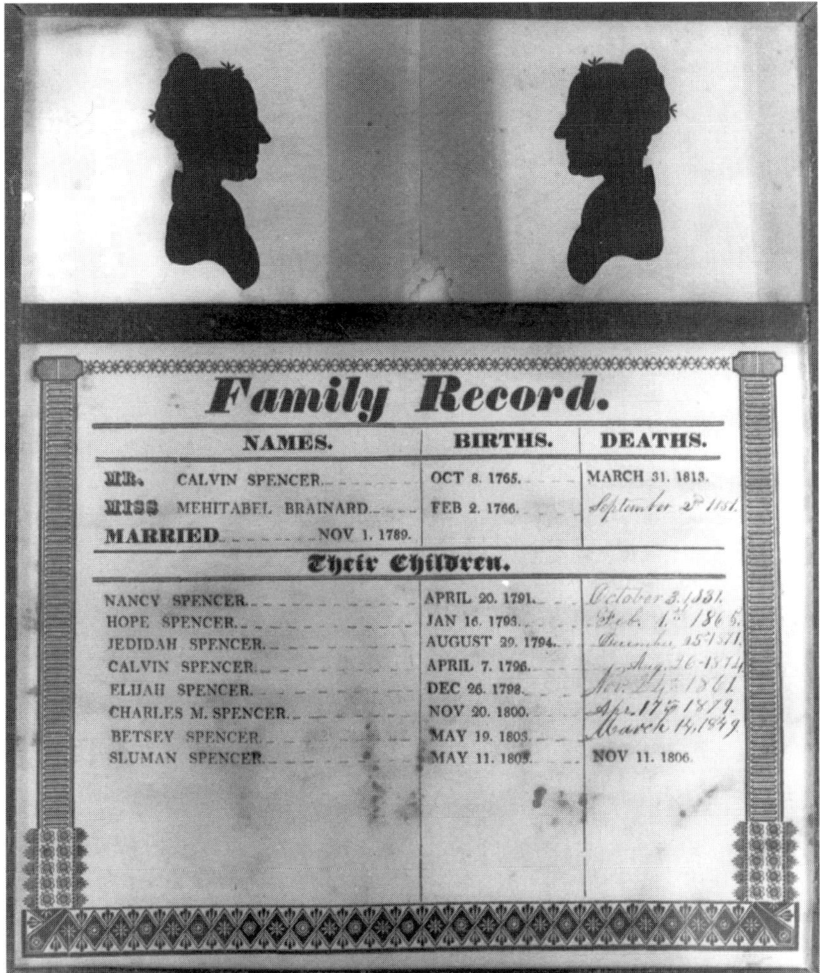

Family Record.

NAMES.	BIRTHS.	DEATHS.
MR. CALVIN SPENCER	OCT 8. 1765.	MARCH 31. 1813.
MISS MEHITABEL BRAINARD	FEB 2. 1766.	September 2nd 1851
MARRIED NOV 1. 1789.		

Their Children.

NAMES.	BIRTHS.	DEATHS.
NANCY SPENCER	APRIL 20. 1791.	October 3, 1831
HOPE SPENCER	JAN 16. 1793.	Feb. 1st 1865
JEDIDAH SPENCER	AUGUST 29. 1794.	December 25 1871
CALVIN SPENCER	APRIL 7. 1796.	Aug. 26-1874
ELIJAH SPENCER	DEC 26. 1798.	Nov. 24th 1861
CHARLES M. SPENCER	NOV 20. 1800.	Apr. 17th 1879
BETSEY SPENCER	MAY 19. 1803.	March 14, 1849
SLUMAN SPENCER	MAY 11. 180[illegible].	NOV 11. 1806.

Figure 16 Profiles and family record. Calvin Spencer and Mehitabel Brainard. Attributed to the Letterpress Artist. Connecticut, probably prior to 16 February 1830. The Connecticut Historical Society, Hartford, Connecticut.

CHECKLIST OF FAMILY RECORD AND PROFILE COMPOSITIONS ATTRIBUTED TO THE LETTERPRESS ARTIST, CIRCA 1828–1834

1. **Bradley.** The profile of Elizabeth M[orris] Bradley, "aged 19," dated 1829.[70] Wife of Elizur Thompson, below.

2. **Bradley/Phelps.** The family record and paired profiles of Uriel Bradley (1804–1887), of Meriden, Conn., and Phebe Gaylord Phelps (1799–1893), of Burlington, Conn., married 1827,[71] and five children listed, born 1829–1837, residents of various towns in Connecticut, including Burlington, Durham, and Plainville.[72] AARFAC.

3. **Chapin/King.** The family record (profiles missing) of Albert Chapin (b. 1807) and Lorinda King (1808–1839), married 1831, and three children listed, born 1831–1835, of Enfield, Conn.[73] Taken 1831. NEHGS.[74]

4. **Colton/Watson.** The family record and paired profiles of Benjamin Colton (1798–1882), a shoemaker and farmer, and Eliza Watson (1801–1880), married 1828, and four children listed (with later generations and notations added in ink). Colton was born in Chester, Mass.,[75] and later resided at Warehouse Point, East Windsor, Conn.[76] Taken 1828. Private collection.

5. **Eager.** The profile of M. K. Eager, "aged 24," dated 1829.[77]

6. **Eno/Case.** The family record and paired profiles of Chauncey Eno (1782–1845), a farmer, and Amrille [*sic*] (or Amarilla/Amaryllis) Case (1788–1860), married 1807, and

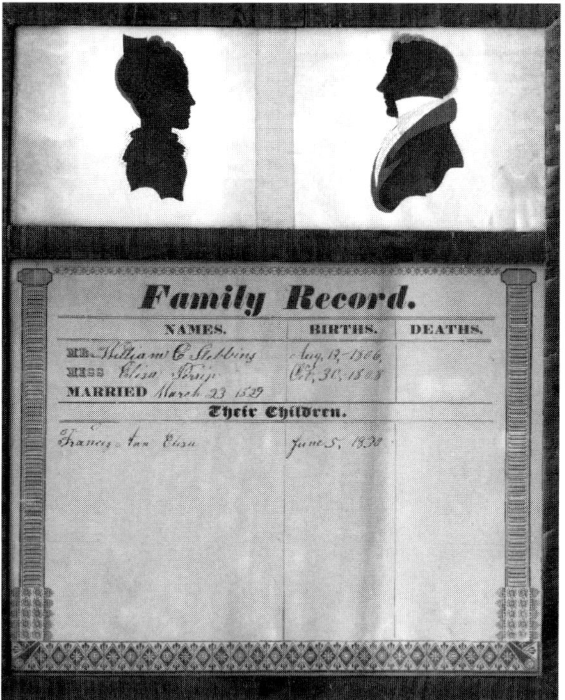

Figure 17 Profiles and family record. William C[arpenter] Stebbins and Eliza Perrin. Attributed to the Letterpress Artist. Connecticut or Massachusetts, probably 1829. Private Collection.

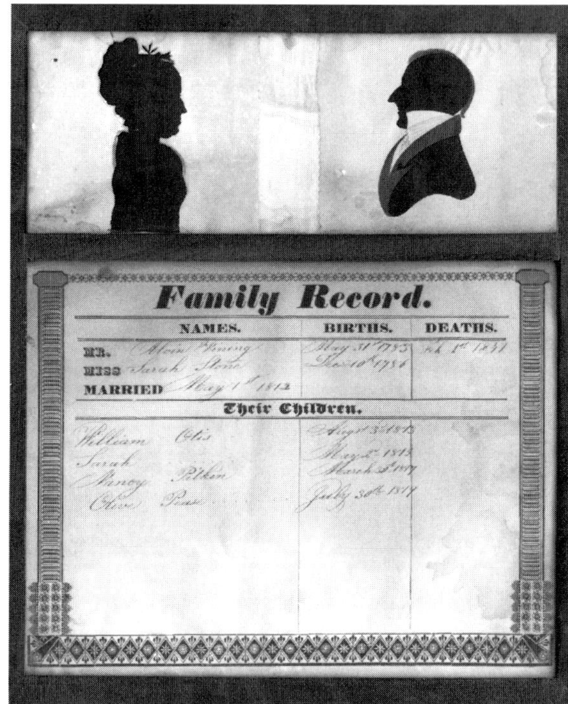

Figure 18 Profiles and family record. Alvin (or Alven) Vining and Sarah Stone. Attributed to the Letterpress Artist. Connecticut or Massachusetts, circa 1828–1830. Private Collection.

five children listed, born 1809–1820, of Simsbury, Conn. Eno was a member of the Connecticut General Assembly in 1828 and a justice of the peace in Simsbury in 1834.[78] Taken circa 1828–1834. CSL.[79]

7. Fish. The family record and paired profiles (with unusual watercolor embellishments, including outstretched arms holding blue books) said to be of a Fish family of Rockport, Mass.[80]

8. Foot/Goodyear. The family record and paired profiles of Uriah Foot (1780–1849)[81] and Esther Goodyear (1789–1861),[82] married 1809, and four children listed, born 1810–1822, and a niece, born 1809, of Hamden, Conn. Taken circa 1829–1830. Private collection.

9. Graham. Profile of Andrew Gilbert Graham (or Gilbert A. Graham) (1814–circa 1850), aged twenty, of New Britain, Conn., and later a merchant of Hartford.[83] Dated 20 March 1834 by handwritten inscription. CHS.

10. Halladay/Noble. The family record and paired profiles of Edmund Tobin Halladay (or Halliday) (1799–1852), a farmer,[84] and Caroline Noble (1806–1840), of Suffield, Conn., married 1827. Edmund married there, secondly, 1840, Clarissa Kendall.[85] Taken between 26 March 1829 when a son, Horace Halladay, was born (listed on family record) and prior to 4 June 1832 when another son, Calvin Halladay, was born (not listed).[86] Private collection.

11. Lynn/Coe. The family record and paired profiles of Samuel W. Lynn (b. 1799) and Sarah Coe (b. 1805), of Durham, Conn., who later "removed to Ohio."[87] The family record states that the couple was married 24 January 1830; the vital records of Durham place that event as having taken place on the same date one year earlier.[88] Private collection.

12. Owen [?]. Unidentified Owen family record and profiles, of Suffield, Conn., described as "Family record. Owen record and silhouettes," in an exhibition at the "Hostess House," 12–14 October 1920, during the 250th anniversary celebrations of the founding of Suffield.[89] On loan in 1920 from Amos B. Crane and John Crane; present location unknown.

13. Scovill/Catlin. The family record and paired profiles of John Scovill (or Scoville) Jr. (1800–1879) and Maria M. Catlin (1808–1870), married 1818, and one child listed, Mindewell Mina (profile inserted), born 1829, of Harwinton, Conn. John Scovill was the older brother of Alvah Scovill, below. According to Charles R. Eastman, John Scovill "traveled extensively in the south as a young man, but afterwards engaged in business with his brother

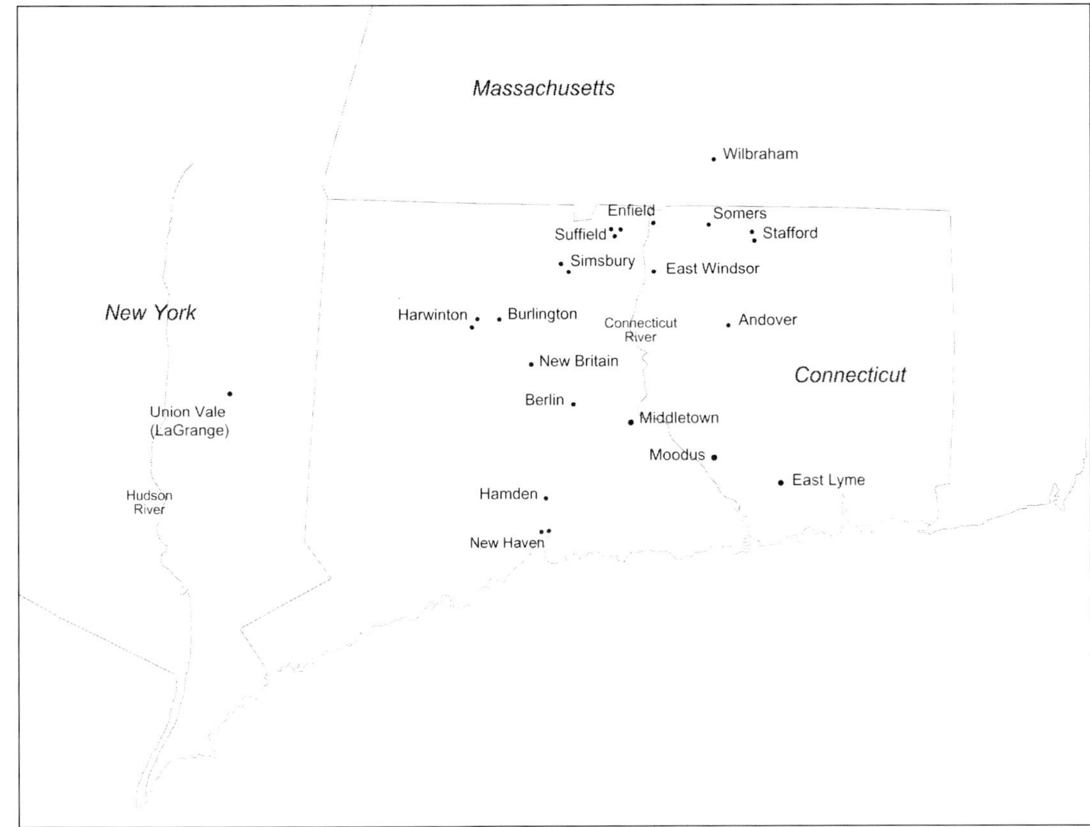

Figure 19 Geographic distribution of works attributed to the Letterpress Artist.

Alvah. He was a 'black Republican' and a strong Abolitionist."[90] Taken post 27 July 1829. NYSHA.

14. Scovill/Hinsdale. The family record and paired profiles of Alvah Scovill (or Scoville) (1802–1847) and Emily Hinsdale (1809–1865), married 1829, and one child listed, born 1833, of Harwinton, Conn.[91] NYSHA.

15. Sikes. Profile of Rufus Sikes (1798–1836), aged thirty, of Suffield, Conn.[92] Dated 1829. Private collection.

16. Sisson/Hall. The family record and paired profiles of Addi (or Addie) Bigelow Sisson (1803–1873),[93] a farmer and distiller, and Huldah Hall (1807–1888), married 1829, and four children listed, born 1830–1839, of Simsbury, Conn., at the time of the 1840 census.[94] Taken 1829–1830. Private collection.

17–19. Smith/Lewis; Smith/Moore. The family record and paired profiles of William Smith (1771–1838) and his first wife, Sally Lewis (1776–1810), married 1796, and four children listed, born 1797–1805, and his second wife (no profile), Lucretia Moore (born 1790), married 1812, and five children listed, born 1816–1822, of Berlin, Conn. Dated 7 November 1829, Berlin. Illustrated in *Shades of Our Ancestors*.[95]

20. Smith/Wetmore. The family record and paired profiles of Samuel Beers Smith (1790–1843) and Emily Wetmore (1795–1852), of Middletown, Conn. Born in Mechanicstown, Dutchess County, N.Y.,[96] Samuel Beers Smith removed to Middletown where he was married 16 April 1815, by the Reverend Daniel Huntington, to Emily Wetmore.[97] Illustrated in *Old-Time New England*.[98]

21. Spencer/Bigelow. The family record and paired profiles of Deacon Elijah Spencer (1798–1861) and Mary Bigelow (1803–1866),[99] married 1824, with seven children listed, born 1826–1843, of Moodus, Conn. Spencer was the son of Calvin and Mehitabel (Brainard) Spencer; see below. Taken prior to 16 February 1830. CHS.

22. Spencer/Brainard. The family record of Calvin Spencer (1765–1813) and duplicate profiles of Mehitabel Brainard (1766–1851), married 1789, and eight children listed, born 1791–1805, of East Lyme (later Flanders), Conn. According to Lucy Abigail Brainard, Calvin Spencer died a "martyr" in 1813 as the result of contracting yellow fever from burying a fellow victim of the disease; Mrs. Spencer was considered "'A Mother in Israel,' and her advice was frequently sought by ministers from all parts of this state."[100] Taken probably at the same time as the Spencer/Bigelow family record above. CHS.

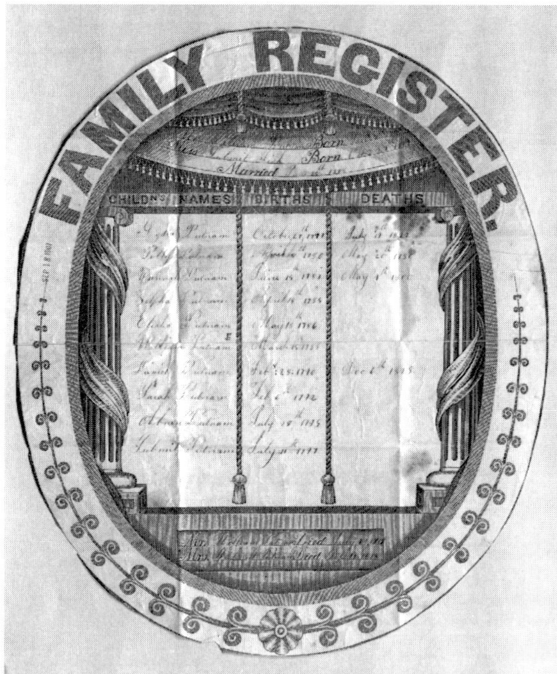

Figure 20 Family register. William Putnam and Submit Fisk. Massachusetts, circa 1820. New England Historic Genealogical Society.

23. Sprague/Birge. The family record and paired profiles of Benjamin Sprague (1791–1865), farmer, of Andover, Conn.,[101] and Julia Birge (1803–1841), of Bolton, Conn., married 1823. Benjamin Sprague married, secondly, 1842, Lois West, of Vernon,[102] and married, thirdly, 1846, Sarah Buckland, of Bolton.[103] Private collection.

24. Stebbins/Perrin. The family record and paired profiles of William C[arpenter] Stebbins (1806–1861) and Eliza Perrin (b. 1808), of Wilbraham, Mass., married 1829.[104] Private collection.

25–26. Stebbins/Smith; Stebbins/Smith. The family record and paired profiles of Austin Bliss Stebbins (1802–1852), a manufacturer and farmer,[105] and his first wife, Susan Smith (1804–1842), and his second wife (third profile inserted), Electa (or Alecta)[106] Smith (1804–1886), of Stafford, Conn., and of Granby, Mass., at the time of the 1830 census.[107] Private collection.

27. Thompson. Profile of Eliza Thompson, "aged 21," dated 1830. Northeast Auctions catalogue, p. 15.

28. Thresher/Snow. The family record and paired profiles of Alfred Thresher (or Thrasher) (1782–1854) and Mercy Snow (1783–1861), married 1813, and two children listed, born 1814–1818. The son of Ebenezer and Hannah (Blodget/Blogget) Thrasher, Alfred Thresher was born in Stafford, Conn.[108] Private collection.

29. Vincent/Fowler. The family record and paired profiles of Richard Vincent (b. 1801), a farmer, and Helen Fowler (b. 1810), married 1828, and two children listed, born 1829 and 1830, of Union Vale, Dutchess County, N.Y. Taken between 7 October 1830, when their second son, Leonard Vincent, was born (listed on family record), and prior to about 1832, when their third son, DeWitt Vincent, was born (not listed). The 1850 census shows the Vincent family in Union Vale with the following children: Joseph J., aged twenty-one; Leonard, aged eighteen; Dewitt, aged sixteen; Mary T., aged fourteen; and Phebe, aged twelve.[109] Private collection.[110]

30. Vining/Stone. The family record and paired profiles of Alvin (or Alven) Vining (1793–1847) and Sarah Stone (b. 1786), married 1812, and four children listed, born 1813–1819, originally of East Windsor, Conn.,[111] and of Wilbraham, Mass., at the time of the 1830 census.[112] The record of births is as follows: William Otis Vining, born 3 August 1813, Sarah Vining, born 2 May 1815, Nancy Pitkin Vining, born 30 March 1817, and Olive Pease Vining, born 30 July 1819. Private collection.

31. Wood/Richardson. The family record and paired profiles of Asa Wood (b. 1785) and Betsey Richardson (b. 1789), married 1806, and one child listed, born 1807, of Somers, Conn.[113] Dated 1829. Private collection.

32. Woodruff. Profile of Eliza Woodruff, "aged 28," dated 1830. Northeast Auctions catalogue, p. 33.

NOTES

[1]The author wishes to acknowledge Georgia Brady Barnhill, Peter Benes, Everett Blodgett, Paul S. D'Ambrosio, Vincent DiCicco, Jane Domenico, Russell and Corinne Earnest, Nancy Finlay, Robert F. Gibson III, W. Lehman Guyton, Henry B. Hoff, C.G., F.A.S.G., Judith Ellen Johnson, David Allen Lambert, Nel and Helen Laughon, Kelly Nolin, Carolyn Sheppard Oakley, Oscar Poriss, Blume J. Rifken, Betty Ring, Gary Boyd Roberts, Robert W. and Sandra J. Rodman, Timothy Salls, Debra Elizabeth Schaffer, Lewis W. Scranton, Andrew B. Searle, Nancy R. Skinner, Scott C. Steward, Hiram Trinidad, Mary Webb, and Paul T. and Karen M. Wendhiser. An earlier version of this essay appeared in *The New England Historical and Genealogical Register* 153 (1999): 387–406.

[2]Charles R. Stark, *Groton, Connecticut, 1705–1905* (Stonington, Conn.: Palmer Press, 1922), p. 93.

[3]Ibid., p. 89.
[4]Gloria Seaman Allen, *Family Record: Genealogical Watercolors and Needlework* (Washington, D.C.: DAR Museum, 1989), catalogue for an exhibition at the DAR Museum, 30 January–14 May 1989, p. 2.
[5]See Peter Benes, "Decorated Family Records from Coastal Massachusetts, New Hampshire, and Connecticut," *Families and Children: 1985 Annual Proceedings of the Dublin Seminar for New England Folklife* (Boston: Boston University Scholarly Publications, 1987), pp. 91–147.
[6]John A. Schutz, *A Noble Pursuit: The Sesquicentennial History of the New England Historic Genealogical Society, 1845–1995* (Boston: New England Historic Genealogical Society, 1995), pp. 1–14.
[7]George C. Groce and David H. Wallace, *The New-York Historical Society's Dictionary of Artists in America, 1564–1860* (New Haven: Yale University Press, 1957), p. 496 (hereafter cited as *Dictionary of Artists*).
[8]Andrew N. Adams, *A Genealogical History of Henry Adams of Braintree, Mass., and His Descendants; also John Adams of Cambridge, Mass., 1632–1897* (Rutland, Vt.: Tuttle Company, 1898), p. 304.
[9]Allen, *Family Record*, facing p. 1, from a private collection.
[10]Ibid., and *Vital Records of Westminster, Massachusetts, to the End of the Year 1849* (Worcester: Franklin P. Rice, 1908), p. 211.
[11]David Allen Lambert, "The Family of Job Hill of Peterborough, New Hampshire," vertical file at the New England Historic Genealogical Society.
[12]Lillian Drake Avery, *A Genealogy of the Ingersoll Family in America, 1629–1925* (New York: Grafton Press, 1926), p. 32.
[13]Private collection.
[14]Cleveland Abbe and Josephine Genung Nicols, *Abbe-Abbey Genealogy: In Memory of John Abbe and His Descendants* (New Haven: Tuttle, Morehouse and Taylor Co., 1916), p. 308.
[15]Suzanne L. Flynt, *Family, Home and Place: Nineteenth-Century Prints* (Deerfield, Mass.: Memorial Hall Museum, Pocumtuck Valley Memorial Association, 1990), p. 4. Also, family record printed by Hiram Ferry and filled out for Jeremiah Ward (1765–1847) and his wife, Hannah Ward (1774–1839), in the possession of the New England Historic Genealogical Society, MSS 494.
[16]A checklist of circa 1845–1873 family registers by Nathaniel Currier and later Currier and Ives appears in Harry T. Peters, *Currier and Ives: Printmakers to the American People*, 2 vols. (Garden City, N.Y.: Doubleday, Doran and Co., 1931), p. 240. See the treatment by Georgia Brady Barnhill elsewhere in this volume.
[17]Connecticut Historical Society (hereafter cited as CHS).
[18]James Pierce Root, *Root Genealogical Records, 1600–1870, Comprising the General History of the Roots in America* (New York: R. C. Root, Anthony and Co., 1870), pp. 416–17.
[19]Rev. William Hamilton Hannum, "William Hannum of New England and Some of His Descendants," *New England Historical and Genealogical Register* 90 (1936): 261–62.
[20]Russell and Corinne Earnest, "Fraktur for New Englanders," *New England Ancestors* (fall 2001): 20–23 (hereafter "Fraktur for New Englanders").
[21]The New York Genealogical and Biographical Society, file 1 (F5518). Gift of Janet McKay Cowing.
[22]Justin Coy Bugbee, comp., *The Family of Edward Bugbee* (n.p., n.p., 1982), p. 90.
[23]The Stebbins monograph was clearly intended for private consumption: "The Editors of the following Account think it needless to make any Excuse or Apology for publishing the following Pedigree; as it is design'd only for the Use of themselves and their Families, and therefore have none to make an Excuse or Apology to." *A Genealogy of the Family of Mr. Samuel Stebbins and Mrs. Hannah Stebbins, his Wife, from the year 1707, to the year 1771, With their Names, Time of their Births, Marriages and Deaths of those that are deceased* (Hartford: Ebenezer Watson, 1771), New England Historic Genealogical Society, CS 71 S81.
[24]"Fraktur for New Englanders."
[25]NEHGS, rare book Y51.
[26]NEHGS, MSS C2335.
[27]Connecticut Vital Records, Norwalk: Births, Marriages, Deaths, 1651–1850 (Barbour Collection, Connecticut State Library, 1925), p. 7. See also Frances Baxter, *The Baxter Family: Descendants of George and Thomas Baxter* (New York: Tobias H. Wright, 1913), pp. 63–64.
[28]Susan Whitney Dimmock, *Births, Marriages, Baptisms and Deaths from the Records of the Town and Churches in Coventry, Connecticut, 1711–1844* (New York: Baker and Taylor Company, 1897), p. 8.
[29]John Cogswell Badger, *Giles Badger and His Descendants* (Manchester, N.H.: John B. Clarke Company, 1909), p. 22.
[30]Dimmock, *Coventry Vital Records*, p. 8.
[31]Connecticut Vital Records, Lebanon: Births, Marriages, Deaths, 1700–1854 (Barbour Collection, Connecticut State Library, 1920), p. 87.
[32]Connecticut Vital Records, Glastonbury: Births, Marriages, Deaths, 1690–1854 (Barbour Collection, Connecticut State Library, 1927), p. 124.
[33]S.V. Talcott, *Talcott Pedigree in England and America* (Albany: Weed, Parsons, and Company, 1876), p. 228.
[34]*The Huntington Family in America: A Genealogical Memoir of the Known Descendants of Simon Huntington from 1633 to 1915* (Hartford: Huntington Family Association, 1915), pp. 702, 707.
[35]NEHGS, MSS c 1840.
[36]Robert F. Gibson III, "Family Records of Isaac Packard of Albany," *The New York Genealogical and Biographical Record*, 127, no. 1, pp. 17–21.
[37]NEHGS, sgcra 15.
[38]David B. Pilsbury and Emily A. Getchell, *The Pillsbury Family: Being a History of William and Dorothy Pillsbury (or Pilsbery) of Newbury in New England and Their Descendants to the Eleventh Generation* (Everett, Mass.: Massachusetts Publishing Co., 1898), p. 51 (hereafter cited as *Pillsbury Family*).
[39]*Vital Records of Chelmsford, Massachusetts, to the End of the Year 1849* (Salem, Mass.: Essex Institute, 1914), p. 428.
[40]*Vital Records of Lowell, Massachusetts, to the End of the Year 1849*, vol. 4 (Salem, Mass.: Essex Institute, 1930), p. 240.
[41]*Pillsbury Family*, p. 104.

[42]Connecticut Vital Records, Pomfret: Births, Marriages, Deaths, 1705–1850 (Barbour Collection, Connecticut State Library), p. 64.
[43]James H. Smith, *The History of Chenango and Madison Counties, New York* (Syracuse: D. Mason, 1880), pp. 171, 245–246. Dresser later practiced law with John C. Clark in Bainbridge, N.Y., and sometime after the death of his family removed to New York City.
[44]NEHGS, MSS c2336.
[45]Diane L. Fagan Affleck, "Textile Commemoratives and Broadsides from New England's Mid-Nineteenth Century," *Textiles in New England II: Four Centuries of Material Life: 1999 Annual Proceedings of the Dublin Seminar for New England Folklife* (Boston: Boston University, Scholarly publications, 2001), pp. 105–211.
[46]NEHGS, Gen I t179; see also Scott C. Steward and John Bradley Arthaud, eds., *A Thorndike Family History: Descendants of John and Elizabeth (Stratton) Thorndike* (Boston: Newbury Street Press, 2000), photographs between pp. 248–249.
[47]NEHGS, Gen H 306, sub group I, series A.
[48]See checklist of Letterpress Artist compositions.
[49]Ellen G. Miles, *Saint-Mémin and the Neoclassical Profile Portrait in America* (Washington, D.C.: National Portrait Gallery and the Smithsonian Institution Press, 1994).
[50]Gloria Wall Bicha and Helen Benjamin Brown, *The Benjamin Family in America* (Racine, Wash.: Gloria Wall Bicha, 1976), p. 44.
[51]Lewis G. Knapp, *In Pursuit of Paradise: History of the Town of Stratford, Connecticut* (West Kennebunk, Maine: Phoenix Publishing, 1989), p. 4.
[52]1800 Federal Census, Fairfield County, Conn., NARA M32-1, p. 44. Courtesy of David Allen Lambert.
[53]These pieces generally measure 12½ inches high and 10½ inches wide.
[54]At least two examples cited herein, Thresher-Snow and Vining-Stone, contain no letterpress entries and were completed by hand.
[55]There are two "cutting" formats among the work of the Letterpress Artist, implying that the artist alternated styles or more than one cutter plied this trade.
[56]One example, Vincent-Fowler, represents a family that lived in Dutchess County, N.Y.
[57]Banton is identified by David C. Dearborn, F.A.S.G., a descendant, in "The Banton Family of Maine" (1975–1987) typescript (vertical file) at NEHGS; a copy of Banton's handbill is owned by Old Sturbridge Village, Sturbridge, Mass. The authenticity of the Banton handbill has been questioned by curator Lynne Bassett, who believes it is a modern museum interpretation by Old Sturbridge Village staff.
[58]Groce and Wallace, *Dictionary of Artists*, n. 7, p. 120.
[59]Ibid., p. 512.
[60]Dana K. Ball, "William Chamberlain, Silhouettist of Loudon, N.H." (ca. 1980s), typescript, Johnson Family Papers, AAS.
[61]The "Puffy Sleeve Artist" was active in 1830 and 1831, and examples of this unidentified artist's work have been found in New Hampshire, Vermont, and Massachusetts. The "Red Book Artist" appears to have been active at about the same time. See Marna Anderson, *A Loving Likeness: American Folk Portraits of the Nineteenth Century* (Princeton, N.J., 1992), catalogue for an exhibition at the Gallery at Bristol-Myers Squibb, 4 April–17 May, 1992, pp. 44–49.
[62]The family register of William Putnam (1755–1819) and Submit Fisk (1758–1818), and their ten children, of Worcester, Massachusetts, New England Historic Genealogical Society, MSS 480. This unusual family register was donated by Ozora S. Davis of New Britain, Conn., to NEHGS on 16 September 1907 with the following note attached: "A stranger seeking financial aid and fumbling around in his pockets pulled out the enclosed family register which he said he got in an old abandoned house somewhere in Massachusetts. I presume it is utterly worthless and yet it may fit somewhere into your library."
[63]Identical type styles are found in both of the following type foundry catalogues: *Specimen of Modern Printing Types and Stereotype Cuts from the Boston Type and Stereotype Foundry* (Boston: T. R. Marvin, 1826) and *Specimen of Printing Types and Ornaments from the Letter-Foundry of Elihu White, No. 11 Thames-Street, New-York* (Sleight and Robinson Printers, New York, 1829), AAS.
[64]Peter Benes, "Machine-Assisted Portrait and Profile Imaging in New England after 1803," *Painting and Portrait Making in the American Northeast: 1994 Annual Proceedings of the Dublin Seminar for New England Folklife* (Boston: Boston University University Scholarly Publications, 1995), pp. 138–50 (hereafter cited as "Portrait and Profile Imaging").
[65]"Joseph Steward and the Hartford Museum," *Connecticut Historical Society Bulletin*, 18 (1953): 1–16.
[66]For other examples of these unusual attractions and their affiliation with profile cutters, see "Portrait and Profile Imaging." At the Hartford Museum the public was invited to receive electrical treatments: "The Electrical Aparatus will give each visitor a *shock*, if requested." The museum further claimed that "*Felons* and *numbness* cured by electricity: certificates of this are satisfactory." *The Connecticut Courant*, 5 January 1830, Hartford, Conn. The same advertisement was printed in the *Connecticut Mirror* on 9 January 1830, "Early American Newspapers," microfilm at Boston Public Library.
[67]Ibid.
[68]Ibid.
[69]"Joseph Steward," p. 9.
[70]New Hampshire Weekend American Auction catalogue, March 2001, Northeast Auctions, Ronald Bourgeault, auctioneer, p. 15 [hereafter Northeast Auctions catalogue]. *Vital Records of New Haven, 1640–1850, Part 1* (Hartford: Order of the Founders and Patriots of America, 1917) p. 521.
[71]Connecticut Vital Records, Burlington: Births, Marriages, Deaths, 1806–1852 (Barbour Collection, Connecticut State Library, 1927), p. 24.
[72]Oliver Seymour Phelps and Andrew T. Servin, *The Phelps Family of America and Their English Ancestors*, 2 vols. (Pittsfield, Mass.: Eagle Publishing, 1899), p. 452. This genealogy gives Phebe Phelps's year of birth as 1803. The Phelpses

evidently lived in Baltimore, Maryland, at the time of their eldest child's birth in 1829 and subsequently returned to Connecticut.

[73]Gilbert Warren Chapin, comp., *The Chapin Book of Genealogical Data with Brief Biographical Sketches of the Descendants of Deacon Samuel Chapin*, 2 vols. (Hartford: Chapin Family Association, 1924), p. 802.

[74]Gift of Mr. and Mrs. Lyndon Haynes, of Medfield, Massachusetts (NEHGS, MSS c 2260).

[75]*Vital Records of Chester, Massachusetts, to the year 1850* (Boston: NEHGS, 1911), p. 30.

[76]Information on overleaf of family record. See also, George Woolworth Colton, *Quartermaster George Colton* (Lancaster, Pa.: Wickersham Printing Company, 1912), p. 286.

[77]Courtesy of Raccoon Creek Antiques, Bridgeport, N.J.

[78]Douglas Richardson, *The Eno and Enos Family in America: Descendants of James Eno, of Windsor, Connecticut*, 2d ed. (Grass Valley, Calif.: Richardson Reprints, 1985), p. 271.

[79]Negative photostat in Special Genealogical File at Connecticut State Library. Reproduced 7 August 1936 from the original then in the possession of Mrs. H. E. Ellsworth of Simsbury, Conn.

[80]Clipping of an undated advertisement from Martha Boynton Antiques, Townsend, Mass.; courtesy of Vincent DiCicco.

[81]Abram W. Foote, *Foote Family: Comprising Genealogy and History of Nathaniel Foote of Wethersfield, Conn., and His Descendants*, 2 vols. (Rutland, Vt., 1907; reprint, Hughson, Calif.: Laura Belle Foote Beekman and Clarence William Beekman, 1974), p. 171.

[82]Grace Goodyear Kirkman, *Genealogy of the Goodyear Family* (San Francisco: Cubery and Co., 1899), p. 214.

[83]Helen Graham Carpenter, *The Reverend John Graham of Woodbury, Connecticut, and His Descendants* (Chicago: Monastery Hill Press, 1942), pp. 449–50.

[84]Lucius M. Boltwood, *History and Genealogy of the Family of Thomas Noble of Westfield, Massachusetts* (Hartford: Case, Lockwood and Brainard Company, 1878), p. 452.

[85]Connecticut Vital Records, Suffield: Births, Marriages, Deaths, 1674–1850 (Barbour Collection, Connecticut State Library, 1928), p. 97.

[86]Ibid. The Halladays later had two further sons, Albert and George K., as recorded in the vital records for Suffield, but not in the family record.

[87]J. Gardner Bartlett, *Robert Coe, Puritan: His Ancestors and Descendants, 1340–1910* (Boston: n. p., 1911), p. 188.

[88]Connecticut Vital Records, Durham: Births, Marriages, Deaths, 1708–1852 (Barbour Collection, Connecticut State Library, 1923), p. 49.

[89]*Celebration of the Two Hundred and Fiftieth Anniversary of the Settlement of Suffield, Connecticut* (Suffield, Conn.: Suffield General Executive Committee, 1921), p. 97.

[90]Charles R. Eastman, ed., *Scoville Family Records, Part III, Harwinton (Conn.) Branch* (Cambridge, Mass.: n.p., 1911), p. 29.

[91]Ibid.

[92]Arthur M. Sikes Jr., comp., *Richard Sikes and His Descendants: The First Six Generations* (Suffield, Conn.: Sykes Family Association, 1992), p. 75.

[93]Joan and David Sisson, *Descendants of Richard and Mary Sisson: Ten Generations from 1608* (n. p., n.p., 1999), p. 323.

[94]1840 Federal Census, Hartford County, Conn., NARA M704-23, p. 150.

[95]Alice Van Leer Carrick, *Shades of Our Ancestors: American Profiles and Profilists* (Boston: Little, Brown and Company, 1928, reprinted as *A History of American Silhouettes: A Collector's Guide, 1790–1840,* Tokyo: Charles E. Tuttle Co., 1968), facing p. 136.

[96]Frederick Kinsman Smith, *The Family of Richard Smith of Smithtown, Long Island* (Smithtown, N.Y.: Smithtown Historical Society, 1967), p. 263.

[97]Connecticut Vital Records, Middletown: Births, Marriages, Deaths, 1651–1854 (Barbour Collection, Connecticut State Library, 1923), I–Z, p. 414.

[98]H. Monmouth Smith, "George Smith of Stratford, Connecticut: Some Relics from His Family," *Old-Time New England* 36 (April 1946): 78.

[99]Loring L. Bigelow, ed., *The Bigelow Family Genealogy, Volume 2, Seventh and Eight Generations of John Biglo (1617–1703) of Watertown, Massachusetts* (n.p.: Bigelow Society, 1993), p. 248.

[100]Lucy Abigail Brainard, *The Genealogy of the Brainerd-Brainard Family in America, 1649–1908* (Hartford: Hartford Press, 1908), pp. 59–60.

[101]Connecticut Vital Records, Andover: Births, Marriages, Deaths, 1848–1851 (Barbour Collection, Connecticut State Library, 1924), p. 12.

[102]*Vital Records of Bolton, Connecticut, to 1854 and Vernon to 1852* (Hartford: Connecticut Historical Society, 1909), p. 187.

[103]Ibid., p. 140.

[104]Ralph Stebbins Greenlee and Robert Lemuel Greenlee, *The Stebbins Genealogy*, 2 vols. (Chicago: n.p., 1904), p. 572.

[105]Ibid., p. 577.

[106]Connecticut Vital Records, Stafford: Births, Marriages, Deaths, 1719–1850 (Barbour Collection, Connecticut State Library, 1921), p. 126 (hereafter *Stafford VRs*).

[107]1850 Federal Census, Hampden County, Mass., NARA M19-63, p. 327.

[108]*Stafford VRs*, p. 136.

[109]1850 Federal Census, Dutchess County, N.Y., NARA M432-496, 206, and Sheridan E. Vincent, comp., *Vincent Family Records* (Rochester, N.Y.: Sheridan E. Vincent, 1979), p. 43.

[110]Illustrated in Blume J. Rifken, *Silhouettes in America: A Collectors' Guide* (Rutland, Vt.: Paradigm Press, 1987), p. 90.

[111]Connecticut Vital Records, East Windsor: Births, Marriages, Deaths, 1768–1860 (Barbour Collection, Connecticut State Library, 1925), pp. 69, 92.

[112]1830 Federal Census, Hampden County, Mass., NARA M19-63, p. 203.

[113]Connecticut Vital Records, Somers: Births, Marriages, Deaths, 1734–1850 (Barbour Collection, Connecticut State Library, 1922), p. 112.

The Family in Portraiture

Lauren B. Hewes

RECENTLY CHILDREN at a Northborough, Massachusetts, preschool were asked to draw pictures of their families. The usual enthusiasm for crayons and paper was indulged and the resulting artwork was placed on view in a public corridor. There were, of course, the standard pictures of mother and father with assorted siblings and pets, but a number of drawings also illustrated what have been termed non-traditional families. There were images with only one parent, or the second parent placed in a separate house to one side, pictures which included grandparents as the central adults, and images with multiple father and mother figures. Parents picking up their children at the end of the day made observational comments about the divorce rate, the appearance of half-brothers and half-sisters in the drawings, and the fact that the children had shown even the most unusual household combinations without bias or prejudice. In a sense, the drawings reflected the flexibility and variety of family life in late-twentieth-century New England.

Can we use nineteenth-century portraits to draw similar conclusions about the structure of families in America before the Civil War? Portraits created by both amateur and professional painters have been regularly used by researchers to investigate many aspects of American life, including the history of decorative arts, stylistic changes in costume and hairstyle, and developments of art patronage and connoisseurship.[1] Could they also provide the genealogist with specific information on familial relationships or serve as accurate representations of particular households?

Portraits have sometimes been used by genealogists as illustrations to family histories. But the ability of artwork to stand alone as the sole documentation of a family structure is questionable and, upon investigation, brings to mind the old adage: "Nothing is as simple as it looks." This essay will examine family portraits made in the United States during the first half of the nineteenth century, codify the compositional formats regularly used by painters of this period, and illustrate the caution needed when solely using visual examination to determine facts about the families and individuals depicted. The resulting analysis will underscore the importance of written documentation, which—where it exists—should always be taken in consideration with the visual record.

Historians, genealogists, and art historians are justly intrigued by the seemingly endless combinations of relationships which define nineteenth-century family life. The historian Jane C. Nylander has noted:

> Many early New England families extended far beyond the nuclear family that is the late twentieth-century norm. Indeed the very concept of family differed widely from that held today, embracing everyone who lived within the same household, . . . old or young widows; children and step-children; elderly grandma'ams and grandsirs; maiden aunts and uncles; nieces and nephews; young men preparing for college; unsettled single people in their twenties; students of law, medicine, or divinity; hired men and hired girls; apprentices, servants, and slaves; orphans; and cousins of all ages might be grafted onto the basic family structure. . . . Whether they were related to each other or not, by living, working, sleeping, and eating together in a single household, people were considered to be members of that family.[2]

Nylander stresses that home life primarily centered around a pair of parents and their assorted children, but that the possibilities for expanded combinations of family members who might also reside in the house varied widely from circumstance to circumstance.

Examination of nineteenth-century census records, diary accounts, and correspondence provides excellent documentation of the complexities of family life outlined by Nylander. Such a domestic scene is hinted at in turn-of-the-century correspondence between Mary (Craigie) Foster (1751–1815) and her brother Andrew Craigie Jr. (1754–1819) which chronicles the Foster household's constant adjustments to a steady and ever-changing stream of family members and guests. Mary Foster was in charge of a large home in Cambridge, Massachusetts, which was also occupied by her spouse and their children, her elderly mother, and Betsy and Bossenger Foster, two teenaged children from her husband's first marriage. Additionally, business associates often boarded with the family and distant relatives made extended visits. A harried Mrs. Foster closed one letter to her brother by noting: "Do not read this with a Critical eye, as it will not Bear it. You know I am often in a hurry which is the case now being Sunday Morning. Mama Craigie's love to you, Miss Betsy desires not to be forgot & the boys are as Noisy as ever."[3]

Although the written record supports their existence, the numerous individuals who made up these complicated and yet typical household situations were rarely depicted together in painted portraits.[4] Most often paintings were commissioned to depict only the very heart of the household: a pair of parents and their children. These portraits of families were carefully constructed by artists and sitters working together to create a public image of domestic life suitable for hanging in the best parlor. Poses and costume were selected with care, and props were often included not only to add artistic flair, but also to illustrate personal characteristics of the sitters or to feature particular objects of which the family was especially proud.

The fact that the majority of painted portraits from the first half of the nineteenth century focus on the core family group and do not reflect the multitude of individuals who actually resided together under one roof is contrary to Nylander's assertion that all the occupants of a house were considered family. There are several ways of explaining the apparent incongruity between extant portraits and the domestic hustle and bustle presented by the written record. On a practical level, portraits were expensive additions to the household furnishings. Artists charged for the time it took to record each likeness or for the quantity of works commissioned or by the number of figures included. This consideration would make purchasing images of every member of the household prohibitive. In addition, many households were affected by cyclical changes and seasonal comings and goings, as students returned home, hired hands moved on, or elderly parents went to live with another child. By focusing on the central family group, omitting the nephews, grandfather, or older single uncles who resided under the same roof, the head of the house made an unconscious assertion about who, for posterity's sake, should be considered part of the family. The extant portrait record reminds the viewer that no matter where life or illness or household demands took them, the primal connections between parents and children, and between siblings, would remain constant.[5] Painted portraits record a moment in time, capturing a family at a single point in its development. By hanging such imagery in their home for the extended family, visitors, and hired staff to see, the heads of a household visually reinforced and perpetuated the importance and lasting nature of these primary family relationships.

Any analysis of family portraits should begin with an understanding of the basic formats employed by artists to depict families. The strictures defined by these formats are helpful for grouping such images but must be used with care as, typical of any creative production, exceptions and variations exist. All portraiture, whether family images or not, falls into two obvious categories: single-figure compositions and group portraits. Images in both of these categories should be considered family portraits. While single-figure works may seem contrary to the plural nature of the term "family," an examination of the way in which such works were commissioned and displayed indicates that they were perceived by sitters as a complete set of objects intended to illuminate and memorialize the family structure.

Probate and household inventories document the location in the home, usually the most formal room available, where many sitters chose to display their family portraits. Research done with probate records of the period can be frustrating due to the lack of specification and the repeated use of the term "picture," which seems to have stood for everything on the wall, from painted portraits to silhouettes to framed engravings.[6] Portraits were rarely described as such, but when they were noted, they were usually given a high monetary value by estate assessors. For example, a family portrait owned by Isaiah Thomas Sr. (1749–1831) was assessed for $20 in 1831 (when $10 could buy a good horse) and was recorded as hanging in a first-floor room which contained the "Best bed and Pillows."[7] Commentary provided in period journals and letters also indicates that family likenesses were prominently displayed in formal areas of the home. After a visit to see a professional painter, an aspiring artist in Massachusetts noted in her journal: "The eldest daughter is a Portrait Painter —she is as I had anticipated an eccentric person and one whose ideas range in scenes of wild unheard of grandeur, altogether a creation of eccentricity. . . . I was admitted into the best room and found what is usually discovered. Her portraits were very fine and her drawings by crayon also."[8] The "best" room, be it bedroom or parlor, was a space carefully constructed and maintained by the family to reflect their social position and financial status. Painted portraits, along with fashionable draperies and furniture, helped to create an atmosphere of permanence and importance in such rooms.[9]

The placement of a single figure set against a neutral or decorative background was the most common format used by artists to depict individuals in the nineteenth century. A family might commission pendant pairs showing mother and father or multi-part sets of images with each adult and child standing alone as a separate painting. Pendant pairs were usually commissioned together and were designed to hang side-by-side or, at the very least, near each other in the same room. The creation of such pairs permitted a family to display and venerate the propagators of the entire family tree. Artists encouraged this format, as the attraction of two commissions clearly outweighed an order for only one. Such encouragement is documented in a letter from the artist Alonzo Slafter (1801–1864) to a potential patron, James Beattie (1776–1866) (*Figure 1*), a Ryegate, Vermont, farmer and itinerant peddler. In mid-1840, Beattie had written to Slafter in New Hampshire expressing interest in having his portrait painted and inviting the artist to Ryegate. Slafter answered him promptly, stating:

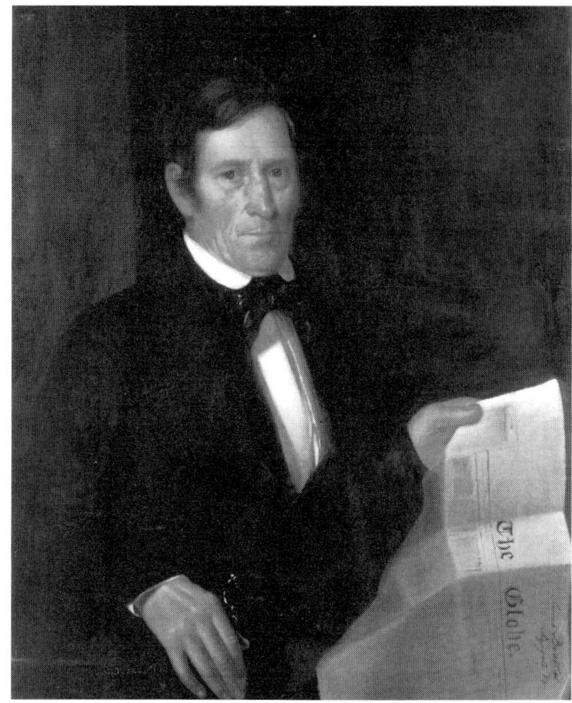

Figure 1 James Beattie (1776–1866). Alonzo Slafter (1801–1864). Ryegate, Vermont, 1840. Oil on canvas; 35½ × 29¼ inches. Inscribed lower left: "Painted by Alonzo Slafter" and lower right, in the image: "James Beattie, Ryegate, Vt." Shelburne Museum (27.1.1-189), Gift of Mrs. James H. Woods. © *Shelburne Museum, Shelburne, Vermont.*

> Friend Beattie, I Received your Communication of the 22nd and in reply inform you that I shall be at leisure after the next week. I do not like to make a journey for the purpose of Executing a single likeness, as, I should be delayed in the drying of the work equivalent to the Time requisite for two portraits, besides the labor and inconvenience of packing and unpacking materials. Are there any others to be painted in your family? If two or more, write me when and I am yours to command.[10]

The two men must have reached an agreement, as Slafter also painted a portrait of the peddler's wife, Margaret Jane (Gillespie) Beattie (d. 1861) (*Figure 2*).

In creating pendant likenesses, artists used compositional elements, such as identical drapery swags, matching furniture, or complementary poses to indicate when two separate canvases were meant to hang together as a pair. Such visual clues can be helpful when trying to match portraits to one another. However, one unusual commission, well-documented by the sitter, resulted in the production of a pair of likenesses which, although created at the same time, were, in fact, painted by different artists. In 1809 Reverend Stephen Peabody (1741–1819) decided

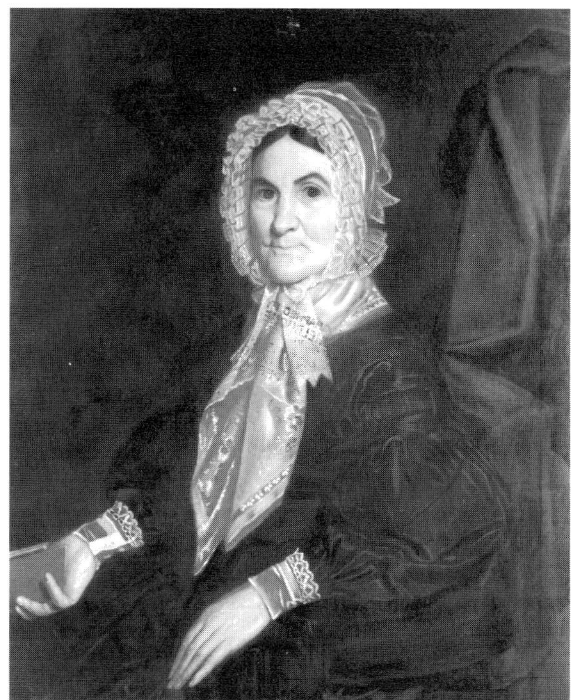

Figure 2 Margaret Jane (Gillespie) Beattie (d. 1861). Alonzo Slafter (1801–1864). Ryegate, Vermont, 1840. Oil on canvas; 35½ × 29¼ inches. Shelburne Museum (27.1.1-190), Gift of Mrs. James H. Woods. © *Shelburne Museum, Shelburne, Vermont.*

to commission portraits of himself and his second wife to hang in New Hampshire's Atkinson Academy, a school he had founded in 1787. He recorded the entire transaction in great detail in his diary. One of Peabody's relatives recommended the fashionable Boston portrait painter Gilbert Stuart (1775–1828) and so the reverend and his wife visited this artist's studio. Peabody noted in his diary:

> He shewed us some inimitable likenesses, but asks 100 dollars a piece. I cannot go to his price. We then inquired for a man by the name of Johnston who took likenesses of Governor Phillips and his family, found that he was in Dorchester. . . . He has a shop in Boston and agreed to take our portraits for 30 dollars a piece.[11]

Mrs. Peabody's family insisted that she be painted by Stuart and agreed to pay the $70.00 difference in costs. The parson decided to allow this, but to have his own likeness taken by John Johnston (1752–1818), noting, "They say Johnston is equally good if it were not for drink. I shall risk his taking mine."[12] The resulting images (*Figures 3 and 4*) hung together in Atkinson Academy for many years, until they were separated by descendants. Without the documentation provided by Peabody in his diary, historians would be unaware that these two visually dissimilar images were intended by the sitters to be a pair. Taken alone, the reverend's portrait is just another image of a New England clergyman in his white tab collar and robe. Knowing the circumstances of its creation changes our perception of Peabody. He was not only the prominent cleric illustrated by his portrait, but was also a husband and the head of a family, as indicated by the pairing of his likeness with that of his wife.

Often pendant pairs of portraits were accompanied by additional canvases, each depicting an individual child. Such sets of images, taken together as a multipart family portrait, could be made up of a large number of paintings, usually with mother and father meant to hang together and the images of the children each designed to hang independently. This type of commission must have been especially desired by painters, as the larger the family, the more likely the artist was to stay in one place and earn a greater payment for his or her efforts. For those who maintained studio space, a steady parade of family members would help secure the month's expenses and temporarily relieve the ever-constant need to drum up new business. The painter Ethan Allen Greenwood (1779–1856) recorded the details of several multisitter family commissions in his journal. He noted in March of 1813, "Agreed with Mr. Whittemore of West Cambridge to paint 10 likenesses of his family for $150.00. One daughter ill & couldn't sit up in bed but ten minutes at a time, a difficult job."[13] He completed eleven portraits by the end of the month and continued into April with other branches of the family. By the middle of April, Greenwood was finishing up with the last of the Whittemore clan, commenting:

> Began Miss W.'s likeness in such an attitude as she chose, next day having changed her mind in the course of the night, as a woman is very liable to do, wished her portrait begun anew, in a different attitude & I accordingly began it on another canvas.[14]

The artist eventually completed more than twenty portraits for members of the Whittemore family, including an image of Rebecca (Tufts) Whittemore

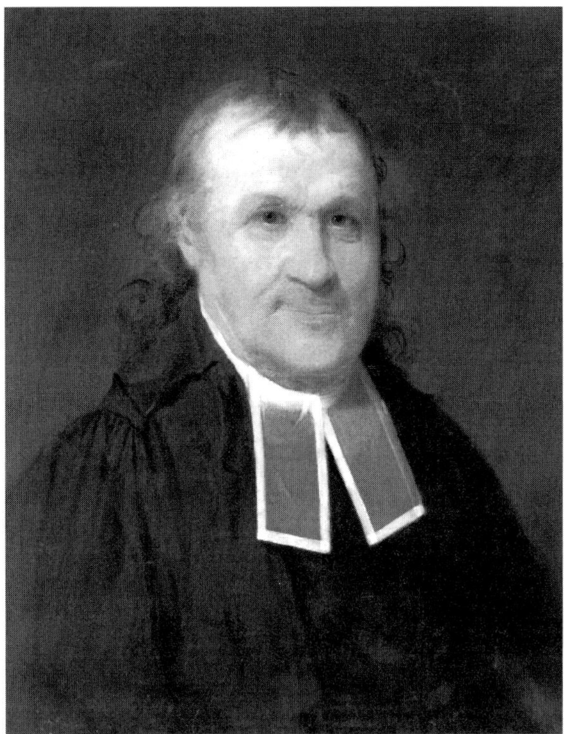

Figure 3 Stephen Peabody (1741–1819). John Johnston (1752–1818). Boston, Massachusetts, 1809. Oil on canvas; 29¼ × 24½ inches. American Antiquarian Society, Gift of Mr. and Mrs. James B. Thompson, 1982.

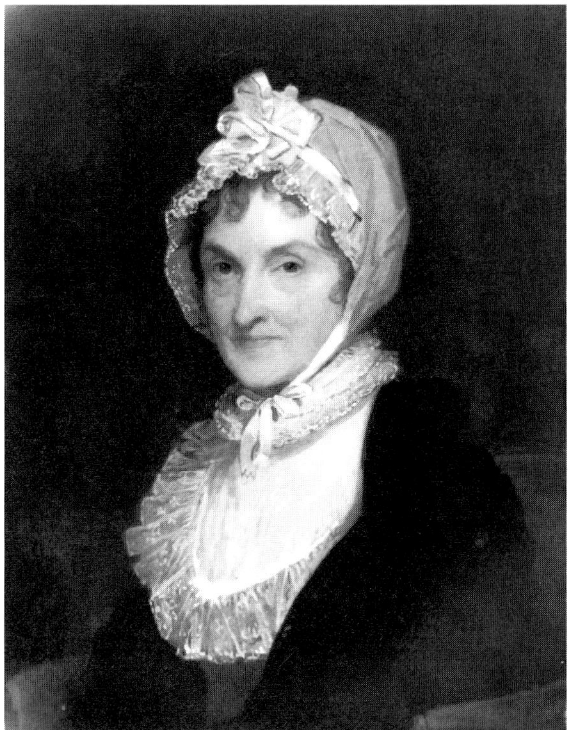

Figure 4 Elizabeth (Smith) (Shaw) Peabody (1750–1815). Gilbert Stuart (1775–1828). Boston, Massachusetts, circa 1809. Oil on panel; 36¾ × 21¼ inches. During the sittings for this portrait, Mrs. Peabody wrote to her son, "Mr. Stewart [*sic*] was very polite, appeared sensible, and entertaining. . . [but] I felt so disagreeably to set down and be looked at, and to look up in a stranger's face, that I fear little of my true lineaments will be seen." [cited in Charles Merrill Mount, *Gilbert Stuart* (New York: W. W. Norton, 1964), p. 286]. Arizona State University Art Museum; gift of Oliver B. James.

(ca. 1782–1833) (*Figure 5*).[15] Artists were not the only beneficiaries of these multiple-canvas commissions. Such arrangements allowed patrons to assess the skill of a painter, to first evaluate his abilities on portraits of the mother and father before committing to the financial obligation of numerous likenesses.[16] Also, the resulting set of pictures, all from the same artist's hand, became a sort of visual suite and, whether they were displayed together or scattered throughout the house, they formed an image of the family united by design.

For the researcher, one of the most challenging problems with large sets of family paintings is that, over time, they tend to be split up by descendants. Images were often willed to individual children and then given to their heirs, who gradually lost track of other branches of the family. This was the case with a set of four likenesses of the Goddard family of Nashua, New Hampshire. Painted in 1837 by the itinerant artist Horace Bundy (1814–1883), the set included four images: Nathan W. Goddard (b. 1800), his wife Mary (b. 1806), and their two oldest children, John and Franklin.[17] The paintings hung in the Goddard home through most of the first half of the nineteenth century, while Nathan Goddard ran a prosperous jewelry business in Nashua. The Goddards eventually had six children, and Franklin lived into the 1880s.[18] The exact provenance of the portraits is unknown from about 1860 to the mid-twentieth century. Somehow they left New Hampshire and were split up. In the 1950s, the images of the adult Goddards were owned by a New York folk art collector and in 1964 the canvases of the two

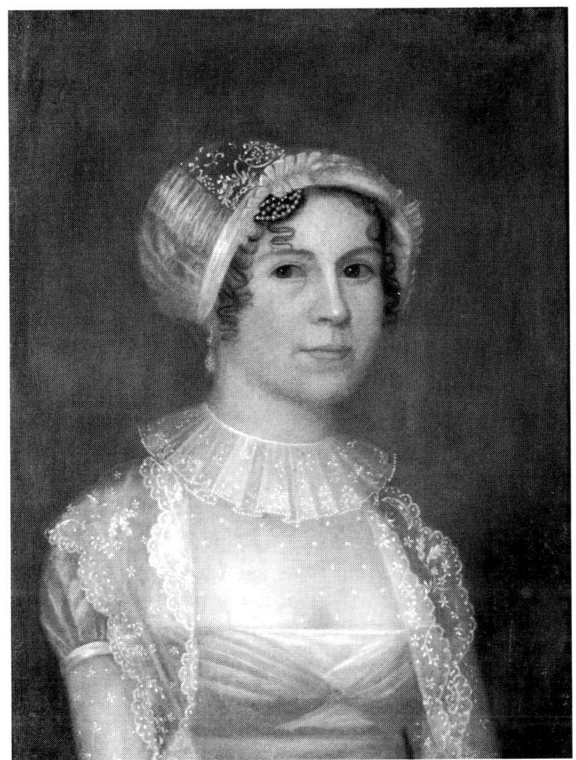

Figure 5 Rebecca (Tufts) Whittemore (1782?–1833). Ethan Allen Greenwood (1779–1856). West Cambridge, Massachusetts, 1812. Oil on canvas; 25¾ × 19¾ inches. Old Sturbridge Village (20.1.30/B23725). *Photograph by Thomas Neill.*

boys were offered for sale by a central Massachusetts antiques dealer.[19] All four images are today owned by public institutions and, in fact, were reunited briefly at an exhibition in 1992.[20] Unfortunately, untold numbers of family portrait sets remain separated from each other and undocumented. Artists' journals such as Greenwood's are invaluable sources for identifying family portrait suites painted in this period and for documenting the intricate web of family connections followed by painters in search of such commissions.[21]

A second popular format used by artists to depict families in the nineteenth century was actually a variation of the standard pendant pair. Two canvases, one with the mother and another with the father, were designed as usual, but included the depiction of the children, particularly infants, posing with the adults. Sometimes children would be separated by gender, boys placed with their father and girls shown with their mother.[22] Fairly often, the father was shown alone surrounded by attributes of his profession, while the children appeared on the same canvas as the mother. For example, the circa 1806 canvas by William Jennys (1774–1859), which depicts Vermont attorney Cephas Smith Jr. (1760–1815) at work at his desk, is paired with a likeness of his young wife holding their daughter (*Figures 6 and 7*). The adults are seated in matching chairs and the use of identical drapery unites the two canvases visually. There were benefits to this format for both the sitter and the artist. The painter had two canvases to work on simultaneously, creating a more efficient and thereby more attractive commission. The artist's ability to cope with the design complexities of multiple figures may have been challenged, but was not too greatly taxed as the whole family was not shown together. The sitters received a pair of canvases which, although they featured multiple likenesses, took up much less wall space than the numerous multi-part suite format used by the Whittemores. The added attraction of being able to show family members in different settings or involved in diverse tasks also allowed the art patron to commemorate in one commission not only the family's private role, but also to stress the patriarch's public position.[23]

If multi-figure pendant pairs would not suffice, the next logical composition style was the group portrait. These likenesses, images with all of the members of the family united together on a single canvas, are perhaps the works most thought of when the term "family" is applied to painting. Group portraits, usually more expensive than all previous formats described, could be extremely large, such as the almost seven-foot-by-eight-foot image of the Moore family by Erastus Salisbury Field (1805–1900) (*Figure 8*), or small and intimate, such as the watercolor of the Haight family attributed to Nicolino Calyo (1799–1884) (*Figure 9*). To the painter, group likenesses were the ultimate portrait commission. They took longer to complete and were compositionally more complex because the placement of each figure had to be carefully planned in advance and sittings arranged around the family's schedule.[24] An artist's ability to render objects such as furniture, decorative items, and window treatments was also often

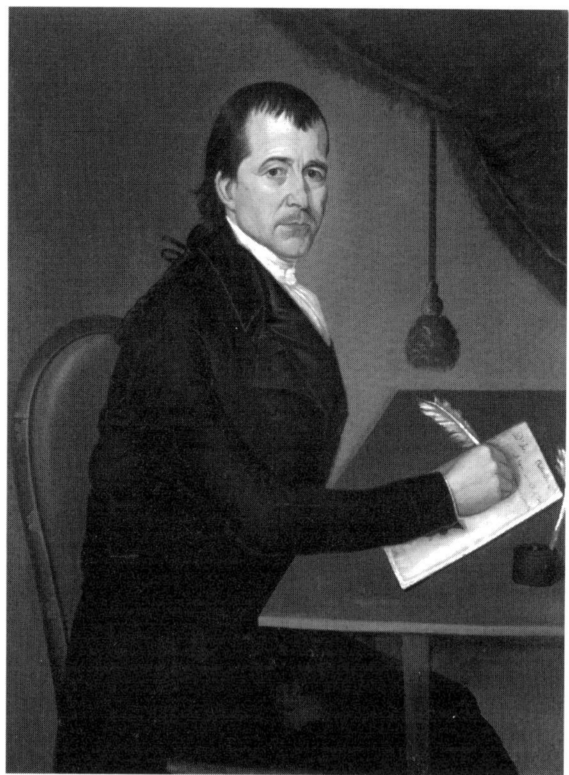

Figure 6 Cephas Smith Jr. (1760–1815). William Jennys (1774–1859). Rutland, Vermont, circa 1806. Oil on canvas; 41¼ × 31½ inches. Courtesy, Museum of Fine Arts, Boston; Emily L. Ainsley Fund, M. Theresa B. Hopkins Fund, A. Shuman Collection, and Lucy Dalbiac Luard Fund (1974.135). *Reproduced with permission. © 2002 Museum of Fine Arts, Boston. All Rights Reserved.*

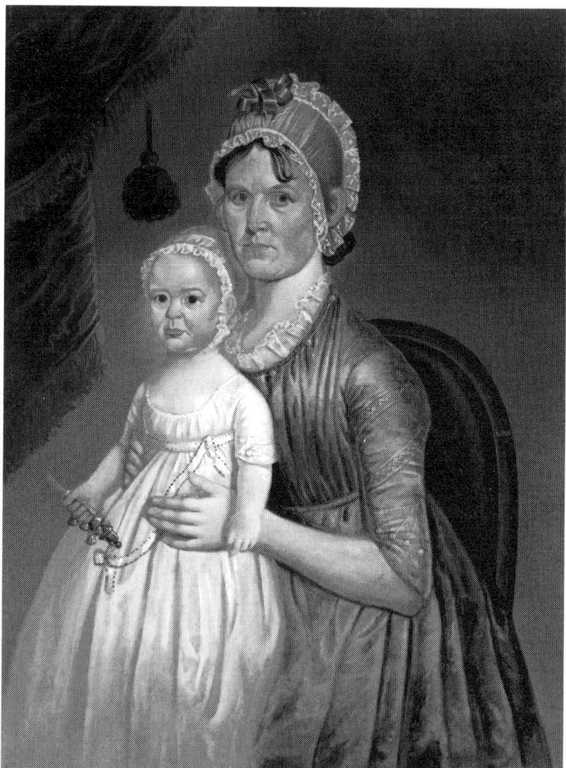

Figure 7 Mary (Gove) Smith (b. 1775) with Baby Mary. William Jennys (1774–1859). Rutland, Vermont, circa 1806. Oil on canvas; 41¼ × 31½ inches. Courtesy, Museum of Fine Arts, Boston; Emily L. Ainsley Fund, M. Theresa B. Hopkins Fund, A. Shuman Collection, and Lucy Dalbiac Luard Fund (1974.136). *Reproduced with permission. © 2002 Museum of Fine Arts, Boston. All Rights Reserved.*

exercised in group portraits, as many of these images also featured specific details of the household interior. This is illustrated by the Haight portrait, which is set in the family's library. Based on the level of detail, it is likely that the Haights worked closely with the artist to select the location and many of the particulars. The room is appointed with expensive furnishings and is filled with mementos from the Haights' European travels. The adjoining greenhouse, shelves of books, a reproduction of Antonio Canova's *The Three Graces,* and a map of Italy spread on the table all work together to communicate to the viewer the family's obviously cultivated tastes.[25]

Inferring facts about families shown in group portraits solely from the work's appearance, however, can be misleading. In Field's portrait of the Moore family, for example, one might reasonably assume that Joseph Moore (1804–1855) and Almira (Gallond) Moore (1807–1892) were the parents of all four children depicted. In fact, a review of the family history reveals that the girl and youngest boy were the children of Almira's recently deceased sister, Louisa (Gallond) Cook (1816–1838).[26] The personal relationships of aunt and uncle to niece and nephew are not clarified by Field in the portrait, but the inclusion of these children in a major family endeavor such as this large-scale likeness indicates that they were easily absorbed into the heart of the Moore clan.

The Moores, like the Haights, are shown surrounded by their finest possessions. The details of

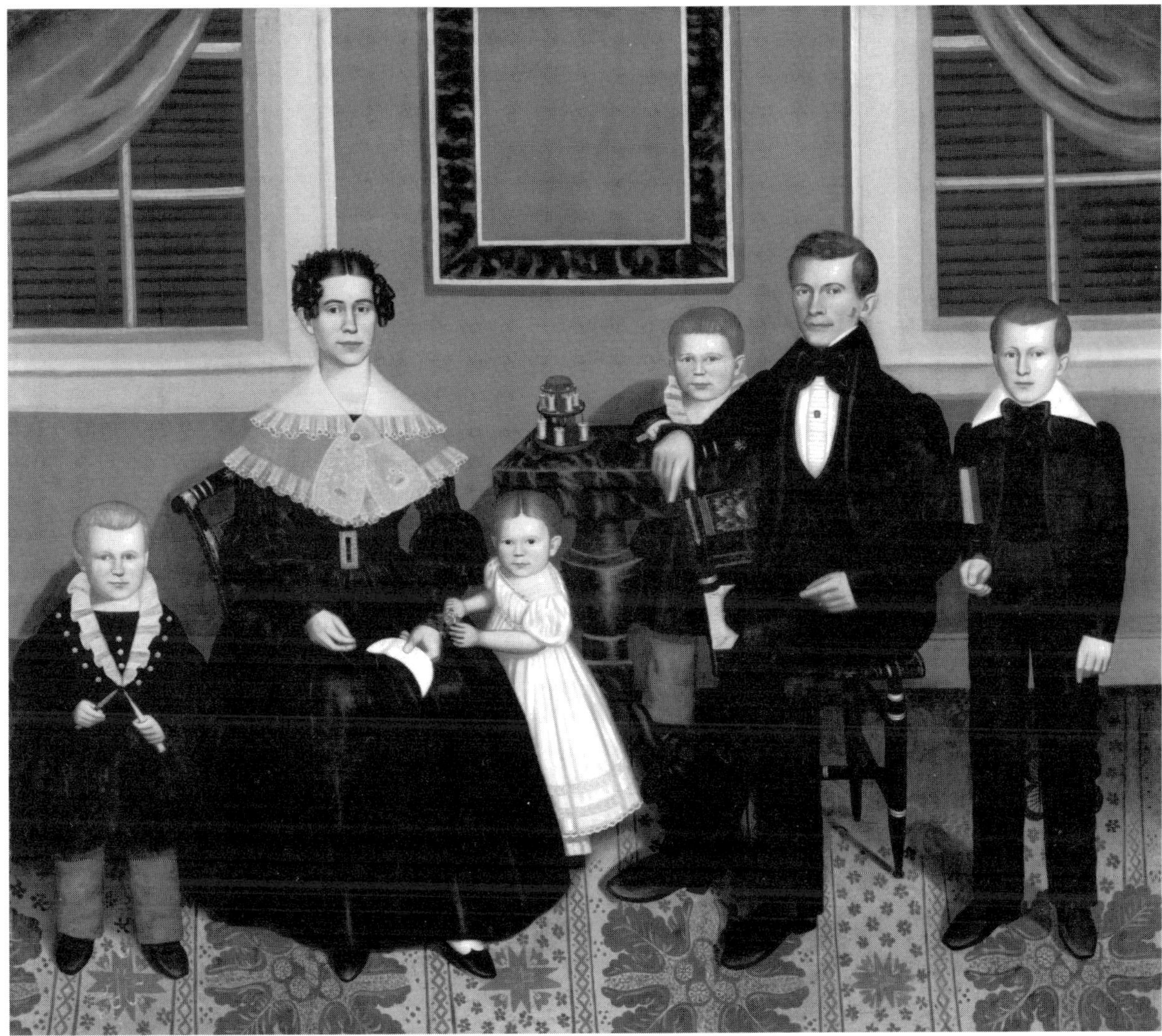

Figure 8 Joseph Moore (1804–1855) and his family. Erastus Salisbury Field (1805–1900). Ware, Massachusetts, 1839. Oil on canvas; 82¾ × 93¼ inches. The brooch and buckle worn by Mrs. Moore, the fancy-painted side chair, and Joseph Moore's dental tools all descended with this portrait. Courtesy, Museum of Fine Arts, Boston; M. & M. Karolik Collection of American Paintings (1815–1865, 58.25). *Reproduced with permission. © 2002 Museum of Fine Arts, Boston. All Rights Reserved.*

the family's front parlor are all rendered with painstaking accuracy, from the pattern of the ingrain carpet to the warm tones of the burl-framed mirror.[27] The specificity of group portraits often tempts art historians and genealogists to draw conclusions about more general concepts of American life. Issues of consumerism, social position, and developments of taste have all been investigated using this type of portraiture as source material.[28] This practice is perfectly acceptable as long as details of the family are firmly documented by the written record, tempering the amount of assumption. A degree of caution is required as it is known, for example, that some artists provided elegant chairs or fancy dresses for their sitters, allowing those who could not afford such finery to be painted as if they could.[29] Even the Reverend Stephen Peabody (see *Figure 3*) borrowed an expensive clerical robe from

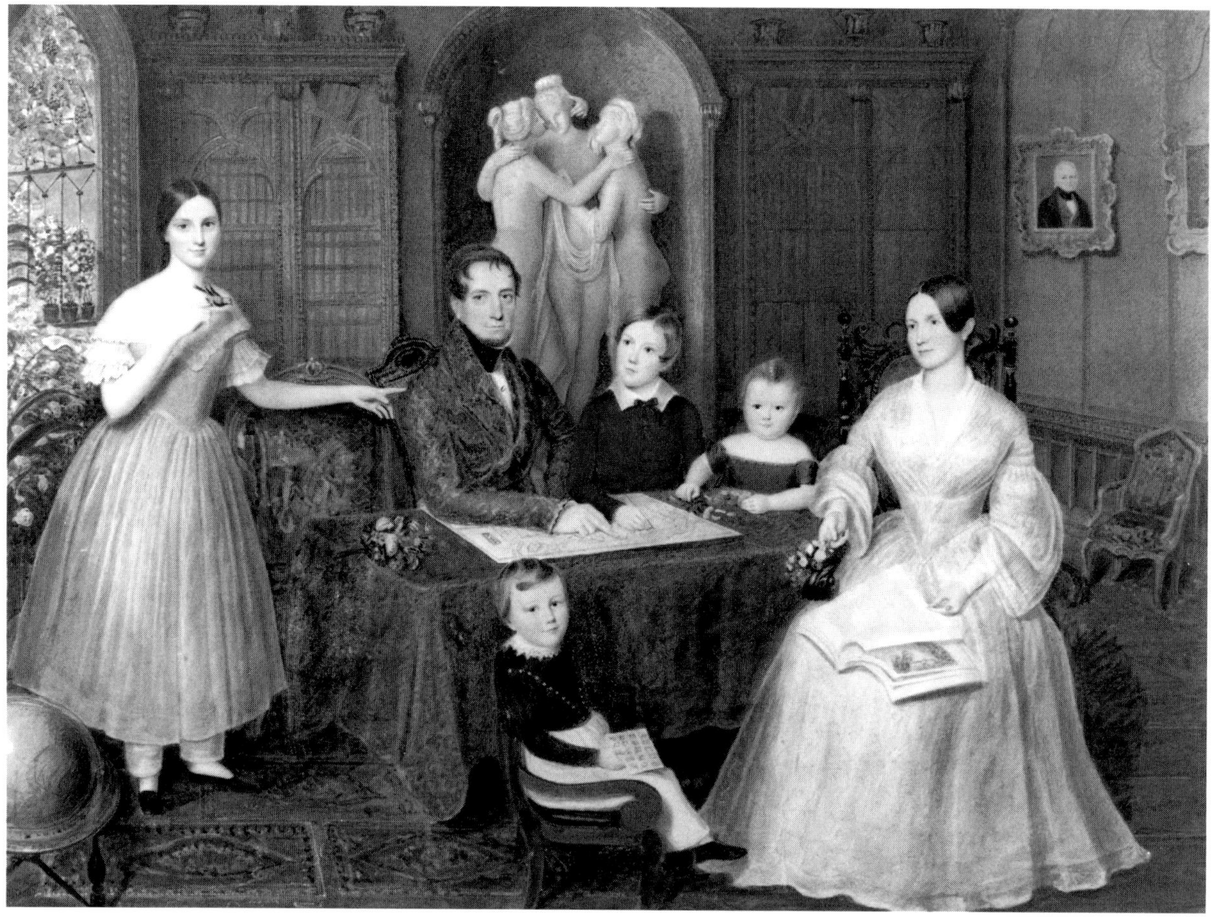

Figure 9 The Richard K. Haight family. Attributed to Nicolino Calyo (1799–1884). New York, New York, circa 1848. Gouache on paper; 20 × 15 inches. Museum of the City of New York, Bequest of Elizabeth Cushing Iselin (74.97.2). *Copyright by The Museum of the City of New York. Used by permission.*

a colleague, as he considered his own not fine enough.[30] Such occurrences may have been quite common and, if unknown to the viewer, can lead to incorrect assumptions about the sitter's financial situation or taste in dress.

There are several variations on the standard group portrait where only a portion of a family is represented. Two oft-used compositional types include canvases depicting a mother with her offspring, such as the charming portrait of Fanny (Negus) Fuller holding her twin boys (*Figure 10*), and portraits that focus only on children, such as the miniature of the three youngest members of the Foster family (*Figure 11*). Portraits like these, which commemorate motherhood and childhood, gained in popularity as the century wore on and reflect the increased attention to the life, education, and importance of children that developed in the nineteenth century.[31] Fanny Fuller had seven children, but the twins were her last, born when she was thirty-nine years of age.[32] This image, while not inclusive of all of her offspring or the several step-children she also helped to raise, nevertheless records Fuller's maternal success at delivering two babies at once and serves as a celebratory visual record of the end of her childbearing years.[33]

The Foster miniature depicts the three children of Alfred and Lydia Foster of Worcester, Massachusetts. The children, Dwight (1828–1884), Mary (1830–1900), and Rebecca (1832–1927) are posed in an interior with ten-year-old Dwight reading at a table as Mary arranges flowers and Rebecca stands

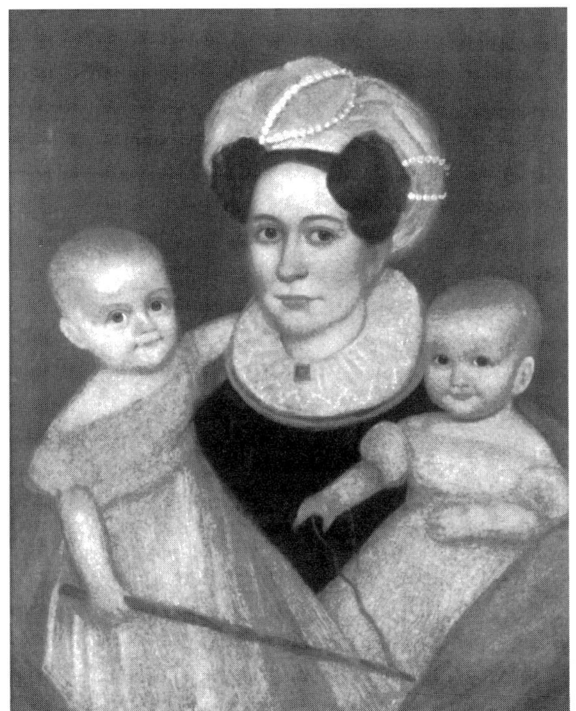

Figure 10 Fanny (Negus) Fuller (1799–1845) and her sons Francis Benjamin (1838–1915) and John Emery (b. 1838). Augustus Fuller (1812–1873). Oil on canvas; 30 × 25 inches. Deerfield, Massachusetts, circa 1838–1839. The artist Augustus Fuller was just nine when his widowed father married Fanny Negus. He was twenty-seven when he painted this portrait of his step-mother and twin brothers, and in the midst of a fairly profitable career as an itinerant portrait painter. Around 1833, Fanny wrote to her husband, "we all wish verry [*sic*] much to see Augustus, we hear he paints fine." (Fanny Fuller to Aaron Fuller, 31 May circa 1833, Fuller/Negus family papers, The Pocumtuck Valley Memorial Association Library, Deerfield, Massachusetts). The Charles P. Russell Collection of Deerfield Academy, Deerfield, Massachusetts.

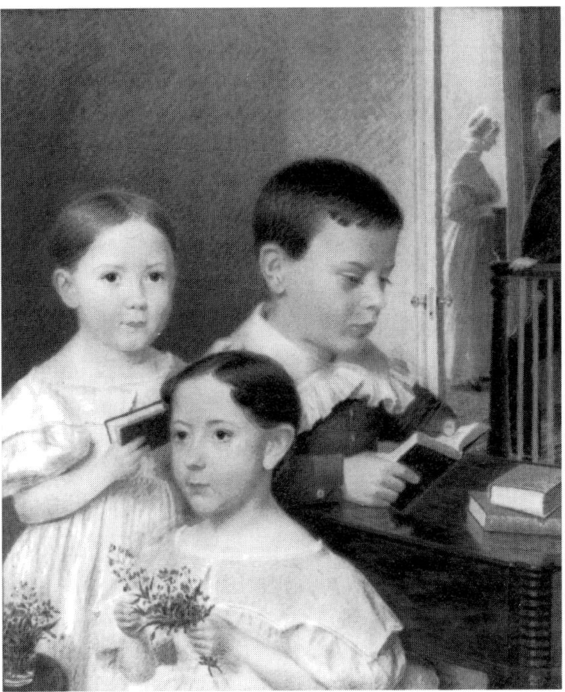

Figure 11 The Foster children. Eliza Goodridge (1798–1882). Worcester, Massachusetts, 1838. Watercolor on ivory; 4 1/16 × 3 3/8 inches. American Antiquarian Society, Bequest of Dwight Foster Dunn, 1937.

nearby. Their parents appear as indistinct figures moving through the background. This portrait was not commissioned by the Fosters but was instead a gift from the artist, Eliza Goodridge (1798–1882), to the children's mother. It was intended to mark the Fosters' tenth wedding anniversary and, according to the artist, was meant to serve as a visual reminder to the parents of their successes and hopes for their children. In a letter accompanying the miniature, Goodridge wrote:

> Will you, my good friend, on this tenth anniversary of your wedding accept this picture? . . . [W]hen the second tenth shall arrive may it find you possessed of all you now enjoy, may the legitimate fruits of such a period of time wisely spent be added to them, and may the originals of this picture, then beginning to take their place in the busy scenes of life (God willing), be to you all the fond Christian parent can desire.[34]

From this letter it becomes apparent that the miniature, which was preserved in the family and passed down through three generations with great care, was intended not only to capture the fleeting likenesses of three children, but also to serve as an icon of sorts, an artistic manifestation of the potential of childhood and the value it brought to a marriage.

Like Dwight Foster and his sisters, most children in group portraits were shown holding books or Bibles to reflect their education and piety. They played with toys or held flowers to signify their gender, innocence, and youth and (perhaps more practically) to entertain and distract them while the artist painted their likenesses.[35] Paintings of small children are numerous before the era of the daguerreotype, as portraits were the only way to preserve the ever-changing features of the youngest members of the family. Some portrait painters encouraged parents to secure images of their offspring before the babies grew up, or, in some cases, lest the children should perish. One artist even ran the following morbid, yet persuasive, poem with his newspaper advertisements:

My paintings are fine, the likenesses true;
The pencil was dipt in nature's own hue;
All glowing and lifelike, you may there behold,
Each delicate feature of both young and old.
Then call on the painter, don't let it be said
"I don't feel quite able," till that loved one is dead.[36]

One of the most unusual group images of children produced in this period was painted around 1860. The children of the Carryl family (*Figure 12*) are all shown at play in a well-appointed parlor. Once again, however, visual information can be misleading as an evaluation of Carryl family records reveals that this painting is in fact a posthumous one, painted after the death of the eldest boy, Oscar, aged eleven. He is shown with three siblings, each of whom is depicted at his age at death. Edward, the infant on the floor, and Gordon, on the rocking horse both died in 1857. Thaddeus, holding the hoop, died in 1859 and Oscar in 1861.[37] The details of the commission of this portrait are unknown, but the artist most likely worked from daguerreotypes and descriptions of the children to create a memorial piece which was surely treasured by the Carryls.[38]

All of the portrait formats described here have in common that they depict families or members of families and, while they cannot reliably tell genealogists everything about the composition of a household or the relationships between individuals, the images are valuable in other ways. On a practical level, for instance, the descent of the objects themselves can offer succinct and exacting genealogical information. Many family portraits, so significant to those depicted, were passed respectfully down through each generation. Tracking the provenance of family portraits provides detailed information on patterns of inheritance and the overall structure of a family tree. The portraits of the Beatties, for example, were given in the 1860s to their eldest son Thomas, who later presented them to his daughter May. In the early 1920s, she bestowed the paintings, along with the dress worn by her grandmother and other family memorabilia, to her daughter Margaret, who outlived all of her siblings and, as the only remaining member of the fourth generation of this family, eventually gave the whole group of objects and papers to a public institution.[39] Such caches of family mementos are tremendous windfalls for the researcher. When several aspects of a family's life, such as portraits, a fancy dress, and a bundle of letters, are preserved as a unit, the objects and documents work together to better amplify that family's existence.

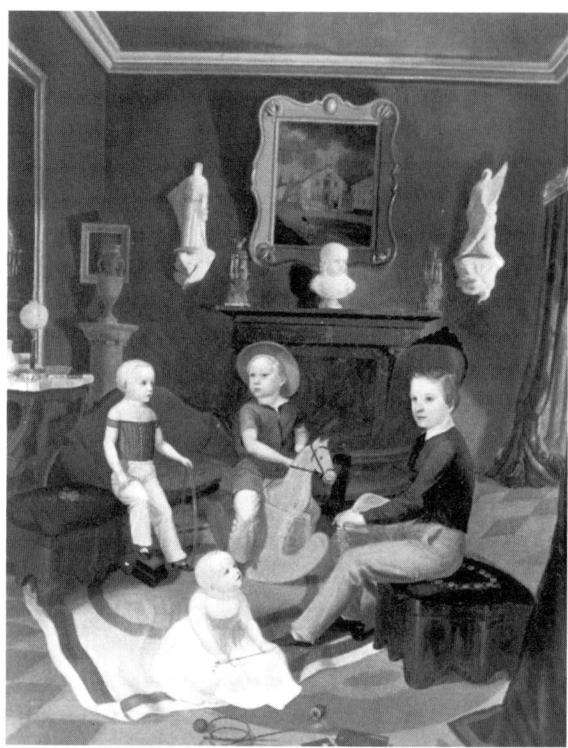

Figure 12 The Carryl children. Attributed to Louis Ransom (1831–1926). Salisbury Center, New York, after 1861. Oil on canvas; 47½ × 38¼ inches. The portrait bust on the mantle depicts a fifth Carryl child, Victoria, who predeceased all of her brothers, dying in 1845, more than fifteen years before this portrait was painted. Fruitlands Museum (G.1975.286). *Published courtesy of Fruitlands Museums, Harvard, Massachusetts.*

While portraits are not the single best source of information on nineteenth-century family life, they have been and should continue to be used by historians and genealogists to give family history and American life a human face. Their ability to illuminate and enliven lists of names and hierarchical charts is incomparable. Portraits, like nothing else before the camera, record for us the physical traits of those pompous great-uncles, famous soldiering relatives, and scholarly grandmothers of our past. For this alone, family portraits will always be valued as ancestral objects. The nineteenth-century portraits which hang in our homes and museums today become more distant links to the past with every passing generation, and yet we continue to be intrigued by these likenesses, pointing out noses, prominent chins, hair color, or expressions that have reappeared in successive generations. In 1846 the American poet Walt Whitman (1819–1892) commented on the human tendency to admire these images, writing: "There is always . . . a strange fascination in portraits. We love to dwell long upon them—to infer many things from the text they preach—to pursue the current of thoughts running riot about them. . . . For the strange fascination of looking at the eyes of a portrait sometimes goes beyond what comes from the real orbs themselves."[40] Our ability to imagine and speculate is endless. Family portraits are simply one more piece of the endless puzzle of human relationships and events that form our nation's history.

NOTES

[1]This use of portraits as interpretive material is noted by Ellen Miles in her introduction and commentary to *Painting and Portrait Making in the American Northeast: 1994 Annual Proceedings of the Dublin Seminar for New England Folklife* (Boston: Boston University Scholarly Publications, 1995), pp. 11–16.

[2]Jane C. Nylander, *Our Own Snug Fireside: Images of the New England Home, 1760–1860* (New Haven: Yale University Press, 1993), pp. 21–22.

[3]Mary (Craigie) Foster to Andrew Craigie Jr., 20 April 1783, Andrew Craigie Papers, 1717–1854, Manuscript Collection, American Antiquarian Society, Worcester, Mass. Another set of family papers which documents a complex family structure is the Negus Family Papers, 1808–1844, Pocumtuck Valley Memorial Association Library, Deerfield, Mass. Copies are available through the Archives of American Art and quoted extensively in *Meet Your Neighbors: New England Portraits, Painters and Society, 1790–1850,* ed. Caroline F. Sloat (Sturbridge, Mass.: Old Sturbridge Village, 1992).

[4]There are exceptions, such as a watercolor of three generations of the Talcott family and an oil portrait of the women of the Ege-Galt family of Virginia (both illustrated in Beatrix Rumford, *American Folk Portraits: Paintings and Drawings from the Abby Aldrich Rockefeller Folk Art Center* [Williamsburg, Va.: Colonial Williamsburg Foundation, 1981], pp. 109–10, 221–22). Also rare are portraits which show household help. Samuel Colman's portrait of the Yeatman children includes Miss Boggs, the family's governess, but her face is obscured by a large bonnet (illustrated in Nancy C. Muller, *Paintings and Drawings of the Shelburne Museum* [Shelburne, Vt.: Museum, 1976], p. 42).

[5]Such strong family connections are well documented throughout the nineteenth-century written record. One example of many is found in an 1837 letter from Lydia Foster (1806–1887) who writes to her newly married sister: "I have hardly recovered from the excitement of the few weeks previous to your leaving us. . . . I cannot yet realize that you are not where a short walk would enable me to see you, believe me that my affection for you is strong as it should be towards an only sister and your absence is deeply felt by us all." (Lydia [Stiles] Foster to Mary [Stiles] Newcomb, 17 November 1837, Foster Family Papers, 1740–1884. Manuscript Collection, American Antiquarian Society.)

[6]See Jack Larkin, "The Faces of Change: Images of Self and Society in New England, 1790–1850," in *Meet Your Neighbors,* pp. 10, 20.

[7]Probate inventory of Isaiah Thomas Sr., Worcester County Probate Records, 1831. Copy in the Thomas Family Papers, 1815–1887, Manuscript Collection, American Antiquarian Society. The portrait depicted Isaiah Thomas's son and was painted by Ethan Allen Greenwood (1779–1856) in 1818. The probate inventory for the North Front Room also includes a bureau, washstand, assorted linens, and two drawings with needlework.

[8]Ellen Triphosa Harrington (1830–1900), Journal, Shrewsbury, Mass., 26 February 1847. (Journal no. 3, pp. 249–50), MS no. 128.3, Museum Archives, Shelburne Museum, Shelburne, Vt.

[9]Nylander, *Our Own Snug Fireside,* pp. 251–54. One nineteenth-century woman called her seldom-used best room a "store-room for household treasures."

[10]Alonzo Slafter to James Beattie, 24 July 1840, MS no. 27.1.189, Museum Archives, Shelburne Museum.

[11]Stephen Peabody Diaries, 1767–1814, 1 September 1809, Manuscript Collection, American Antiquarian Society.

[12]Ibid., 13 October 1809.

[13]Cited in Georgia Brady Barnhill, "'Extracts from the Journals of Ethan A. Greenwood': Portrait Painter and Museum Proprietor," *Proceedings of the American Antiquarian Society* 103, pt. 1 (April 1993): 114, appendix p. 12. Greenwood's journal entry is for 4 March 1813.

[14]Ibid., p. 114. Greenwood's journal entry is for 20 April 1813.

[15]Ibid., appendix pp. 12, 14. According to Greenwood's journal, in May of 1813 he also produced portraits of Rebecca's

husband William (1761–1842) and the couple's daughters Caroline and Hannah. The locations of most of the Whittemore family portraits are, unfortunately, unknown. According to *The Inventory of American Paintings Executed before 1914* (Washington, D.C.: Smithsonian Institution, on-line catalogue), Greenwood's portrait of William Whittemore as well as a portrait of Thomas Jefferson Whittemore (1797–1872) were owned privately in the 1970s.

[16]Barnhill, "'Extracts from the Journals of Ethan A. Greenwood,'" appendix p. 12. This is probably how the Whittemore commission developed, as, according to his accounts, Greenwood completed a likeness of Henry Whittemore on 3 March 1812, one day before receiving the larger proposition to paint the rest of the family.

[17]The set may have included a fifth image, as it is unknown whether Bundy painted a likeness of one-year-old Nathan William Goddard during the 1837 sittings. The Goddard paintings are all illustrated in *Meet Your Neighbors*, pp. 97–99.

[18]Ibid., p. 98.

[19]The likenesses of the parents were sold from the Elizabeth and Eliot Orr collection on 9 August 1969 by Richard Bourne Auctions, Hyannisport, Mass. They were purchased at this sale by Mr. and Mrs. Josiah Kirby Lilly III. (Thanks are due to Curator Jennifer Yunginger, who gleaned this information for me from the files of Heritage Plantation, Sandwich, Mass.) The images of the boys were purchased in 1964 by Old Sturbridge Village from C. A. Carpenter of Shrewsbury, Mass. (Thanks are due to Lynne Z. Bassett for checking the provenance files on behalf of the author.)

[20]*Meet Your Neighbors*, organized by Old Sturbridge Village.

[21]Some artists, like Erastus Salisbury Field (1805–1900), spent their entire careers following up on possible family connections. See Mary Black, *Erastus Salisbury Field, 1805–1900* (Springfield, Mass.: Museum of Fine Arts, 1984).

[22]Two portraits by Winthrop Chandler (1747–1790), depicting Ebenezer Craft and his family, serve as wonderful eighteenth-century examples of such images. On one canvas, son Samuel stands near his father while on the other, two well-dressed girls are seated with their mother. These images are illustrated in Richard H. Saunders and Virginia M. Westbrook, *Celebrating Vermont: Myths and Realities* (Middlebury, Vt.: Christian A. Johnson Memorial Gallery, Middlebury College, 1991), pp. 29, 128.

[23]This separation was not usually possible in group portraits which tended to illustrate a family gathered in one room or united around a central task.

[24]The smallest family members' intolerance for lengthy sittings also had to be accommodated. One sitter in a portrait group painted by Horace Bundy in the 1850s recalled that the youngest siblings kept running away and hiding during the painting sessions. See Lauren B. Hewes, "Horace Bundy: Itinerant Portraitist," *Magazine Antiques* 146, no. 4 (October 1994): 486–87.

[25]Wendy A. Cooper, *Classical Taste in America, 1800–1840* (Baltimore, Md.: Baltimore Museum of Art and Abbeville Press, 1993), p. 101. The pair of portraits hanging on the wall of the library could be ancestral likenesses, a common ploy used by artists to include deceased or absent family members in a group portrait.

[26]Black, *Erastus Salisbury Field*, p. 106. The children are Louisa Ellen Cook and her brother Frederick.

[27]Ibid., p. 29. Many of the pieces of furniture, costumes, and jewelry shown in the portrait were retained by the sitters and descended to the heirs along with the painting.

[28]For publications which use portraits in this manner see, David Jaffee, "The Age of Democratic Portraiture: Artisan-Entrepreneurs and the Rise of Consumer Goods," in *Meet Your Neighbors*, pp. 35–46; John Michael Vlach, *Plain Painters: Making Sense of American Folk Art* (Washington, D.C.: Smithsonian Institution Press, 1988); and Gerald W. R. Ward and William N. Hosley, eds., *The Great River: Art and Society of the Connecticut Valley, 1635–1820* (Hartford: Wadsworth Atheneum, 1985).

[29]Colleen Cowles Heslip, *Between the Rivers: Itinerant Painters from the Connecticut to the Hudson* (Williamstown, Mass.: Sterling and Francine Clark Art Institute, 1990), p. 23.

[30]Stephen Peabody Diaries, 21 October 1809.

[31]For more on perceptions of childhood in this period, see Anita Schorsch, *Images of Childhood: An Illustrated Social History* (New York: Mayflower Press, 1979), and Sandra Brandt and Elissa Cullman, *Small Folk: A Celebration of Childhood in America* (New York: E. P. Dutton, 1980).

[32]*Meet Your Neighbors*, pp. 95–96.

[33]A few years after the birth of the twins, Fanny (Negus) Fuller became an invalid after contracting pulmonary tuberculosis. See *Meet Your Neighbors*, p. 96.

[34]Eliza Goodridge to Lydia (Stiles) Foster, 14 February 1838, Foster Family Papers, 1740–1884.

[35]For more on the props used in portraits of children, see Jennifer A. Yunginger, *Is She or Isn't He: Identifying Gender in Folk Portraits of Children* (Sandwich, Mass.: Heritage Plantation, 1995).

[36]*West Troy Advocate*, no date, excerpted on a broadside promoting the work of Horace Bundy, 27 March 1851. Dodges and Noyes, Printers, Nashua, N.H., New Hampshire Historical Society, Concord (No. F2903). Illustrated in Lauren Hewes, "Horace Bundy: Portraits Painted from Daguerreotypes," in *Painting and Portrait Making in the American Northeast*, p. 253.

[37]Yunginger, *Is She or Isn't He*, p. 68.

[38]For more on the unique subgroup of posthumous family portraiture, see Phoebe Lloyd, "Posthumous Mourning Portraiture," in *A Time to Mourn: Expressions of Grief in Nineteenth-Century America*, ed. Martha V. Pike and Janice G. Armstrong (Stony Brook, N.Y.: Museums at Stony Brook, 1980), pp. 70–89.

[39]Curatorial object files, 27.1.1-189, 190, Shelburne Museum.

[40]Walt Whitman, *Brooklyn Daily Eagle*, 2 July 1846, reporting on John Plumbe Jr.'s New York gallery of daguerreotype portraits, cited by Margaret C. S. Christman, *1846: Portrait of the Nation* (Washington, D.C.: Smithsonian Institution Press, 1996), p. 160.

Tokens of Love and Sorrow: New England Portrait Miniatures and Mourning Jewelry

Elle Shushan

> Twenty Shillings Reward shall be given to any one who shall bring to Mr. Luke Vardy at the Royal Exchange near the Town Hall, a little painted Picture of a Young Lady, under a Crystial [*sic*] in a Shagreen Case lined with Green with Silver Clasps which hath been lost. *Boston Gazette,* 5–12 September 1726.[1]

> A Burying-Ring marked N. Hubbard, Esq; Ob. 10 Jan. 1747–8. Aet. 69, lost in Boston. The person who has found the same, and brings or sends it to the Printer, shall be well rewarded. *Boston Gazette,* 15 November 1748.[2]

SUCH WAS THE value of these most intimate treasures that advertisements beseeching their return appeared in colonial newspapers beside reports of stolen silver punch bowls and runaway servants. Both miniatures and mourning rings were traditions brought to British North America from England. They became part of the fabric of life in New England from the earliest days, and both closely reflect the ties that bound family members and friends and the larger outlines of genealogical remembrance as expressed through small-scale painting and jewelry. Like silver objects, inscriptions and markings found on miniatures and mourning jewelry were sometimes genealogically specific, referring not only to the portrayed subject but to sequence of its ownership.

Miniatures

Miniature portraits were taken to commemorate landmarks in a life: childhood (after the threat of infant mortality had passed), engagement or marriage, a change of location of a family member, and more than occasionally, death. Miniatures, the most private form of portraiture, differed from full-size oil portraits which were made to embellish public rooms in homes for all to see, and by extension, to admire. Miniatures were reserved for the eyes of the recipient. Often depicting only the face, therefore free from the distractions of clothing and other accouterments, the essence of the subject was revealed. Many times framed with a lock of the sitter's hair to make the gift even more intimate, this handheld likeness provided candid communication between the subject and the viewer.

English and American portrait miniatures descend from the illustrations in medieval illuminated manuscripts. The missing links in this process appear to be the self-portrait of artist John Siferwas with John, Lord Lovell, in the *Lovell Lectionary,* circa 1400, and the portrait of Geoffrey Chaucer in Thomas Hoccleve's *The Regiment of Princes.*[3] The first fully detached portrait miniatures in England began during the reign of Henry VIII. In 1525 Gerard Hornebolte, court painter to the Regent of the Netherlands, was brought to England with his family, all of whom were artists, to work as manuscript illuminators. His son Lucas Hornebolte's miniature of Henry VIII, now in the Fitzwilliam Museum, Cambridge, England, is widely considered the first English portrait miniature as presently defined.[4] This new art form, distinct from other forms of portraiture, was called "limning" after illumination, the field from which it grew. Both the term and the discipline remained in use well into the nineteenth century in America.

From the very beginning, portrait miniatures were considered as precious as jewels. Elizabeth I kept hers in her private bedroom, each wrapped separately, bearing the name of the sitter.[5] She also appreciated the quality of the miniature, concerning herself about her images and appointing Nicholas Hilliard as her portrait painter of choice. But as much as Elizabeth appreciated Hilliard, she was too thrifty to pay him a retainer which would have made his talents exclusive to the throne. This helped change the role of miniatures when Hilliard, a freeman of the Goldsmiths' Company, opened a shop in Fleet Street,

London, in the early 1570s. Not only aristocrats but gentry and even ordinary citizens of means could now have a miniature taken by the same man who painted the queen. At a time when portraiture was not common, Hilliard's miniatures began to chronicle Elizabethan life.[6] In fact, during this time miniatures by Hilliard and his successor, Isaac Oliver, were by far the most distinguished portrait form available, virtually the only one based on academic training.[7]

The first image of the portrait miniature as a wearable jewel appeared about 1560. A miniature attributed to Levina Teerlinc, depicting Katherine Grey, Lady Hertford, holding her child and wearing a miniature of her husband, is the earliest evidence of the fashion.[8] An unidentified lady called "Lady Walsingham," painted by George Gower in 1572, is the earliest full-sized portrait showing the miniature worn as a jewel.[9] Miniatures set within a jeweled locket and hung on a chain around the neck or from the waist were a recurring fashion in life and portraiture for the next two hundred fifty years.[10]

In New England, miniatures were in evidence during the middle of the seventeenth century. Elizabeth Eggington of Boston had her portrait painted by an unknown artist in 1664. This portrait, now in the Wadsworth Atheneum, is among the earliest images of the portrait miniature in America.[11] The frame of the miniature is set with gems or decorated with enamel and adorned with pendant pearls, much like Lady Walsingham's of almost one hundred years earlier. Elizabeth Eggington was a granddaughter of the Reverend John Cotton (1585–1652).[12] A Puritan, Cotton had fled from Boston, England, to Boston, Massachusetts, in 1633 and wrote over fifty books before his death in 1652. After his death, his widow Sarah (Story) Cotton married Rev. Richard Mather, another Puritan minister of eminence and patriarch of the Mather clan in America.[13] Young Elizabeth Eggington, who died the year this portrait was painted, was a child of substance by early colonial standards. Her other jewelry, including a pearl necklace, a pendant pearl at the neck, and a gold ring, "testify to the fact that hers was a family of wealth,"[14] in other words, early American aristocracy worthy of a miniature.

John Smibert (1688–1751), a Scotsman, painted the first documented portrait miniatures in New England. Originally from Edinburgh, Smibert studied in London at Sir Godfrey Kneller's Great Queen Street Academy and had taken the "Grand Tour" to Italy, making him the most highly trained artist in the colonies when he arrived in Boston in 1729. By 1734, when Smibert painted Samuel Browne of Salem in both oil on canvas and in miniature, in oil on copper, the artist's clientele included a number of the wealthiest families in New England. The Browne family commissioned at least twelve portraits by Smibert, including a miniature of Samuel's brother, William. The miniature of Samuel Browne, with a gold case by the prominent Boston goldsmith Jacob Hurd, stayed in family hands until the twentieth century.[15]

Miniature painting in New England nevertheless remained in its infancy until John Singleton Copley (1738–1815), the son of Anglo-Irish immigrants in Boston, remade the visual image of its upper classes in the much-coveted style of the English aristocracy. Copley, with no formal instruction, began painting accomplished miniatures in oil on copper before adopting the popular English standard of watercolor on ivory with equal proficiency. Many times he copied a miniature from his own large portrait of the same sitter.[16]

Among Copley's most enthusiastic early patrons were the Oliver family of Massachusetts. Almost two-thirds of recorded Copley miniatures are of members of that family.[17] Interestingly, the first of these miniatures—Massachusetts lieutenant governor Andrew Oliver—was painted in oil on ivory, a process which fought the positive qualities of the ivory.[18] But Copley's miniature of Oliver's second wife, Mary Sandford, was painted in oil on copper covered with a sheet of gold leaf,[19] a process exclusive to Copley (*Figure 1*). His earliest miniatures, painted when Copley was just seventeen, were executed on the used printmaking plates of his stepfather, Peter Pelham.[20] Seventeen of the thirty-five miniatures attributed to Copley are oil on copper. Of these, five have the unique gold ground.[21]

The recently discovered thirty-sixth miniature by Copley (*Figure 2*) appeared in London, possibly carried there for a British relative of the sitter. The smallest recorded Copley miniature, it measures just 1 17/32 inches (3.9 cm) high. The underlayer of gold is visible in the eyelashes and nostrils. Set in a gold

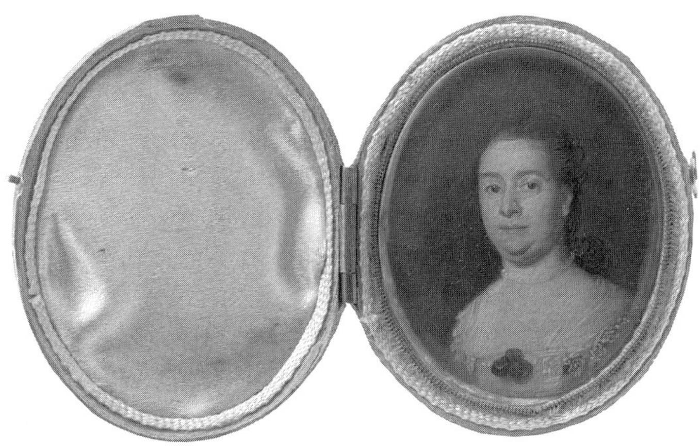

Figure 1 Mary (Sandford) Oliver. Miniature by John Singleton Copley (1738–1815). Boston, Massachusetts, circa 1759. Oil on gold-leafed copper blank. 1¼ inches (4.5 cm) high. Yale University Art Gallery, Mabel Brady Garvan Fund. 1955-5-12.

locket with plaited hair within the glazed reverse, it dates circa 1758–1760. Although the identity of the sitter is still unknown, it is intriguing to compare the physical resemblance to Mary Sandford Oliver.

In 1775 Irish miniaturist and goldsmith John Ramage (ca. 1748–1802) arrived in Boston. His stay was brief. A Loyalist, Ramage enlisted in an Irish regiment to fight for the British and by 1776 had moved with his regiment to Halifax. Ramage brought with him beautiful gold miniature cases of a style popular in Ireland at the time, elaborately embellished with scallops and brightwork.[22] His miniatures, painted in brilliant jewel tones and set in these splendid cases, continued the high standard of miniature painting begun by Copley. Ramage, who had trained at the Dublin Society Schools, was also proficient at genre and "fancy pieces" on ivory, introducing a more sophisticated quality to home-grown mourning scenes. Ramage quickly moved on to British-occupied New York, where he elegantly chronicled on ivory the British participants in the Revolution, much as Charles Willson Peale was doing with the Continental Army in Philadelphia.

Before the Revolution, Boston had been the artistic center in New England. But with the fighting, the exodus of talent began. Copley, a Loyalist, had abandoned America for London in 1774. His half brother, the gifted Henry Pelham, followed in 1776. Ramage was followed in Boston by the first real generation of indigenous American miniaturists. These native artists, like Copley, were self-taught. But, unlike Copley, few had the talent to live off their craft. They advertised as gilders, teachers, even barn painters. Samuel King (1748/9–1819), the Newport portrait and miniature painter, presented Dr. Isaac Senter a bill which not only included Dr. Senter's portrait, but additional charges for painting and gilding his chaise, painting his sulky, and gilding picture frames.[23] Portrait painter and miniaturist John Johnston (1753–1818), called by the *Massachusetts Centinel* of 4 November 1789 "one of the two best portrait painters in th[at] metropolis [Boston]," also painted patterns on silk for schoolgirl needlework.[24]

Richard Jennys appeared in Paul Revere's day books in 1764 when he was charged "for gold bracelet and glass—for gold picture frame with glass."[25] This entry indicates that Jennys was painting miniatures, though none has yet been identified. Jennys made his living by running a dry-goods store, but in 1776 he was still advertising as a portrait painter.[26] Nevertheless, many of the names of the miniaturists working in New England during the Revolution are lost, though examples of their works remain. A fine portrait miniature (ca. 1775–1780) of the printer and publisher Isaiah Thomas Sr. (Worcester Art Museum) must have been painted in Massachusetts. The quality is exceptional for this period, but the identity of the artist remains a mystery.[27]

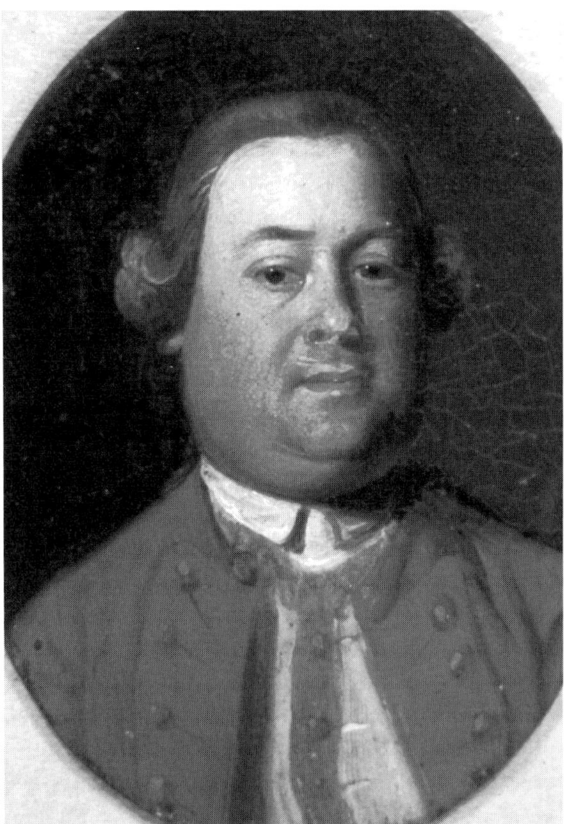

Figure 2 Unknown Gentleman. Miniature by John Singleton Copley (1738–1815). Boston Massachusetts, circa 1759. Oil on gold-leafed copper blank. This recently discovered portrait is the eighteenth known oil on copper miniature by Copley, and the sixth with a gold ground. 1 17/32 inches (3.9 cm) high. Private collection.

With the end of the Revolution, miniaturists of reputation reappeared in Boston. Joseph Dunkerley (active 1778–1788) arrived in America as a soldier in the British Army, deserting to join a Massachusetts artillery regiment. He left that post in 1778,[28] staying in New England only until 1788. An artist of some talent, he attracted a clientele which included many of the élite of Revolutionary Massachusetts. Much of his better work has been mistaken for miniatures of Copley, whom he copied. Many times Copley reproduced his own portraits "In Littel," but in the case of Mr. and Mrs. Ebenezer Storer II of Boston, that assignment went to Dunkerley. Copley's pastel portraits of the Storers, taken in the late 1760s, were copied by Dunkerley in about 1785 onto tiny discs of ivory (*Figure 3*). That Ebenezer Storer II (1729–1807) was a substantial gentleman is revealed in these portraits, with Storer in a damask dressing gown and his wife's dress trimmed with pearls. By the time Dunkerley copied the original pastel portraits, his wife, Elizabeth Green (1734–1774), had been dead for over ten years, and Storer had married Hannah Quincy Lincoln. Probably one of Elizabeth Green Storer's three adult children commissioned the copies of the pastel portraits.[29] These diminutive treasures, only one inch high, were then set in gold bracelet clasps. These miniatures would probably have been made for a daughter to wear. The style of hairweaving establishes that the bracelets were again updated during the mid-nineteenth century, indicating that they remained treasured remembrances for several generations.[30]

During the time Dunkerley was in Boston, he advertised a drawing school with John Hazlitt (1767–1837), a younger brother of the writer William Hazlitt, which they intended to start in 1785. John Hazlitt, then eighteen, had already established himself as a miniaturist in Salem and Dorchester. Hazlitt returned with his family to England in 1787, exhibiting at the Royal Academy from 1788 to 1819.[31]

Who, besides the aristocrats of the region, was likely to patronize miniature painters? Immediate family members continued to be one source of patronage. Sarah Sanford (ca. 1760–1829), who married Job Perit/Peret (ca. 1751–1794) at Trinity Church in New Haven on 17 November 1782,[32] was painted in 1790 by Reuben Moulthrop (1763–1814) (*Figure 4*). The focal point of the portrait is a proudly displayed miniature of a child hung around Mrs. Peret's neck; she lost three of her four children in infancy. But the subject of the miniature, Elizabeth Sanford Perit (1785–1858), lived to marry Elihu Munson, the son of Dr. Eneas Munson. Dr. Eneas Munson, a founder of the Yale Medical School, became the second husband of the subject of this painting, Sally (Sanford) Perit.

This portrait is one of a very small group of signed and dated examples of Moulthrop's work. It was painted in Hartford. The miniature within the portrait appears to be by William Verstille, the leading miniaturist in Connecticut at this time.[33]

Mariners were enthusiastic sitters for miniatures which were often the only images of them remaining

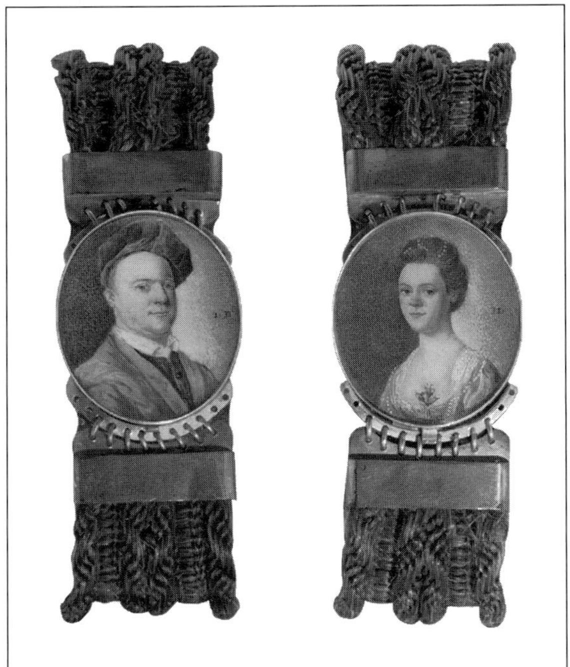

Figure 3 Ebenezer Storer II (1729–1807) and Elizabeth (Green) Storer (1734–1774). Miniatures by Joseph Dunkerley (active in America 1778–1788), signed, circa 1785, after pastel portraits by John Singleton Copley, 1767–1769. 1¼ inches high. Yale University Art Gallery; John Hill Morgan, B.A. 1893 Fund.

with their families during long periods of separation. They frequently sat for these images before leaving on voyages and had additional ones painted in distant ports of call. Father and son Adam and Timothy Wellman of Salem were both sea captains.[34] Adam Wellman (1744–1786) was also a Revolutionary soldier. Though he married Margaret Lambert in 1767, Adam spent part of that year and the following as master of the schooner *Thomas*, sailing to the West Indies and Dominico. He would have left a miniature behind for his bride and taken one of her with him. Margaret died in 1773 leaving three children. In 1776 Wellman married a widow, Mercy (Mascoll) Stevens (ca. 1738–1828), daughter of shipwright Joseph and Ruth (Purchase) Mascoll and widow of Thomas Stevens. Immediately, Adam Wellman joined the Revolution as a lieutenant on the schooner *Success*, a privateer. Later, he was commissioned commander of the privateer schooner *Jackall*. Adam and Mercy (Mascoll) Wellman had eight or more children between them—his three with Margaret, at least three of Mercy's by her first husband Thomas Stevens, and two of their own. In 1786 Captain Wellman died of fever at Port-au-Prince.[35] His charming miniature (ca. 1780–1785) by an unknown folk artist shows the captain in his environment: a seascape behind him, a ship bearing the American flag, and a rowboat heading toward it (*Figure 5*). The reverse has hair designed as a wheat sheath, tied with seed pearls, with the initials "A W" placed on top.[36]

Adam's son Timothy Wellman III (1776–1823) followed him to sea, joining the Salem Marine Society in 1796 and the East India Marine Society in 1803. During the War of 1812, Timothy, like his father before him, was a privateer. His miniature was painted in Cronstadt, Russia, in 1803 (*Figure 6*) and brought home as a trophy of his exotic journeys.[37] In 1823 Wellman sold his ship while abroad and sailed for Salem with a Captain Cheever. And, like his father and his elder half brother Adam Wellman Jr. (ca. 1773–1800), Timothy Wellman perished on a sea voyage.[38]

One Boston native began painting with no apparent instruction in the new British style of using large pieces of ivory. William Lovett (1773–1801) appears to have had a healthy career in the area by the mid-1790s. The enchanting double portrait miniature of Rebecca and Debra Hovey (Worcester Art Museum) displays a remarkable use of the glowing qualities of ivory. The Hovey twins, born in 1793, were the daughters of General Amos and Deborah (Steward) Hovey of Salem, Massachusetts.[39] Reverend William Bentley mentioned the death of Debra on 11 July 1798 during a smallpox epidemic. This may well have been her posthumous portrait.[40] Lovett worked in Boston and the surrounding areas. His clientele was affluent. Many of his miniatures were set in expensive gold cases ordered from England with cobalt glass surrounding a central hair reserve. The portrait of master mariner and privateer Penn Townsend (1772–1846), in the Peabody Essex Museum, compares favorably with miniatures known to have been painted by Lovett, as does the portrait (now at the Newport Historical Society) of Abraham Touro (1777–1822), benefactor of the Massachusetts General Hospital in Boston and Touro Synagogue in Newport.

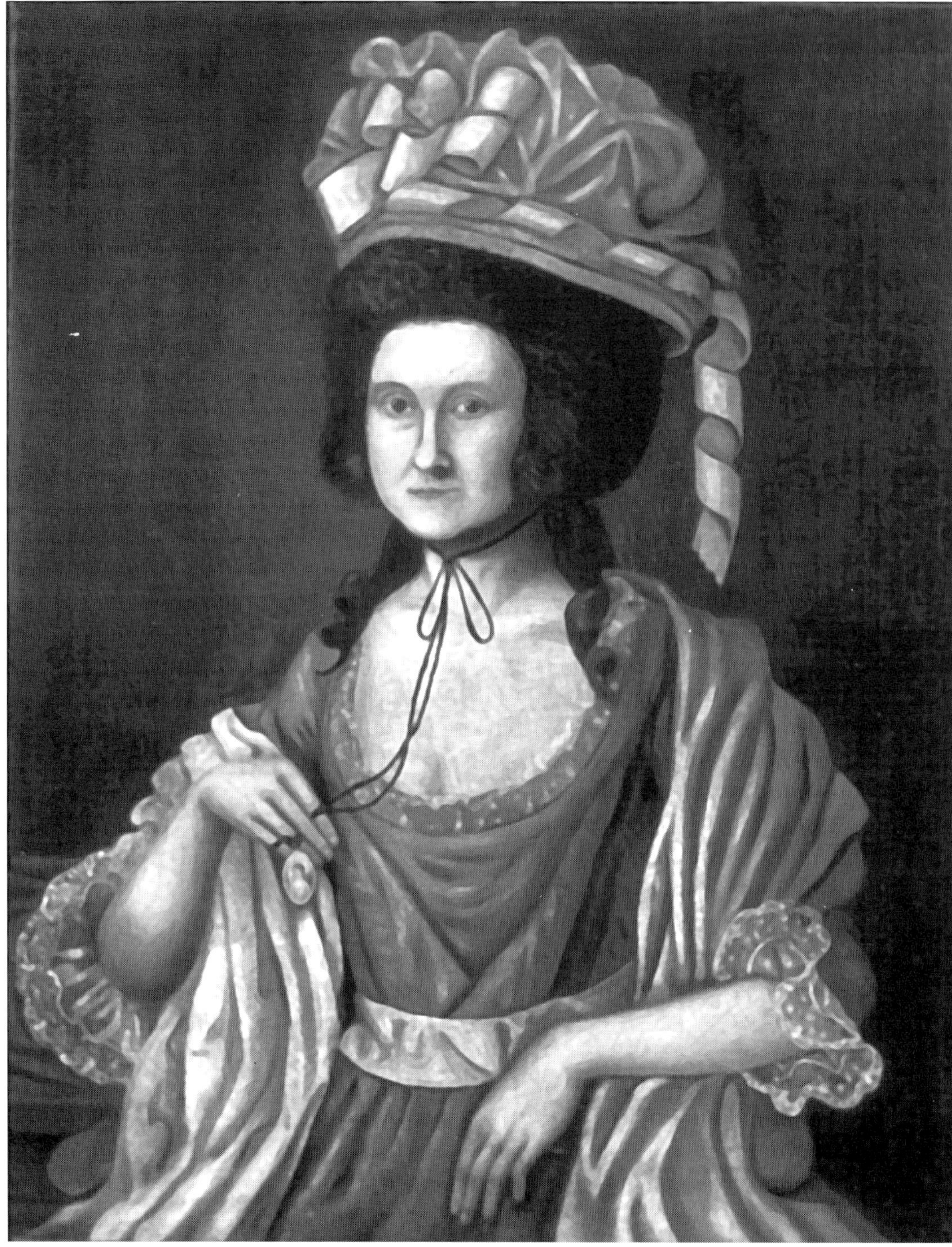

Figure 4 Sally (Sanford) Perit (1760–1829). Portrait by Reuben Molthrop (1763–1814), oil on canvas, Hartford, Connecticut, signed and dated 1790. Mrs. Perit is wearing a miniature of her daughter, Elizabeth Sanford Perit (1785–1858), probably painted by leading Connecticut miniaturist William Verstille (1757–1803). 36¼ inches high. The Metropolitan Museum of Art, Gift of Edgar William and Bernice Chrysler Garbisch, 1957.

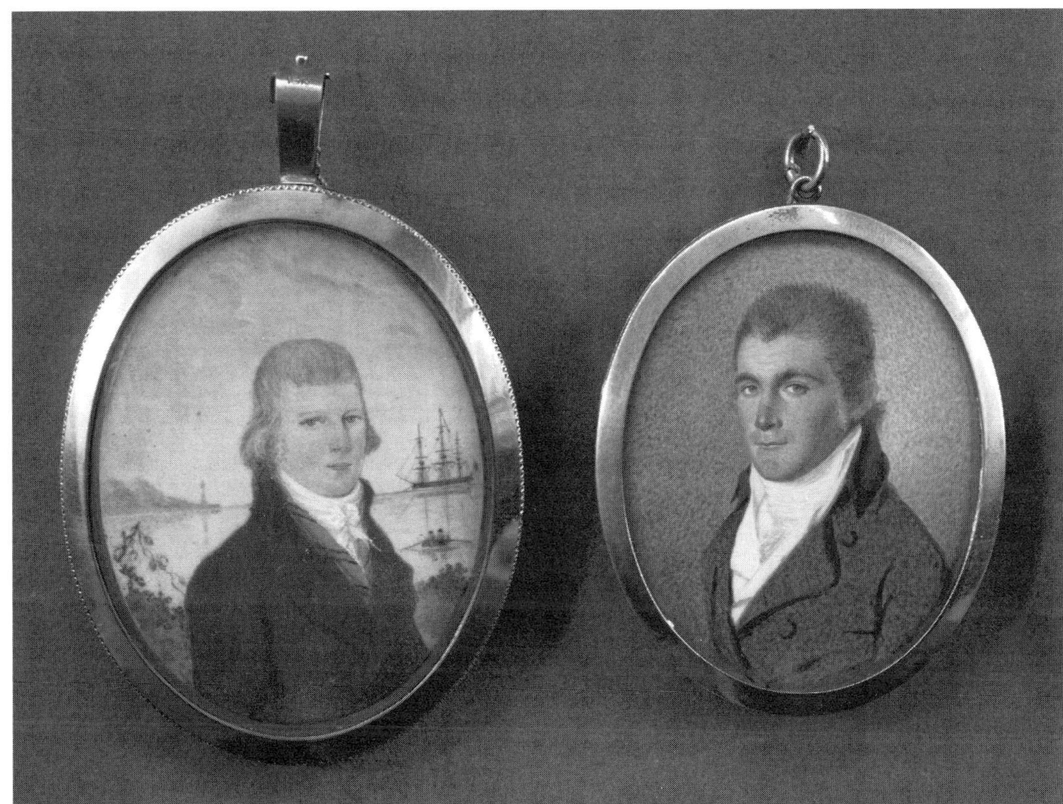

Figures 5 and 6 Left: Captain Adam Wellman (1744–1786). Miniature by an unknown American artist. Massachusetts, circa 1780–1785. Peabody Essex Museum. Right: Captain Timothy Wellman (1776–1825). Miniature by an unknown continental artist, painted in Cronstadt, Russia, 1805. Peabody Essex Museum. Both father and son, captains from Salem, Massachusetts, were lost at sea. *Photographs courtesy of Peabody Essex Museum.*

Lovett died at twenty-eight, leaving little information about himself and a body of work only now coming to light. It was discovered recently that he cooperated with the erratic, but wildly talented Boston-born artist Benjamin Trott (ca. 1770–1843). Two paintings were found in Virginia painted in 1793, signed "Trott and Lovett" on the reverse.[41] The characteristics of Trott's later style correspond closely to those of the known work of Lovett. Trott was working in Boston as late as 1793 when he advertised in the *Columbian Centinel* as a miniaturist and a maker of "Devices in Hair" and announced a drawing school he was planning.[42] Few works by Trott are known from this period.

Some key miniatures of this period are by artists who remain unidentified. Abigail Lopez (1771–1851) of Newport, Rhode Island, was nineteen when she married Isaac Gomez of New York City. This union merged two of the richest and most influential Sephardic Jewish families in America. Abigail's father, Aaron Lopez, the owner of thirty ships carrying molasses, rum, and slaves, was known as "The Merchant Prince" of Newport.[43] Aaron took Sarah, the daughter of his business associate, Jacob Rodriguez Rivera, as his second wife. Their son, Joshua, in turn married the daughter of Isaac Touro, leader of the synagogue in Newport to which Lopez and Rivera were the major contributing founders.[44] Isaac Gomez was a member of the wealthiest Jewish family in New York.[45]

One hundred fifty years after her marriage, the miniature taken of Abigail (Lopez) Gomez was still in her family, but her identity had been long forgotten (*Figure 7*). In 1953, when Hannah R. London wrote *Miniatures of Early American Jews,* all that was known about the miniature was that it was "a Miss Gomez, a member of Miss (Florence) Dreyfous' mother's family." In 1999 the miniature again appeared, this time in a small auction house in England. It had been consigned there by a family who said her name was "Miss Lopez." Armed with the Lopez-Gomez connection and the Dreyfous ancestry, researchers found that Abigail Lopez had married Isaac Gomez in 1790. A direct descendant of that union was Florence Dreyfous's mother.[46] And Abigail, still lovely in her white lace gown, set in a beautiful American gold case, had her full identity returned.

In 1805 the Englishman Robert Field (1769–1819) arrived in Boston. Called by Dale Johnson the most accomplished of the foreign-born miniaturists painting in America,[47] Field set a new standard for this genre in Boston. A favorite artist of Martha Washington, Field had remained a Loyalist and in 1808 finally left Boston for Halifax. His sophisticated portraits depicted Federal America at its most elegant. Joseph Ruggles (1781–1819) (*Figures 8 through 10*), who had been painted in the year of his birth by an unknown primitive miniaturist, was painted in 1808 by Field. This stylish miniature shows an aristocratic man in his prime. Ten years later, the same sitter, now facing his final days, was again painted by the leading miniaturist in Boston. This time the job went to Henry Williams, who, with his occasional partner, William M. S. Doyle, replaced Field in popularity, if not talent.

In other parts of New England, there were few academic, or even attributable, miniaturists before 1800. In Newport, Rhode Island, Samuel King was helping a young Edward Greene Malbone (1777–1807), who would become America's preeminent miniaturist. Malbone, the third of six children of Newport merchant John Malbone Jr., by one Patience Greene,[48] began his career in Providence in 1794 at the age of seventeen, moving within two years to Boston,[49] returning to Newport for family occasions. Some of Malbone's sitters had strong roots to Newport. Mary Gould Almy was born there in 1735 and was a lifelong resident—and a lifelong Loyalist. When she married Benjamin Almy in 1762, both considered themselves British. But when war broke out, Mary remained

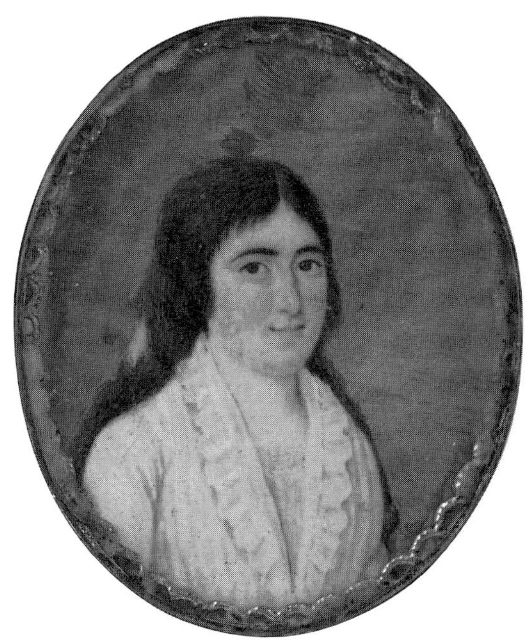

Figure 7 Abigail (Lopez) Gomez (1771–1851). Miniature by unknown American artist, probably Newport, Rhode Island, circa 1790. A daughter of the "Merchant Prince" of Newport, Abigail was nineteen when she married Isaac Gomez of New York City, uniting two of the richest and most powerful Sephardic families in America. 1 15/16 inches high. Private collection.

faithful to England, while Benjamin went to fight for his new country. Early in the war, the British occupied Newport. There, in 1778, they were attacked by the Americans and their French allies. During this time, Mary kept a journal for her husband documenting in the most graphic terms the horrors of the battles and suffering she and her children were forced to endure. In 1881 her harrowing journal was published in *The Newport Historical Magazine.*

The Almy family were early and enthusiastic patrons of Malbone. According to family tradition, this portrait of the aging, but still spirited Mary (Gould) Almy (*Figure 11*) was painted when she was sixty-six. In 1957, when it was shown at the Museum of Fine Arts, Boston, in its exhibition *New England Miniatures, 1750–1850,* it was still in the possession of her descendants.[50] Miniatures by Malbone of Mrs. Almy's son, James Gould Almy, and his wife, Myra (Elliot) Almy, painted at the same time, are in the collection of the Metropolitan Museum of Art.

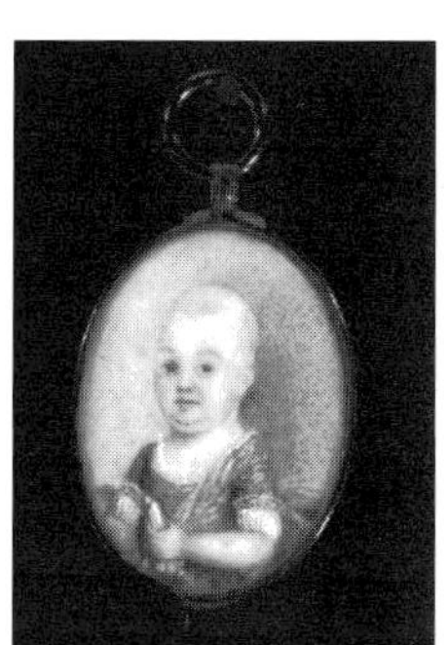

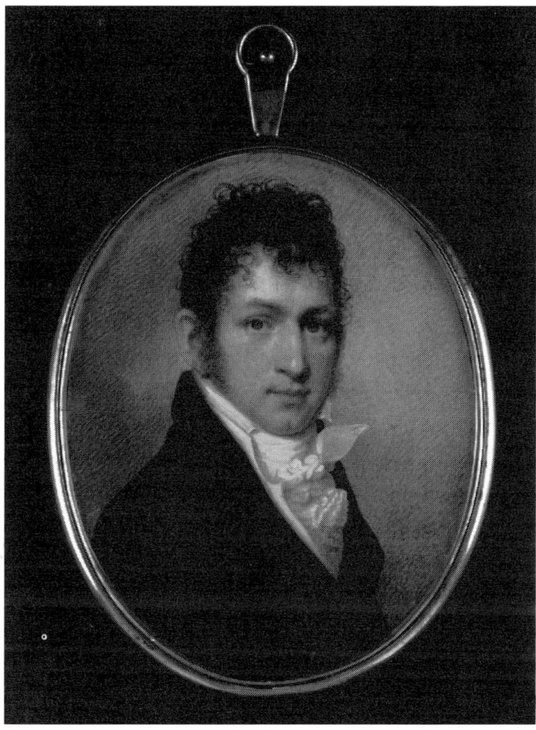

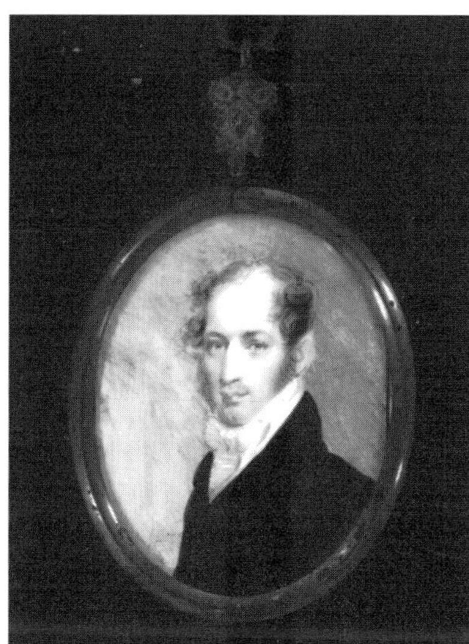

Figures 8, 9, 10 Joseph Ruggles (1781–1819). Three miniatures, at the three stages of life. Left: unknown American artist, Boston, circa 1781. 1⁵⁄₁₆ inches high. Center: by Robert Field (1769–1819), Boston, signed and dated 1808. 3⅛ inches high. Right: by Henry Williams (1787–1830), Boston, signed and dated 1819. 3⅛ inches high. Left and right: Collection of M. Donald Hayes. Center: Collection of George and Annette Klabin.

Without training, by the age of twenty-three, Malbone had become the most accomplished miniaturist in America. Malbone painted in New York, Philadelphia, and Charleston. He provided instruction to friends John Wesley Jarvis, Joseph Wood, Anson Dickinson, Charles Fraser, and William Dunlap, all of whom became exceptional artists. In 1806 Malbone contracted tuberculosis, dying the next year at the home of his first cousin Robert Mackay in Savannah at the age of twenty-nine.[51] It is impossible to exaggerate Malbone's contribution to American miniature painting.

Another self-trained artist, Thomas Young (1765–1821) was one of the few other Rhode Island miniaturists[52] until 1831, when Richard Morrell Staigg (1817–1881) arrived in Newport from England. Promoted by Boston artist Washington Allston, who had also encouraged Malbone, Staigg was given rudimentary instruction in the art of miniature painting by Gilbert Stuart's daughter Jane Stuart (1812–1888). Staigg, who eventually exhibited at the Paris Salon and the Royal Academy, had a distinguished clientele, including Edward Everett and Daniel Webster.[53]

In Connecticut, Isaac Sanford (fl. 1783–1822) advertised in the *Connecticut Courant* of 1794 that he did painting of all descriptions, clock and watch making, was a jeweler, engraver, and silversmith, made swords and buttons, set miniatures, and sold hardware, dry goods, and groceries.[54] William Wadsworth (fl. 1798–1810), who advertised from the house of Isaac Sheffield of New London, stated that in addition to miniatures he painted mourning pieces, made mourning rings, and also produced "paintings of Hair."[55]

Elkanah Tisdale Jr. (1768–1835) of Lebanon, Hartford, and Norwich, Connecticut, and New York City, son of Elkanah and Abigail (Tisdale) Tisdale of Lebanon,[56] was the first highly polished Connecticut miniaturist. Tisdale probably helped the self-taught Anson Dickinson (1779–1852),[57] who was called by

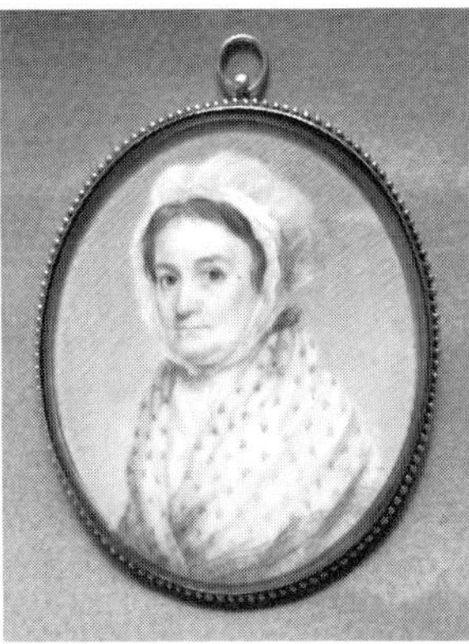

Figure 11 Mary (Gould) Almy (1735–1808). Miniature by Edward Greene Malbone (1777–1807), Newport, Rhode Island, circa 1797–1798. Mrs. Almy and her family were early patrons of the young artist. She was a spirited sixty-six years old when Malbone took this portrait. 2 9/16 inches high. Private collection.

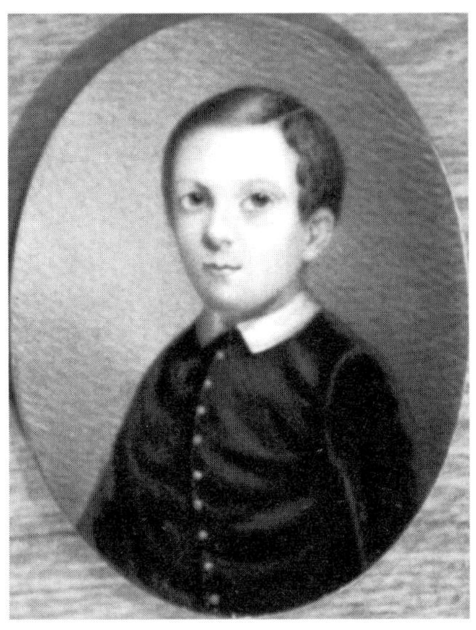

Figure 12 William Briggs Dennis (1845–1851). Miniature painted at the hour of his death by his uncle, Edgar Dennis (1823–1852), New London, Connecticut, 1851. 2 7/16 inches high. Collection of Dr. and Mrs. Louis Schwartz.

Dunlop in 1811 "the best miniature painter in New York."[58] Dickinson was almost continually on the road as an itinerant artist.[59] His portraits of the sturdy, prosperous citizens of Litchfield remain a substantial chronicle of Federal-era life in Connecticut. His literal depictions of the members of his immediate family (private collection) truly demonstrate the blunt reality of personal portraiture.

Dickinson was followed by another notably talented artist, Nathaniel Jocelyn (1796–1881) of New Haven, and the team of Thomas H. Parker (b. 1801), originally of Sag Harbor, Long Island, and Charles William Eldredge (1811–1883) of New London. Parker and Eldredge, who began as teacher and pupil, traveled and painted together in New York, Connecticut, and as far north as Vermont. One of the very few miniatures signed by both artists is of Henry Gallup Dennis (1813–1891) of New London (private collection), painted in 1834, the year Dennis married Abigail Mercer Holt (1814–1858). William Briggs Dennis, the fifth of their seven children, was born on 19 March 1845 and died 31 January 1851, aged almost six. His doleful posthumous miniature (*Figure 12*) was painted by his uncle, Edgar Dennis (1823–1852), who appears in standard references only as "Sixteen-year old artist at New London in August 1850," due to a mistaken age in the 1850 census, where he was enumerated as an artist, aged sixteen (he was actually twenty-six), in his father's household, a few doors from brother Henry G. Dennis.[60] The touching inscription on the miniature's backing paper reads "Wm Briggs Dennis/ . . . 1845/ . . . 1851/ 6 years/ Painted by Edgar Dennis 8 AM/ 1851."

By the middle of the nineteenth century, miniature painting in New England was one hundred years old. The style had changed from tiny, densely colored oil-on-copper gems by Smibert and Copley to the small, simple, and straightforward early ivory pieces of Ramage and Dunkerley, to the translucent treasures of Lovett, to the exquisite Federal pieces by Robert Field. As the 1830s approached, miniature painting became more substantial. The brilliant jewels of the colonial and Federal periods gave way to smaller versions of oil portraits. The oval format was abandoned for a much larger rectangle, and the luminous properties of ivory ignored in favor of a much darker palette, meant to emulate oils. These miniatures in new sizes and shapes decorated rooms on walls, tables, and pianos, becoming in the process public art of a sort and forsaking the intimacy of the early pieces.

Brilliantly talented miniaturist Washington Blanchard kept a studio in Boston from 1831 to 1843. Born in Cambridge, Massachusetts, in 1808, Washington was the son of Francis and Hannah Blanchard.[61] Though virtually forgotten today, Washington Blanchard was clearly a prominent artist in his own time. His impressive list of sitters included Henry Clay, Albert Gallatin, New York governor Silas Wright Jr., and vice president John C. Calhoun. In 1835 a Beverly, Massachusetts, native, four-year-old Henry Larcom Abbot, and his pet bird, a cedar waxwing,[62] sat together for Mr. Blanchard (*Figure 13*). His parents must have treasured the touching portrait. Henry grew up and in 1856 married Mary Susan Everett in Cambridge, Massachusetts. Over 100 years after his miniature was painted, Henry's daughter presented it to his grandson, passing it on to a fourth generation. Within the green leather miniature case was a handwritten note: "Henry Larcom Abbot, painted in 1835 by Mr. Blanchard of Boston. Given to me by my father, signature is tucked in behind the miniature. I now give it to his grandson, my dear Henry D. Abbot. January 1939, Elinor Everett Abbot."

The new style of these miniatures heralded their own final demise when the fashion for diminutive portraits became almost photo-realistic. As soon as photography became affordable, painted miniatures in turn reverted to their beginnings, becoming a luxury item for statesmen and aristocrats. A few artists, such as the exceptional Richard Morrell Staigg, continued working. Some, like the underrated Alvan Clark (1804–1887), turned to other professions. Still others, like Stock and Russell, followed the public fascination by taking up photography themselves.

Mourning Rings and Brooches

The warning "Memento Mori" (Remember that you must die) was a direct address from the grave and expressed what is probably the most popular epitaph in the English language. Various versions of this epitaph had appeared in Great Britain since the Middle Ages. Memento mori was already the dominant message in 1376, when Edward the Black Prince was buried in Canterbury Cathedral. Similar epitaphs, intended as a warning to all, can also be found throughout New England in a somewhat less elegant form:

Stop here my friends and cast an eye,
As you are now, so once was I.

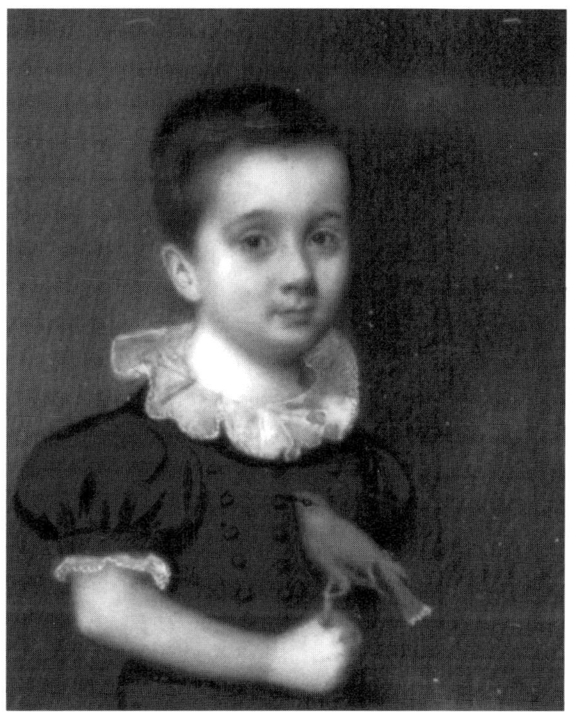

Figure 13 Henry Larcom Abbot (born 1831). Miniature by Washington Blanchard (1808–after 1849), Boston, Massachusetts, 1835. 3 1/8 inches high. The Metropolitan Museum of Art, Lois and Arthur Stainman Philanthropic Fund Gift, 2001.

As I am now, so you will be,
Prepare for Death and follow me.[63]

In reality, death was never very far from everyday life and therefore was treated accordingly. From the earliest settlements in New England until well into the nineteenth century, most people were in some stage of public mourning for most of their adult lives. In the late eighteenth and early nineteenth centuries, Reverend William Bentley of Salem recorded a death on virtually every page of his diary, as had Judge Samuel Sewall of Boston roughly a century before.

Mourning rings were as much a warning to those remaining behind as a remembrance of those gone before. The evolution of mourning jewelry followed approximately the same dates as miniatures. The wearing of mourning rings originated in the Middle Ages when the rings belonging to the deceased were distributed among, and worn by, relatives and friends.[64] Memento mori rings created for the occasion evolved from this custom in the sixteenth century with all the time-honored symbols of death apparent in their design: skulls, coffins, crossbones, shovels, and worms. Changes in style of the gold work followed the fashion of the day, but the tradition and content of mourning rings remained. Even the simplest contained the name of the departed and the date of the death. Many times they were enameled in black or white and often embellished with a reminder, a skull or skeleton set under a crystal, that death was ever imminent.

By the late seventeenth century, the custom of bequeathing money for rings became a mark of affluence and the required standard among wealthy English families.[65] The custom of gifts for honored mourners quickly crossed the Atlantic. Judge Samuel Sewall chronicled every internment he attended for over fifty years. Sewall, who received the customary gifts of gloves and scarves at funerals with regularity, first mentioned receiving a burying ring on 12 November 1687 at the funeral of "Mis[tress]" Elisa Saffin: ". . . Bearers: had Scarfs and Rings. Rings given at the House after coming from the Grave."[66] The custom flourished to the extent that in 1758 Dr. Samuel Buxton of Salem bequeathed his heirs a quart tankard filled with mourning rings.[67] In 1763 one of a series of laws was passed in Massachusetts in a futile attempt to check funereal extravagance: "Whereas, the giving of scarves, gloves, wine, rum and rings at funerals is a great and unnecessary expense and while practiced will be detrimental to the province, and tend to the impoverishing of many families. . . ." The act goes on to say that the penalty for such pretense at funerals would be fifty pounds.[68]

Again following the tradition brought from England, many early American mourning rings were marked. Since 1576 the Goldsmiths' Company in London had recognized only twenty-two carat as acceptable for wrought gold. For reasons now lost, mourning rings were the only item legally required to be marked—but not always. It was only in 1798 that eighteen-carat gold was recognized by the Goldsmiths' Company,[69] so a ring of less than twenty-two carats would not have been marked until that time. This change in regulations explains why, despite the law, so many English mourning rings are unmarked; without a mark, it is therefore almost impossible to state positively a ring's country of origin. Gold was scarce in colonial America, the only available source being coins such as the British sovereign or the Portuguese johannes[70] which were easily attainable in port cities. Though they were alloyed at the time of manufacture, the goldsmith refined them during the melting process, producing articles of twenty carats or higher.

From the late seventeenth century on through the colonial period, the greatest number of surviving American gold objects are mourning rings.[71] The earliest example known to have been made in New England was wrought by Jeremiah Dummer (1645–1718) of Boston for the funeral of James Lloyd. The inscription states: "Iames Lloyd. Obyt. 21. Augt 1693."[72] Only a year later Dummer's future brother-in-law, the Boston goldsmith John Coney, executed a simple gold ring decorated outside with an engraved death's head. The inside bears this inscription: "SC obt: 17: April: 94 AEt: 36." The ring carries the maker's mark "IC" within a rectangle. This ring is believed to have been made in memory of the goldsmith's wife, Sarah (Blackman/Blakeman) Coney,[73] who died on that day.[74]

Funeral customs were practiced in New England regardless of political persuasion. Richard Dana (1700–1772), an original member of the Sons of Liberty, was born into wealth in Cambridge, Massachusetts. After graduating from Harvard in 1718, he studied law in Marblehead and then practiced in Charlestown before settling in Boston and marrying Lydia, the sister of his colleague, Judge Edmund Trowbridge, in 1737. His son Francis Dana followed Richard's political lead, also joining the Sons of Liberty and serving with John Adams in London and Paris. Richard Dana, a staunch but prosperous patriot, had his portrait taken by John Singleton Copley about 1770. Only a few years later, "His death in Boston . . . was at the time regarded as a severe if not irreparable loss to the Colonial cause."[75] When Dana died in 1772, Nathaniel Hurd made an unadorned gold ring, engraved on the inside: "Richard Dana Esq. Ob 17 May 1772 AEt 72." The ring bears Hurd's maker's mark, "NH" within a rectangle.[76]

As always, ring styles followed closely the lead of England. By 1730, though still using the memento mori iconography of the Stuart period, the flamboyance of early Georgian rococo influenced even

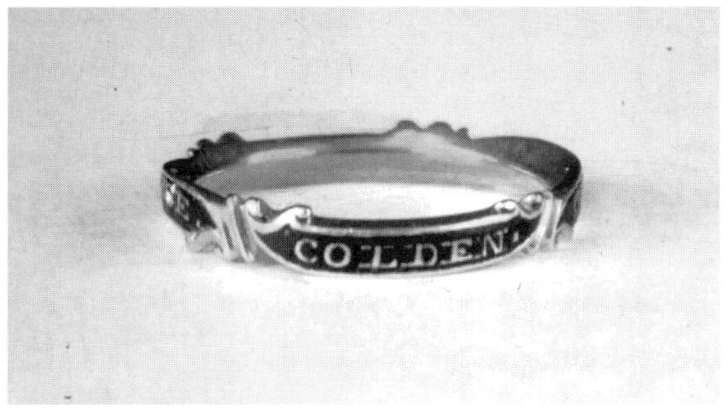

Figure 14 Gold and enamel mourning ring in memory of Alice Colden, wife of Cadwaller Colden (1688–1776), colonial Lieutenant-Governor of New York 1760–1775. The enamel on the ring reads: "Alice./Colden./ob: 17 Jany/1762./AE 72." Collection of Elle Shushan.

mourning customs. The fashion for funeral rings became a scroll band (*Figure 14*), many times with openwork and often set with stones. The cartouches on the outside were filled in with either black or white[77] enamel around the outside with the name of the deceased, the date of death, and the age at the time of death in gold around the ring. In keeping with the tradition of "Remember that you must die," the center stone was many times a crystal shaped like a coffin with a skeleton of paper resting beneath.

While many of the rings of simple gold bands adorned with death's heads and engraved on the inside bear New England makers' marks, most of the cast scroll rings bear no mark of any kind. It is probable that the majority of these rings were imported from England as components, then finished to order as required. Charles Dutens, jeweler, advertised in New York in 1751 that he had "just imported from London, by Capt. Richards . . . fine white and black for Mourning Rings, with Death Heads and Skeletons to put under. . . ."[78] This arrangement would enable him to supply his patrons with the kind of service Jeremiah Andrews, jeweler, advertised in 1774: "Mourning rings made in the newest Fashion, and with greatest Dispatch."[79]

Along with rings, mourning pendants and brooches became popular as the focus of Federal-period mourning turned to salvation after physical death. Along with the remembrance of the deceased came sepia paintings on ivory of widows in classical gowns weeping over tombs topped by urns or broken columns, all

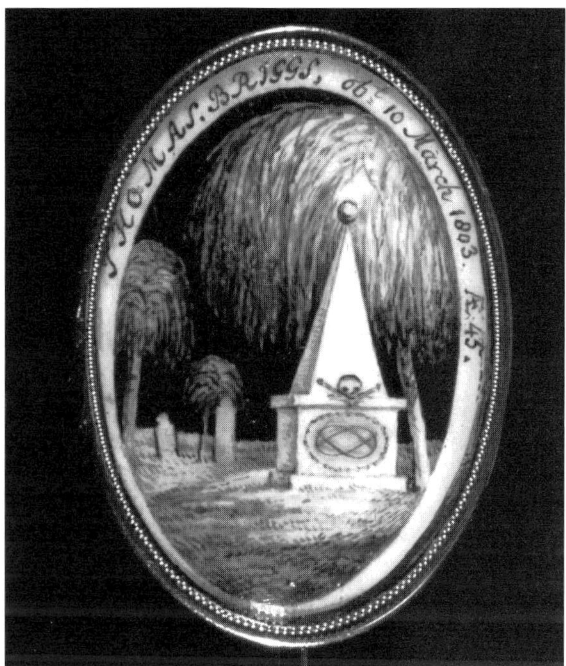

Figure 15 Gold mourning brooch in memory of rope maker Thomas Briggs. Salem, Massachusetts, circa 1803. $2\frac{1}{8}$ inches high. Collection of Betty Ring.

set in a willow or cypress grove with sleeping lambs under the trees. Heavy with the new symbolism of death, these scenes were often painted with a pigment made from the hair of the deceased. The threat "Remember that you must die" was replaced with "Forgive the wish that would have kept thee here."

Many of the finest miniaturists of Federal America painted mourning allegories in addition to portraits. John Ramage was one of the first in America to paint these sepia pictures. His memorial to John Forman in 1789 depicts a widow in classical dress sitting under a tree, weeping over a tomb with the inscription "Sacred will I keep thy dear remains."[80] Flying toward heaven is a cherubic soul carrying the motto "To Bliss." Ramage's sample cards of mourning scenes and hair work are now in the New-York Historical Society.

Samuel Folwell (ca. 1765/68–1813), best known for his engaging faces painted on silk-work pictures, also painted miniatures, worked in hair, and painted beautiful, brightly colored mourning scenes; he was active as far north as New Hampshire. A great many other miniaturists advertised fancy pieces and mourning scenes. But as such items were almost never signed, the majority are virtually impossible to attribute.

Archibald Robertson (1765–1835) of Aberdeen, Scotland, arrived in America in 1791. He and his brother Alexander founded the Columbian Academy of Painting in New York City. There the brothers taught the usual painting and drawing, but also the making of hair devices and silk painting. Robertson's miniature of Timothy Treadwell Smith (collection of Betty Ring) has a mourning scene also by Robertson on the reverse. Painted in sepia tones, with a combination of watercolor and dissolved hair, it depicts a woman weeping on a tomb topped with a broken column. The ubiquitous weeping willow stands in the background. Around the border, where an English memorial would have had enamel, is a rim of black paint with white writing: "Timothy Tredwell Smith OB^{t} 24th October 1803 AE. 55 years 9 M^{o} & 7 days."[81]

As accomplished as it was, Timothy Treadwell Smith's memorial was not of the standard in painting or execution that was being produced in England. Many families of substance, who required the best money could buy, still ordered the finest from London. Joseph Barrell of Charlestown, Massachusetts, ordered with regularity from Stephen Twycross of London, giving specific instructions on both the scenes that should be painted and the jewelry into which they should be set.[82] One of the specially designed brooches in memory of Barrell's sister-in-law was made for his young son, Charles.[83] In this case the brooch was probably meant more as a relic than a piece of jewelry.

After the 1798 English act allowing gold wares to be manufactured at a lower standard,[84] mourning rings became affordable and available to everyone. The style changed as well, from thin "D" shaped bands to "cigar" bands. America, of course, followed suit. Many times the enamel on the exterior, applied at the time of manufacture, said "In Memoriam." When the ring was purchased, the name and dates of the deceased were then engraved in the interior. This accounts for the disparity of sometimes decades between the date stamp and the date of death. Other rings contained smaller versions of the scenes on ivory set in brooches and pendants.

As remembrance of the dead was paramount in the ritual of mourning, relics were required even if homemade. Lucretia Carew (1778–1862) of Norwich, Connecticut, was a daughter of Daniel and Lucy (Perkins) Carew. Mrs. Lucy Carew kept a school offering instruction in needlework, drawing, and painting.[85] In 1800 Lucretia worked a silk memorial to her sister, Mrs. Lucy Tillinghast, with the painted faces of Lucretia, her parents, and brother attributed to John Brewster (1766–after 1846) (the Museums at Stony Brook, New York). At the same time, Lucretia probably created a wearable emblem of her grief, a naïve mourning locket (collection of Betty Ring). The front, painted in watercolor on ivory, depicts a kneeling woman in classical dress pointing toward an urn-topped tomb. The background has both a weeping willow and a cypress grove. This scene, which fits quite tightly in its gilt-metal locket case, was possibly a stock item sold by rural jewelers, with an empty back, to be personalized as needed. The reverse of this piece is made of cut gilt paper, laid over a field of light brown hair. The center is an urn with a band around the circumference with the inscription: "Memory of Mrs. Lucy Tillinghurst died at Providence Aug. 27 1800."

Federal-era mourning customs required strict conformity to ritual. Widows and close family members wore black for a year. Mirrors were draped in black crepe. Because any kind of shine was prohibited, jewelry, with the exception of pearls, black garnets, jet, and mourning commemoratives, was forbidden. Mourning brooches and lockets, with their ivory scenes on one side and the woven hair of the deceased on the other, took on the significance of a reliquary.

A most unusual mourning brooch was created for Thomas Briggs who was born in Little Compton, Rhode Island, in 1758 and died in 1803 (*Figure 15*). A rope maker by profession, Briggs moved to Salem, Massachusetts, where he married Anna Vincent. Their only child, Anna Briggs, married Jabez Baldwin, a jeweler with the largest stock in Salem. When Thomas Briggs died, he was buried in his private cemetery.[86] The gold brooch was a vertical oval with beaded bezel containing a mourning scene painted on ivory. Written in ornate script letters on the top edge of the ivory is "Thomas Briggs, ob^{t} 10 March 1803 AE 45." The picture shows a cemetery scene with several willows. The large tomb in the foreground bears a death's head on the front over a piece of Briggs's hair, tied in a rope knot in reference to his profession. It can be assumed that this unique reliquary was created by Briggs's soon-to-be son-in-law, jeweler Jabez Baldwin.

But even with the dawn of enlightened mourning, old habits continued to remain. The death from smallpox of Dudley Pettibone Jr. (1771–1793),[87] of Simsbury, Connecticut, inspired a most unusual mourning pendant, made of silver. On one side is a modern mourning scene with cherubs; the Angel Gabriel leads the soul to Heaven, surrounded by the motto: "O Death Where Is Thy Sting? O Grave Where is Thy Victory?" The other side, however, bears all the iconography of a century earlier: wheat sheaths, an hourglass, a death's head, and, at the bottom "Memento Mori," and the question, ever potent, ever ominous: "Behold He Taketh Away. Who Can Hinder Him? Who Can Say? What Doest Thou?"

NOTES

[1]George Francis Dow, *The Arts and Crafts of New England, 1704–1775* (Topsfield, Mass.: Wayside Press, 1927), p. 5.
[2]Ibid., p. 61.
[3]Richard Walker, *Miniatures: 300 Years of the English Miniature Illustrated from the Collections of the National Portrait Gallery* (London: National Portrait Gallery Publications, 1998), p. 7.
[4]For a complete history of the early miniature in England, see John Murdoch et al., *The English Miniature* (New Haven: Yale University Press, 1981).
[5]Roy Strong, *Artists of the Tudor Court: The Portrait Miniature Rediscovered, 1520–1620* (London: Victoria and Albert Museum, 1983), p. 9.
[6]Ibid., p. 12.
[7]Patrick J. Noon, *English Portrait Drawings and Miniatures* (New Haven: Yale Center for British Art, 1979), p. viii.
[8]Katherine Coombs, *The Portrait Miniature in England* (London: Victoria and Albert Publications, 1998), p. 26, fig. 7.
[9]Strong, *Artists of the Tudor Court,* p. 64, plate 61.
[10]Another portrait of circa 1560, in Italy, attributed to Alessandro Allori, depicts Francesco I de Medici holding a portrait miniature of his sister, who was about to marry. The importance of the private relationship between the sitter in the painting and the sitter in the miniature is pointed out by Karen Schaffers-Bodenhausen and Marieke Tiethoff-Spliethoff in *The Portrait Miniatures in the Collection of the House of Orange-Nassau* (The Hague: Waanders Publishers, 1993), pp. 14–15, plate 6.
[11]Carol Aiken, "The Emergence of the Portrait Miniature in New England," *Painting and Portrait Making in the American Northeast: 1994 Annual Proceedings of the Dublin Seminar for New England Folklife* (Boston: Boston University Scholarly Publications, 1995), pp. 37–39, fig. 1.
[12]*Appleton's Cyclopaedia of American Biography,* ed. James G. Wilson and John Fiske, 6 vols. (New York: D. Appleton and Company, 1887–1891): 1:752–53; Robert Charles Anderson, *The Great Migration Begins: Immigrants to New England, 1620–1633* (Boston: New England Historic Genealogical Society, 1995), 1:484–87.
[13]*Appleton's Cyclopaedia,* 4:251–52.
[14]Martha Gandy Fales, *Jewelry in America: 1600–1900* (Woodbridge, Suffolk, England: Antique Collectors Club, 1988), p. 21, color plate 7.
[15]Ibid., "John Smibert," pp. 122–23.
[16]For an excellent discussion of Copley's miniatures, see Erica E. Hirshler, "Copley in Miniature," in Carrie Rebora [Barratt] et al., *Copley in America* (New York: Metropolitan Museum of Art, 1995), pp. 117–24.
[17]Robin Jaffee Frank, *Love and Loss: American Portrait and Mourning Miniatures* (New Haven: Yale University Press, 2000), p. 61.
[18]Ibid.
[19]Ibid.
[20]Theresa Fairbanks, "Gold Discovered: John Singleton Copley's Portrait Miniatures on Copper," *Yale University Art Gallery Bulletin 1999,* p. 77.
[21]Ibid., p. 75.
[22]For a discussion of the influences of Ramage's gold casework techniques, see Elle Shushan, "The Art of High Living: Miniature Goldwork by John Ramage," *The Catalogue of Antiques and Fine Art* (Winter 2001): 170–71.
[23]Frank H. Goodyear Jr., *American Paintings in the Rhode Island Historical Society* (Providence: Rhode Island Historical Society, 1974), p. 24.
[24]Davida Tenenbaum Deutsch, "John Johnston: An Artist for the Needleworker," *Magazine Antiques* 152, no. 5 (November 1997). Johnston was a portrait painter living in Water Street, Boston, according to the earliest Boston directory. Ann Smith Lainhart, ed., *First Boston City Directory (1789), Including Extensive Annotations by John Haven Dexter (1791–1876)* (Boston: New England Historic Genealogical Society, 1989), p. 62.
[25]Quoted by Barbara Neville Parker, "Miniature Painting in New England," *New England Miniatures, 1750–1850* (Boston: Museum of Fine Arts, 1957), p. 13.
[26]William Bright Jones, "The Portraits of Richard and William Jennys and the Story of Their Wayfaring Lives," *Painting and Portrait Making in the American Northeast: 1994 Annual Proceedings of the Dublin Seminar for New England Folklife* (Boston: Boston University Scholarly Publications, 1995), p. 71.
[27]Susan Strickler, *American Portrait Miniatures: The Worcester Art Museum Collection* (Worcester, Mass.: Worcester Art Museum, 1989), p. 117.
[28]Frank, *Love and Loss,* p. 77.
[29]Ibid., p. 79.
[30]Ibid., p. 81.

[31]George C. Groce and David H. Wallace, *The New-York Historical Society's Dictionary of Artists in America, 1564–1860* (New Haven and London: Yale University Press, 1957), pp. 194, 303–4.

[32]Donald Lines Jacobus, *Families of Ancient New Haven,* 3 vols. (Baltimore: Genealogical Publishing Company, 1972), 3:1596.

[33]Metropolitan Museum of Art, New York.

[34]Rev. Joshua Wyman Wellman, D.D., *Descendants of Thomas Wellman of Lynn, Massachusetts* (Boston: Arthur Holbrook Wellman, 1918), pp. 168–73; *Massachusetts Soldiers and Sailors of the Revolutionary War . . . ,* 17 vols. (Boston: Wright and Potter, State Printers, 1892–1908), 16: 831, 853. For Captain Wellman's wife, Mercy (Mascoll) Stevens, see Sidney Perley, *The History of Salem, Massachusetts,* 3 vols. (Salem, Mass.: Sidney Perley, 1924–28), 2:179n.

[35]*Portraits of Shipmasters and Merchants in the Peabody Museum of Salem* (Salem: Peabody Museum, 1939), pp. 139–40.

[36]Peabody Essex Museum, Salem, Mass.

[37]Ibid.

[38]Wellman, *Descendants of Thomas Wellman,* pp. 140, 141.

[39]*The Hovey Book: Describing the English Ancestry and American Descendants of Daniel Hovey of Ipswich, Massachusetts* (Haverhill, Mass.: Lewis R. Hovey, 1913), pp. 178–79.

[40]Strickler, *American Portrait Miniatures,* p. 92.

[41]Anne A. Verplanck, "Benjamin Trott: Miniature Painter" (master's thesis, College of William and Mary, 1990), p.14.

[42]Ibid., p. 15.

[43]Richard Brilliant, *Facing the New World: Jewish Portraits in Colonial and Federal America* (New York: Jewish Museum under the auspices of the Jewish Theological Seminary of America, 1997), p. 51.

[44]Ibid.

[45]Ibid., p. 13

[46]The author is grateful to D. Brenton Simons, for his assistance on "Miss Lopez." See also Malcolm Stern, *First American Jewish Families: 600 Genealogies 1654–1988* (Baltimore: Ottenheimer Publishers, Inc., 1991), pp. 85, 175.

[47]Dale T. Johnson, *American Portrait Miniatures in the Manney Collection* (New York: Metropolitan Museum of Art, 1990), p. 117.

[48]Richard LeBaron Bowen, "Godfrey Malbone's Armorial Silver," *Rhode Island History* 9 (1950): 37–51, 84–94, reprinted in *Genealogies of Rhode Island Families from Rhode Island Periodicals,* 2 vols. (Baltimore: Genealogical Publishing Company, 1983, hereafter cited as *RIFP*), 2: 834–59, 857–58.

[49]Johnson, *American Portrait Miniatures,* p. 148.

[50]Parker, *New England Miniatures,* catalogue entry 6.

[51]William Dunlap, *A History of the Rise and Progress of the Arts of Design in the United States,* 2 vols. (1834; reprint, New York: Dover Publications, 1969), 2:14–21; *RIFP,* 2:857.

[52]Goodyear, *American Paintings,* p. 29.

[53]Johnson, *American Portrait Miniatures,* p. 204.

[54]Philip H. Dunbar, "Portrait Miniatures on Ivory, 1750–1850. From the Collection of the Connecticut Historical Society," *Connecticut Historical Society Bulletin* 29, no. 2 (1964): 100. Isaac Sanford may have been the person of this name born at New Haven, Conn., 22 March 1763, son of Moses and Mary (Robinson) Sanford, but who is not carried forward in Carlton E. Sanford, *Thomas Sanford, The Emigrant to New England: Ancestry, Life, and Descendants, 1632–4,* 2 vols. (Rutland, Vt.: Tuttle Company, 1911), 1:129.

[55]Dunbar, "Portrait Miniatures," p. 99.

[56]Rosa D. Tisdale, *Meet the Tisdales: Descendants of John Tisdale of Taunton, Massachusetts, 1634–1980* (Baltimore: Gateway Press, 1981), pp. 403–4.

[57]Mona Leithiser Dearborn, *Anson Dickinson: The Celebrated Miniature Painter, 1779–1852* (Hartford: Connecticut Historical Society, 1983), p. 6; see also Elinor V. Smith, *Descendants of Nathaniel Dickinson* (n.p.: Dickinson Family Association, 1978), p. 329.

[58]Dunlap, *Arts of Design,* 2:217.

[59]Dearborn, *Anson Dickinson,* p. 11.

[60]Groce and Wallace, *Dictionary of Artists in America,* p. 17; 1850 U.S. Census, New London County, Conn., City of New London, roll no. 49, p. 153/305, nos. 781–1173 (lines 9–16), nos. 784–1178 (lines 30–37). Children of a head of household were generally listed in descending order of age; Edgar, his name clearly written as "16, Artist," appears on line 33, between sisters Sarah A., 38, and Frances, 18. Perhaps the error arose when the enumerator made his fair copy. Edgar's 1823 birth (to Henry and Sarah [Briggs] Dennis) and 1852 death appear in New London vital records and the *New London Weekly Chronicle* (issue of 15 April 1852), p. 29, respectively. For W. B. Dennis's death, see *New London Weekly Chronicle* (issue of 5 February 1851), p. 19.

[61]Vital Records of Cambridge, Mass., For the Year 1850, vol. one: Births (Boston: n.p., 1914), p. 67.

[62]The author wishes to express her thanks to H. Barbara Weinberg, Alice Pratt Brown Curator of American Paintings and Sculpture at the Metropolitan Museum of Art, for the identification of the species of bird.

[63]E. R. Shushan, *Grave Matters* (New York: Ballantine Books, 1990), p. viii.

[64]Harold Newman, *An Illustrated Dictionary of Jewelry* (London: Thames and Hudson, 1981), p. 208.

[65]Samuel Pepys bequeathed one hundred twenty-eight rings for distribution at his funeral in 1703. Nigel Llewellyn, *The Art of Death: Visual Culture in the English Death Ritual, c. 1500–c. 1800* (London: Reaktion Books, published in association with the Victoria and Albert Museum, 1991), p. 86.

[66]Samuel Sewall, *The Diary of Samuel Sewall, 1674–1729,* 2 vols., ed. M. Halsey Thomas (New York: Farrar, Straus and Giroux, 1973), 1:153.

[67]Fales, *Jewelry in America,* p. 24.

[68]*Temporary Laws and Acts of Massachusetts* (Boston, 1763), pp. 15–16.

[69]Anthony B. L. Dove, "Some Observations on Gold and Its Hallmarks," *Antique Collecting* (September 1986).

[70]Peter J. Bohan, "American Gold, 1700–1860," monograph based on a loan exhibition, Yale University Art Gallery, 2 April–28 June 1963, p. 5.

[71]Ibid., p. 18.

[72]Fales, *Jewelry in America,* p. 23.

[73]Bohan, "American Gold," pp. 41–42.

[74]See Thomas Hills, *The Parentage and English Progenitors of Nathaniel Coney of Boston, Massachusetts* (Boston: David Clapp, 1906), p. 4; Donald Lines Jacobus, Blackman [note], *The American Genealogist* 10 (1933–1934): 260–61; and Julie Helen Otto, "Some Account of the Descendants of the Reverend Adam Blackman of Stratford, Connecticut (1990–present)," at the New England Historic Genealogical Society. Mrs. Sarah Coney (d. 1694) was a first cousin of the sisters Ann (Atwater) Dummer and Mary (Atwater) Clark, John Coney's subsequent wife.

[75]Conversation with Carrie Rebora Barratt, Metropolitan Museum of Art, regarding Richard Dana, whose portrait by John Singleton Copley is on loan to the museum.

[76]Elizabeth Ellery Dana, *The Dana Family in America* (Cambridge, Mass.: Wright and Potter, 1956), pp. 473–74, 486.

[77]White enamel purportedly signified a child or an adult who died chaste. While a large number of white enamel rings are for children or young women, this symbolism has never been proven conclusively.

[78]Dow, *The Arts and Crafts of New England*, pp. 69–70.

[79]Ibid., p. 64.

[80]John Hill Morgan, *A Sketch of the Life of John Ramage, Miniature Painter* (New York: New-York Historical Society, 1930), facing p. 40.

[81]That this sophisticated locket made in New York in 1803 has paint on paint where one would expect enamel work adds support to the theory that most of the finest of the enamel work was imported from England during colonial and early Federal times.

[82]Martha Gandy Fales, "Federal Bostonians and their London Jeweler, Stephen Twycross," *Magazine Antiques* 131, no. 3 (March 1987).

[83]Ibid.

[84]Dow, *The Arts and Crafts of New England*, p. 1.

[85]Betty Ring, *Girlhood Embroidery: American Samplers and Pictorial Needlework, 1650–1850*, 2 vols. (New York: Alfred A. Knopf, 1993), 1: fig. 24.

[86]Benjamin F. Browne, "Youthful Recollections of Salem," *Essex Institute Historical Collections* 49, no. 4 (October 1913).

[87]I. Fayette Pettibone, *Genealogy of the Pettibone Family* (Chicago: Brown, Pettibone and Kelly, 1885), p. 18.

SECTION IV

Representations of Passage

One Moment in Time: The Family Portrait Mourning Piece, a Unique American Form

Betty Ring

MARTHA WILLIAMS was born in Stonington, Connecticut, on 27 July 1791.[1] Probably when she was seventeen in the summer of 1808, she was sent to the Misses Patten's school in Hartford where she worked a remarkable mourning piece that recorded her family for generations to come (*Figure 1*).[2] Martha's majestic monument is dedicated to her four grandparents who died between 1784 and 1808. Grouped around it are her parents and eleven siblings, from twenty-six-year-old Isaac to two-year-old Emily, while a garland cascades over Martha's shoulder and into the baby's hands.[3]

Martha did this during the final phase of the so-called schoolgirl needlework era that arose with the Renaissance and ended with the advent of the industrial revolution. Needlework was then an essential subject in every girl's formal education, and the products of this instruction survive in abundance from the two centuries between 1640 and 1840. Silk-on-silk embroidery in the neoclassical taste was the last important form to develop before the focus on "accomplishments" diminished; and while subjects from classical literature were widely favored, such as scenes depicting "The Parting of Hector and Andromache," they were soon outnumbered by the urns, willows, and weepers appropriate to mourning embroideries. These emerged first in Europe, and English examples were usually dedicated to heroic, historic, or fictitious characters such as Lord Nelson, Shakespeare, or Charlotte mourning Werther. This fashion did not flower in America until 1800, however, and the impetus appears to have been the death of George Washington.[4] Yet lustrous memorials to Washington had scarcely appeared when American schoolmistresses began preparing patterns for dedication to deceased family members of their students, and these personal memorials soon vastly outnumbered American embroideries commemorating heroes.

The majority of American mourning pieces picture a monument with one female figure who was usually intended to represent the needleworker. Much more exceptional are memorials that portray the entire bereaved family, and the most remarkable aspect of these records is the necessary effort that was required of the schoolmistress in gathering correct information so that her pattern would accurately convey how the family related in age to each other when the death occurred. Obviously these projects were the product of the teacher's taste and talent. In most cases, only the embroidery was performed by the student,[5] while characteristic patterns, painting, and a consistent style in stitchery have made work from various schools discernable.

Although occasional images of identifiable members of large families are known on work from Pennsylvania,[6] New York,[7] Massachusetts,[8] New Hampshire,[9] and Maine,[10] Connecticut teachers are particularly noted for this custom.[11] At present, the best known many-peopled mourning pieces survive from the rival academies kept in Hartford by the Misses Patten and Mrs. Lydia Royse, and in both cases their embroidered memorials were

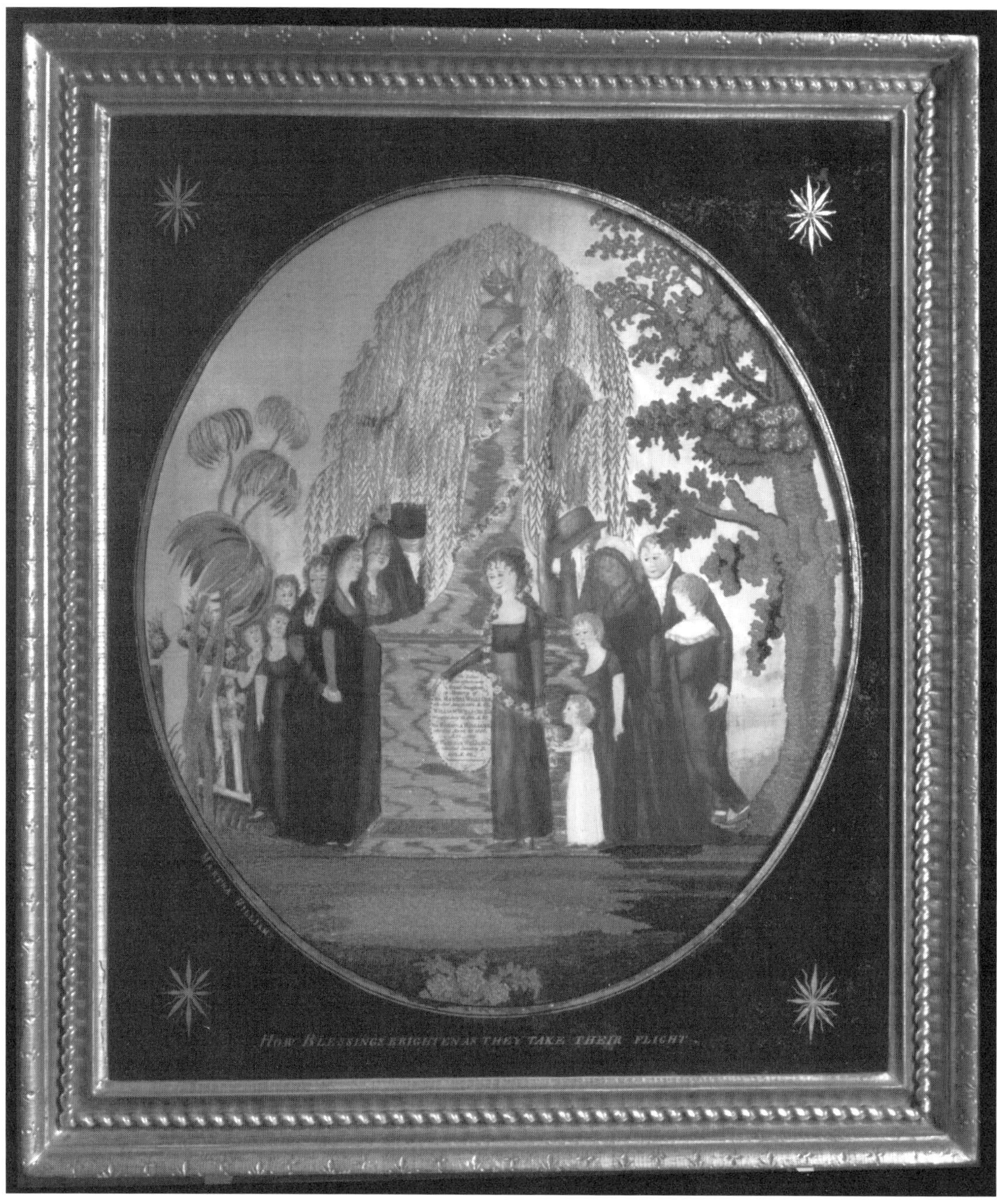

Figure 1 Mourning piece inscribed on the glass at left beside the oval "MARTHA WILLIAMS." And beneath the oval: "HOW BLESSINGS BRIGHTEN AS THEY TAKE THEIR FLIGHT." Inscribed in ink on the plinth: "The Tribute/ of an affectionate/ Grand-Daughter,/ in Memory of/ Mrs. MARTHA WILLIAMS,/ who died June 16, 1784 AE. 67. WILLIAM WILLIAMS, Esq/ who died July 27, 1801, AE. 86/ Mrs. REBECCA WILLIAMS,/ who died March 20, 1806,/AE, 82. and/ Mr. WAREHAM WILLIAMS,/ who died January 31, 1808./ AE, 82." Silk, chenille, watercolor, and ink on silk; oval 21¾ × 19 inches; overall within the original frame 29¾ × 25¾ inches. The painted figures appear to represent, at right, the maker's parents, Isaac (1758–1844) and Phebe Williams (1761–1822) of Stonington, Connecticut, with their children Cyrus (1783–1863), John (1793–1872), Martha (1791–1812), Eunice (b. 1797), and Emily (b. 1805); on the left, Isaac (b. 1781), Lucy (1785–1862), Sally (1787–1875), Rebecca (b. 1789), Jerusha (b. 1795), Phebe (b. 1799), and Fanny (1801–1869). Private collection.

worked during the first decade of the nineteenth century.[12] As found in the Williams memorial (see *Figure 1*), the mourners on the Patten pieces are consistently painted with the occasional exception of an appliquéd hat or shawl. The drooping foliage of their willow trees usually have some visible branches; often they include rounded palm trees or tilted conifers, and a leafy shrub may nestle in the chenille-worked foreground. Who painted the mourners, often with sheer veils, remains unknown.

There is convincing evidence that schoolmistress Lydia Royse was an artist who drew the patterns and painted the figures and backgrounds on her students' needlework. Typical of her compositions is the memorial to Julia and Dolly Cowles (*Figure 2*) where the kneeling figure is believed to represent

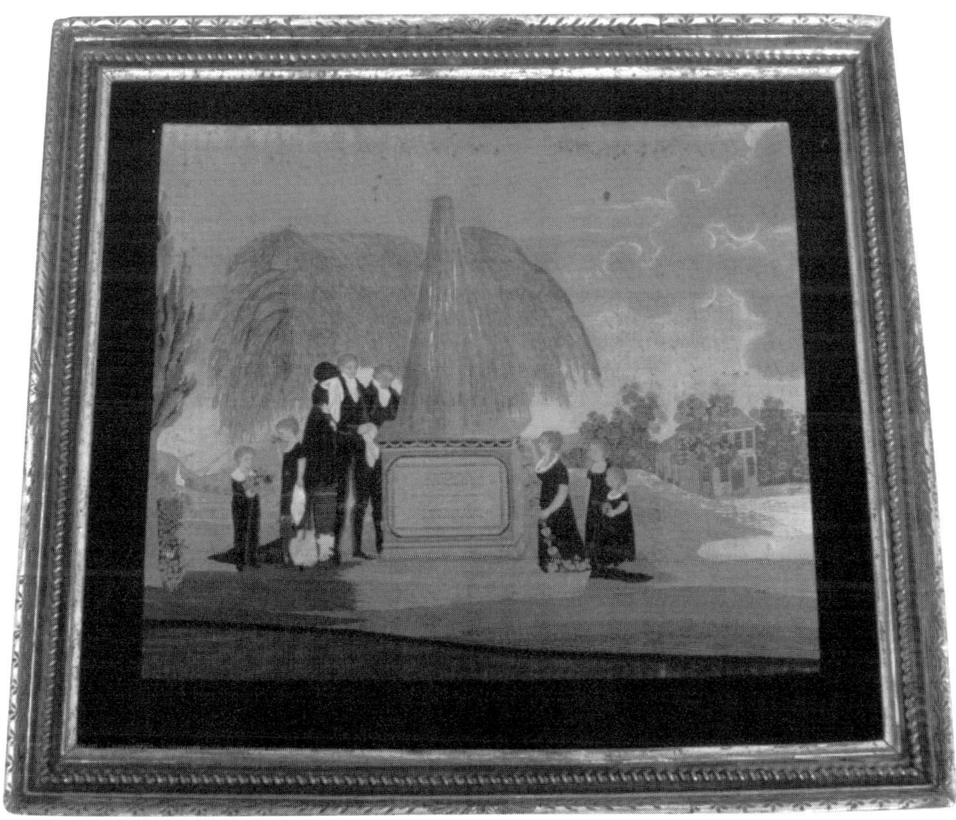

Figure 2 Mourning piece, circa 1805. Attributed to Jeanette Cowles (1792–1809), the third daughter of Zenas Cowles (1762–1835) and Mary Lewis Cowles (1766–1836) of Farmington, Connecticut, and dedicated to her older sisters. Inscribed on the plinth: "In Memory of Julia Cowles, Ob. May 15th, 1803, AEt 18 and Dolly Cowles, Ob. September 25th, 1803, AEt 16. So swiftly fly the raptures of our prime, swept by the tempest of destroying time." Silk, chenille, watercolor, and ink on silk with appliquéd silk and velvet; 22⅛ × 26 inches within a black velvet mat that may be a replacement for an earlier glass with painted decoration; overall within the original frame 27 × 30¾ inches. Beside the monument at left are Jeanette's parents with her brother Edward (1789–1864), sister Emily (1796–1876), and brother Lewis (1800–1825). White spots reflect the loss of appliquéd silk from the mother's and Emily's dresses. On the right is Jeanette kneeling beside the monument with sister Elizabeth (1798–1823) and the second Julia (1803–1859). Julia (1785–1803), the eldest daughter, attended Sarah Pierce's school in Litchfield, Connecticut, in 1797 and 1798. See *The Diaries of Julia Cowles* (New Haven: Yale University Press, 1931) where Jeanette's embroidery is the frontispiece. At the time of her death, Julia was engaged to John Treadwell of Farmington. His sister Mary (b. 1786) worked a very similar memorial dedicated to their elder sister (illustrated in Ring, *Girlhood Embroidery*, fig. 251). Private collection.

their sister Jeanette, the needleworker. The women's garments are delicately appliquéd silk while the men's and boys' suits are embroidered. Possibly Jeanette Cowles attended the school kept by Lydia Royse because of long-standing ties between the Bull and Cowles families. Jeanette Cowles and Lydia Bull Royse were descended, respectively, from the brothers Thomas Bull (1646–1708) and Joseph Bull (d. 1712), sons of Thomas Bull (1605–1684), the founder of the Bull family in Hartford.[13]

Like her older sisters, Jeanette Cowles died in her teens, and her embroidery still hangs in the house that received it when she returned from boarding school. Her father, Zenas Cowles, was a prominent farmer and merchant of Farmington; and upon his marriage in 1785, he moved into Old Gate, the Palladian mansion provided by his father Solomon Cowles.[14] Zenas and Mary (Lewis) Cowles had ten children between 1785 and 1809, and they were survived by three sons and two daughters, but only Emily (1796–1876) and Thomas (1809–1884) had descendants. The mansion and the mourning piece descended in the male line to the present owners.

It has been impossible to determine the school that first introduced this very personal style of mourning piece in Hartford. There was, in fact, another distinctive group produced in or near Hartford, and both their male and female mourners have appliquéd garments. At least three of these have been published.[15]

Considering the expense of tuition and boarding, in addition to costly materials, charges for painting, and extravagant frames, these ambitious compositions were clearly regarded as important documents of heirloom quality, and presumably they were also intended to impress the student with the importance of recording family history. Despite the extreme delicacy of work on silk, and the fragility of their thin decorative glass, the excellent condition of many of these memorials attests to their cherished existence for nearly two centuries.

NOTES

[1]The author is indebted to William N. Hosley Jr., director, Antiquarian and Landmarks Society, Hartford, Conn., for the opportunity of including the Cowles memorial.

[2]Connecticut Vital Records, Stonington: Births, Marriages, Deaths, 1658–1854 (Barbour Collection, Connecticut State Library, 1918), p. 285.

[3]Martha's grandfathers, William Williams (1716–1801) and Wareham Williams (1727–1808) were first cousins. Her father, Isaac Williams (1758–1844), son of William, married Phebe Williams (1761–1822), daughter of Wareham. They had three sons, and Martha was fourth among their nine daughters. Their twelve children all lived to adulthood, and all married except Fanny (1801–1869), the eleventh child. Martha was the first to die. She married her first cousin, Henry Chesebrough (1784–1869) on 27 January 1812 and died 19 March 1812, aged twenty. On 18 July 1813, Henry married Martha's elder sister, Sally Potter Williams (1787–1875), and their five children were born in Stonington. In 1834 Henry Chesebrough moved to Onondaga, N.Y., and finally settled in Wisconsin in 1844. His eldest daughter, Martha Williams Chesebrough (b. 1815) was married to Gilbert A. Woods (b. 1812), at Fleming, N.Y., in 1837. Evidently Martha Williams's mourning piece descended with the heirs of her namesake, and it hung undisturbed in Woodlawn, the Woods homestead near Pulaski, N.Y., until the contents were sold on 7 September 1996. See Richard Anson Wheeler, *History of the Town of Stonington, County of New London, Connecticut* (Mystic, Conn.: Lawrence Verry, 1900), pp. 665–70, 673. See also Anna Chesebrough Wildey, *Genealogy of the Descendants of William Chesebrough of Boston, [and] Rehoboth, Massachusetts* (New York: T. A. Wright, 1903), pp. 498–99.

[4]For numerous memorials dedicated to Washington, see *Magazine Antiques* 119, no. 2 (February 1981): 402–19.

[5]In this regard, on 20 January 1806, an enlightening note was written by Miss Ruth Patten to Providence student Susan Jenckes Winsor concerning "the detention of your picture" and explaining that "Miss Pomeroy has completed the needlework elegantly—the frame is done and waits only for Schipper's arrival." (Manuscripts, Connecticut Historical Society). This was Gerritt Schipper, ornamental artist, who evidently drew the pattern and would normally return to add painting after the embroidery was completed. Miss Pomeroy's task was probably to remove the picture from a working frame and mount it on a stretcher for framing. This unpublished and formerly unlocated needlework picture, described as "Liberty" in Susan Winsor's will, has recently emerged.

[6]Samuel Folwell (1764–1813), an ornamental artist of Philadelphia, drew patterns for countless Washington memorials and occasionally decorative pieces depicting entire families, but very few personal memorials. For his Goodman family mourning piece with five figures, now at the Metropolitan Museum, see Georgiana Brown Harbeson, *American Needlework* (New York: Coward-McCann, 1938), opp. p. 82.

[7]A New York memorial picturing nine members of the Watkins family is illustrated in Anita Schorsch, *Mourning Becomes America* (Clinton, N.J.: Main Street Press, 1976), plate 7/136.

[8]Examples from Abby Wright's school in South Hadley, Mass., are illustrated in *Magazine Antiques* 130, no. 3 (September 1986): 486, plates 5 and 6.

[9]For a Jaffrey, N.H., memorial of 1829 with ten figures, see Betty Ring, *Girlhood Embroidery: American Samplers and Pictorial Needlework, 1650–1850* (New York: Alfred A. Knopf, 1993), p. 247.

[10]Portland, Maine, memorials appear in *Magazine Antiques* 134, no. 3 (September 1988): 518–19, plates 9 and 10.

[11]One of the earliest and finest Connecticut examples with four family members was worked in 1800 by Lucretia Carew (1778–1862) and probably at her mother's school in Norwich, but no related memorials have been published. Ring, *Girlhood Embroidery*, p. 23. Another exceptional example with twelve figures was executed in print work by Anna Maria Holmes at Sarah Pierce's Litchfield Academy about 1822. See Jean Lipman and Alice Winchester, *The Flowering of American Folk Art* (New York: Viking Press in cooperation with the Whitney Museum of American Art, 1974), p. 86, fig. 110.

[12]The spinster sisters, Sarah (1761–1843), Ruth (1764–1850), and Mary Patten (1769–1850), taught from about 1785 until 1825 and were guided by their widowed mother, Ruth (Wheelock) Patten (1740–1831), a daughter of Eleazer Wheelock (1711–1779), founder of Dartmouth College. The young widow, Lydia (Bull) Royse (1772–1832), first advertised her school in the *Connecticut Courant* on 17 June 1799, and it continued until 1818. For more about these women and work from their schools, see Ring, *Girlhood Embroidery*, pp. 202–17. For the Pattens, see also Peter Haring Judd, *The Hatch and Brood of Time: Five Phelps Families in the Atlantic World, 1720–1880* (Boston: Newbury Street Press, 1999), pp. 345–46.

[13]Lucius Barnes Barbour, *Families of Early Hartford, Connecticut* (Baltimore, Md.: Genealogical Publishing Co., 1977), pp. 96–105; Calvin Duvall Cowles, *The Cowles Families in America* (New Haven, Conn.: Tuttle, Morehouse and Taylor Co., 1929), pp. 122–23.

[14]See the Farmington home of Zenas Cowles (pronounced Kolz) in *The Great River: Art and Society of the Connecticut Valley, 1635–1820*, ed. William N. Hosley Jr. and Gerald W. R. Ward (Hartford, Conn.: Wadsworth Atheneum, 1985), p. 107.

[15]*Connecticut Historical Society Bulletin* 25 (April 1960): 57; Betty Ring, *American Needlework Treasures* (New York: E. P. Dutton in association with the Museum of American Folk Art, 1987), p. 85, fig. 137; Schorsch, *Mourning Becomes America*, fig. 48/170.

"By this you see we are but dust": The Gravestone Art and Epitaphs of Our Ancestors

Laurel K. Gabel

New England's old tombstones are not only artful reminders of our ancestral past; they are also frequently the source of genealogical data far beyond our expectations.[1] Somber slates and crumbling sandstones speak to us through the mute power of carved images and long forgotten symbols of family connections, confirming relationships, suggesting religious beliefs, and presenting life events honorable or cataclysmic enough to have been commemorated on stone. The carved messages still beg our attention: "Stop and note as you pass by," "He was born . . . ," "She died . . . ," "Here Lyes . . . ," "Remember me!" Although it is possible that fewer than half the population of New England in the seventeenth and eighteenth centuries ever had permanent gravemarkers, thousands of these chiseled records have withstood the ravages of weather, pollution, vandalism, and neglect to validate the lives and deaths of a select minority. The surviving gravestones have much to teach us about our ancestors and the world they lived in.

The slate headstone for Henry and Jane (Dummer) Sewall in Newbury, Massachusetts, provides an early example of one such family record preserved on stone (*Figure 1*).

Mr. HENRY SEWALL (SENT BY
Mr. HENRY SEWALL, HIS FATHER
IN YE SHIP ELISABETH & DORCAS
CAPT. WATTS COMMANDER)
ARRIVED AT BOSTON 1634.
WINTERED AT IPSWICH. HELPD
BEGIN THIS PLANTATION, 1635
FURNISHING ENGLISH SERVANTS
NEAT. CATTEL, & PROVISIONS.
MARRIED MRs. JANE DUMMER,
MARCH YE 25, 1646.
DIED MAY, YE 16, 1700.
AETAT. 86. HIS FRUTFULL
VINE, BEING THUS DISJOIND,
FELL TO YE GROUND JANUARY
YE 13 FOLLOWING; AETAT 74.
PSAL..27.10

The noted judge and diarist Samuel Sewall (1652–1730),[2] son of the above Henry and Jane, kept a detailed ledger book of accounts which includes an entry for the purchase of his parents' gravestone.[3] On a page dedicated to Boston stonecarver William Mumford (1641?–1718), Sewall entered: "1701. Octr. 20. By a Grave-Stone for my dear Father & Mother, £2 10 –" (*Figure 2*). Judge Sewall provided Mumford with the informative text for the gravestone inscription and saw to the placement of the slate marker within a year of his parents' death. Not all gravestones were erected by immediate relatives of the deceased, however, nor were all erected so

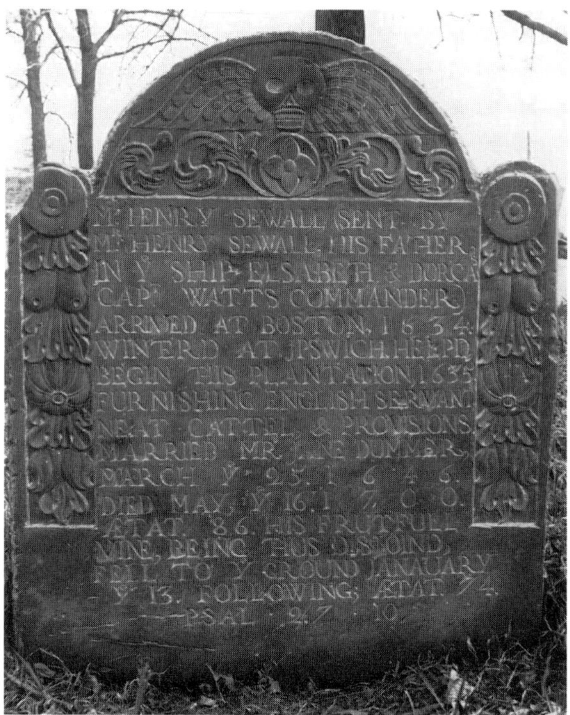

Figure 1 Gravestone of Henry and Jane (Dummer) Sewall, Newbury, Massachusetts. William Mumford (1641–1718); slate. Boston, 1701. Photograph by Harriette Merrifield Forbes, from the Daniel and Jessie Lie Farber Collection of Gravestone Photographs. Courtesy, American Antiquarian Society.

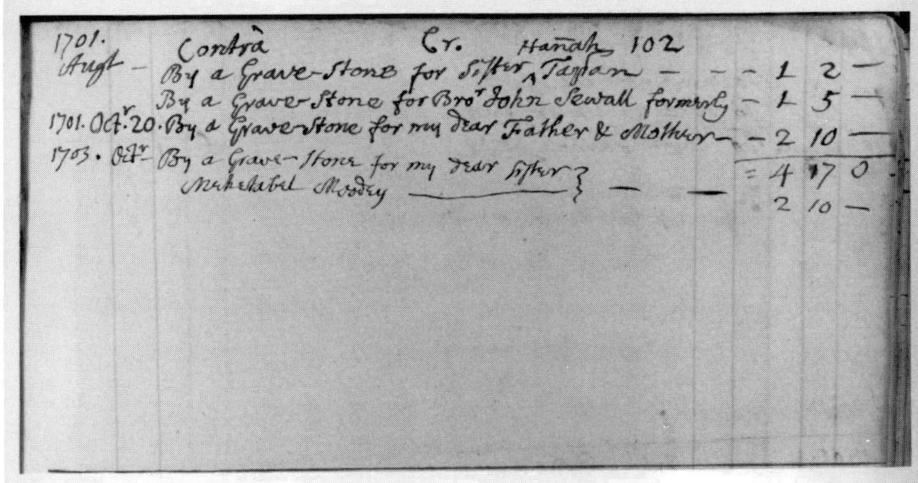

1701. Contra Cr. Hannah 102
Augt – By a Grave-Stone for Sister Tappan – – – 1 2 –
By a Grave-Stone for Brot John Sewall formerly – 1 5 –
1701. Octr 20. By a Grave-Stone for my dear Father & Mother – – 2 10 –
1703. Octr By a Grave-Stone for my dear Sister Mehetabel Moodey – – = 4 17 0
2 10 –

Figure 2 Samuel Sewall's ledger book entry 20 October 1701 showing payment to William Mumford for Sewall family gravestones. New England Historic Genealogical Society.

soon after death; it is not uncommon to find late-nineteenth- and twentieth-century markers honoring much earlier generations.

A tabular summary of genealogical information, in a style often found in family Bibles or on printed or pen-and-ink family records, was occasionally inscribed on stone. The late-eighteenth century headstone of Major John Farrar in Shrewsbury, Massachusetts, includes a chart-like mortality register, which gives death dates and ages for seven children of John and his wife Hannah Brown. The fact that none of the children lived beyond the age of three is a stark reminder of the high child mortality rates of the period. The headstone was most likely ordered by the surviving widow and produced by a local carver within two years of the major's death in 1793. Both the timing of the purchase and the source of the information lend credibility to the integrity of the inscription (*Figure 3*).[4]

As is frequently demonstrated with architecture, silver, needlework, and furniture, gravestone art also reflects the prevailing styles of a particular time and place. The early gravestones of western Vermont are of a design and stone material quite different from the markers found in Newport, Rhode Island, or New Haven, Connecticut. The slates of Boston differ from the sandstone gravemarkers produced in the Connecticut River Valley. Finding a gravestone at odds with the area's prevailing designs or stone materials is a valuable clue for the genealogist. In most instances, an out-of-place gravemarker was obtained from the geographical area of a previous home or from the area where surviving family members were settled. When families moved on, they often found it convenient to have the stone made to order by a local carver in their new town. For example, the Connecticut carving design and red sandstone of the Clarissa Button (ca. 1787–1805) and Jacob Grosvenor (ca. 1767–1793) gravemarkers, out of place in their central New York state locations, strongly suggest links to the Kimball family carvers from Pomfret, Lebanon, and New London, Connecticut. The Button and Grosvenor families were, in fact, from the locations suggested by their gravestones, part of the late-eighteenth-century Connecticut migration into that Mohawk River valley area of upstate New York.[5] In Maine the appearance of a group of gravestones bearing a design long associated with a western Massachusetts carver named Elijah Sikes (ca. 1772–1855), proved to be the link between two generations of the migrating Sikes family. Their distinctive gravestone carvings confirm residencies in Massachusetts, Maine, Vermont, and Ohio.[6] In rare situations, a unique stone can be explained by some genealogical link to the stonecarver who created it. In one such circumstance, the unusually elaborate heraldic marker for five-month-old Bartlett Adams Jr., who died in 1806, was explained by the fact that

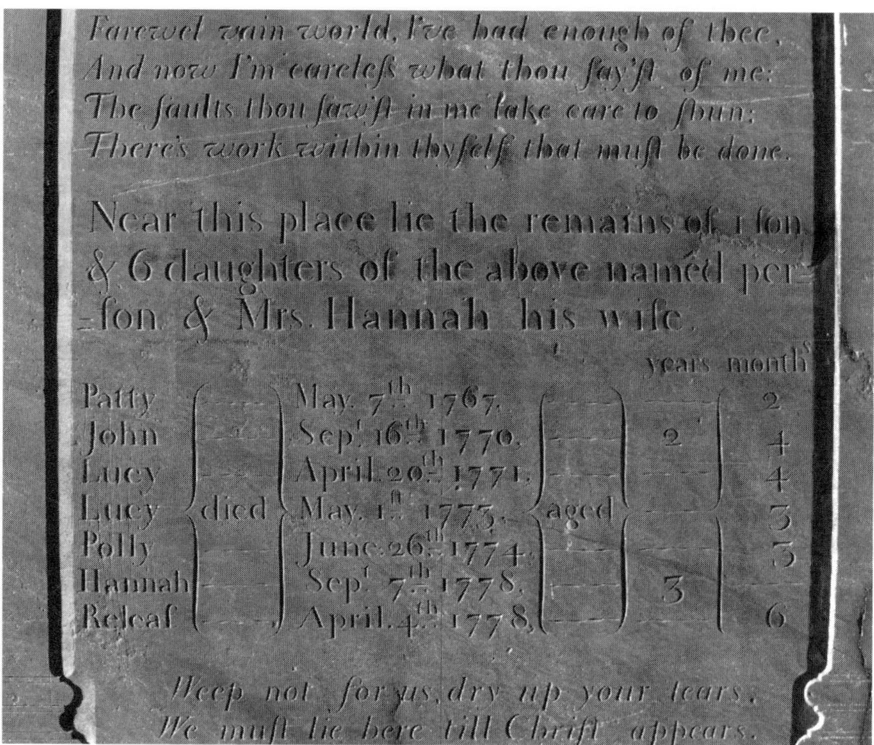

Figure 3 Detail. Mortality chart from the gravestone of Major John Farrar, Shrewsbury, Massachusetts. Probably carved in one of the Park family shops; slate. Worcester County, Massachusetts, circa 1793. From the Daniel and Jessie Lie Farber Collection of Gravestone Photographs. Courtesy, American Antiquarian Society.

the special stone was created by his father, the Portland, Maine, stonecarver Bartlett Adams (1776–1828).

In several instances, gravestone evidence has helped to trace a carver's movements from one area to another. The distinctive gravestone artistry of Zerubbabel Collins (1733–1797) heralded this carver's migration from Connecticut to Vermont;[7] several Soule family carvers left a trail of gravestones to mark their itinerant routes;[8] and gravestone carver John Gaud (1692/93–1750), whose intemperate habits and mounting debts may have precipitated his flight from Boston in the 1720s, was found again in Connecticut, where his identifiable gravestones furnished the evidence of his relocation.[9]

Gravestones, of course, were routinely transported over major overland trade routes and, more frequently, by water. Because of this, some of the finest examples of New England gravestone carving appear in relatively faraway places such as Charleston, South Carolina; Long Island, New York; Halifax, Nova Scotia; or Barbados, West Indies. The beautifully carved gravestone for Captain George Lee, who died in 1737, is one of many New England slates which survive in St. Michael's Cathedral yard in Bridgetown, Barbados.[10] Captain Lee's gravestone was carved in Boston (probably by Nathaniel Emmes) and shipped via well-established trade routes to its Bridgetown destination. The stone is the only known record of George Lee's date and place of death.[11]

With the exception of a few unique stones,[12] all gravemarkers record basic vital data: usually the name of the deceased, a date of death, sometimes a birth date or, more typically, the person's age at death. This age may be expressed in years, months, and days—or, for infants, simply hours.

When used on late-seventeenth- and early-eighteenth-century gravestones, titles such as *Mr.* or *Mrs.*, *Gentleman*, or *Esquire* denoted a particular social standing within the community. The significance of such prefixes diminished with increased

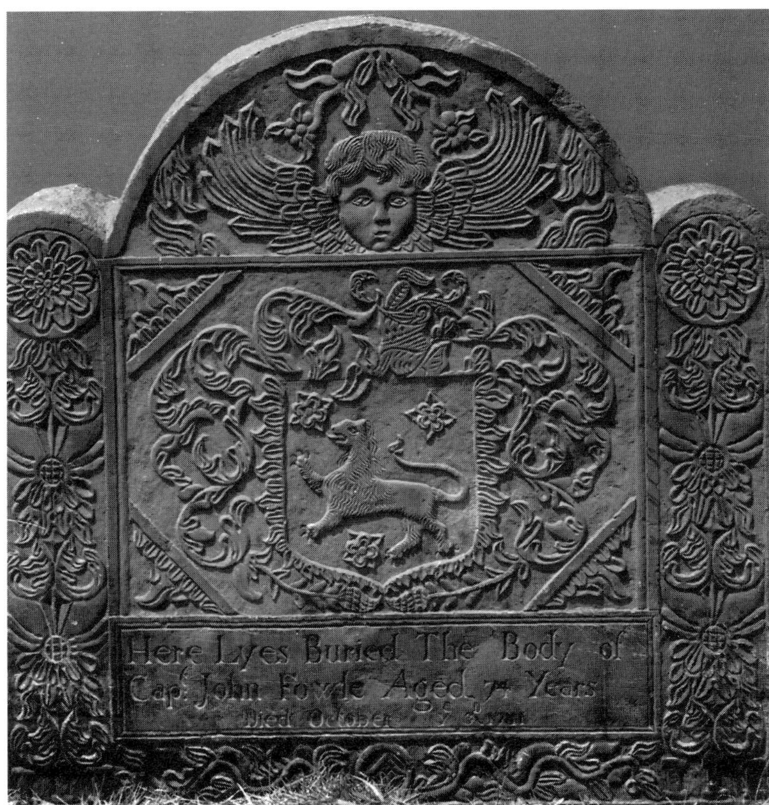

Figure 4 Gravestone of Capt. John Fowle, Charlestown, Massachusetts. Possibly Joseph Lamson (1658/9–1722); slate. Charlestown, Massachusetts, circa 1711. From the Daniel and Jessie Lie Farber Collection of Gravestone Photographs. Courtesy, American Antiquarian Society.

use, as more and more people attained the perceived accoutrements of an elevated respectability. Armorial tomb markers were also seen as indicators of social aristocracy and economic prosperity. More than two hundred heraldic gravestones, produced by at least twenty-five different local carvers, survive in New England. Although a large percentage of these carvings lack any verifiable authenticity, the earliest examples, especially those known to have been in place prior to about 1725, are more likely to be genuine. Such coats of arms may be of help in establishing valid ties to some of England's titled and well-documented families (*Figure 4*). Heraldic tomb markers were fairly evenly divided between the members of Puritan and Anglican congregations as well as between Tory and Patriot families, the defining influence appearing to be wealth, prominence, and family history—real or imagined—rather than any specific political or religious affiliation.[13] According to the late heraldist Harold Bowditch, "from 1750 to 1775 there was hardly a family of wealth or social distinction but could show its family arms engraved and used as a book-plate, or painted by some of the numerous herald-painters who flourished during that period."[14]

The large table stones and raised box tombs, erected for the educationally or economically élite, were usually topped with solid ledger slabs of sandstone, slate, or marble, which were then inscribed with detailed biographical information or genealogical data accumulated over multiple generations. Although these horizontal tomb ledgers are very difficult to photograph and the badly weathered surfaces are now nearly impossible to read, their detailed inscriptions are likely to have been transcribed at some point in the past.[15]

References to familial relationships, such as son, daughter, wife, relict, or widow, appear most often on gravestones of women and children, whose identities were typically linked to a male family member.[16] Men were more likely to be defined by their achievements. Inscriptions for children may omit the usual introduction of "Here Lyes Buried the Body of . . ." or "Sacred to the Memory of . . ." in favor of a shorter inscription which begins with the child's name and, in many instances, the first names of his father and mother: "John Jones, son of Mr. Samuel Jones and Mary his wife" or "Sarah, infant daughter of William and Rachel Jones." It is not unusual to find birth order mentioned on gravestones: "John, first-born son of . . ." or "Mary, last-born daughter of. . . ." Children's gravestones are often smaller in size and less elaborately carved than those of adults. They frequently duplicate footstone motifs or other more conservative, less contemporary designs.

A few headstone inscriptions aim to supply statistical documentation of a particularly long or fruitful life. When Hephzibah Prentice died at Cambridge in 1741/2, the relict of Mr. Solomon Prentice was in her eighty-ninth year and "Thair had Desended From her 140 Persons of whom 92 [?] Remained When She Died."[17] The classical marble gravestone which Nathaniel Hodgkins, Senior (1761–1839), carved circa 1801 for one-hundred-year-old Daniel Tyler, Junior, is a record of the exact date and place of his birth ("born in Groton [Connecticut] . . . 1701 O.S."),[18] his date of death, age in years, months, and days, acknowledgment of his three wives, the number of children born from these marriages, the number of children alive at the time of their father's death, and the number of descendant grandchildren and great-grandchildren. Mary (Loomis) Buell's gravestone in Litchfield, Connecticut, likewise bequeaths a statistical account of her long life as the wife of Dr. John Buell.[19] Mary died in 1768, "AEtat 90, having had 13 children, 101 Grand Children, 274 Great G. Children, 22 Great G. G. Children, 410 Total. 330 Survived her."

Extreme old age was occasionally acknowledged in the stone's iconography as well. The gravestone carvers Nathaniel and/or Henry Emmes portrayed the Honorable John Wheelwright, Senior (1664/5–1745), of Wells, Maine, with a furrowed brow, perhaps to reflect his long life and distinguished years as a lawyer. In *Figure 5*, Jonathan Allen (1766–1836), a Bernardston, Massachusetts, area carver, used his chisels to depict the wonderful toothless and corrugated face of ninety-seven-year-old Esther (Judd) Webster, widow of Mr. Jonathan Webster, who died in 1782.[20]

More typically, long life and celebrated unions were eulogized in the tablet inscription, which often included milestone dates, important life events, or biographical details. The following epitaph is found for Eleazer and Elizabeth (Divol) Houghton, the parents of nine children:[21]

Here/Lies the Bodies of
Mr. ELEAZER HOUGHTON
& Mrs. ELIZABETH his wife:
He died Feb. 20, 1790 in the
Hundredth Year of his age.
& she died June 27, 1785
in the 92 Year of her age.

They was born in Lancaster & mov'd
to Lunenburg, in the Year 1726.
They Liv'd together a married life
Sixty nine Years and upwards.
He liv'd a peaceable & pious Life;
& never had a Law-suit in all his Life;
By this you see we are but dust,
Prepare for death and follow us.

An example of multiple gravestone purchasers is recorded on the headstone of Joanna (Bellows) Wetherbee or Watherbe, the second wife and widow of Captain Ephraim Wetherbee. Joanna, who "departed this life" at Charlestown, New Hampshire, in August 1762, lies under a headstone carved by William Park (1705–1788) of Groton, Massachusetts, "Erected by Rachal Putnam, Jonathan Watherbe, Abigail Willard, Susanna Little, Joanna Heywood and Samuel Watherbe, all Children to the above Mrs. Joanna Watherbe." This somewhat unusual acknowledgment conveniently documents the married names of Mrs. Wetherbee's four surviving daughters.[22]

Occasionally an epitaph or some other added message provides further insight or clues to a less than obvious relationship. A shared stone for Thomazin Collecutt or Collicutt (widow of immigrant Richard Collicott, who arrived at Massachusetts in 1632)[23] and her granddaughter, Bethiah Gookin, readily provides the married name of Thomazin's daughter. Elisabeth (Newberry) Bissell's[24] gravemarker also

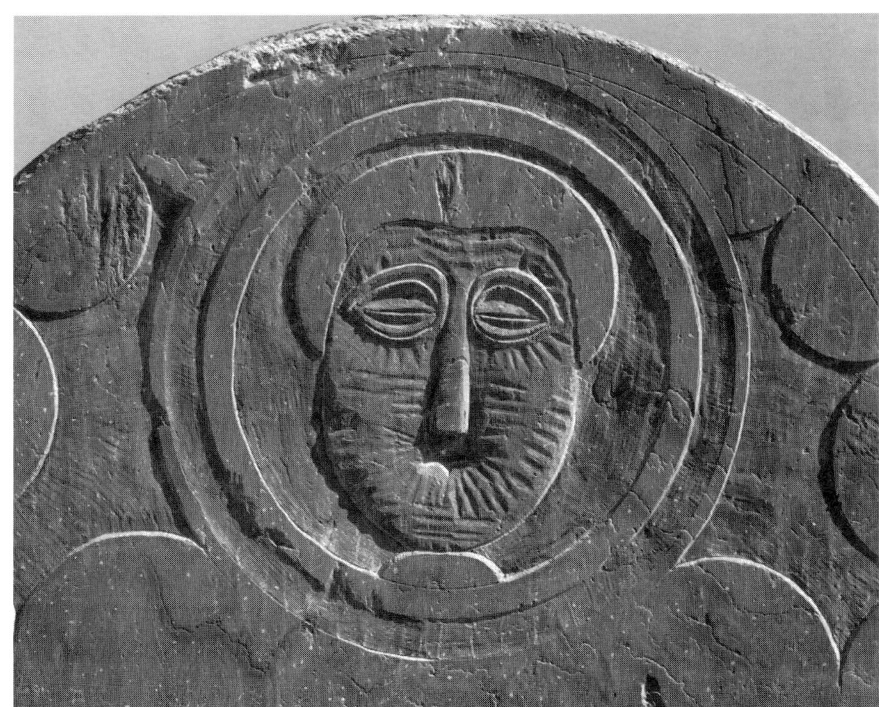

Figure 5 Detail. Gravestone of Esther Webster, Bernardston, Massachusetts. Jonathan Allen (1766–1836); dark gray slate. Bernardston, Massachusetts, circa 1782. From the Daniel and Jessie Lie Farber Collection of Gravestone Photographs. Courtesy, American Antiquarian Society.

includes an added inscription, ". . . In Memory of Her Father, CAPT. ROGER NEUBARY [*sic*] Who Died In the King's Servis In the Spanish Westenges [*sic*] [i.e., West Indies], May the 6, 1741 Aged In ye 35th Year," leaving us a record of Elisabeth's maiden name, her father's name, age, military rank, and place of service, as well as the place and date of his death. According to the published vital records of Windsor, Captain Newberry died "on his return from Carthegene to Jemeca [*sic*]" during the Cuban Expedition.[25] Apparently, the paternal notation on Elisabeth (Newberry) Bissell's gravemarker was something of a family tradition. Her mother, Elizabeth (Wolcott) Newberry, had a similarly inscribed gravestone: "In memory of Mrs. Elizabeth, Relict of Capt. Roger Newberry, who died in the Cuba Expedition, A.D. 1740 [*sic*], in the 35th year of his age; eldest daughter of the Hon. Roger Wolcot [*sic*], Esq., sometime Governor of Conn."[26]

In Westford, Massachusetts, the double gravestone for Jacob and Abigail Wright, who both died in 1761,[27] carries the appended inscription: "erected by Widow Ruth Bats [*sic*]." Ruth (Wright) Bates was the daughter of Jacob and Abigail (Stevens) Wright and the widow of Capt. Oliver Bates, who had died on 4 July 1775 of wounds suffered at the battle of Concord Bridge.[28] Widow Bates's added "credit line" tells us that her parents' gravestone was purchased after her husband Oliver's death in 1775 and before Ruth's subsequent second marriage to Henry Richardson in 1784.[29] Both the stone for Oliver Bates and the marker for Ruth's parents, Jacob and Abigail Wright, who died fourteen years earlier, were most likely ordered at the same time. Such delays in ordering headstones were not infrequent. Gravestones for husband and wife were often acquired a year or two after the death of the surviving spouse, and it was fairly common to order more than one set of stones at the same time: markers for children whose deaths had occurred many years earlier, gravestones for both parents and perhaps the maiden aunt who lived out her last years in their household, or a marker for a young first wife and her unnamed infant buried in the same previously unmarked grave. It was also common to record earlier deaths, especially those of children, on the lower portion of a gravestone erected for parents or siblings.

Particularly valuable to family historians are gravemarkers that mention a wife's parentage. Occasionally these elusive matrilineal relationships are recorded on stone rather than paper: "Mrs. Elizabeth Tedder . . . wife of Valentine Tedder and Daughter to Mr. Samuel and Mrs. Sarah Dodd,"[30] a 1769 Marblehead gravestone; Mary Smith and her child, Mary being the "wife of Mr. Jeduthan Smith & Daughter of Thom's Kimberly Esq. & His Wife Ruth";[31] or from Hebron, Connecticut, ". . . the Corpse of Mrs. Abigail Peters. a Second Consort of ye Revd. Mr. Samuel Peters. a Daughter of Samuel Gilbert Esqr. by Mrs. Abigail his wife. Born Janr. 31st 1752 & Married June 25, 1769 & died July 14, 1769. a wedding Changed to Lamentation ye greatest Greif in all creation a mourning. . . ."[32] Young wives, especially those who died soon after marriage, were often buried with their parents or with their husband's family, rather than in a newly established area by themselves. And it was not unusual for a widowed parent to live out his/her final days in the household of a married daughter or son, often far from the ancestral home. In these situations, one may find a gravestone in a regional design and material foreign to the local area. Those who died from some virulent epidemic, such as yellow fever or smallpox, were occasionally interred in an isolated area apart from the principal burying ground, as was the case for Timothy Hall of Durham, Connecticut, whose ". . . monument [was] erected over an empty Tomb . . . as his remains was inter'd neare the Hospital in this Town" following his death in 1771. Israel Reed (Harvard, Massachusetts, died 1822) was also isolated by his death from smallpox, one of many such victims whose final resting places were far removed from the established burying grounds or populated town centers.

Also of genealogical interest are the carved accounts of second or multiple marriages, such as the gravestone of "Hannah . . . wife of Samuel Livermore, Esq. formerly ye wife of Mr. Daniel Harrington (died 1765, Waltham, Massachusetts)"; or Polly Rhoades who died at Mill River, Massachusetts, in 1855 at the age of eighty-six, "being the widow of 5 husbands," all of whom are enumerated by name on the gravestone: "David Rockwell, Capt. Alpheus Underwood, Deac. Amos Langdon, Hezekiah Butler, and James T. Rhoades"; or Mary Lynde of Southold, New York (died 1724), whose three previous husbands are identified in full on her headstone: "Peter Bradly, Lt. Coll. Thomas Yovngs [Youngs], Nathll. Lynde." Reverend John Woodbridge, "who was born at Springfield . . . 1702 & died . . . 1783 in the 81st Year of his Age, . . . son of ye Venerable and Rev. John Woodbridge of Springfield Parish," and himself "late minister of the Gospel of Christ" in South Hadley, Massachusetts, faces eternity flanked by his two wives: "Mrs. Tryphena [Ruggles], His first wife [who] died Jan. 10, 1749 In her 42nd year," and "Mrs. Martha [(Clark) (Strong)] His 2nd Wife [who] died Aug. 20th 1783 in her 58th year" (*Figure 6*).[33] Before migrating from Connecticut to Vermont and then on to Ohio in 1820, the gravestone carver Elijah Sikes produced a similar family grouping on the Brooklyn, Connecticut, headstone for Captain Benjamin Peirce [Pierce] and three of his wives: Hannah Smith (died 1736 in her 24th year), Naomi Richards (died 1757 in her 42nd year), and Sarah Mills (died 1759 in her 41st year), and a son, Rufus, "by [his] 2nd wife," who died in December, 1741.[34]

Infants and children, always particularly vulnerable to childhood epidemics and accidents, account for some of New England's most powerfully graphic gravestone art. A superb example, carved by a still unidentified Connecticut artist, portrays the "Four Lovely and promising Sons of Mr. Appleton & Mrs. Lydia Holmes," all of whom died within weeks of one another in the winter of 1794–1795, East Glastonbury, Connecticut (*Figure 7*).

> Appleton died Feb. 24th AD 1795 in the 9th Year of his Age
> Ozias died Feb. 23d AD 1795 in the 7th Year of his Age
> Burridg died Dec. 20th AD 1794 in the 12th Year of his Age
> Calvin died Feb. 25th AD 1795 in the 12th Year of his Age

The two slightly different sized profiles on the left represent Appleton and Ozias who were nine and seven years old at the time of their deaths. Burridg

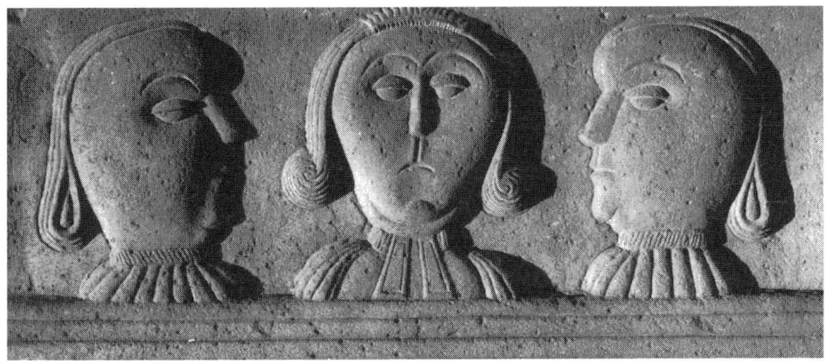

Figure 6 Detail. Gravestone of Reverend John Woodbridge and his wives, Tryphena (d. 1749) and Martha (d. 1783), South Hadley, Massachusetts. Longmeadow School (perhaps Stebbins family); red sandstone. Longmeadow, Massachusetts, circa 1783. From the Daniel and Jessie Lie Farber Collection of Gravestone Photographs. Courtesy, American Antiquarian Society.

and Calvin, shown facing one another as mirror images on the right, were twins, joined again by death during their twelfth year. In the center of the four profiles is a family tree with its truncated limbs providing graphic validation of this Holmes genealogy. The intact, fruit-bearing limbs symbolize the surviving sons and daughters of Appleton and Lydia (Goodrich) Holmes. On the right, in their order of birth, a limb for each male: Richard, Elijah, Solomon, and Israel, followed by severed fused branches for the twins Burridg and Calvin, and individual cut limbs for Appleton and his younger brother, Ozias. The branches growing out of the left side of the tree represent daughters: Florinda, Rocksena (whose severed branch tells us that she did not survive, but for whom there is no gravestone), a second, more fortunate Rocksena, born three years later, and Lydia Goodrich, the youngest female.

Ye living mortals see in earthly bloom
Four lovely offsprings lie beneath this tomb.
The afflicted mother weeps from day to day,
To see thoes lovely branches torn away.
But whilst you weep the Lamb on Calvary slain
Feeds the young branches which shall sprout again.
Whilst God the FATHER who all heaven supplies,
Shall wipe the sorrows from the parent's eyes.

There are numerous gravestones erected to the memory of six or more children in one family, parents made childless by migrating epidemics of "throat distemper," "children's plague," or "minor pox."[35] In Grafton, Vermont, a single gravestone, engraved by a local artist, Moses Wright Jr. (birth and death dates unknown; active as a gravestone carver from circa 1790 to 1812), represents the tragic story of fourteen children born to Thomas and Rebecca (Gilson/Gibson) Park. Thirteen of the infants died at or shortly after birth, and another, Thomas, Junior, did not survive childhood. As is often the case, the words of the epitaph reinforce the tympanum design, first for the children and then for their mother:

Youth behold and shed a teer,
Se fourteen children slumber here.
Se their image how they shine,
Like flowers of a fruitful vine.

Behold and see as you pass by,
My fourteen children with me lie,
Old or young you soon must die,
And turn to dust as well as I.[36]

These infant deaths may have resulted from a blood-group incompatibility (Rh negative factor), a medical condition that could be successfully managed today.[37] Think about the human tragedy behind these fourteen little circle faces, so graphic on their gravestone. In an age when such tragedies were often seen as manifestations of God's disfavor, the anguish and guilt that accompanied these unexplained deaths must have been catastrophic to the parents.

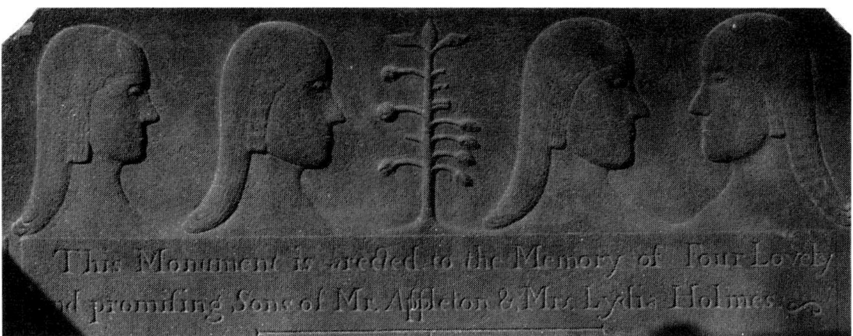

Figure 7 Detail. Gravestone of Appleton, Ozias, Burridg, and Calvin Holmes, East Glastonbury, Connecticut. Maker unknown; red sandstone. Connecticut River Valley, circa 1794–1795. From the Daniel and Jessie Lie Farber Collection of Gravestone Photographs. Courtesy, American Antiquarian Society.

Clues suggesting inherited characteristics or medical patterns that repeat over several generations are occasionally alluded to in gravestone inscriptions. Multiple births are one common example. The "four twen [*sic*] infants" born to Jacomiah and Mercy (Phillips) Palmer on 25 November 1795 were given the appropriately descriptive names of Wonderful, Admirable, Remarkable, and Strange.[38] These quadruplets, who lived only twelve hours, are buried in Farm Cemetery, Danby Four Corners, Vermont. Phinetta and Pamela, twins born to the same parents a few years later, survived to perpetuate their inherited predisposition for multiple births.

Evidence of medical disabilities, chronic diseases, or genetically transmitted conditions may also be mentioned, or perhaps subtly depicted, on a gravestone. "Deaf and dumb," "sightless from birth," "always an invalid," and "insane" are just a few of the more startling descriptions recorded on stone. Medical speculation may be prompted by the carving on Captain Anthony Gwyn's handsome gravestone (Newburyport, Massachusetts, 1776) (*Figure 8*). Do the enlarged knuckles and the elderly merchant's use of a walking stick indicate that Captain Gwyn suffered from some crippling arthritic infirmity? Or, as is more likely the case here, does the deformity simply result from the gravestone carver's inability to render a complex hand position?

Along with the necessary documentation of names and dates, gravemarkers often focus on the most noteworthy, unusual, or particularly memorable events in the life of the deceased. For many males this meant military service. The passionate patriotism and political intensity of the time are frequently recorded in the tablet inscriptions or epitaphs. It is not unusual, for example, to find information about the soldier's military unit, the name of his commanding officer, and mention of a specific military campaign. King Phillip's War in the 1600s, the French and Indian Wars and Revolutionary War of the eighteenth century, the War of 1812, and the cataclysmic Civil War resulted in thousands of collective gravestones, each one documentary evidence of individual sacrifice.

Claimed by some as the first martyr to the cause of American independence, William French died in March of 1775, a victim of the "Westminster Massacare [*sic*]." William's Westminster (Vermont) gravestone, one of many such examples, reflects the fervor of the times.

> In memory of WILLIAM FRENCH
> Son to Mr. Nathaniel French. Who
> Was Shot at Westminster March ye 13th,
> 1775, by the hands of Cruel Ministerial tools
> Of Georg ye 3d, in the Corthouse at a 11 a Clock
> At Night in the 22d year of his Age.
>
> HERE WILLIAM FRENCH his Body lies,
> For Murder his Blood for Vengence Cries
> King Georg the third his Tory Crew
> tha with a Bawl his head Shot threw.
> For Liberty and his Country's Good
> he Lost his Life his Dearest blood.

Captain Daniel Malcom is interred at Copp's Hill Burying Ground in Boston under a stone pockmarked by bullet strikes, said to be the result of a targeted

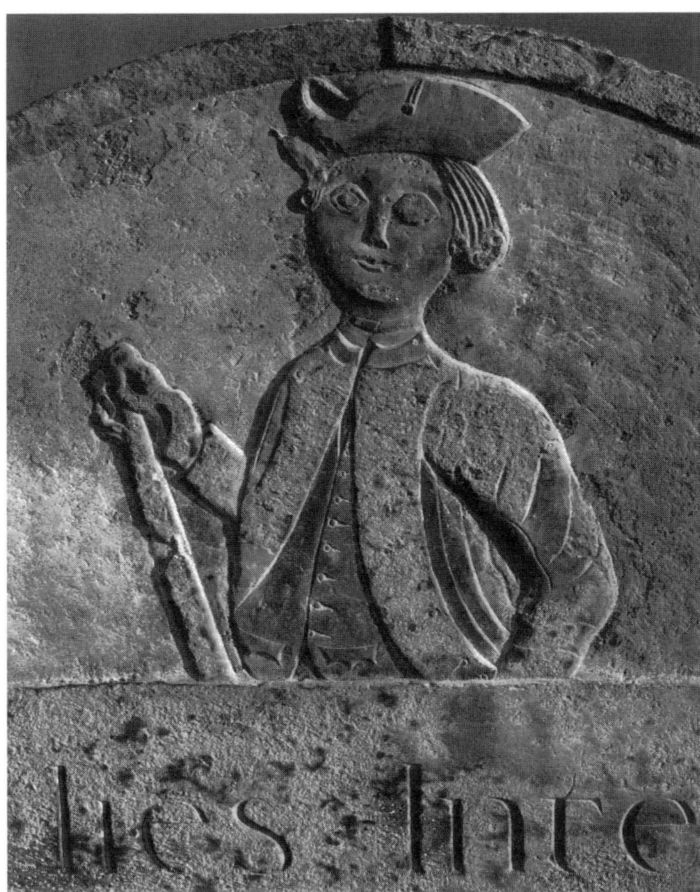

Figure 8 Detail. Gravestone of Captain Anthony Gwyn, Newburyport, Massachusetts. Lamson family carvers; light gray slate. Charlestown, Massachusetts, circa 1776. From the Daniel and Jessie Lie Farber Collection of Gravestone Photographs. Courtesy, American Antiquarian Society.

British response to his revolutionary protests and his politically provocative epitaph. Malcom was an active Son of Liberty, one of the fifteen patriots named on Paul Revere's famous Liberty Bowl.[39]

> Here lies buried in a
> Stone Grave 10 feet deep
> Capt. Daniel Malcom [,] Marcht [Merchant]
> who departed this Life
> october 23d 1769
> Aged 44 years.
> a true son of Liberty
> a Friend to the Publick
> an Enemy to oppression
> and one of the foremost
> in opposing the Revenue Acts
> on America.[40]

Perhaps identifying with the heroic sentiment of Ebenezer Cox's 1768 gravestone in Hardwick, Massachusetts, Samuel Fisher (1732–1816) used the space at the bottom of the stone to advertise himself as the carver. Very few seventeenth- and eighteenth-century gravestones were ever signed or initialed, making the infrequent documented examples especially notable. Signed stones may indicate special effort on the part of the carver and were used by some as a way to advertise their wares.

> In Memory of Capt.
> EBENEZER COX who Died
> March ye, 2nd, 1768. in ye
> 42nd, Year of his Age.
> Beneath this Stone a noble Captain's laid

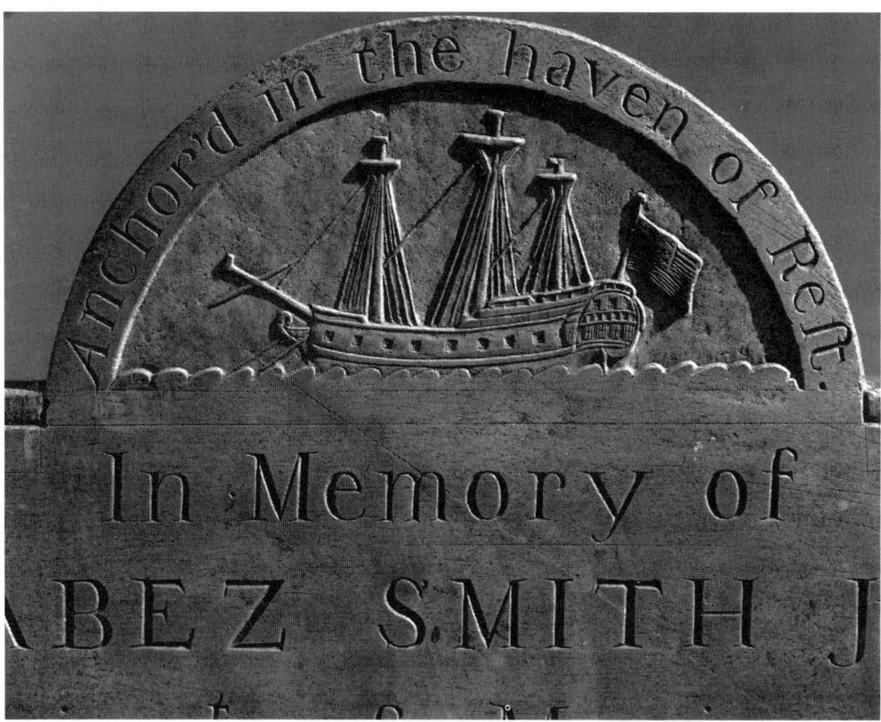

Figure 9 Gravestone of Lieutenant Jabez Smith Jr., Boston, Massachusetts. Maker unknown (possibly John Homer); gray slate. Boston, Massachusetts, circa 1780. From the Daniel and Jessie Lie Farber Collection of Gravestone Photographs. Courtesy, American Antiquarian Society.

which for his King & Country was Display'd
his Courage that no Terrors Could Disarm
Nor when he fac'd ye, Foe his fear Alarm
But now he's Conquer'd & ye, silent grave
Can boast that power ye, French could never have
Under his care his Soldiers were Secure
Equal with them all hardship's he'd Endure
In Six Campains Intrepid trod ye, Field
Nor to ye, Gallic Power would ever Yield
At last he's gone we hope where wars do cease
To spend a whole Eternity in Peace.

Made by
Samuel Fisher
In Wrentham

The impressive gravestone of Jabez Smith Jr. still draws the admiration of visitors to Boston's old Granary Burying Ground (*Figure 9*). Smith (son of Jabez and Amy [Avery] Smith of Groton, Connecticut), a lieutenant of marines aboard the twenty-eight-gun Continental frigate *Trumbull*,[41] died at Boston on 28 June 1780 at the age of twenty-nine, following a fierce naval engagement between the British letter of marque *Watt* and the ill-fated *Trumbull*. The slate gravestone featuring a carved ship flying the American flag documents when and where the young lieutenant was born, his military affiliation and rank, the name and perhaps the design of his ship, its home port, and when and where Lieutenant Jabez Smith Jr. was finally "Anchored in the Haven of Rest."

Typical of many war-related epitaphs, Doctor Abiah Perkins's gravestone in Hanover, Connecticut, lays angry blame at the enemy's feet but concludes with a prayer for peace.

To the worthy Memory
of Doctr, Abiah Perkins
who after enduring Im-
prisonment Chains Hunger
and ye, barbarous Insults of
cruel Britons, Departed
this life Aug.st 31st, AD 1782
Age'd 27: in ye Bloom of
youth a Martyr to his

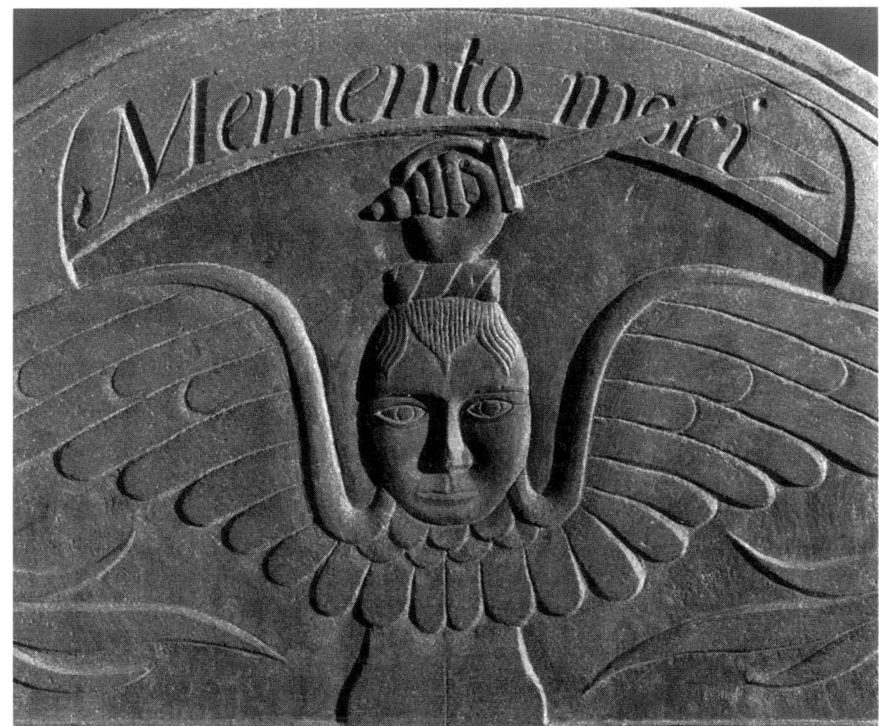

Figure 10 Detail. Gravestone of Benjamin Chamberlin, Pepperell, Massachusetts. Thomas (ca. 1745–1806) or John (1731–1793) Park; gray slate. Groton, Massachusetts, circa 1778. From the Daniel and Jessie Lie Farber Collection of Gravestone Photographs. Courtesy, American Antiquarian Society.

Country's Cause.
Great God, forgive our
proud imperious foe,
Whose cruel usage caus'd
his early death,
May we be still & tre[m]bling
learn to know
Thy will was done when
he resign'd his breath.

Some stones, like those for Lieutenant Joseph Spauldin, who died at Bunker Hill, Benjamin Chamberlin (*Figure 10*), "who departed this life in the Continental Army at Valley forge in the year 1778 in ye 17th year of his age," or Captain Jonathan Willson who was killed at Concord's fight, include iconography indicating that the men fought in the Revolution. The heraldic-like crest, composed of a clutched fist brandishing a sword, appears to have been initiated by one of the Park family carvers and was used in New England almost exclusively on gravestones produced by craftsmen working in or around the Harvard/Groton area of Massachusetts, the site of one of the Northeast's most productive slate sources in the second half of the eighteenth century.

Along with the numerous testimonials for men "killed in the service of [their] country" at Fort Stanwix or Peekskill, Concord or Bunker Hill, many gravestones of the late 1760s and 1770s allude to the effects of English occupation and war on New England's civilian population. Abigail (Soley) Codman, the daughter of Captain John and Dorcas Soley, died in Haverhill when, as her gravestone explains, "She was drove from Charlestown in April, 1775 by ye cruel hand of oppression." Elderly Abigail (Bowen) Kendrick[42] also "left her pleasant habitation in Newton and come to her Daugher [*sic*] Dana's in Groton on account of ye civil War." She died at Groton in the autumn of 1775 at the age of seventy-six, removed at last "to that place where ye wicked cease from troubling and ye weary are at rest." A surprising number of women, children, and elderly withdrew to safer ground during the upheaval of occupation and revolution. Death records or gravestone evidence, missing from the last known town of residence, may appear in outlying districts where other relatives often provided safe haven for families in danger.

Charles Pratt Marston, an "Infant son of John Marston, Esq. and Mrs. Elizabeth Marston of Boston," was one of many who died away from home in 1775 "while British Forces held his native Town." Young Charles's gravestone, which was carved by the Boston stonecutter Henry Christian Geyer (ca. 1757–1785), refers to the severe disruptions resulting from British occupation of the town. Nine-month-old Charles Pratt Marston was the namesake of Charles Pratt, first Earl of Camden, a famous British jurist who defended the grievances of the American colonists against the policies of King George III and was persecuted for his views. Charles Pratt Marston was the son of John Marston, owner of Boston's Bunch of Grapes tavern, where much of the clandestine business of the Sons of Liberty was conducted. Marston was a noted Revolutionary and another one of the fifteen patriots whose names appear on Revere's Liberty Bowl. The child's epitaph concludes with these politically revealing lines:

> Then shalt thou rise where dwells immortal Love
> And with great CAMDEN live in brightest Realms
> above
> Lord Camden a great friend to America
> & after whom the child was nam'd.[43]

Occasionally, one finds the strongly held religious convictions of the deceased proclaimed in an epitaph or depicted by gravestone iconography. James Park (1741–1778), whose unyielding religious faith was forged in his native Scotland, leaves posterity little doubt as to his beliefs.

> He died no Libertine, there is two extremes,
> the world has always run into, since ye fall of Adam.
> 1st Papists here have exceded in boundlesse domination & tyranny over ye consciences of men: & what ever is contrary to ye lawlesse decrees of there Councells & Popes, is an unexpiable heresie & cannot be purged but by fire & fagot. 2 Whoever refuse subjection of conscience to that Enemy of Christ, & to that woman-mistress of witchcraft, on whose skirts is found ye Blood of ye martyres of Jesus, is Presently an heretick, & his arguments answered with burning-quicke, this tyranny over conscience we disclaime; yet for that ought not ye other extremity of wild toleration to be imbraced.

The intricately carved stone for the *Christian Rabbi* Judah Monis (1683–1764),[44] an Italian Jew educated in the academies of Leghorn and Amsterdam, who for forty years taught Hebrew to the scholars at Harvard, presents a most unusual narrative (*Figure 11*).[45] Although "by Birth and Religion a jew," as the stone tells us, he "embrac'd the Christian Faith & was publickly baptiz'd at Cambridge, AD 1722." The word "RESURGAM" carved across the tympanum arch accompanied by an image of three budding plants sprouting from death's symbolic skull, confirms the Christian belief in the rebirth of Judah Monis's soul. The gravestone was carved by William Park, a staunch Presbyterian from Scotland.

> Here lies buried the Remains of RABBI
> IUDAH MONIS, M.A. late HEBREW
> Instructer at HARVARD College in
> Cambridge in which Office He continued 40
> years. He was by Birth and Religion a jew but
> embrac d the Christian Faith & was publickly
> baptiz d at Cambridge AD 1722 and
> departed this Life April 25, 1764, Aged
> 81 years 2 months and 21 days

Monis's epitaph provides a biblical interpretation for the rabbi's conversion.

> A native branch of Jacob see!
> Which, once from off its olive brok,
> Regrafted, from the living tree — Rom. XI. 17–24
> Of the reviving sap partook
> From teeming Zion's fertile womb, — Isai. LXVI. 8.
> As dewy drops in early morn, — Psal. CX. 3.
> Or rising bodies from the tomb, — Iohn V. 28, 29
> At once be Isr'els nation born! — Isai. LXVI. 8

It was not unusual for gravestones of college graduates such as Judah Monis to be inscribed entirely in Latin: Thomas Sewall (1692/3–1716), "Collegii Harvardini,"[46] Obadias Pease (1746–1766), "Collegio Yalensi,"[47] Eleazari Wheelock (1711–1779), "Collegii Dartmuthensis."[48] In addition to some use of Latin, ministers were often memorialized with large, more elaborate markers and were more likely to have prominent portrait-like images on their gravestones. In one well-preserved example, carver William

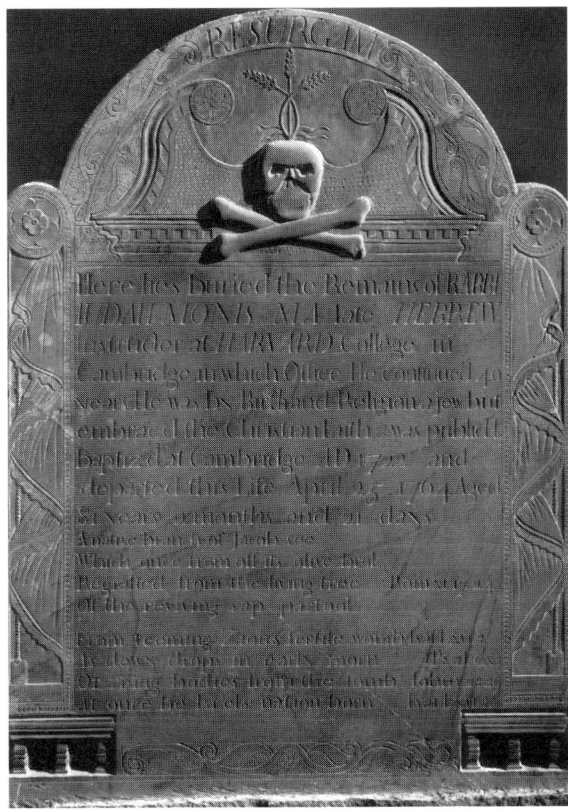

Figure 11 Gravestone of Rabbi Judah Monis, Northborough, Massachusetts. William Park (1795–1788); gray slate. Groton, Massachusetts, circa 1764. From the Daniel and Jessie Lie Farber Collection of Gravestone Photographs. Courtesy, American Antiquarian Society.

Young (1711–1795) portrayed what is clearly meant to be Reverend Silas Biglow (ca. 1738–1769) preaching to the faithful from his Paxton (Massachusetts) pulpit (*Figure 12*). The Park family carvers (William, John, and Thomas Park) were locally renowned for the handsome portrait medallions which they produced in great numbers for area clergymen. These oval busts and cameos, more stylized representations than any true portrait, represent the only known portrayal of the memorialized individuals. Studying the gravestone likeness of Reverend Nathan Holt (Peabody, Massachusetts, 1792) (*Figure 13*) with the details of his minister's robe, clerical collar, and curled wig so carefully portrayed, one is understandably led to conclude that Reverend Nathan Holt's steady gaze, kindly mouth, and double chins are also faithfully rendered. But this is not necessarily the case. There is a sameness to many of the carved "portrait" faces, not unlike the rather formulaic portraits produced by itinerant sign painters, limners, and folk artists of the day who were known to have repeated a similar pose, costume, and general facial features on a whole series of different paintings.

Numerous carved portrait-style figures of the eighteenth century—women in fashionable gowns (*Figure 14*), men in stylish finery or proudly posing in their best military attire—undoubtedly represent the deceased individuals, but probably do not actually resemble them. Gravestone carvers tended to follow their own stylistic conventions when rendering soul effigies or representative human likenesses on gravestones. These stylistic conventions differed from carver to carver and were altered over time so that a single practice did not always prevail. The Park carvers and their many followers, for example, almost always portrayed men with stylized wigs or parted hair, their "Everyman's" face supported by elaborate wings. Park figures of women and children, on the other hand, usually appear wingless, with slightly smaller, bonneted heads staring out of a portal or niche frame. The inclusion of garment buttons almost always indicates that the deceased was a man or boy; women are seldom portrayed with button embellishments. On the numerous double stones commemorating husband and wife, the winged head of the man is usually on the left side of the marker, with his wingless wife in her niche on the right. In other locations, individual carvers might practice a different convention or prefer to make no differentiation between the stones for males and females. It most parts of New England, however, women and children were linked and often memorialized somewhat differently from men.

Unlike the aforementioned winged faces and portraits, the ubiquitous winged skull motif which adorns so many New England gravestones was a fairly gender-neutral design that sufficed for both men and women. Universally understood as a symbol of death, the skull was thought to house the soul whose heavenly flight might be aided by metaphorical wings. Angels or soul effigies, as faces-with-wings are sometimes called, eventually replaced the more foreboding skull stones, only to be quickly displaced by classical urn and willow designs which became

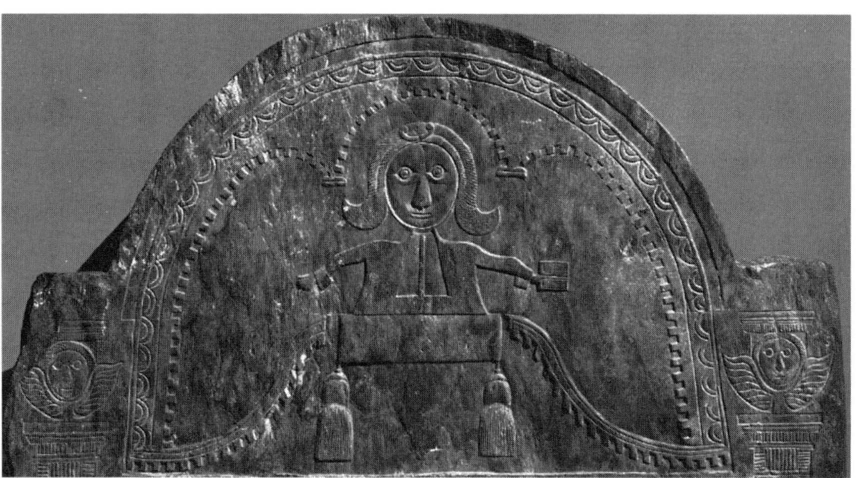

Figure 12 Detail. Gravestone of Reverend Silas Biglow, Paxton, Massachusetts. William Young (1711–1795); slate. Worcester, Massachusetts, circa 1769. From the Daniel and Jessie Lie Farber Collection of Gravestone Photographs. Courtesy, American Antiquarian Society.

almost universal in the early 1800s. When "Madam Mary Cushing, Relict of Rev. Job Cushing and eldest daughter of Rev. John Prentice" died in 1798, her grave was soon marked by a fashionable urn and willow style marker. Her husband, whose death had occurred almost forty years earlier, received a similarly fashionable stone on his adjacent grave (*Figure 15*).[49] Reverend Job Cushing's estate, however, included a payment to gravestone carver George Allen Jr. (1742/3–1764), for another headstone and footstone which had apparently been placed on the grave shortly after his death in 1760. The present urn/willow marker certainly bears no resemblance to George Allen Jr.'s known work, and the classical urn design is inconsistent with the 1762 probate payment date. As is sometimes the case, Reverend Mr. Cushing's earlier stone was updated when the widow's stone was ordered. Buried beneath the Reverend Job Cushing's replacement stone was found the beautiful and well-preserved original (*Figure 16*): an expressive winged face framed by elaborate border carvings. The rose motif of the headstone border is matched on the paired footstone. Grinning skulls and winged faces, which had been reminding generations of New Englanders that "as I am now, so you will be," were being replaced by the more intellectual appeal of classical urns and weeping trees which emphasized memory rather than death, surviving mourners rather than the deceased.

As we learn more about the men who carved these gravestones (there were few women carvers until the twentieth century), we are finding evidence of extensive and surprisingly widespread carving networks. In almost all known instances, eighteenth-century gravestone carvers learned their occupation from a relative or close family associate and then passed on their knowledge (and tools) to a son, grandson, son-in-law, or nephew who showed an early aptitude or interest in following the trade. While it is true that multiple generation shops were responsible for a majority of the more ornate and sophisticated gravestones, many truly original and striking folk designs were produced by carvers with little or no training who worked independently in comparative isolation far from the populated coastal settlements. Most carvers chose to live in fairly close proximity to their stone source or to some major waterway or trade route that would make this necessary raw material accessible. Along with the various chisels, mallets, wedges, and smoothing stones that made up a carver's occupational estate, valuable stone quarry rents, mineral rights, and carving shops were also passed from one generation of carvers to another. In most instances, apprentice sons began carving in the style

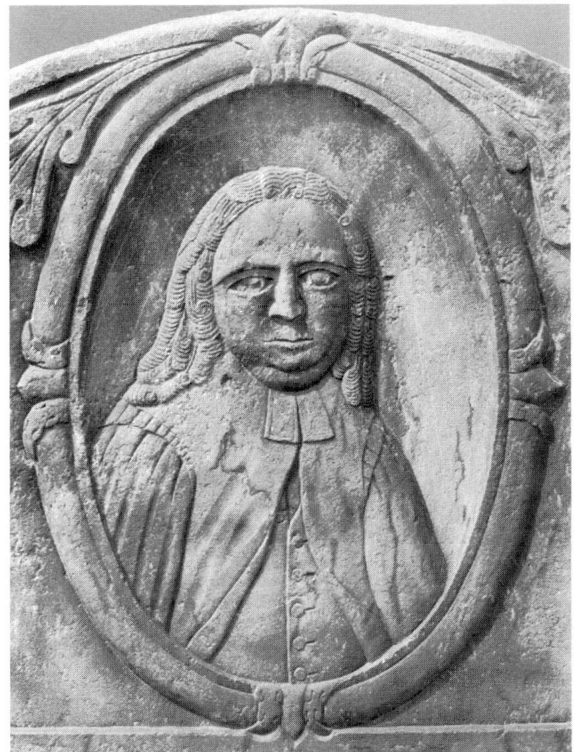

Figure 13 Detail. Gravestone of Reverend Nathan Holt, Peabody, Massachusetts. Park family carvers; gray slate. Groton, Massachusetts, circa 1792. From the Daniel and Jessie Lie Farber Collection of Gravestone Photographs. Courtesy, American Antiquarian Society.

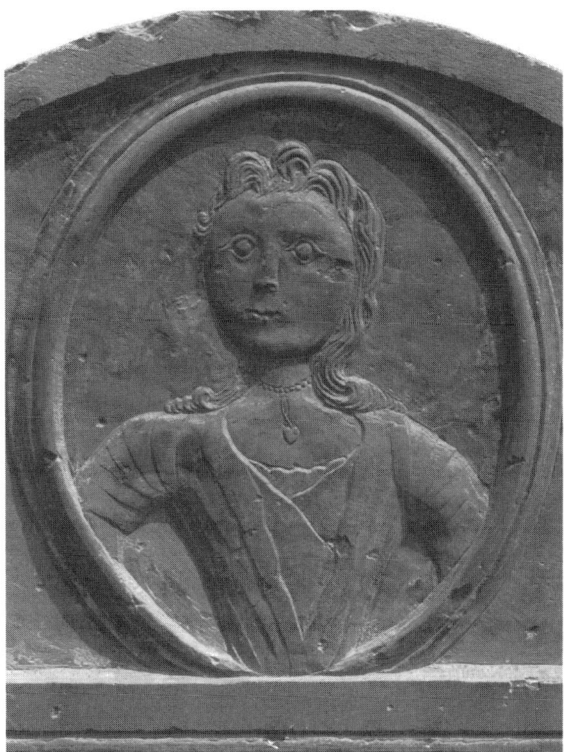

Figure 14 Detail. Gravestone of Patience Watson, Plymouth, Massachusetts. Probably William Codner (1709–1769); gray slate. Boston, Massachusetts, circa 1767. From the Daniel and Jessie Lie Farber Collection of Gravestone Photographs. Courtesy, American Antiquarian Society.

of their parent and teacher, although modifications often evolved as skill was attained, and several second or third generation carvers went on to develop strongly independent styles. The process of identifying the body of work belonging to a particular carver does not rely solely on matching a design to a named carver. Since the same designs and lettering styles were frequently shared by several carvers or workshops, successful research involves a great deal of field study, genealogical and probate searches, and historical analysis.

When genealogical roots lead back to a foreign shore, useful information about these origins is occasionally included in a gravestone epitaph. In New England, the details of parish, county, and country of birth seem to be particularly prevalent on stones for Ireland's sons and daughters: Patrick Gregory from the "parish of Iver in the county of Donagall in the Kingdom of Ireland"; William Sinclair "Born in Ireland in the county of Down in ye parish of Drumbloo. He lived in New England 24 years" (thus providing an estimated year of immigration); Robert Giffen, "born in the Parish of Bellewilling in ye County of Antrim & Kingdom of Ireland . . ."; Elisabeth Crawford, "born in Machrefelt in the County of Londonderry and Kingdom of IreLand." Other nationalities are also frequently found. A handsome marble gravestone for John J. Stickelmire, which identifies him as "a native of Germany and late forman of the Chelmsford Glass Manufactury," was signed by James Hay, one of a family of Scottish stone carvers who migrated to Nova Scotia. In Newport, Rhode Island, the beautifully carved headstones of the colony's early Jewish population include multilingual memorials that attest to the community's scattered roots. Such stones

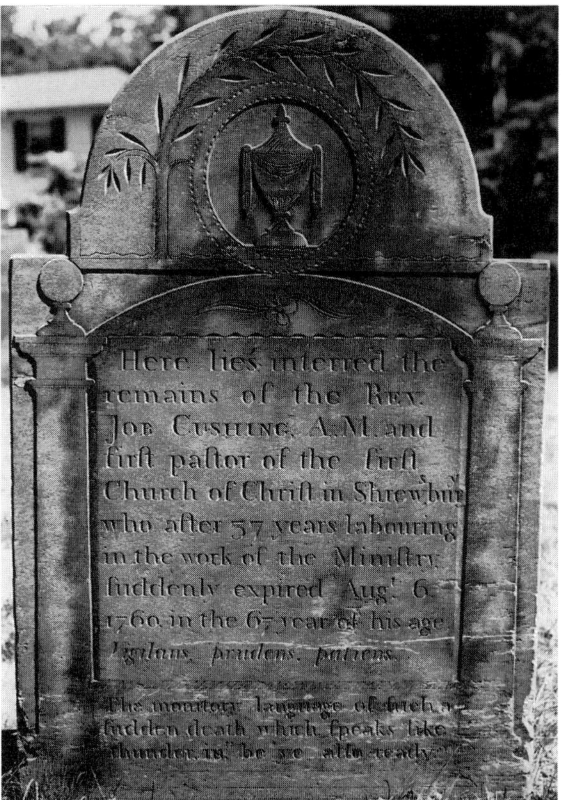

Figure 15 Reverend Job Cushing, Shrewsbury, Massachusetts. Maker unknown; gray slate. Worcester County, Massachusetts, circa 1798. From the Daniel and Jessie Lie Farber Collection of Gravestone Photographs. Courtesy, American Antiquarian Society.

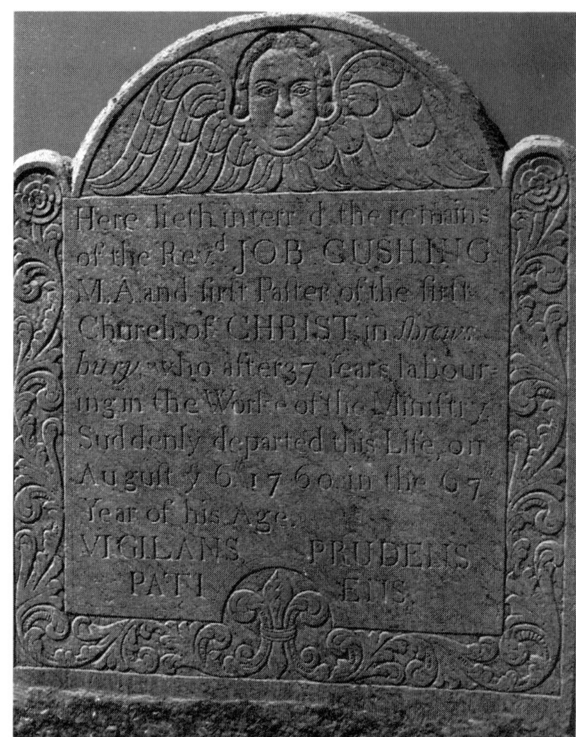

Figure 16 Reverend Job Cushing, Shrewsbury, Massachusetts. George Allen Jr. (1742/3–1764?); probably phyllite. Rehoboth, Massachusetts, circa 1762. From the Daniel and Jessie Lie Farber Collection of Gravestone Photographs. Courtesy, American Antiquarian Society.

have inscriptions in Latin, Hebrew, Spanish, Portuguese, and English (*Figure 17*).

African-Americans were also represented in Colonial and post-Colonial gravesites. The gravestone for Quash Gomer in the segregated area of the Ancient Burying Ground in Wethersfield, Connecticut, states that this former slave was "a native of Angola in Africa, brought from there in 1748." When he died in 1799 at the age of sixty-eight, Quash Gomer was a free man, having purchased his freedom from owner John Smith in 1766 for £25. Quash Gomer and Elenor Smith were "married together on the 3d day of Novr. AD 1766 by the Revd Samuel Auchmuty Missionary of New York." Wethersfield vital records present the births of ten children to Quash and Elenor (Smith) Gomer between 1769 and 1792.[50] While such well-defined origins or organized family groups for African-Americans are rare in New England, other genealogical information such as age, military involvement, or exceptional attributes may appear on the gravemarkers of blacks. In Norwichtown, Connecticut, for example, Boston Trowtrow's gravestone (died 1772, aet 66) honors him as "Govener of ye Affrican Trib"; and Florio Hercules, who died in New London in 1749, is described on her gravestone as the "wife of Hercules Governour of The Negroes."[51] Venture Smith (died 1805 "in ye 77th year of his Age"), the "son of an African King . . . [who] was kidnapped & sold as a slave but by his industry . . . acquired Money to purchase his Freedom" lies next to his wife Marget (died 1809) in an East Haddam, Connecticut, burying ground. More typically, epitaphs for black servants or slaves tended to refer to the emotional relationship between these

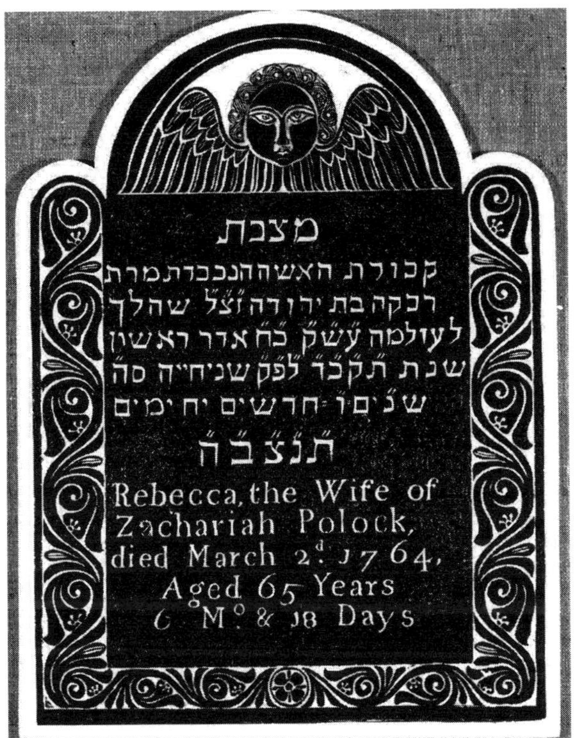

Figure 17 Gravestone of Rebecca Polock, Newport, Rhode Island. William Stevens (1710–?); slate. Newport, Rhode Island, circa 1764. Rubbing by Sue Kelly and Anne Williams, from the Daniel and Jessie Lie Farber Collection of Gravestone Photographs. Courtesy, American Antiquarian Society.

subordinates and their masters or employers, rather than to the black man's origins or familial relationships. The epitaph for seventy-seven-year-old Caesar, a beloved slave of the Maxcy family of Attleboro, Massachusetts, is a stunning example.

> In memory of
> CAESAR
> Here lies the best of slaves
> Now turning into dust:
> Caesar the Ethiopian craves
> A place among the just.
> His faithful soul has fled
> To realms of heavenly light,
> And by the blood that Jesus shed
> is changed from Black to White.
> Jan. 15 he quitted the stage
> in the 77th year of his age
> 1780

Through the further study of gravestones, historians and genealogists are continuing to uncover the rich history and social customs of African-American communities in eighteenth-century New England.

Perhaps an occupation, avocation, or other noteworthy talent may be an ancestor's defining legacy. Miriam Wood (Dorchester, Massachusetts, 1706), "formerly ye wife of John Smith," we learn, was a "woman well beloved of all her neighbors . . . ," and esteemed "for her care of small folks education." From the *New England Primer*, children learned their alphabet in addition to life's larger lessons: "As runs the Glass Man's life doth pass" or "Youth forward slips, Death soonest nips," for "I in the Burying Place may see, Graves shorter there than I; From Death's Arrest no Age is Free, Young children too may die." These reminders of life's uncertainty often appeared on gravestones as well. The epitaph of Joanna Winship (Cambridge, Massachusetts, 1707), the "Good school Dame," appropriately repeats the cadence of the Primer verses which she no doubt taught.

> This good school Dame no longer school must keep,
> Which gives us cause for children's sake to weep.

The worn stone of Boston schoolmaster John Procter Jr., who died in 1773, includes a symbol of his occupation in the form of a quill pen inconspicuously carved above the stone's tablet inscription. Procter's probate account includes a payment of £2/8/0 to gravestone carver John Homer, presumably for the modest stone in King's Chapel Burying Ground.[52] Anticipating his death, the Connecticut gravestone carver Josiah Manning (1725–1806) proudly chiseled his occupation on the back of his own headstone: "This Monument I made in ye year 1800: in my 76th year. JM." Manning is buried in Windham, Connecticut, where he died in 1806.

The skeletal figure of Death and a winged Father Time struggle for supremacy on John Foster's magnificent early gravestone (*Figure 18*). An unnamed carver, recognized only as "The Old Stonecutter," produced the allegorical scene for the thirty-three-year-old Dorchester mathematician and printer, who died in 1681. Foster's will expressed an explicit desire

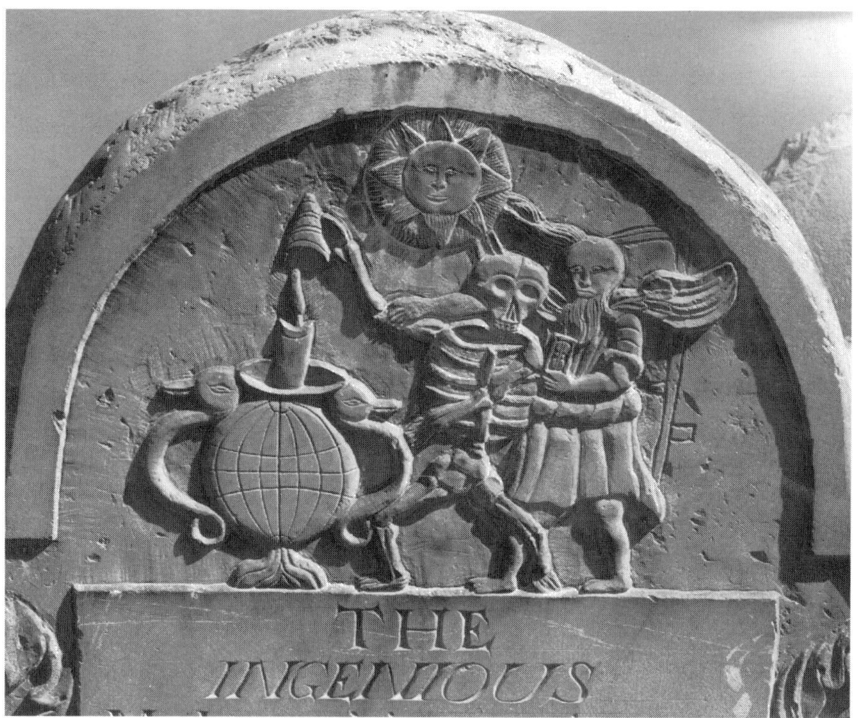

Figure 18 Detail. Gravestone of John Foster, Dorchester, Massachusetts. Maker unknown; gray slate. Boston or Charlestown, Massachusetts, circa 1681. From the Daniel and Jessie Lie Farber Collection of Gravestone Photographs. Courtesy, American Antiquarian Society.

for a handsome gravestone. The inscription includes a popular literary exercise of that day in the form of an anagram of Foster's name ("I shone forth") as well as a couplet written in Latin by Increase Mather and the answering response composed by Foster himself:

> Living thou studiest the stars, dying, mayst thou Foster, I pray,
> mount above the skies and learn to measure the highest heaven.
>
> I.M.
>
> I measure it and it is mine; the Lord Jesus has bought it for me;
> nor am I held to pay aught for it but thanks.
>
> J.F.[53]

A multitude of Americans must descend from the more than three thousand souls helped into the world by midwife Elizabeth Phillips, whose gravestone at Phipp's Street Burying Ground in Charlestown (Massachusetts) informs the viewer that she was "born in Westminster Great Britain, commissioned by John Lord Bishop of London . . . 1718 to ye office of Midwife, came to this country in 1719 . . . brought into this world above 3000 children" before dying in 1761 at the age of seventy-six. Not far away in the town of Dorchester, Daniel Davenport's gravestone identifies him as the "sexton gravedigger," who "buried 1837 persons" before he himself was allowed to rest in 1852.

The gravemarker for Benjamin Thompson (ca. 1642–1714) is one of many beautiful stones by carver James Foster (1651–1732) of Dorchester, Massachusetts. In a mixture of fractured Latin and English, Thompson is eulogized as Roxbury's

> Learned Schoolmaster & Physician, & Ye
> Renouned Poet of N:Engl: Obiit Aprilis, 13
> Anno Dom 1714 & Aetatis Suae, 72
> Mortuus Sed Immortalis. He That Would
> Try What Is True Happiness Indeed Must Die

Ebenezer Dexter of Marlborough, Massachusetts, who died 4 May 1769 in his fortieth year,[54] although

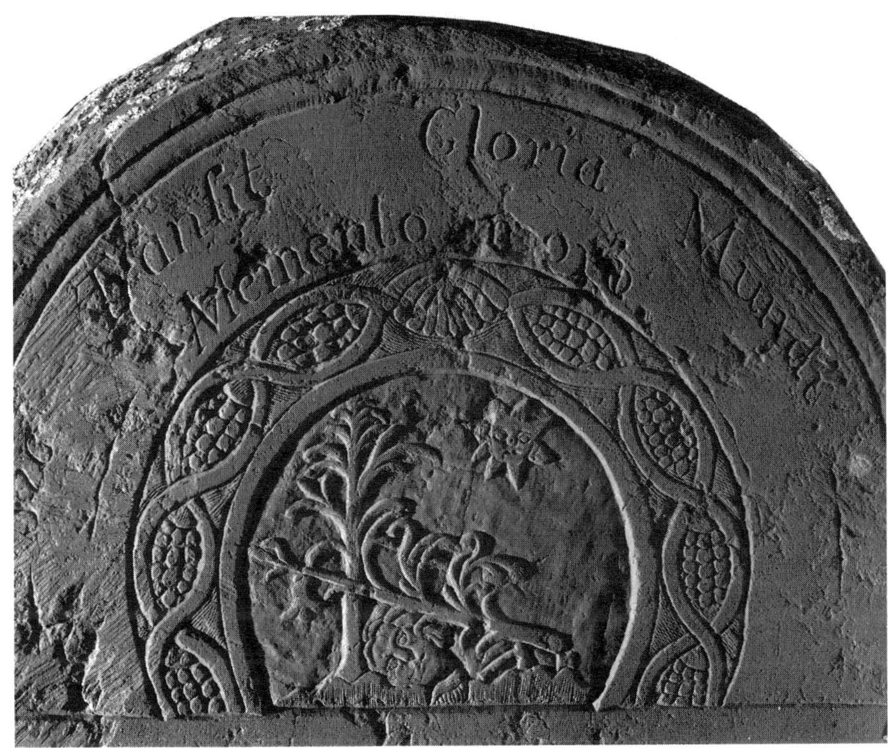

Figure 19 Detail. Gravestone of John Stockbridge, Hanover, Massachusetts. John New (1722–1811); red slate. Abington, Massachusetts, circa 1768. From the Daniel and Jessie Lie Farber Collection of Gravestone Photographs. Courtesy, American Antiquarian Society.

also lauded as an "Eminent Physician," received no special treatment. His epitaph makes clear that he is "as Subject unto Death even as other men."

Gravestones often document or graphically depict deaths that were especially "sudden, premature, awful, [or] violent," as in the case of John Stockbridge, whose gravestone establishes him as the "Son of Coll. David Stockbridge descended by ye Mother's side from the Eldest Daughter of the Hon. John Cushing, Esq. whose mortality has rendered the male issue of that Branch of that Respectable Family extinct," and whose death in 1768 was "providentially occasioned by the Fall of a tree" (*Figure 19*). Three-year-old John Bowers, "The first Born and only son of Mr. John Bowers and Mrs. Lydia his wife," in 1776 "was drowned in a tan pit,"[55] only to be followed in death by a later brother, Aaron, who "was instantly killed by a stack of boards" (*Figure 20*). The idea that these deaths might represent punishment for a dangerously tender attachment to the child or for some other unrepented sin is suggested in the epitaph chosen for Aaron's stone:

> Parents dear, your idols all take down
> Lest God should still upon you frown.

Many who survived infancy and the early years of childhood were claimed by "turning over of a cart," "drowning," "being burned in a fire," "froze to death," "dragged by a horse," "casually shot," or in one case a "powder mill [that] caught fire and blew up."

Young Jonathan Blood of Pepperell died as a result of "a cart wheels going over him." Friends John Cloyes and Abraham Rice, who died in "a sudden and Awful manner" after being struck by lightning, share a gravemarker in Framingham, Massachusetts; Jonas Farnsworth, who lies under an impressive Masonic stone, died "Suddenly by a stroke of the sun"; brothers James, John, and Edward Brown, ages ten, eight and a half, and six, were "burned in [their] house." For Chow Manderien, a nineteen-year-old native of

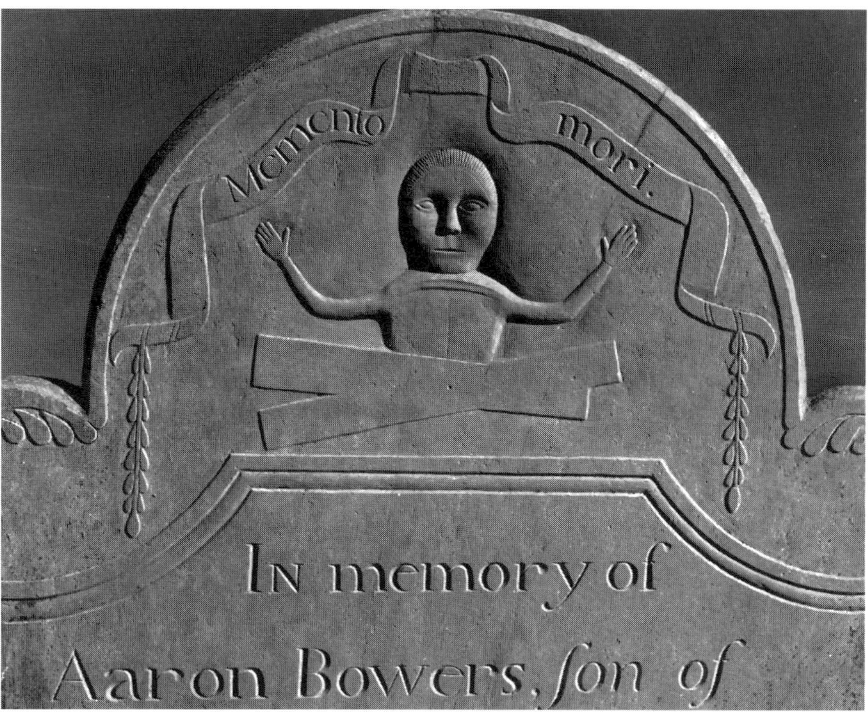

Figure 20 Detail. Gravestone of Aaron Bowers, Pepperell, Massachusetts. Ithamar Spauldin (1767– ?); gray slate. Concord, Massachusetts, circa 1791. From the Daniel and Jessie Lie Farber Collection of Gravestone Photographs. Courtesy, American Antiquarian Society.

China, death was "occassioned on the 11th, Sept. 1798, by a fall from the mast of the ship, *Mac*, of Boston." His stone was erected "by his affectionate master, John Boit, Jr.," a mate on an American ship that discovered the Columbia River in 1792.[56] Lieutenant Moses and Susannah (Hastings) Willard, "first Settlers of this Town" (Charlestown, New Hampshire), are shown side by side on their gravestone. "He was kill'd by the Indians June 16, 1756 in the 54th year of his age and she departed this Life May 5, 1797 in the 88th year of her age. What render'd their lives remarkable was their being bereft of two of their elder daughters by the Indians one of whom had her famuly [*sic*] with her and continued in captivity till after his death." [57]

Fraternal symbolism survives on a surprising number of eighteenth- and early-nineteenth-century New England gravestones (*Figure 21*). The first and most influential of the early fraternal groups was Masonry, or Ancient Free and Accepted Masonry, as it is more officially known. The Masons were active in both Philadelphia and Boston by the year 1738, and they are known to have played a significant role in the final formation of our democratic government. The Odd Fellows, another popular fraternal group, established themselves in Baltimore in 1819. The Society of the Cincinnati, founded 13 May 1783 by George Washington and other officers of the Continental Army, was the first American hereditary order.[58] The modern temperance movement began in the early nineteenth century with as many as ten or eleven major societies in existence by 1830. Sometimes a gravemarker inscription (or an inconspicuous symbol) identifies the deceased as a member of one of these fraternal or hereditary brotherhoods. A rewarding amount of personal information may occasionally be found in the records of the early secret societies and in their offshoots that proliferated in the nineteenth century.[59]

Suicide, murder, or mayhem, although not commonly alluded to on gravestones, add footnotes to family history. An explicit example comes from Rutland, Massachusetts, where lies "ye body of Mr. Daniel Campbell born in Scotland came into New

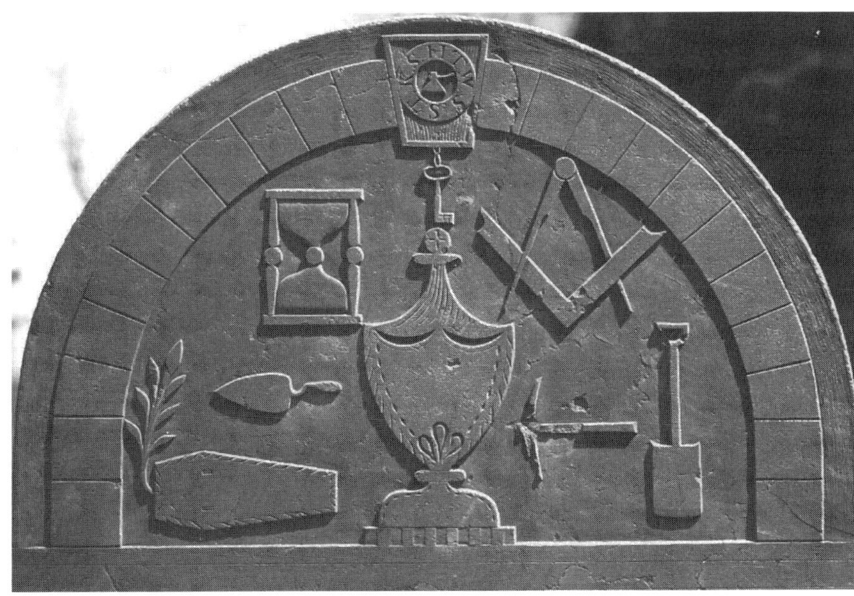

Figure 21 Detail. Lieutenant Jonas Farnsworth, Groton, Massachusetts. Maker unknown; gray slate. Middlesex County, Massachusetts, circa 1805. From the Daniel and Jessie Lie Farber Collection of Gravestone Photographs. Courtesy, American Antiquarian Society.

England anno 1716 was murdered on his own farm . . . by Ed Fitzpatrick an Irishman on March ye 8th anno dm 1743/4 in ye 48 year of his age." Two grave stones in New Boston, New Hampshire, document the murder/suicide of seventeen-year-old Sevilla (1836–1854), the daughter of George and Sarah (Battles) Jones, "murdered by Henry N. Sargent," whose own nearby grave confirms that he was indeed the "murderer of Sevilla Jones," before he took his own life. Careful reading and interpretation of epitaphs may reveal details that are omitted from family chronicles or official records:

> Lo! where this silent marble weeps,
> Our neighbor, friend & brother sleeps;
> Insanity & death are near alli'd,
> He gave the wound by which he di'd.[60]

The epitaph and iconography of the uniquely personal gravestone erected for Harriet (Ruggles) Loomis (Newbury, Vermont, 1861) provide an outstanding example of the genealogical value of cemetery art. Harriet's gravestone documents her final hours of life at the tiny Evangasimba Mission station, Corisco, West Africa (*Figure 22*). The marble gravemarker, carved at Middletown, Connecticut, by a Scottish immigrant named James Craig (1830–1886), provides the clues needed to unravel Harriet's remarkable story. The identities of "Perley" and "Betsey," the significance of the longitude and latitude coordinates carved on the gravestone, the meaning of "Henry Leister, emigravit, July 17 1861" and the date "Jan. 11, 1865" carved on a rock at the bottom of the tropical scene suggested the research which pieced together the incredible lives of the three people mentioned on the stone: a school teacher/missionary who traveled from her home in Vermont to New York, Missouri, and finally to the tiny island of Corisco, West Africa; her earnest, but controversial and often disruptive missionary husband, the Reverend Chauncey Loomis, M.D. (1819–1894), and their infant son, sacrificed by his father at birth when it seemed that the child's death would prolong his mother's life. The gravestone inscription quotes Harriet's dying words; the carved scene of Evangasimba and the brig *Ocean Eagle* was copied from her sketch of the missionary station; the personal and intentionally enigmatic message from Chauncey Loomis to his wife is inscribed in Benga, the tribal language of Corisco.[61]

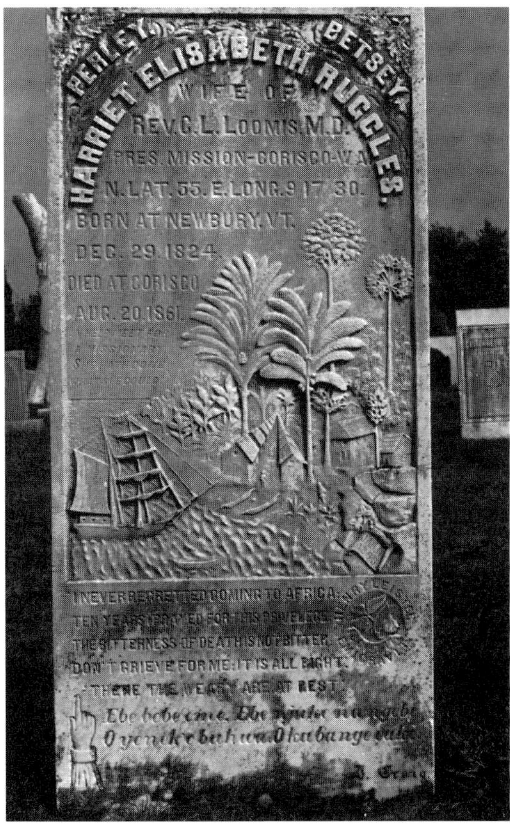

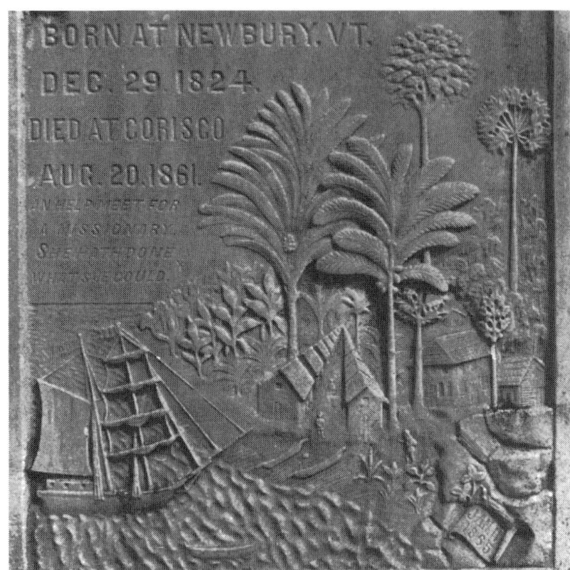

Figure 22 *Left:* Gravestone of Harriet Elisabeth Ruggles Loomis, Newbury, Vermont. *Right:* Detail. Carved rendition of a sketch made by the deceased. James Craig (1830–1886); marble. Middletown, Connecticut, 1865. From the Daniel and Jessie Lie Farber Collection of Gravestone Photographs. Courtesy, American Antiquarian Society.

The art and the epitaph of Harriet's gravestone tell the lost story of her life and death.

Gravestones are an irreplaceable archive of America's social and political history, religious beliefs, and artistic styles. As enduring documentation of individual lives and family histories, they often contain vital information and personal art that is not available from other sources. "STOP and note as you pass by." "He was born . . . ," "She died . . . ," "Here Lyes . . .": the artful footnotes of our past.

NOTES

[1]The author wishes to acknowledge information and assistance provided by the following: Jill Cunninghis, Jessie Lie Farber, Dorothy Flanders, David Gradwohl, Cornelia Jenness, Ann Jones, Barbara Jones, Diane E. Kaplan, Robert Miller, Virginia Moore, Roberta O'Keefe, Beatrice Peirce, Cecile Pimental, Travi Prugno, Mary Wilson, and Rosie Wilson, with special thanks to Nat Shipton, D. Brenton Simons, and Helen Schatvet Ullmann.

[2]M. Halsey Thomas, ed., *The Diary of Samuel Sewall, 1674–1729,* 2 vols. (New York: Farrar, Straus and Giroux, 1973). Dumas Malone, ed., *Dictionary of American Biography* (New York: Charles Scribner's Sons, 1935), 16:610–12.

[3]Samuel Sewall Ledger and Account Book (New England Historic Genealogical Society [hereafter NEHGS], MS/Cb/230), pp. 101–2.

[4]The births of their children are also recorded in the published vital records of Concord and Shrewsbury, Massachusetts. *Concord, Massachusetts Births, Marriages, and Deaths, 1635–1850* (Concord, Mass.: Thomas Todd, 1895). *Vital Records of Shrewsbury, Massachusetts, to the end of the year 1849* (Worcester, Mass.: Franklin P. Rice, 1904), p. 34.

[5]Lois Kimball Mathews, *The Expansion of New England: The Spread of New England Settlement and Institutions to the Mississippi River, 1620–1865* (Boston: Houghton Mifflin Co., 1909), pp. 155, 158.

[6]Marjorie Waterfield, "Elijah Sikes: He Left a Trail of Tombstones!", personal correspondence, August, 1995. Robert Drinkwater, personal correspondence, 1992–1998. Reverend Ralph Tucker, personal correspondence, 1995.

[7]Ernest Caulfield, "Connecticut Gravestones IX: The Collins Family," *Markers VIII: Journal of the Association for Gravestone Studies* (Worcester, Mass.: Association for Gravestone Studies, 1991), pp. 128–40.

[8]Peter Benes, *The Masks of Orthodoxy: Folk Gravestone Carving in Plymouth County, Massachusetts, 1689–1805* (Amherst: University of Massachusetts Press, 1977), pp. 123–32.

[9]Theodore Chase and Laurel K. Gabel, *Gravestone Chronicles I: Some Eighteenth-Century New England Gravestone Carvers and Their Work* (Boston: NEHGS, 1990; reprinted and expanded, Boston: NEHGS, 1997 [hereafter cited as *Gravestone Chronicles I*]), pp. 135–38.

[10]Theodore Chase and Laurel K. Gabel, *Gravestone Chronicles II: More Eighteenth-Century New England Carvers and an Exploration of Gravestone Heraldica* (Boston: NEHGS, 1997 [hereafter cited as *Gravestone Chronicles II*]), pp. 542, 543, 603 and *Gravestone Chronicles I*, p. 125, n. 50.

[11]The author is indebted to Helen Schatvet Ullmann, C.G., for her search for any record of George Lee's date or place of death.

[12]There are a few early gravemarkers whose tablet inscriptions intentionally omit any name or date. Representative of this unusual format is a stone in Newton, Mass., probably carved in the early 1700s: "He thats here interrd needs no versifyi[ng]/ a Vertuos life will keep ye name from dyi[ng]/ he'll live though poets cease thir scribling [ ]/ when yt this stone shall mouldred be by e/tira [?]."

[13]Theodore Chase and Laurel K. Gabel, "Headstones, Hatchments, and Heraldry," *Gravestone Chronicles II*, p. 516. Betty Ring, "Heraldic Embroidery in Eighteenth-Century Boston," *Magazine Antiques* 141, no. 4 (April 1992): 623.

[14]Harold Bowditch, "Early Water-Color Paintings of New England Coats of Arms," *Publications of the Colonial Society of Massachusetts* (Boston: Colonial Society of Massachusetts, 1942–1946), 35:174.

[15]Local libraries and historical societies may have nineteenth-century manuscript transcriptions or inventories done during the WPA years or at the time of the country's centennial or bicentennial. Most early graves were marked at the head and foot with a carved headstone and a smaller, less ornate footstone. In New England the body was most often positioned with the feet of the deceased toward the East, "for the trumpet shall sound, and the dead shall be raised incorruptible" to face the new day—from 1 Corinthians 15:52. Individual headstones and their accompanying footstones are more modest (and infinitely more numerous) than table tombs and provide equally valuable information.

[16]In addition, in some areas of Massachusetts (and probably other locations as well), the gravestones of women and children were linked by a common tympanum design. In one study of seven hundred pre-1800 gravestones produced by carvers John Ball and Paul Colburn, there was clearly one design used for women and children and a different design employed for men: 98.5 percent of the wingless face-in-an-arch style stones were for women or for children under the age of sixteen; 76 percent of the winged faces were on stones for men or boys over the age of sixteen. *Gravestone Chronicles I*, pp. 230–31.

[17]C. J. F. Binney, *The History and Genealogy of the Prentice, or Prentiss Family in New England, etc., from 1631–1883* (Boston: C. J. F. Binney, 1883).

[18]The published vital records for Groton, Connecticut, state that Daniel Tiler Jr. was born 22 February 1700/1701. If correct, this means that he was born in 1700 "old style"—in disagreement with the gravestone that says he was born 1701 "old style." Connecticut Vital Records, Groton: Births, Marriages, Deaths, 1704–1853 (Hartford: Connecticut State Library, Barbour Collection, 1918), p. 148.

[19]Mary Loomis and John Buell were married at Windsor, Connecticut, 20 November 1695. Connecticut Vital Records, Windsor: Births, Marriages, Deaths, 1637–1850 (Hartford: Connecticut State Library, Barbour Collection, 1929), p. 46.

[20]Wayne Hilton Webster (the eleventh generation), "The Indomitable Spirits, a Webster Family Anthology, 1590–1990," MS at Bernardston, Mass., Public Library.

[21]John W. Houghton, *The Houghton Genealogy: Descendants of Ralph and John of Lancaster, Massachusetts* (New York: Frederick H. Hitchcock, 1912), pp. 303, 309.

[22]Ethel Wetherbee Mazza, *John Wetherbee of Marlboro and Stow, Massachusetts*, 2 vols. (Somersworth, N.H.: New Hampshire Printers, 1991), 1:6–7.

[23]Robert Charles Anderson, *The Great Migration Begins: Immigrants to New England, 1620–1633*, 3 vols. (Boston: NEHGS, 1995), 1:439–46.

[24]Edward Payson Jones, "Genealogy of the Descendants of John Bissell of Windsor, Connecticut, by 1640," MS at NEHGS.

[25]Connecticut Vital Records, Windsor: Births, Marriages, Deaths, 1637–1850 (Hartford: Connecticut State Library, Barbour Collection, 1929), pp. 204–5. A more substantial account of Captain Newberry's activities in the Cuban Expedition is found in J. Gardner Bartlett, *Newberry Genealogy: The Ancestors and Descendants of Thomas Newberry of Dorechester, Massachusetts, 1634* (Boston: J. Gardner Bartlett, 1914), pp. 58–63 [hereafter cited as *Newberry Genealogy*].

[26]*Newberry Genealogy*, p. 61.

[27]*Vital Records of Westford, Massachusetts, to the end of the year 1849* (Salem: Essex Institute, 1915), pp. 321, 322 [hereafter cited as *Westford VR*].

[28]Information from the Wright gravestone enables us to correct an error in Reverend Edwin R. Hodgman's *History of the Town of Westford* (Lowell, Mass.: Morning Mail Company, Printers, 1883), which erroneously records Ruth Wright Bates's parents as Ebenezer and Hannah Wright. Oliver Bates's service record is found in *Massachusetts Soldiers and Sailors of the Revolutionary War*, 16 vols. (Boston: Wright and Porter, 1896), 1:797.

[29]*Westford VR*, p. 134.

[30]*Vital Records of Marblehead, Massachusetts, to the end of the year 1849*, 3 vols. (Salem: Essex Institute, 1904), 2:421.

[31]Donald Lines Jacobus, *The Genealogy of the Kimberly Family* (Menasha, Wisc.: George Banta Publishing Company, 1950), pp. 22–23.

[32]James Slater, *The Colonial Burying Grounds of Eastern Connecticut and the Men Who Made Them* (Hamden, Conn.: Archon Books, 1987), p. 194.

[33]Louis Mitchell, *The Woodbridge Record: Being an Account of the Descendants of the Reverend John Woodbridge of Newbury, Massachusetts* (New Haven: n. p., 1883), p. 32.

[34]According to Frederic Beech Pierce, *Pierce Genealogy, Being the Record of the Posterity of Thomas Pierce, an Early Inhabitant of Charlestown, And Afterwards Charlestown Village (Woburn)* (Worcester, Mass.: Press of Charles Hamilton, 1882), p. 52, Captain Benjamin Pierce had four wives, the last being Sarah Holt whom he married in 1762. The gravestone for "Widow Sarah Peirce" who died in 1797 at the age of seventy-nine is in Hampton, Conn.

[35]"Throat distemper," which killed over 5,000 people (more than half of them children), began as diptheria but eventually also included scarlet fever as well. For a thorough description and discussion of the epidemic "throat distemper" or "children's plague" that swept New England between 1735 and 1740, see Dr. Ernest Caulfield's "A History of the Terrible Epidemic, Vulgarly Called the Throat Distemper, as it Occurred in His Majesty's New England Colonies Between 1735 and 1740," in *Yale Journal of Biology and Medicine* (New Haven, 1938–1939), 11:219–72, 277–335; and Bryan F. LeBeau, "'Angelical Conjunction' Revisited: Another Look at the Preacher-Physician in Colonial America and the Throat Distemper Epidemic of 1735–1740," *Journal of American Culture* 18, no. 3 (fall 1995): 1–12. Minor pox was probably chicken pox.

[36]A narrative of the Park family tragedy is found in Victoria Miles, *Raising Rebecca: An Exploration of Life, Death, and Gravestone Art in Early Vermont* (Grafton, Vt:. Grafton Historical Society, 1998).

[37]The fact that thirteen of the children died within days of their birth strongly suggests Rh incompatibility as the cause of death. Rh incompatibility was not known to be the cause of this syndrome until after 1940. Modern immunologic techniques have essentially eliminated Rh incompatibility as a cause of neonatal death in industrialized countries. *The Columbia Encyclopedia, Fifth Edition* (New York: Columbia University Press, 1993).

[38]Horace Wilbur Palmer, comp., *Palmer Families in America (Vol. I): Lieutenant William Palmer of Yarmouth, Massachusetts and his Descendants of Greenwich, Conn.* (1966; reprint, Salem, Mass.: Higginson Book Co., n.d.). Jacomiah Palmer (1761–1847) m. 1787 Mercy Phillips, Danby Corners, Vt.; children: Daniel Palmer, b. 1788, Enoch Palmer, b. 1790, Bazaliel Palmer, b. 1791, Silas Palmer, b. 1793, Wonderful Palmer, b. 1795, Admirable Palmer, b. 1795, Remarkable Palmer, b. 1795, and Strange Palmer, b. 1795, Rena Palmer, b. 1797, Phinetta Palmer, b. 1800, and Pamela Palmer, b. 1800.

[39]The famous Revere bowl was commissioned in 1768 by the fifteen Boston merchants whose names are engraved on the rim: "Caleb Hopkins, Nathl. Barber, John White, Willm Mackay, Danl. Malcolm, Benjn. Goodwin, John Welsh, Fortescue Vernon, Danl. Parker, John Marston, Ichabod Jones, John Homer, Willm Bowes, Peter Boyer, Banja. Cobb." It was dedicated "To the Memory of the glorious NINETY-TWO: Members of the Honbl. House of Representatives of the Massachusetts-Bay, who, undaunted by the insolent Menaces of Villains in Power, from a Strict regard to Conscience, and the LIBERTIES of their Constituents, on the 30th of June 1768, Voted NOT TO RESCIND." The bowl includes such symbols as a Liberty Cap and banners bearing the words "Magna Charta" and "Bill of Rights" and a torn page labeled "Generall Warrants." Within a circle on the bowl are the words "No. 45" and "Wilkes and Liberty." The Sons of Liberty were supporters of John Wilkes (1727–1797), a noted English journalist and member of Parliament. In issue no. 45 of Wilkes's periodical, the *North Briton,* he was openly critical of the policies of King George III toward the American colonies. He opposed the taxation of the colonies and championed freedom of the press and the rights of the electorate. John Homer is one of the fifteen names on the Revere Liberty Bowl. Although it is possible that the Boston gravestone carver John Homer was the one whose name appears, it is perhaps more likely that another John Homer, a wealthy ship owner and merchant, was the man so honored. Merchant John Homer became a Tory sympathizer and removed to Nova Scotia during the British evacuation of Boston in March, 1776.

[40]Boston merchant Daniel Malcom was the focus of a near riot in October of 1766, when customs officials broke into his warehouse in search of illegal goods or other incriminating evidence that would show that he had violated the hated Navigation Acts. An angry mob came to Malcom's defense and the king's men were forced to retreat.

[41]The twenty-eight-gun frigate *Trumbull,* named after Connecticut's popular Governor Jonathan Trumbull, was constructed according to an Act of Congress on 13 December 1775. The ship was built on the Connecticut River at Chatham by John Cotton and launched in the summer of 1776, although it did not actually go to sea until April 1780. The ship depicted on Lieutenant Smith's gravestone does not appear to be an accurate portrayal of the *Trumbull.* For a more complete account of the ship's turbulent history, see John F. Millar's *American Ships of the Colonial and Revolutionary Periods* (New York: W. W. Norton and Company, 1978), pp. 278, 284–86; *The American Navies of the Revolutionary War,* introduction by Richard B. Morris (New York: G. P. Putnam's Sons, 1974), p. 114; and E. B. Potter, *The Naval Academy Illustrated History of the United States Navy* (New York: Galahad Books, 1871), p. 26.

[42]Elizabeth Ellery Dana, *The Dana Family in America* (Cambridge, Mass.: Wright and Potter, 1956), pp. 258–59.

[43]Other Sons of Liberty pointedly named children after the English heroes of their cause. Nathaniel Barber (another one of the fifteen names on the Revere Liberty Bowl) named a son Wilkes (brother to another son named Oliver Cromwell and to a sister Catharine Macaulay).

[44]Dumas Malone, ed., *Dictionary of American Biography,* 11 vols. (New York: Charles Scribner's Sons, 1934), 7: 86–87.

[45]Judah Monis, an Italian Jew who had come to Cambridge by way of Jamaica and New York, was probably educated in the Jewish academies of Leghorn and Amsterdam. He was admitted to the master's degree at Harvard in 1720 at a time when most universities of Christendom admitted no Jew to a degree, "on account of the religious tests and oaths that

went with" a degree. In 1722 Monis was formally converted to Christianity at an impressive public ceremony in the college hall and within a month was chosen "Instructor of the hebrew Language" at Harvard College for a year, with an annual salary of £50. At one point the Harvard Corporation asked Monis to revise his teaching methods "which were thought so tedious as to be discouraging." Judah Monis's appointment was renewed and his salary raised annually for forty years, until his resignation in 1769. Samuel Eliot Morison, *Three Centuries of Harvard* (Cambridge: Harvard University Press, 1942). See also David M. Gradwohl, "Judah Monis's Puzzling Gravestone as Reflection of His Enigmatic Identity" (American Culture Association Conference, San Diego, California, April 1999), which explores Monis's origins, his celebrated and conflicted Judeo/Christian identity, his subsequent marriage and academic life at Harvard, and his final days in Northborough, Mass.

[46]Clifford K. Shipton, ed., *Sibley's Harvard Graduates: Biographical Sketches of Those Who Attended Harvard College in the Classes 1713–17* (Boston: Massachusetts Historical Society, 1942), pp. 282–83.

[47]Francis Olcott Allen, *History of Enfield, Connecticut*, 3 vols. (Lancaster, Pa.: Wickersham Publishing Company, 1900), pp. 1651, 1873.

[48]Malone, *Dictionary of American Biography*, 10 (pt. 1): 58–59.

[49]James S. Cushing, *The Genealogy of the Cushing Family* (Montreal: Perrault Printing Co., 1905; reprinted 1979, by Helen Grant Cushing), pp. 48–49.

[50]The author is indebted to Helen Schatvet Ullmann for this information from the Wethersfield Vital Records, book 2, page 21a. In 1784 Connecticut passed an act granting all Negro and mulatto children their freedom on reaching twenty-five years of age. Not until 1848 were all slaves emancipated in Connecticut. Gladys G. Macdonough, *The Stone and the Spirit: A Walking Tour Guide to the Ancient Burying Ground in the Wethersfield Village Cemetery* (Wethersfield, Conn.: Wethersfield Historical Society, 1987), p. 29.

[51]William D. Piersen, *Black Yankees: The Development of an Afro-American Subculture in Eighteenth-Century New England* (Amherst: University of Massachusetts Press, 1988), pp. 117–40; and Orville H. Platt, "Negro Governors," *New Haven Colony Historical Society, Papers 6* (1900): 117–128, tables 9–10.

[52]Suffolk County Probate Records 73:595, Massachusetts Archives, Dorchester, Mass.

[53]John Foster (born 1648) was Boston's first printer and engraver. He compiled an early almanac and engraved the seal of Massachusetts. A man of many interests and talents, he was also an amateur astronomer and author of a book about comets.

[54]*Vital Records of Marlborough, Massachusetts, to the end of the year 1849* (Worcester, Mass.: Franklin P. Rice, 1908), p. 356.

[55]The tanning process in practice in the Colonies in the 1760s required the animal skins to be immersed repeatedly into a pit of lime, then an alkaline bath (frequently made by combining hen dung, potash or salt, and water), and finally into the tanning pit, a deep vat of water and bark that produced the ooze known as tannin. Tannin, or tan, was usually produced from the bark of oak, ground or chopped into a coarse powder. The average square, above-ground, tanning vat measured about five feet on a side. The entire tanning process could take anywhere from six months to several years. Peter C. Welsh, *Tanning in the United States to 1850* (Washington, D.C.: Smithsonian Institution, 1964), pp. 15–24, 75–76.

[56]Howard Mumford Jones and Bessie Zaban Jones, eds., *The Many Voices of Boston* (Boston: Little Brown, 1975), p. 137, quoting in part from Chiang Yee, *The Silent Traveller in Boston* (New York: Norton, 1959), pp. 178–84. John Boit Jr. probably erected the gravemarker for Chow Manderien at the same time that he placed a gravestone for his father John Boit Sr. who died three months later, in December 1798.

[57]Susannah Johnson Hastings, *A Narrative of the Captivity of Mrs. Johnson* (Bowie, Md.: Heritage Press, 1990).

[58]George Washington served as the first president-general of the Society of the Cincinnati from 1783 until his death in 1799. The founding officers of the order "possess[ed] high veneration for the character of that illustrious Roman, Lucius Quintus Cincinnatus; and being resolved to follow his example, by returning to their citizenship, they think they may with propriety denominate themselves—The Society of the Cincinnati." Bryce Metcalf, *Original Members and Other Officers Eligible to the Society of the Cincinnati, 1738–1938* (Strasburg, Va.: Shenandoah Publishing House, 1938), pp. 1–2.

[59]By the beginning of the twentieth century, nearly half of the entire population of the United States, men and women, belonged to at least one secret order or fraternal benefit society. "Death and funerary regalia held special importance in the complex rituals and secret initiations of fraternalism and this regalia was also an integral part of the etiquette and ceremony of fraternal burials." Laurel K. Gabel, "Ritual, Regalia, and Remembrance. Fraternal Symbolism and Gravestones," *Markers XI: Journal of the Association for Gravestone Studies* (Worcester, Mass.: Association for Gravestone Studies, 1994), pp. 1–27. In addition to all of the various Masonic and Odd Fellow organizations, some of the more popular early-nineteenth-century fraternal societies include the United Ancient Order of Druids (1830), Improved Order of Red Men (1834), Ancient Order of Hibernians (1836), Order of Sons of Herman (1840), Sons of Temperance (1842), United American Mechanics (1845), Free Sons of Israel (1849), Knights of Jericho (1850), International Order of Good Templars (1850), and Knights of Pythias (1864).

[60]Nathan Cutting, 1803, Westminster, Mass.

[61]Laurel K. Gabel, "I Never Regretted Coming to Africa: The Story Behind the Harriet Loomis Gravestone," *Markers XVI: The Journal of the Association for Gravestone Studies* (Greenfield, Mass.: Association for Gravestone Studies, 1999), pp. 176–211.

SECTION V

Patterns of Inheritance and Acquisition

Sterling Memories: Family and Silver in Early New England

Barbara McLean Ward and Gerald W. R. Ward

When Elizabeth Curwen of Salem, Massachusetts, wrote her will in 1717, she dispersed the silver objects in her possession among her children and grandchildren. In doing so, not only did she recognize that these pieces of plate, as silver objects were known, would provide her family with tangible reminders of her, she also took pains to note the connection of these items to an earlier family member. She gave to her son, Henry Gibbs, the "Great Silver Tankard which his grandfather Sir Henry Gibbs sent me as a present," and to her grandson Henry Gibbs she gave her "Silver sugar box which his great-grandfather Sir Henry Gibbs sent me also as a present."[1] It was clearly important to her to pass these items on to Sir Henry's namesakes and to tell the recipients that the original giver had been honored with a knighthood. Why did she choose to make silver objects act as the carriers of family memory?

For centuries the silversmith's craft has been about art, money, and memory. Working with fabulously responsive metal—a material, moreover, with intrinsic value—the silversmith produced beautiful, durable, and often useful works of art. These please the eye and serve the purposes of the silversmith's own generation, but they also, in a way probably not exceeded by any other type of small, portable object, have become records of family ties and lasting legacies for future generations.

The special role of silver in acting as a vehicle for communicating family prestige and honor and transmitting these qualities to the next generation derives largely from its properties as a metal. Silver's malleability and ductility allow it to be fashioned by many different techniques into almost any shape or form that the silversmith desires. Unlike pewter, which is generally cast in molds, silver challenges a craftsman's imagination each time he or she sets out to make a new object. Among the metals, silver is the most reflective, bouncing back approximately 95 percent of incident light—nearly as much as new-fallen snow. It is easily engraved, and many silver objects bear inscriptions that record the history of their ownership, a gift, or a bequest.[2]

Silver's intrinsic worth has always made it a significant repository of wealth. Being fashioned of one of the precious metals, a silver tankard or teapot retained the current value of its metal. Even when old and out of fashion, it could be returned to the melting pot to provide its owner with its value in bullion. Silver objects were often specified individually in wills, with children and relatives designated to receive a particular cup or tankard as a remembrance. When Elizabeth Curwen made her bequests, she was not only creating memory, she was transferring wealth and status to her heirs. As William Fitzhugh of Virginia observed in 1688, "I esteem it as well politic as reputable to furnish myself with an handsome cupboard of plate which gives myself the present use and credit, is a sure friend at a dead lift without much loss or is a certain portion for a Child after my decease."[3] The safety net of intrinsic worth was a two-edged sword, however. While many family heirlooms were retained because of their value, many were sacrificed by later generations in need of ready cash.

Because of its high cost and the scarcity of specie in the American colonies, the ownership of silver in any quantity was confined to a small proportion of the population. While many households might contain one or more silver spoons or small items of silver jewelry, perhaps only 5 percent of the population owned significant amounts of hollowware. As a luxury good, therefore, silver has always connoted wealth, but it has also had a special relationship with the concept of family, especially in the seventeenth century. During the first century of settlement, people who considered themselves to be of a high social station, although perhaps not great wealth—ministers in New England, for example—owned silver in quantities disproportionate to their total estates. The Reverend Solomon Stoddard, even though he lived on the frontier in Northampton, Massachusetts, owned a standing silver salt (*Figure 1*) made in Boston that was decorated with gadrooning in the latest fashion.[4] Henry Flynt, tutor at Harvard College for fifty-five years, owned a vast array of plate because each year his students presented him with a gift. His collection became so comprehensive, in fact, that his students finally decided to give him a silver chamber pot, reasoning that it was the only article in silver that he did not yet own.[5] However, as the eighteenth century progressed, silver became more of a consumer commodity whose ownership primarily reflected wealth.[6]

As a family object, perhaps the most important quality of silver has been its durability. Although it tarnishes with exposure to oxygen and other common gases, silver is a noble metal and survives most conditions and environments well. Unlike the much softer metal alloy pewter, silver does not wear out with regular use; and, unlike glass and ceramics, silver dents, rather than shatters, when accidentally dropped. Silver is not subject to worm disease, like wooden furniture, and generally endures dampness and temperature extremes. Furthermore, it does not fray or fade under daily use like clothing, textiles, or upholstered furniture.

Bright, shiny things attract people, and this enhanced silver's display function within the relatively dark domestic interiors of the first generation of colonial Americans. When arrayed upon a cloth atop a seventeenth-century cupboard, for example, silver vessels provided sparkle and flashes of light, drawing attention to themselves and thus underlining the owner's social status and wealth. Because the silver objects that were owned by the first Europeans in America were made in their own native lands, these objects displayed the status the family had enjoyed in the mother country, a status the family usually hoped to maintain in their new home. In the early eighteenth century it was considered fitting for representatives of the crown in foreign countries and in the colonies to own and display £3,000 in silver plate in their homes.[7] Governor Charles Knowles of Louisburg even took some of his silver with him in 1747 when he spent several weeks in Boston recruiting (and impressing) sailors to fight against the French. He placed the silver on display in the shop of Jacob Hurd, Boston's most prominent silver- or goldsmith, undoubtedly so that the local populace would be persuaded of his importance. Upon seeing the plate, shopkeeper Benjamin Walker recorded in his diary, "Att mr. Hurds Gold Smith [shop] in Cornhill Street I see ye finest Sight of Silver plate belonging To Gouernour Charles Knowles of Lewisburg on Cape Briton some part of his Sideboard, such fine Crafte work & Variety I can't Enumerate & It's sd he has much more."[8] The ability of silver to convey means and meaning across generations was widely understood in early America. Authority was even more firmly established if confirmed by one's lineage. When Massachusetts royal governor William Burnet died in 1729, he owned more than 1,172 ounces of plate, including "ffour silver Gilt antient family Cups with covers."[9]

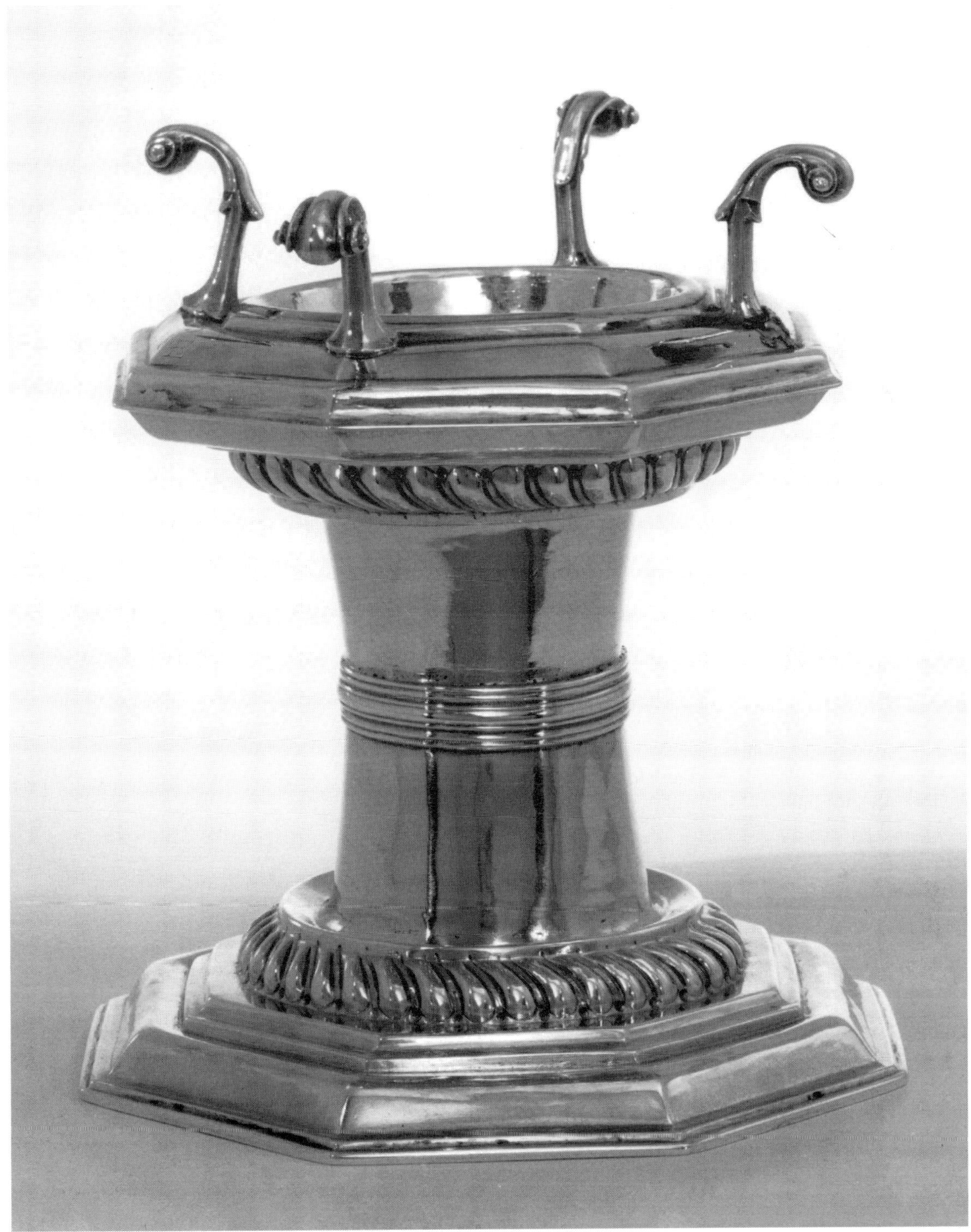

Figure 1 Standing salt. John Allen (1671/72–1760) and John Edwards (circa 1671–1746). Boston, Massachusetts, circa 1696. Silver; 5¾ inches high. The Metropolitan Museum of Art. Gift of Sarah Hayward Draper, 1972. (1972.204).

Family objects of this type were often identified as such with armorial engraving. Although only a small number of early Americans had any official right to use coats of arms, beginning in the late seventeenth century, many wealthy individuals who commissioned silver objects worked with the silversmith to select arms associated with their surnames from printed sources such as John Guillam's *Display of Heraldry* (first published in the seventeenth century and reissued many times), the 1724 (6th) edition of which was frequently used in this country. In doing so, these colonists were aligning themselves with the officials of the new royal government that replaced the old charter government and confirming their allegiance to English manners, customs, and hierarchy.[10] An interesting example of this reliance on Guillam's book is a teapot (*Figure 2*) given to tutor Henry Flynt as a gift from his students in 1738. It bears a coat of arms with three flint stones, as described in Guillam (*Figure 3*). Flynt subsequently gave the teapot to his niece, Dorothy (Quinsey) Jackson, daughter of his sister Dorothy (Flynt) Quinsey.[11]

The fashion for adopting coats of arms became particularly strong in New England during the middle decades of the eighteenth century, when wealthy colonial families sought increasingly to identify themselves with the landed English gentry. In 1729 John Vassall, a sophomore, and William Vassall, whose father had made his fortune in the West Indies, were admitted as "fellow-commoners" of Harvard College. The designation of fellow-commoner was reserved for students whose parents paid fees

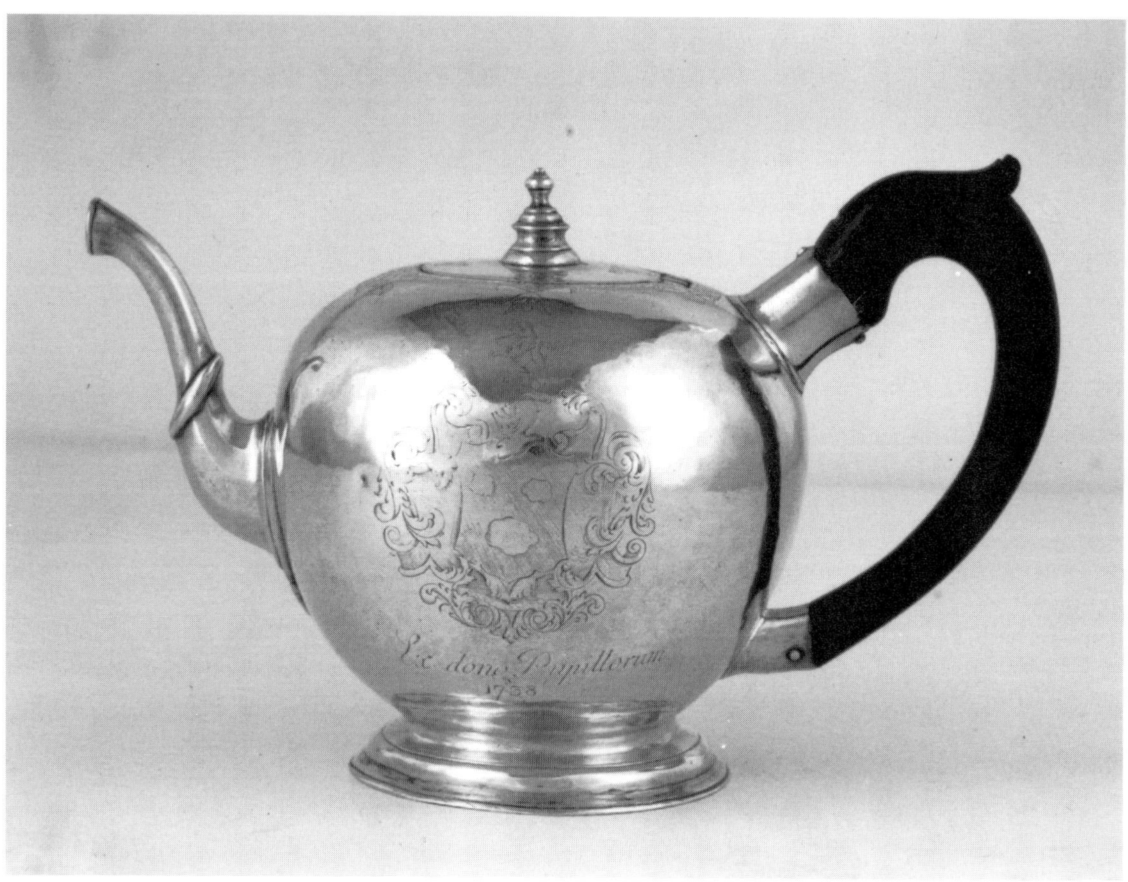

Figure 2 Teapot. Jacob Hurd (1702/03–1758). Boston, Massachusetts, 1738. Silver; 5¾ inches high. Edward Jackson Holmes Collection, Bequest of Mrs. Holmes (65.385). Courtesy, Museum of Fine Arts, Boston.

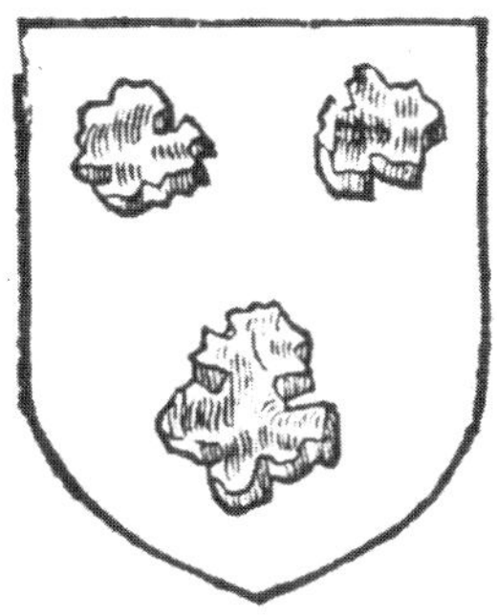

Figure 3 Flint family arms. From John Guillam, *Display of Heraldry* (London, 1724), chap. 6, p. 110.

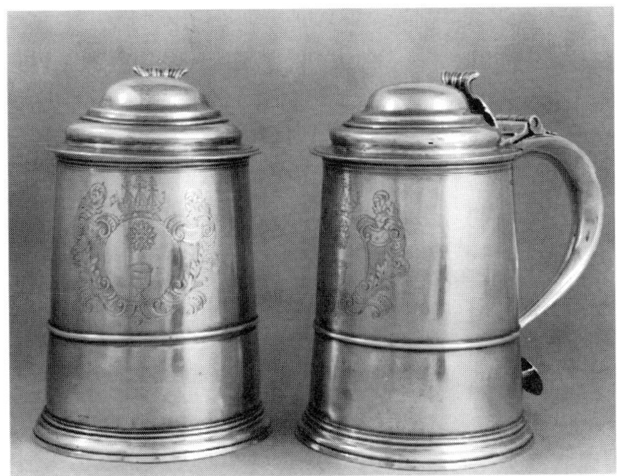

Figure 4 Pair of tankards. Joseph Kneeland (1700–1740). Boston, Massachusetts, 1729. Silver; 6¾ inches high. Courtesy of the Fogg Art Museum, Harvard University Art Museums, Loan from Harvard University (874.1927): Gift to Harvard College from William Vassal, Class of 1733, 1729. © *President and Fellows of Harvard College.*

that were approximately twice those paid by regular students. These students received special privileges and ranked above all undergraduates, eating at the fellows' table. The fellows' table was noteworthy not only because of the status of the men who sat there, but also for its fine linen and silver. Each fellow-commoner was required to present the college with a piece of plate worth at least £3. This plate was used at the fellows' table and displayed for all of the students to see.[12] The Vassall brothers presented two tankards (*Figure 4*), made by Joseph Kneeland of Boston and engraved with the Vassall family coat of arms, as their gifts to the college. The tankards also bear Latin inscriptions commemorating the brothers' status as fellow-commoners.[13] Because the brothers drank from them every day at the fellows' table, the tankards provided an effective vehicle for displaying the Vassall family's social status to the other students; the tankards continue to remind visitors to the Fogg Art Museum of the family's importance to Harvard College.

As well as being attractive and recognizable reminders of family origins, coats of arms could display the social power implicit in the merger of great families through marriage. The impressive cluster column candlesticks (*Figure 5*) made by Jeremiah Dummer of Boston in the 1680s bear four coats of arms, one at each corner of the base, representing four great New England merchant families—Lidgett, Clarke, Usher, and Jeffries—and were originally made to commemorate the marriage of David Jeffries and Elizabeth Usher in 1686 and may have been given to the couple by Elizabeth's grandfather, Colonel Peter Lidgett. In 1713 their son, David Jeffries, married Anne Clarke, and at that time the Clarke arms were probably added.[14]

These candlesticks, like many other seventeenth- and eighteenth-century silver objects, also bear engraving of the owners' initials—in this case "D I E" for David and Elizabeth Jeffries, the letter *I* being commonly used both as an *I* and a *J* at the time—in the traditional form for a married couple, with the first initial of the last name placed in the superior position flanked by the first letter of the bride's and groom's names. Sometimes initials, of either a couple or an individual, are accompanied by a date, usually the year in which the piece was acquired. On larger objects this same information is often present and is joined in many instances by an engraved coat of arms. Ciphers became fashionable during the 1760s and continued in use until the end of the century.

As this pair of candlesticks demonstrates, keeping alive the memory of the status of a woman's family and her female ancestors was often just as important as displaying the status of a man's ancestral family. In New England, movable goods frequently passed through the female side of the family, while real property most often passed through the male line. There are numerous examples of both patrilineal and matrilineal descent of silver objects noted in probate records, but one way that a couple could

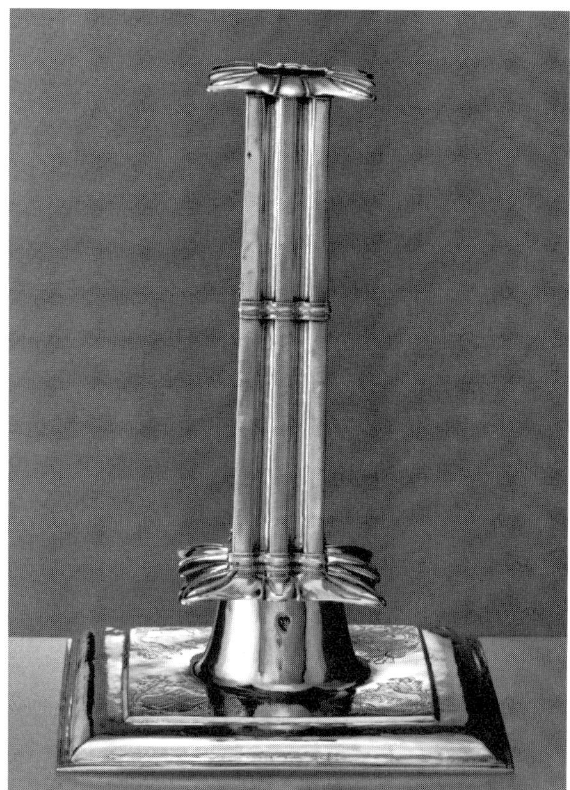

Figure 5 Candlestick. Jeremiah Dummer (1645–1718). Boston, Massachusetts, ca. 1680–1890. Silver; 10 13/16 inches high. Yale University Art Gallery; Mabel Brady Garvan Collection (1935.234 or 1953.22.1).

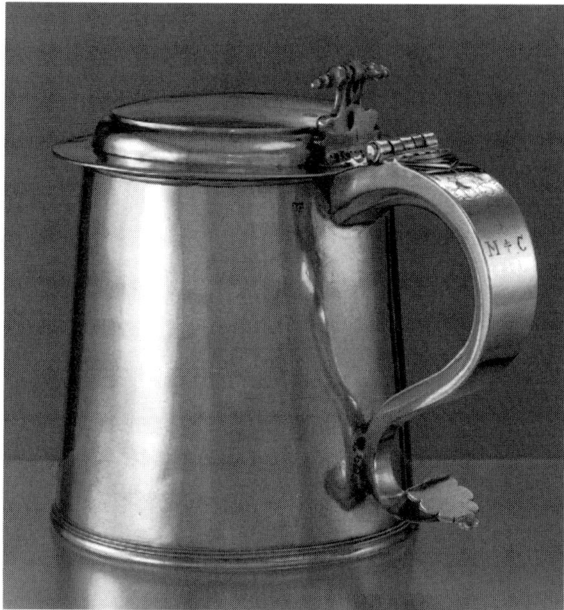

Figure 6 Tankard. John Coney (1655/56–1722). Boston, Massachusetts, circa 1690. Silver; 7 1/8 inches high. Yale University Art Gallery; Mabel Brady Garvan Collection (1931.323).

make sure that visitors were aware of the complete web of their kin relationships was to display objects bearing the initials and arms of the wife's family. The large silver tankard (*Figure 6*) that Mary (Shrimpton) Gibbs gave to her daughter Mary (Gibbs) Cotton bears the arms of the Shrimpton family in foliate mantling and was used to display her family origins and the origins of generations of her descendants. The tankard continued to descend through the female line, following the daughter of each owner, Martha (Cotton) Thayer, Catherine (Thayer) Abbot, Martha (Abbot) Cram, Catherine Abbot (Cram) Folsom, and finally to Anna Abbot Folsom.[15] In some cases, these objects could include meaningful connections to other members of a woman's birth family, as in the case of the three silver tea services that Thomas Welles had made for his three daughters. Two of the three sets survive (*Figure 7*) and are

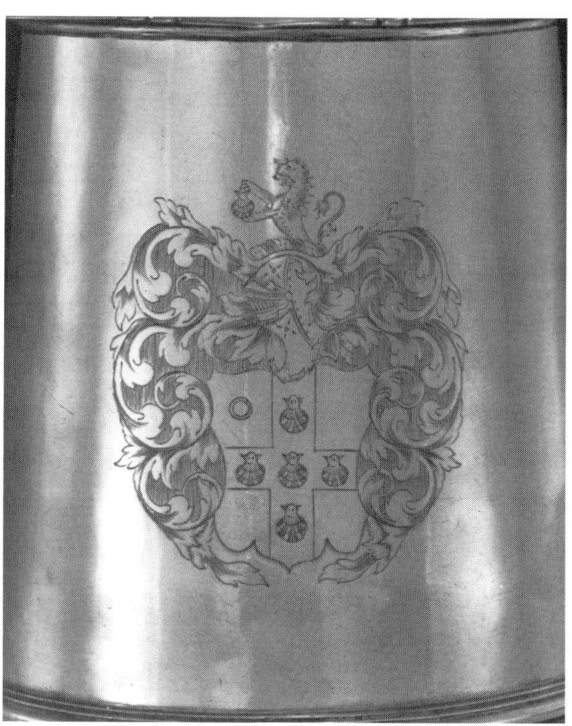

Figure 6A Detail of coat of arms on Coney tankard in *Figure 6*. Yale University Art Gallery; Mabel Brady Garvan Collection (1931.323).

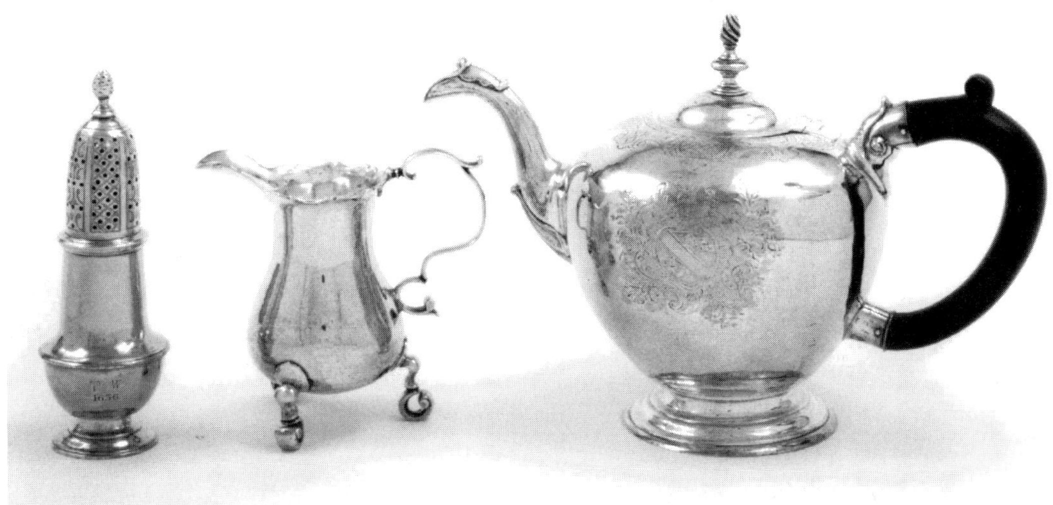

Figure 7 Tea set. John Coburn (1724–1803). Boston, Massachusetts, circa 1753. Silver; teapot 6½ inches high. Courtesy of Historic Deerfield. *Photograph by Amanda Merullo.*

almost identical in appearance to one another. Both were made by John Coburn, and both sets include a teapot, a sugar caster, and a cream pot, and both are engraved "TW." The form of the sets, as well as the inscription linking both sets to the women's father, made the link between them clearly evident. The fact that the sets are identical may also indicate Thomas Welles's desire to provide equally for each of his daughters.[16] Mary Storer also established connections between her female kin by presenting them with identical objects. She gave a cann (*Figure 8*) to each of her infant granddaughters, Mary Smith, born in 1757 to Elizabeth (Storer) Smith and her husband Isaac Smith, and Mary Storer "Junr" born in 1758 to Ebenezer and Elizabeth (Green) Storer. Both canns bear the Storer arms and crest on the body within an elaborate rococo mantling, creating a tangible kinship link between the two Marys. The canns were made by Samuel Edwards, brother-in-law of Isaac Smith, but may have been engraved by a specialist.[17]

Other pieces of silver are engraved with coats of arms in which the woman's family arms are combined with her husband's family arms, as is the case on a beautifully engraved salver made by Thomas Edwards of Boston that bears the arms of Allen impaling Parker, a tankard (*Figure 9*) by Benjamin Burt bearing the arms of North impaling Pitson, and the pair of silver standing cups made by Daniel Henchman with the arms of Hancock impaling Henchman that Lydia (Henchman) Hancock presented to the First Church in Boston on 4 September 1773.[18]

Many pieces of silver were engraved to commemorate family threshold events, such as births, marriages, anniversaries, and deaths. A set of three porringers with keyhole handles by William Swan of Boston engraved "K . . . C" were made for Katharine Chandler prior to her marriage to Levi Willard in 1755 probably as part of her dowry.[19] A similar set of three porringers by Samuel Gray of Boston bears the initials "S A M" for both the bride and groom, Samuel and Mary (Gyles) Atkins.[20] A tankard by Benjamin Burt of Boston bears the inscription "The Gift of John North/ to his Wife, Elizabeth/ 1756." Anthony N. B. Garvan suggested that porringers were given not only as birth and marriage gifts, but sometimes also to commemorate the birth of the last child a couple expected to have.[21] John and Elizabeth North were married in 1746, and it is interesting to speculate on whether or not this tankard may have been an anniversary present or a presentation related to the birth of a child.[22] A particularly interesting object

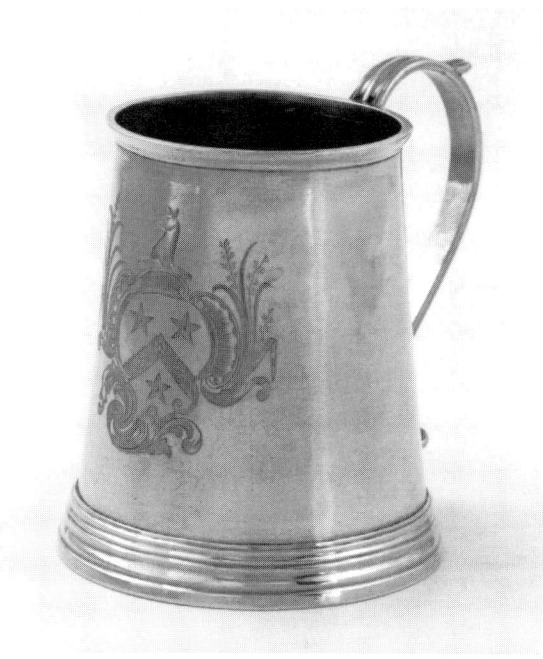

Figure 8 Cann. Samuel Edwards (1705–1762). Boston, Massachusetts, 1758. Silver; 3¾ inches high. Gift of the Estates of the Misses Eunice McLellan and Frances Cordis Cruft (42.384). Courtesy, Museum of Fine Arts, Boston. *Reproduced with permission. © 2002 Museum of Fine Arts, Boston. All Rights Reserved.*

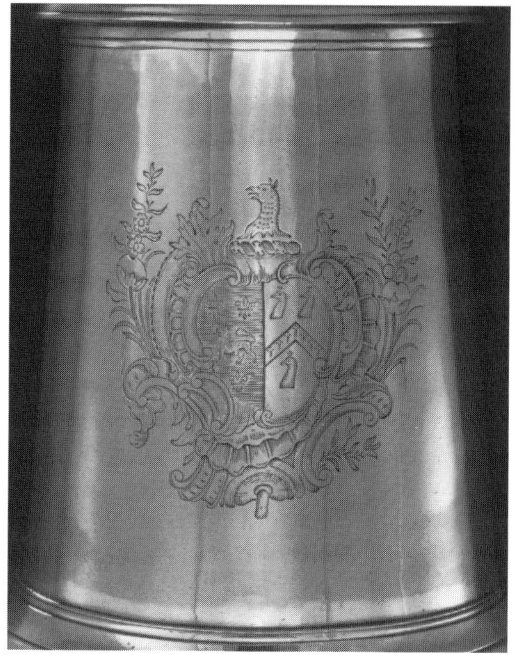

Figure 9 Detail of tankard. Benjamin Burt (1729–1805). Boston, Massachusetts, circa 1756. Silver; 8⁵⁄₁₆ inches high. Yale University Art Gallery; Mabel Brady Garvan Collection (1930.1297).

honoring the birth of a child is the large basin by Edward Winslow that Adam Winthrop presented to the Second Church in Boston for the baptism of his son Adam on 18 August 1706. The basin bears a long Latin inscription and an improper version of the Winthrop coat of arms.[23]

Some engraved inscriptions were put in place by an object's maker on the direction of the original owner, but as countless objects attest, later generations have added their own inscriptions over time. For instance, a tankard by John Coney made about 1700 for Captain John Rawlins descended to his daughter who later passed it on with the inscription, "Love Rawlins Pickman./ to her great niece./ Martha Pickman Codman./1864."[24] Often inscriptions turned silver objects into permanent documents of family history and have made them ideal transmitters of family memories and genealogical information from generation to generation. For example, a tankard made by John Burt of Boston in the early eighteenth century was later engraved on the underside of the base to commemorate the marriage of William and Frances Mackay in 1775. Later, when it was given by one of their descendants and her husband to their granddaughter, it was again engraved, this time on the body, "F.B.T. 2nd/ from / T.C.S. & F.B.S. 1885."[25] A porringer (*Figure 10*) made by Jacob Hurd about 1740, now in the Museum of Fine Arts, Boston, bears the initials "D * F" in the center of the handle, "MI" added above, "S.W" below, and "OWH" twice on the rim on opposite sides of the handle. The first owner has not been positively identified but may have been a member of the Flynt family. Dorothy (Flynt) Quinsey was the grandmother of Mary Jackson, who married Oliver Wendell. Mary Jackson passed the porringer on to her daughter Sarah Wendell, who married Abiel Holmes. The porringer then was given to their son Oliver Wendell Holmes, and later he gave it to his son, Oliver Wendell Holmes Jr.[26]

Sometimes, when the record is extensive or unusual, these inscriptions can provide the genealogist with clues that are helpful in tracing members of a

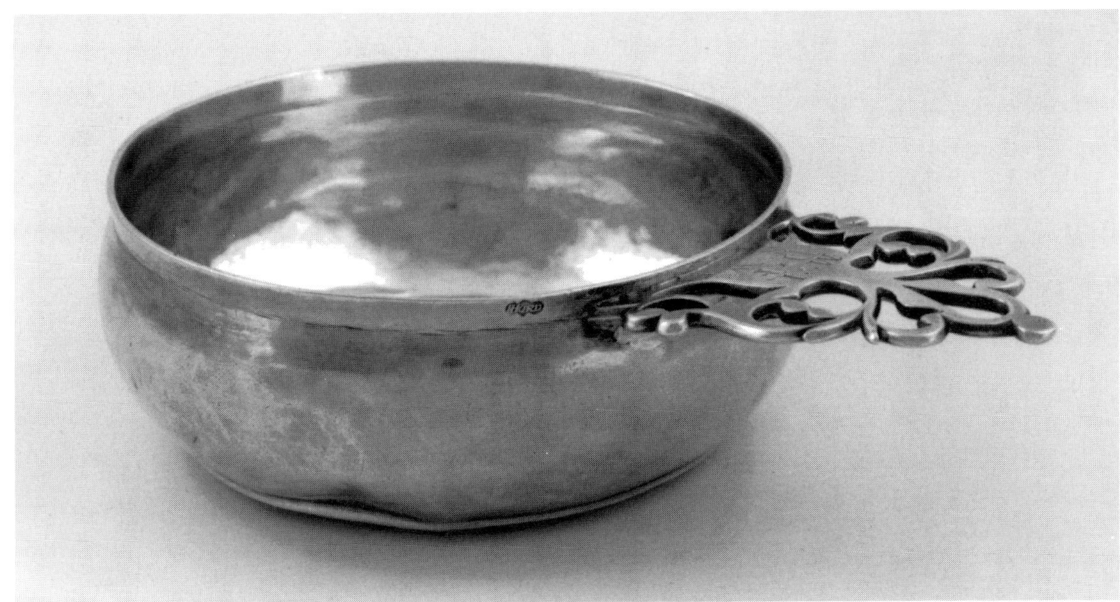

Figure 10 Porringer. Jacob Hurd (1702/03–1758). Boston, Massachusetts, 1730–40. Silver; 1⅞ inches high. The Edward Jackson Holmes Collection, Bequest of Mrs. Holmes (65.387). Courtesy, Museum of Fine Arts, Boston. *Reproduced with permission. © 2002 Museum of Fine Arts, Boston. All Rights Reserved.*

particular family. One example is the tankard made by Jeremiah Dummer now in the collection of Historic Deerfield that remained in the Williams family for more than six generations. It is inscribed "M C/ to/ TW/ to/ EW/ to/ SWW/ to/ EJW/ to HSW." It was given by Mary Jackson Cook to Thomas Williams and may have originally been owned by Mary's husband's grandfather, Gregory Cook. Thomas Williams (1718–1775) then gave the tankard to his second wife Esther Williams, who bequeathed it to her grandson Stephen West Williams. His son, Edward Jenner Williams, passed it on to his son Henry Smith Williams.[27] A tankard by Knight Leverett (*Figure 11*) in the Museum of Fine Arts, Boston, bears a succession of conjoined initials, which the family believed to be a record of the marriages of William Johnson to Martha Pierce in 1702, Sarah Johnson to Ralph Cross in 1728, Ralph Cross Jr. to Miriam Atkinson in 1757, and William Atkinson to Ruth Stacey in 1785, William Atkinson Jr. to Sophia A. Thompson. The tankard then passed to their son William Thompson who apparently did not marry. He seems to have given the tankard to his cousin Charles R. Cross who married Marianna Pike in 1873, adding their initials in the traditional form. The last owner of the tankard, Charles R. Cross Jr., presented the tankard to the museum in 1922.[28] A particularly unusual engraved salver (*Figure 12*) was made by William Hunter of London for Theodore Atkinson of Portsmouth, New Hampshire, in 1751. Over the next twenty years, Atkinson had the salver engraved on the underside (*Figure 12A*), probably by local silversmith William Cario Jr., with the names, dates of death, and ages of death of forty-eight of his friends, relatives, and acquaintances who lived in the Portsmouth area. The criteria for inclusion on the list remain elusive, as many of Atkinson's closest family members are not included. Nonetheless, the salver remains a fascinating and curious effort by an influential lawyer and politician to record this information for posterity.[29]

While silver displayed in the home represented "family" in the domestic sphere, silver gifts and bequests to New England churches formed a second significant way in which silver was used to establish and perpetuate a sense of family identity, or to commemorate the loss of a loved one. In 1740 Mrs. Hannah How presented a beaker to the New South Church in Boston in memory of her deceased husband, Mr.

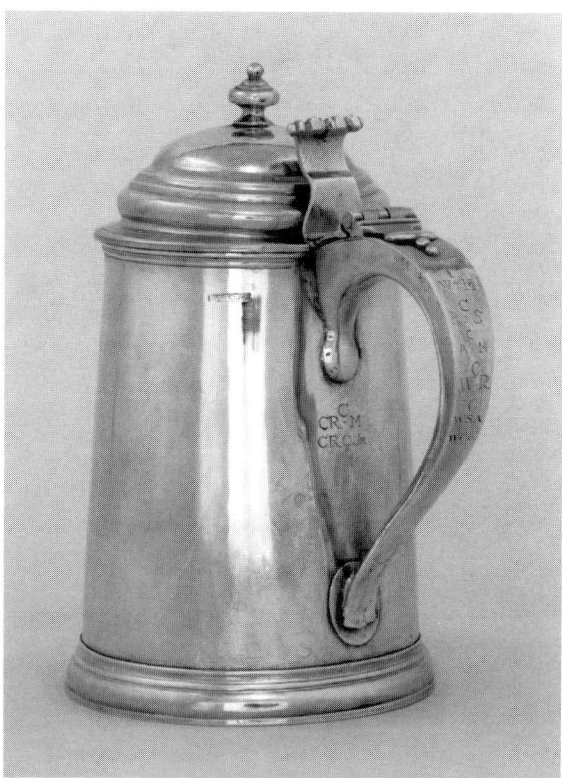

Figure 11 Tankard. Knight Leverett (1702/03–1753). Boston, Massachusetts, ca. 1735. Silver; 8⅗⁄16 inches high. Bequest of Charles R. Cross (22.584). Courtesy, Museum of Fine Arts, Boston. *Reproduced with permission. © 2002 Museum of Fine Arts, Boston. All Rights Reserved.*

Abraham How; and many times when women gave pieces of plate to the church they were identified as the wives or daughters of male parishioners.[30] For instance, a two-handled cup made for the Hollis Street Church in Boston is inscribed "Presented/ to the Church in Hollis Street by/ Mrs. A. Fox, daughter of the/ late Dean Thomas Bayley/Feby 1st 1813," and a set of six tankards by Paul Revere is engraved "The Gift of/ Mary Bartlett Widow of Ephm Bartlett/ to the third Church in Brookfield/ 1768." John Williams's gift of an engraved silver tankard (*Figure 13*) to the church in Deerfield in 1832 preserved the memory of the important associations of his ancestor. The tankard had been inscribed "Presented/ by the Directors of the Banks of the/ United States, North America, and Pennsylvania/ To John Williams Esquire, of Deerfield/ in the State of Massachusetts/ Justice of the Peace, / in consideration of/ Services rendered their Institutions/ A.D. 1801," and another inscription indicating Williams's gift to the church was added.[31]

Sometimes late in life in anticipation of death, relatives would make bequests in their wills that ensured that their memories would be perpetuated in silver. Lieutenant Governor William Stoughton of Massachusetts wrote in his will: "Unto my niece Sarah Tailer, I give as a particular remembrance of me twelve pounds to buy a piece of plate." Sarah converted the bequest into a beautiful and very fashionable chocolate pot by John Coney, which she had inscribed "The gift of Wm Stoughton Esquire/ To Mrs Sarah Tailer : [1]701."[32] Most commonly, however, rings and spoons served as mementos of the deceased and were often broadly distributed to family and friends, along with hats, gloves, and scarves. When Captain George Curwen of Salem died in 1684, the family distributed sixty gold mourning rings to Curwen's friends. Mourning rings of the seventeenth and early eighteenth centuries were usually simple and often engraved with winged death's heads.[33] A brief inscription commemorating the deceased was engraved inside the ring. As the eighteenth century progressed, enameled rings, with inscriptions on the outside face of the band, became more common. Some rings were set with coffin-shaped cut crystals, which, in a few instances, were placed over enameled representations of a skeleton. In the nineteenth century, mourning jewelry was often made using not only silver and gold, but also braided and curled hair from the deceased loved one.

While a piece of plate engraved with reminders of one's family bestowed status upon the recipient, it could also carry a burden. There are perhaps few stories about the history of silver objects that more tellingly convey the significance of silver objects for New England families than the story of the monumental two-handled covered cup (*Figure 14*) presented to Edward Tyng by the merchants of Boston in 1744. The cup is inscribed: "To Edward Tyng Esq/ Commander of ye Snow/ Prince of Orange/ As an Acknowledgement of/ his good Service done the/ Trade in Taking ye First/ French Privateer/ on this Coast the 24th of June/ 1744. This Plate is presented by Several of ye Merchants/ in Boston New/ England." The

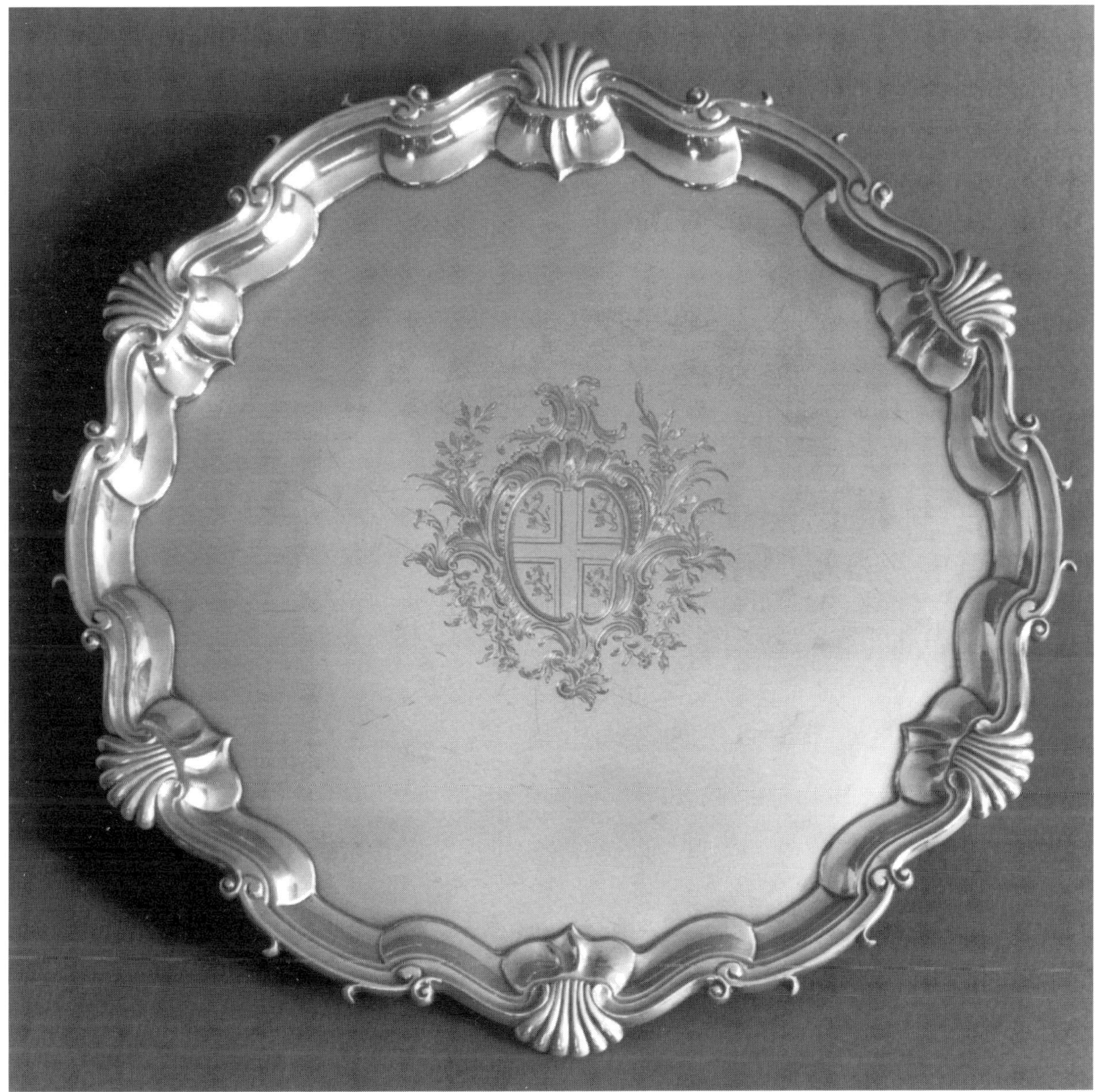

Figure 12 Salver. William Hunter, London, England, 1740/51. Silver; 14½ inches in diameter. Gift of Martha Williams Pike (1939.2). New Hampshire Historical Society.

cup subsequently passed to Edward's son, William. In 1775 an angry mob stole the cup and a "laced hat" from William's house because of his Loyalist sympathies. According to a contemporary account, the thieves, who were Revolutionary soldiers, said that they "have only taken these things as pawns to make the owner behave better." In fact, the cup never was returned to William Tyng, who, the soldiers believed, had failed to live up to its legacy. After the Revolution was over, and the patriots had emerged victorious, the cup was returned to William's mother-in-law by an act of the Provincial Congress.[34] The responsibility to live up to one's family and the heroic deeds of one's ancestors could be a weighty one, indeed.

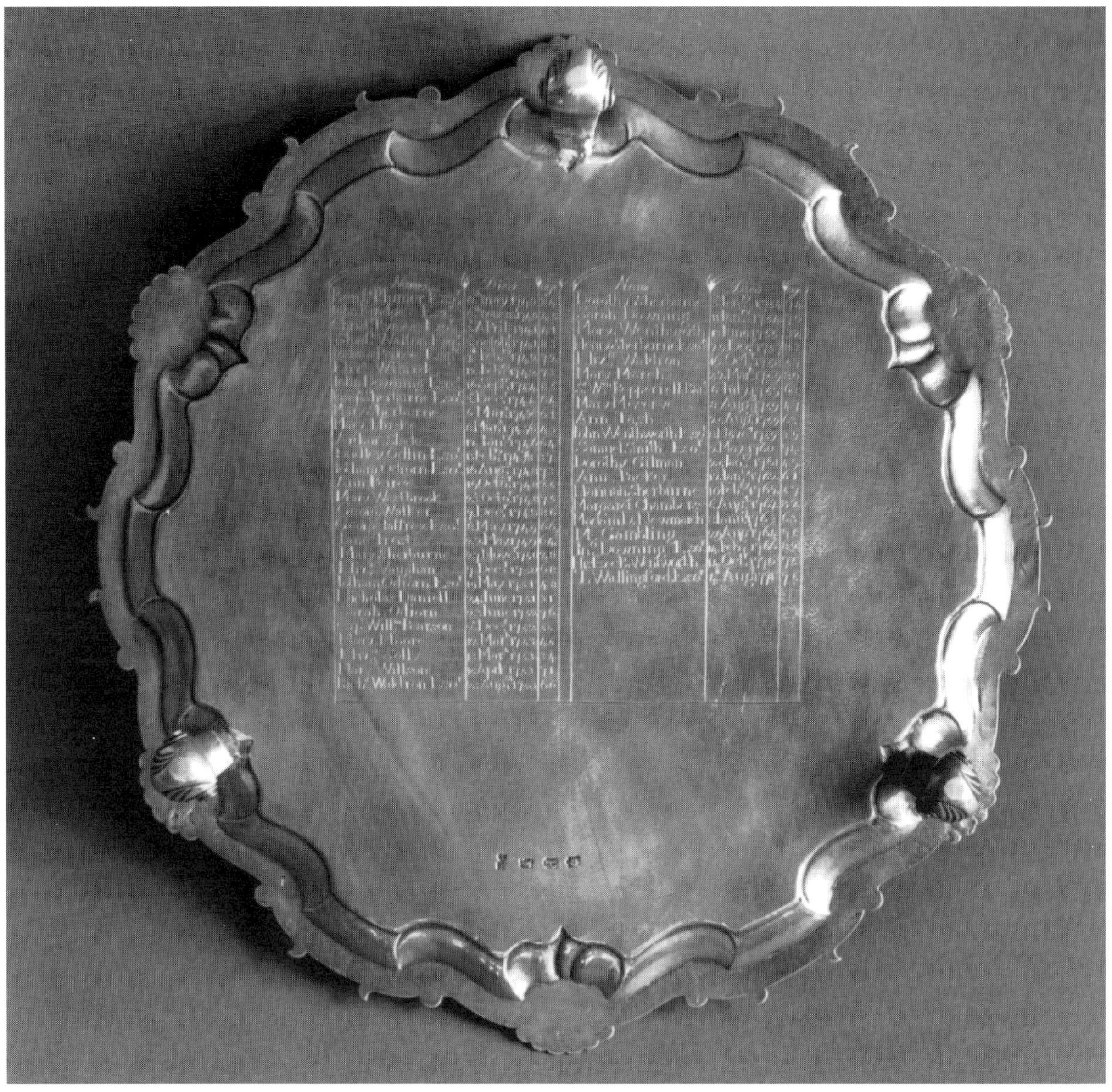

Figure 12A Detail of reverse of salver in *Figure 12.* Engraving probably by William Cario Jr. (1739–1804), of Portsmouth, New Hampshire. New Hampshire Historical Society.

NOTES

1 Gerald W. R. Ward, "'An Handsome Cupboard of Plate': The Role of Silver in American Life," in *Silver in American Life*, ed. Barbara M. Ward and Gerald W. R. Ward (New York: American Federation of Arts, 1979), pp. 36–37.

2 William A. Lanford, "'A Mineral of that Excellent Nature': The Qualities of Silver as a Metal," in *Silver in American Life*, pp. 3–9.

3 "Letters of William Fitzhugh," *Virginia Magazine of History and Biography* 2, no. 3 (January 1895): 271.

4 Barbara McLean Ward, "Silver," in *The Great River: Art and Society of the Connecticut Valley, 1635–1820*, ed. William N. Hosley and Gerald W. R. Ward (Hartford, Conn.: Wadsworth Atheneum, 1985), p. 279.

5 Walter Muir Whitehill, "Tutor Flynt's Silver Chamber-pot," *The Colonial Society of Massachusetts Transactions, 1947–1951*, 38: 360–63. *Harvard Tercentenary Exhibition: Catalogue of Furniture, Silver, Pewter, Glass, Ceramics, Paintings, Prints, Together with Allied Arts and Crafts of the*

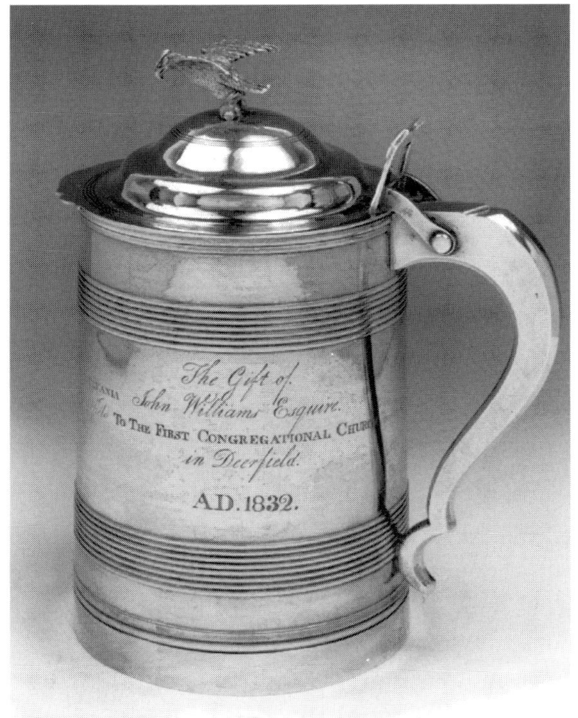

Figure 13 Hooped tankard. Samuel Williamson (1772–1843). Philadelphia, Pennsylvania. Silver; 8 1/8 inches high; 4 7/8 inches in diameter at base. Courtesy of Historic Deerfield. *Photograph by Amanda Merullo.*

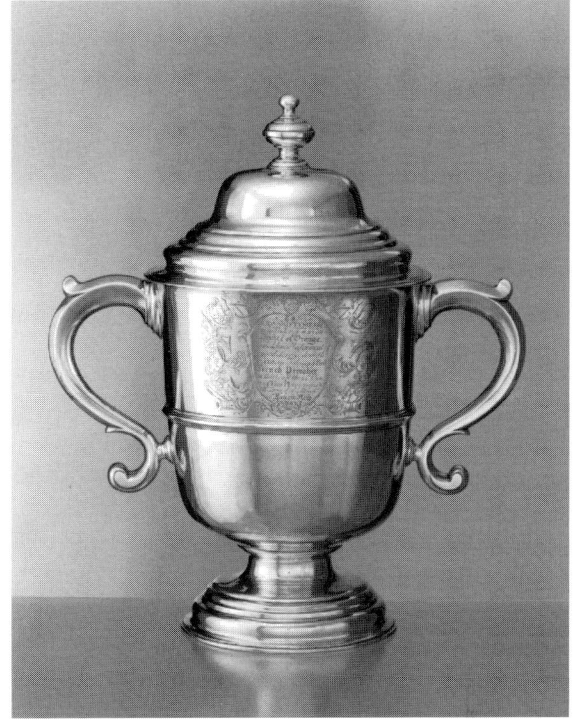

Figure 14 Two-handled covered cup. Jacob Hurd (1702/03–1758). Boston, Massachusetts, 1744. Silver; 15 1/16 inches high. Yale University Art Gallery; Mabel Brady Garvan Collection (1932.48).

Period, 1636–1836 (Cambridge, Mass.: Harvard University Press, 1936), pp. 27, 29, 30, 37, 38, 103.

6 Gerald W. R. Ward, "Silver and Society in Salem, Massachusetts, 1630–1820. A Case Study of the Consumer and the Craft" (Ph.D. diss., Boston University, 1984), pp. 16–59.

7 J. F. Hayward, *Huguenot Silver in England, 1688–1727* (London: Faber and Faber, 1959), p. 78.

8 Barbara McLean Ward, "The Craftsman in a Changing Society: Boston Goldsmiths, 1690–1730" (Ph.D. diss., Boston University, 1983), p. 183; Diary of Benjamin Walker, vol. 1743–49, 7 October 1747, Massachusetts Historical Society, Boston, Mass.

9 B. Ward, "The Craftsman in a Changing Society," p. 178.

10 Ibid., p. 175; Patricia E. Kane, "Artistry in Boston Silver of the Colonial Period," in *Colonial Massachusetts Silversmiths and Jewelers*, ed. Patricia E. Kane (New Haven: Yale University Art Gallery, 1998), pp. 50–51. Although Kane emphasizes the use of coats of arms by newly arrived merchants such as Peter Lidgett, the practice was quickly adopted by prominent old New England families.

11 Kathryn C. Buhler, *American Silver, 1655–1825, in the Museum of Fine Arts, Boston*, 2 vols. (Boston: Museum of Fine Arts, distributed by the New York Graphic Society, Greenwich, Conn., 1972), 1:220–21.

12 Samuel Eliot Morison, *Harvard in the Seventeenth Century, Part I* (Cambridge, Mass.: Harvard University Press, 1936), pp. 58–60, 94–95.

13 *Harvard Tercentenary Exhibition*, pp. 36, 112–13, plate 23.

14 Kathryn C. Buhler and Graham Hood, *American Silver: Garvan and Other Collections in the Yale University Art Gallery* (New Haven: Yale University Press, 1970), pp. 14–16. Later engraving indicates that the candlesticks were given by John Jeffries, a descendant of David and Anne (Clarke) Jeffries, to "Dr. B. Joy Jeffries in 1876."

15 Buhler and Hood, *American Silver . . . Yale*, pp. 32–34.

16 Barbara McLean Ward, "Women's Property and Family Continuity in Eighteenth-Century Connecticut," in *Early American Probate Inventories: 1987 Annual Proceedings of the Dublin Seminar for New England Folklife* (Boston: Boston University Scholarly Publications, 1989), p. 78.

17 Buhler, *American Silver . . . Museum of Fine Arts, Boston*, 1: 246.

18 The salver is in the collection of the Winterthur Museum. See Ian M. G. Quimby, *American Silver at Winterthur* (Charlottesville: University Press of Virginia, 1995), pp. 105–6. The tankard is in the collection of the Yale University Art Gallery. See Buhler and Hood, *American Silver . . . Yale*, pp. 163–64. The pair of standing cups are on loan to

the Museum of Fine Arts, Boston, from the First and Second Churches in Boston. See E. Alfred Jones, *The Old Silver of American Churches* (Letchworth, England: Privately printed for the National Society of the Colonial Dames of America at the Arden Press, 1913), pp. 26–27.
[19]Buhler, *American Silver . . . Museum of Fine Arts, Boston*, 1:269.
[20]Ibid., 1:261.
[21]Anthony N. B. Garvan, "The New England Porringer: An Index of Custom," *Annual Report of the Board of Regents of the Smithsonian Institution . . . for the Year Ended June 30, 1958*, Publication 4354 (Washington, D.C.: United States Government Printing Office, 1959), pp. 543–52.
[22]Buhler and Hood, *American Silver . . . Yale*, pp. 163–64.
[23]Jones, *Old Silver of American Churches*, pp. 40–41, 43; plate 16. The basin is on loan to the Museum of Fine Arts, Boston, from the First and Second Churches in Boston.
[24]Buhler, *American Silver . . . Museum of Fine Arts, Boston*, 1:51.
[25]Ibid., 1:149.
[26]Ibid., 1:216.
[27]Henry N. Flynt and Martha Gandy Fales, *The Heritage Foundation Collection of Silver* (Deerfield, Mass.: Heritage Foundation, 1968), pp. 51–53.
[28]Buhler, *American Silver . . . Museum of Fine Arts, Boston*, 1:193.
[29]*The Decorative Arts of New Hampshire: A Sesquicentennial Exhibition* (Concord: New Hampshire Historical Society, 1973), pp. 54–55, figs. 102 and 103.
[30]Buhler, *American Silver . . . Museum of Fine Arts, Boston*, 1:122; Jones, *Old Silver of American Churches*, pp. 72–73.
[31]Flynt and Fales, *The Heritage Foundation Collection of Silver*, pp. 48–49.
[32]Buhler, *American Silver . . . Museum of Fine Arts*, Boston, 1:59–61.
[33]Ward and Ward, *Silver in American Life*, p. 121; Martha Gandy Fales, "The Early American Way of Death," *Essex Institute Historical Collections* 100, no. 2 (April 1964): 75–84.
[34]Kevin L. Stayton, "Captain Tyng's Trophy," *Portfolio* 3, no. 2 (March/April 1981): 44–45.

The Abigail Ball Box: The History of an Initialed Object

Abbott Lowell Cummings

AMONG MANY CUSTOMS brought by English settlers to America from the Old World was that of marking with personal initials certain household objects. When correctly identified, these initials are of vital importance to students of decorative arts in supplying both period and provenance of an object. Such pieces can also be of great interest to genealogists for more than a single reason: first, in terms of family history, they enrich our knowledge of individuals whose profiles might otherwise be limited entirely to vital statistics. Second, in those cases where factual information is lacking, initials can help clarify or confirm relationships. Furthermore, initialed objects of furnishing are easier to trace from one generation to another. Modern historians recognize now from such records as wills and inventories and from well-known histories of specific pieces that a majority of household items descended matrilineally in a society that was otherwise decidedly patriarchal.

The "A B" Box and Its Maker

The wooden box with carved decoration, initialed "A B" for Abigail Ball of Springfield, Massachusetts, and Durham, Connecticut, now owned by the Connecticut Historical Society in Hartford, is of particular interest because it furnishes clear and precise information in the several areas of significance outlined above. This box, designed to sit on a table or chest (*Figure 1*), would have held any number of useful and cherished small articles belonging to a housewife, although an earlier generation of antique collectors assumed, mistakenly, that such boxes contained but a single item, the "great Bible" of colonial

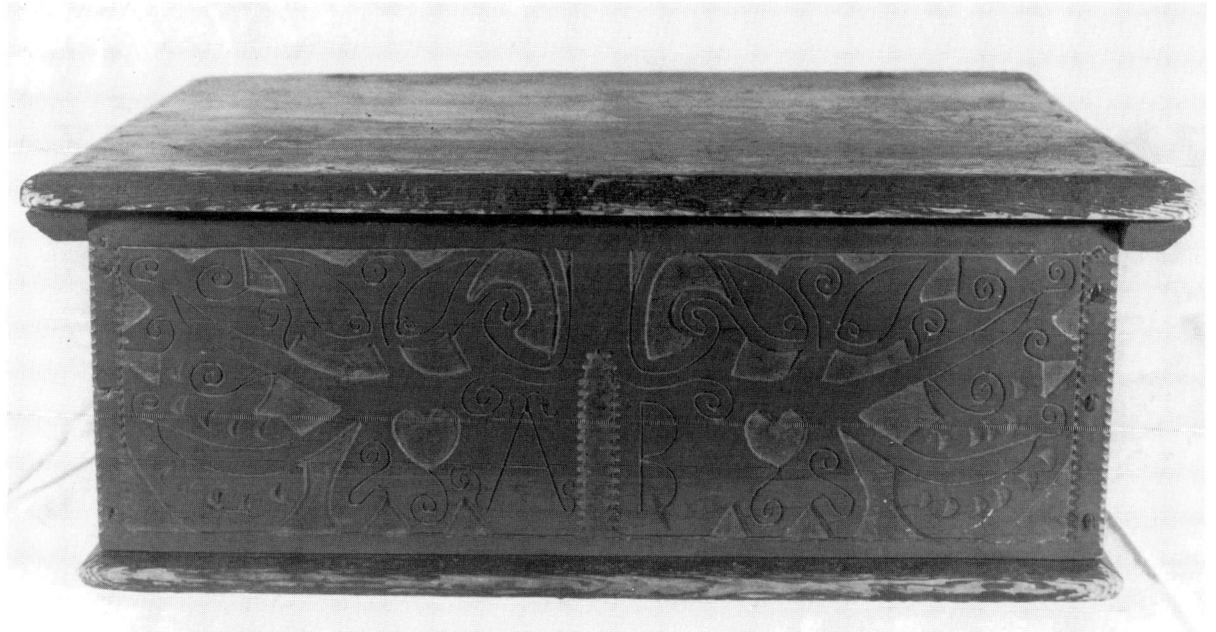

Figure 1 Box. Maker unknown. Springfield, Massachusetts, area, circa 1710. Initialed "A B" for Abigail Ball. Photograph by Peter Zaharis, 1957. The Connecticut Historical Society, Hartford, Connecticut.

inventories. Regrettably, the misnomer "Bible box" has persisted.

The object itself is not large. The body of the box measures 21⅜ by 17½ inches, and the total height, including lid, is 8¾ inches. The materials are beech, oak, and pine, and the surface preserves its original coat of red paint or stain. For a broader understanding of the subject, we look to standard historical sources concerning the material culture of the Connecticut River Valley. Attempts in the 1930s by early furniture historian Clair Franklin Luther to categorize more than one hundred chests of the late seventeenth and early eighteenth century which could be traced to the area in terms of style were not entirely successful.[1] He saw them basically as belonging to a single genre, which he labeled the "Hadley" tradition. Patricia E. Kane of the Yale University Art Gallery is the first modern scholar to have redirected attention to the matter of classification.[2] She has demonstrated convincingly, and as one might well expect, that correlations in design and carving among these associated chests must be integrated with and measured against similarities and differences of construction, and in the process one realizes at once that we are dealing with a significantly enlarged phenomenon of groups and subgroups which represents different individuals or "schools" of furniture making.

For the simpler six-board boxes which are stylistically related to the chests one is limited largely to a more conventional analysis in terms of the decorative motifs and their execution. In this respect, the "A B" box would seem to fall into Patricia Kane's "Group 5: Scribed Line Type" for which she posits four subgroups, the first of which is subgroup 5a. Two chests in this category not only have distinctive stylistic affinities with the "A B" box, but have histories which link the first probably and the second definitely to the Springfield, Massachusetts, area and thus command our attention. The first is a joined chest initialed "P W" in the Winterthur collection which in light of its later history may well have come out of the Warner family of Springfield. The chest itself has been closely studied by Philip M. Zea of the Society for the Preservation of New England Antiquities and compared with the "A B" box. "Both objects," he writes, "have the same flat style of carving with broad, poorly drawn leaves and gouge highlights. Like the 'P W' chest, the ["A B"] box is made of beech, oak, and pine."[3]

The second of the two chests was illustrated by Luther in his original publication and numbered 77. Unlike virtually all chests of the "Hadley" type, this example is a plain six-board chest, the front of which is decorated with creased mouldings and provided with a single oak drawer, the face of which bears the carved decoration. While the carved initials "M S" on the drawer front are rendered quite differently from those of the "A B" box, there are marked similarities in the incised decoration, suggesting the same individual "hand."

According to Luther, the "M S" chest could be traced to a Springfield family and, indeed, was still privately owned in that city when first inspected by him on 23 September 1930.[4] The initials, he was informed, stood for Miriam Stebbins; and on the basis of the family history of the piece, furnished to him by the then owners (who were descendants), the present writer has been able to discover that while unrelated by blood, an interestingly close family relationship nevertheless existed between Abigail Ball and Miriam Stebbins. Such relationships are always of interest to the art historian in that closely allied clients, it is argued, would often patronize the same artist (or artisan). The family connection between the two young women is so complex that attempts to compile a graphic chart have proved almost impossible (*Figure 2*). Abigail Ball, born at Springfield 18 August 1682, and Miriam Stebbins, born there 8 October 1707, though contemporaries, were not close in age and were actually of two different generations.[5] In purely descriptive terms the relationship was as follows: Abigail Ball was daughter of Samuel Ball (1648–1689) and his wife Mary _____ (d. 1727), and granddaughter of Francis Ball who died in 1648 and his wife, Abigail Burt, whom he married in 1644.[6] Miriam Stebbins was daughter of Benjamin Stebbins (1676–1748) and his wife, Martha (Blackman) Ball, married in 1701; granddaughter of Lieutenant Joseph Stebbins (1652–1728) and his wife, Sarah Dorchester, married in 1673; and great-granddaughter of Lieutenant Thomas Stebbins (d. 1683) and his wife Hannah Wright, all of the Springfield area. The picture becomes complicated only

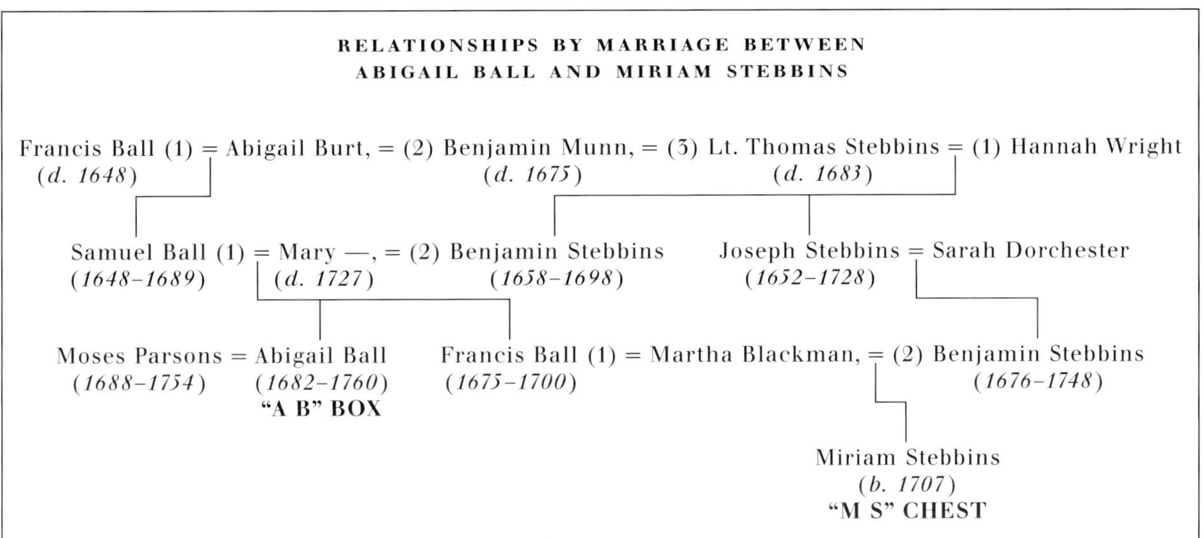

Figure 2 Relationships by marriage between Abigail Ball and Miriam Stebbins.

when we realize, beginning with the first generation, that Abigail (Burt) Ball, having remarried in 1649 as her second husband Benjamin Munn who died in 1675, married for a third time in 1676 Lieutenant Thomas Stebbins, Miriam's great-grandfather. In the next generation, Lieutenant Thomas's son, Lieutenant Joseph Stebbins, had a brother Benjamin (1658–1698) who married as his second wife in 1690 Samuel Ball's widow, Mary. And as if that were not enough, Abigail's brother, Francis Ball (1675–1700), had married Martha Blackman in 1699 before (as widow Martha Ball) she married Benjamin Stebbins in 1701 and became the mother of Miriam! Thus, while Abigail was, strictly speaking, no more than a young aunt by marriage to Miriam, the intertwining pattern of second and third marriages among earlier generations, we may assume, created a very real closeness between these two families in a Connecticut River Valley community considerably smaller than it is today.

If the "A B" box and the "M S" chest were made by the same obviously skilled person, one moreover who would have been well known to both parties, a likely candidate can be suggested, for whom no example of actual work has yet been documented. While Abigail Ball was born at Springfield, as we have noted, her father, Samuel Ball, removed thereafter to Northampton; and Abigail's marriage in Springfield 20 January 1709/10[7] was to Moses Parsons, son of Joseph Parsons of Northampton, born there 15 January 1687.[8] In his undated will, proved at Northampton 9 December 1729, Joseph Parsons refers to his "3d part of the homelot & Meadow at Springfd"; and the probate inventory of his estate, taken 30 December following, includes a "Right of Commons . . . upon ye Right hand ye Way to Westfeild [*sic*]," both of which items hint at Parsons family interests in or near Springfield. Moses and Abigail (Ball) Parsons and their immediate families, in other words, can be associated with both Springfield and Northampton. Of more direct importance, and while we have no specific reference to the trade or calling of Moses Parsons's father, Joseph, his inventory contains an impressive array of joinery tools. Grouped and scattered throughout the inventory are the following items, all related to the skilled woodworker:

To: Part of a square 18d   to a broad Ax: 5s
  to: 2. Narrow axes. 8s . . . a Small Gimlet 6d
To an Old Tenant Saw: 4s,   To one Handsaw: 12s
  to one ax: 6s . . .
To Hammer: 2s   to 2:Auls: 12d: one file 2s./6d
  Compases: 12d
To one old hammer: 12d: ditto: 6d: . . .
To an Inch & a half Auger: 4s   to an Inch Auger: 2s:
  to: 2: old ditto. 3s
To an Old drawing Knife: 2s   spoke shave: 18d:
  one Gouge: 2s

To a smal Chisel: 12d   to a stone Hammer: 3s./6d . . .
To a Leather staking Line: 18d: to: 2: broad Links: 8d
To a Rabiting Plain: 12d   to several other Jonery toolls: 8s
To Chisel: 12d   to an Old Frew [froe]: 2s: to a joynting Iron: 3s: to: 3: old Chisels: 2s
To a brest wimble stock: 3s: to a screw, Turning Gudgin [*sic*]: 3s . . . to a Peck [one word unclear] ax, on mortising: ax: 4s[9]

There are as well a few contemporary references to activities which would seem to indicate beyond question that Joseph Parsons was a woodworker. Both the mid-nineteenth-century antiquarian Sylvester Judd and James Russell Trumbull, late-nineteenth-century historian of Northampton, cite factual information from an account book of Joseph Parsons to which they then had access, but which cannot now be found. Parsons charged the town in 1694 in connection with repairs to the meetinghouse for "'sawing two stocks for Preamady' [*sic*] (pyramid), for carting two great beams and for 'work in underpinning ye meeting house,'"[10] in addition to which, Deerfield historian, George Sheldon, tells us that Parsons contracted in 1691 to build a gristmill on the Mill River in the South Meadows.[11] One can suggest, therefore, that Joseph Parsons may well have been the person who made and carved the "A B" box for his prospective daughter-in-law about the time of her marriage in 1710, and later, the chest for her niece by marriage, Miriam Stebbins. At the very least, researchers should be on the lookout for more specific evidence that Joseph Parsons of Northampton made furniture as well as engaging in building activities.

The "A B" Box and Its Line of Descent

Within less than a year of their marriage, Moses and Abigail Parsons joined his uncle, Samuel Parsons, and other Northampton families in a group migration to Durham, Connecticut, under the leadership of the Reverend Nathaniel Chauncey. Here their first son, Moses Parsons Jr., was born 19 October 1710,[12] and here Moses and Abigail (Ball) Parsons spent the rest of their lives. Of the lands which they acquired there, one tract, described as a "farm," was conveyed to Moses by his father Joseph Parsons of Northampton 3 April 1712[13] and was about a mile in depth. In addition, Joseph's will, probated 9 December 1729, bequeathed to his son Moses "all my Rights of Lands at Durram," valued at £80, together with £20 in movables.[14]

Mention of movables raises an important question with respect to property rights in Colonial New England. Moses and Abigail had a (recorded) total of six children born at Durham, three sons and three daughters. Completely in keeping with eighteenth-century law and custom, the estate of Moses Parsons was distributed among these children and the widow following his death at Durham without a will on 26 September 1754, aged sixty-seven years.[15] The instrument of distribution is fully characteristic of numberless other such documents filed in Connecticut during the eighteenth century which reveal certain tacit assumptions: first, that title to all movables or personal estate was vested in the male head of the family, and this included whatever the wife may have brought to the marriage of her own or from her father's household; and second, that the widow received for the balance of her life, or until remarriage, the use only of one-third of the real estate while one-third of the personal property was hers with provision of terminal use, or (sometimes) in terms of outright possession.

The sons invariably received the bulk of the parental lands and occupational equipment and in terms of personal estate little more than such obvious "manly" items as their father's clothing. For the daughters the situation was quite different: the will or instrument of distribution provided that they should inherit the greater share of all movables related to housekeeping (often taking into account what they may already have received as a marriage "portion"), while any amount of land they received was modest indeed compared with their brothers' shares.

The distribution of Moses Parsons's estate, which would have included the box bearing the carved initials of his wife, Abigail Ball, is dated 14 October 1754 and contains no surprises: the widow, Abigail, was to have life use of one-third part of the "Houseing &

Lands . . . also one third part of the Household stuff beding & furneture of the House," which at her death "or Sooner, if she shall Secause, [shall] belong to her . . . thre daughters" or their legal representatives. The greater part of the lands, together with the husbandry tools, was distributed to the two surviving sons, Moses Jr. and Samuel Parsons. As for the three daughters, already recognized as having remainder rights in the widow's thirds, it was stipulated that "two third parts of the House Hold Stuff, beding & furneture of ye House shall belong unto the sd. thre daughters to be Equally divided betwen them," together with a minor portion of the lands.[16] The original instrument of distribution is of further interest in its signatures: the two sons and the two living sons-in-law signed their names, as did the widow, Abigail (Ball) Parsons. The latter signature is in a firm, interesting hand, commensurate, one might argue, with her upbringing and social position in the Springfield area. The youngest daughter, Elizabeth, alone among the women in this generation, signed her name. The other two daughters made their marks, including the oldest, Abigail Bates, identified as a widow living then at Haddam. Unfortunately, this evidence does not permit us to distinguish positively between various degrees of literacy in the eighteenth century, defined as reading only, writing only, and signature literacy only—or some combination of these abilities.

Interest centers in the oldest daughter, Abigail, named for her mother. For whatever method the three daughters selected to make their division of movables, either their own two-thirds or their mother's third at her death, which occurred at Durham 4 December 1760,[17] daughter Abigail not unnaturally in light of her own married initials apparently received the box marked "A B," an assumption based on the fact that the box is next found in the possession of *her* daughter, Ann (Bates) Walkley.

Abigail, daughter of Moses and Abigail, had been born at Durham 10 February 1713/4, as their third child,[18] and was married in the adjoining town of Haddam 7 January 1741/2 to Samuel Bates,[19] son of James and Hannah (Bull) Bates, born at Haddam 20 December 1712.[20] Samuel Bates does not seem to have been unusually conspicuous in the community but left, nevertheless, a substantial estate totaling £3,105 at his premature death 14 May 1750, aged thirty-eight years.[21] There were only four children, two sons and two daughters, the last son, Moses Bates, "born after the death of his father," as the Durham church records report.[22] The widow, Abigail, was made guardian of the minor children.[23] When the probate court made its distribution 17 May 1754, she received her third part dower interest in the farm and "Moveables" to the value of £213. "Moveables," defined only in terms of monetary value, were set off also to the children as follows: to Samuel, "Eldest Son," £47; to Moses, "Youngest Child," £9; to Anne, "Eldest Daughter," £187-19-0; and to Abigail, "Second Daughter," £188-18-0.[24] It is clear from these records that some six months prior to the distribution of her father's (Moses Parsons) estate in October 1754, the widow Abigail (Parsons) Bates could be described as "well situated," though by no means wealthy.

All of this helps explain the next important event in her life and the legalities attendant upon it. Having devoted herself, apparently, to the raising of her children and the safeguarding of their portions in the inherited estate, and after the youngest child had reached majority, the widow Abigail Bates entered into a second marriage 30 November 1772 at Durham.[25] The second husband, Ensign Simeon Parsons, was an important and relatively well-to-do member of the Durham community, at least one of whose sons (by his first wife), named Noah, baptized early in 1738, was educated at Yale where he became a tutor.[26] There was also a family connection. Ensign Simeon Parsons, born at Northampton 16 September 1701,[27] was a son of that Samuel Parsons, uncle of the first Moses, who had removed with other Northampton families to Durham about 1710, and was thus first cousin to Abigail, though once removed.

On the day of her marriage to Ensign Simeon Parsons (and presumably before the ceremony) Abigail (Parsons) Bates executed a will which could easily be interpreted as a prenuptial agreement, signed with her mark. While this instrument appears never to have been submitted to probate, it has survived, nevertheless, among the family papers of her descendants and is indicative of those occasional situations in which the eighteenth-century woman was in a position to dispose of property in her own right. It is a brief document and bequeaths "to my two Daughters Ann the wife of Jonathan Wackly and Abigail the wife of John Johnson all my personal Estate to be equally divided between them having heretofore," she continues, "given to my two Sons Samuel & Moses their Portion of my Estate."[28]

Ensign Simeon Parsons died 6 January 1781, aged eighty years, and Abigail (Parsons) (Bates) Parsons, his widow, 15 July 1791, aged seventy-eight years.[29] One might expect that Abigail Ball's carved box would have been taken as part of her portion by Abigail Ball's granddaughter and namesake who married John Johnson and lived out her life in Durham. Rather, it was the oldest and somewhat more peripatetic daughter, Ann, to whom the box descended. Born at Haddam 17 November 1744,[30] she was married at Durham 17 September 1767 to Jonathan Walkley of that town.[31] Baptisms of the first three of their children, all daughters, are recorded there,[32] to which, from Jonathan's Bible, can be added the births of three more daughters and only a single male child, Stephen Walkley, born 8 January 1782.[33] Shortly before 1787 Jonathan removed with his family to Granville, Massachusetts, where baptism of the next-to-the-last daughter, Phoebe, was recorded on 8 July of that year.[34] The family remained at Granville for only two or three years. On 4 April 1791, in the year of Abigail (Parsons) (Bates) Parsons's death, Jonathan Walkley, described as of Granville, purchased land in Southington, Connecticut, in that part of town known as South End and moved there with his family shortly thereafter.[35] The "A B" box may have been delivered to Anne (Bates) Walkley during this year of her mother's death, or it may have been given to her as part of her marriage "portion" at an earlier date. If so, it had traveled to Granville before coming to rest in Southington where it would remain until the middle of the twentieth century.

Three years after his arrival in Southington, Jonathan Walkley sold his initial purchase and acquired in 1794 a nearby farm on which he lived for the balance of his life, located just below the early burying ground in South End.[36] The mid-eighteenth-century house which had stood on the property was replaced by the present house, erected by Jonathan's son Stephen for the whole family in 1808, as the latter's diary and account book reveals.[37] Jonathan Walkley remained head of this household, which was augmented by Stephen's wife, Olive Newell, daughter of Amos and Lucy (Root) Newell of South End, whom he married 23 May 1811.[38]

By now the carved box with its stylistic reminders of preceding generations must have seemed old-fashioned. Yet there is highly suggestive evidence that it remained plainly on view among the furnishings of Stephen's newly built house, having achieved, perhaps, a certain iconic status. When well along in years, Stephen and Olive's first son, Dr. Nelson Walkley, born 22 March 1812,[39] and living then in Troy, Ohio, recorded 6 March 1877 a number of his childhood recollections which included the following statement: "With regard to the old white Oake box . . . some one asked aunt Anne Clark in my presence once when I was a child what the Initials A. B. carved on it stood for & she said Abigail Ball & that she was [his] Grand Mothers Grandmother & that the box was more than 100 years old."[40] Anne Clark was the third daughter of Jonathan and Anne Walkley, baptized at Durham 13 August 1775[41] and married at Southington 16 March 1794 to Avery Clark of a nearby farm in South End.[42] Neither a degree of seniority in the family nor the first initial of her name had managed to secure for Anne (Walkley) Clark the possession of this family relic. Rather, with the opening of the nineteenth century the pattern of descent of "moveables" in New England would alter dramatically, and yet consistently with changing attitudes about the succession of title to personal property.

Jonathan Walkley's household was unusual in being composed entirely of daughters and only one son. When Stephen married in 1811, there were but two unmarried daughters still living at home, Phoebe, born 8 April 1785, and Rebecca, the youngest daughter, born 22 April 1788.[43] Shortly after the death of Anne (Bates) Walkley, 24 November 1809,[44] her husband Jonathan executed a will on 25 January 1810. He bequeathed to son Stephen "all my estate both real and personal excepting the legacies hereafter mentioned," whereupon, in a continuing eighteenth-century tradition, he provided that the two daughters still at home, Phoebe and Rebecca, should have "all my household furniture to be equally divided between them." Elsewhere in this same will he states that he had given "their portion" to the "rest of my children," meaning thereby the other married daughters.[45]

Jonathan Walkley's death did not occur until 4 April 1819,[46] and as long as the two unmarried daughters lived at home with their brother, the question of an actual division was presumably postponed. Phoebe died unmarried 24 October 1826,[47] thereby taking herself out of the equation, while Rebecca, having reigned for some time as the undisputed "maiden aunt," startled the family by making a late marriage in 1837 and going to live first at Prairieville and then Waukesha, Wisconsin.[48] Concerning a seventeenth-century Bible which had come down in the family, Dr. Nelson Walkley, reminiscing, was "inclined to think that in 1837 when aunt Rebecca took her 'plunder' & went out west that she took it with her[.] I know," he continues, "that there was considerable talk about the bibles[.] Father thought that as he was the only male Walkly of the family he ought to have them[.] But Aunt Rebecca said that all the Household matters belonged to the girls & insisted on having one of the old bibles."[49]

This reported conversation of about 1837 is the last reminder we have in the Walkley family of commonly understood eighteenth-century perceptions by an eighteenth-century woman, born in 1788. Within just a few years there would be a lingering, traditional after-melody of such customs among the next generation of women but intermixed with more modern practices. Important changes in attitudes about women's property rights were occurring in a rapidly industrialized New England, subjected as well to the disruptions of the Civil War, and these changes would be reflected in the next transfer of ownership of the "A B" carved box. Clearly, it did *not* go "out west" with Aunt Rebecca but remained in the Walkley house in Southington's South End. In the absence of any more counterclaims, it devolved, more or less by default, upon Jonathan and Anne Walkley's only son, Stephen. His wife Olive died 15 January 1858, aged seventy years,[50] and Stephen's remaining years were spent between two living daughters who had married and were then established in homes of their own in nearby Plantsville (part of Southington), in one of which he died 28 March 1866.[51]

At some point during this period or at the time of its sale about 1864, Stephen Walkley's South End home was broken up. The dispersal of its contents is a matter of interest, combining as we have noted, concepts reminiscent of the eighteenth century with newer, nineteenth-century attitudes. Some two-thirds of the household effects that had survived in the family, mostly from the married life of Stephen and Olive Walkley, were distributed in varying amounts among their then three living daughters by an understanding for which we have no record. The fate of the remaining third, which included the carved box, introduces an entirely new element into this hitherto traditional pattern of a woman's inheritance of "moveables."

Of Stephen and Olive's eight children, the youngest, Stephen Walkley Jr., born at South End 27 June 1832,[52] early established for himself important professional and intellectual goals. While his education proceeded no higher than Southington's Sally Lewis Academy, he had keen bookish interests and strong antiquarian leanings. As early as 1859, the 4 April issue of the (short-lived) *Southington Press* carried a front-page article signed by "S. W. JR." entitled "Fragments from the History of Southington." From these simple beginnings he went on to become the official historian of the Civil War's Seventh Regiment of Connecticut Volunteers (in which he had served) and whose extended historical record he published in 1905.[53] One is not surprised, therefore, to learn that of the remaining roughly one-third of the household contents of the Walkley home in South End, Stephen Walkley Jr. secured (though by what agreement with his sisters we are not informed) almost without exception all the earlier, eighteenth-century items, including the box marked "A B"—those items, in other words, of obvious interest to a nineteenth-century antiquarian.

From this time forward, quite in keeping with later nineteenth-century attitudes towards male primacy, Abigail Ball's box passed through three generations of the Walkley family from father to son. When following the Second World War the male lines finally became extinct among the numerous descendants of Jonathan and Anne (Bates) Walkley, and the box itself had become part of an estate with several heirs, it was two Walkley women of the eighth generation removed from Abigail Ball who again took control of the situation. And in a gesture not only typical of the leading position taken by their gender in the modern preservation movement, but also redolent of long, deeply ingrained attitudes among New England women about rights of stewardship over household objects or "moveables," it was they who in 1972 persuaded other members of the family, male and female, to relinquish individual proprietary rights in this now much-acclaimed family heirloom in favor of a secure, museum-based future at the Connecticut Historical Society.

NOTES

[1]Clair Franklin Luther, *The Hadley Chest* (Hartford, Conn.: Case, Lockwood and Brainard Company, 1935).

[2]Patricia E. Kane, "The Seventeenth-Century Furniture of the Connecticut Valley: The Hadley Chest Reappraised," *Arts of the Anglo-American Community in the Seventeenth Century*, ed. Ian M. G. Quimby (Winterthur, Del.: Winterthur Museum, 1974), pp. 79–122.

[3]Philip Martin Zea, "The Fruits of Oligarchy: Patronage and Joinery in Western Massachusetts, 1630–1730" (master's thesis, University of Delaware, 1984), p. 96.

[4]Clair Franklin Luther Papers, Society for the Preservation of New England Antiquities, Boston, Mass.

[5]All vital data in this paragraph are found in the original Springfield Vital Records. Holbrook microfiche, Archive Publishing (Division of Holbrook Research Institute), 4 Mayfair Circle, Oxford, Mass.

[6]Latter-day family members have suggested that the initials "A B" on the box stood for Abigail Burt, who was much too early for the style of the object. This suggestion, put forward around the turn of the twentieth century, can be found among family papers preserved by descendants of Moses and Abigail (Ball) Parsons in the Walkley line. Citations from these various documents throughout the present essay will hereafter be identified as Family Papers. The collection as a whole is now privately owned.

[7]Springfield Vital Records.

[8]Henry Parsons, *Parsons Family[,] Descendants of Cornet Joseph Parsons[,] Springfield, 1636—Northampton, 1655*, 2 vols. (New York: Frank Allaben Genealogical Company, ca. 1912; New Haven, Conn.: Tuttle, Morehouse, and Taylor Co., ca. 1920), 1:54.

[9]Hampshire County Probate Records, Northampton, Mass., box no. 110, no. 12.

[10]James Russell Trumbull, *History of Northampton, Massachusetts*, 2 vols. (Northampton, Mass.: Gazette Printing, 1898, 1902), 1:121n. For earlier citation of the same information, see Sylvester Judd MS, Northampton Volume 1, pp. 32–37, 81–83, Forbes Library, Northampton, Mass. The author is grateful to Philip Zea for having brought these references to his attention.

[11]George A. Sheldon, *A History of Deerfield, Massachusetts*, 2 vols. (Deerfield, Mass.: Pocumtuck Valley Memorial Association, 1895–1896), 1:269, 578.

[12]Proprietors Records, see William Chauncey Fowler, *History of Durham, Connecticut . . .* (Hartford, Conn.: Town of Durham, 1866), p. 340.

[13]Durham Land Records, 2:178.

[14]Hampshire County Probate Records, box no. 110, no. 12.

[15]Gravestone, Old Cemetery, Durham, Conn. (Hale Collection, Connecticut State Library, Hartford, Conn., Cem., 1:15).

[16]Connecticut Probate Records, Connecticut State Library, Hartford, Conn., Middletown District, file 2528 (hereafter cited as CPR).

[17]Gravestone, Old Cemetery, Durham, Conn. (Hale Collection, Connecticut State Library, Hartford, Conn., Cem. 1:15).

[18]Fowler, *History of Durham*, p. 341 (Proprietors' Records); see also p. 253 for baptism.

[19]Haddam Land Records, 5:277, Haddam, Conn., Town Clerk.

[20]Ibid., 2:10.

[21]Gravestone, Old Cemetery, Durham, Conn. (Hale Collection, Connecticut State Library, Hartford, Conn., Cem. 1:10).

[22]Fowler, *History of Durham*, p. 291.

[23]CPR, Colchester District, file 152.

[24]CPR, Middletown District, file 327. The "Moveables" are not itemized in the instrument of distribution.

[25]Fowler, *History of Durham*, p. 332 (Church Records).

[26]Ibid., pp. 274, 112. Noah Parsons completed his degree in 1757: *Catalogue of the Officers and Graduates of Yale University in New Haven, Connecticut, 1701–1924* (New Haven: Yale University, 1924), p. 766.

[27]Parsons, *Parsons Family*, 1:77.

[28]Family Papers.

[29]Gravestones, Old Cemetery, Durham Conn. (Hale Collection, Connecticut State Library, Hartford, Conn., Cem. 1:17).

[30]Haddam Land Records, 5:277.

[31]Fowler, *History of Durham*, p. 392 (Town Records).

[32]Ibid., pp. 318, 321, 325 (Church Records).

[33]Family Papers.

[34]Congregational Church Records, Granville, Mass.

[35]Southington Land Records, 3:177, Southington, Conn., Town Clerk.

[36]Southington Land Records, 4:179.

[37]Family Papers.

[38]Congregational Church Records, Southington, Conn., transcription included in Heman R. Timlow, *Ecclesiastical and other Sketches of Southington, Conn.* (Hartford, Conn.: Case, Lockwood and Brainard, 1875), p. 246.

[39]Stephen Walkley's Bible (Family Papers, hereafter cited as Walkley Bible).

[40]Family Papers. In further support of the attribution of the initials to Abigail Ball, Stephen Walkley Jr. wrote about

1900: "That it [the box] was owned by Abigail Ball is proved by the fact that my father was told so by his mother Anne Bates who was her granddaughter, and was sixteen years old when Abigail Ball died, and therefore would probably not be mistaken in such a matter." (Family Papers).

[41]Fowler, *History of Durham,* p. 325 (Church Records).

[42]Timlow, *Sketches of Southington,* p. 240.

[43]Walkley Bible.

[44]Gravestone, South End Cemetery, Southington, Conn.

[45]CPR, Farmington District, file 2828.

[46]Gravestone, South End Cemetery, Southington, Conn.

[47]Walkley Bible.

[48]See letters written back to her family in Connecticut. Rebecca (Walkley) (Potter) Finch had made a subsequent second marriage as well (Family Papers).

[49]Letter of Dr. Nelson Walkley, Troy, Ohio, 23 July 1877 (Family Papers).

[50]Gravestone, South End Cemetery, Southington, Conn.

[51]Ibid.; see also Family Papers.

[52]Walkley Bible.

[53]*History of the Seventh Connecticut Volunteer Infantry[,] Hawley's Brigade, Terry's Division[,] Tenth Army Corps[,] 1861–1865,* comp. by Stephen Walkley (n.p., n.d.) (date is supplied from the preface).

SECTION VI

Patterns of Family Legacies

Preserving a Legacy

Jane Cayford Nylander

IN THE YEARS after the Civil War, many New England women found that they lacked opportunities for matrimony and were saddled with large old family houses filled with the treasures and detritus of previous generations.[1] Some of these women had grown up knowing grandparents and maiden aunts who had been born in the eighteenth century and from whom they learned to cherish both things and stories, things that were meaningful in the family narrative and in the larger story of New England. In some families the historical consciousness extended to extraordinary minutiae. A combination of Yankee thrift, conservatism, and penury sometimes came together to perpetuate an earlier lifestyle for many of these women. They were willing to live with old things in old ways: their refusal to install indoor plumbing, gas, and electricity in their old houses and their resistance to new fashions in clothing and furnishings resulted in an extraordinarily high degree of preservation of old houses and their old-fashioned furnishing schemes along with attics and sheds, trunks, chests, boxes, and drawers crammed full of letters, old clothes, spinning wheels, teacups, and interesting other old things.

Some of these women were actively involved in the growing antiquarian movement in late-nineteenth-century New England, busying themselves identifying things worth saving, recording historical information, organizing loan exhibitions of antiquarian material, and founding and developing local and regional historical societies in which the things they valued would be protected and preserved. In Lexington, Massachusetts, as well as in nearby Concord, where there were old families and acquisitive antiquarians, the local historical societies were founded in 1886. Both organizations were soon headquartered in historic houses that featured domestic displays, growing collections of museum and library materials, and exhibitions designed to memorialize the events of 1776.

So it was not a unique situation nor was there a lack of local interest, then, when Ellen Adelia Robbins Stone's widowed mother died in 1890 at the age of seventy-three. Ellen's sister Mary had died in 1884 and their great aunt Caira in 1881. Inheriting the combined possessions of all of these women, Miss Stone had both a huge responsibility and also a wonderful opportunity. Her mother's will provided her with a life tenancy in the old family homestead, the Stephen Robbins House, on Massachusetts Avenue in East Lexington, Massachusetts (*Figure 1*), but she had inherited outright ownership of the furniture, silverware, and personal effects "for her sole use and disposal forever."[2] As the last of her generation, she was the only one left who knew the stories associated with the chairs and tables, the cups and saucers she now used every day. She could identify the family pictures. She was the one who remembered what her grandparents Eli and Abigail Robbins had told her about her great-grandfather Stephen's fur business and which baby clothes had been his. She alone knew that their horse had been named "Humility" and that he was "left all day hitched to a ring on the left of the big tree [and that] any one of the family wanting to go anywhere just took Humility to get there."[3] She knew the sad story of her great-uncle

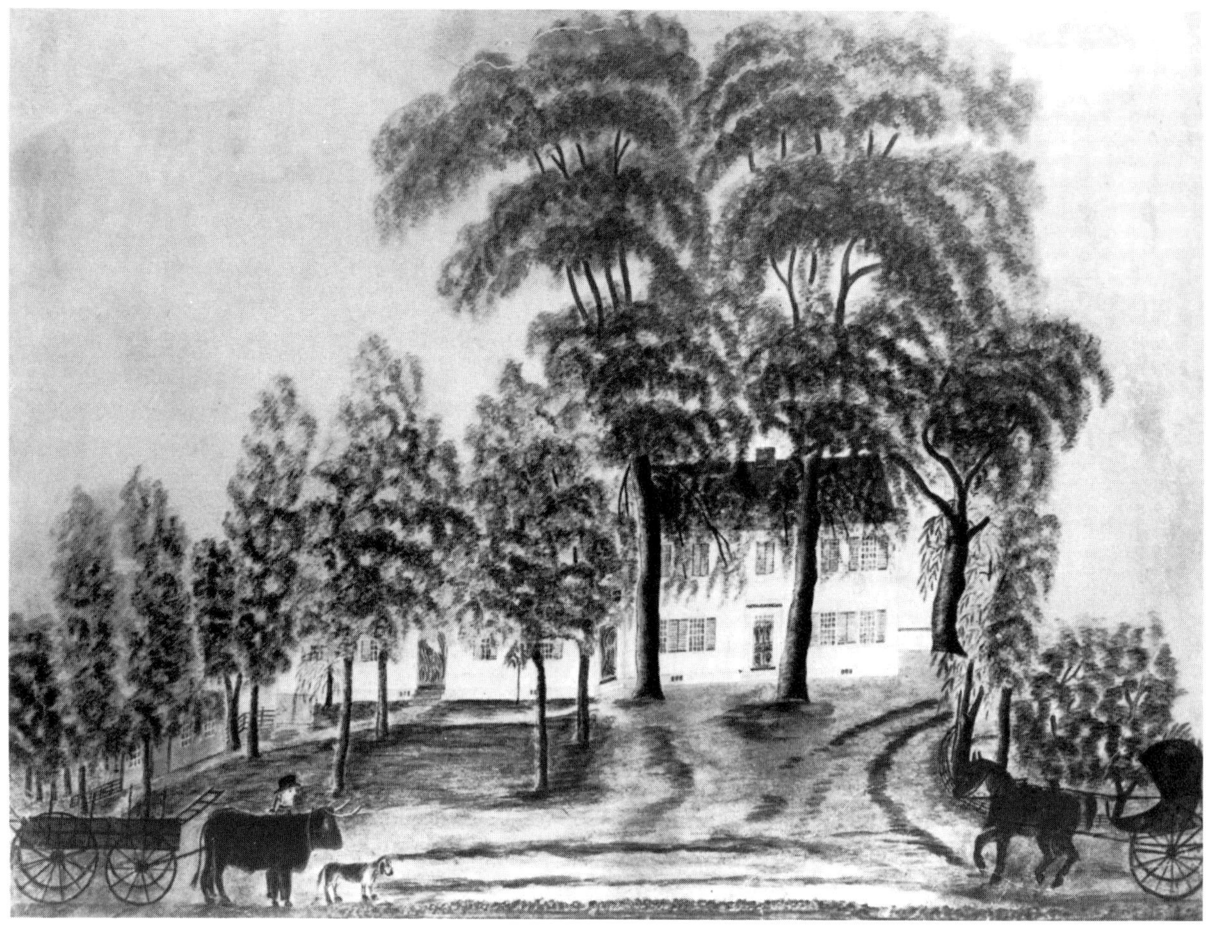

Figure 1 The Stephen Robbins House, Massachusetts Avenue, East Lexington, Massachusetts. Watercolor by Caira Robbins (1791–1881), daughter of Stephen and Abigail Robbins, circa 1810. Courtesy of the Society for the Preservation of New England Antiquities.

Lot Robbins, a dancing master and penmanship teacher who was one of the first patients admitted to McLean's Hospital for the insane in the old Barrell Mansion in Somerville and who lived there for fifty years. She could now open the chest of his clothing that her great-grandmother Abigail had locked when her youngest son departed and which had not been opened for more than sixty years. Ellen was now the only one who recalled her great aunt Caira's stories of attending Mrs. Haswell's Academy in Charlestown in 1810, could find her diary and letters, and remembered which of the dresses now carefully packed away were the ones Caira had worn when she traveled to New York and "walked down Broadway" in 1812.[4] Her attic (*Figure 2*) and drawers were full. The challenge was what to do with it all; who would care?

Apparently Ellen Stone was not an active member nor an officer in any museum or historical society. Her only published historical work, a selection of her great-aunt Caira's letters and diaries, appeared in the *Proceedings of the Lexington Historical Society* in 1907, a time when Ellen was intensely concerned about the disposition of her heirlooms. Perhaps surprisingly, she only placed a few of the family things at the Lexington Historical Society during her lifetime; family photographs and manuscripts, including much of her own incoming correspondence, were given there later by her executors.

Whatever may have driven her decision not to entrust most of her treasures to the local historical society, today's students of New England life during the years from 1740 to 1840 are greatly indebted to

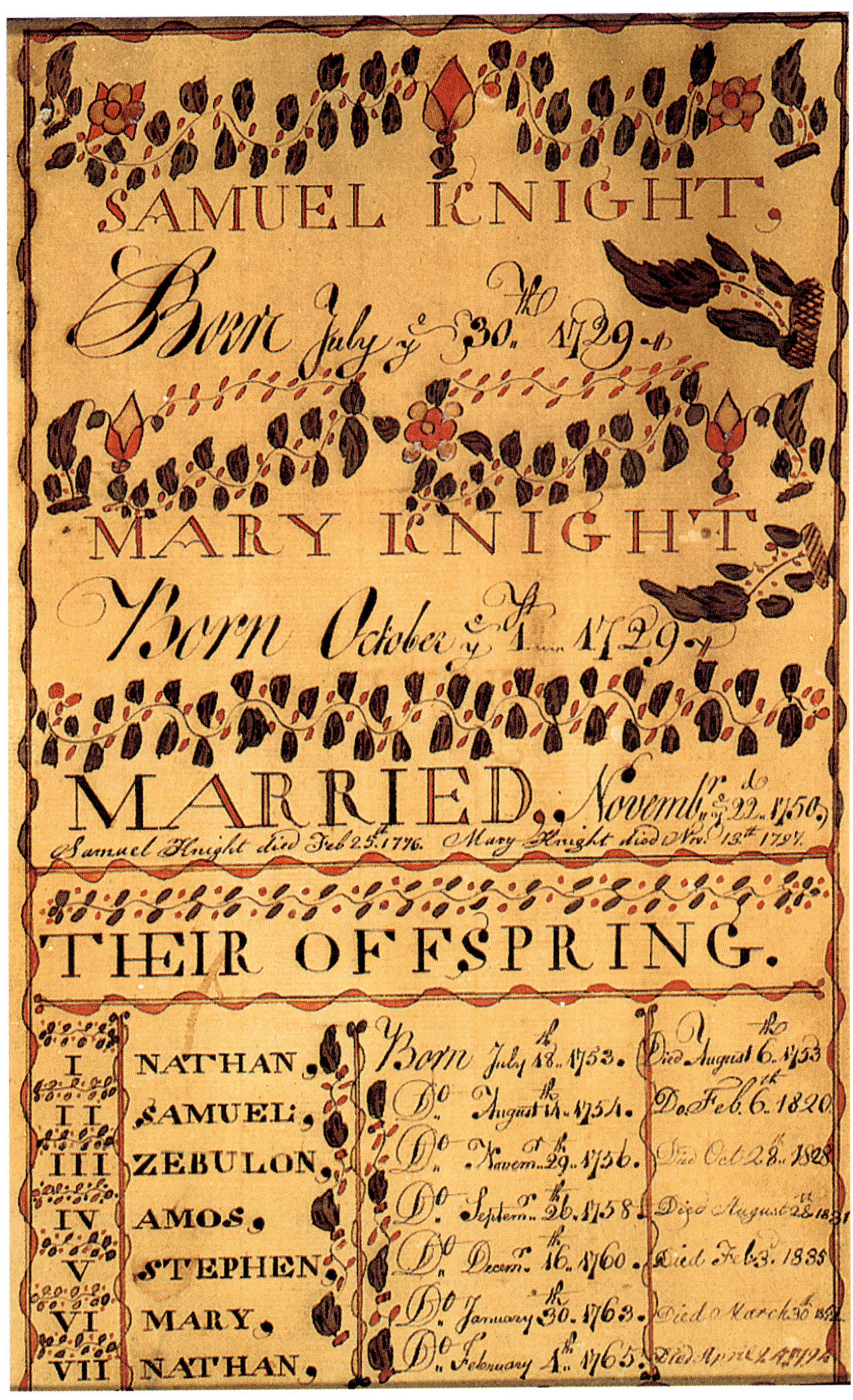

Family record. Samuel Knight and Mary Knight. Falmouth, Maine, circa 1780. Watercolor. Courtesy, Winterthur Museum.

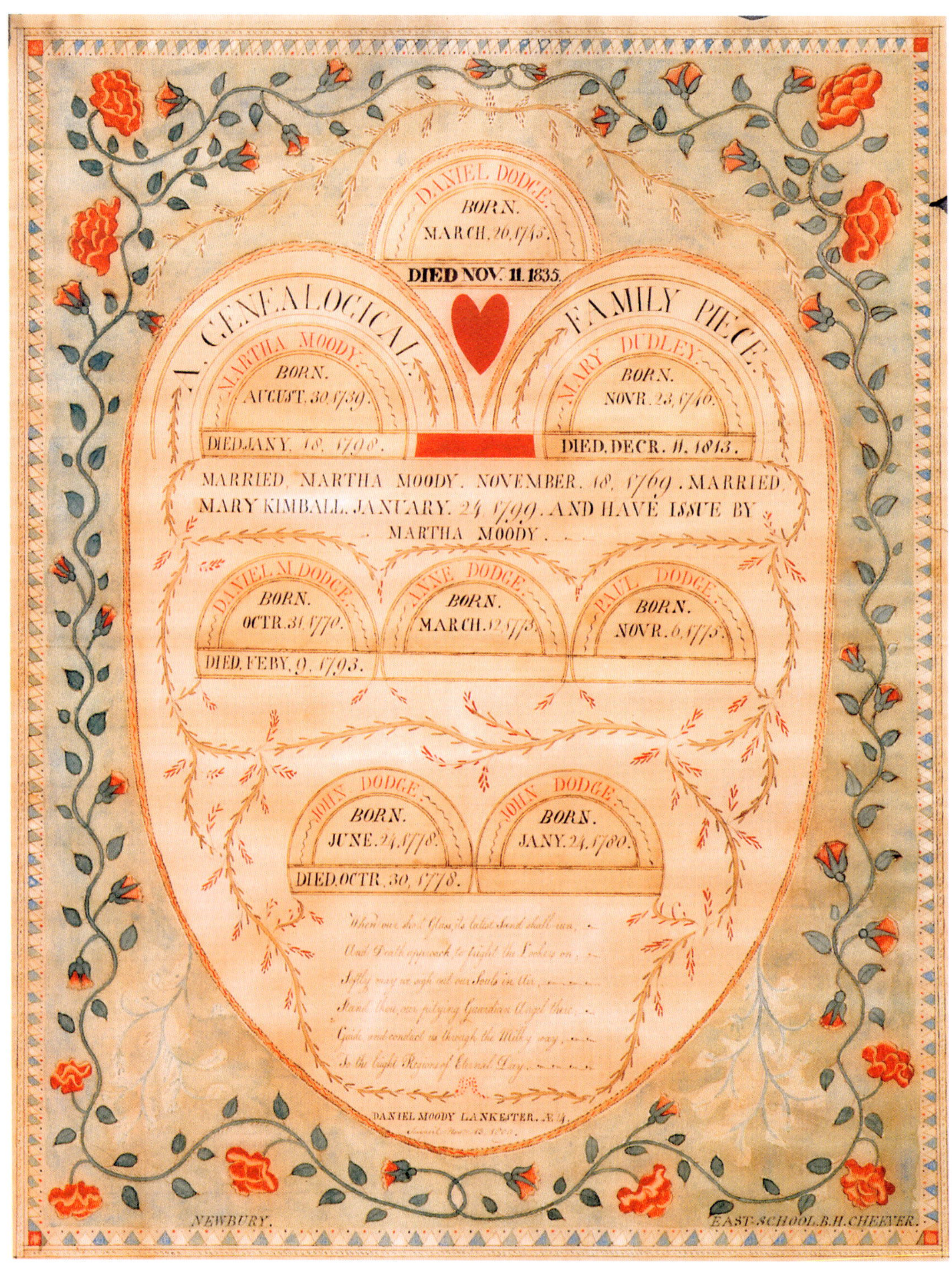

Family Register. Daniel Dodge and Martha Moody. Daniel Dodge and Mary Kimball. "Daniel Moody Lankester, Newbury East School, B. H. Cheever." Newbury, Massachusetts, 1809. Watercolor. New England Historic Genealogical Society.

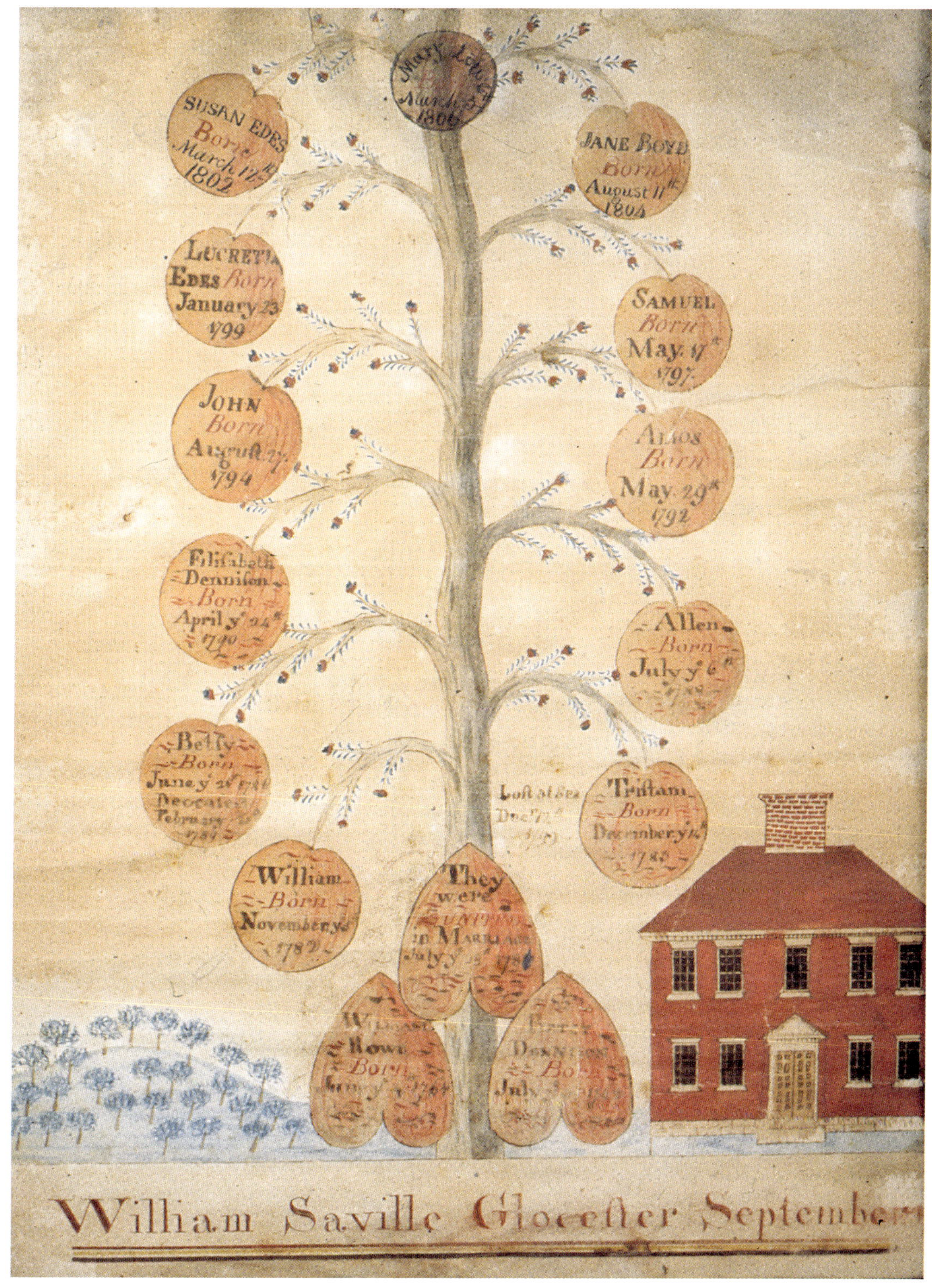

Family register. William Rowe and Betsy Dennison. "William Saville Glocester September 17 [ ]." Gloucester, Massachusetts, circa 1790. Watercolor. Sandy Bay Historical Society.

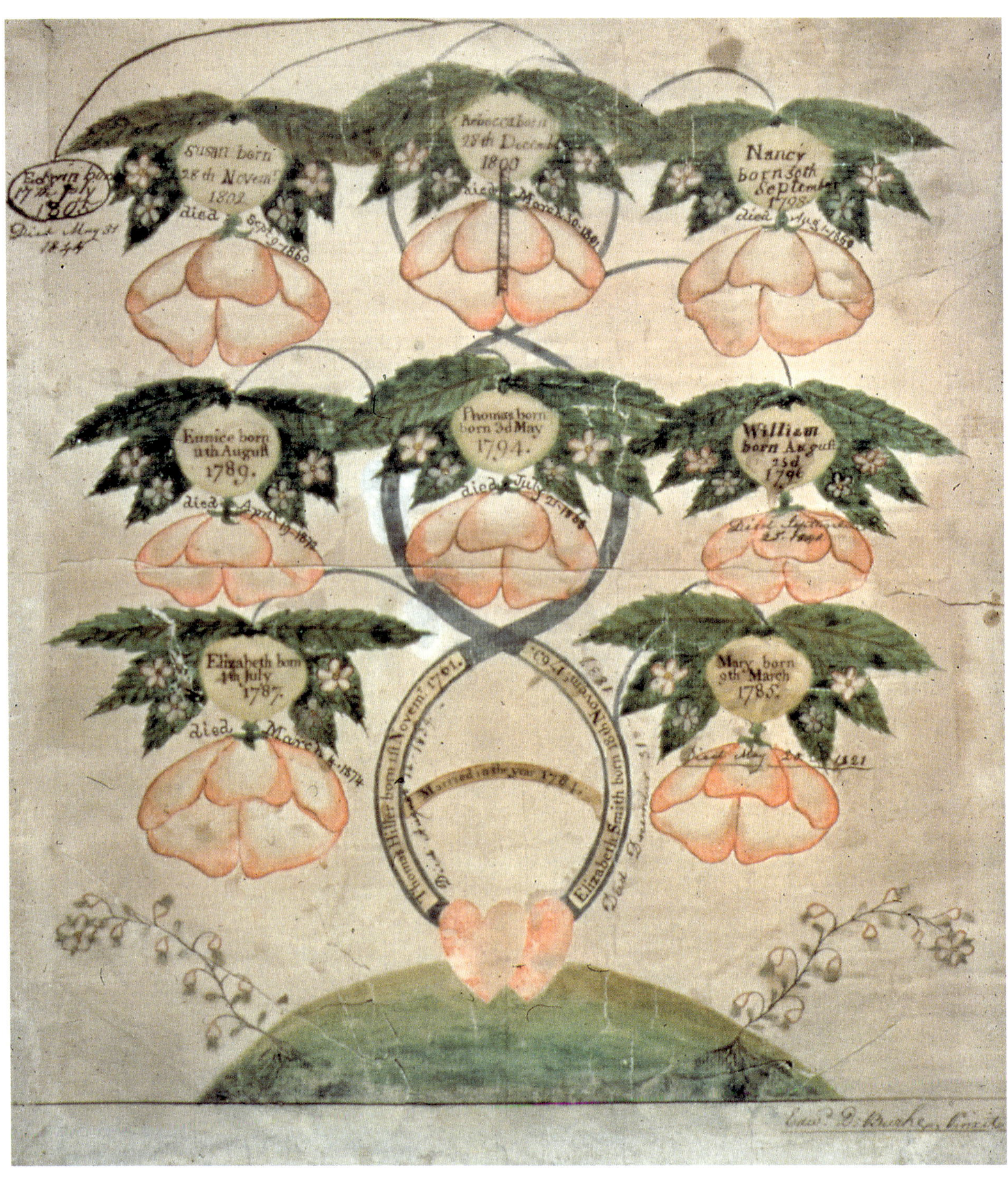

Family register. Thomas Hiller and Elizabeth Smith. "Edw.d D. Burke, Pinxit." Nantucket, Massachusetts, circa 1794–1796. Watercolor. Courtesy of the Nantucket Historical Association.

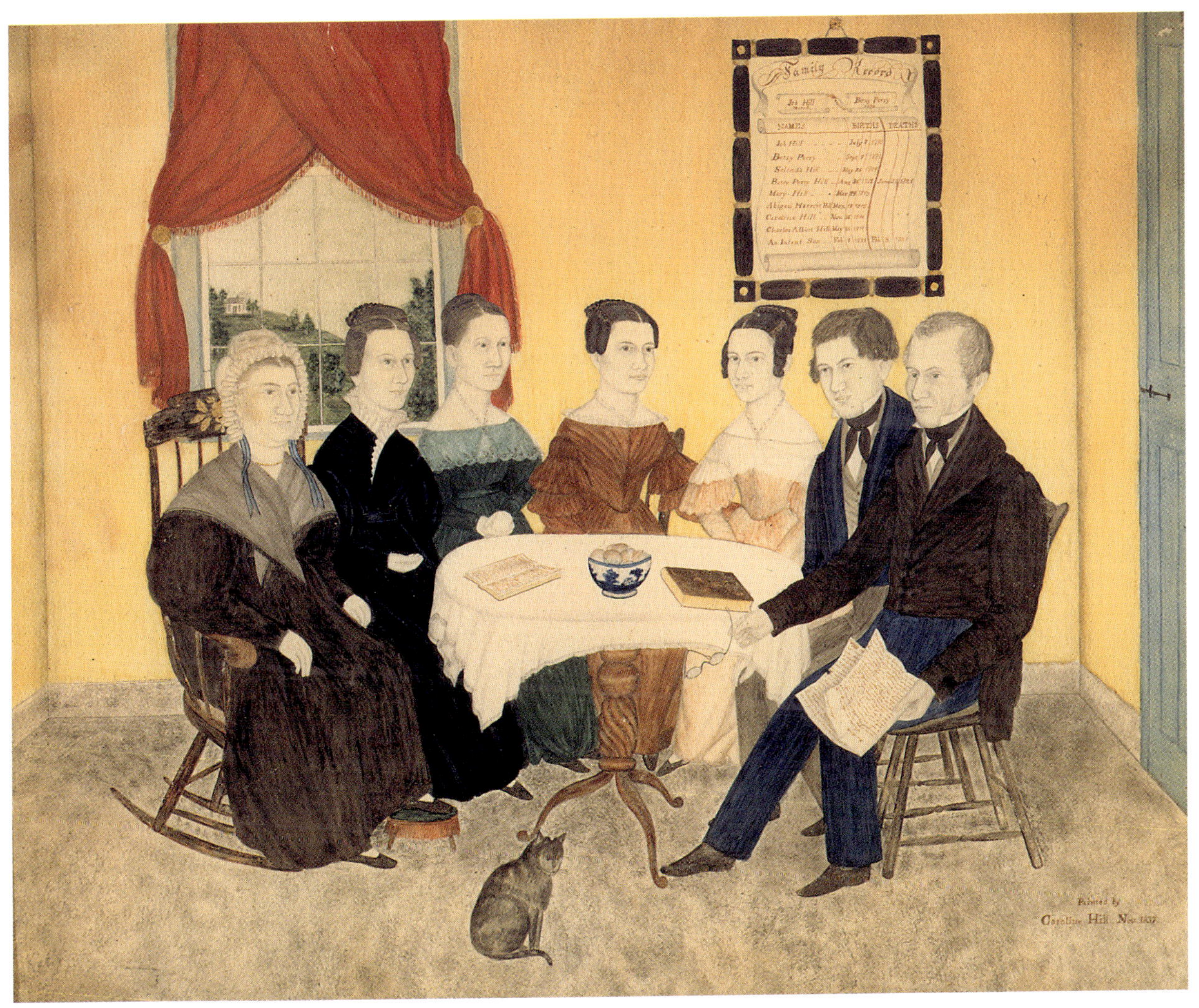

Family Portrait. Job Hill and family, by Caroline Hill, aged twenty-one. Peterborough, New Hampshire, 1837. Ink and watercolor on paper. Collection of the Peterborough Historical Society.

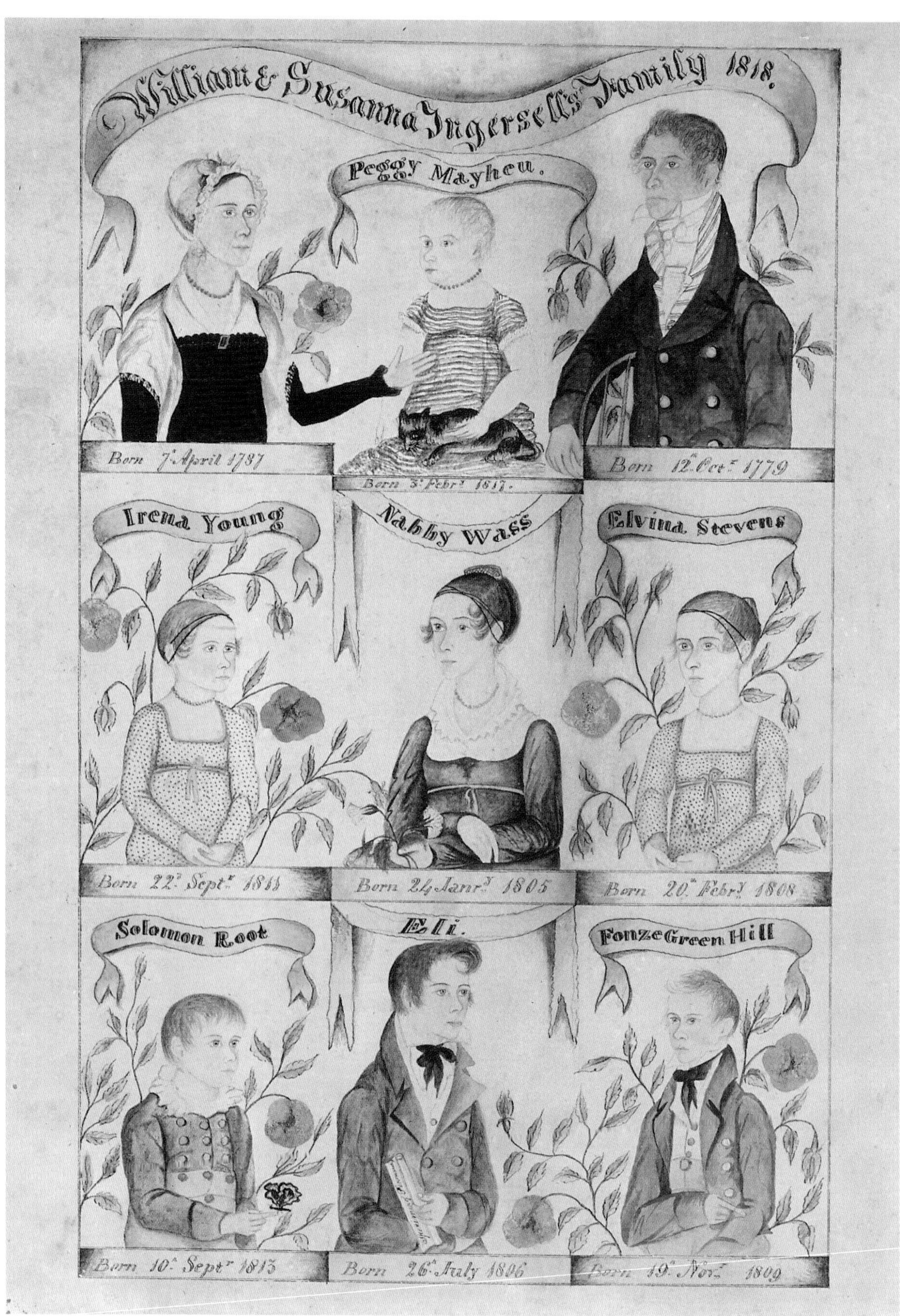

Family record. William Ingersell and family. Artist unknown. Columbia, Maine, 1818. Ink and watercolor on paper. Private Collection.

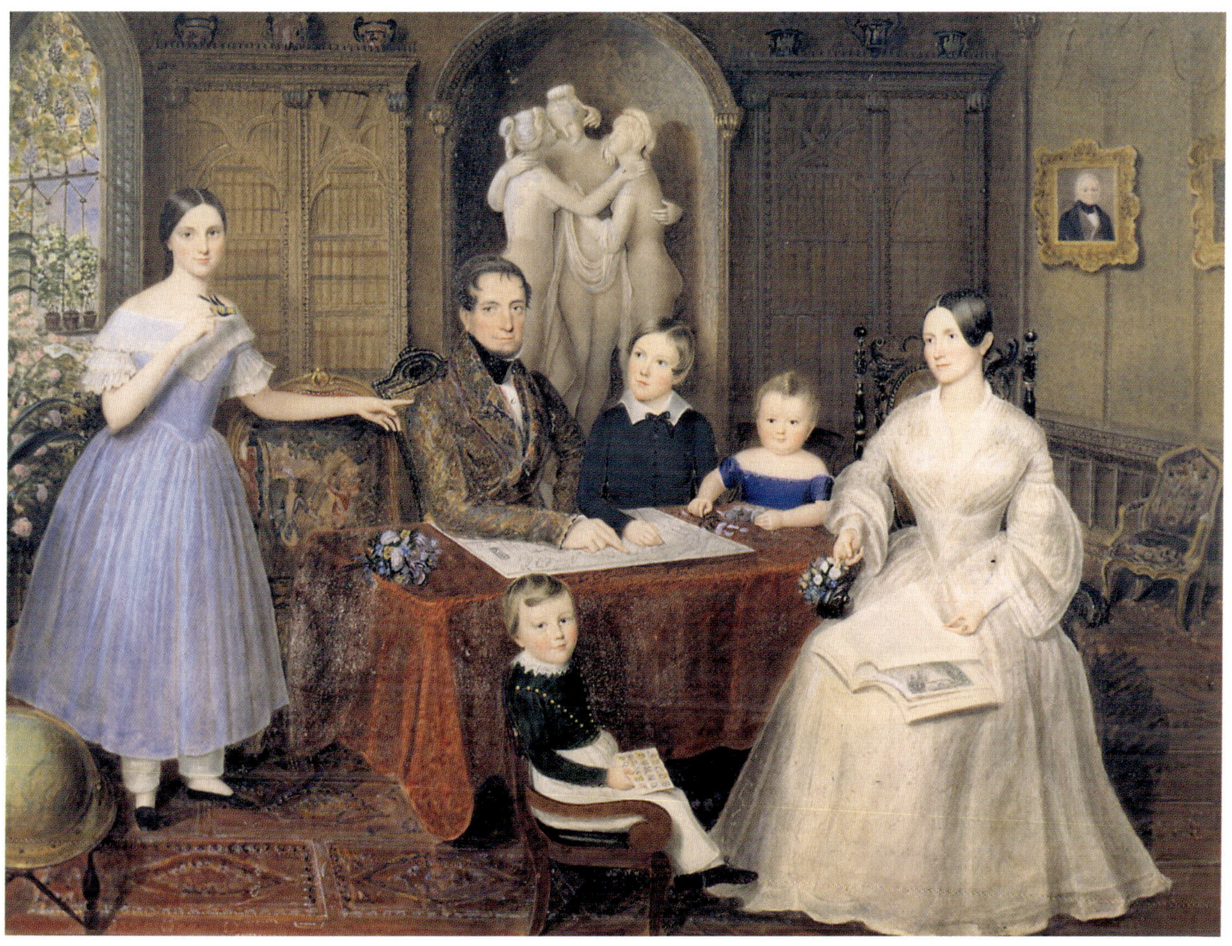

The Richard K. Haight Family. Attributed to Nicolino Calyo (1799–1884). New York, New York, circa 1848. Gouache on paper; 20 x 15 inches. Museum of the City of New York, Bequest of Elizabeth Cushing Iselin, (74.97.2). *Copyright by The Museum of the City of New York. Used by permission.*

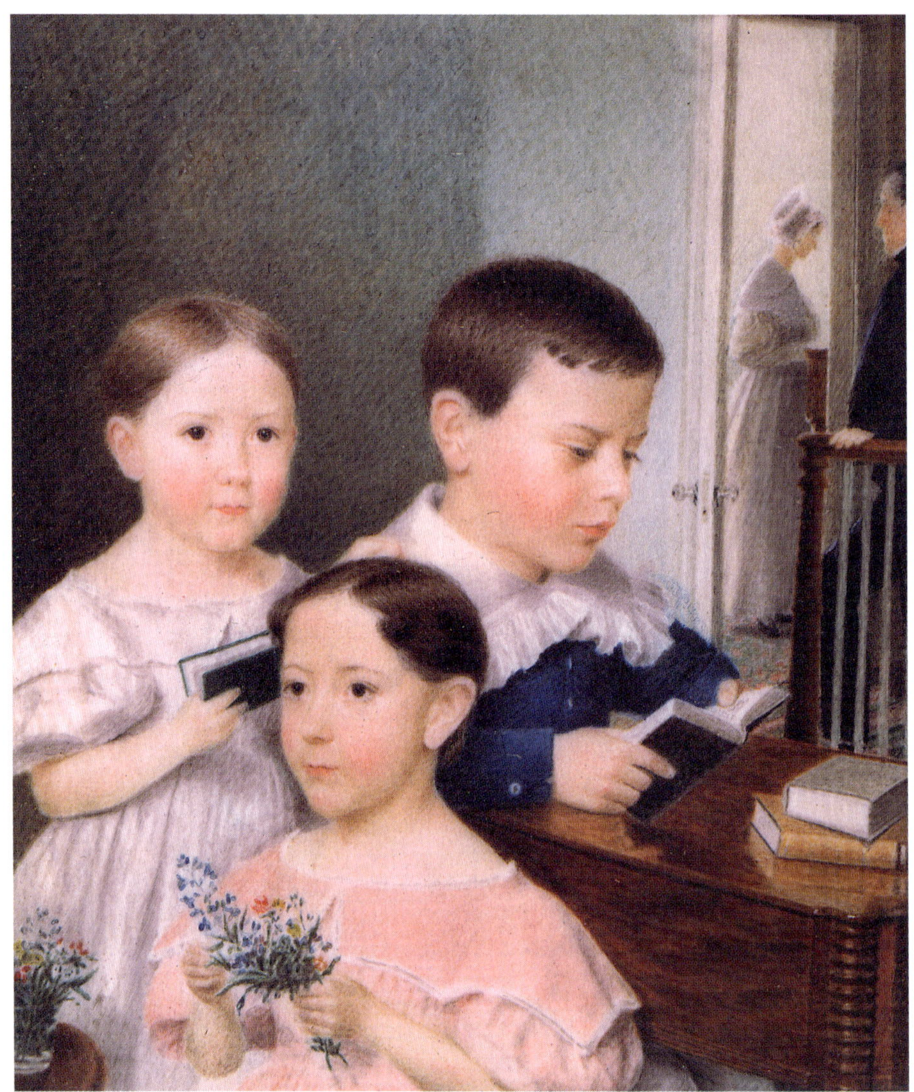

The Foster children. Eliza Goodridge (1798–1882). Worcester, Massachusetts, 1838. Watercolor on ivory; 4 1/16 x 3 3/8 inches. American Antiquarian Society, Bequest of Dwight Foster Dunn, 1937.

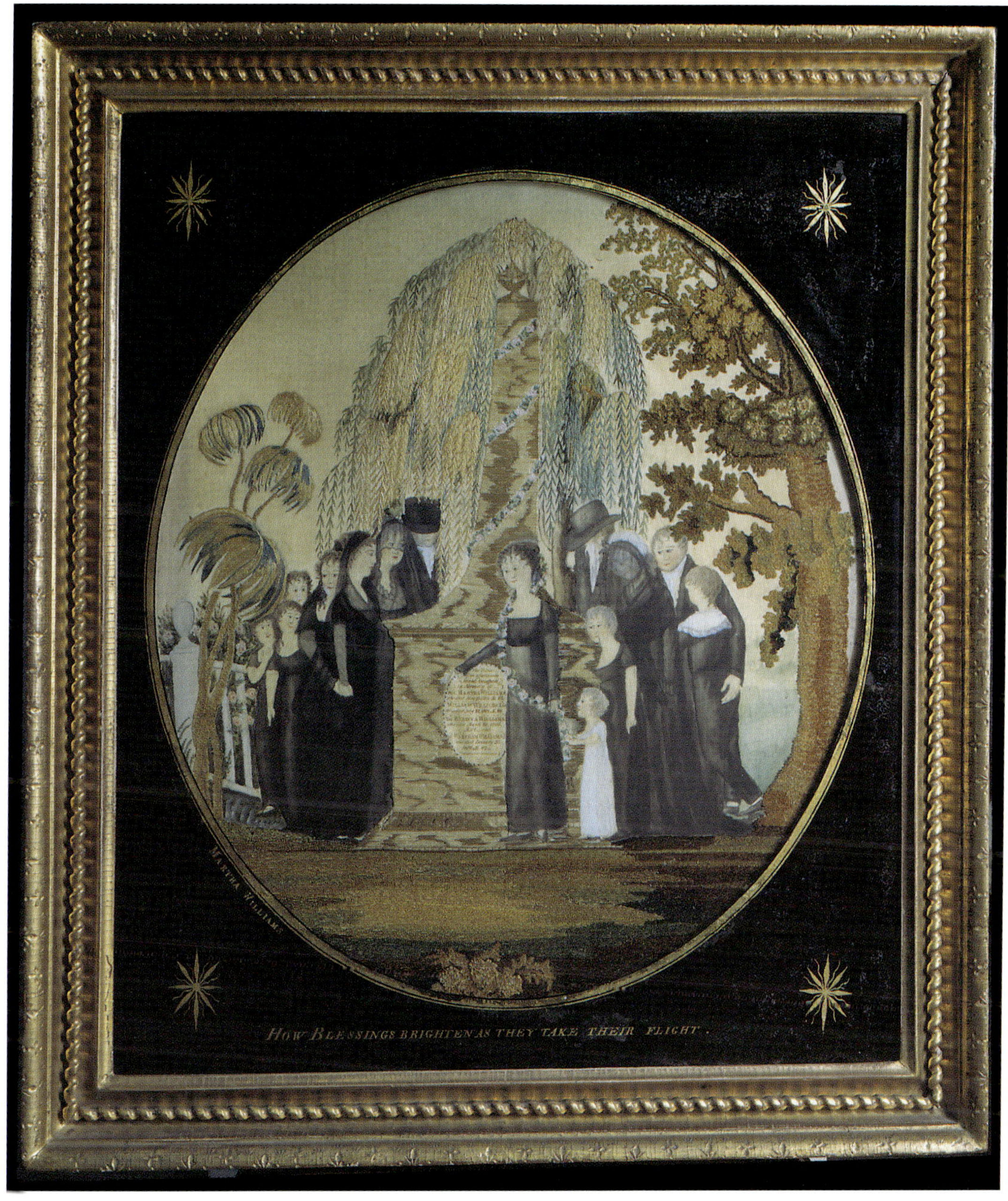

Mourning piece inscribed on the glass at left beside the oval "MARTHA WILLIAMS." And beneath the oval: "HOW BLESSINGS BRIGHTEN AS THEY TAKE THEIR FLIGHT." Inscribed in ink on the plinth: "The Tribute/ of an affectionate/ Grand-Daughter,/ in Memory of/ Mrs. MARTHA WILLIAMS,/ WHO DIED June 16, 1784 AE. 67. WILLIAM WILLIAMS, Esq/ who died July 27, 1801, AE. 86/ Mrs. REBECCA WILLIAMS,/ who died March 20, 1806,/ AE, 82 and/ Mr.WAREHAM WILLIAMS,/ who died January 31, 1808./AE, 82." Silk, chenille, watercolor, and ink on silk; oval 21 x 19 inches; overall within the original frame 29 3/4 x 25 3/4 inches. The painted figures appear to represent, at right, the maker's parents, Isaac (1758–1844) and Phebe Williams (1761–1822) of Stonington, Connecticut, with their children Cyrus (1783–1863), John (1793–1872), Martha (1791–1812), Eunice (b. 1797), and Emily (b. 1805); on the left, Isaac (b. 1781), Lucy (1785–1862), Sally (1787–1875), Rebecca (b. 1789), Jerusha (b. 1795), Phebe (b. 1799), and Fanny (1801–1869). Private collection.

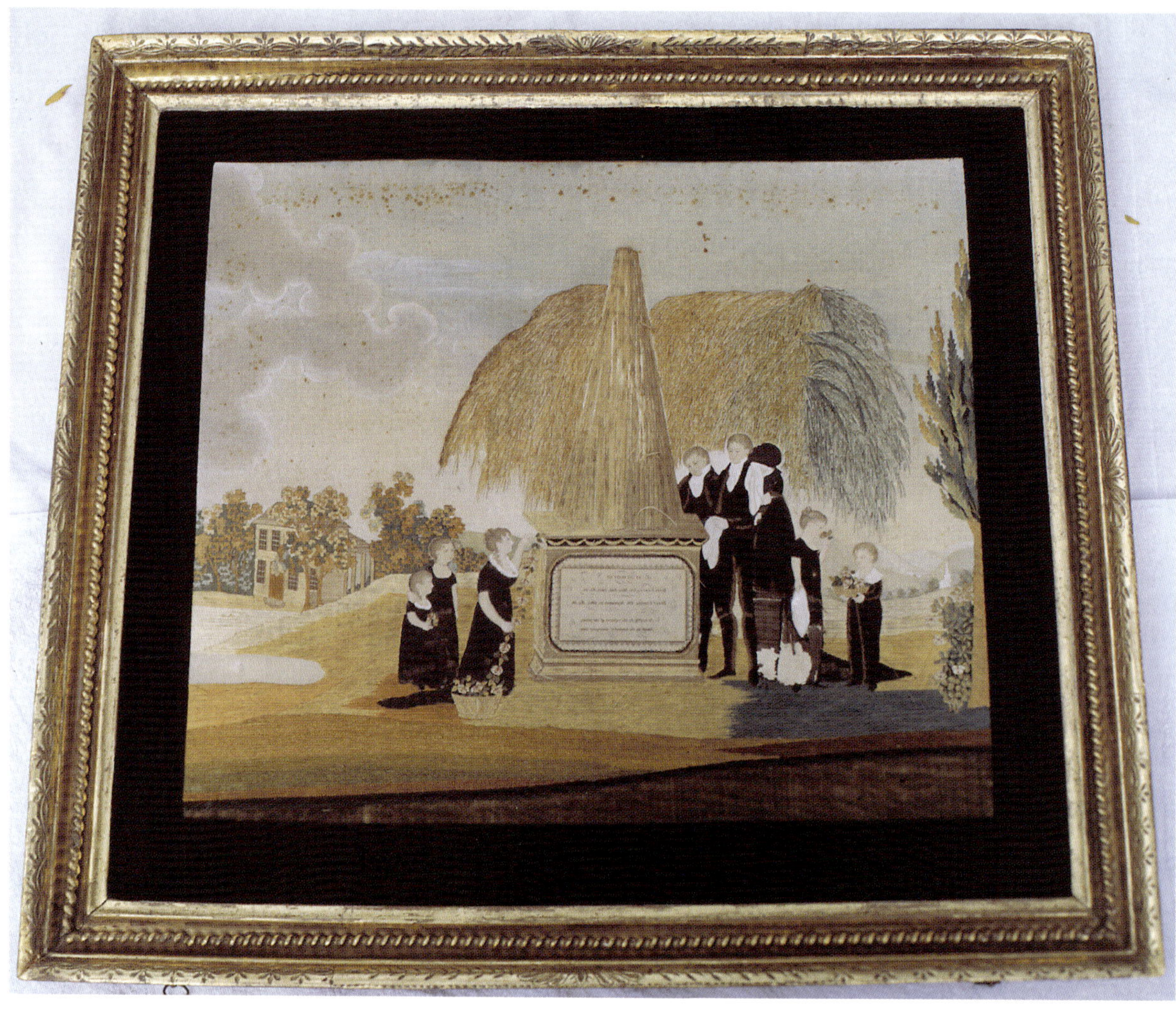

Mourning piece, circa 1805. Attributed to Jeanette Cowles (1792–1809), the third daughter of Zenas Cowles (1762–1835) and Mary Lewis Cowles (1766–1836) of Farmington, Connecticut, and dedicated to her older sisters. Inscribed on the plinth: "In Memory of Julia Cowles, Ob. May 15th, 1803, AEt 18 and Dolly Cowles, Ob. September 25th, 1803, AEt 16. So swiftly fly the raptures of our prime, swept by the tempest of destroying time." Silk, chenille, watercolor, and ink on silk with appliquéd silk and velvet; 22 1/8 x 26 inches within a black velvet mat that may be a replacement for an earlier glass with painted decoration; overall within the original frame 27 x 30 3/4 inches. Beside the monument at left are Jeanette's parents with her brother Edward (1789-1864), sister Emily (1796–1876), and brother Lewis (1800–1825). White spots reflect the loss of appliquéd silk from the mother's and Emily's dresses. On the right is Jeanette kneeling beside the monument with sister Elizabeth (1798–1823) and the second Julia (1803–1859). Julia (1785–1803), the eldest daughter, attended Sarah Pierce's school in Litch-field, Connecticut, in 1797 and 1798. See *The Diaries of Julia Cowles* (New Haven: Yale University Press, 1931) where Jeanette's embroidery is the frontispiece. At the time of her death, Julia was engaged to John Treadwell of Farmington. His sister Mary (b. 1786) worked a very similar memorial dedicated to their elder sister (illustrated in Ring, *Girlhood Embroidery*, fig. 251). Private collection.

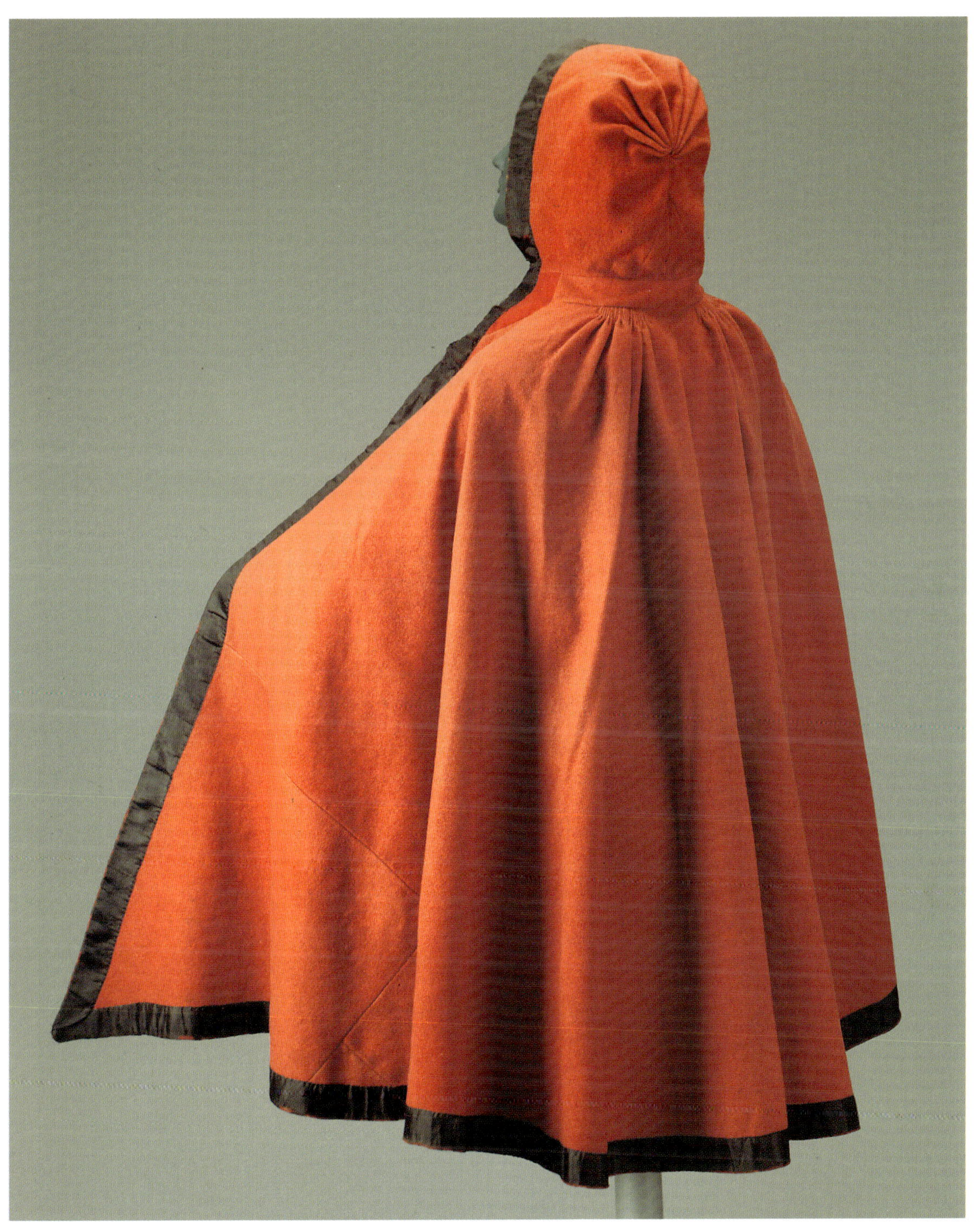

Red riding hood. Belonging to Abigail Winship Robbins (Mrs. Stephen Robbins) (1759–1850), circa 1780–1800. Courtesy, Museum of Fine Arts, Boston. *Reproduced with permission. Museum of Fine Arts, Boston.*

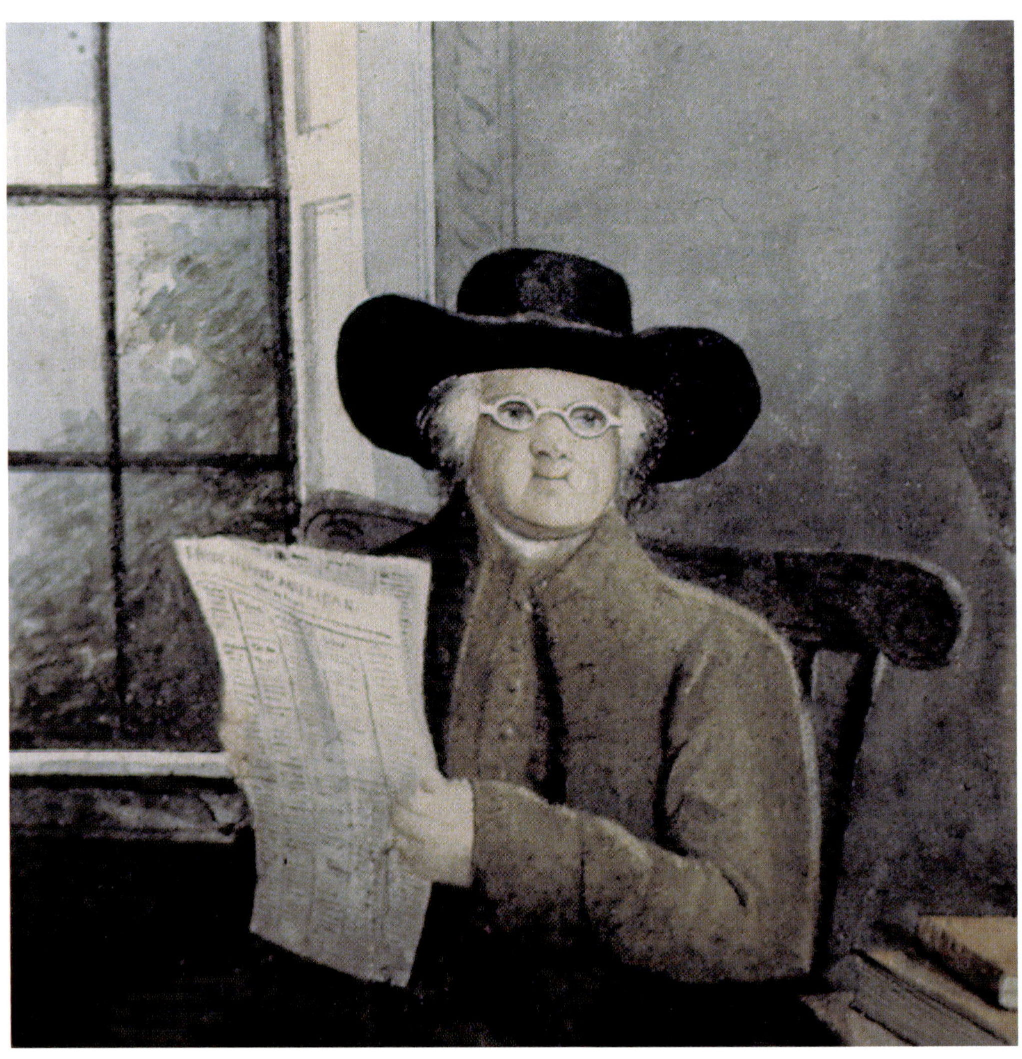

Moses Brown. Joseph Partridge (1792–circa 1833). Providence, Rhode Island 1823. Watercolor on paper; 4 1/2 x 4 1/2 inches. Inscribed: "J.P. - x II 1823" lower right; signed "Moses Brown's" in the subject's own hand on a piece of paper attached below the painting, and inscribed on the reverse of the painting: "Moses Brown was born 9 mo 23 1738. Departed this earth 9 mo 6 1836. Aged 97 years 11 months & 3 days." Private collection.

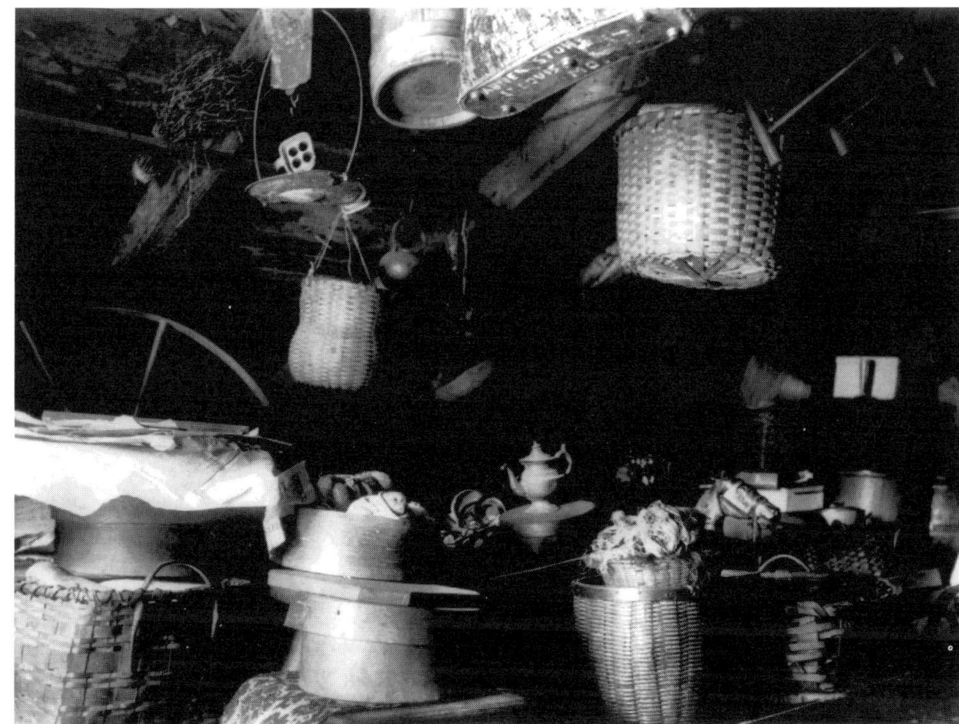

Figure 2 "Interior of Miss Stone's Garrett about 1900–1910. Old Robbins Homestead." Courtesy of the Society for the Preservation of New England Antiquities.

Ellen Stone for her saving ways, the gifts she made to stable institutions, and the knowledge she passed along with her family heirlooms. She had listened carefully to her aunt and her mother, learning from them the identities of the things they cherished and how to manage the family homestead. When she listened, she remembered. Not only did she preserve and document the material culture of the family, she preserved a historic house and a way of life (*Figure 3*). Apparently, she became more and more eccentric as the years passed, eschewing new clothing in favor of that she found in the attic. She lived alone in the old homestead for fifty-four years after her mother's death without a furnace, a bathroom, or gas service. She made use of a hand pump at the kitchen sink and only had electricity installed in 1942, when she was eighty-five years old.

Both Miss Ellen Adelia Robbins Stone and her mother, also Ellen A. R., were interested in much more than their family heirlooms. They were both active in the movements to promote higher education and secure suffrage for women. They were also concerned with ways in which they could serve people in need and in their community. They were avid readers and book collectors as well as advocates of literacy. Miss Stone worked as a nurse in hospitals in the Midwest and in England; she also traveled widely for pleasure, passing some winters in Jamaica, Hawaii, North Carolina, and other places "at the south," spending pleasant summer months at least one year in Jackson, New Hampshire, and once visiting Niagara Falls on a journey with Susan B. Anthony.[5] Mrs. Stone's will provided a trust fund for Ellen's comfortable maintenance in the old homestead and left small cash legacies to distant cousins, but she also looked beyond Ellen's lifetime and made certain that the homestead itself and her additional real estate and financial resources were used to do good in ways she had long espoused. Mrs. Stone bequeathed one-half an acre of land to the town of Lexington to support a public reading room and named Lucy Stone, Ednah D. Cheney, William I. Bowditch, Eva Channing, Henry B. Blackwell, Alice Stone Blackwell, Samuel E. Sewall, Harriet Pitman,

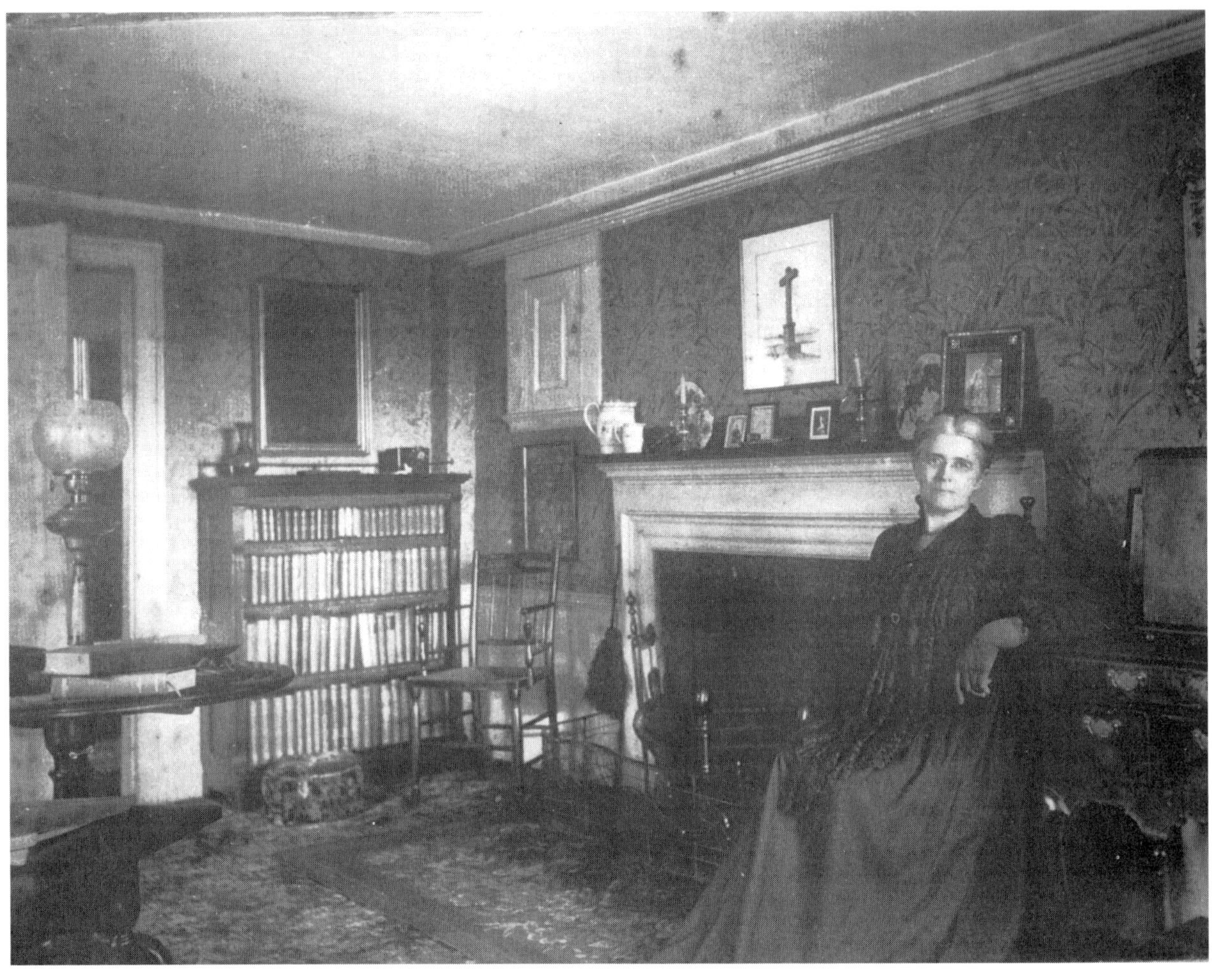

Figure 3 "Miss Ellen Stone, Nov. 1890. Room to the left of the front door." From the collections of the Lexington Historical Society.

Alice W. DeNormandie, and Thomas Wentworth Higginson as trustees responsible for a bequest of ten thousand dollars to be used "at their discretion for improving the condition of women . . . by promoting superior education and changes of laws so as to remove the unjust inequalities of their sex" and a further sum which was to be turned over to the town of Lexington, the interest of which was to be employed "in aiding needy and deserving young women of Lexington in getting a good school education." After Ellen Jr.'s death in 1944, the surviving and successor trustees used these funds and others from the younger woman's estate to establish "the Ellen A. Stone Scholarships for women in the College of Liberal Arts at Boston University."[6]

Ellen Stone's first recorded gifts of Robbins family material to a museum or historical society were those of a portrait of Nathaniel Gerry to the Essex Institute in Salem in 1889 and of fifteen additional items the following year. It is unclear at this time how her attention was first drawn to the Institute, although Gerry was born in Salem and that association may have seemed appropriate. Why, then, she chose to give pieces of wrapping paper and a bar of soap to the Institute the next year or why she turned to other organizations for other gifts until 1908 and 1913 when she made additional large gifts to the Salem institution is unclear.

The majority of things given by Miss Stone to the Essex Institute were articles of clothing, textile

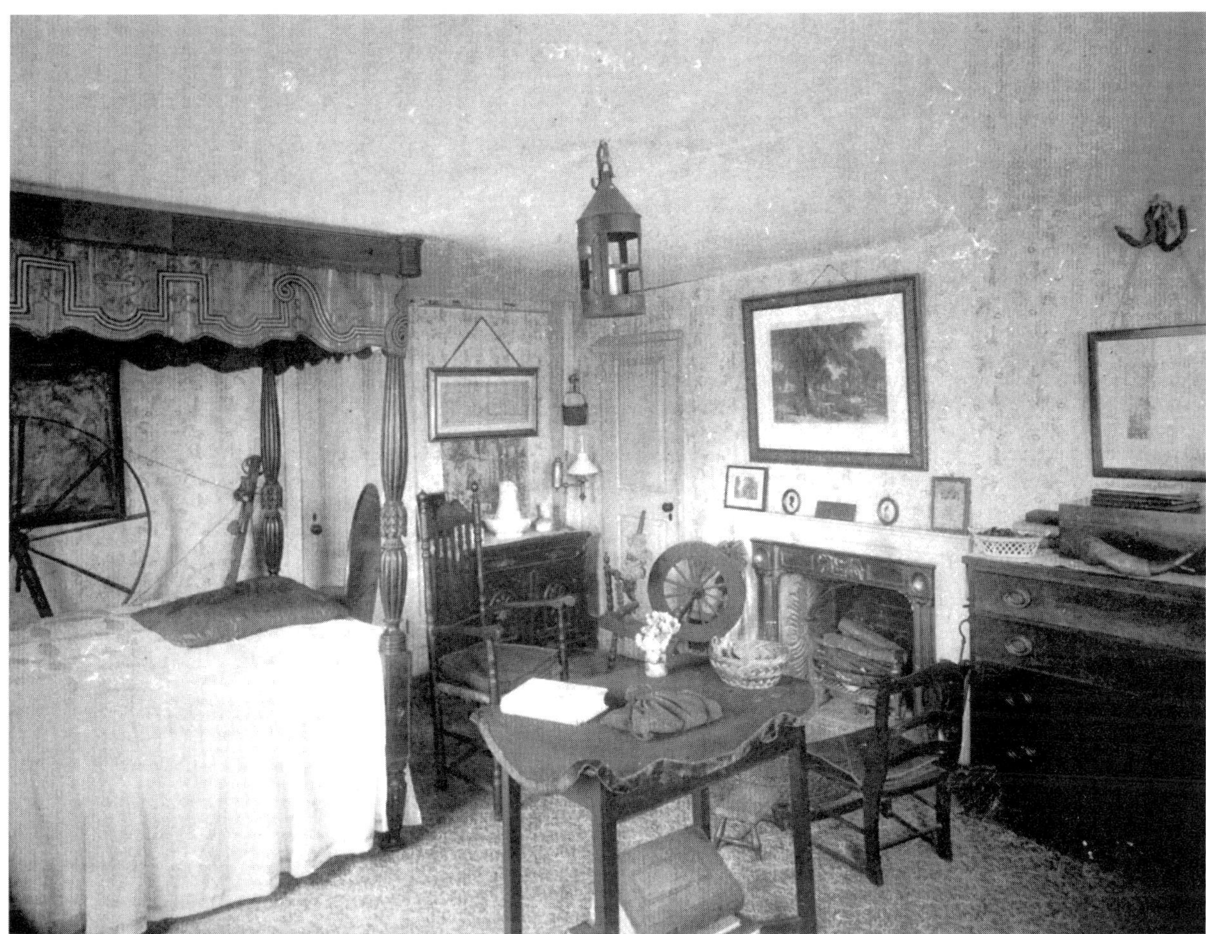

Figure 4 "Caira's Bedroom, in Stephen Robbins house, Nov. 1890." From the collections of the Lexington Historical Society.

samples, and sewing notions such as tape, thread, and buttons. The Institute also received and catalogued more than twenty various types of writing and wrapping paper, slate pencils, and other stationery items, toys, shaving materials, small boxes, medicines, four pieces of ceramics, some bottles, and the bar of soap. There were no gifts of furniture or other portraits, the kinds of things most sought by those memorializing important men, furnishing house museums, or setting up period rooms. Other than the Gerry portrait, there was nothing associated with anyone of national historical significance or with Salem as a city.

Probably the most interesting of Ellen Stone's gifts to the Essex Institute were the textiles. These included a remarkable early-eighteenth-century woolen bed valance that had been used in the Robbins House during the 1890s on a bed of the Federal period (*Figure 4*) that Miss Stone later gave to the Society for the Preservation of New England Antiquities (SPNEA). The gifts also included nearly one hundred samples of fabric, most of which were identified by name, use, and date. Many of these were mounted in winged glass cases by George Francis Dow, the Institute's early-twentieth-century curator; their labels conveyed Miss Stone's identifications of those that had been used for men's or women's clothing or for household use, probable dates of manufacture, and their place of origin, if she knew it. These remained on display until well into the 1980s; there was no other textile display of such rich documentation and detail in New England during those years.

In 1899 Miss Stone presented a group of 138 pieces of Robbins family clothing to the Textile Department of the Museum of Fine Arts in Boston (MFA). Nearly 25 percent of this material had belonged to Miss Stone's unmarried great-aunt Caira, the youngest child of Stephen and Abigail Robbins. Born in 1791, at the time of the French Revolution, her name derives from *Ça Ira,* the stirring refrain of a French patriotic song. It may have been her unusual name or it may have been the story associated with Caira's clothing that attracted the attention of Alice Morse Earle, the antiquarian author who illustrated in her monumental book on costume in early America the salmon pink lutestring gown with the sea green silk hat and matching slippers that Caira herself had identified as "The Dress I made to walk down Broadway in."[7] The MFA gift included clothing for men, women, and children, both high-style garments and examples of everyday clothing. Of the clothing of Miss Stone's grandmother Abigail Robbins (1759–1850), the MFA received dresses of plum-colored silk and blue and white gingham, a black silk redingote, and a red riding hood (*Figure 5*). In addition were a black silk hood trimmed with Ipswich lace "to wear over a turban," black and green silk traveling veils, a muslin apron, white silk stockings marked "A," a white linen short gown, cambric kerchiefs, black satin high heeled shoes without their buckles, a pair of "carpet saver" slippers made of warp faced striped carpet, white kid and black silk mitts, and a chemise. Her eighteenth-century stays (*Figure 6*) of glazed yellow wool are bound with white kid and measure twenty-seven inches around the waist and thirty-two at the bust. Miss Stone also gave the MFA Caira's pastel (*Figure 7*) and watercolor boxes and a small example of her painting on velvet. Although these art supplies may have seemed appropriate gifts for an art museum to Miss Alice Gray, the textile curator at that time, they have remained in the textile and costume department to this day, valued for their documentation as well as their design.

Miss Stone must have been concerned about giving so many things to the MFA; perhaps she had already made promises of future gifts to the Essex Institute. In any case, Miss Gray assured Miss Stone that things she gave to the Museum of Fine Arts would be "in the best shape, for their best preservation, cleaned, etc. and have the best of care in a fireproof building, receipts given, etc.," and she coaxed her to give more things, "for instance . . . wall-papers are very desirable for the Museum . . . and I shall beg of you samples of all your early calicoes."[8] In another letter Miss Gray assured her that "there will be plenty for the Essex Institute after the Museum has had the things mentioned."[9] In her view, other gifts would be all right as long as she, Miss Gray, had first choice.

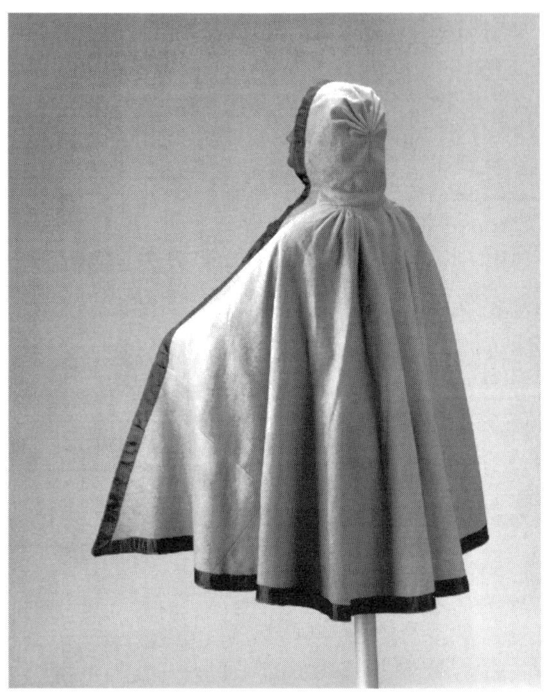

Figure 5 Red riding hood. Belonging to Abigail Winship Robbins (Mrs. Stephen Robbins) (1759–1850), circa 1780–1800. Courtesy, Museum of Fine Arts, Boston. *Reproduced with permission. © 2002 Museum of Fine Arts, Boston. All Rights Reserved.*

Ironically, in 1907, more than one hundred pieces of the Robbins family clothing were loaned by the Museum of Fine Arts to the Essex Institute. There they were displayed for more than sixty years in glass cases on headless forms or on flat mounts. The pieces are still in remarkably good condition and the family histories supplied by Miss Ellen Stone align with current scholarly considerations of date and attribution. Because many of the items in the collection were precisely dated or the names and dates of the original owners are known, they are useful in helping to establish chronologies of items such as baby caps and shirts, those things which often appear in local historical or private family collections

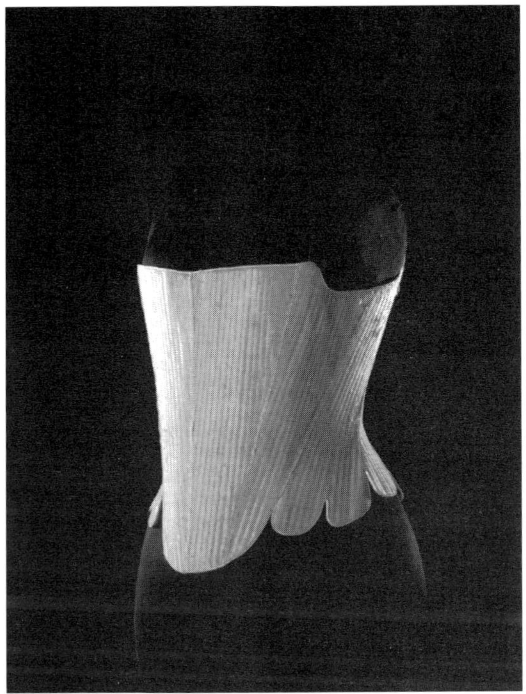

Figure 6 Stays. Used by Abigail Winship Robbins, circa 1780–1790. Courtesy, Museum of Fine Arts, Boston. *Reproduced with permission. © 2002 Museum of Fine Arts, Boston. All Rights Reserved.*

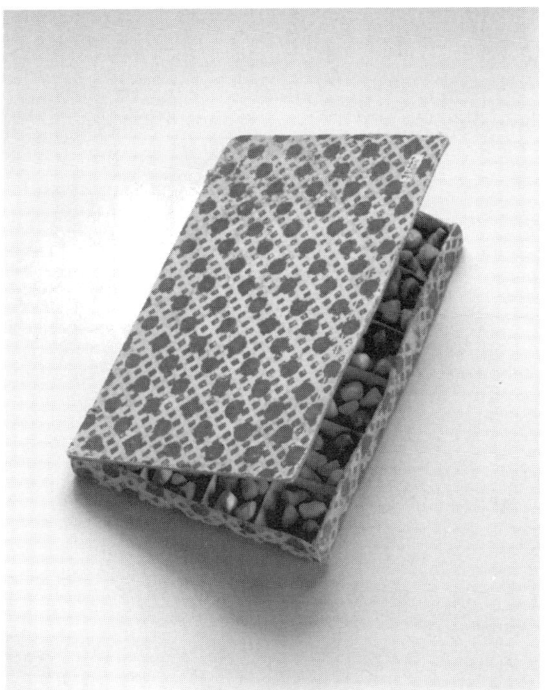

Figure 7 Pastel box. Used by Caira Robbins. English, circa 1810. Courtesy, Museum of Fine Arts, Boston. *Reproduced with permission. © 2002 Museum of Fine Arts, Boston. All Rights Reserved.*

in large quantities but just as often lack any specific attribution of ownership or accurate date. While handstitched white cotton or linen infant clothing is abundant in New England clothing collections, few examples are as firmly dated in the mid-eighteenth century as those of Stephen Robbins who was born in 1758 (*Figure 8*).

In the spring of 1899, "after twenty three years of service at the Fine Art Museum in Boston," Alice A. Gray moved to Ipswich, Massachusetts, where the Whipple House had been acquired by the Ipswich Historical Society the previous year. Reportedly, she "felt the charm of our ancient mansion so powerfully that she relinquished in a large measure her work at the Fine Art Museum and became the custodian of our house. She brought to her new position . . . the devotion of an antiquary, the skill in arrangement learned by long experience, and exquisite taste [and] a great store of ancient furniture as well, and many decorative adornments."[10] Miss Gray moved into the Whipple House with her friend and housekeeper, Miss Julia Gutberlett. She furnished some rooms for her own use and others for public view. Suggesting that they were kindred spirits, Miss Gray wrote to Miss Stone, "I fancy that your family and mine are twins in that respect. Our things are the burdens of our lives."[11] Drawing on the relationship developed when Miss Stone gave so many Robbins family materials to the Museum of Fine Arts earlier that same year, Miss Gray convinced Ellen Stone to send "a fine collection of antiques from her marvelous old home in East Lexington"[12] down to Ipswich to help furnish the Whipple House.

The things were soon safely delivered although they were somewhat damp as a result of being shipped from Lexington to Ipswich in an open wagon on a rainy day. Miss Gray wrote to Miss Stone that the president of the Society, the Reverend "Mr. Waters was delighted with the furniture—and we sent it at once to the Cabinet makers to be repaired and polished. The bedstead is too wide for the bedroom it will go into, the 'E. A. Stone bedroom,' but he will cut

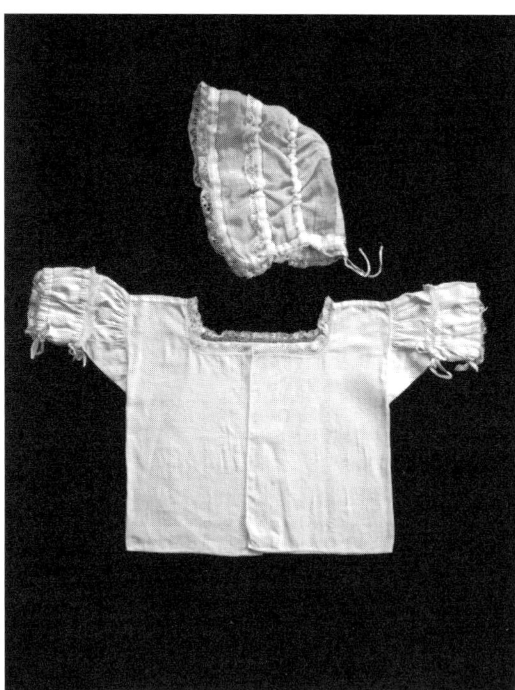

Figure 8 Shirt and Cap. Worn by Stephen Robbins (born 1758). Courtesy, Museum of Fine Arts, Boston. *Reproduced with permission. © 2002 Museum of Fine Arts, Boston. All Rights Reserved.*

it down in width without injuring at all the style of the bedstead. The candlestand has been mended, scraped, and polished already and is a beauty. You will be surprised when you see how finely they look when all finished."[13] Indeed, the completed arrangements of homelike settings were greatly admired. Visitors in the summer of 1901 included Alice Morse Earle and her sister, Frances Clary Morse, as well as Halliday, the photographer, who wrote "there is nothing that can touch it." Miss Gray's arrangement of the kitchen at the Whipple House was illustrated in volume three of Esther Singleton's *Furniture of Our Forefathers* and in the *New York Tribune* 28 July 1901 review of the Singleton books.[14] Despite the widespread admiration of the rooms she had created and the influence they were having on antiquarian taste throughout the Northeast, Miss Gray seems to have felt ambivalent about her efforts. She wrote to Ellen Stone, "Now you and I spend ourselves and all our reserve force in old pots and kettles, chests & chairs. I asked myself what's the good?—and had no answer, only we can't help it, the Lord made us so, but we must try."[15]

Miss Stone's gift to the Ipswich Historical Society is recorded in the "Register of Donations" on 20 August 1899 as a "large number of Household articles from the house of her great grandfather and grandmother Stephen and Abigail Winship Robbins of Lexington, Mass." Among them were five pieces of glass, two pictures, and nine pieces of "bedding" and homespun linen, 21 pieces of "pottery" primarily creamware, pearlware, and transfer printed wares as well as single pieces of redware and stoneware, and seven pieces of furniture, including an arm chair "that was one of a set used in the sitting room in the Robbins's House in Lexington" (*Figure 9*). All of the pieces were described and a few of the ceramics were attributed to manufactories such as Bow or Wedgwood, based on marks. Some of the bed and table linens were identified by marked initials, such as A.R., S.R., and A., but the obvious associations with Miss Stone's great-grandparents Stephen and Abigail Robbins were not recorded in the register. The few family associations that were recorded were those of the sitting room chairs, the "best set" of china belonging to Mrs. Stephen Robbins (*Figure 10*), and a "'Mourning Piece' painted by Miss Caira Robbins of Lexington about 1810."[16] Apparently there was no concern on the part of the donor or the historical society's officers that the Robbins family things had no historical association with the town of Ipswich or that items from Lexington might have been of greater interest to the Lexington Historical Society.

The rooms at the Ipswich Historical Society were uniformly admired, especially after being published again in *The House Beautiful* in September 1903. The kitchen also served as the source for the installation of a colonial kitchen in the State Historical Society of Wisconsin where the blackened old oak beams and spacious fireplace were reproduced as part of a setting for the display of "Such articles of the olden time as would have been daily needed in a kitchen of our forefathers in colonial days."[17] Perhaps not surprisingly, some of the items displayed in the Wisconsin colonial kitchen were the gift of Miss Ellen Stone. Her house was still full and she was eager to place

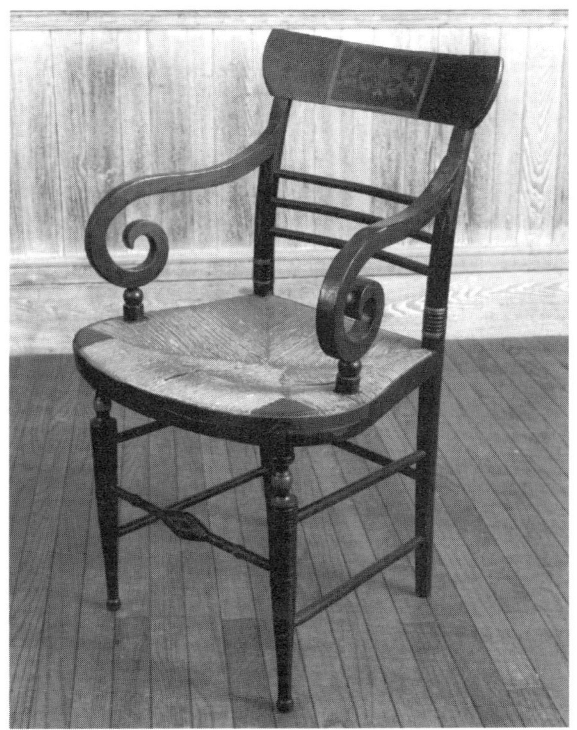

Figure 9 Arm Chair. From the sitting room of the Stephen Robbins House, East Lexington, Massachusetts. Circa 1820–1830. Ipswich Historical Society.

her family treasures in settings where they would be useful and instructive. Somehow her name and address had been shared with those setting up the rooms in Madison and she was glad to help.

It was probably through the Ipswich Historical Society that Miss Stone came to know William Sumner Appleton, for they were both made honorary members of that organization in 1899 and for several years thereafter; they were also members of the Essex Institute in Salem. Soon after Appleton and several friends founded the Society for the Preservation of New England Antiquities in 1910, Ellen Stone was invited to become a member of that organization, as well. Appleton served as corresponding secretary of the Society which was soon recognized as the nerve center of preservation and antiquarianism in New England. Appleton kept track of threats to historic buildings, located significant collections of family heirlooms, and befriended both old families and new collectors as potential donors. For SPNEA he

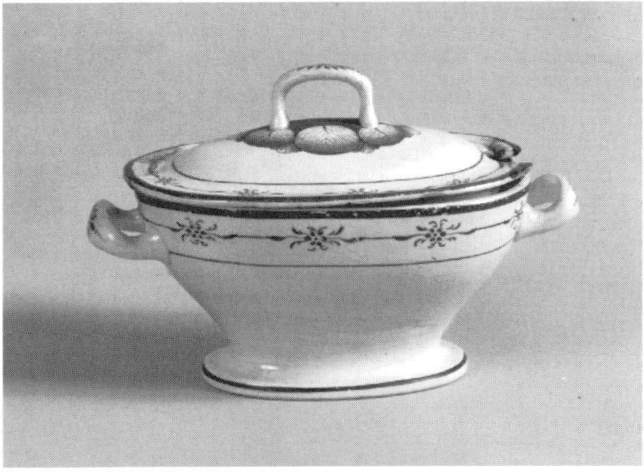

Figure 10 Gravy Tureen. From Abigail Winship Robbins's "Best China." English, Wedgwood, circa 1790–1800. Ipswich Historical Society.

voraciously collected books, photographs and postcards, clothing and textiles, household furnishings of all kinds, tools, and a wide variety of antiquarian treasures. He also began to collect old houses.

The first house acquired by SPNEA was the Swett-Ilsley House in Newbury, which was to be financed through operation as a tearoom. SPNEA's second house, the Fowler House in Danvers, was acquired in 1912 with the intention of furnishing it and exhibiting it as a museum. Before the year was out, Miss Stone wrote to Appleton, asking to visit "the old house recently opened by the N. E. Society for the Preservation of N. E. Antiquities [*sic*]," saying, "I should like to visit the place with the idea of seeing what its needs might be and if I could in any way contribute items."[18] Appleton must have responded promptly, for only five days later Miss Stone wrote again enclosing a check intended "to show my interest in the general objects of the Soc'y by becoming an associate member. As I myself live in an old N. E. Homestead and am the last of a long line, I should be very glad to talk with some one who has the needs of the Soc'y. at heart, not with a view to disposing of my house or land but rather the preservation of many objects which might seem to suit a Museum."[19] Miss Stone called on Sumner Appleton at the Society's headquarters, then located in one-half of a room at 20 Beacon Street in Boston, at three o'clock on Friday, 3 January 1913. Apparently they had a cordial conversation and she must have impressed him with what she had to offer. It is unclear whether or not Appleton visited her in Lexington before she left for a winter visit to the South, but he wrote to her in June, noting that she had asked him to remind her that perhaps she "would turn over to the Society a part of [her] collections." Knowing that she might prefer to have things exhibited, Appleton continued, "I believe I warned you that whatever was turned over to us would have to be packed away for the time being, against the time when we might have a house to show them in, but I hope this will not discourage you from giving things to us for you have such a wonderful lot of good things, and I can't help hoping that a good proportion of them will find their way here." Undaunted, Appleton continued, "P.S. You may remember that I was to suggest to you the advisability of your bequeathing all your antique personal property to three antiquarians, let us say, Mr. Dow, myself and one other, such property to be divided between institutions in the same way that you are now doing. You asked me to remind you of this also, and accordingly, I am now doing so in the hope that you will choose to follow my advice, for I feel it would be a great loss to have such of your personal antiques as you may die in the possession of exchanged through the auction room." Despite Appleton's entreaties, Miss Stone was interested in seeing her things on display as well as considered useful, and she never did write a will making certain that all of her treasures would be placed in the hands of responsible antiquarians like him.

By 1913 Miss Gray was gone and Miss Stone's ties to Ipswich had died with her. The Essex Institute was in a favorable situation in Miss Stone's eyes. The Institute's museum was in the hands of Curator George Francis Dow who had just completed furnishing the Ward House on the Institute grounds and the installation of three period rooms in the exhibition galleries of the main building. He could offer both display space and a fireproof building, whereas Appleton still lamented SPNEA's lack of either.

Fortunately, the Society acquired the Harrison Gray Otis House as its headquarters in 1916 and six years later was able to connect it with two brick rowhouses in which it established "The New England Museum." Appleton wasted no time in convincing Miss Stone that SPNEA was now a suitable place for her treasures. During the years from 1917 to 1933 SPNEA accessioned more than 1,500 things as gifts from Ellen Stone. A few items were returned as "worthless" or "too motheaten," but over the years Miss Stone gave SPNEA things that reflected the interests of both the donor and the recipients, SPNEA's founder William Sumner Appleton and its Curator, George Francis Dow who left the Essex Institute in 1919 to join the tiny staff at SPNEA.

Among the first gifts to SPNEA from Ellen Stone during the years from 1917 to 1919 were "a wonderfully extensive and representative collection, one of the very best the Society has ever received." The gifts included "articles of costume; fabrics; hats and bonnets; books, announcements, railroad tickets; horn combs; carpet bags; thirteen glass lamps; ten candlesticks; pasteboard boxes; baskets; wall paper; printed cotton table cover; ink wells; rocking foot stool; farming implements; kitchen utensils; door latches and hardware; nine Windsor chairs; glass bottles; knives and forks; carpenter's tools; oil painting; wallets; fifty-five pieces of pottery ware; twenty-six pieces of glass ware; etc., etc."[20]

At SPNEA, as in Salem, the largest quantity of things given by Ellen Stone over the years was in the category of textiles and clothing, with more than 250 identified textile fragments and 178 pieces of clothing and millinery. The collection also includes 35 architectural fragments and pieces of hardware, 64 pieces of ceramics, and 27 pieces of glass, ranging from mason jars to handblown syllabub glasses and an engraved tumbler made in Germany between 1790 and 1810 (*Figure 11*). There are 35 assorted lighting devices, 65 baskets, 34 boxes, 42 tools for domestic textile manufacture, some tinware, a few measuring devices, and a number of handsome baskets for which the original household purpose was identified, but there was almost no furniture—only the nine Windsor chairs. In addition, there are many items that document housekeeping procedures and family management such as a container of redding "for polishing brick hearth after it has been washed," matted cobwebs for stopping bleeding, netting used for a sieve, rotten stone used with oil and lots of elbow grease for cleaning brasses, mosquito netting, cork and paper "tapers" used as float lamps or night

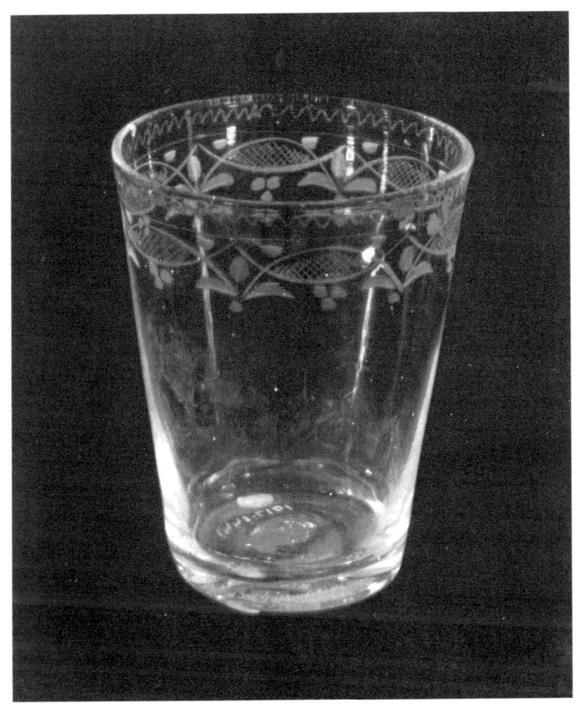

Figure 11 Tumbler. German, circa 1790–1810. Courtesy of the Society for the Preservation of New England Antiquities.

lights, wrapping paper, sticks of twist, toothbrushes, and a bar of soap in its original wrapper (*Figure 12*).

Looking into the SPNEA accession records for Miss Stone's gifts, one finds a host of interesting and useful objects ranging from fourteen skeins of linen thread that Miss Stone asserted to have been kettle dyed at home and extending to the small clothes [knee breeches] of her great-grandfather Stephen Robbins, a successful furrier who had "died in 1849, wearing these small clothes at the time of his death, long after everyone else had changed with the fashions."[21] With the small clothes came half a dozen pairs of cotton, linen, wool, and silk stockings, worn by Stephen Robbins with his small clothes—homemade linen ones "for very hot summer weather," a "blue and white week day working stocking" of cotton, "machine woven," "winter worsted . . . for dress he wore white silk," "machine made . . . summer or medium weight. In winter he wore fleece-lined stockings" and his linen "summer stocking for hottest weather . . . 1800–1825." The differentiation between the stocking types is the kind of minutiae that has

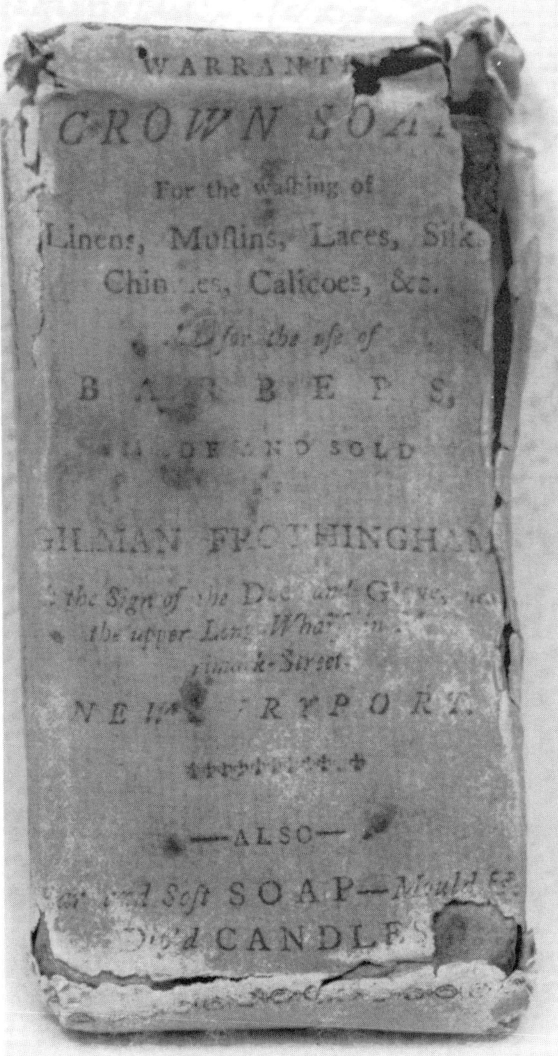

Figure 12 Soap in original wrapper. Newburyport, Massachusetts, circa 1790–1800. Courtesy of the Society for the Preservation of New England Antiquities.

seldom been recorded and is now especially valued. Ellen Stone selected and documented the items she gave to New England museums where meticulous accession records preserved the information.

Among Miss Stone's gifts are some things that hint at the appearance of the interiors of the Robbins House during her great-grandparents' lifetime. The kitchen wallpaper (*Figure 13*) with its black and white block-printed leaves on a cinnamon-colored ground was made in Boston by Moses Grant Jr. between 1811 and 1817. The warm brown background would have

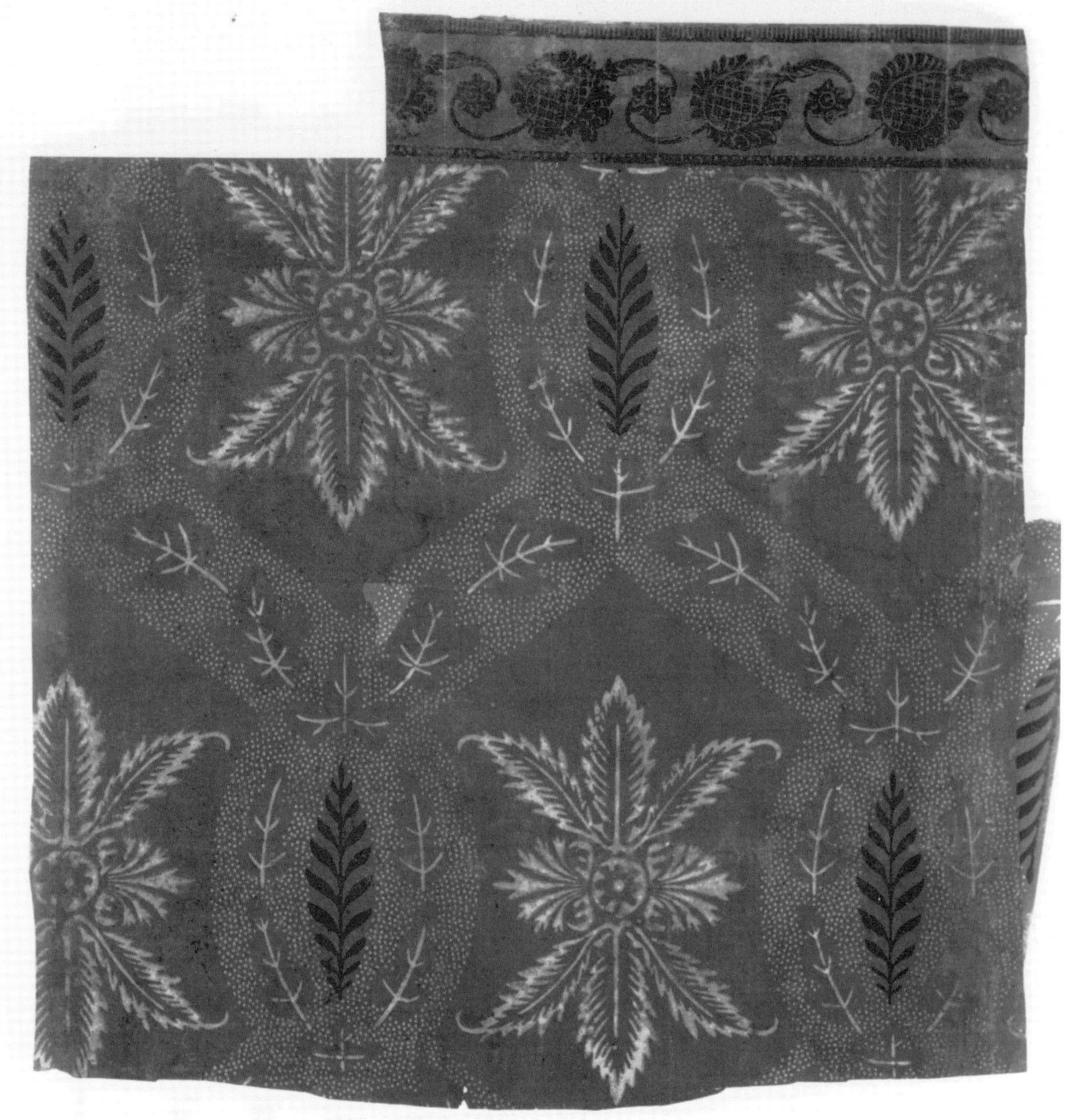

Figure 13 Wallpaper used in the kitchen of the Robbins House, Boston, Massachusetts. Made by Moses Grant Jr. and Co., circa 1811–1817. Courtesy of the Society for the Preservation of New England Antiquities.

given a pleasant glow to the kitchen at the same time that it disguised smoke stains and fly specks. At the window in this room hung a modest bleached linen sash curtain, heavily patched, and just large enough to cover the lower half of the window. Other examples of stylish wallpapers used in the Robbins House during the early nineteenth century include a pillar and arch design suitable for a hallway, simple block designs, and handsome borders. These are illustrated in *Wallpaper in New England*.[22]

In contrast to these wallpapers, the simple window curtains said to have been used in the Robbins household in the late eighteenth or very early nineteenth century are much less sophisticated in design. The curtains include straight hanging copperplate printed cotton panels that were used at the upper entry window. These and several other types were made of single widths of material and hung from tiny linen tape loops. Since the loops are too small for either an iron or wooden curtain rod to be used for support, the curtains probably hung from a drawstring or wire that was attached to nails or hooks at each side of the window. According to Miss Stone, one curtain (*Figure 14*) "was woven at home, the size of the window it was meant for. The way was to set this aside until the stenciler came to the neighborhood. Designs and colors were selected and the stenciling done." One can readily see that this curtain was spun, woven, and hemmed before it was printed, for the design does not extend onto the back of the hems. However, it is hard to believe that this curtain was stenciled or that there was much choice of color available. In all probability the curtain was block printed by an itinerant or local linen stamper, who used the common, but imported, dyestuffs, indigo and madder, for the colors.

A remarkable linen curtain from the Robbins House (*Figure 15*) has striped designs created with red, gold, and blue warp threads alternating with undyed bleached linen. The design was enlivened by clouded blue effects that were created either by being painted on the warp after it was set on the loom but before weaving or by dipping bundles of the warp thread part way into the dye pot before the warping was completed. This latter technique is known today as "ikat"; if that is how this textile was created, no other early New England examples are now known.

Not all of the Robbins family material that is presently in museum collections came directly from Miss Ellen Stone. She gave some things to her cousins Ida and Caira during the first decade after her mother's death in 1890. In turn, they gave additional material to SPNEA in 1931 when they emptied their house, now the Arlington Town Offices, at 672 Massachusetts Avenue in Arlington, and moved permanently to Lausanne, Switzerland.

Among the items given to SPNEA by Ida and Caira in 1931 was a four-post bed that they correctly thought dated about 1820 to 1825. Sumner Appleton wrote to the sisters that "the Trustees . . . were delighted with it. We now have five four-posters and yours is by far the finest. In fact it is one of the most sumptuous in its hangings that I have ever seen."[23] Appleton inquired specifically about whether or not the bed itself had originally been used by Stephen Robbins in the house where Ellen Stone was then living in Lexington. The sisters replied that yes it had been; he was their great-uncle. Indeed, it is the same one upon which the early-eighteenth-century red valance had been hung in the 1890s (see *Figure 4*, p. 205). Upon receipt of Appleton's letter, Ida and Caira apparently had second thoughts about the gift record and way the bed had come to them, for they asked to add Miss Stone's name to theirs in the SPNEA accession record as a donor of the bed, since she had originally given it to them.

This bed came to SPNEA with a full set of "red tapestry" hangings that Caira wrote to explain were "modern and were made by A. H. Davenport thirty years ago. The valance is a copy of the original one which was of moreen of a rather dark blueish-green and trimmed with a green and white braid in addition to having the border of guimp." She suggested that "Miss Stone may still have a piece of the original valance that she lent us to have copied. This would be worth inquiring about for the pattern was unusually attractive and ought not to be lost."[24]

This set both Appleton and Dow off on a tear to try to find Ellen Stone to get her to document the story and to locate the original bed hanging. They had not heard from her in over a year. Apparently they had both forgotten that she had given the original valance to the Essex Institute in 1908 when Dow was working there and she had given the blue-green one (*Figure 16*) that had served as a model for the Davenport reproduction bed hangings to SPNEA in 1917. It was already safe in SPNEA's own collections. Unfortunately they never obtained any more information from Miss Stone about either valance or the whereabouts of the related hangings.

Without question the earliest and most stylish articles of household furnishing that Miss Stone gave to any museum are these bed valances, referred to by her as being of moreen, a type of eighteenth-century embossed woolen textile often confused with harateen. The valances predate the bed on which Miss

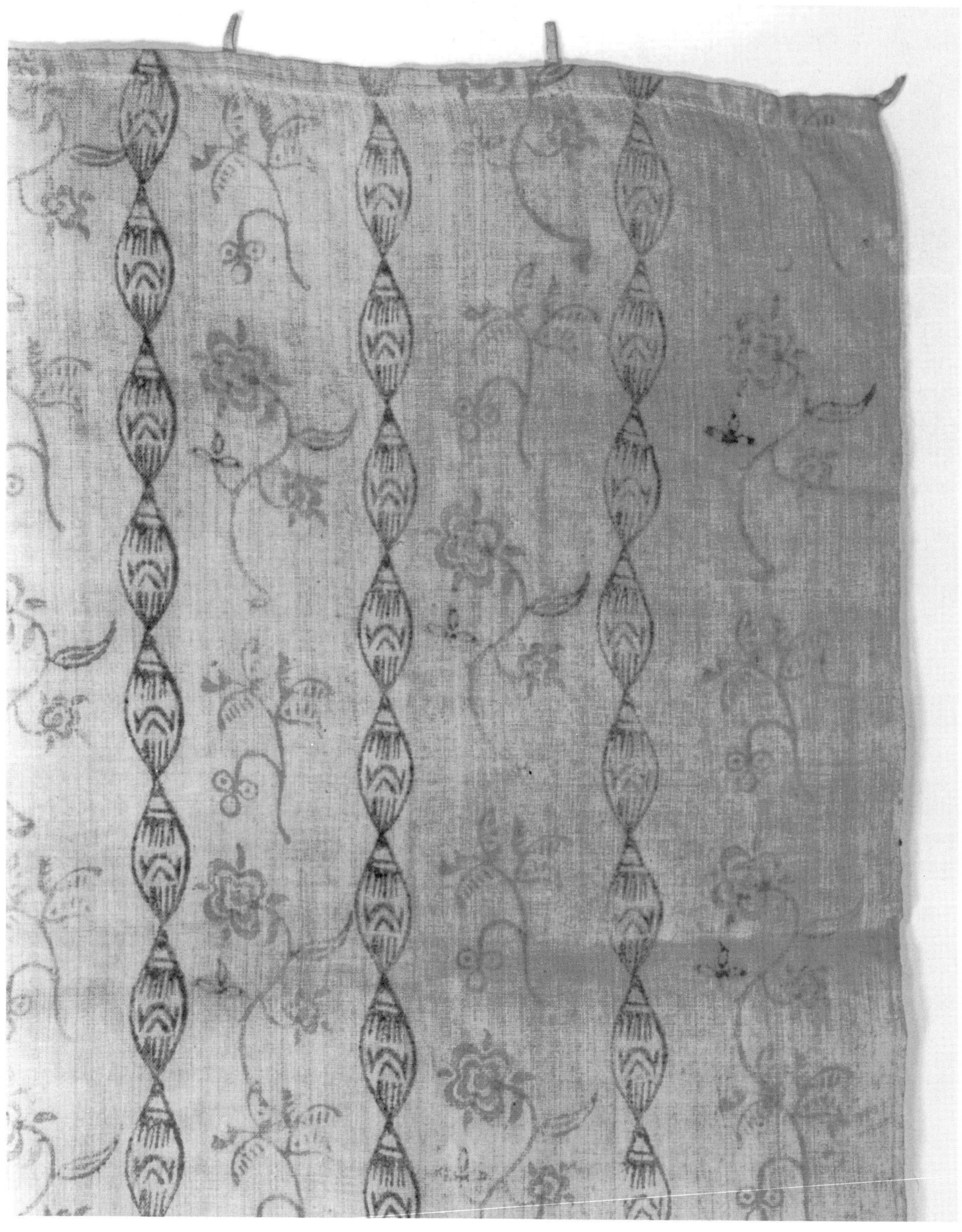

Figure 14 Window curtain. Probably Lexington, Massachusetts, circa 1790–1820. Courtesy of the Society for the Preservation of New England Antiquities.

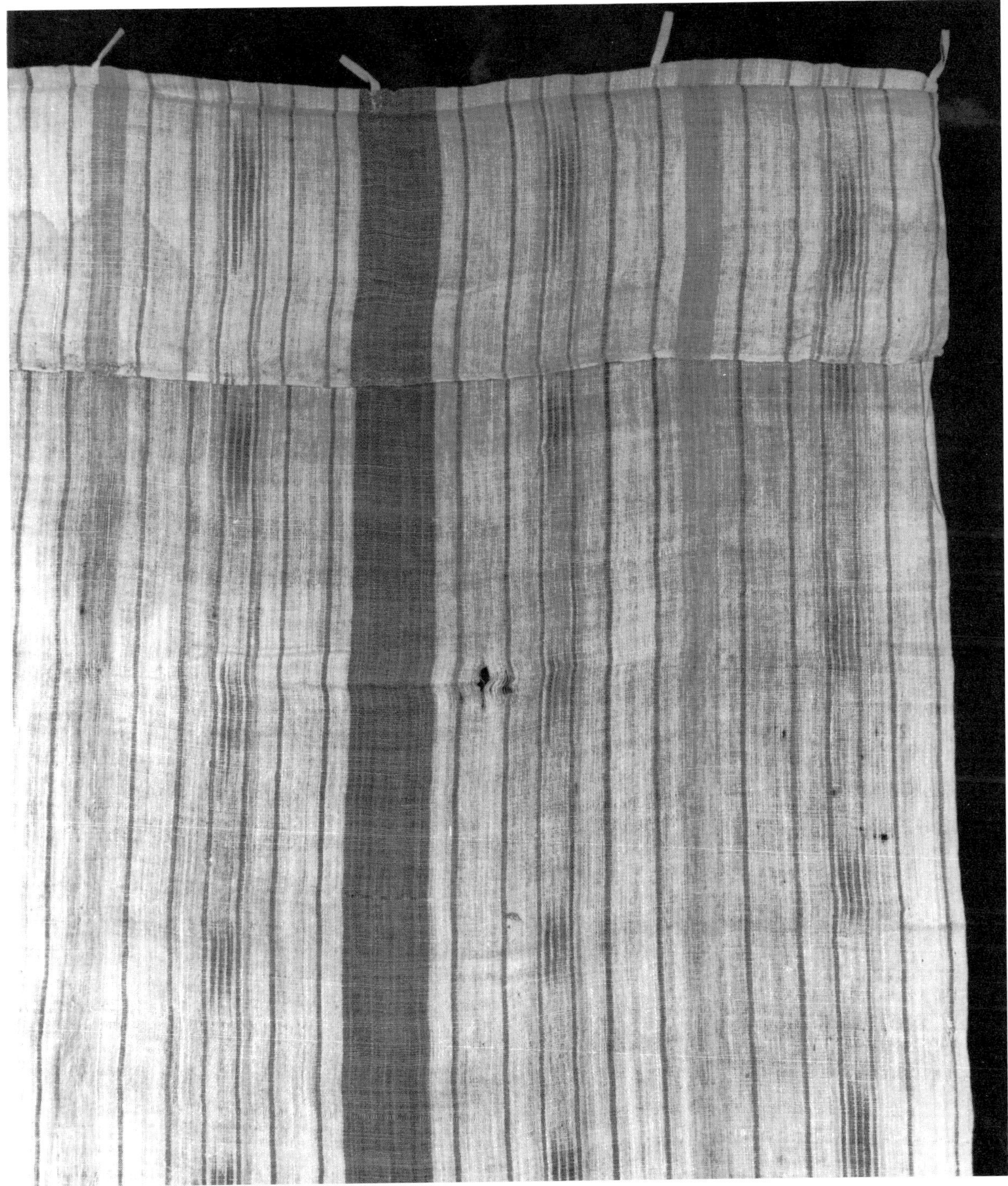

Figure 15 Window curtain. Probably Lexington, Massachusetts, circa 1770–1810. Courtesy of the Society for the Preservation of New England Antiquities.

Figure 16 Bed valance. Probably Boston, Massachusetts, circa 1740–1755. Courtesy of the Society for the Preservation of New England Antiquities.

Stone had used them, and they certainly predate Stephen Robbins Jr. himself. The older one must have been fifty or sixty[25] years old and the blue one must have been more than forty years old when Robbins bought his homestead in Lexington on 1 May 1786.[26] The valances are the earliest with any bit of New England history that are now known, and yet we do not yet know anything about the house in which they were first used, their first owner, the kind of beds on which they were displayed, or the identity of their makers. We can speculate that they could have been made by a fashionable upholsterer in London and sent to Boston in response to an order for something in the latest taste. Alternatively, they could have been made in Boston by a professional upholsterer copying something lately imported or copying a printed illustration of a similar design. They could also have been made by a skilled needlewoman in Boston or Lexington for herself or for a paying customer. The complex shaping and patterns of applied scrollwork suggest a familiarity with sophisticated London taste, but the pieces are made of readily available, although very expensive, British materials. Both valances were made and decorated by a skilled hand, but knowing none other quite like them, and without a story from Ellen Stone, we know no more.

Most tantalizing is the record that Miss Stone gave the Ipswich Historical Society for something identified as "Bed Hangings. Blue Moreen, trimmed with blue and white gimp. (These are very worn and hardly worth keeping.)"[27] Most of Miss Robbins's gifts are still in the possession of the Ipswich Historical Society, but these bed hangings are nowhere to be found and no photographs of them have yet been located. The description suggests that they may have been a set of bed curtains that matched the valance now in SPNEA's collection and that the scrolling decoration seen on the valance may have also been used on the matching curtains. Without pictures of the Ipswich installation, we will probably never know.

Undoubtedly, the Stephen Robbins House contained many things that Ellen Stone did not pass along to museums or historical societies. She gave very little furniture and almost nothing that was made after mid-century. The things she valued were largely from the women's sphere. She gave clothing from earlier generations, but none of her own and little of her mother's. She gave textiles, china, and glass, the tools and equipment of housekeeping. They were old things that had been used in her time, about which stories had been told time and again. They were not new things, products of Victorian fashion and industry.

Looking at the collections today, one finds many dimensions that may not have occurred to Ellen Stone. For the most part, the value of these things is in their association with the reliable information that she provided with each piece. Stephen Robbins's 1758 infant shirt and cap are now standards against which other unidentified baby clothes can be dated. The pile

Figure 17 Textile fragment. England, circa 1815–1830. Courtesy of the Society for the Preservation of New England Antiquities.

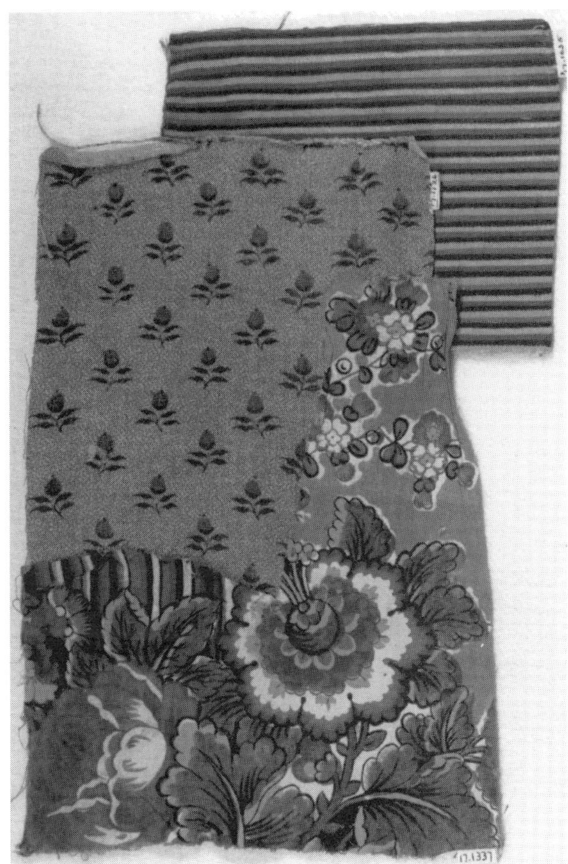

Figure 18 Textile fragments. England, late eighteenth century. Courtesy of the Society for the Preservation of New England Antiquities.

of old stockings helps us understand seasonal differences. The wrapping paper and the bar of soap illustrate original packaging and the ways of shopkeepers.

We are now able to visualize many simple tools and accessories of housekeeping and daily life—the tiny waxed paperboard circles holding short lengths of candlewick which were floated on a thin layer of oil in a cup or bowl of water to provide a safe night light in a sickroom or to soothe a frightened child, the nature of the "redding" that was used to restore the color of bricks on a heavily used hearth or fireplace surround, the shape and size of a goose feather basket, a clothes basket, or a gathering basket as opposed to just any old basket.

Thanks to Ellen Stone we can illustrate the many kinds of printed cottons that were called "patch" in the New England vernacular and we are certain that this word was used for many different designs, only a few of which simulated handsewn patchwork. In the Robbins family, a slipcover for a sofa was made of this "typical piece of patch, which simulates a piece of patch" (*Figure 17*). Within the piles of fabric swatches that she gave to be preserved are samples of woolen goods used for men's winter vests (*Figure 18, upper right*), women's petticoats and winter gowns, children's summer dresses, a pillar print of chintz that was used for window curtains (*Figure 18, bottom*), a stormont used for gowns (*Figure 18, center*), and three different kinds of mattress ticking (*Figure 19*). She gave things that are now rare, but were typical in their time, like Abigail Winship Robbins's short gown, stays, and red riding hood.[28] Among her gifts are things that reveal the taste of

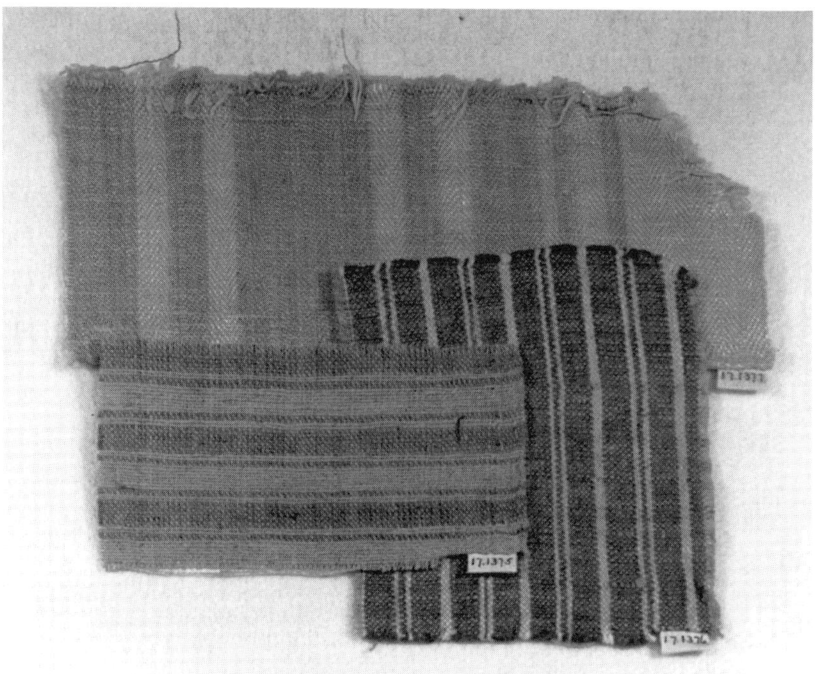

Figure 19 Fragments of ticking. England or Massachusetts, circa 1760–1830. Courtesy of the Society for the Preservation of New England Antiquities.

her ancestors, their "best china" and parlor furniture, their wallpaper and window curtains, and their clothing. The same items reveal changing patterns of household consumption and newly available goods as the influence of the consumer society and the industrial revolution came to Lexington.

We also have some sense of the Robbins family. Because their profiles by Rufus Porter are at the Lexington Historical Society, we know what Stephen and Abigail Robbins, their son Eli, and their daughter Caira (*Figure 20*) looked like;[29] because we have some of their clothing, we know how large or small they were; because we have Caira's watercolor, we know what their house looked like; because we have the sitting room chairs, the "best china," samples of the wallpaper, and some of the window curtains, we can imagine the interior of that house in which six of Stephen and Abigail's children grew up and where two died. Because Ellen Stone published selections from Caira's diary and letters, we know that her sister Abigail, who was nicknamed Nabby, attended Mrs. Rowson's school in 1805, and it may well have been there that she completed her watercolor memorial (*Figure 21*) to her brother Martin who had died in 1792 at the age of four. Thirteen years after his death, when Nabby needed to select a subject for a fashionable mourning piece, she chose a composition with a mourning female figure standing over a footed sarcophagus on a small hill above the river of life. The iconography of the piece is part of a fashionable formula of the period, but Nabby, like many New England schoolgirls, chose to inscribe the piece in memory of a family member rather than to Shakespeare, George Washington, or some distant relative. Instead she chose to memorialize her younger brother even though it was long after any formal period of mourning for him would have been observed. The family association was the most important.

For Ellen Stone these things had been a source of continuing interest and concern. Thanks to her careful stewardship of family treasures and her meticulous documentation, we can learn much about a single family and through them about the material culture of many New England families.

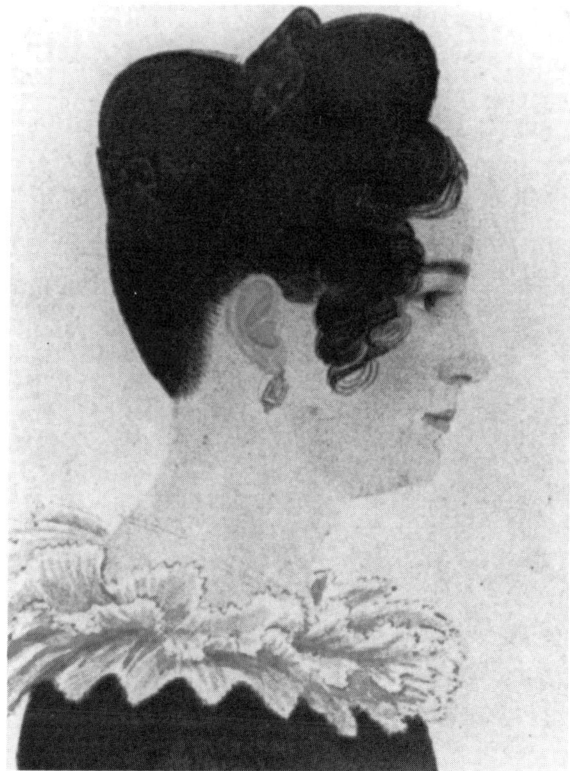

Figure 20 Caira Robbins (1791–1881). Attributed to Rufus Porter (1792–1884). Lexington, Massachusetts, circa 1815–1820. Watercolor. From the collections of the Lexington Historical Society.

NOTES

[1]The author would like to acknowledge the extraordinary help of the following colleagues in the preparation of this paper: At the Society for the Preservation of New England Antiquities, Melinda Linderer, Registrar; Lorna Condon, Curator of Library and Archives; Rebecca Aaronson, Library and Archives Assistant; and Jamie Lee, Photographer. In Lexington, S. Lawrence Whipple, and at the Lexington Historical Society, George Comtois and numerous volunteers; at the Museum of Fine Arts, Boston, Anne Coleman and the late Larry Salmon; at the Ipswich Historical Society, Elizabeth Redmond, Jim Kyprianos, and Robert Stone; at the Peabody Essex Museum, Paula Richter; and at the State Historical Society of Wisconsin, Christiana Gomez Frye. The author is also grateful to Abbott Lowell Cummings and the late Robert Harrington Nylander who first awakened her interest in Ellen Stone and taught her to trust the information she conveyed with her gifts to museums. The author is always grateful to Richard Nylander for his intimate knowledge of the SPNEA collections and related files, for his thoughtful reading and good suggestions through many drafts, and for his unwavering support and love which both enrich our family and our understanding of the families of so many who have gone before us.

[2]Last Will and Testament of Ellen A. Stone of Lexington, Middlesex County, 1888, docket no. 28949, East Cambridge, Mass.

[3]Inscription on reverse of photograph of a drawing of the Robbins House, SPNEA Library and Archives, Boston, Mass.

[4]Alice Morse Earle, *Two Centuries of Costume in America*, 2 vols. (New York: Macmillan, 1903), 2:798.

[5]"Diary and Letters of Caira Robbins, 1794–1881," *Proceedings of the Lexington Historical Society* 4 (1905–1910): 76.

[6]Last Will and Testament of Ellen A. R. Stone, 1888, and related probate documents, 1888–1944.

[7]Earle, *Two Centuries of Costume in America*, 2:798.

[8]Alice A. Gray to Miss Ellen A. R. Stone, n.d., Lexington Historical Society Collection, Lexington, Mass.

[9]Ibid.

[10]"Proceedings at the Annual Meeting, December 4, 1899," *Publications of the Ipswich Historical Society* 8 (Salem, Mass., 1900): 19.

[11]Alice A. Gray to Miss Stone, 6 June 1901, Lexington Historical Society Collection, Lexington, Mass.

[12]"Proceedings at the Annual Meeting, December 4, 1899," p. 21.

[13]Alice A. Gray to My dear Miss Stone, 31 August 1899, Lexington Historical Society Collection, Lexington, Mass.

[14]"Proceedings at the Annual Meeting, December 2, 1901," *Publications of the Ipswich Historical Society* 11 (Salem, Mass., 1902): 39.

[15]Alice A. Gray to Ellen A. R. Stone, Sauquoit, N.Y., 28 September 1901, Lexington Historical Society Collection, Lexington, Mass.

[16]Register of Donations to the Ipswich Historical Society, 1899–1961, Ipswich, Mass.

[17]"President's Report, Dec. 7, 1903," *Publications of the Ipswich Historical Society* 12 (Salem, Mass., 1904): 40.

[18]Ellen A. R. Stone to William Sumner Appleton, 18 December 1912, SPNEA Library and Archives.

[19]Ellen A. R. Stone to William Sumner Appleton, 23 December 1912, SPNEA Library and Archives.

[20]*Old-Time New England* 10, no. 1, ser. 20 (1919): 35.

[21]SPNEA, Accession Record 1917.815.

[22]Richard C. Nylander, Elizabeth Redmond, and Penny J. Sander, *Wallpaper in New England* (Boston: SPNEA, 1986).

[23]William Sumner Appleton to Misses Ida F. and Caira Robbins, 16 November 1931. Carbon copy in SPNEA Library and Archives.

[24]Caira Robbins to Mr. Appleton, 22 October 1932, SPNEA Library and Archives.

[25]Reinier Baarsen, Gervase Jackson-Stops, Phillip M. Johnston, and Elaine Evans Dee, *Courts and Colonies: The William and Mary Style in Holland, England, and America* (New York: Cooper-Hewitt Museum, 1988), pp. 188–89. Both valances are discussed in Abbott Lowell Cummings, comp. *Bed Hangings* (Boston: SPNEA, 1961), figs. 9 and 14. See also Linda Wesselman Jackson, "Beyond the Fringe: Ornamental

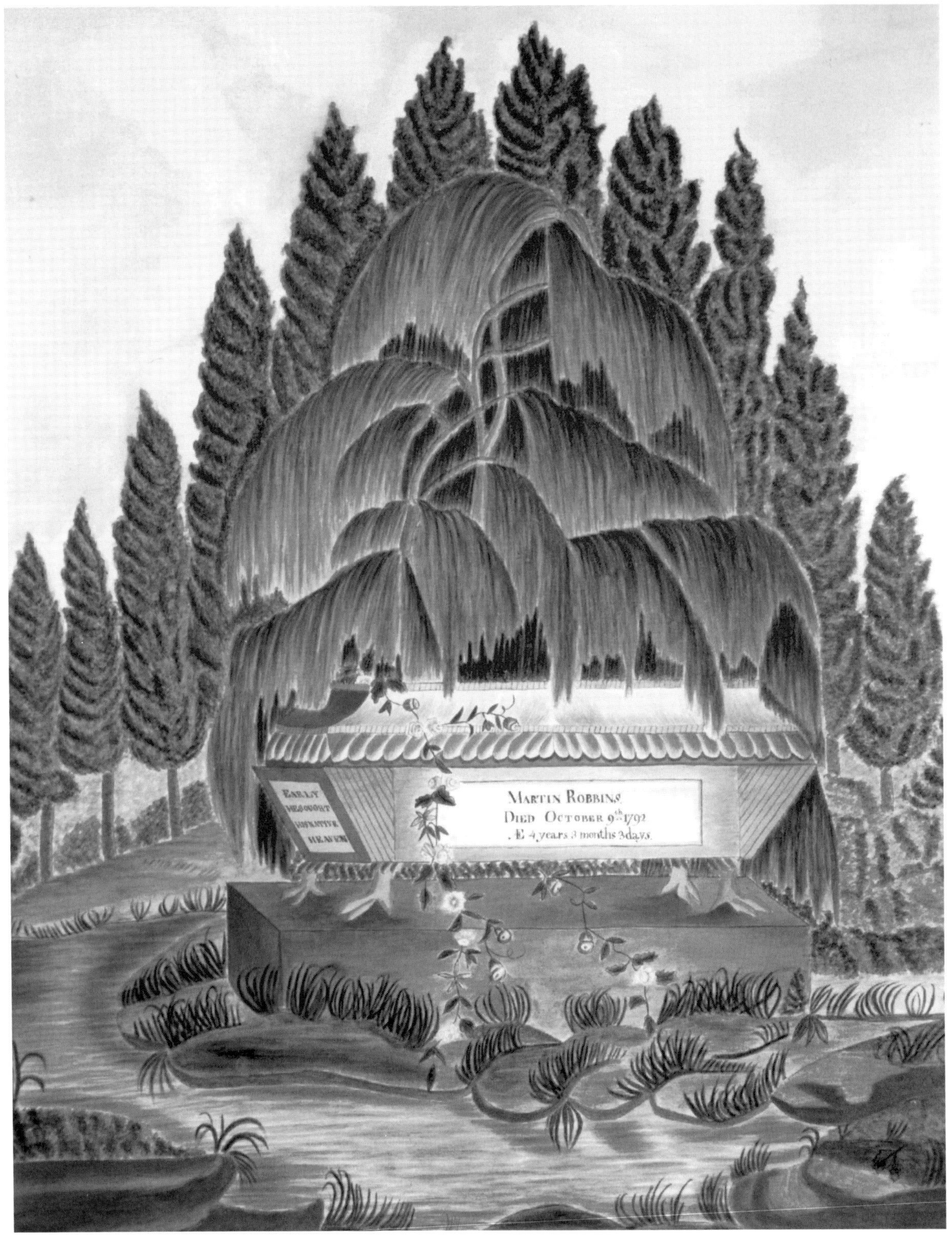

Figure 21 Memorial to Martin Robbins (1788–1792). Abigail Robbins. Probably worked at Mrs. Rowson's Academy, Boston, Massachusetts, circa 1805. Watercolor. Courtesy of the Society for the Preservation of New England Antiquities.

Upholstery Trimmings in the Seventeenth, Eighteenth, and Early Nineteenth Centuries," in *Upholstery in America and Europe from the Seventeenth Century to World War I*, ed. Edward S. Cooke Jr. (New York: Norton, 1987), plate 7, p. 138.

[26]Middlesex Deeds, Lib. 97, folio 430, Middlesex County Courthouse, Cambridge, Mass.

[27]Register of Donations to the Ipswich Historical Society, 1899–1961.

[28]For more on red riding hoods see the author's "Hooded Cloak" no. 257 in *The Great River: Art and Society of the Connecticut Valley, 1635–1820*, ed. William N. Hosley and Gerald W. R. Ward (Hartford, Conn.: Wadsworth Atheneum, 1985), pp. 387–88.

[29]Dean T. Lahikainen, *Lexington Portraits, 1734–1884* (Lexington, Mass.: Lexington Historical Society, 1977), Caira, p. 40; Eli, pp. 42–43; Hannah (Mrs. Eli), pp. 44 and 52–53.

Commemorating Colonial New England's First Families: The Triumph of the Pilgrims

Jeremy Dupertuis Bangs

Introduction: Founders of Empire

IN THIS CHAPTER some of the imagery which is used to objectify sentiment commemorating the Pilgrims will be examined so that associative meaning connected with similar imagery of other specific topics can be identified.[1] In art historical terms, we shall examine not only the iconography but also the iconology of Pilgrim commemorations, seeking to identify the significance that a depiction gains through repetition of the forms familiar from depictions of other events.

Nineteenth-century writers described the Pilgrims as the embodiment of virtue, the promulgators of social improvement, and the penultimate stage in the history of progress leading up to themselves.[2]

> America is the continent best fitted to receive new ideas. Nevertheless, it would be a great mistake to think that the republic appeared at once in that chosen land of liberty and democracy. Below Franklin, below Washington, were great social movements, as below our soil there are other strata more primitive and more solid, indispensable to the firm constitution of the planet. It was necessary for the republican movement of America that the human conscience should vindicate its liberty by means of the Reformation in Europe. It was necessary that in addition to that vindication of conscience there should come a morality more austere than Luther's, the morality of Calvin; and a church more democratic than the German, the church of Geneva. It may be said, therefore, that from the middle of the sixteenth century to the end of the eighteenth century the republican initiation of America is not delayed for a moment; and it commenced before the Pilgrims landed on the shore of the new continent, in the struggles and the sorrows of the Old World. In England the Reformation is divided into two religious movements, the one aristocratic, the other democratic. To the second belonged Hooper, who seemed only to live in his preaching, and who died smiling on his bed of burning coals like a child sleeping upon roses. From these martyrdoms rose the Puritans, an object of terror to kings, because they would have no aristocracies in the church, and without aristocracies in the church there could be none in society or the state. The great Protestant Elizabeth of England called the Christians who sought for truth simply in the word of God more dangerous than the Catholics themselves. The liberty of preaching is the liberty of thought, and this is the Divine Word communicated to all souls. In this universal illumination of dark places vanished the shadow of the ancient secular power. Therefore it is that James I, in closing the conference at Hampton Court, seeing that he could not persuade the Pilgrims with pedantic rhetoric, exclaims, shrugging his shoulders, 'Then we shall hang them.'
>
> And there, at the mouth of the Humber, many families left the soil of their country, the shores they loved, the society of their fellow-citizens, all that sustains and embellishes life, to preserve the purity of their souls, the idea of their God, the austerity of their worship, in the one asylum then offered to free consciences—republican Holland. The cavaliers who pursued them boldly among the fogs, and who succeeded in taking prisoners their wives and their children, when they spurred their horses thus into the sea to detain them, did not know that these poor fugitives bore with them in their frail vessel the immortal spirit of a new world and a new humanity, the gospel of social redemption, the complement and the crown of the religious redemption.
>
> Next they set sail from Leyden, from Amsterdam, accompanied by sacred melodies, by canticles like those intoned in the departure from Egypt. They set out through the immensity of the ocean, defying the hurricanes and the storms, to rear a new temple in the bosom of a new nature, each for all and all for each, brethren in belief as in virtue; and before disembarking in Massachusetts Bay, before setting foot on the shore of Plymouth, they drew up the democratic contract which was to be the first fundamental charter of the republic in America. From the middle of the sixteenth century to the twentieth year of the seventeenth century, and from that date to the end of the eighteenth century, the initiation of Americans into the austere republican discipline has not been delayed at any point. Nevertheless, more than

> a century elapses between each one of these great movements—between the ardent speech of Calvin and the holy pilgrimage of the Puritans, between the arrival of the Puritans in America and the proclamation of the republic; and even when it was proclaimed in the North, many years passed before the idea traversed the continent, before it crossed the isthmus of Panama, scaled and descended both slopes of the Andes, illuminating two hemispheres, creating that collection of democracies, which, in spite of their convulsions, make America the continent of the republic, as Europe, in spite of its revolutions, still continues the continent of monarchy."[3]

Such enthusiasm, expressed by a Spanish republican, Emilio Castelar, more than one hundred twenty-five years ago, confronts us almost embarrassingly with our contemporary rejection of any grandiose and simple belief in historical determinism, or of belief in assumptions of the superiority of what was once New England's dominant religious and ethnic background—confronts us with our doubt in the face of such assurance that society is improving and that progress is inevitable. It was still possible in 1887 to see the culmination of all history in the rise of American democracy: "The whole course of the Protestant reformation, from the thirteenth century [*sic*] to the nineteenth, is coincident with the transfer of the world's political center of gravity from the Tiber and the Rhine to the Thames and the Mississippi. . . . The voyage of the Mayflower was not itself the greatest event in this migration; but it serves to mark the era. . . ."[4]

We are rather amazed to read what virtues and impulses toward social improvement have been attributed to the Pilgrims. For example, in 1874 Eugene Lawrence remarked that

> Purity, gentleness, discretion, were practiced by Bradford, Carver, and their associates; they melted at the voice of sorrow, and forgot none of the duties of charity; and a natural refinement grew up among them that added to the vigor of the race. But possibly the congregation of Scrooby might have failed wholly to maintain their lasting influence had they not discovered, in an age of dense ignorance, the necessity of universal education. It was upon knowledge and religion that they founded their state. Puritanism has become everywhere the herald of popular instruction. The school was planted in Massachusetts as early as the church. To teach and to be taught was the chief aim of its ever-progressive people. At length the common-school system of education was perfected and confirmed by the experience of New England; the grand machinery of national instruction was set in motion that now covers the land from sea to sea. Every state has obeyed the precepts of Robinson and Bradford, and Colorado and California found their prosperity on their public schools."[5]

But of course important inventions and perfections were part of the lives of these people, about whom James Thacher remarked, "While the establishment of a colony and an Independent Church was their primary object, it was ordained, that our fathers should be the founders of an empire."[6]

Objects of Veneration

Such deeds proclaimed to have been of supreme historical importance undoubtedly call for public commemoration, yet it almost defies the imagination when the specific topic of giving form and focus to the public effort is faced. Would it help to know what the Pilgrims looked like? Probably not. Piety and virtue would not necessarily appear in portraits of the Pilgrims, even if we had any besides that of Edward Winslow, the well-fed diplomat whom the conventional painter shows with a smile.[7] If he had a lean and muscular jaw or a little more hair, we would still see nothing of the urgent zeal for democracy and universal education we have just heard about. Unsurprisingly, commemorating the Pilgrims has inspired no new forms. Instead, their story has been conceived in terms already familiar in European religion and politics. We heard a hint of that already in Castelar's passing reference to the Exodus of the Israelites from Egypt.

Significant in this respect are the objects of veneration: Plymouth Rock, the Mayflower Compact, Pilgrim possessions, and Burial Hill, together with the commemorative forms of processions and costumed presentation, and, of course, the Thanksgiving meal. It is not irrelevant to America's self-righteous image as savior of the world, apostle of democracy, that parallels can be drawn referring to the Miracle of the Rock, to Christ's sacrificial death, or to the persecutions of the early church, to relics of the saints, to ceremonial religious processions, and to Communion. R. J. Slater, writing for school children in

1965, was clear about this religious identity: "The word 'rock' is defined by an 1847 edition of Webster's Dictionary as a 'firm or immovable foundation.' It is significant that Plymouth Rock has remained associated in the thought of Americans as symbolizing a foundation which cannot be forgotten, 'and that Rock was Christ.' I Cor. 10:4."[8] The political interpretation was put into words in the poetic opening declamation for the dramatic Pilgrim Tercentenary Celebration in 1921: "To me the Pilgrims come, on me they stand,/ As one by one they land./ Here they will work out their salvation. For this have I been waiting, waiting./ Of me, the rock in the ooze, they have made a cornerstone/ of the Republic."[9]

The Rock in the Ooze

Plymouth Rock (*Figure 1*) itself is insignificant and unimpressive when compared with the symbolic historical weight it is asked to support. As a rock, its company is illustrious, including that struck by Moses in the desert, preserving the chosen people through its life-giving water. In fact, there are so many significant rocks one might almost wonder whether any self-respecting religion can do without one. Peter was the rock on which Christ founded his church; the rock from which Elijah ascended later became a shrine of Islam. Jacob's rock pillow somehow found itself in the throne of England at Westminster Abbey (as well as somewhere in Israel); the mosque at Mecca enshrines the Ka'aba, another rock; the devotees of a major Oriental religion pour oil on sacred rocks representing erect penises.[10] England has Augustus Toplady's Rock of Ages, and at Coventry Cathedral there is a new baptismal font with a label that informs the visitor that it was carved from "an ancient rock from Bethlehem" (not one of those new rocks). The religion of eloquence has its rock enshrined in Ireland, to say nothing of the proto-New Age pet rocks of a few years ago and the still ubiquitous amethyst crystals.

The problem with Plymouth Rock is not that its story is unauthenticated; the problem is that the rock is too small. Even telling ourselves that there are enough fragments for a much larger rock, distributed throughout the country by souvenir takers of earlier times, provides little comfort.[11] As the foundation stone of democracy, that rock has always been too small. Artists, however, have provided a solution.

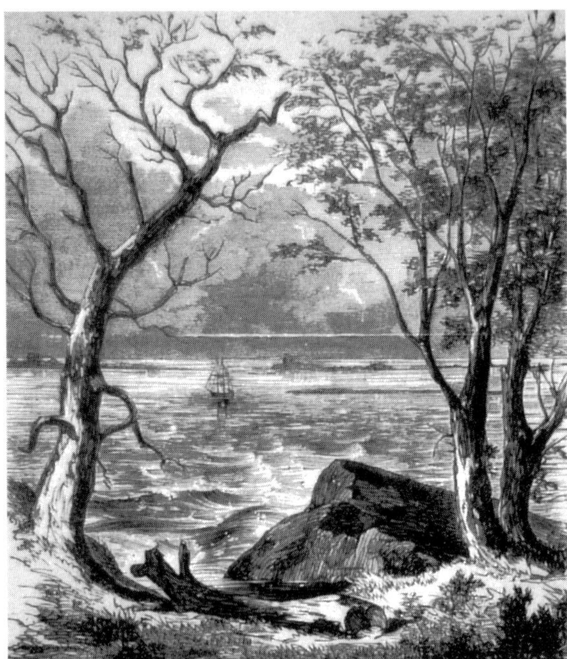

Figure 1 "Plymouth Rock." Nineteenth-century stereotype. Hezekiah Butterworth, *Zig-Zag Journeys, The British Isles* (Boston: Estes and Lauriat, 1889), p. 58. Plimoth Plantation.

The earliest known depiction of it appears on a map by Thomas Jefferys published in London 29 November 1774 (*Figure 2*).[12] The rock is depicted already inscribed with the date 1620 ("MDCXX"). Pilgrim men, women, and children dressed in old-fashioned costumes of about 1660 bring baggage ashore from a late-seventeenth-century sailing vessel as they are met by an Indian whose trading intentions are indicated by a dead beaver. A figure, allegorical perhaps, points inland, while a wealth of fish rounds off the rococo composition

The narrative elements reappear in subsequent depictions of the "Landing," most notably in the large painting (circa 1813–1816) by Henry Sargent (1770–1845) in Pilgrim Hall (*Figure 3*). The rock itself is not emphasized, but we might think either that the Pilgrims are standing on it (as in an anonymous painting circa 1820, also in Pilgrim Hall) or that it is represented by the impressive cliff on the right of the composition. Examination of this imaginary rockface,

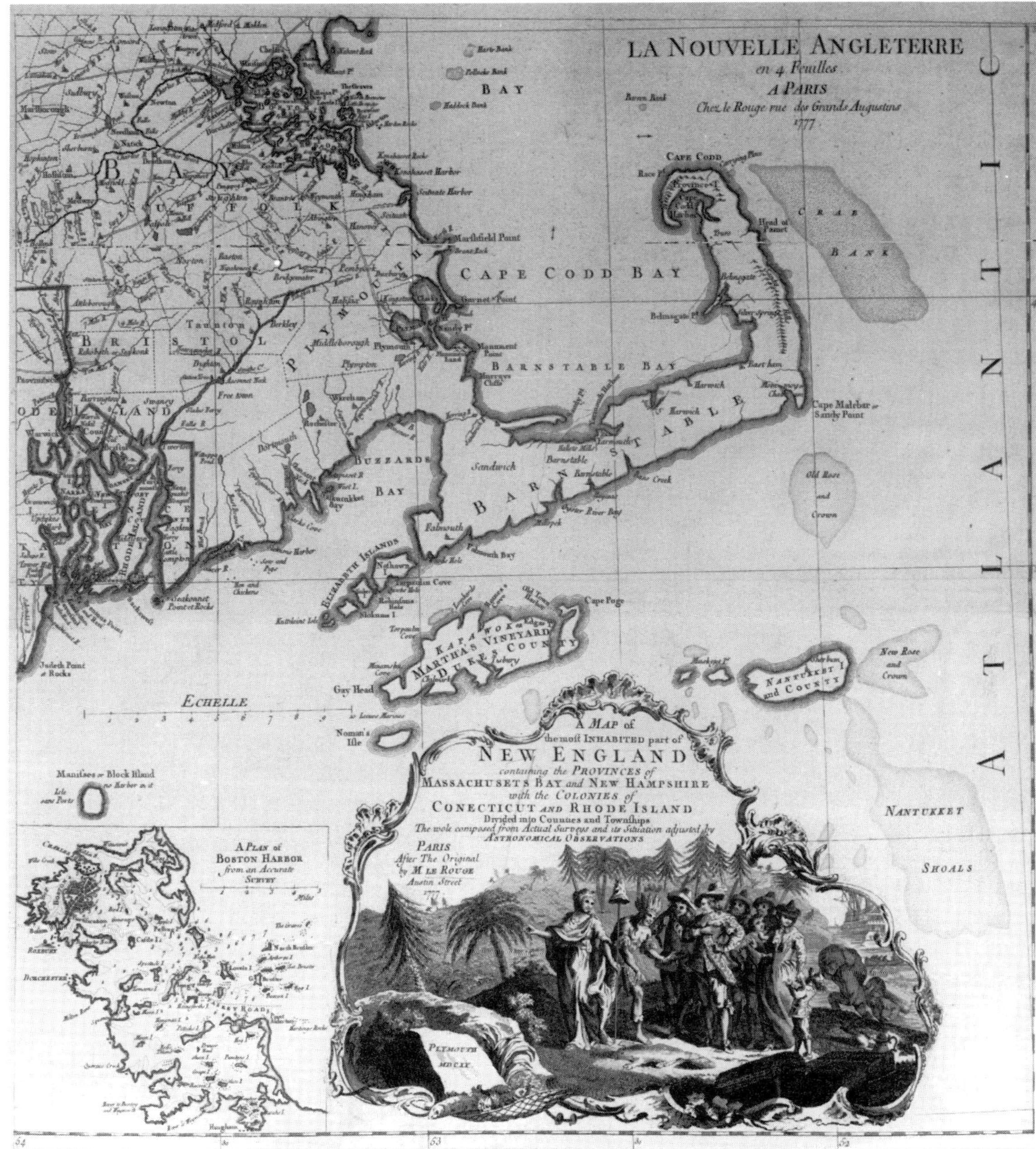

Figure 2 Plymouth Rock. From Thomas Jefferys (1720?–1771), *A Map of the most Inhabited part of New England*, lower right sheet. London, 29 November 1774. 19 × 19 inches. Ectype by George Le Rouge, Paris, 1777. New Hampshire Historical Society. *Photograph by Daniel Farber.*

which is nowhere to be discovered around Plymouth, leads quickly to recognition that explains its rugged familiarity. It reminds us of the Rock of Gibraltar (*Figure 4*), which for many decades was the bastion that protected English (and American) enterprise in the Mediterranean. The mental imagery dissolves and runs together. We have at Gibraltar a mighty fortress, and as such it reminds us of Divine Providentiality, perhaps even insuring the Godly virtue of Prudence (and recalling the trademark of Prudential Insurance

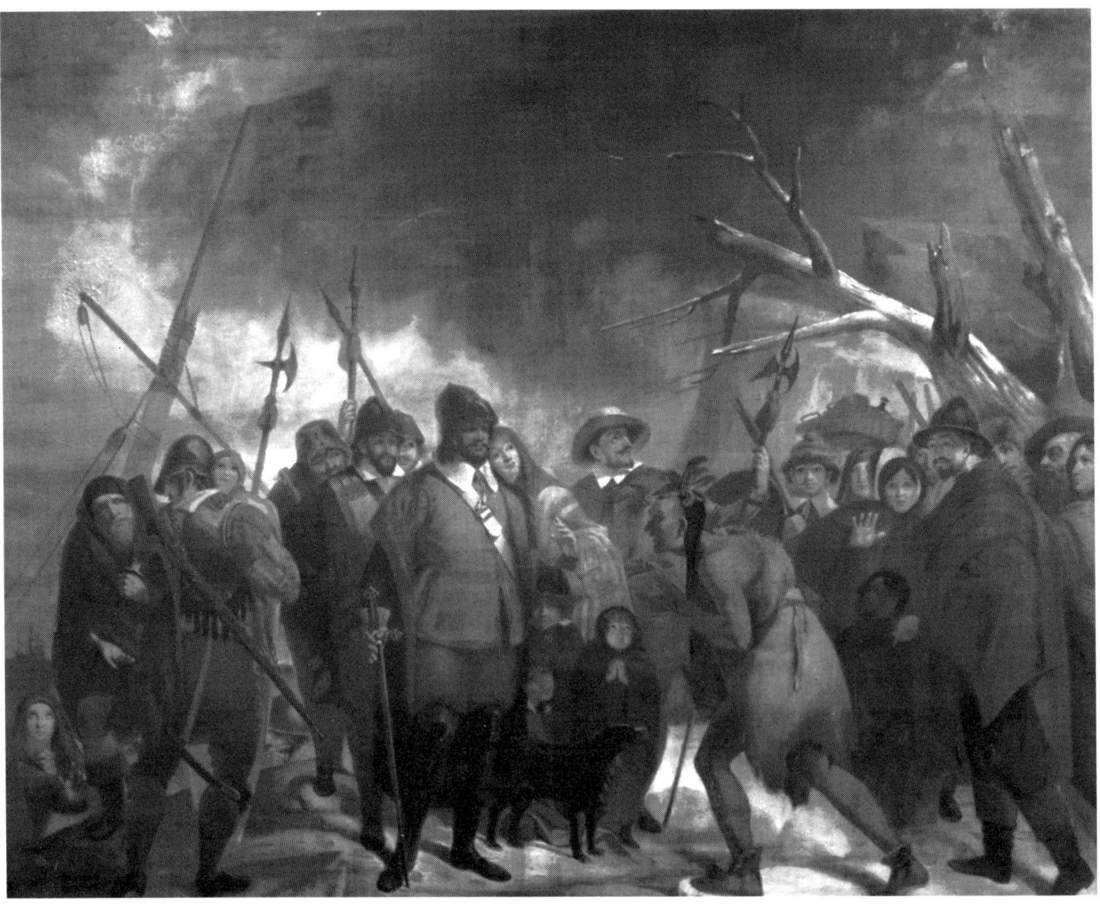

Figure 3 *The Landing of the Fathers.* Henry Sargent (1770–1845). Boston, 1803. Undated copy, circa 1813–1816. Oil on canvas, 13 × 16 feet. Courtesy of Pilgrim Hall Museum, Plymouth, Massachusetts.

located in Providence, Rhode Island, a company no doubt as firm-principled as the Pilgrims). Gibraltar presents several views, some more imposing than others. Plymouth Rock could accommodate them. The unconscious visual reference became literally a cliché, with the same engraving plate copied by the stereotype process and used in one nineteenth-century publication after another. A comparison of the limited number of standardized views of Gibraltar with the few depictions of Plymouth Rock that appeared in the second half of the nineteenth century shows that the stereotypical shape of Gibraltar provided the model for the depicted shape of Plymouth Rock.[13] Imputation of grandeur in this roundabout artistic way will not, however, repay anyone who has traveled from the well-educated states of Colorado or California to mingle with the ever-progressive folk of Massachusetts and see the Rock itself. The usual visitor's response to an encounter with the Rock remains one of disappointed expectations, and the vacationing social scientist can have no more amusing relaxation than to spend a few minutes listening on Plymouth's waterfront to comments about Plymouth Rock, mostly reducible to "Is that all?" We have no solution to the problem that the Rock is too small, but at least we can leave it sitting quietly under its triumphal arch, to which we shall later return.

In this picture there is, however, more that is familiar than the Rock of Gibraltar. An arrangement in a picture, derived from another picture generally agreed to belong within the canon of fine art, can subtly suggest that what is portrayed in the derivative picture is very important. If great deeds should be commemorated with great art, does it follow that

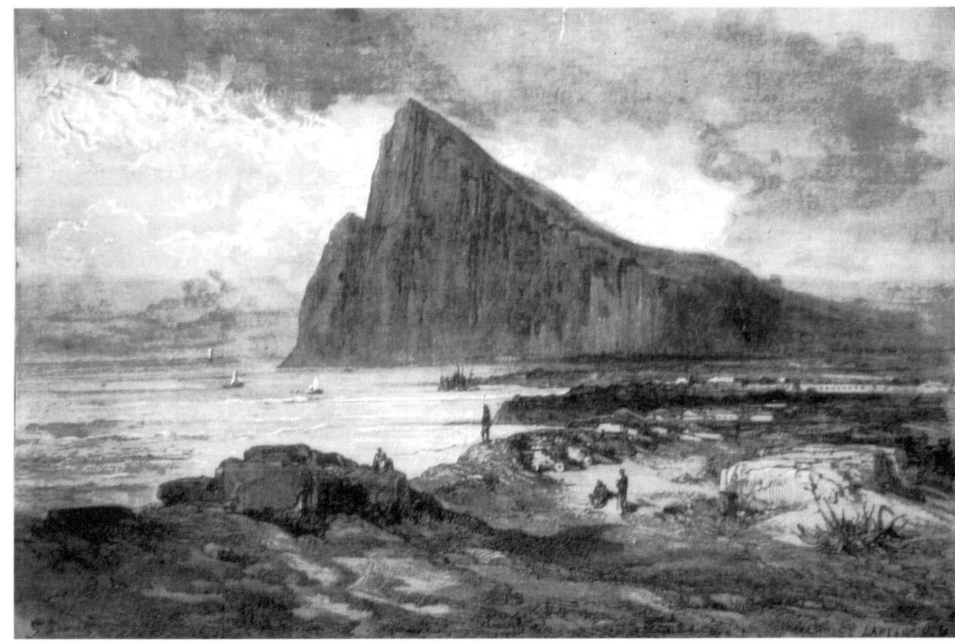

Figure 4 Rock of Gibraltar. Signed "Laplante". From: Hezekiah Butterworth, *Zig-Zag Journeys, The British Isles* (Boston: Estes and Lauriat, 1889), p. 49. Steel engraving. Plimoth Plantation.

great art makes the deeds it commemorates great? What we see here is borrowed—the compositional grouping of the landing Pilgrims is the reversed arrangement of the militia members seen in Rembrandt's *Night Watch* (Rijksmuseum, Amsterdam) (*Figure 5*). Some individual figures in the Landing take the poses of Rembrandt's militia, such as Sargent's man holding a pike, centrally behind the approaching Indian, who is copied from the standard bearer in Rembrandt's group. As a young man Henry Sargent had gone to England, where he studied under Benjamin West from 1793 to 1797, then returned to Boston. West collected paintings and drawings by Rembrandt; and both West and John Singleton Copley, another American painter working in England to whom Sargent had letters of introduction from Jonathan Trumbull, were to some extent influenced by Rembrandt. Although many works by Rembrandt were available in reproductive engravings and mezzotints, it is possible that while he was in England Henry Sargent also went to Amsterdam and became acquainted with the *Night Watch* at first hand.[14]

Thinking of history with the aid of poet or painter is commonplace, but the nineteenth century particularly saw the creation of grand paintings intended to visualize the past of heroes for nations either new or newly self-conscious.[15] In the painting by Robert W. Weir (1803–1889) in the Capitol at Washington (with a large copy at Pilgrim Hall), which shows Pilgrim devotions on board the *Speedwell* preparatory to departure from Delfshaven, the woman in fine clothes at the left is borrowed generally from paintings by Rubens and Van Dyke.[16] The presence of this fine lady elevates the event commemorated to the level of romantic fiction. This must be an identifiable heroine, because she looks like something from an illustration to a novel by Sir Walter Scott.

Great art could be asked to lend a hand in various ways. The same solution to compositional problems found by Rembrandt for his group portrait of *The Syndics of the Amsterdam Drapers' Guild* (Rijksmuseum, Amsterdam)—a decision about how to show everyone's face in a portrait group, all apparently engaged in something together at a table and all on the side away from the viewer—does admirably if we have to imagine the signing of the Mayflower Compact.[17] Pilgrim Hall's painting of this subject, circa 1900, by Percy Moran (1862–1932) achieves a sense

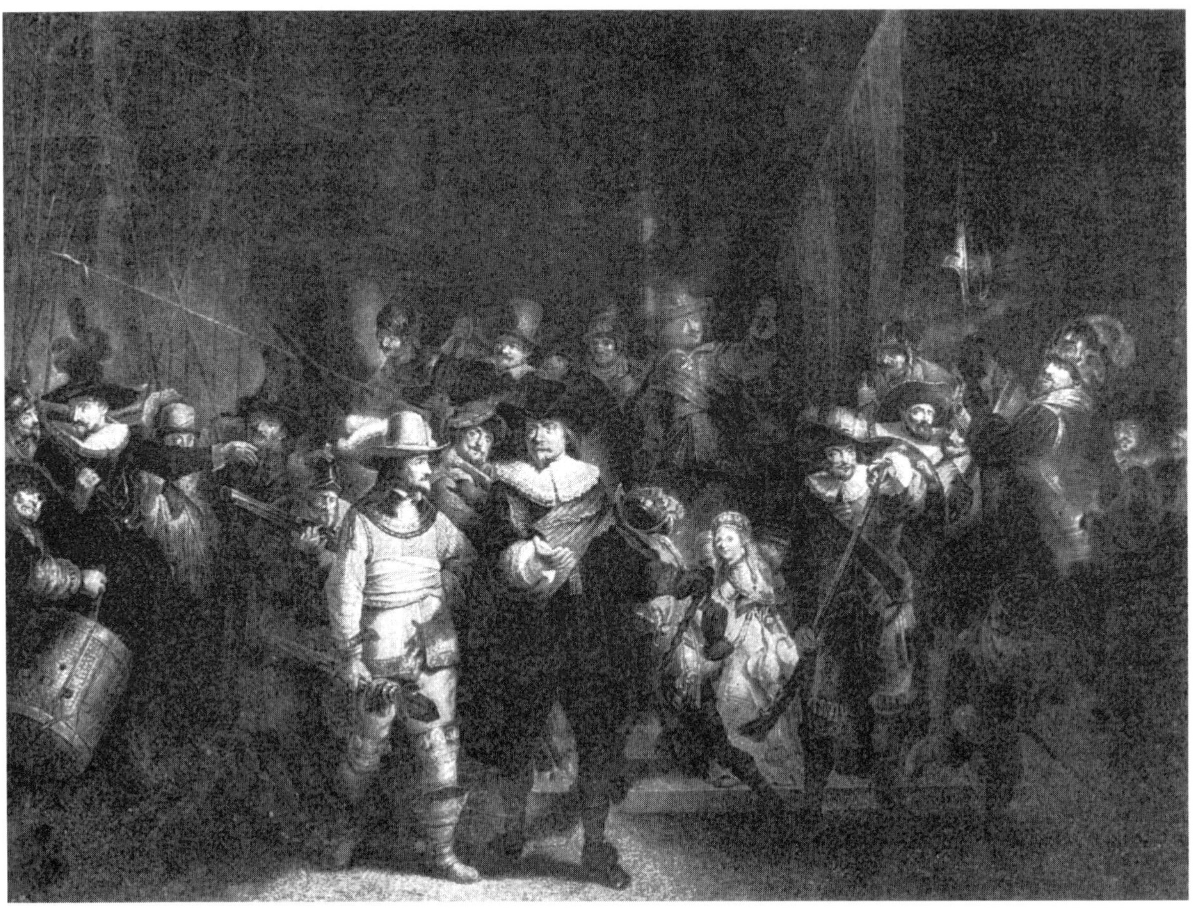

Figure 5 *Night Watch.* Rembrandt van Rijn (1606–1669). Steel engraving, from P. L. Muller, *Onze Gouden Eeuw,* 1896 (reversed). Author's collection.

of grandeur for the event that is partly dependent on the unconscious association with the Rembrandt painting, which we know is great art. It is nearly impossible to reconstruct a ship's cabin from what is seen in Moran's painting, unlike some other attempts at depicting the event. Allyn Cox's sketch version for the mural he painted in the United States Capitol in the early 1980s sets the transverse table in a ship's cabin which is just like that of *Mayflower II* except that the walls and windows have been enlarged greatly to accommodate numerous signatories around the table.[18] Inspiring this painting was the actual furniture arrangement in the replica of the *Mayflower II,* built in 1957. Connecting the event unconsciously with Rembrandt's composition had resulted in a particularly inconvenient transverse table placement in the cabin of the replica *Mayflower,* but it felt right, because everyone had seen something like it, and no one really remembered where. This unnautical table arrangement remained in *Mayflower II* until the author redesigned the cabin furnishings in the late 1980s.

A lithograph of a painting from 1858 by the Dutch artist Johan Schwartze (1814–1874) depicting a religious service held by the Pilgrims (Pilgrim Hall Museum) is another example where repetition of a general arrangement and some individual poses implies that the Pilgrim topic depicted participates in the importance associated with another event. This painting was lost at sea on the way to America, when the ship carrying it was attacked by the Confederate ship *Alabama* during the Civil War, but its appearance had already been recorded in a lithograph by August Allebé (*Figure 6*).[19] Reproduced in

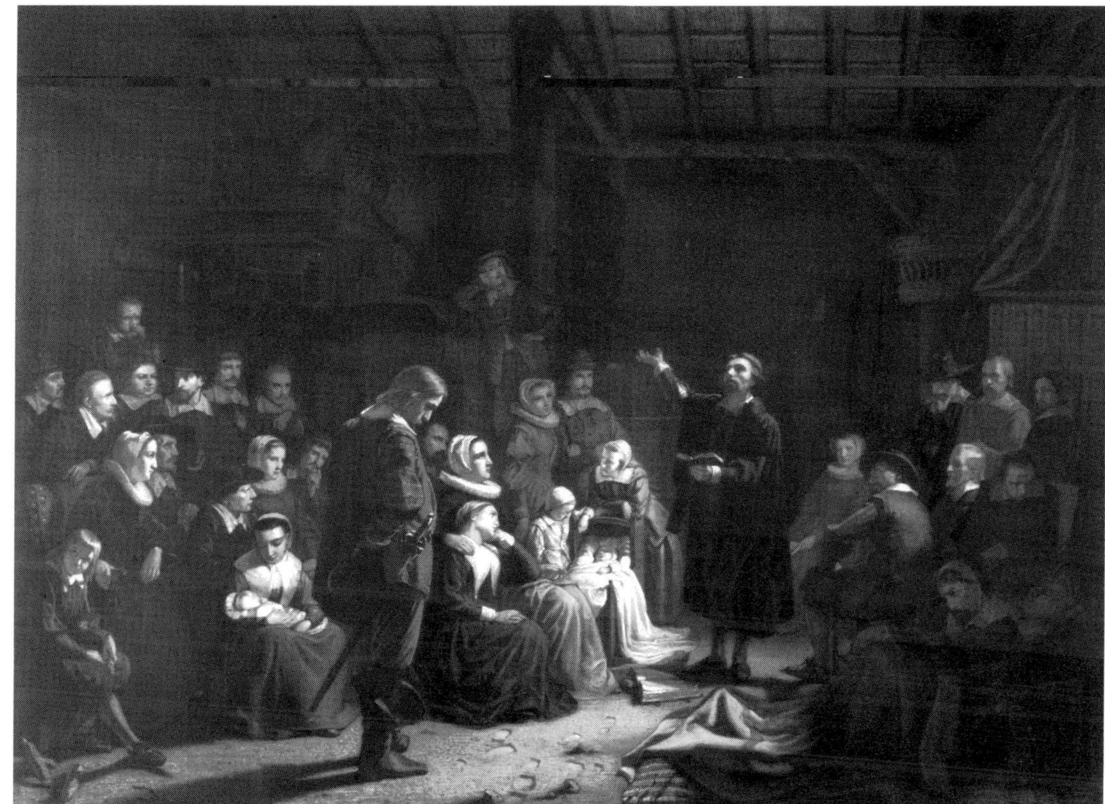

Figure 6 *The Pilgrim Fathers Holding their first meeting for Public Worship in North America.* August Allebé. After a painting of 1858 by the Dutch artist Johan Schwartze (1814–1874). Lithograph. Courtesy of Pilgrim Hall Museum, Plymouth, Massachusetts.

books about the Pilgrims, the picture has been identified as depicting a church service in John Robinson's Leiden house, or a religious service being held on the *Mayflower*, but also as showing a service held in Plymouth in New England. If it represents Leiden, we can identify the representation of the minister John Robinson a little right of center, holding a Bible, his hand raised in a rhetorical gesture. If the picture is thought to represent the *Mayflower* or Plymouth, the religious leader must then be Elder William Brewster. The artist evidently intended his picture to represent a service in the common "blockhouse" erected by the Pilgrims in Plymouth.[20] This figure (Brewster) and the grouping of the people around him were already familiar in the nineteenth century from various lithographic representations of Martin Luther at the Reichstag in Worms, uttering his famous statement "Here I stand, I can do no other."[21] One engraving of that subject includes a standing soldier with one arm akimbo, who could have been the model for the standing soldier seen from the back in Schwartze's painting, presumably Myles Standish.[22] The composition of the group as a whole is derived from a painting first exhibited in Amsterdam four years earlier, Johannes Hinderikus Egenberger's portrayal of *The Conference at The Hague* in 1611 between the Remonstrants (followers of Jacobus Arminius) and the Contraremonstrants (followers of Franciscus Gomarus). This painting (*Figure 7*) was number 122 in the Historical Gallery which Jacob de Vos Jacobszoon commissioned between 1850 and 1863 to illustrate Dutch national history from the first through the nineteenth century.[23]

The Pilgrims' place as the crowning achievement of the progress of the Reformation, mentioned by Castelar and Fiske, is here given visual form. The

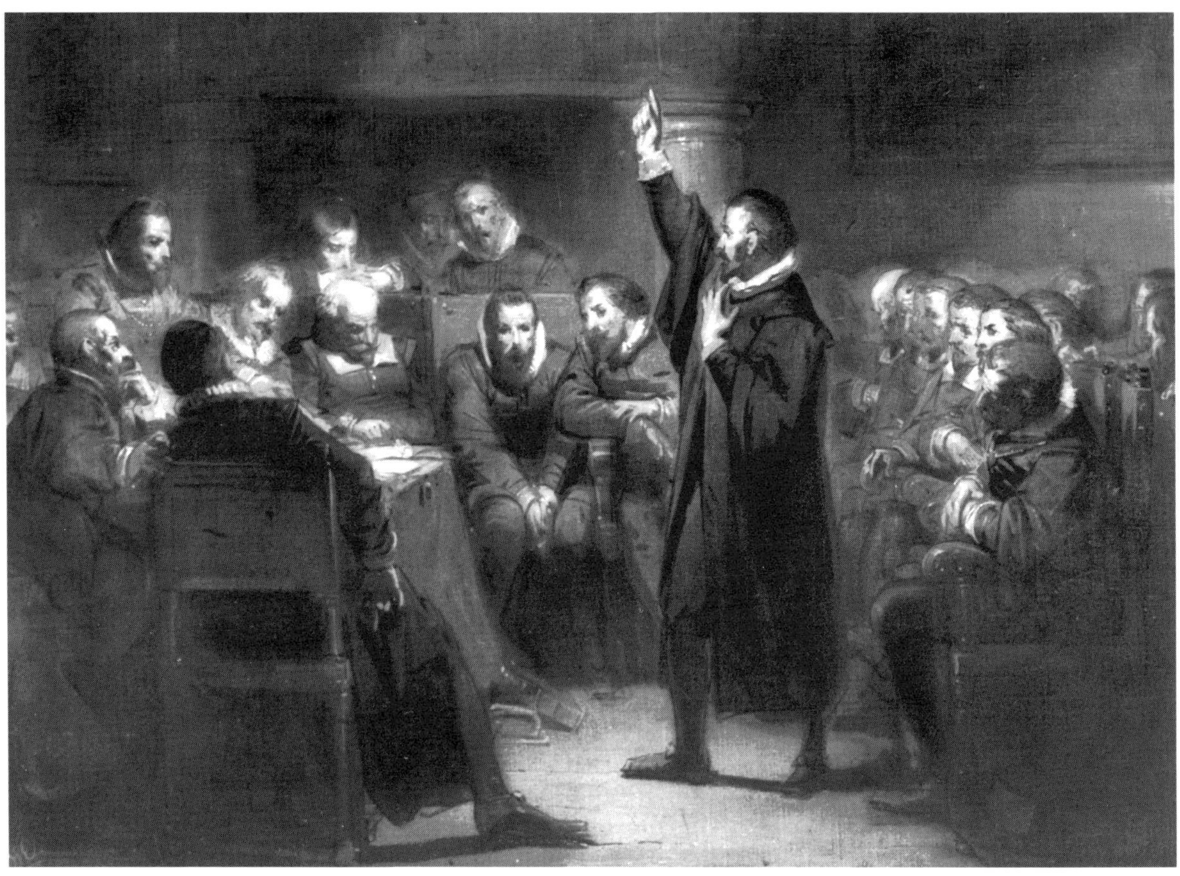

Figure 7 *The Conference at The Hague in 1611 between the Remonstrants and the Contraremonstrants.* Johannes Hinderikus Egenberger. Amsterdam, circa 1850. Oil on canvas, 40 × 55 cm. Amsterdam Historical Museum.

rhetorical gesture, with the extended arm and raised hand, is specifically associated with preachers, and not so frequently, for example, with politicians. This pose was what identified the representation of Eloquence in an eighteenth-century guide to allegorical visual rhetoric, by H.-F. Gravelot and C.-N. Cochin, *Iconologie.* The expected gesture had been established during the sixteenth century in Cesare Ripa's influential codification of allegorical personification.[24] The pose was well known in the nineteenth century from a portrait of John Wesley (National Portrait Gallery, London), but it may also have been a customary gesture employed by many preachers who had learned to use it in order to be recognized as being eloquent.[25] The isolation of the figure is consistent with the rise of individual commemorative statues, where a gesture and an attribute (the book) are all that identify a well-known historical figure. The Pilgrim religious leader looks somewhat like the once famous Luther memorial statue in the market square at Wittenberg designed by Karl Friedrich Schinkel and Johann Gottfried Schadow.[26] Schwartze had studied in Dusseldorf under Schadow, among others.

The outstretched, pointing hand of Eloquence is seen again in the eighty-one-foot-high granite statue of "Faith" by Hammatt Billings, commissioned as a "Monument to the Forefathers" in 1853 and finally dedicated at the summit of a hill in Plymouth in 1889 (*Figure 8*). Echoing the commemoration of Protestant religious leaders, the statue's other hand clasps a book identified as the Bible. While the colossal size of the statue immediately recalls fragments in the Capitol museum in Rome, the analogy with the canon of great art continues in the sources for the allegorical figures of Morality, Freedom, Education,

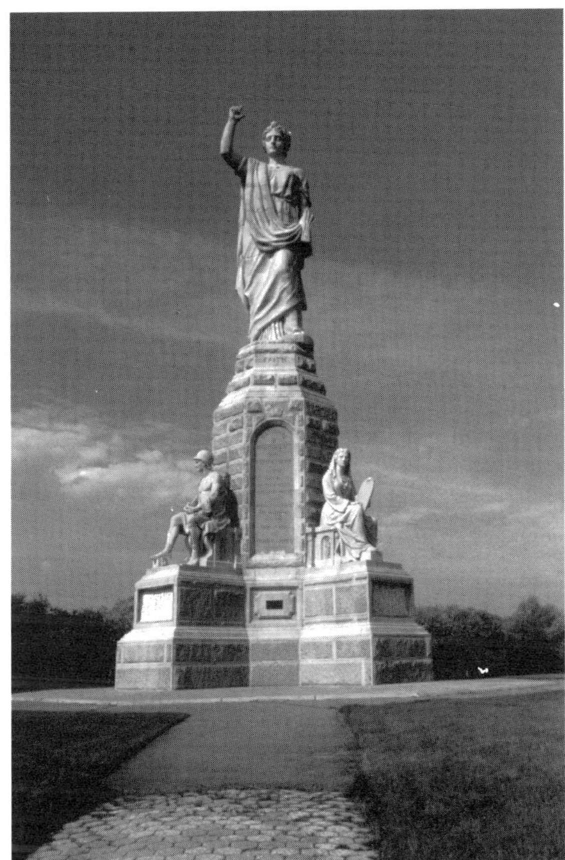

Figure 8 "Faith." Hammatt Billings (1818–1874). Granite, height 81 feet. Plymouth, Massachusetts. Courtesy of Pilgrim Hall Museum, Plymouth, Massachusetts.

and Law, which are seated on the arms of a cross that forms the massive foundation of Faith. "Freedom," for example, obviously combines aspects of Michaelangelo's statues of Lorenzo and Giuliano de' Medici in the tomb chapel in the Basilica of San Lorenzo in Florence. Parts of "Lorenzo" reappear in the figure of Law, where, however, the familiar head should remind one of the ancient bronze statue of St. Peter seated, in the nave of St. Peter's in Rome.

Seats of Authority

A specialist in the history of decorative arts can easily forget that to someone without similar training the furniture once possessed by Pilgrims is also, in itself, something of a bust. Edward Winslow's chair is not more interesting in appearance than numerous English chairs of the time. The same can be said of Governor Carver's and Elder Brewster's chairs. As far as turned chairs go (meaning chairs whose parts have been turned on a lathe), it is not difficult to point out others more interesting in design. Clearly these Pilgrim possessions derive their major attraction from association with famous people.[27] Romantic imagination enables us to picture for ourselves Winslow or Brewster sitting in their chairs. The Romantic imagination, however, visualized the past through pictures and went beyond the sedentary patriarchs.

Longfellow's poem "The Courtship of Miles Standish" had provided a romantic story that eclipsed in popular memory everything that Bradford wrote, even if carping historians early objected to the poet's claim that John Alden and Priscilla rode home on his bull.[28] But this was not enough. Plymouth's own Jane G. Austin invented a story called "The Wife of John Carver," which adds sentimental imagery to be recollected in the presence of the governor's chair.[29] According to Austin, Katherine Carver was adored by the Carvers' servant, John Howland. When the governor was on his dying bed, with his wife seated in the great chair by his side, and after Carver's death as well, Howland did everything possible to lighten her sorrow. Governor Bradford, a widower hoping for the arrival of his second wife, advised, even commanded, Howland to marry the widow Carver, which he might have done had she ever been able to rise from that chair. She felt herself dying, and when Howland brought up the subject of marriage with her, she replied,

> "But how could you, John—how should you even dream of such a matter? And I had thought to see you wedded to Elizabeth before I died."
>
> "Elizabeth?"
>
> "Yes, Elizabeth Tillie, who loves you, and has loved you for all these weary months; and you never saw it?"
>
> "Nay, dame, I thought not of her, at any rate," replied Howland sadly and abstractedly. Mistress Carver, her short-lived indignation changing to milder feelings, sat looking at him for a while, then said kindly:
>
> "Think not overmuch of my reproaches but now. I might as well have answered you more kindly; for you did not mean to wound me, and I am not so rich in love that I should trample upon an honest heart, though it may be that I could not so much as think of accepting it; but John, it is true that I am soon to

leave you, and I fain would see the two I love best happy together before I die. John, you said you would do much for my pleasure."

"God knows I would, Katherine," groaned the young man.

"Then you will marry Elizabeth?"

"Oh, mistress, will no less satisfy you?"

"Naught else would give me half the pleasure, or add to the delight I have in following my husband."

A long silence followed, and then John Howland laid his cold and trembling hand upon his mistress's knee.

"I am all yours, lady," said he. "Do with me as will best pleasure yourself."

"Thank you dear friend. Shall I speak for you to Elizabeth?"

"An you will. But profess not that I love her other than as a kind friend and sister. Let her not mistake."

"I shall ask her, as I have asked you, to do this for the love and satisfaction of a dying woman who holds you two dearer than any now on earth."

Jane G. Austin tells us that Howland had a hard time with this, and she describes his remarking to Mistress Carver, "Oh, Katherine, if you had bid me die for you, it had been easier." Nonetheless, everything worked out happily in the end, and John and Elizabeth were married by Master Winslow in Katherine Carver's bedroom just minutes before she died. The genealogist will know how rare is such insight into the motivations of courtship; unfortunately this is entirely the product of Austin's imagination. We are left with the image of the widowed matchmaker seated in the great chair, and since we do not have any better picture of her, when we look at Carver's empty chair we can think of someone sitting in it commandingly, like Cornelia Claesdr. Vooght in the portrait from 1631 by Frans Hals (Rijksmuseum, Amsterdam).

The Triumph of the Pilgrims

It went almost without saying in the nineteenth century that Roman architecture suitably accompanies the idea of a republic, while Greek architecture somehow means democracy.[30] Both styles, moreover, proclaim the reassuring solidity and virtues of institutions architecturally clad in them, such as Pilgrim Hall Museum or Massachusetts banks. The triumphal arch has more specific connotations. The Romans commemorated military victories by constructing these archways. Processions of soldiers carrying armor taken from defeated enemies, loot from cities they had ransacked, and captives whose future was slavery marched beneath them. The processions themselves are depicted on several monuments. In the fifteenth century Andrea Mantegna's series of paintings, *The Triumphs of Caesar,* published as an edition of engravings, was widely known in the courts of Europe.[31] Virtues, Death, Fame, and Time became the subject of triumphs with the series of Petrarch, in which Chastity conquers Love, Death conquers Chastity, Fame conquers Death, and Time conquers Fame.[32] These were often visualized as imaginary processions, some of which are preserved to us in tapestries of the highest quality, most of which have faded.[33]

It was the Emperor Maximilian who commissioned the most elaborate imaginary procession designs.[34] His triumphal arch was, in fact, an extraordinarily large woodcut composition (over ten feet high) designed by Albrecht Dürer (*Figure 9*).[35] Its allegorical depictions made known the virtues, victories, political biography, and ancestry of the emperor. There was also a woodcut procession forming part of the propagandistic concept. Depictions of troops and captives, representations of the lands of the empire, and allegorical images on triumphal wagons follow each other in a parade that never happened. Maximilian, as Keizer of the Holy Roman Empire, made his triumphal procession as the Caesar of his age. Certain woodcuts in the series indicate that Maximilian also wanted to be understood as the reincarnation of early heroes such as King Arthur, Godfried of Bouillon (Crusader King of Jerusalem), and Odobert, King of Provence. The costumed drama presented to us as the woodcut portrayal of a parade illustrated the idea that people of the present (in the early sixteenth century) identified themselves in terms of the virtues of heroic ancestors (*Figure 10*).

Real processions took place also. Following old Burgundian precedent, Maximilian, his grandson Charles V, and Charles V's son Philip II made triumphal progresses from city to city throughout their Netherlandish (and other) territories.[36] The parades consisted of the rulers and their accompanying noblemen and liveried servants, gaily costumed soldiers, musicians, choirs, clergy, and groups from the

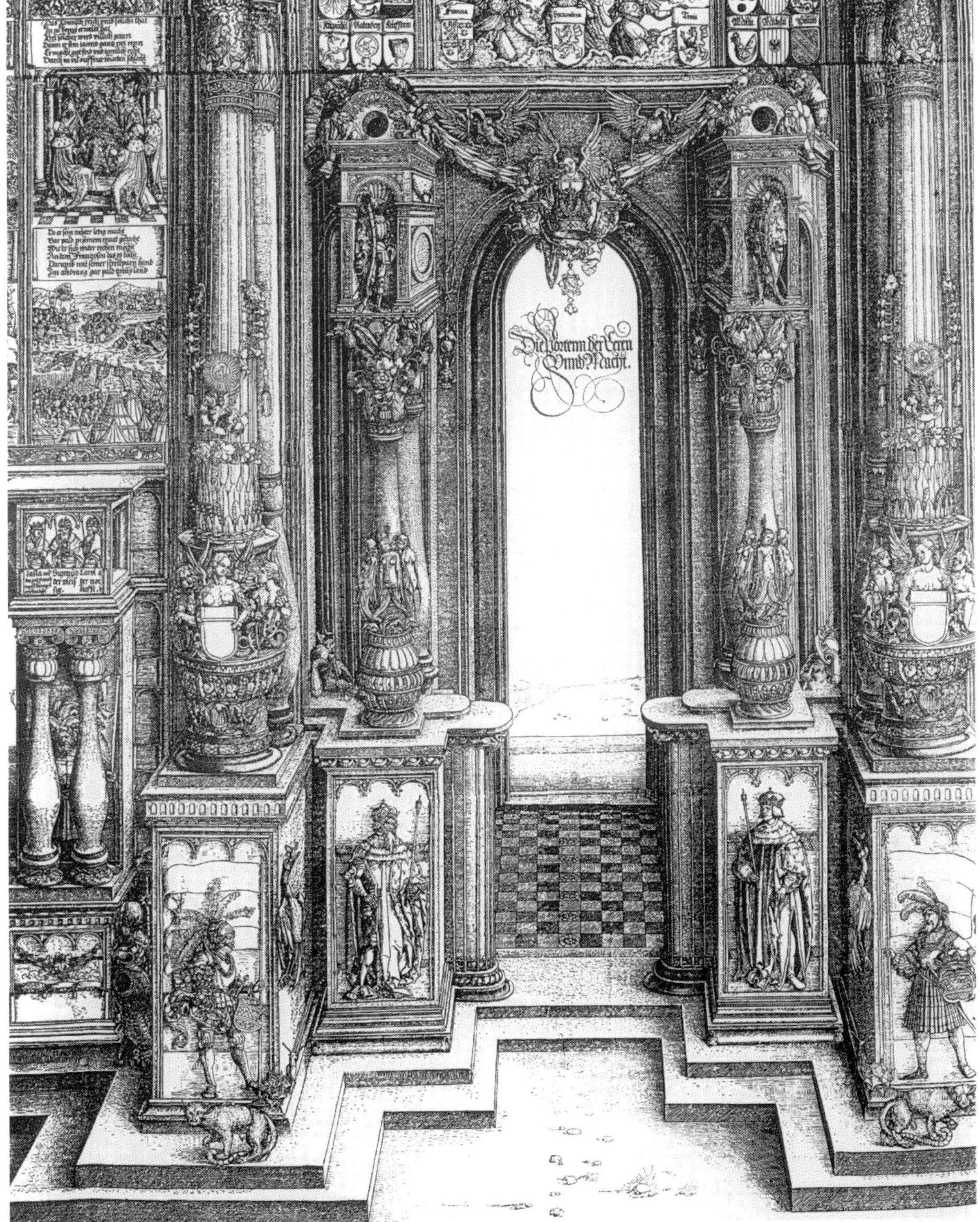

Figure 9 The Triumphal Arch of Maximilian (detail). Albrecht Dürer (1471–1528). Germany, 1517. Woodcut. From: *Maximilian's Triumphal Arch, Woodcuts by Albrecht Dürer and Others* [Dover reprint, 1972; from *Jahrbuch der kunsthistorische Sammlungen des Allerhochsten Kaiserhauses, 1885–1886*].

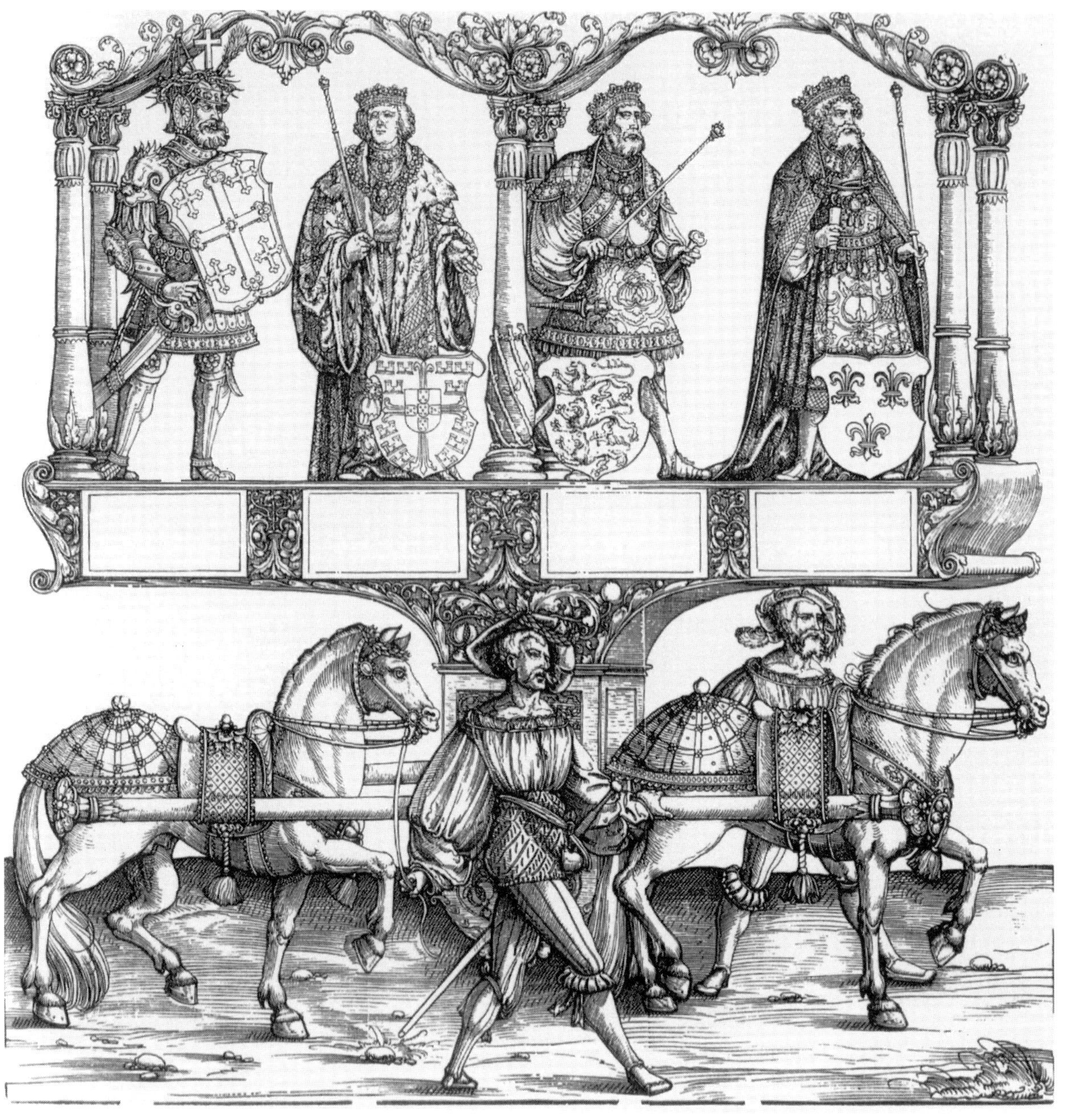

Figure 10 The Triumph of Maximilian (detail), Odobert King of Provence, King Arthur of England, King John of Portugal, Godfried of Bouillon King of Jerusalem. Hans Burgkmair (1473–1531). Woodcut, 1526. Plimoth Plantation.

city being visited, such as the guilds and the various local militia companies. Temporary triumphal arches were erected at several places along the route, offering an impressive entry to the city and leading from one part of the town to another. At points where the parade was to pause, stages were built on which historical plays were performed, indicating parallels from the Bible or from classical history to call attention to the ruler's virtues. These so-called Joyous Entries were not mere circus parades coming through town at random. The processions formally constituted the time at which the new ruler confirmed the traditional, chartered rights and privileges of the individual cities, and when, in response, the representatives of the citizens acknowledged their allegiance to the new ruler. The Joyous Entries, in other words, marked the beginning of a new period in government, when the legal foundations of the society were commemorated and reaffirmed. The Joyous Entries invariably ended in a formal high mass with display of all the local church's relics.

Perhaps it is no more than curious that every August in Plymouth, Massachusetts, on Fridays a gaily costumed group begins on the waterfront at the triumphal arch over Plymouth Rock commemorating the ancestral entry into town and walks solemnly in procession to the top of Burial Hill to hold prayer in the vicinity of the relics of their saints. There may be more to it, however; we have here a continuation of a polemical tradition which allows us to identify ourselves in terms of the virtuous and victorious beliefs we attribute to our ancestors, and which by implication our enemies (or at least those people not in our group) do not have. In this context, comparing Bradford to Moses, which has become so common it is boring, can imply that we as Americans are leading the world out of its past bondage of ignorance into the Promised Land of the American Way of Life. We begin with a reaffirmation of the principles of government associated with the Mayflower Compact and Plymouth Rock and end with a religious observation at the shrine of the ancestors. This imagery is potent and it has an ancient tradition. It is unsurprising that some people, who consider their ancestors to have been the conquered, object. It is also unsurprising that the canopy over the Rock looks like a small temple, with reminiscences of a triumphal arch. The previous canopy looked even more like a triumphal arch, calling to mind specifically the arch built at Antwerp in 1635, although the architectural elements are commonplace and no direct derivation can be assumed.[37]

Netherlandish Chambers of Rhetoric (secular guilds of poets, playwrights, and actors) held what can be called proto-national competitions, in which the chambers of several cities from Brabant, Flanders, Zeeland, and Holland met together in one town, where they performed their plays while taking part in a long procession.[38] These processions were formally derivative of the Joyous Entries of the princes. Typically the content of the plays performed along the parade route consisted of a story from biblical, classical, or imaginary local antiquity whose moral was to be understood as referring to contemporary events. At the Reformation, local heroes for the Protestant Netherlands included those who had risen up in revolt against Roman oppressors long before the area was converted to Christianity. The actors could be dressed in old-fashioned clothing, generally from about a century earlier, and the public understood that the ancient past was like that. The moral point, that the present should continue the virtuous example set by the ancestral past, was clear.[39]

Polemical Triumphal Entries continued for centuries. A procession is depicted in a carved frieze from 1542 on the choir stalls in the church at Dordrecht in Holland which equates Charles V with an early defender of Rome and simultaneously shows the triumph of the doctrine of transubstantiation over heresy, trampled underfoot by an allegorical wagon representing the Roman Catholic church.[40] Countering that, the University of Leiden opened in 1575 with a procession whose single triumphal wagon symbolized the triumph of Holy Scripture (*Figure 11*). There was, however, a boat with allegorical figures of the nine muses.[41] One of Rubens's major tapestry designs about forty years later repeats the theme from Dordrecht, which itself was derived from Titian's *Triomfo della Fede* (woodcuts published in 1517), with the triumphant Catholic church riding high over heresy and displaying the consecrated host.[42]

Triumphal processions were by no means restricted to the Low Countries or the sixteenth century. James I's entry into London is well known, with woodcut illustrations preserving some of its impressive display (*Figure 12*). An aspect of the transition when James I died is that the Turkish ambassador presented Charles I with one hundred fifty slaves (mostly Englishmen enslaved by the Turks), as well as some lions, panthers, and other animals. The animals, at least, were paraded in London, providing an early link between the traditions of triumphal entries and the circus parades of the nineteenth and twentieth centuries, where baroque wagons continue to appear.[43] Throughout Europe, great artists, including Rubens and Romeyn de Hooghe, designed temporary triumphal arches. Arising out of this tradition, a less impressive classical arch was considered appropriate

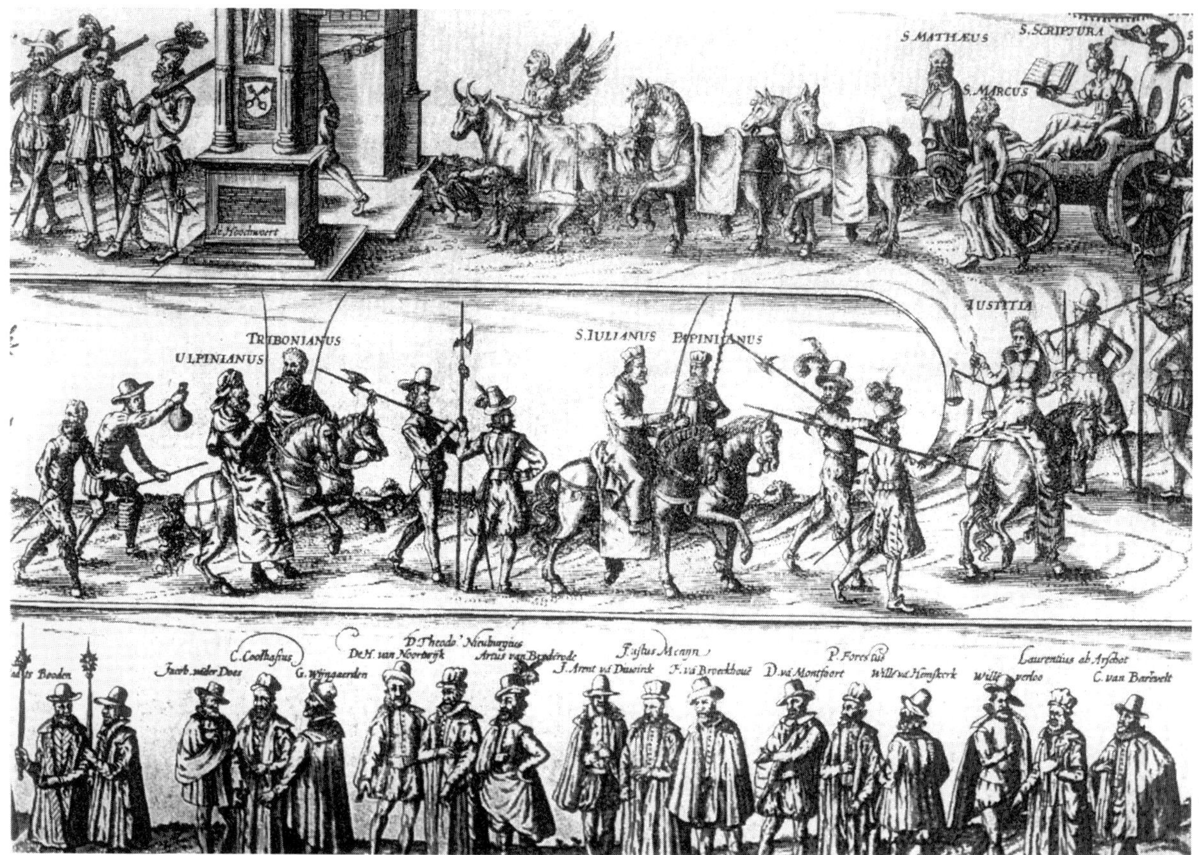

Figure 11 The Triumph of Scripture: Procession at the opening of the University of Leiden in 1575 (detail). Artist unknown. Engraving, 1614. Plimoth Plantation.

in the late eighteenth century when George Washington entered Boston.

Numerous illustrations show how clearly people of the seventeenth century imagined themselves in terms of Roman or biblical precedent, for example, the anonymous engraving in which a Roman commander points directions to a troop of soldiers with harquebuses (*Figure 13*) (formerly collection of the author, now Plimoth Plantation collection). There is no clear period at which this self-conception becomes less urgent, although eighteenth-century costumed pageant processions, like that commemorating the two-hundredth anniversary of the founding of the University of Leiden, where triumphal wagons were replaced with sleighs for the February weather, appear considerably more fun.[44] A serious program nonetheless underlies the arrangement from 1775 in Leiden, with allegorical representations next to costumed actors representing historical figures, next to actors whose costumes indicate a different period and identify them, for example, as "Greek knights." We can probably discover self-important pedantry in later pageantry, as well. In America's 1876 centennial celebrations, for example, Jefferson was compared with Moses, and processions were arranged incorporating wagons on which were tableaux vivants. That these historical pageants came forth from a centuries-old European tradition was overlooked by Terence Ranger and Eric Hobsbawm, who wrote that "one use of history was unique to pageantry and to the early twentieth century: the belief that history could be made into a dramatic public ritual through which the residents of a town, by acting out the right version of their past, could bring about some kind of future social and political transformation."[45]

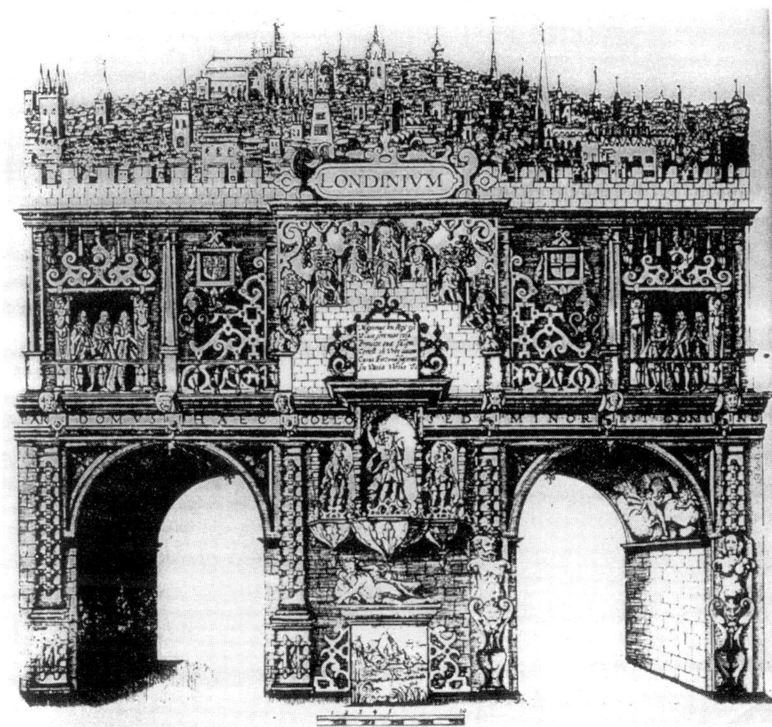

Figure 12 Triumphal Arch of King James I. 1603. Artist unknown. Engraving. (From Robert Adams, *The Lost Museum,* p. 34). The Huntington Library, San Marino, California.

The element of amusement and high jinks seen in the Leiden commemoration of 1775 carried through into nineteenth- and early-twentieth-century historical pageants and parades. In 1905, two hundred sixty-nine students of the University of Leiden in historic costume participated in a reenactment of "The Triumphal Entry of King-Stadholder William III into The Hague in 1691 after his Return from England." The great deed of the past commemorated in this triumphal-entry-like parade was itself a triumphal entry. This was one of many pageants of the late nineteenth and early twentieth centuries, when great attention was given to what was considered historical accuracy. Many had an explicit political point to make, and the rise of such parades in the second quarter of the nineteenth century is traced to the nationalism of newly independent Belgium, where the future was celebrated with a direct recollection of the heroic Burgundian past. Rising nationalism in Switzerland, Germany, and Italy was accompanied by a similar use of politically motivated pageantry in which triumphal floats represented both the past, interpreted with what was claimed to be historical accuracy, and the future.[46]

Historical accuracy was to be a major concern in the 1921 celebrations held in Plymouth to commemorate the Pilgrims. According to David Glassberg, "As pageant production grew more historically and technically sophisticated, audiences looked to each episode for the accuracy of details or for the power of its special effects but not for an overall historical interpretation. . . . George Pierce Baker traveled to Holland and Great Britain to conduct original research for his Pilgrim tercentenary pageant of 1921, but those critics present at the performance in Plymouth had more to say about the lighting—300 kilowatts flowing in 300 separate lines through 15 miles of wire—than about Baker's dramatic story of the Pilgrims' struggles in the Old and the New World."[47] Quoting somewhat negative critical comments, Glassberg does not cite Frederick W. Bittinger, who reported, "Probably this pageant was the greatest event of that sort ever

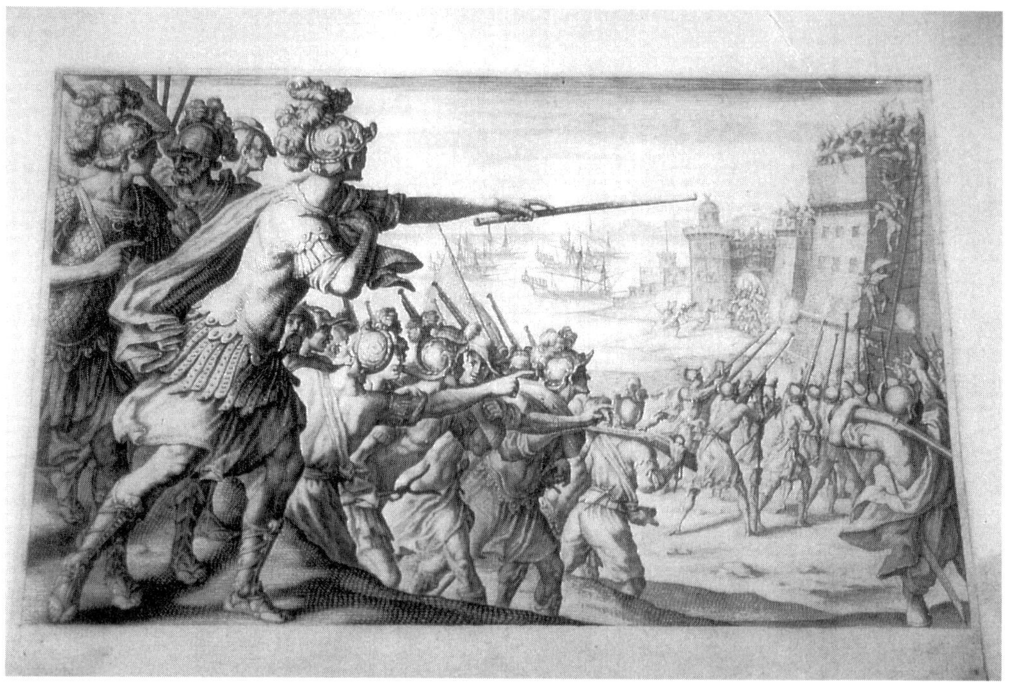

Figure 13 Roman heroes inspiring a seventeenth-century seige. Artist unknown. Engraving. Plimoth Plantation.

attempted with non-professional actors anywhere in this country."[48] Bittinger described the cast in quasi-symbolic terms: "The actors in the spectacle, which was one of the largest events in pageantry ever attempted in this country, were many of them, descendants of the old time peoples they portray, and the cast embraced the sons and daughters of many nations, descendants from the sea kings of the Norse land, Danes, Hollanders, English, Indians of real native stock, and even [*sic*] countrymen of Christopher Columbus."[49] The various historical episodes, which were the equivalent of the separate dramatic performances along the route of a Burgundian triumphal entry, included a representation of the royal progress of the Scottish King James VI from Scotland to England where he became James I.

> Throngs of people press around the royal train, paying their respects to their sovereign, and the mass blocks the road of the royal party. It is here, after a small scuffle where a subject strives to approach His Majesty, that one of the leaders of the Puritans makes an attempt to present a petition to the King, claiming to represent a thousand subjects, at least. King James receives the petition grudgingly and after a half promise of consideration tells one of his following, "I will harry them out of this land." To the skirl of the bagpipes the retinue and King James move away. . . .[50]

Under "historical accuracy" the royal progress was presented as the moment of the abrogation of liberty, rather than the time of confirmation of traditional liberties and privileges; and the famous "harrying" statement from the Hampton Court Conference is brought forward ten months to be used as a response to the Millenary Petition. In a later scene from the 1921 pageant, the University of Leiden appears. "The Third Episode opens with the Pilgrims safe in Holland and introduces the 'march of the Dutch Cities of Charity—April 1609.' Each city group is represented by dress and its distinctive banner, while the professors of Leyden appear, each bearing a torch as emblematic of the 'more light' shed by them as distinguished from their predecessors."[51] Thus was echoed at Plymouth the triumphal entry which opened the University of Leiden in 1575, when the professors themselves took part.

A disadvantage of pageants is that they come to an end. Just as the Disney company's Epcot Center perpetuates the foreign pavilions of a world's fair, open-air museums could be used to preserve and continue the pageants' pleasant and structured confrontation with the past.

First-Person Fun

Attempts to identify one's own national history as arising out of a noble golden age in a primitive past are seen throughout Europe in the seventeenth century, continuing into later times and including America, especially during the nineteenth century, but still seen, for example, in the popular late-twentieth-century reevaluation of Native American precontact culture.[52] While examination of the lives of the contemporary peasantry, as shown to the wealthier classes in seventeenth-century paintings, does not bear out an interpretation of idyllic conditions, pastoral poetry and painting related to it suggest that in some more perfect past shepherds and shepherdesses often had good weather and a carefree time. The view of actual peasants as near savages was conducive to recognizing them from a distance as examples of the noble savage. Experiencing an idealized agricultural ambience in which such nobility and simplicity could thrive in the imagination was not at all impossible. Marie Antoinette achieved it in her open-air village at Versailles, which featured a working dairy and the chance for first-person conversation with the people who lived there (even though one knew that many of them really went home at night). It is Versailles, therefore, which is the ideological ancestor of open-air museums that go beyond the preservation of ancient buildings and incorporate an imaginary participation in the life of the exotic past. This is not a negative remark, because for such museums the philosophical association with Jean-Jacques Rousseau may be more flattering than an identification with the ideas of George Santayana and the inclination to consider them the places where those who are ignorant of history are forced to repeat it.

To summarize, this essay suggests that the Pilgrims have been like a screen on which people could project whatever they wanted to have as their own ancestral virtues to justify their own points of view. Something that strikes us quite favorably about them, even more than their role in the development of democracy, is their decision to leave Europe rather than get sucked into yet another war. In this, their migration is admirable, like that of the Russian Mennonites in the nineteenth century. Others might notice that the Pilgrims' search for freedom to practice their own religion is meritoriously similar to the migration of Catholics to Maryland or of the Mormons to Utah; or that their concern to avoid economic hardship and terrorist reprisals raises them to the same worthy company as the Irish and Haitian refugees and even that of German Jews before 1940, although the Pilgrims' persecution was minor by comparison. Selecting any one aspect of their reality is unavoidably a distortion of their experience. Throughout America's national history, various isolated ancestral Pilgrim strengths have been chosen for fighting battles that sometimes are no longer our issues, such as when one author observed that in Pilgrim times ministers did not take two weeks off for vacation,[53] or when another author could remark approvingly that

> At the period of which we write—and long after it—women had work to do, and much of it. They spun the wool and the flax into thread, they wove it into cloth, and they made it up into garments for their husbands. So it was in Solomon's day, so it was in Caesar's day, and so it was in Bradford's day. . . . But all is changed, and within half a century, to such an amazing extent as to have created a revolution in social life. Steam and machinery have destroyed the occupations of women, and in a degree those of men.[54]

We have, since then, come to terms with the steam engine, which may be visited in any number of museums.

A century ago the Pilgrims were held up righteously as exemplars of anti-Catholicism, which, indubitably, they were. That historical models could teach anything on this point to some of America's Pilgrim admirers of the period is, however, definitely questionable. Alice Carey's 1854 article about the Pilgrims is followed by an editorial assuring the reader that America really has nothing to fear from Catholics.[55] Titled "The Religious Scarecrow of the Age," it begins, "Have we reason to fear the Pope in this country? Of course we do not mean his questionable holiness, personally, but the system which he represents and names—Popery itself. Of himself personally or officially, it would be a very grave joke for us to entertain a single anxiety. He sits in the Vatican, only the shadow of what he once was—the impersonation of decrepitude, smothered under the obsolete and grotesque habiliments of a long gone age, and mumbling from a toothless mouth the language of mere imbecility."[56] People could rejoice then in response to such an obsolete and grotesque formulation. It was an age before concern about weighing one's words for politically correct inoffensiveness in the scale of potential future retribution. Descendants could be glad their Pilgrim ancestors had raised the banner of "No Pope Here!" Nowadays, although the Pilgrims are not usually praised for anti-Catholicism, the name of the Pilgrims is used to cast a haze of respectability over any number of enterprises, from the Plymouth nuclear power plant called "Pilgrim 2," to the Plymouth business called "Pilgrim Rubbish Disposal" and the downtown Boston pornography movie house called "The Pilgrim."

It is pleasant to discover not all views of the Pilgrims and Puritans rigid with inherited piety. In 1865 J. W. de Forest described a visit to something like Plimoth Plantation.[57] In the midst of a long narrative he describes the effects of first-person interpretation on the visitors:

> At that tantalizing instant a stout squat fellow, in scarlet doublet and breeches, leaped out from behind the pillory, and completely smashed the precious vessel [a bottle of strong drink] with his cane. The Doctor dropped the empty butt of it, and rushed shrieking toward us, dreadfully punished in the rear by the hobnailed shoes of the part in red breeches. The latter then proceeded to inform us, in horrible obsolete English, that he was constable, and would permit no interference with the rascally varlets in the pillory.

After a long day in the village, the visitors departed, receiving a final greeting from the governor.

> "Go, and let this day be a warning unto ye for all the days of your life, lest a worse thing come upon ye."
>
> "I kinder reckon it will be, and no mistake," muttered Major Slick, as we hurried away toward our landing-place. . . .
>
> 'Puritans be darned!' thundered the Major. 'I'm glad the confounded hard-headed old critters have died out. This generation an that couldn't git along together nohow. I don't like to take my religion so stiff as they mixed it."
>
> "Fact is," continued the Major, philosophically, "men of one century hain't no kind of business in another century. I see some good in death that I never saw before!"
>
> "Agreeing unanimously in this conclusion, we returned with great satisfaction to the comfortable temporalities of Nahant, thanking heaven that we were well rid of the forefathers of whom we were not worthy!"

NOTES

[1]The author wishes to give his thanks to Peggy Baker, Director, the Pilgrim Society, for permission to reproduce pictures in its collection; to James W. Baker, Pilgrim historian, who generously allowed the use of his unmatched library on the topic of Pilgrim commemorations; and to Karin Goldstein, former Curator, Pilgrim Hall Museum, who provided helpful information about paintings and artists. This article is a revised and expanded version of a paper presented to a conference on new research about the Pilgrims and related topics, held at Plimoth Plantation in 1992, organized by the Colonial Society of Massachusetts and the Pilgrim Society. It was written before the publication of two related books: John Seelye's *Memory's Nation: The Place of Plymouth Rock* (1998); and Ann Uhry Abrams, *The Pilgrims and Pocahontas: Rival Myths of American Origin* (1999).

[2]For analysis of such literature, see Lawrence Buell, *New England Literary Culture: From Revolution through Renaissance* (Cambridge and New York: Cambridge University Press, 1986), pp. 191ff., Part 3, "Reinventing Puritanism: The New England Historical Imagination"; pp. 193–213, ch. 8, "The Concept of Puritan Ancestry." Buell wrote (p. 201) that "the Puritans' habit of seeing history in typological terms as fulfillment of biblical prophecy was perpetuated, with the creation of the republic identified as the millennial fulfillment toward which the preceding crises pointed." The tendentious reading of history is well expressed in the title of a book by Joseph Dillaway Sawyer, *History of the Pilgrims and Puritans, Their Ancestry and Descendants, Basis of Americanization*, 3 vols., ed. William Elliot Griffis (New York: Century History Co., 1922).

[3]Emilio Castelar, "The Republican Movement in Europe," *Harper's New Monthly Magazine* 45 (June–November 1872): 47–60; 215–24; 372–85; 581–92; 722–32; 849–60. Castelar makes "Then we shall hang them" out of King James I's reported statement, "If this bee al that they have to say, I shall make them conform themselves, or I wil harrie them out of

the land, or else doe worse." (*The Summe and Substance of the Conference Which it pleased his excellent Maiestie to have with the Lords Bischops, and others of his Clergie . . . at Hampton Court, Jan. 14, 1603;* cited in Henry Martyn Dexter and Morton Dexter, *The England and Holland of the Pilgrims* [Boston and New York: Houghton, Mifflin and Company, 1905], p. 342.)

[4]John Fiske, *The Beginnings of New England; or, The Puritan Theocracy in its Relations to Civil and Religious Liberty* (Boston and New York: Houghton, Mifflin and Company, 1889, reprinted 1899), p. 49. The lectures which form this book were first delivered at Washington University, St. Louis, Missouri; hence the reference to the Mississippi.

[5]Eugene Lawrence, "Genesis of the New England Churches," *Harper's New Monthly Magazine* 50 (December 1874–May 1875): 124–31. This interpretation is at variance with the modern claim that the Pilgrims originated home schooling.

[6]James Thacher, *History of the Town of Plymouth: From Its First Settlement in 1620, to the Year 1832* (Boston: Marsh, Capen and Lyon, 1832), p. 14.

[7]For a discussion of a second portrait of Edward Winslow and a spurious portrait of William Bradford, see Jeremy D. Bangs, "Towards a Revision of the Pilgrims: Three New Pictures," *New England Historical and Genealogical Register* 153 (1999): 3–28. A spurious portrait of Myles Standish is published in Jonathan King, *The Mayflower Miracle: The Pilgrims' Own Story of the Founding of America* (Newton Abbot and London: David and Charles, 1987), color illustration between pp. 54 and 55: "Captain Myles Standish, Oil by Daniel Mytens, Flemish School. Reproduced by kind permission of National Geographic Society, Washington, U.S.A." The portrait in fact depicts Wolstenholme, as was indicated in the *National Geographic* article where this illustration was originally used in Ivor Noel Hume's, "Martin's Hundred." In that article, the portrait was provided with a white rectangle indicating a clothing detail like an item recovered archaeologically at Martin's Hundred; peculiarly, the white rectangle is retained in the book by King.

[8]R. J. Slater, *Teaching and Learning America's Christian History, The Study of Basic Principles from Volume One of the Text, The Christian History of the Constitution of the United States of America* (San Francisco: Anaheim, California, Foundation for American Christian Education, 1965), p. 195.

[9]Frederick W. Bittinger, *The Story of the Pilgrim Tercentenary Celebration, at Plymouth in the Year 1921* (Plymouth, Mass.: Memorial Press, 1923), p. 46.

[10]Some of these parallels have been remarked before; see, for example, Benson J. Lossing, *The Achievements of Four Centuries; or, the Wonderful Story of our Great Continent within and beyond the States, The Marvellous and Unparalleled Progress of The Hemisphere of Republics, from the Landing of Columbus to the Present time, Historical, Statistical, and Descriptive [. . .] the Whole Forming a Grand Cycloramic View of the Western World,* 2 vols. (New York: Gay Brothers and Company, 1890), 1:64: "Still 'Pilgrim Rock' —which some have rather irreverently called the 'Yankee Blarney Stone'—is, for an outsider, what really makes Plymouth what it is—a kind of hallowed ground. Apart from the tradition which makes it mark the spot where the Pilgrims first set foot upon the New England shore, there is nothing noteworthy about this rock. [. . .] Neither, for the matter of that, is there anything specially notable in the look of the Irish Blarney Stone or in that of the still more sacred Black Stone in the Kaaba at Mecca. . . ."

[11]A four-page collection of advertisements (in the author's collection of ephemera), on which the date June 1860 appears, includes a notice for "Plymouth Rock Jewelry" offered by Crosby, Hunnewell, and Morse (successors to Samuel T. Crosby and Co.). The company is said to "have removed to the new and elegant store, No. 240 Washington Street, to which they invite their former customers and the public generally. Having in their possession a large piece of the veritable Plymouth Rock, which is now so difficult to obtain, they will sell specimens in its original state, or will manufacture the same into Brooches, Studs, Seals, Keys, Charms, &c., &c., making a handsome and valuable ornament."

[12]The title is *A Map of the most Inhabited part of New England, containing the Provinces of Massachusetts Bay and New Hampshire, with the Colonies of Conecticut* [sic] *and Rhode Island, Divided into Counties and Townships: The whole composed from actual Surveys and its Situation adjusted by Astronomical Observations.* It is reproduced in: W. W. Ristow, ed., *Thomas Jefferys, The American Atlas, London, 1776* (Amsterdam: Theatrum Orbis Terrarum, 1974; Series of Atlases in Facsimile, 6th ser., vol. 6).

[13]Both Gibraltar and Plymouth Rock are seen as illustrations in Hezekiah Butterworth, *Zig-Zag Journeys, The British Isles* (Boston: Estes and Lauriat, 1889), pp. 49–58. The series *Zig-Zag Journeys* was published circa 1880–1890. Reuse of some of the same clichés is found in numerous other publications, such as Rupert van Wert, *Van Wert's Travels in Foreign Lands* (Chicago and New York: Belford, Clarke and Co., 1884). As chief curator at Plimoth Plantation Museum, the author added to its print collection a small group of such engravings illustrating the visual parallel of Gibraltar with Plymouth Rock.

[14]On Henry Sargent, see George C. Groce and David H. Wallace, *The New-York Historical Society's Dictionary of Artists in America, 1564–1860* (New Haven: Yale University Press, and London: Oxford University Press, 1957), p. 557; J. De Wolf Addison, "Henry Sargent: A Boston Painter," *Art in America,* 17 (1928–1929): 279–284. On the influence of Rembrandt on West and Copley, see Christopher White, David Alexander, and Ellen d'Oench, *Rembrandt in Eighteenth-Century England* (London: Yale Center for British Art, 1983; exhibition catalogue), p. 21 and nos. 8 and 55 (figs. 39, 40); David Alexander, "Rembrandt and the Reproductive Print in Eighteenth-Century England" in *Rembrandt in Eighteenth-Century England* (New Haven: Yale Center for British Art, 1983), pp. 46–54.

[15]See H. van de Waal, *Drie Eeuwen Vaderlandsche Geschied-Uitbeelding* (The Hague: Martinus Nijhoff, 1952) with English summary; Roy Strong, *Recreating the Past: British History and the Victorian Painter* (New York: Thames and Hudson, 1978); Werner Telesko, ed., *Der Traum vom Gluck,*

Die Kunst des Historismus in Europa (Vienna and Munich: Christian Brandstatter Verlag, 1996; exhibition catalogue, Kunstlerhaus und der Akademie der bildenden Kunste, Vienna, 13 September 1996–6 January 1997). Further, see David Lowenthal, *The Past is a Foreign Country* (Cambridge and London: Cambridge University Press, 1985); Ekkehard Mai and Anke Repp-Eckert, *Historiemalerei in Europa, Paradigmen in Form, Funktion und Ideologie* (Mainz: Verlag Philipp von Zabern, 1990); Werner Hofmann, *Luther und die Folgen fur die Kunst* (Munich: Prestel-Verlag, for the Hamburger Kunsthalle [exhibition catalogue, 11 November 1983–8 January 1984], 1983), pp. 506–521, "Protestantische Historie."

[16]Although the costume generally looks like some worn in portraits by Rubens of Helena Fourment and Susan Fourment, those paintings had inspired not only numerous other paintings and prints in the nineteenth century but also actual clothing. A direct connection of Weir's figure with a particular source is therefore elusive. For comparison, see Eugene Deveria's painting *A Notable Lady from the Period of Louis XIII* (Quimper, Musee des Beaux-Arts) illustrated in Telesko, *Der Traum vom Gluck*, p. 668, no. 23.4; Franz Hanfstaengl, photograph of a "contemporary" in Telesko, *Der Traum vom Gluck*, p. 507, no. 16.4. This sort of costume was one of a few identified in the nineteenth century as "Elizabethan." For numerous examples, see Joseph Nash, *The Mansions of England in the Olden Time*, 4 vols. (London: T. M. Lean, 1839–1849), Speke Hall.

[17]The major study of Rembrandt's painting of the Syndics of the Cloth Guild is H. van de Waal, "*The Syndics* and their Legend," which is chapter 12 in H. van de Waal, *Steps towards Rembrandt* (Amsterdam and London: North-Holland Publishing Company, 1974), pp. 247–92.

[18]The sketch is published in Mary B. Sherwood, *Pilgrim: A Biography of William Brewster* (Falls Church, Va.: Great Oak Press of Virginia, 1982), illustrations between pp. 128 and 129.

[19]Charles Hubert de Stuers, *Het Lithografisch Werk van August Allebé, Beschrijvende Catalogus met Inleiding* (Utrecht: De Ploeg, 1929; diss. Utrecht, 1929), p. 99, no. 28. The lithograph was made in 1860, drawn by Allebé on commission from Schwartze, printed on Chinese paper by the Parisian firm of Bertauts, Rue Cadet 11, as stated on the stone, below the image. De Stuers catalogues the lithograph as: "The Pilgrimfathers Holding their first meeting for public worship in Noord-Amerika." Postcards of the lithograph were published in 1960 by the verger of Amsterdam's Oude Kerk, A. Stout, who numbered the figures depicted and identified them each with the name of a specific *Mayflower* passenger. His source for these identifications is unknown.

[20]In King, *The Mayflower Miracle*, p. 103, the picture is captioned: "Once the Pilgrims had built their Community Hall they were able to hold their first full prayer service on shore." This is consistent with the information accompanying the painting when it was exhibited in Amsterdam at the Arti et Amicitiae exhibition of works by "Living Masters" in 1858, no. 160. After a brief historical identification of the Pilgrims and their 1620 emigration to America, the viewer learned that "A common blockhouse was built and being finished on a Saturday, the next day it was consecrated by a first religious celebration in America." (Information from the Rijksbureau voor Kunsthistorische Documentatie, The Hague.)

[21]The earliest example of a depiction of Luther in this pose is a sculpture from 1752–1753 by Johann Daniel Schnorr (1717–1784), illustrated in Jutte Strehle, ed., *Luther mit dem Schwan, Tod und Verklarung eines grossen Mannes* (Berlin: Verlag Schelzky and Jeep for the Lutherhalle Wittenberg, 1996; exhibition catalogue 21 February–10 November 1996), p. 92, no. 21. Luther in his study extending the arm of eloquence is seen in a lithograph from 1817 by Sigfried Detlef Bendixen; illustrated in Strehle, *Luther mit dem Schwan*, p. 103, no. 53. Ten years later, Franz Schnorr's lithograph repeats the general pose, but has Luther holding a book in his left hand, rather than an open book on a lectern, as in Bendixen's version; see Strehle, *Luther mit dem Schwan*, p. 97, no. 30. Schnorr's print was the evident model for a lithograph by Fr. C. Wentzel, published in 1883. Wentzel's version has the heavenward gaze also seen in Schwartze's earlier Pilgrim painting; see Gerhard Seib, ed., and Christian Rietschel, *Luther in Portrait, Druckgrafik 1550–1900* (Marburg/Lahn: Jonas Verlag fur Kunst und Literatur, for Stadt Bad Oeynhausen, 1983), p. 56, no. 51. A drawing of Luther before the Reichsdag at Worms, by Wilhelm von Kaulbach, has the Reformer standing off-center to the left, with his left arm extended and his hand in the gesture of eloquence and his right hand holding a book, all quite like Schwartze's Pilgrim religious leader; see Hofmann, *Luther und die Folgen fur die Kunst*, pp. 510–11, no. 387. A similar composition and pose are seen in K. F. Lessing's 1842 painting of Jan Hus before the Council at Constance; Gotz Pochat, "Friedrich Theodor Vischer: Gedanken zur Form und Funktion der Historienmalerei im 19. Jahrhundert," E. Mai and A. Repp-Eckert, *Historienmalerei in Europa: Paradigmen in Form, Funktion und Ideologie* (Mainz am Rhein: P. von Zabern, 1990), pp. 253–61, specifically p. 255, fig. 1. Lessing was one of the Dusseldorf artists under whom Schwartze studied, besides with Schadow and with Leutze, who is best known in America for his painting of *Washington Crossing the Delaware*.

[22]Joachim Kruse and Minni Maedebach, *Luthers Leben in Illustrationen des 18. und 19. Jahrhunderts* (Coburg: Joachim Kruse, 1980; exhibition catalogue 23 April–5 October 1980, Kunstsammlungen der Veste Coburg), p. 92, no. 33.5: Luther before the Reichstag at Worms, unsigned engraving, Germanisches Nationalmuseum Nurnberg, Inv.-Nr. H.B. 25770,5; Kapsel 1249a.

[23]Dedalo Carasso, ed., *Helden van het Vaderland, Onze Geschiedenis in 19de-eeuwse Taferelen Verbeeld, De Historische Galerij van Jacob de Bos Jacobszoon, 1850–1863* (Amsterdam: Amsterdams Historisch Museum and Van Soeren and Co., 1991), p. 99, no. 122. The caption continues the descriptive propaganda of the victorious Contra-Remonstrant party, stating inaccurately that "Some preachers departed from the established teaching that

people called the 'orthodox'. . . At the head of the dissidents stood Arminius." In fact the Contraremonstrants supported an innovation on the point of predestination, not found in Calvin, while Arminius expounded and elaborated traditional teachings. On Arminius, see Carl O. Bangs, *Arminius: A Study in the Dutch Reformation* (2d ed., Grand Rapids: Francis Asbury Press/Zondervan, 1985).

[24]The first edition of Ripa was in 1593, with many subsequent editions. Throughout Europe, this became a handbook for artists composing histories and allegories. The first alphabetized arrangement of the allegorical personifications was in the Dutch translation: see Jochen Becker (intro.), *Cesare Ripa, Iconologia of Uytbeeldinghe des Verstandts* (Amsterdam: Dirck Pietersz. Pers, 1644; facsimile edition, Soest: Davaco publishers, 1971), pp. 394–97 for "Welspreeckentheyt. Eloquenza," particularly p. 495, where the personification of eloquence is described as holding a book in the right hand, with the left hand raised and the index finger extended. Further, see H.-F. Gravelet and C.-N. Cochin, *Iconologie par Figures, ou Traite Complet des Allegories, Emblemes, etc. A L'Usage des Artiestes, en 350 Figures* (Paris: Luttre, n.d.; facsimile edition, Geneva: Minkoff Reprint, 1972), no. 9, Eloquence. Gravelet and Cochin is cited in J. Traeger, "Kaiserliche Inkarnationen: Napoleon-Bilder, von Jacques-Louis David zu Heinrich Heine," Mai and Repp-Eckert, *Historiemalerei in Europa*, p. 147, fig. 10.

[25]The Wesley portrait appears, among other places, in Alfred Cobban, ed., *The Eighteenth Century: Europe in the Age of Enlightenment* (New York: McGraw-Hill, 1969), p. 323. A similar pose characterizes the central figure in the 1791 drawing by Jacques-Louis David, depicting the *Oath of the Tennis Court;* illustrated in the same volume, p. 324, and in Hofmann, *Luther und die Folgen fur die Kunst*, p. 519, fig. 393b. Washington Allston's painting of *Belschazzar's Feast* (1817–43, unfinished; Detroit Institute of Arts) depicts the prophet Daniel in the pose of Eloquence, with his left arm extended, hand open, but the right arm is down and the hand is in a fist. Among the unfinished parts of the painting is the fist. This painting is illustrated in William H. Gerdts and Mark Thistlethwaite, *Grand Illusions, History Painting in America* (Fort Worth: Amon Carter Museum, 1988), p. 23, fig. 13.

[26]On the rise of individual commemorative statues, see W. Telesko, "Der Denkmalskult im 19. Jahrhundert," in *Der Traum vom Gluck*, pp. 251–55; the Luther monument by Johann Gottfried Schadow and Karl Friedrich Schinkel is illustrated on p. 252; see also, W. Schulz, *Martin Luther, Fuhrer zu den Lutherstatten* (Berlin: Stiftung Deutschlandhaus Berlin, 1982), p. 113, fig. 32; Hofmann, *Luther und die Folgen fur die Kunst*, p. 515, fig. 389b.

[27]Famous people, on the other hand, might themselves become more attractive by association with these chairs. Calvin Coolidge sat in Governor Bradford's chair in 1921, thereby achieving identification with the traditional values honored at the celebration of the Pilgrims' tercentenary. This political theater was one of the aspects of the Pilgrim leaders' chairs featured in a very interesting exhibition titled "Great Chairs, Great Leaders," organized by Karin Goldstein, Curator of Collections, Pilgrim Hall. The tradition of providing outsize chairs (thrones) for political leaders is discussed in Theodor H. Lunsingh Scheurleer, "De Stoel van den Stadhouder," *Oud-Holland* 63 (1948): 189–204.

[28]C. Wyllys Elliott, "'The Good Old Times' at Plymouth," *Harper's New Monthly Magazine* 54 (December 1876–May 1877): 180–96.

[29]Jane G. Austin, "The wife of John Carver," *Harper's New Monthly Magazine* 40 (December 1869–May 1870): 231–39.

[30]The moralizing approach to architecture was consistent with the common identification of simplicity, as exemplified by the New England meeting house, with purity.

[31]Andrew Martindale, *The Triumphs of Caesar by Andrea Mantegna in the Collections of Her Majesty the Queen at Hampton Court* (London: Harvey Miller, 1979).

[32]On the topic of Triumphs in general, see Werner Weisbach, *Trionfi* (Berlin: G. Grote'sche Verlagsbuchhandlung, 1919). Further, see Roy Strong, *Splendour at Court* (London, 1973); Strong, *Art and Power: Renaissance Festivals 1450–1650* (Woodbridge: Boydell, 1984); Strong, *The Tudor and Stuart Monarchy: Pageantry, Painting, Iconography* (Woodbridge: Boydell, 1995); Barbara Wisch and Susan Scott Munshower, *"All the world's a stage . . ." Art and Pageantry in the Renaissance and Baroque, Part 1, Triumphal Celebrations and the Rituals of Statecraft, Part 2, Theatrical Spectacle and Spectacular Theatre*, 2 vols. (University Park, Penn.: Department of Art History, Pennsylvania State University, 1990; Papers in Art History from the Pennsylvania State University, vol. 6); Jean Jacquot, ed., *Les Fetes de la Renaissance*, 3 vols. (Paris: Editions du Centre national de la recherche scientifique, 1956, 1960, 1975).

[33]For example, Anna G. Bennett, *Five Centuries of Tapestry from the Fine Arts Museums of San Francisco* (Rutland, Vt.: Charles E. Tuttle, for the Fine Arts Museums of San Francisco, 1976), pp. 86–89, no. 17; pp. 96–101, nos. 19–21; Bertrand Jestaz and Roseline Bacou, *Jules Romain, L'Histoire de Scipion, Tapisseries et Dessins* (Paris: Ministère de la Culture et de la Communication, Éditions de la Réunion des musées nationaux, 1978; exhibition catalogue Grand Palais, 26 May–2 October 1978).

[34]The series of woodcuts has been republished (reduced to 47 percent of the original size): Stanley Appelbaum, *The Triumph of Maximilian I, 137 Woodcuts by Hans Burgkmair and Others* (New York: Dover, 1964); this has information about earlier editions. A good recent study is Larry Silver, "Paper Pageants: The Triumphs of Emperor Maximilian I," Wisch and Munshower, *Art and Pageantry in the Renaissance and Baroque*, 1:292–332.

[35]The woodcuts of the triumphal arch have been republished (reduced to 79 percent of the original size): *Maximilian's Triumphal Arch, Woodcuts by Albrecht Dürer and Others* (New York: Dover, 1972); this has information about earlier republication.

[36]Von Roeder-Baumbach, *Versieringen bij Blijde Inkomsten Gebruikt in de Zuidelijke Nederlanden Gedurende de 16de en 17de Eeuw* (Antwerp, 1943); John Landwehr, *Splendid Ceremonies, State Entries and Funerals in the Low Countries,*

1515–1791, A Bibliography (Nieuwkoop: B. de Graaf and Leiden: A. W. Sijthof, 1971).

[37]A depiction by Caspar Geratius of the Antwerp arch designed by Peter Paul Rubens was published in Antwerp by Iohannes Meursius in 1641; see Landwehr, *Splendid Ceremonies*, no. 99. This arch was to celebrate the entry of Archduke Ferdinand of Austria.

[38]Besides publications mentioned in Landwehr's bibliography, see Jeremy D. Bangs, *Cornelis Engebrechtsz's Leiden: Studies in Cultural History* (Assen: Van Gorcum, 1979), pp. 107–12, chap. 11, "The 'Joyous Entries' of Maximilian and Charles."

[39]This topic is thoroughly studied in Van de Waal, *Drie Eeuwen vaderlandsche Geschied-Uitbeelding*. Representing the old days by using clothing from only a couple generations back explains the costumes in the anonymous painting, ca. 1820, of the *Landing of the Pilgrims* (Pilgrim Hall), in which several of the figures wear coats and hats of a style from the late eighteenth century. As Pilgrim historian James Baker has pointed out, this 1820 concept of the past accounts for the nineteenth-century invention of the Pilgrim buckled hat, a detail that did not exist in the seventeenth century, but which became one of the attributes of the imaginary Pilgrim in the twentieth century.

[40]Jeremy D. Bangs, *Church Art and Architecture in the Low Countries before 1566* (Kirksville: Sixteenth Century Journal Press, 1997; Sixteenth Century Essays and Studies, vol. 37), pp. 76–79.

[41]An anonymous engraving depicting the inaugural pageant of the University of Leiden, 8 February 1575, is reproduced in R. E. O. Ekkart, *Athenae Batavae, De Leidse Universiteit, The University of Leiden* (Leiden: Universitaire Pers Leiden, 1975), pp. 14–15. An example of the engraving is in the collections of Plimoth Plantation. An image related to this triumph of Scripture is seen as the title page of the officially sanctioned Dutch Reformed translation of the Bible, the "Staten Vertaling" (States General's Translation, roughly equivalent to the King James Version), published in Leiden in 1637. The title text is placed on an apparent tablet in front of the architectural surroundings of a triumphal arch. Triumphal arch imagery appears commonly on title pages in the sixteenth century. The boat with Muses in the 1575 Leiden triumph calls attention to the fact that, although the Oxford English Dictionary gives a different etymology for the word "float" meaning a parade wagon, it probably comes from the use of decorated barges in triumphal entries with a water-borne component, such as the Leiden triumph, and that of the Earl of Leicester in the Hague in 1586, as well as various celebrations in Venice, London, and elsewhere.

[42]For the woodcuts, see Weisbach, *Trionfi*, p. 95, fig. 41. The tapestry series is in the Convent of the Descalzas Reales, Madrid. One panel is illustrated in Herman Liebaers et al., *Flemish Art: From the Beginning till Now* (New York: Arch Cape Press, 1985), p. 458.

[43]See *Jacobi Franci Historische Beschreibung aller denckwürdigen Historien, so sich hin und wider in Europe, in hoch und nider Teutschland, auch in Franckreich, Schott- unnd Engeland, Hispanien, Indien, Hungarn, Polen, Siebenbürgen, Wallachen, Moldaw, Türcken &c. vor und hierzwischen nechstverschiener Franckfurter Fastenmesse, biss auff Herbstmesse dieses 1625. Jahrs verlauffen und zugetragen* (Frankfurt am Mayn: Sigismundum Latomum, alias Meurer, 1625), p. 5.

[44]A 1778 etching of the 1775 parade by Simon Fokke after a design by Johannes le Francq van Berkhey is illustrated in Ekkart, *Athenae Batavae*, pp. 50–51, no. 80.

[45]Terence Ranger and Eric Hobsbawm, *The Invention of Tradition* (Cambridge and New York: Cambridge University Press, 1983), p. 4; see also pp. 9–10, 16, 35.

[46]Nineteenth-century triumphal processions in Germany and Austria are discussed by Werner Telesko, "Der Triumph- und Festzug im Historismus," *Der Traum vom Gluck*, pp. 290–96, including an illustration (p. 293) of a float from 1879 allegorically representing railroads, derived from the triumphal wagons imagined for Keiser Maximilian.

[47]David Glassberg, *American Historical Pageantry: The Uses of Tradition in the Early Twentieth Century* (Chapel Hill: University of North Carolina Press, 1990), pp. 265–66. On the tercentenary pageant, see Joseph Dillaway Sawyer, *"The Pilgrim Spirit" Shown in the Pilgrim Pageant Staged at Plymouth, Massachusetts, July and August, 1921, Supplemented by An Illustrated Portrayal of the Separatists' Struggles from Spiritual and Bodily Bondage to Freedom* (New York: Century History Co., 1921).

[48]Bittinger, *The Story of the Pilgrim Tercentenary Celebration*, p. 52.

[49]Ibid., p. 43.

[50]Ibid., p. 48.

[51]Ibid., p. 49. Regarding "historical accuracy," it is curious that among the Dutch towns in this scene one discovers (p. 65) the German town of Emden. Professor Albert Eekhof of the University of Leiden was an invited guest at the first performance, writing later (p. 68) that he "felt the pageant was of a remarkable historical accuracy and [I] was very proud of the tribute paid to my city and University of Leyden."

[52]Besides the analysis in Van de Waal, *Drie Eeuwen Vaderlandsche Geschied Uitbeelding*, and in Telesko, *Der Traum vom Gluck*, see Lowenthal, *The Past is a Foreign Country*.

[53]"We find no record of summer vacations among the ministers of those times." A. Carey, "Plymouth, the Pilgrims and Puritans," *National Magazine* 5 (1854): 508–22.

[54]Elliott, "'The Good Old Times' at Plymouth," p. 196.

[55]Carey, "Plymouth, the Pilgrims and Puritans."

[56]A. Stevens, "The Religious Scarecrow of the Age," *National Magazine* 5 (1854): 523–28.

[57]J. W. de Forest, "Visit to the Isle of the Puritans," *Harper's New Monthly Magazine* 31 (June–November 1865): 561–70.

S E C T I O N V I I

Genealogy and Historical Research

On the Importance of Genealogical Methodology in Researching Early New England Folk Portraitists

Arthur B. and Sybil B. Kern

DURING THE PAST twenty-six years we have been actively engaged in research and writing relative to American folk art of the eighteenth and nineteenth centuries. The majority of our twenty projects have centered on the identification of little-known portraitists, their work, lives, and the gathering of information concerning the subjects of their paintings. What very early became clear was the importance of genealogical methodology in these endeavors. To illustrate this, we have selected six of the portrait painters we investigated and will review the steps taken in our research.

Benjamin Greenleaf

One of the earliest of our studies was on Benjamin Greenleaf. He had first been called to general attention by a 1947 article by renowned art historian Jean Lipman. In this publication, which included a checklist of his ten known portraits, Greenleaf was identified as the noted educator and mathematician of this name from Bradford, Massachusetts.[1] This identification, except for occasional rumblings of disbelief from Bradford historians, had been accepted without question.

We became interested in Greenleaf in 1974 on coming upon a pair of his reverse paintings on glass. At the time we knew nothing about the artist and consulted Groce and Wallace's *Dictionary of Artists in America, 1564–1860*.[2] There we found him described as a portrait painter on glass, born in Haverhill, Massachusetts, "from 1814 to 1836 . . . a preceptor of Bradford Academy, Bradford (Mass.), and it was during these years (until about 1825) that he painted his known portraits on glass." This and other biographical material concerning his service in the state legislature, his founding of the Bradford Teachers Seminary, and his writing of mathematics textbooks was derived from the previously noted Lipman article and from the *Dictionary of American Biography*.[3] What puzzled us was the fact that nowhere in the latter's lengthy treatment of Greenleaf is there any mention of his having been a portrait painter. Nowhere in the Bradford community, where he lived and taught for about fifty years, is there a trace of his activity as a painter. Furthermore, the years from 1814 to 1817 were particularly busy ones for the educator, as indicated by the fact that the number of students at Bradford Academy increased from 10 to 147 during that period. Yet those same years were the ones in which the painter of this name was producing his greatest number of portraits while traveling through Maine, New Hampshire, and Massachusetts. Finally, in her article on Greenleaf, Lipman fails to give any reason for her conclusion that artist and educator were one and the same.[4]

But if the painter was not the educator, who was he? Reviewing publications on early American folk art, we found a clue. Clara Endicott Sears, in *Some American Primitives*,[5] reproduced a letter from a historian in which reference is made to the portrait painter Benjamin Greenleaf as being of Phippsburg, Maine. Also suggesting a Maine origin for the artist was a 1956 letter from the curator of the Bowdoin College Museum of Art in Brunswick, Maine, stating, "The only information we have uncovered is undoubtedly familiar to you—namely that Benjamin Greenleaf, painter of primitive portraits, is said to have lived in Phippsburg—down the river from Bath, about 1810 to 1817."[6]

With these two references suggesting that the artist had lived in Maine, we next turned to a review of federal census indexes for Maine. From these we found a Benjamin Greenleaf at Wiscasset, Lincoln County, Maine (close to Phippsburg) in 1810; in 1820 not one, but two Benjamin Greenleafs resided in Wiscasset. Pursuing this lead, we consulted a published genealogy of the Greenleaf family and found that a Benjamin had been born 8 September 1759 in Westport (near Wiscasset) to Samuel and Hephzibah (Preble) Greenleaf.[7] Wiscasset vital statistics recorded the marriage of this Benjamin to Rachel Arnold of Pownalborough, Maine, on 7 January 1784. The couple resided in Wiscasset, where they raised ten children; Benjamin Jr. was born there 7 April 1786.

Since the known Greenleaf portraits had been painted between 1804 and 1818, either father or son could have been the artist. Lincoln County land and probate records indicate that the elder Greenleaf was an active farmer and landowner between 1784 and 1842. Busy operating his farm and buying land, at the same time raising ten children, he seemed an unlikely choice for our artist. In contrast, according to town and county records, his son owned no property and only sporadically paid a poll tax. Of the two, Benjamin Greenleaf the son would more likely have been the itinerant artist.

There were, however, three disturbing problems with the hypothesis that Benjamin Greenleaf Jr. of Wiscasset was the painter. First, in 1804—the date of the portrait of Dr. Cotton Tufts, Greenleaf's earliest known painting—Benjamin Greenleaf Jr. of Wiscasset would have been only eighteen years of age. Would one so young be summoned all the way from Maine to distant Weymouth, Massachusetts, for so important a commission—to paint a leading physician and one of the founders of the Massachusetts Medical Society?[8] Second, Benjamin Greenleaf Jr. died in 1849 at the age of sixty-three, thirty-one years after the last known portrait was painted. Finally, we were unable to find any primary evidence of his having been a painter.

It was the discovery of the 1803 portrait of Jacob Goold (*Figure 1*) that led to the establishment of the artist's correct identity. A study of the genealogy of the Goold family proved, without question, that the artist was originally from Hull, Massachusetts—not the educator from Bradford, nor the young man from Wiscasset.

Jacob Goold, the son of Captain John and Lydia (Jacobs) Goold, and grandson of Robert and Elizabeth (Bosworth) Goold, was born in Hull on 10 January 1720. He lived most of his life in nearby Weymouth, where he died 13 May 1804, about one year after his portrait was painted. Another son of Robert Goold and his second wife, Sarah, and half-brother to Captain John Goold, was Joseph, who married Mary Prince. Their son Joseph, who was Jacob Goold's cousin, married Hannah Binney of Hull on 7 June 1739;[9] and their daughter, Mary, was wed to John Greenleaf of Boston on 27 April 1768.[10] The first child of John and Mary (Goold) Greenleaf, born in Hull on 13 January 1769, was Benjamin.[11]

That this Benjamin Greenleaf was the limner was verified through further genealogical investigation. On 26 July 1781 his widowed mother married Lieutenant Nicholas Phillips of Weymouth who, in turn, died on 8 August 1797.[12] A search of probate records disclosed two bonds, one naming Mary (Goold) (Greenleaf) Phillips guardian of the children and the second stipulating that the signers were responsible for her carrying out her duties.[13] The latter states the following: "Know All Men by these Presents, That we Mary Phillips, Widow, Elnathan Bates, Gentleman, both of Weymouth and Benjamin Greenleaf, of Dorchester, Painter, all in the county of Norfolk. . . ." That this Benjamin Greenleaf was a portrait painter is supported by the fact that Elnathan Bates, one of

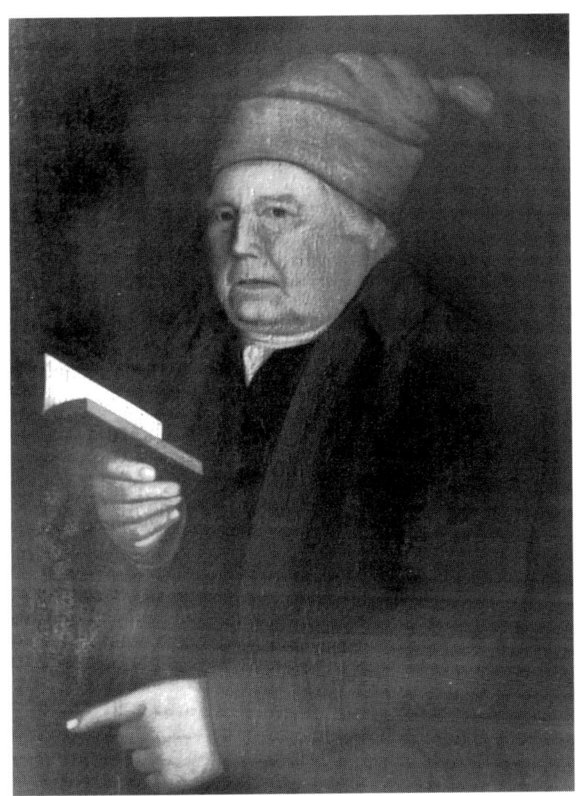

Figure 1 Jacob Goold. Benjamin Greenleaf (1769–after 1818). Weymouth, Massachusetts, 1803. Oil on canvas, laid down on wood panel; 29 × 21¾ inches. Inscribed with blunt instrument on reverse: "Jacob Goold now Ag. 84. Benjamin Greenleaf Painter 1803." Courtesy of the Society for the Preservation of New England Antiquities.

the signers of this document, was painted by Greenleaf in 1814.[14] An additional piece of evidence is that the signature of Benjamin Greenleaf on this same document is identical to that on his portrait of Mary Ann Cushing Nichols. On 20 November 1779 Greenleaf married Abigail Greenleaf Rhodes, also a resident of Dorchester;[15] he died of apoplexy in Weymouth on 10 January 1821.[16]

From his earliest known portrait of Jacob Goold, painted in 1803, to his last known works of 1818, more than sixty portraits can now be attributed to Benjamin Greenleaf. All, with the exception of the few on wood panel and on canvas, are reverse paintings on glass. In most instances the subject is identified by an inscription on the stretcher, backing board, or on an attached label. Genealogical research of each of these, utilizing a variety of sources including published family genealogies, vital records, town records, census records, and cemetery records, led to our uncovering a chain that started with Jacob Goold, prominent citizen of Weymouth, and relative of the artist, as well as five other Goolds who sat for Greenleaf. The next link in the chain was Cotton Tufts, another leading member of the Weymouth community and undoubtedly a friend of Jacob Goold. These were followed by many other portraits, painted between 1806 and 1812, of persons living in Weymouth and the nearby towns of Hingham, Braintree, and Newton. Most of the subjects in these four towns were related to each other or to the artist. In 1813 Greenleaf was active in Hopkinton and Hanover, New Hampshire, these subjects being linked to each other, to Greenleaf, or to some of those he had painted in Massachusetts. In 1815 he was back in Weymouth, judging from his portrait of Elnathan Bates. The year 1816 finds him active in eastern Maine, particularly in Bath, Paris, and Portland; once again, marital connections played a major role in his obtaining these commissions.

Greenleaf's portrait of Dr. Samuel Adams of Bath (*Figure 2*) is of particular significance. Our search for information concerning this prominent physician led to his diary in the collection of New York's Fifth Avenue Public Library. The entry therein for 21 November 1816 reports: "Had my likeness taken today by a Mr. Greenleaf who came to our house on Monday last." On 14 December he writes: "Mr. B. Greenleaf's board is settled up to this day—Ballance [*sic*] of all accts—Board to begin anew from this morning." These diary entries not only confirm Greenleaf's presence in Bath in 1816, but also document the practice common to itinerant artists of the eighteenth and nineteenth centuries of temporarily residing at the homes of their subjects. Judging from the length of Greenleaf's stay, he probably remained with Dr. Adams while doing the portraits of the doctor as well as his relatives and neighbors. For several of our other subjects, the personal diary was an equally valuable source of information.

Early in 1817 Greenleaf was in the Boston area, for it was then that he did the portrait of Mary Ann Cushing Nichols as well as those of several other children of that town. Later in 1817 and 1818 he was back in Maine where he painted, among others, the

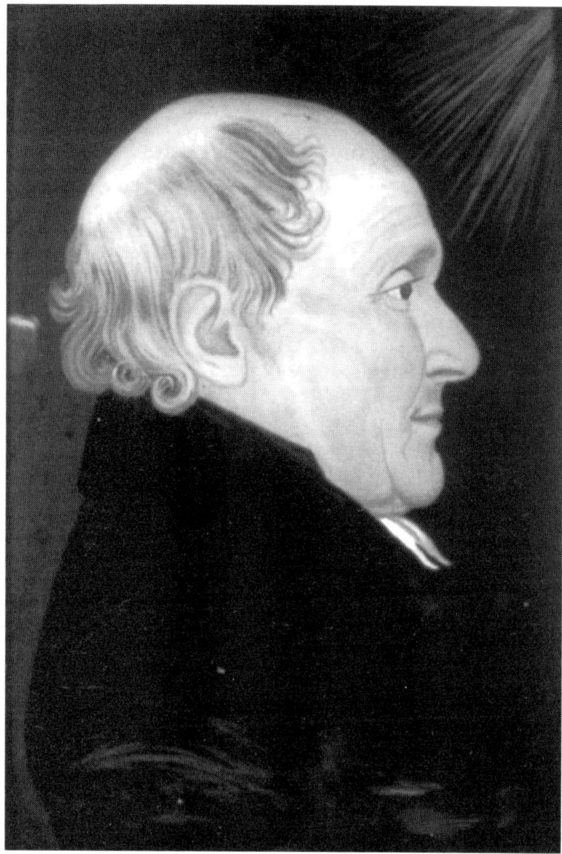

Figure 2 Dr. Samuel Adams. Benjamin Greenleaf (1769–after 1818). Bath, Maine, 1816. Reverse painting on glass; 29 × 21¾ inches. Inscription on the original backing (now missing): "The portrait of Doctor Samuel Adams AE 72, Painted at Bath by Benjamin Greenleaf, November 1816." The Corning Museum of Glass, Corning, New York.

portrait of Dummer Sewall, a very important resident of Bath, who was related to or associated with many of Greenleaf's earlier subjects.

Review of newspapers from those towns in which the artist worked failed to uncover any advertisements by him. This is not surprising, since the strong links formed by friendship and marital connections made these unnecessary for him to obtain commissions.

J. A. Davis

General knowledge of the work of J. A. Davis goes back to 1923 with the publication of an article by Frederick Fairchild Sherman in which are pictured three stylistically similar unsigned watercolor and pencil portraits.[17] Because these were found in Norwich, Connecticut, Sherman first attributed them to James Sanford Ellsworth and later to Alexander Emmons, both of whom were folk artists who had worked in that area. It was not until fifty years later that Gail and Norbert Savage reported on approximately forty portraits by this same hand; three of these bore the signature "J. A. Davis."[18] A 1974 exhibition at the Art Institute of Chicago included fifty-one portraits that could be attributed to this artist; since then, at least a hundred more have been discovered. Despite this large body of work, the identity of the artist remained a mystery.

The catalogue for this 1974 exhibition[19] suggests that J. A. Davis might have been Joshua A. Davis or Joshua N. Davis, both listed as portrait painters in the Providence (Rhode Island) city directories for 1852 to 1856. However, we quickly discarded these possibilities—not only do the dates not correspond to the known period of the artist's activity, but we were unable to find any evidence to support the consideration of either Joshua Davis.

We then sought the name "J. A. Davis" in earlier years of the Providence city directory, and in the 1830 through 1860 census indexes for Rhode Island and Connecticut—the two states in which Davis's subjects lived—but without success. Equally disappointing were a search for advertisements by the artist in local newspapers, the hunt for a useful published genealogy for the Davis family, and the study of town histories and vital statistics. Finally, the name "Jane A. Davis" was discovered in *Benn's Index of Rhode Island Graves*. Even more interesting was the fact that on reviewing the microfilm we found not the expected death notice, but the marriage notice reprinted from the *Manufacturers and Farmers Journal*: "February 4, 1841. In Warwick, Monday last by the Reverend Job Manchester, Mr. Edward N. Davis of Norwich, Conn. married Miss Jane Anthony, daughter of Giles Anthony, Esq., of Warwick." This raised the exciting possibility that Jane (Anthony) Davis might be the artist J. A. Davis.

Using the four names available—Jane Anthony, Jane (Anthony) Davis, Giles Anthony, and Edward N. Davis—we conducted a search of vital statistics, but without success. At the time, only a sketchy genealogy for the Anthony family could be found; so hoping for a lead we reviewed published genealogies of other prominent Rhode Island families. After many failures, these efforts were finally rewarded; in the volumes of the Greene family genealogy[20] we again found the name of Jane (Anthony) Davis. The first child of Giles and Sarah Robinson (Greene) Anthony of Warwick, Rhode Island, she was born 24 September 1821 and was said to have married Edward Nelson Davis on 1 February 1840. This last date is erroneous since the marriage was reported in 1841 by two Rhode Island newspapers, the previously noted *Manufacturers and Farmers Journal* and the 3 February 1841 issue of the *Republican Herald*. The genealogy gives no date of death but does note that on 25 June 1856, Jane's husband married her double first cousin, Eliza Greene. On consulting the Index of Deaths, Providence, 1851–1870, we found the following entry: "Davis, Jane A.—33 years. April 28, 1855." Her date of death was confirmed by both her cemetery record at Providence's Swan Point Cemetery and her death certificate found at the State Office Building in Providence. Her death certificate also records her death at the early age of thirty-three years from "consumption."

At this point we had established that Jane (Anthony) Davis was born in Rhode Island in 1821 and that she died there in 1855. These dates are significant since study of the dated portraits by J. A. Davis indicated that the artist's active period was between 1838 and 1854. On the basis of time, therefore, Jane (Anthony) Davis could have been J. A. Davis. Furthermore, she was a resident of Rhode Island and her husband was from Norwich, Connecticut, the two areas in which practically all of the artist's known sitters had lived and where most of the paintings had been found.

Realizing that all published facts had seemingly been exhausted, we started a search for Jane Anthony's living descendants, using (among other sources) city directories, cemetery listings, and probate records. Finally we made a most exciting discovery in the library of the New England Historic Genealogical Society—a family record for Edward and Jane (Anthony) Davis, compiled by their grandson, Edward Davis Anthony (1869–1948) of West Barrington, Rhode Island. This established the correct Davis line to follow and led us to a granddaughter of Jane's younger sister, Sally Ann.

The granddaughter had two letters addressed to Jane Anthony at the Warren Ladies Seminary in Warren, Rhode Island. The first, written by Jane's mother, Sarah Robinson (Greene) Anthony, was dated 24 May 1838, shortly after the school term had commenced; the second, from her maternal grandmother, Barbara (Low) Greene, was dated 6 June 1838. Significantly, there are no dated portraits by J. A. Davis before 1838, the year that seventeen-year-old Jane, away from home for the first time, attended the Warren Ladies Seminary. This suggests that she may have begun her serious painting while at the school and that the subjects of these early works could have been classmates, faculty, male students from the nearby Warren Academy, or local neighbors. That opportunity was present is evident from the school catalogue for the year ending 1838, found at the George Hail Memorial Library in Warren. The name of Jane Anthony of Warwick appears in the record of students, but only for the May through August term; drawing and painting are listed under tuition fees as available at an extra charge of three dollars.

The next phase of our research involved a review of those paintings by J. A. Davis that are dated and where the subject is identified by an inscription. The purpose of this was to determine whether there was a relationship between the subject and Jane (Anthony) Davis, thereby supporting the hypothesis that she was the artist. Starting with the earliest of the watercolors by J. A. Davis, the five painted in 1838 and 1839, a possible connection between subject and Jane Anthony could be demonstrated. George B. Sisson, the son of James and Sarah Sisson, was born in Warren on 22 July 1795, according to Warren vital records. On 13 January 1838 he married Eliza Ann Mason in Warren's St. Mark's Church, and the 1840 census shows him residing in Warren. Young Jane may possibly have boarded with the newlyweds. Not only was George B. Sisson in the right place at the right time, but, in addition, there was intermarriage between the extended Sisson and Greene-Anthony families.[21] The portrait of Samuel M. Demeritt, who was born in Barrington, New Hampshire, on 7 May 1811, is inscribed on its back with his name, age, and the words "By J. A. Davis July 23 & 24 1838," obviously written at a much later time; he was a schoolteacher and may have been teaching in Warren at the time

Jane Anthony was a student there. According to Warren vital records, Margaret Sharkey, whose portrait is dated 1839, was born in Ireland to James and Catherine Sharkey and died in Warren on 26 November 1901 at the age of eighty. In 1838, when Jane Anthony was at the Warren Ladies Seminary, she and Margaret Sharkey were the same age, and the two may possibly have been friends. Stephen N. Tingley was the subject of two almost identical 1839 portraits. He was born in 1816, the son of Benjamin and Polly Tingley of Cumberland, Rhode Island; his sister, Almira Amanda (Tingley) Wheaton, was the wife of the Methodist minister Reverend James Wheaton.[22] Significantly, three girls by the name of Wheaton were at the Warren Ladies Seminary with Jane.[23]

The double portrait of Jacob and Mary Withington (*Figure 3*) was painted in 1840. The New Hampshire 1840 census shows Jacob Withington as a resident of Manchester; both he and his wife are recorded there in the 1850 census. There is nothing to suggest that Jane was an itinerant artist, but there are several reasons why the Withingtons might have come to the Rhode Island area. First, Lydia Tingley, wife of Thomas Withington of Attleboro, Massachusetts (a town bordering on Rhode Island), was the sister of Benjamin Tingley, grandfather of the Stephen N. Tingley who had sat for the artist just one year earlier.[24] Second, Jacob Withington's brother, Samuel, and his family also lived in Attleboro in 1840.[25] Finally, and perhaps most important, Lydia (Claflin) Withington, Samuel's daughter-in-law, died in Attleboro in October 1840,[26] and Jacob and Mary may have been visiting there during Lydia's terminal illness.

On 1 February 1841, about four months after the Withington portraits were painted, Jane Anthony was married in Warwick, Rhode Island, to Edward Nelson Davis, the son of Hannah (Stafford) Davis of Providence and the late John Davis. John's will had been drawn up in 1825 at Warwick, where his family may have been neighbors of the Anthonys. After her husband's death in 1829, Hannah and her two sons, Edward and Benjamin, moved to Providence, where she is listed in the 1830 city directory. Both sons are listed in the 1838/1839 directory, but neither in 1841. By then, as indicated in the previously mentioned wedding notice, Edward was living in Norwich, Connecticut.

Jane was married to Edward by his uncle, the Reverend Job Manchester, pastor of the Old Baptist Church of the Warwick circuit, which included Cumberland, Rhode Island, and Plainfield, Norwich, and Voluntown, Connecticut. This is of particular importance since many of J. A. Davis's sitters, as well as relatives of Jane Anthony, were associated with the Baptist church or closely related Methodist-Episcopal churches within this circuit.

There are no dated portraits attributable to J. A. Davis between that of the Withingtons in September 1840 and the one of Caroline Frances Phillips of November 1842. This gap can be explained by the fact that Jane (Anthony) Davis would have been quite busy during this period making preparations for her wedding, the move from Rhode Island, and then the birth of her first child, Harriet Aspinwall Davis, on 10 January 1842.[27] According to the Rhode Island census of 1840, the Phillips family was living in Coventry, which lies about ten miles from Warwick, Jane Anthony's original home, and about twenty miles from Norwich, where Jane (Anthony) Davis lived at the time the portrait was painted.

An exciting discovery was a group of five J. A. Davis portraits, one of which has an inscription that identifies the subject as Jonathan E. Bowen and the date of execution as 1843. The 1850 Connecticut census lists Jonathan, then twenty-seven years of age, as a farmer born in [Thompson] Connecticut, and his wife, Mary, born in [Glocester] Rhode Island; vital statistics at the Thompson Town Hall (Marriages, Town of Thompson, 1840–1854), give the marriage of Jonathan E. Bowen and Mary Sayles, both of Thompson, as 12 February 1843. Since Jonathan was married in 1843 (the same year the portraits were done), and since Jonathan's is the only one of the five in which the subject is identified by an inscription on the face of the painting, it is likely that the portraits were commissioned in celebration of the wedding. Framed together with the portrait of Jonathan was that of a young woman, the backing board of which bears the pencil inscription in a later hand: "Ellis Bowen and Lydia Bowen / Jesse Bowen's father." Non-contemporary inscriptions are often erroneous. This subject identified here as Lydia is more likely Jonathan E.'s bride, Mary Sayles. Jonathan E. Bowen (whose middle name was Ellis) had

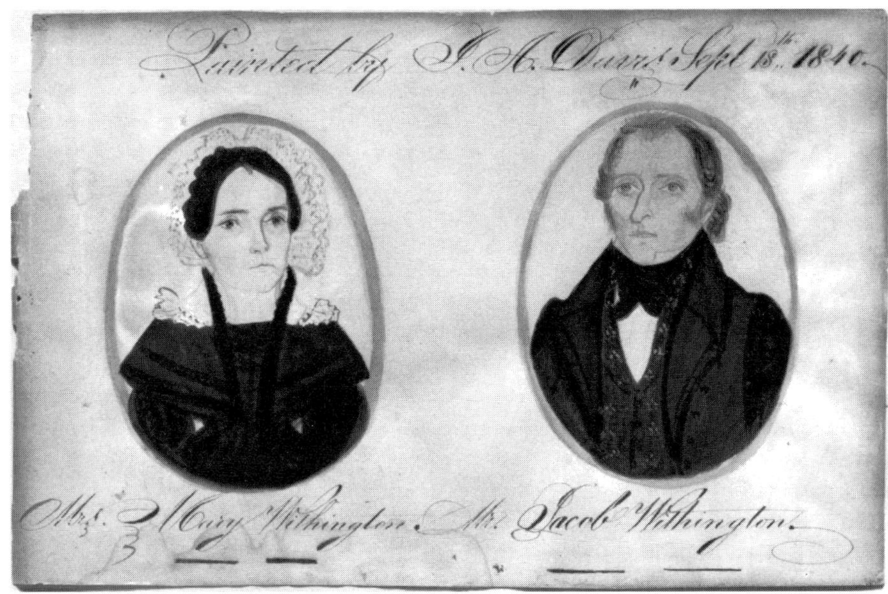

Figure 3 Jacob and Mary Withington. Jane (Anthony) Davis (1821–1855). Probably Rhode Island or Massachusetts, 1840. Watercolor and pencil on paper; 5 × 7¾ inches. Inscribed in ink on top of front of paper: "Painted by J. A. Davis September 18th 1840," and at bottom of paper: "Mrs. Mary Withington, Mr. Jacob Withington." This painting is unique among Davis's work in presentation of the subjects within painted ovals. Private collection.

a sister Lydia, who died the year he was married; by his wife Mary (Sayles) he was father of Jesse. A third portrait has on its backing board the same type of pencil inscription, identifying the subject as Millard Bowen, Jesse's grandfather (*Figure 4*). The fourth, on its backing board, is identified as "Lucy Bowen / Millard Bowen's wife," and the fifth is inscribed "Jane Bowen" near the top of the backing board and "Ellis Bowen's sister" near the bottom. The relationships among the family members are clarified by the 1850 Connecticut census, by Clarence Winthrop Bowen's genealogical history of families in the area of Woodstock, Connecticut,[28] and by a volume at the Thompson town hall (Town of Thompson, Births, Deaths, Marriages, vol. 3, 1847–1868). Millard Bowen (his first name incorrectly spelled "Willard" in the genealogy), born 11 February 1784, died 6 October 1852, a farmer of Thompson, married Lucy—as his second wife; she died 8 June 1857. Lydia, their first child, was born at Thompson in 1815 and died 30 June 1843. "Ellis" was Jonathan E., the son of Millard, brother of Lydia and Jane[29] and father of Jesse P., who was not born until 1845, after the portraits were executed. Since Jonathan's portrait is dated 1843, and the five are stylistically identical, it can be assumed that they were all painted at this time in Thompson, about thirty miles from Norwich. Attesting to the close relationship between Jane (Anthony) Davis and this Bowen family is the fact that William Bowen, listed in the 1850 census as residing at the home of Millard Bowen (and undoubtedly a relative), married Jeanette Greene, double cousin of Jane (Anthony) Davis. Mary T. Bowen of Warren, whose name was listed along with Jane's among the pupils attending the Warren Ladies Seminary in 1838, may also be linked to this family.

Three portraits of members of the Barber family were painted in 1844. That of Thankful Barber is inscribed with her name and age (forty-nine). By checking records for towns in the Norwich-Plainfield area, we learned from vital statistics of Voluntown, Connecticut, that Thankful Lewis of Rhode Island had been born 5 July 1795, confirming the age given in the inscription; that she had married Jabez Barber of

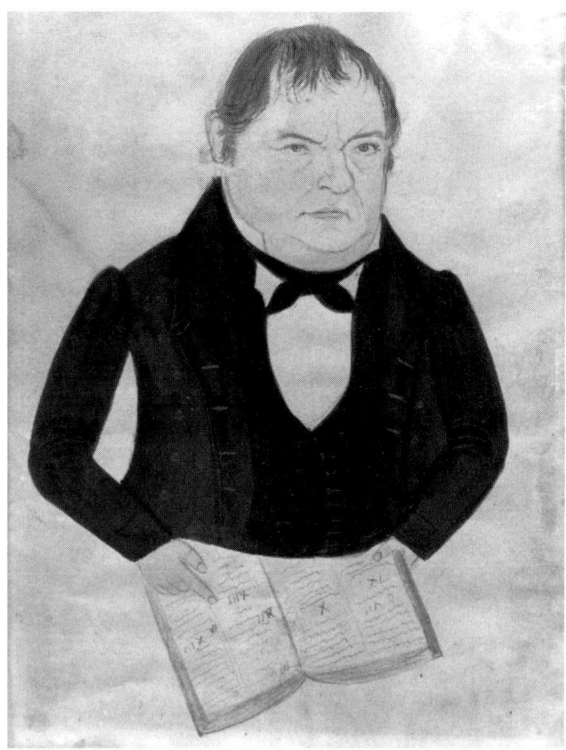

Figure 4 Millard Bowen. Jane (Anthony) Davis (1821–1855). Thompson, Connecticut, 1843. Watercolor and pencil on paper; 8 × 6 inches. Private collection.

Voluntown on 18 September 1814; and that their son John G., subject of the second portrait, was born in West Greenwich, Rhode Island, in 1832. The third portrait carries no inscription, but records at Old Sturbridge Village indicate that the subject was the daughter of Thankful Barber; a death record for Sabra Ann Barber, daughter of Jabez and Thankful, was found in Westerly, Rhode Island.[30]

The portrait inscribed "Hiram Browning, and Wife and Child," attributable to J. A. Davis, is dated (beneath the frame) "October 8, 1844." Hiram, the son of Avery and Mary (Arnold) Browning, was born 6 October 1816 at Exeter, Rhode Island, and married Prudence Barnes, daughter of Avery Barnes of Preston, Connecticut, in March 1839; the family resided on a farm in Preston. Their third child, Ruth Ann, shown with them in the triple portrait, was born 26 August 1844.[31]

Depictions of other Connecticut subjects by J. A. Davis, although not dated, were probably painted during the 1843–1844 period when the artist was active in that state. One is of George Bishop, shown by both the 1840 and 1850 census to be a resident of Ashford, Connecticut. This town lies only about seven miles from Willington, home of Eliza Snow, whose portrait was painted by J. A. Davis in 1844. Another is the double portrait of Eben Davis and his wife (*Figure 5*), which may have been commissioned to celebrate Eben's marriage on 18 September of that year, in Plainfield, Connecticut, to Rhoda Ann Thatcher. In 1820, the year after Rhoda Ann's birth in Plainfield, her father became pastor of the Methodist Episcopal church of East Greenwich, Rhode Island. In 1821 Jane Anthony was born in Warwick, Rhode Island (which abuts East Greenwich); it is quite possible that her parents knew Rhoda Ann's parents through church activities. Reverend Hezekiah Thatcher later was pastor of the Methodist church in Byfield, Massachusetts, where his daughter undoubtedly met Eben Davis; by 1840 the Thatcher family was back in Plainfield,[32] only about ten miles from Norwich, where Jane Anthony was living. A final portrait in this group is that of Mary (Ecclestone) Hoxie, also of Norwich. She married William C. Hoxie of Griswold, Connecticut, on 16 September 1844,[33] and the painting may have been done to commemorate their wedding.

Late in 1844 Edward and Jane returned to Rhode Island and took up residence in Providence. The 1844 Providence city directory includes Edward Davis, a clerk at 85 High Street. In the 1847–1848 directory he is listed at both 55 Westminster Street (his work address) and at 151 High Street (his home address).[34]

The portraits of Lydia Goddard and of James Bixby are each signed and dated "By J. A. Davis / Nov. 10, 1845" on the reverse. James, born in August 1824 at Quadic, Connecticut, later lived in Moosup, adjacent to Plainfield and nearby Webster, Massachusetts. He married Lydia about a year after their portraits were painted. Strong ties to Rhode Island are suggested by his mother's birth there and by his father's name which appears in the Providence city directory from 1858 through 1867.[35]

The final work of this period is inscribed "Portrait of Eunice A. Buss [or Busa] 1829, March 22 / age 16 years / daughter of David and Ar___na (Jones) Boss." A search of Rhode Island and Connecticut records failed to yield anything concerning a Buss or Busa family, but there were numerous Buss families in

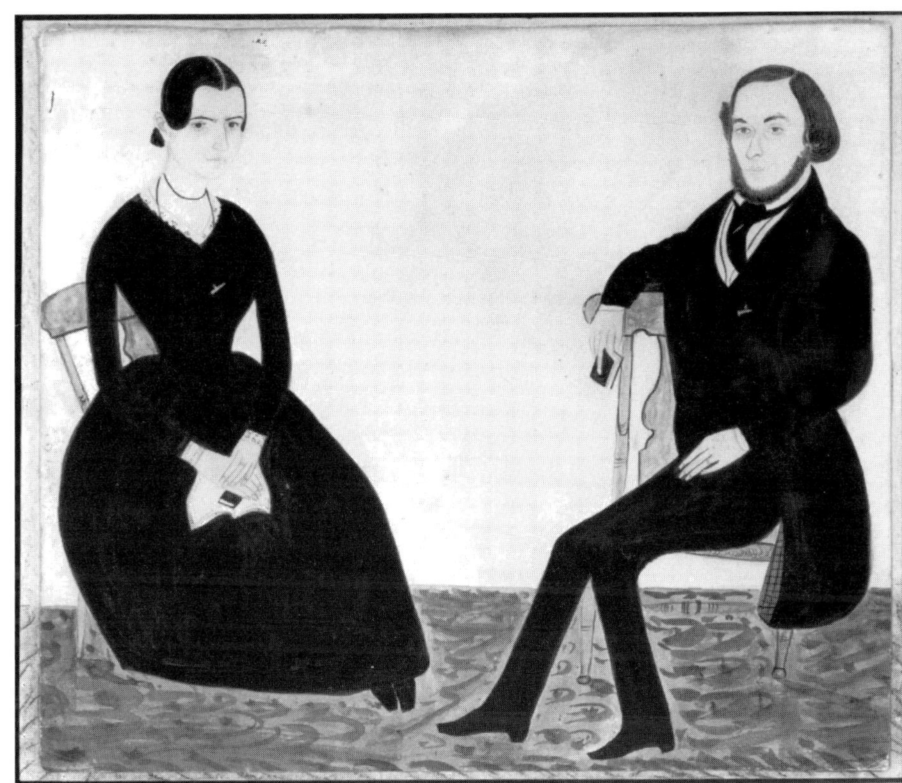

Figure 5 Eben and Rhoda Ann (Thatcher) Davis. Jane (Anthony) Davis (1821–1855). Plainfield, Connecticut, circa 1844. Watercolor and pencil on paper; 13½ × 15¾ inches. Pencil inscription on reverse of primary support: "Eben Davis / He and wife." A later pencil inscription on a fragment of the wood backing: "MR & Mrs EBEN DAVIS OF BYFIELD / MASS / PAINTED BY MR DAVIS BEFORE THEIR MARRIAGE / ABOUT . . . {1860}." Abby Aldrich Rockefeller Folk Art Museum, Williamsburg, Virginia.

both states. Most significant was the discovery of a Jeremiah Boss, his wife Euny Ann, and two children, listed in the 1840 and 1850 Rhode Island census as neighbors on High Street of Edward and Jane (Anthony) Davis. Further investigation revealed that Jeremiah's wife was actually Alcy Ann Manchester of Scituate, Rhode Island, a cousin of Reverend Job Manchester, the minister who was a cousin of Edward N. Davis and who had married him to Jane Anthony. Finally, instead of "1829 / age 16," the inscription should probably read "1816" (Alcy Ann's approximate birth date) and "age 29" (her age when the portrait was painted); the painting would thus date the portrait to 1845, when the Davis and Boss families were neighbors on Providence's High Street.

Another gap in the output of paintings by J. A. Davis occurs between those of 1845 and the ones of 1848. Like the hiatus between 1840 and 1842, this one can be related to an event in the life of Jane (Anthony) Davis. On 26 April 1847 Jane gave birth to her second child, John Edward Davis, in Providence.[36]

In 1848 J. A. Davis did the portraits of James Arnold; his son, Edward Greene Arnold; and the latter's wife and two children. James Arnold was born in Warwick, Rhode Island, in 1791, a contemporary of Giles Anthony, Jane's father.[37] Furthermore, his mother, Sarah Greene, was a distant relative of Jane's mother, and his great-grandfather was a brother of the great-grandfather of Jane's husband. Edward Greene Arnold was born in 1814 and in 1835 married Almaria Corbin, who was born at Woodstock, Connecticut, in 1816.[38] In view of family ties, and the fact that Woodstock is only a short distance from the Connecticut area where the Davises lived between

1840 and 1844, a close relationship probably developed between the two families during this period. Although the occasion for the 1848 portraits is unknown, visits by Jane to the Arnolds' home and vice versa are not unlikely in view of the short distance between Woodstock and Providence.

The last known portraits by J. A. Davis, painted between 1849 and 1854, were all of children and were probably executed in Rhode Island. In 1849 two were done of Ellen Augusta Smith. From the Daughters of the American Revolution records of Rhode Island births, marriages, and deaths, we learned that Jane's brother Edward Anthony had married an Elizabeth Smith. In addition, Joseph Warren Greene married a Mary Augusta Smith.[39] Records of Christ Church, Westerly, Rhode Island, contain an entry for the baptism on 2 December 1845 of Julia Augusta Smith, daughter of Stephen and Marcia Smith. These circumstances may serve to connect some or all of these Smith families to that of Jane (Anthony) Davis and to Westerly, not far from where Jane had lived.

The subject of the portrait *Little Girl with Parrot* was originally identified by descendants as "Annie E. Holland," whose portrait "was done by an itinerant artist who came through the village of Peace Dale (Rhode Island) sometime during the late 1800s." She has recently been correctly identified as Annie M. Sims, daughter of Sprague and Sarah (Holland) Sims. Her death on 5 January 1881, aged thirty-three years, is recorded in the registers of Christ Church, Westerly; Annie's age at death indicates a birth year of 1847. Judging from the appearance of the child in the portrait, this dating would be compatible with an 1849 date of execution.

The last known portrait by J. A. Davis, that of Louella P. Hodges, is dated August 1854. The daughter of Valorous and Hannah (Grover) Hodges, she was born 5 January 1852 in Mansfield, Massachusetts, about fifteen miles from Providence. Her maternal grandmother was Betsy (Brownell) Grover of Providence,[40] and the child may have been visiting her grandmother when the portrait was painted.

All of the above evidence, presented in our 1981 and 1991 articles on the identity of J. A. Davis, clearly established the fact that the artist was Jane (Anthony) Davis. Nevertheless, one thing continued to bother us: the 1838 portrait of Samuel Demeritt, the two of Stephen N. Tingley dated 1839, and the double portrait of the Withingtons painted in 1840 are all inscribed "By J. A. Davis," when Jane Anthony was not yet married. Available evidence suggested that the four inscriptions had been added by individuals other than the artist after her marriage, thus explaining use of the Davis name. This hypothesis has been confirmed by our recent discovery of a typical signed portrait by J. A. Davis, genealogical investigation of which has demonstrated that its inscription must have been added at a later time.[41]

The watercolor in question is that of a full-length standing boy, inscribed "Joseph Wanton Gardner / Born May 31 1836 / Taken Feb. 5 1841 / Aged 4 yrs. 9 mo. / By J. A. Davis" (*Figure 6*). A published 1907 genealogy of the Gardner family yielded the surprising information that Joseph Wanton Gardner was born 26 September 1799.[42] In 1841, when the portrait was painted, he would have been almost forty-two years of age, rather than the four years, nine months indicated by the painting's inscription. We found supporting evidence for the 1799 birth of Joseph Wanton Gardner in several other sources.[43] If the subject was not Joseph Wanton, who was he? He was Joseph Warren, fourth child of Joseph Wanton Gardner, born in March 1836 according to the family genealogy.[44] The Church of the Latter Day Saints International Genealogical Index records the birth of Joseph Warren Gardner at Exeter, Rhode Island, in March 1836. The fact that the name of the father is erroneously inscribed on the painting indicates that it was not placed there by the artist, who would undoubtedly have known the name of her subject; the inscription must have been added later by someone else, probably a descendant.

On 28 April 1855, just eight months following the execution of her last known painting (that of Louella P. Hodges in August 1854), Jane (Anthony) Davis died. She is buried in Providence's Swan Point Cemetery, also the final resting place of Alcy Ann Boss, one of J. A. Davis's subjects.

Joseph H. Davis

Another painter of folk portraits during the early nineteenth century, not related to Jane (Anthony) Davis, was Joseph H. Davis. Despite the fact that a

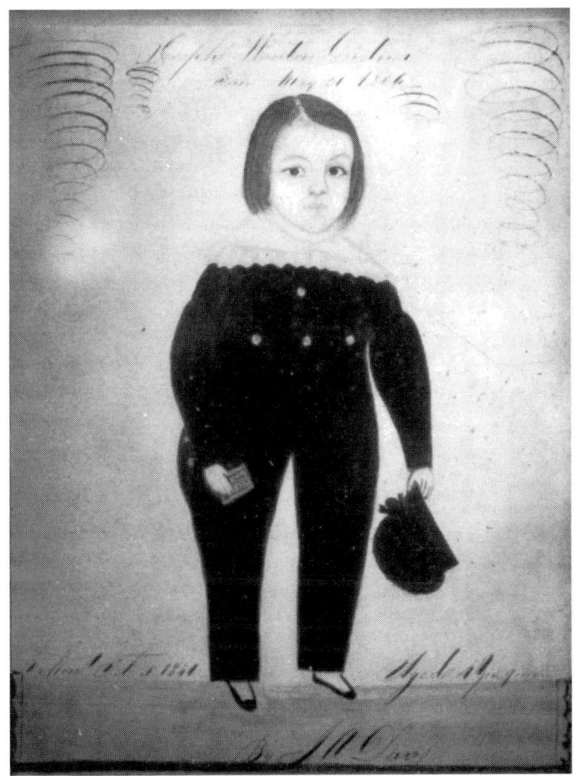

Figure 6 Joseph Warren Gardner. Jane (Anthony) Davis (1821–1855). Exeter, Rhode Island, 1841. Watercolor and pencil; 7½ × 6 inches. Ink inscription at top of front of paper: "Joseph Wanton [*sic*] Gardner / Born May 31 1836," and at bottom, "Taken Feb 5 1841 Aged 4 yrs. 9 mos. / By J. A. Davis." Private collection.

considerable quantity of this artist's work was known, little had been published concerning his life. The challenge of filling this void led to our investigation of the "other Davis."

We again started our research by consulting Groce and Wallace's *Dictionary of Artists in America.* There Joseph H. Davis is described as a prolific primitive "left hand painter" who had produced more than one hundred portraits in New Hampshire and Maine in the years from 1832 to 1837. The sources for this information are the 1943 and 1950 articles by Frank O. Spinney. In the first,[45] Spinney suggests that the painter was Joseph Hilliard Davis of Farmington, New Hampshire, or Joseph H. Davis of Dover, New Hampshire. In the second,[46] he proposes what he felt was a better choice—"Pine Hill Joe" Davis of Newfield, Maine.

However, G. E. Hall of Portland, Maine, in a 1959 letter to a Mr. and Mrs. Sears of the same city, states that he or she had done "some research on the forgotten artist, J. H. Davis, and found that he was of Limington [Maine]." In the 16 August 1959 issue of the *Portland Sunday Telegram,* Esther Wood, Professor of History at Gorham (Maine) College, reports that the artist was a "native of Limington though at various times he used the address of Vassalborough, Maine, and Wilmington, Massachusetts." Esther Sparks, in an exhibition catalogue, mentions as possibilities "the voter in Dover in the 1850s, the confectionery of Dover, the landowner in Farmington in the '40s, or the Davis in Farmington who bought 26 pounds of nails from Clark and Scruton in the last half of 1844," although her first choice is Pine Hill Joe.[47] Finally, Robert L. Taylor, in his publication on early Limington families, includes Joseph H. Davis, the "noted left-hand artist."[48]

Was Joseph H. Davis of Limington the painter? Was it Joseph H. Davis of Newfield, Farmington, Dover, or elsewhere? None of these suggestions was supported by any real evidence. In order to resolve this problem, we conducted two parallel lines of research. We first identified those individuals with the name of Joseph H. Davis living in New Hampshire and Maine between 1830 and 1840, known to be near the place and time of the artist's activity from the inscriptions on his paintings. We next reviewed the subjects of all portraits attributable to Joseph H. Davis; from these were extracted those paintings that carried an inscription in the artist's own hand on the front of the paper, and only those that included the date of execution and name of the subject. Of this group, we considered only those that included the town of residence in the painting's inscription or those for which we could establish this by genealogical investigation. The final result was a total of eighty-five portraits from which the whereabouts of Joseph H. Davis during his years as an itinerant limner could be determined.

Although the surname "Davis" was the fifth most common in New England in 1790,[49] the name Joseph H. Davis was fortunately uncommon during the period under investigation. A study of census indexes and vital records of Maine and New Hampshire—the states where the artist was known to have been active—narrowed the possibilities down to those previously mentioned individuals of Farmington, New Hampshire, and Limington, Maine.

First to be considered was Joseph Hilliard Davis, born in Farmington on 24 January 1820 to James and Rachel (Hilliard) Davis.[50] In favor of this choice was the fact that Farmington is only about ten miles from Lebanon, Maine, home of Sally (Rogers) Chamberlin, and approximately eighteen miles from Dover, New Hampshire, home of Sarah Ann Guppy, both of whose portraits were painted in 1832. Making this possibility unlikely was the fact that Joseph Hilliard Davis was only twelve years of age in 1832. Although the very young Joseph Hilliard Davis may have been unusually gifted, it is unlikely that he was the artist in question. A review of the Strafford County, New Hampshire, Registry of Deeds for the period from 1818 to 1850 disclosed a deed dated 14 January 1847 for the purchase of land by Joseph H. Davis, "a country trader," from Ebenezer Ransom. It is likely that he was Joseph Hilliard and that he was the same Davis of Dover and Farmington referred to by Esther Sparks and Frank O. Spinney. Most significantly, it has not been possible to relate this Davis to any of the subjects of the portraits.

In contrast, the Joseph H. Davis of Limington, born 10 August 1811 to Joseph and Phebe (Small) Davis,[51] who were married there 27 November 1808,[52] was twenty-one years of age when the first portraits were painted in 1832. His paternal grandfather, John, may have been married to Molly Harper,[53] and his maternal great-grandfather, Samuel Small, was married to Dorothy Hubbard;[54] his middle initial may, therefore, have stood for "Harper" or "Hubbard." He lived on his father's farm in Limington, in that section known as Pine Hill; in 1821 his name is included, along with those of his parents and siblings, on a list of those people then residing in the town's fourth school district.[55] The 1830 census index for Maine shows him still living in Limington,[56] about twenty miles from Lebanon, Maine, where the 1832 portrait of Sally (Rogers) Chamberlin was painted.[57] Dover, New Hampshire, where the portrait of Sarah Ann Guppy was done the same year, is just ten miles from Lebanon. Sarah Ann's mother was Hannah (Dame) Guppy of Maine; an interesting possibility is that she may have been related to Bartholomew Van Dame, who was an important link between the painter and many of his subjects.

In his conversations (circa 1950) with residents of Newfield, a town only about eight miles from Limington, Spinney learned of a "Pine Hill Joe" Davis who was remembered as a farmer inclined to suddenly leave his farm to go wandering from town to town "painting pictures of people on little sheets of paper." Spinney refers to the artist as Pine Hill Joe of Newfield rather than of Limington. As he states, however, the identification was based on tradition and legend handed down through several generations. There is nothing to support the contention that Joseph H. Davis lived in Newfield in the 1830s. The Davis of Limington did move there in 1844, and it was this that must have led to the legend's error. The Pine Hill Joe Davis of Limington probably continued to carry the name of Pine Hill Joe when he lived in Newfield. This, plus the intervening years, would explain the confusion.

Review of the 1833 portraits indicated that Joseph H. Davis spent a good deal of time painting in the Dover-Somersworth area of New Hampshire and the Lebanon-Berwick area of Maine. The double portrait of Ira and Fanny Libby was particularly important in establishing the artist as the Joseph H. Davis of Limington. Born in Berwick, Maine, in 1788, Ira Libby married Fanny Langdon of Lebanon and was a deacon in the Freewill Baptist Church of North Berwick.[58] The father and uncle of J. H. Davis of Limington were both active in the nearby Freewill Baptist Church of Limington; another member of the family, Ezra Davis Jr., was one of the first three deacons of the church.[59] As we studied the subjects of Joseph H. Davis, it became apparent that a common interest in the Freewill Baptist Church was an important link between the painter and many of his Maine and New Hampshire subjects. The fact that the church newspaper, the *Morning Star*, was published at Limerick (only five miles from Limington) from 1826 to 1833, and after that in Dover, may explain the artist's greater activity in the first area before 1834, and in the second after 1833.

Numerous marital connections among the Libbys, the Smalls, and the J. H. Davis of Limington helped establish this town as the artist's place of residence. This Davis's maternal great-grandmother was Elizabeth (Libby) Plummer.[60] His mother's sister, Martha Small, was married to Philemon Libby who was given 100 acres of land in Limington by Samuel Small, great-grandfather of the painter.[61] Philemon Libby's son of the same name settled in that part of Limington known as Pine Hill,[62] the area in which Joseph H. Davis lived. The latter's cousin, Samuel Small, married Mary Libby,[63] and a witness to the will of Benjamin Small, J. H. Davis's grandfather, was Abner Libby.[64] Finally, Davis's great-aunt, Sarah Small, married Timothy Waterhouse, son of Joseph and Mary (Libby) Waterhouse.[65]

At or near Limington, in 1834, Davis painted the double portrait of Joseph and Sarah Ann (Libby) Emery (*Figure 7*), daughter of Ira and Fanny Libby.[66] Joseph Emery, born in Limington on 4 July 1808,[67] was only three years older than J. H. Davis, and the two may have been boyhood friends. Also painted in 1834 were the portraits of Oliver and Louisa Fernald of North Berwick.[68] In 1838 S. P. Fernald, probably a relative of Oliver, became pastor of the Freewill Baptist Church in Northwood, New Hampshire,[69] a town in which Davis was active in 1836. In December 1834 he was in Dover, New Hampshire, where he did the portraits of Tobias Bunker and Sally B. Buzzell, whom Buzzell married one year later. Tobias was the son of James and Lois (Foye) Bunker of Durham, about five miles from Dover.[70]

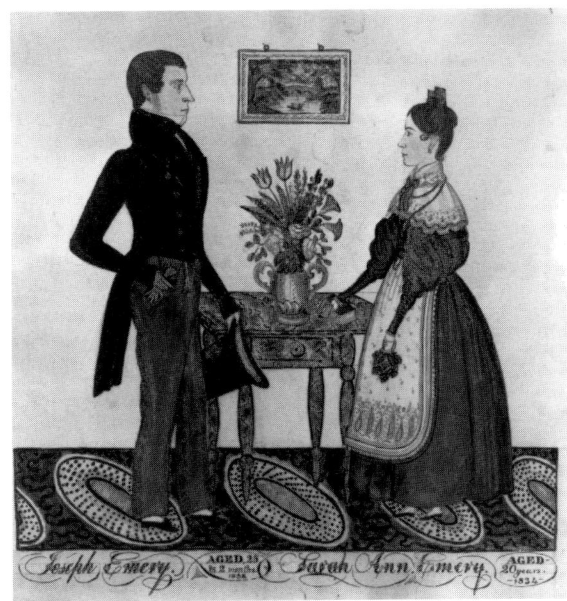

Figure 7 Joseph and Sarah Ann (Libby) Emery. Joseph H. Davis (1811–1865). Probably Limington, Maine, 1834. Watercolor and pencil, on paper; $13\frac{13}{16} \times 13\frac{13}{16}$ inches. Inscribed in ink in lower margin: "Joseph Emery. AGED 25 / & 2 months. / 1834 / Sarah Ann Emery. AGED 20 years. / 1834." Joseph, the son of James and Sarah (Fogg) Emery of Limington, died in nearby Limerick, Maine, on 11 March 1866. As do many folk portraits, this depicts clothing, furniture, floor covering, and other incidentals in great detail. Fenimore Art Museum, Cooperstown, New York.

Among the 1835 portraits painted in New Hampshire were those of the Hayes family[71] of Strafford, about ten miles west of Dover. Joseph Hayes's wife, Lois, was the daughter of Paul and Elizabeth (Davis) Demeritt, suggesting the possibility that she may have been related to the artist. Significantly, Joseph Hayes's father, Wentworth Hayes, was active in the Freewill Baptist Church.[72] In Brookfield, New Hampshire, Davis painted the portrait of William B. Chamberlin. Reflecting the frequent involvement of the subjects of Joseph H. Davis with the Freewill Baptist Church is the death notice that appeared in the *Morning Star*.[73]

In 1836 Joseph H. Davis painted his small portraits exclusively in New Hampshire. One was of John Crockett, deacon of Northwood's Calvin Baptist Church; Daniel Crockett, of Limington, was a member of the Freewill Baptist Church of Buxton, Maine. Following the death of the sister of John Neally (another Davis subject), Neally's friend Bartholomew Van Dame wrote a memorial poem for her that was published in the *Morning Star*. Van Dame—an itinerant schoolteacher, preacher, and reformer, as well as a frequent contributor to the *Morning Star*—visited many of the towns where Davis was active. The diaries of Van Dame, who was also a Davis subject, indicate his friendship with many of Davis's other sitters, and he was undoubtedly a key link between the artist and those whose portraits he painted.

Judging from his dated portraits, 1837 was the last year of Davis's painting activity, and he worked exclusively in New Hampshire. The portrait of Thomas York depicts him reading the *Morning Star* (*Figure 8*).

After our review of the portraits by Joseph H. Davis, certain questions came to mind. Did he have any occupation other than painter prior to 1838? Why did his artistic activity suddenly cease after 1837?

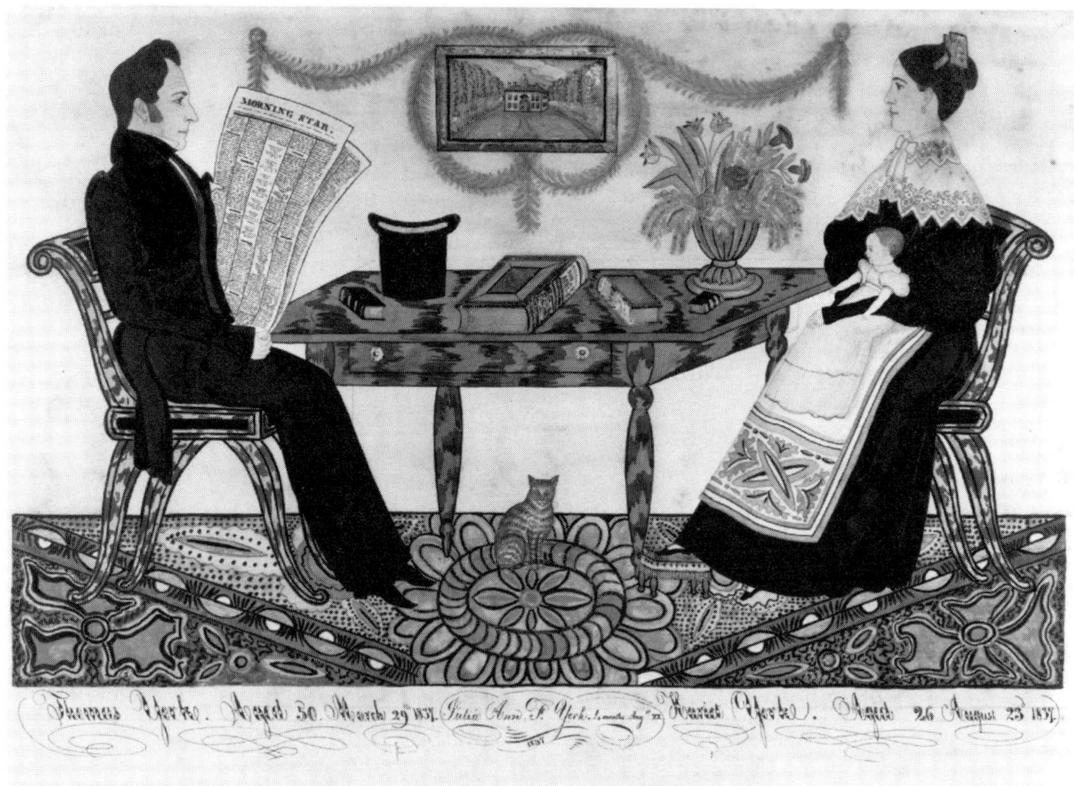

Figure 8 The York Family at Home. Joseph H. Davis (1811–1865). Lee, New Hampshire, 1837. Pencil, watercolor and ink on paper; 11 1/16 × 14 7/8 inches. Inscribed: "Thomas York. Aged 50. March 29th 1837. Julia Ann F. York, 4 months Augst 22 Harriet York. Aged 26 August 23d 1837." Thomas York was born 29 March 1787 in Lee, New Hampshire. His death there on 11 November 1857 is noted in the diary of Bartholomew Van Dame. He is shown reading the newspaper of the Freewill Baptist Church. Abby Aldrich Rockefeller Folk Art Museum, Williamsburg, Virginia.

And, if it was not death that was responsible, what happened to him after he stopped painting?

Since his father was a farmer in Limington, it is likely that the son also worked on the family farm, at least before 1835. Prior to that time his output of portraits was small, probably painted during his occasional trips away from the farm, as described by Spinney. His greatest activity as a painter was from 1835 through 1837. This increased productivity may have been due to the growing responsibility that marriage placed upon the young man. On 5 November 1835 he married Elizabeth Patterson, the marriage record indicating that they were both of Saco, Maine,[74] at the time. Five days later, "Joseph H. Davis of Saco, gentleman" was involved in a land transaction,[75] and on 13 November of that year there was recorded the sale of a parcel of land in Vassalborough, Maine, by Joseph and Elizabeth Davis to Ezekiel Small,[76] a former resident of Limington. These deeds, in addition to the marriage record, indicate that by November 1835 the Davises had moved to Saco.

The reason for the sudden cessation of painting after 1837 is not known. However, the birth of the painter's daughter, Elizabeth Ann, in 1838 or 1839, may have been a factor.[77] Also puzzling is the absence of records of any type indicating the nature of his activity during these years.

Evidence of the resumption of his work as a land trader is seen in February 1840 with the transfer of a parcel of land in Vassalborough from his father to J. H. Davis; at that time the son's place of residence is given as Vassalborough.[78] One month later he sold a piece of land in the same town, the deed recording his occupation as "trader."[79] During the following year he moved to Wilmington, Massachusetts. Deeds dated 31 March 1841 record the purchase of land by Joseph H. Davis of that city[80] and his sale of land to Phillips Academy.[81] By 10 December 1844 he had moved to Newfield, Maine; a deed of that date for his purchase of land there gives his occupation as "yeoman" and his place of residence as Newfield.[82] That he continued to live there through the first part of 1847 is indicated by numerous deeds.[83] His employment in another capacity is apparent from a newspaper announcement in the 13 January 1847 issue of the *Maine Freewill Baptist Repository* signed by Joseph H. Davis, treasurer of the Mount Eagle Manufacturing Company of Newfield. A final deed giving Newfield as his place of residence is dated 7 August 1847.[84] Shortly thereafter he moved back to Saco, for there is a record of the purchase of land on 2 December 1847 by Joseph H. Davis of that city.[85] A deed recorded eight days later now gives his occupation as "manufacturer."[86] Davis next moved to Morristown, New Jersey, his activity as a resident land trader there testified to by numerous deeds filed from 30 June 1848 through 1855.

The years spent by Davis in New Jersey were not limited to land trading. The 7 April 1853 issue of the Morristown newspaper, the *Jerseyman,* reports that "The Democracy of this Township had a meeting . . . and nominated . . . Assessor— Joseph H. Davis." The paper went on to state that his ticket would undoubtedly be elected, since in all probability there would be no organized opposition. The Democratic party in 1853 was the dominant one in Morristown,[87] so it can be assumed that he did win election to the post of assessor. Another significant item was found in the 15 December 1853 issue of the *Jerseyman,* "The subscriber respectfully tenders his thanks to the citizens and Fire Companies of Morristown, whose timely and united exertions saved his Paint Mills from total destruction by Fire on the 1st inst.," signed "Jos. H. Davis, Agent." He must have been either an important employee or the owner of this mill. From the 1860 census we learned that Joseph H. Davis was also busy as a New Jersey inventor. An inquiry sent to the Patent and Trademark Office of the U.S. Department of Commerce yielded a reply that three patents had been issued to him. The first, on 8 August 1854 (patent number 11,476), was "for new and useful improvements in forming the ores of iron into paint by a direct process of different colors."[88]

The final deed filed in Morristown is dated May 1855,[89] and by September of that year Joseph H. Davis had moved to Woburn, Massachusetts, a deed then giving Woburn as his place of residence and his occupation as "gentleman."[90] In November 1858 there is evidence of his continuing activity as an inventor. He then received his second patent, number 22,003, on an arrangement "for transmitting power from any prime motor to a propelling gear or wheel." The United States census of 1860 gives Woburn as his town of residence and his occupation as "inventor." On 31 July 1860 Joseph H. Davis was issued his third patent, number 29,364, on "certain new and useful improvements in chimney flues and radiators for warming apartments."

The last recorded reference to events in the life of J. H. Davis is the listing of his death at Woburn in that town's vital records: "Davis, Joseph H., son of Joseph and Phebe (b. in Limington, Me.), of disease of liver. May 28, 1865; 53y.9m.18d."[91] He is buried, along with his wife, daughter, father-in-law, and mother-in-law, in lot number 305, Cypress Path, Laurel Hill Cemetery, Saco.

Joseph Partridge

Our interest in researching the little-known artist Joseph Partridge was triggered by finding the watercolor portrait of Joseph Chapman (*Figure 9*) with the inscription on its reverse, "Painted by Joseph Partridge / May 15th 1825." At the time we knew of this painter only because of his 1822 watercolor of Providence's President Street at the Rhode Island Historical Society. From a book on paintings in that society's collection we learned that Partridge had been a drawing master in Halifax, Nova Scotia, and this seemed a good place to begin our investigation. Our first stop was at the city's public library, where a search of local newspapers led to the discovery of his advertisement in the 1 September 1817 issue of the *Halifax Journal,* in which Partridge announces that he had recently arrived from England and that he planned to open a school for drawing as soon as there was a sufficient number of students. The advertisement was

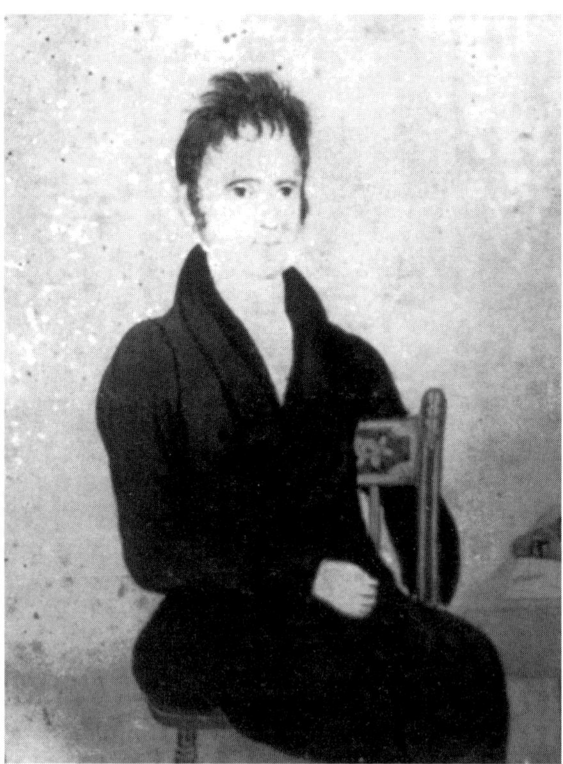

Figure 9 Joseph Chapman. Joseph Partridge (1792–circa 1833). Westerly, Rhode Island, or Boston, Massachusetts, 1825. Watercolor on paper; 8¾ × 6½ inches. Inscribed in ink on a piece of paper attached to the backing board: "Painted by Jos[h] Partridge / May 15th 1825 – / (Aged 41 years)," and in a different hand on another piece of paper "Mr. Joseph Chapman / Born 1784," and in yet another hand, "Mrs. F. M. Nichols, 115 Charles St." Private collection.

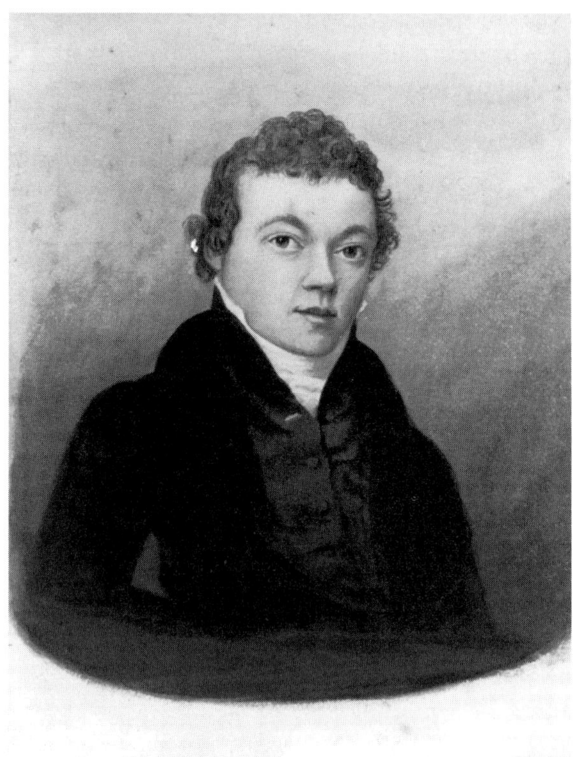

Figure 10 Self-Portrait. Joseph Partridge (1792–circa 1833). Halifax, Nova Scotia, 1819. Watercolor on paper; 7½ × 6¾ inches. Inscribed on the reverse, in 1920, by Harry Piers, then curator of the Provincial Museum, Halifax, Canada: "Watercolor portrait of Joseph Partridge painted by himself, at Nova Scotia, in 1819." History Collection, Nova Scotia Museum, Halifax, Nova Scotia, Canada.

repeated at approximately weekly intervals and in the *Nova Scotia Royal Gazette* on 3 September. The actual opening of his school on 3 November is reported in another advertisement in the former newspaper's 22 October issue.

While in Halifax we found two watercolors by Partridge at the Public Archives of Nova Scotia—his view of the National School, painted between 1817 and 1819, and an 1819 self-portrait (*Figure 10*) at the Nova Scotia Museum.

In the 26 July and 9 August issues of the *Halifax Journal*, Partridge announces his intention to return to England. Although he may have done so briefly, it is more likely that he moved directly from Halifax to Boston. His name appears in the 1821 Boston city directory as a miniature painter on School Street. Surprisingly, no advertisements by him could be found in Boston newspapers of 1820 or 1821 and—with only one possible exception—no paintings can be dated to his Boston stay.

Advertisements in Providence, Rhode Island, newspapers establish Partridge's move to that city. In the 26 December 1821 issue of the *Providence Gazette*, he "Respectfully begs leave to inform the Ladies and Gentlemen of Providence that . . . he intends to give instruction in the various branches of water colouring." Of interest is mention of his ability to do miniature paintings "either from the living or dead subject." Advertisements of 2 February 1822, in both the *Providence Gazette* and the *Providence Patriot*, inform the public that Partridge has opened his drawing academy and that he will be in his room "over No. 17 Cheapside to meet those desiring to enroll."

Early in 1822 he painted the portrait of the Reverend Stephen Gano of Providence. Although unsigned, it can be attributed to Partridge because of advertisements in the 3, 7, 14, and 21 August 1822 issues of the *Providence Gazette* reporting the sale of engravings of Reverend Stephen Gano based on that minister's portrait painted by Joseph Partridge.

Advertisements beginning in April 1822 attest to Partridge's ability to "sketch from nature" and to paint "Gentlemen's Country Seats, Factorys, Stores, &c.&c. . . . also, Anatomical Paintings in all cases of decease." An editorial in the *Providence Gazette* of 8 May 1822 reports on his "talents in sketching and painting rural scenery" and his excellent paintings of a number of Providence's buildings.

On 26 June 1822 Partridge was married in Boston to Mary Kelton of that city.[92] We found marriage notices in both Providence and Boston newspapers. Mary is listed in the Boston city directories of 1818 and 1820 as a tailoress at 3 Pleasant Street, and it can be assumed that the two met during Partridge's residence in that city.

In 1823 Partridge did three portraits of Moses Brown, a Quaker and a most important member of the Providence community. One of these, now in the library of the Religious Society of Friends in London, was sent by Brown's daughter-in-law, Dorcas, to a friend in Liverpool, England, along with a letter in which she states that the portrait had been painted by a young man without the knowledge of the subject; it also mentions that she had a copy that she valued highly.[93] The third, and most completely developed version, was probably retained by the artist (*Figure 11*).

The beginning of Partridge's financial difficulties becomes apparent in his advertisements of 4 September 1822 and 7 May 1823 in the *Providence Patriot,* requesting creditors to leave their accounts for adjustment in the office of Walter R. Danforth. The serious nature of his situation is more evident from minutes of the Providence Town Council meetings found in the library of the Rhode Island Historical Society. On 26 December 1823, John Howland, Providence treasurer, was authorized by William Larned, Overseer of the Poor, to "Pay Thomas Henry two dollars Sixty two cents for a load of wood for Mr. Partridge the Painter."[94] His economic situation worsened; on 24 January 1824, Howland was authorized to "Pay three dollars and Twenty five cents for a load of wood for Partridge the Portrait Painter he being very poor and family suffering."[95] Because he was not a native of Rhode Island, Partridge was brought before the Providence Town Council on 2 February 1824: "He says that he was born in England, left there about eight years ago, and landed first in Canada, came into the United States Decem'r 1819. —Married in Boston,— his Wife belonged in Dedham State of Massachusetts—Has been in this Town upwards of two years—His family now consists of his wife Mary and her grandmother and one child. He says that the maiden name of his wife was Kelton, her father belonged in Wiscasset, Maine—that he never owned any real Estate. . . ."[96] Partridge was then expelled from the state of Rhode Island and given three dollars to assist him in his move to Taunton, Massachusetts.

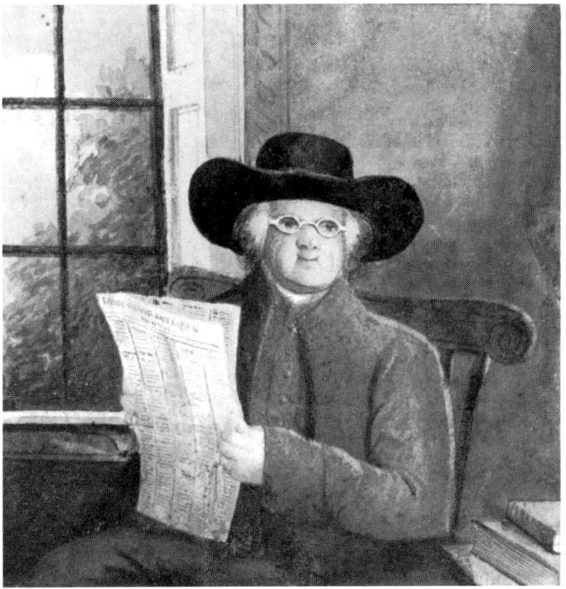

Figure 11 Moses Brown. Joseph Partridge (1792–circa 1833). Providence, Rhode Island 1823. Watercolor on paper; 4½ × 4½ inches. Inscribed: "J.P. – × II 1823" lower right; signed "Moses Brown's" in the subject's own hand on a piece of paper attached below the painting, and inscribed on the reverse of the painting: "Moses Brown was born 9 mo 23 1738. Departed this earth 9 mo 6 1836. Aged 97 years 11 months & 3 days." Private collection.

From 10 March through 9 June 1824 Partridge advertised in the *Taunton Columbian Reporter and Old Colony Journal* that he was teaching watercolor drawing and that his wife would teach the ladies. But he apparently failed again and left Taunton, for from 14 July through 13 October 1824 his mail was listed in the newspaper as unclaimed at the post office. Where he went cannot be stated with certainty, but it was probably Boston or Westerly, Rhode Island, for on 15 May 1825 he signed and dated the previously noted portrait of Joseph Chapman. The two candidates for the sitter are a bank cashier by that name who, according to the 1825 Boston city directory, lived on Summer Street, and Joseph, the son of Joseph and Elizabeth (Kenyon) Chapman, who was born in Westerly according to Rhode Island vital records.[97] In support of the latter is the fact that his stepmother, Eunice (Clarke) Chapman, was the niece of Adam Clarke of Westerly,[98] who may be the subject of another Partridge portrait. Supporting the former identification is the fact that Partridge is known to have been in the Boston area in the summer of 1825, since on 26 August he enlisted for five years as a private in the United States Marine Corps at Charlestown, a suburb of Boston.[99]

Partridge's enlistment papers record his birthplace as England, his age as thirty-three—indicating a birth date of 1792—and his occupation as "anatomical painter." He is described as being five feet four and one-half inches tall, with hazel eyes, brown hair, and a light complexion.

Partridge was assigned to the Charlestown Navy Barracks until 1 January 1827, when he was transferred to the USS *Warren*, which was being built at the Navy Yard at Charlestown. He then spent three years on this ship as it sailed the Mediterranean Sea protecting American merchant ships from Greek-flag pirates. It was during this period that he produced most of his surviving work—twenty-three watercolors including a few portraits, but mainly views of places at which the ship called.

After a few short tours on other ships in the Mediterranean, Partridge was honorably discharged from the Marine Corps on 18 October 1830, with the rank of sergeant.[100] Nothing has been learned of his activity following discharge, but study of the life of Mary (Kelton) Partridge has enabled us to establish the approximate time of her husband's death.

In 1827, with Joseph aboard ship, Mary returned to Providence where, according to the 1828 Providence city directory, she was employed as a preceptress at a school on North Market Street while living at 40 High Street. According to the 1830 city directory, she held the same job and lived at the same address with her grandmother, Mary (Doggett) Baker. The next city directory in which the women appear is the Boston directory of 1834. Mary (Kelton) Partridge is now, for the first time, listed as a widow. From this it is clear that Partridge must have died at some time between his discharge from the Marine Corps in October 1830 and late 1833 or early 1834, when the directory was compiled. Where he died and the cause of his death—at approximately forty years of age—have not yet been determined.

Royall Brewster Smith

Nina Fletcher Little, in a 1963 publication on Maine and its role in American art, refers to Royall Brewster Smith as a relatively unknown artist who was hired by a neighbor, Arthur McArthur, to paint portraits of members of his family.[101] At the time Mrs. Little knew of only two other portraits attributable to Smith. During the following twenty-five years nothing significant concerning his work appeared in the literature other than the infrequent illustration of a portrait by him.

Our interest in this painter was stimulated by the discovery of the portrait of an elderly woman (*Figure 12*) that, although unsigned, had the typical stylistic characteristics of known portraits by Royall Brewster Smith. The resultant research led to thirty-six oil-on-canvas portraits painted by him between 1830 and 1837, plus an interesting personal story that reflects life in Maine during the first half of the nineteenth century. Genealogical investigation of the artist and his subjects was a vital part of the project.

There is little evidence that Smith had any formal training in the arts. Since he had lived in and around Buxton, Maine, for a number of years, he was probably familiar with the work of the well-known portrait painter John Brewster, who was very active in that area. Although there is nothing to suggest any

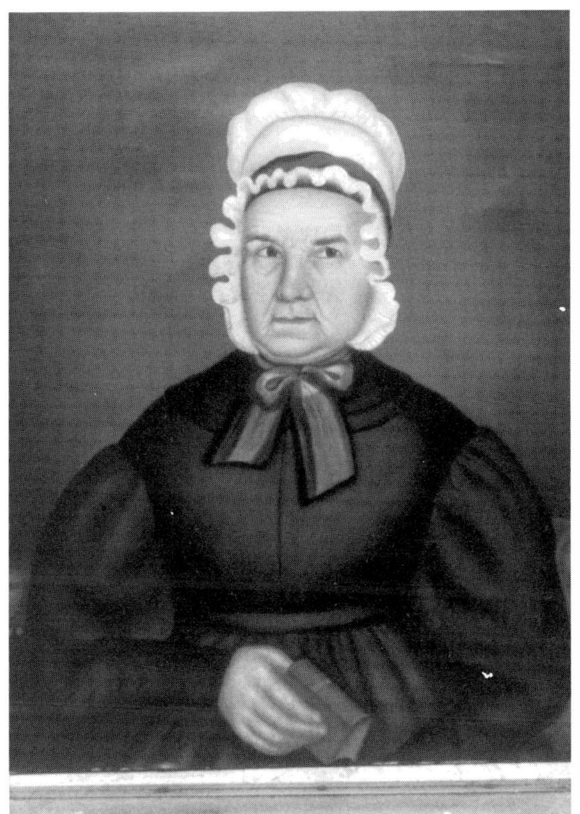

Figure 12 Older Woman With Bible. Royall Brewster Smith (1801–1855). Probably Standish, Maine, circa 1837. Oil on canvas; 31 × 26 inches. The striking similarity between the facial features and those of Nathaniel Marshall Richardson, another of Royall Brewster Smith's subjects, suggests that she was probably Richardson's mother, Anna (Tyler) (Richardson) Waterhouse. She married David Richardson of Limington and had nine children in Limington and Standish, Maine, between 1806 and 1822. In 1822 the Richardsons' home was destroyed by fire, her husband and son Isaac perishing in the flames. In 1825 she married Theophilus Waterhouse of Standish as his fourth wife and was living there in 1837 when her portrait was painted. Private collection.

influence from the older painter, the two families were related in that John Brewster's brother, Dr. Royall Brewster, was physician to the Smith family, and it was he after whom the young painter was named.

Of the thirty-six portraits attributed to Royall Brewster Smith, twenty-one identify the subjects by an inscription on the canvas; the names of an additional six are known as the result of information from descendants. Genealogical investigation of each of these, and of the artist, revealed that all were residents of a small area of Maine that included the towns of Gorham and Limington (*Figure 13*). Further, many were related to each other or to members of Royall's family.

In addition to portraits, Smith is known to have made two undecorated family records. The first, for his own family, includes the names, dates, and places of his and his parents' births; his parents' marriage date; and the names and dates of birth of their children.[102] The second, probably executed by him in late 1826 or early 1827, was for the family of Robert and Mary Davis of South Limington. Attribution of this family record to Royall is based on the large printed initials "R.B.S." on the first of the five sheets; this is supported by the fact that Robert Davis was a first cousin of the Mary Davis who married Royall's older brother Alexander Smith.[103]

Knowing that Royall Brewster Smith had been active in the state of Maine, we began our investigation of his life by visiting the library of the Maine Historical Society in Portland. There, in a 1972 publication, *Recollections of Old Buxton, Maine,* we found four paragraphs devoted to Royall. This work reports that he was born at Buxton in 1801 and died in 1849; that he was an untrained artist and not a full-time painter; that no paintings by him other than those of the McArthurs were known; and that he "and his family are buried in the churchyard at Groveville, behind the Congregational Church."[104]

On a trip to Maine we located the cemetery in Groveville, which proved to be a section of Buxton. There we found a tall monument with the names of Royal B. Smith; his wife, Mary N.; and their two sons. Also inscribed was the date of Royal's death, 29 September 1849, at the age of thirty-five years. This age was at variance with the previously noted family record by Royall that gives his birth date as 1801, so that in 1849 he would have been forty-eight, not thirty-five years of age. To check this discrepancy we examined old birth records in the Buxton town clerk's office and found one for Royal B. Smith that gives his date of birth as 8 November 1814. With that birth date he would have been thirty-five years of age

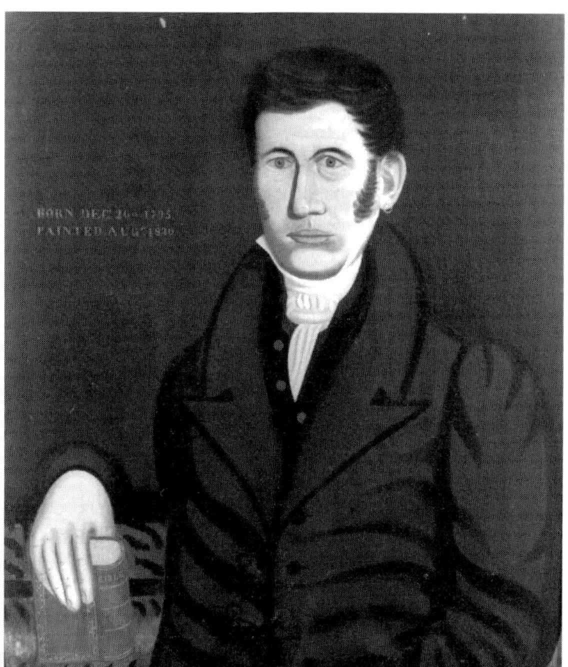

Figure 13 Ira Baker. Royall Brewster Smith (1801–1855). Gorham, Maine, 1830. Oil on canvas; 30 × 25⅛ inches. Inscribed on the front: "BORN DEC. 26th 1795 / PAINTED AUG.st 1830." This and its companion portrait of a woman were donated to the Newark Museum, Newark, New Jersey, in 1950, identified only as "the Beckers." Based on the following, it is believed that the male subject was Ira Baker: 1) the phonetic similarity of *Becker and Baker;* 2) the dates of birth as presented on the portraits are close to those in town records for the Bakers; 3) Royall was related by marriage to Betsy (Hanscom) Baker, Ira's wife; and 4) Ira's cousin, Mary Ann Baker, was married to Theophilus Dame of Gorham, Maine, another Smith subject. *Copyright The Newark Museum / Art Resource, New York.*

in 1849, as inscribed on the tombstone. However, on further study of this birth record we noted that the names of his parents are given as John and Rebecca, but our Royall's mother was Elizabeth. In addition, the names of the brothers and sisters on the tombstone were not those of the artist's siblings. Obviously, the man buried in the churchyard was not the artist, but a man with the same name. Further research led to the record for a Royall Brewster Smith born on 7 August 1801 to Lieutenant John and Elizabeth Smith. Also listed were the correct names of his brothers and sisters. The identity of the Smith buried in the Groveville churchyard was found in a more complete family record prepared by descendants. John McCurdy Smith, brother of the artist, married Rebecca Hill of Buxton on 26 August 1810. That this was the correct couple named John and Rebecca is evident from the fact that the family record gives John McCurdy Smith's date of death as 19 April 1862, the same date recorded in the Buxton town records. Who, then, was the Royal B. Smith buried in the Groveville churchyard? It was the nephew of the painter, the son of his brother John.[105] The burial site of the artist was discovered later as a result of further genealogical investigation.

The artist Royall Brewster Smith was the eleventh of fourteen children of John McCurdy and Elizabeth (McLellan) Smith.[106] He and his sister Margaret were baptized 14 December 1801 at Buxton's Church of Christ.[107] In September 1817 the sheriff brought legal action to seize the Smith farm, and two years later it was taken over. John McCurdy Smith had served in the Continental Army from 4 June 1778 to 6 March 1779, and in his 1818 pension application he stated: ". . . am in reduced circumstances in life and in need of a pension from my country for support. . . . Real estate, none, personal estate, none, no income, no money due me, am supported by charity." The application lists his wife and six of his children as residing with him; Royall, then seventeen years of age, is not included.[108]

Study of probate records then revealed that in September 1820 the selectmen of Buxton declared that "in their judgment John Smith by excessive drinking and idleness [did] so spend, waste and lessen his estate as thereby to expose himself and his family to want and suffering circumstances, and does also thereby endanger and expose the said town of Buxton to a charge or expense for his and their maintenance and support."[109] One month later a guardian was appointed for "John Smith . . . a spendthrift."[110] In May 1821, Elizabeth (McLellan) Smith left her husband and moved with the younger children (including Royall) from Buxton to Limington.[111] Among the expenses listed on 11 October 1821 by John Smith's guardian is an interesting item: "Dr. Royall Brewster's bill for doctering [*sic*] the said Smith family . . . $54.37."[112] Another entry is for payment of seventeen dollars to Alexander Smith for boarding his younger brother Royall, "a sick boy child of the said J. Smith." Royall at this time was twenty years of age. The guardian's later January 1823 report to the probate court for expenses incurred includes two bills from Alexander for continued boarding and care of his younger brother.[113] Not until October 1825 had Royall recovered sufficiently to leave Alexander's home and move back to Buxton.[114]

Copies of letters sent to Royall by his brother George suggest that, following his return to Buxton, Royall traveled to nearby communities as an itinerant. The first, dated 15 December 1831, was mailed to Gorham, Maine; the next two, dated 13 August 1832 and 12 May 1833, were sent to Gorham Corner; the fourth, dated 22 November 1834, went to Sacarappa, Maine.[115] In the second letter George wrote, ". . . I think you had better come down as soon as you can. I think you had better not engage any more work at painting until we can find a shop that will suit you." This advice was not taken; on 11 April 1838 Royall paid for an option to purchase a parcel of land with buildings in Gorham.[116] Six months later, for the sum of one thousand dollars, the property was conveyed to him.[117] His involvement in Gorham town affairs is indicated by his signing of a temperance petition in January 1838.[118]

A review of Gorham town records led us to Royall's November 1840 intention of marriage to Miss Roxana Gowen of Shapleigh, Maine. We could find neither his marriage record nor anything concerning his wife. However, a Gowen descendant who was preparing her family's genealogy informed us that Roxana's mother was an Emery. A published genealogy for this family then yielded the fact that on 30 November 1840 Royal [*sic*] B. Smith had married Roxanna [*sic*], born 19 October 1818 to John and Martha (Emery) Gowen.[119] From the as yet unpublished Gowen genealogy we learned that Royall's father-in-law was buried in the Mount Hope Cemetery of Bangor, Maine. On the outside chance that Royall might also be buried there, we sent a letter of inquiry to the cemetery director. To our delight, the response was positive; Royall was buried in Lot 368 C.G. On visiting the site, we found his tombstone bearing the simple inscription "ROYAL [*sic*] B. SMITH / Aug. 7, 1801. / Dec. 5, 1855" (*Figure 14*). With him are buried his wife, daughter, and grandson.

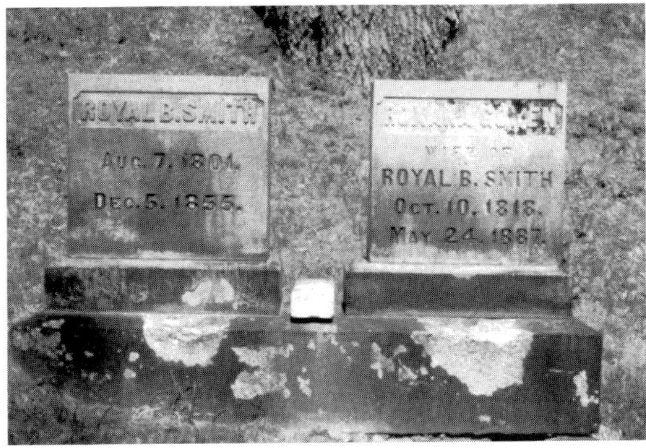

Figure 14 Tombstone of Royall Brewster Smith and his wife, Roxana. Hope Cemetery, Bangor, Maine.

Since Royall B. Smith was buried in Bangor, it appeared possible that he might have lived there prior to his death. Study of city directories supplied the answer. His listing as a carpenter residing on Garland Street, Bangor, in the 1843 directory, indicates that the family had moved from Gorham to Bangor at some time between that year and his wedding in 1840. In 1843 he purchased a parcel of land on Essex Street.[120] The 1846 directory records his residence there and gives his occupation as "painter," living on Harlow Street. In the 1851 directory, Simon Pierce Bradbury, husband of Roxana (Gowen) Smith's sister Mary, is listed as a sculptor with a working address on Harlow Street and residence on Essex Street. It appears probable, therefore, that the Smiths had moved to Bangor to be closer to their relatives—Mary (Gowen) Bradbury and Royall's younger brother George Smith.

Royall is shown as a painter in Bangor city directories from 1846 through 1855. However, there are no known portraits by him after 1837—one year before his purchase of land in Gorham, six years before his first listing in the Bangor directory, and eighteen years prior to his death.

His estate at probate[121] consisted of $1,500 in real estate, $285 in goods and chattels, and $1,301 in rights and credits. The inventory of goods included $123.75 in silverware, books, and so forth, and a shop and tools valued at $161; unfortunately, the nature of his shop and tools is not specified.

An obituary in the 7 December 1855 issue of the *Bangor Daily Whig and Courier* reports, among other things, that Royall "was one of our most industrious and reliable mechanics." Had he been active as a portrait painter, this would probably have been mentioned. Use of the descriptive term "mechanic," along with his listing as "painter" in the directories, plus the use of lettering and grained furniture in many of his paintings, suggested that he had worked in Bangor as a painter of signs, furniture, and houses. This hypothesis is supported by the diary of Daniel Holman, kept from 1846 through 1851. Entries after 1 April 1848 indicate that Holman was in partnership with Royall and that their business focused on house painting, but included other things such as hanging wallpaper, painting vessels, varnishing doors, and setting glass. From this we can conclude that Royall Brewster Smith, who was probably a craftsman early in life and evolved into a portrait painter, in his later years returned to work as a craftsman.

Thomas Ware

The state of Vermont has produced a number of important nineteenth-century naïve or primitive painters of portraits. Among these is Thomas Ware, whose name was for the most part unknown prior to our research. As will be seen, it was genealogical investigation of the artist and his subjects that allowed us to juxtapose their relationships to one another against the setting of life in Vermont during the first quarter of the nineteenth century.

When we started our research, the only mention of Thomas Ware in print was in an 1872 article by Philip Battell[122] on another Vermont portrait painter, Benjamin Franklin Mason. Mason, born in Pomfret, Vermont, was a childhood friend of Ware, and it was during the former's confinement following surgery on his leg at the age of nine years that Ware encouraged him to draw, using engravings in books as his models. Both boys did draw "with chalk and coal, Ware taking to it more boldly as a pleasure, Mason perhaps more carefully as a study." Ware then met Abraham Tuthill, a portrait painter of some note, whose father lived in Pomfret for a few years. From Tuthill he learned the technique of painting in oil and, in turn, passed this knowledge on to his friend, Benjamin. A final reference is the following: "In 1823–1825, he [Mason] was with Ware at school and painting. His friend was already making a local reputation, and had begun to go out."

Thomas Ware was born in Pomfret on 7 August 1803, the son of Dr. Frederick and Jemima (Manning) Ware.[123] His father was born in Wrentham, Massachusetts, and later moved to Pomfret, marrying his first wife, Eunice Emerson, on 25 January 1784. Following her death on 9 May 1785, he married Jemima, the daughter of William and Mary Manning, on 29 September of the same year. Thomas had three half-sisters from his father's first marriage and was the tenth of twelve children from the second.

The whereabouts of Ware's early sketches in ink and pencil, mentioned by Battell, are unknown. In a 1950 publication about Mason and Tuthill, the authors state that they had been unable to locate any work by Thomas Ware.[124] However, at the time of our 1984 report,[125] forty-one portraits, most on wood panel, were known. A signed inscription on the reverse of the panel identifies many of his subjects so that of the forty-one, the identity of thirty-five is known. Because of space limitations, only the most significant of these will be reviewed.

One of the most remarkable is Ware's huge portrait (circa 1820) of members of the Titus Hutchinson family. Measuring 30 by 124 inches, it includes renderings of Titus Hutchinson, his wife Clarissa (Sage) Hutchinson, and their six children. Titus, the son of the Reverend Aaron and Margery (Carter) Hutchinson, was born 29 April 1771 in Grafton, Massachusetts. In July 1776 the family moved to the "Hutchinson farm" in Pomfret. Titus worked on the farm until he reached the age of nineteen, when he began his studies preparatory to entering college. With his father as his instructor, he was able to complete the first two years' work at home and then spent the following two years at Princeton College. On the completion of this course, he began the study of law in the Lebanon, New Hampshire, office of his older brother Aaron Jr. Titus was admitted to the Vermont bar in June 1798, following which he opened his office in Woodstock, just two miles from Pomfret. Very successful in practice, he was appointed in 1813 by President James Madison to the position of United States Attorney for the Vermont district. He retained this office for about ten years and in 1825 was elected a judge of the state supreme court. He continued on the bench for eight years, during the last four years of which he presided as chief judge. He died 24 August 1857. Of interest is the fact that this painting was attributed to "Henry Ware" in the Smithsonian Institution's *Inventory of American Paintings* (1983). On investigation we learned that it had been donated with an attribution to a Henry Ware of Pomfret—obviously in error, since Henry, Thomas Ware's cousin, was not born until 1825, three or four years after execution of the painting.

Three of Titus Hutchinson's sons—Edwin, Oramel, and Henry, born between 1803 and 1806—graduated from the University of Vermont. All were students in their father's office and then were admitted to the Vermont bar. Titus Hutchinson Jr., born in 1809, was a merchant in Woodstock; Clarissa Sage Hutchinson, born in 1814 and named for her mother, resided in Woodstock and died, unmarried, in 1852; and Alexander Hutchinson, born in 1816, was a merchant first in Boston and then in Woodstock and died in 1850 while crossing the Isthmus of Panama on his way to California.[126]

An inscription on the reverse of the portrait of James Chandler Jr. bears the subject's name and age (twenty-one years), the year of execution (1822), and the signature "Thomas Ware." James, the first of eight children of James and Abigail (Vilas) Chandler, was born 20 September 1801 in Alstead, New Hampshire. He was married first in 1831 to Sophia Tuttle, who died in 1837, aged thirty-two; second to her sister Nancy Tuttle, who died in 1847, aged thirty-one; and last to Polly (Stowell) Tuttle. The sitter's father was a farmer who resided in Drewsville, a few miles from Alstead.[127] His wife Abigail was born in Grafton, Massachusetts, in 1775,[128] when the Hutchinson family was still living there. Annis Orr (Chandler) Chamberlain (1795–1865) of the same vicinity—subject of another Ware portrait, circa 1822—was only distantly related to the James Chandler family.

The triggering force for our investigation of the life and work of Thomas Ware was exposure to a group of four oil on wood panel portraits (*Figure 15*). An inscription on a piece of paper held by one of the subjects had been read by a gallery owner as "David and Susan Lake, Painted March 1822. Painted by T. Ware." The other subjects were reported to be the sitter's daughter and mother. Several years later the four paintings appeared at auction, but they were now attributed to "T. Wale" rather than to T. Ware. On consulting Groce and Wallace's *Dictionary of Artists in America*, we found no listing of a T. Ware, but for "T. Wale" there was the following entry: "Portraits in oil on wood. White River Junction, Vt. 1820."[129] The source for this information was Lipman and Winchester's *Primitive Painters in America*.[130] A search of Vermont census indexes for 1820 and 1830 led to no listing of a T. Wale, nor could such a person be found in Vermont vital records nor in any published genealogy. As has been pointed out, the artist's surname was "Ware," not "Wale."

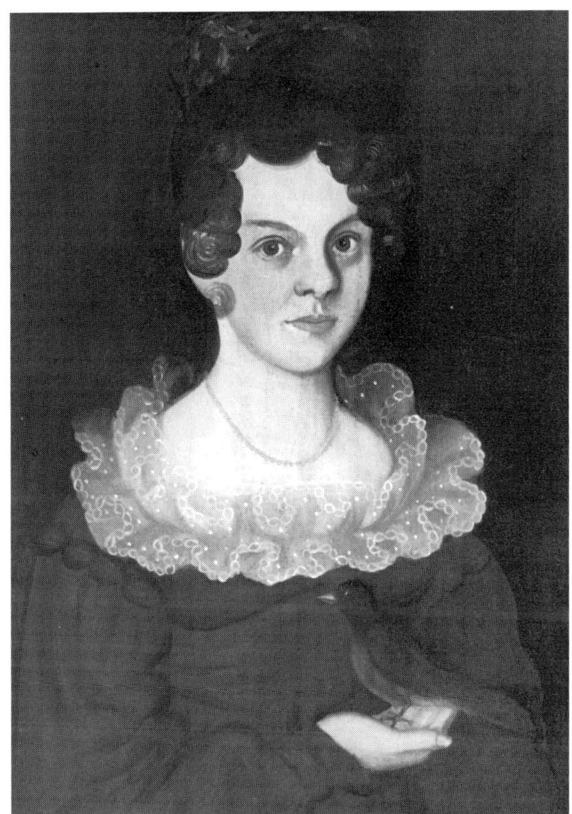

Figure 15 Huldah (Edson) Lake. Thomas Ware (1803–circa 1826). Woodstock, Vermont, 1822. Oil on wood panel; 26 × 19 inches. Private collection.

A similar spelling error became apparent in regard to the subject "David" Lake. We were unable to locate any such person in the census index, but did find four Daniel Lakes, residing respectively in Springfield, Charlotte, Castleton, and Woodstock. Using a magnifying lens, we reexamined a photograph of the painting, and it became clear that what had previously been read as "David" was actually "Daniel."

Since Woodstock is the town closest to White River Junction (reported by Lipman and Winchester to have been the locale of the artist "Wale"), we selected this place for our first visit. At the town clerk's office we found records of the birth on 16 March 1784 of Daniel Lake, son of George Lake, and another for his marriage on 3 June 1806 to Susanna Edson. The names *David* and *Susan,* originally said to have been in the inscription held by Mr. Lake, were obviously *Daniel* and *Susanna.*

There was no published genealogy for the family of Daniel Lake. However, from one of the Edson family we learned that Susanna Edson, third child of Silvester and Susanna (Allen) Edson, was born 5 February 1788 in Hartland, Vermont; and on 3 June 1806 she married Daniel Lake in Woodstock. Daniel was born in Woodstock on 16 March 1784 to George and Sarah (Lovejoy) Lake.[131] From the published history of Woodstock, we learned that Daniel Lake was a farmer and cooper, a man of vigorous frame and great physical strength and industry.[132]

The Edson genealogy reported that there were no children born to Daniel and Susanna (Edson) Lake. Who, then, was the young woman in the portrait, said to be their daughter? Since this painting had descended in the family with the other three, it seemed likely that she was related. Susanna had seven siblings, among whom were sisters Huldah, born in 1792, and Cynthia, born five years earlier. The latter and her husband, Richard Hayes, were painted by Ware in 1823. Lending support to the hypothesis that Huldah is the subject of the portrait in question is the fact that she had married John Lake, Daniel's brother, about 1810. Huldah was the mother of six children, all born in Woodstock, where she died in 1860.

The Smithsonian Institution's *Inventory of American Paintings* lists the portraits of the Lakes, Richard and Cynthia Hayes, and also those of Amaziah and Hannah (Throope) Richmond. A published Throop(e) family genealogy lists only Hannah's date of birth in Bristol, Rhode Island. Much more productive was the Richmond family genealogy.[133] The son of Lemuel and Molly Richmond, Amaziah was born in Middleborough, Massachusetts, on 22 March 1758. He was a farmer in Taunton, Massachusetts, and later lived in Bristol, Rhode Island; Woodstock, Vermont; and finally nearby Barnard, Vermont. He joined the Revolutionary Army at the age of sixteen or seventeen and fought in three different campaigns. Later, when working on a house, Amaziah fractured his leg, which had to be amputated. Soon thereafter he began marketing meat in Woodstock, where he purchased the Killam farm, taking up residence there in 1811.[134] A final comment concerns Amaziah in the Richmond genealogy: "He had sound judgment, strict integrity, was temperate in all things and so regular in his attendance at church meetings that his horse would leave the pasture and go to the church at the ringing of the bell." Hannah, daughter of Billings and Hannah (Morton) Throope, was born 24 January 1763 in Bristol, Rhode Island. She married Amaziah Richmond on 25 November 1780 and had twelve children, the first three born in Bristol and the last nine in Barnard, Vermont. She died in Woodstock on 26 December 1845.[135]

These portraits of the Richmonds led us to another pair of Ware portraits, those of Job Richmond and Mary H. Marcy. Like those of Amaziah and Hannah Richmond, these two were framed together. On the reverse of the portrait of Mary Marcy is the following inscription in black paint: "Mary H. Marcy / Aged 21 years / Painted in 1823, / By Tho. Ware." From the Richmond genealogy we learned that Job was the eighth child of Amaziah and Hannah. He was born in Barnard in 1797 and married Mary H. Marcy in 1827, about four years after their portraits were painted. Following the wedding they moved to Pomfret, in 1837 to Hartland, and in 1843 to the Richmond farm in Woodstock. Job taught school for twenty winters, was a justice of the peace, a selectman, and a captain in the militia—hence the uniform he wears in the portrait. Mary H. Marcy was born in 1802, the third of five children of Joseph and Mary (Cole) Marcy of Middleborough, Massachusetts,[136] also the Richmonds' hometown. She had two children, James Sylvester Richmond (born in 1828), who in 1853 graduated from the medical school then in Woodstock, and Lauriston Amaziah Richmond (born in 1829).

Two other members of the Marcy family, Sylvester and Eliza Throop Marcy, were subjects for Ware in 1823. Sylvester, the son of Joseph and Mary (Cole) Marcy, and brother of Mary H. (Marcy) Richmond, was born 9 August 1799 in Hartland, Vermont. A physician like his father, he died unmarried in 1840. His portrait depicts him preparing medication for a patient. Eliza Throop Marcy, the youngest child of Joseph and Mary (Cole) Marcy, born in Hartland 20 January 1805, was the sister of Sylvester Marcy and of Mary H. Marcy, wife of Job Richmond.

As with Job Richmond, Daniel Tinkham in his portrait (*Figure 16*) is depicted in a striking military uniform. It was donated to the Shelburne Museum along with his enlistment papers as captain in the state militia, family photographs, land deeds, and the record of his deputization as Sheriff of Windsor County, Vermont.[137] Daniel, the son of Isaiah and Susanna (Ellis) Tinkham, was born in Pomfret on 15 October 1794 and died there on 12 March 1874. He married Pamelia/Permelia Atherton on 19 February 1815 in Pomfret, where they had eleven children. Daniel Tinkham ran the grist mill at Snow's store in Pomfret. Martin Snow, another Ware subject, ran the sawmill at this store,[138] and his name is included in an account book kept by Tinkham.

One of Ware's most interesting paintings, from the point of view of its history, is a portrait that many years ago had been identified by family members as "Pamela St. John, daughter of General St. John, a Revolutionary War officer after whom the town of St. Johnsbury, Vermont, was named." However, St. Johnsbury, Vermont, was actually named for a Frenchman, Michel-Guillaume-Jean de Crèvecoeur, whose adopted American name was J. Hector St. John.[139] The subject is believed to be Pamelia (not Pamela) St. John, the sixth of eight children of John and Hannah (Fitch) St. John. She was born 10 April 1800, married John Reed, and died 10 April 1843.[140] Her father, John St. John, was born at Ridgefield, Connecticut, and enlisted in the Revolutionary Army in 1775; his highest rank was captain, not general. Pamelia's portrait was painted between 1824 and 1825 when she was living in Greenfield, New York, where her father died. Greenfield lies only about thirty-five miles from Whitehall, New York, where Ware was living at the time.

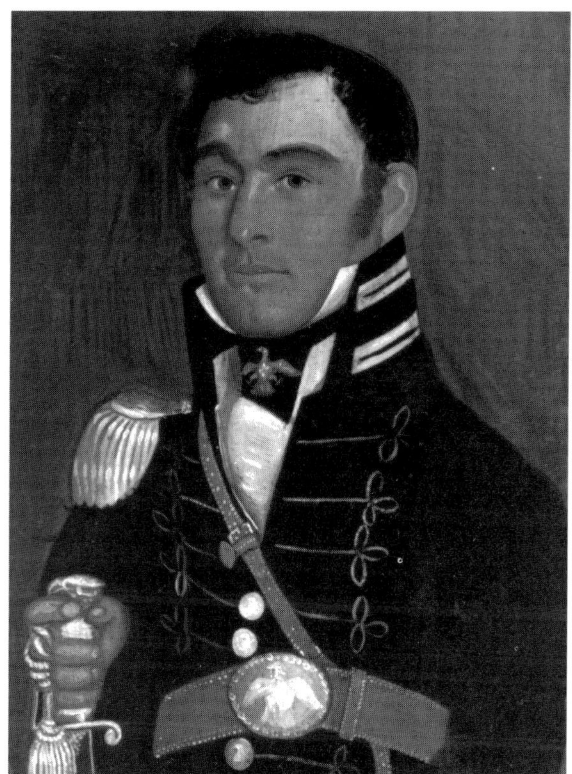

Figure 16 Daniel Tinkham. Thomas Ware (1803–circa 1826). Pomfret, Vermont, circa 1823. Oil on wood panel; 27 × 20½ inches. Shelburne Museum. © *Shelburne Museum, Shelburne, Vermont.*

In summary, all of the portraits by Thomas Ware were painted in the years from 1820 through 1823, with one or two possibly done in 1824 or 1825. He was active as a portrait painter from the age of seventeen to twenty or twenty-one. Almost all subjects were from Pomfret, Woodstock, or Hartland, Vermont, towns no more than fifteen miles from one another. In those few instances where the subjects lived at a greater distance from Ware's area of activity, there is a link connecting the two. Why he stopped painting is not known, nor is it known why he left Vermont to go to Whitehall, New York, about forty-five miles west of Woodstock. One possible intermediary between him and Whitehall is Sarah, daughter of Amaziah Richmond. She moved from Barnard to Brandon, Vermont, and then to Whitehall.[141] Thomas Ware is reported to have died in Whitehall in 1826 or 1827[142] after a short life of twenty-three or twenty-four years. Unfortunately, further information concerning Ware's time in Whitehall is not available; vital records for the town go back only to 1881, fire having destroyed the earlier ones.

Study of paintings by early American folk artists is in itself of great interest. However, a real appreciation and understanding of their work—particularly in the case of portraiture, the most common type of folk art—can only come from knowledge of the lives of the artists and their subjects, how they relate to each other and to the times in which they lived. To arrive at this goal, research in genealogical sources is an especially valuable tool. This review of six early-nineteenth-century folk portrait painters demonstrates some of the genealogical methods used to achieve a true, interesting, and complete picture of their lives and work.

NOTES

[1]Jean Lipman, "Benjamin Greenleaf, New England Limner," *Magazine Antiques* 52, no. 3 (September 1947): 195–97.

[2]George C. Groce and David H. Wallace, *The New-York Historical Society's Dictionary of Artists in America, 1564–1860* (New Haven and London: Yale University Press, 1957), p. 273.

[3]*Dictionary of American Biography*, 20 vols., ed. Allen Johnson and Dumas Malone (New York: Charles Scribner's Sons, 1928–1936), 7:581.

[4]The conclusion that they were the same was based on statements made by two descendants that their ancestors' portraits had been painted by Benjamin Greenleaf of Bradford Academy. Since he was the only well-known person by that name, it is easy to understand why the sitters' descendants might erroneously assume that he was the artist.

[5]Clara Endicott Sears, *Some American Primitives: A Study of New England Faces and Folk Portraits* (Boston: Houghton Mifflin Company, 1941), p. 132.

[6]Carl N. Schmalz Jr. to Thomas Hunter, 10 July 1956, Bowdoin College Museum of Art, Brunswick, Maine.

[7]James Edward Greenleaf, *Genealogy of the Greenleaf Family* (Boston: Frank Wood, Printer, 1896), pp. 339, 361.

[8]*Dictionary of American Biography*, 19:49–50.

[9]George M. Gould, *Genealogical Data Concerning the Descendants of Robert Goold, 1888–1889* (Philadelphia: n.p., 1888–1889), p. 5.

[10]Charles J. F. Binney, *Genealogy of the Binney Family* (Albany: Joel Munsell's Sons, 1886), p. 24.

[11]*Vital Records of Hull, Massachusetts, to the Year 1850*, 2 vols. (Boston: New England Historic Genealogical Society, 1910), 1:21.

[12]*Vital Records of Hull*, 2:139, 312.

[13]Norfolk County, Massachusetts, Probate no. 14450.

[14]The whereabouts of this painting is unknown. A photograph of it is reproduced in the *Bates Bulletin* (Bates Association, September 1909): 10, 11.

[15]*A Report of the Record Commissioners of Boston, Containing Dorchester Births, Marriages and Deaths to the End of 1825* (City Document 59), Boston Record Commission vol. 21 (Boston: Rockwell and Churchill, City Printers, 1890), p. 245.

[16]*Vital Records of Weymouth, Massachusetts, to the Year 1850*, 2 vols. (Boston: New England Historic Genealogical Society, 1910), 2:274.

[17]Frederick Fairfield Sherman, "Three New England Miniatures," *Magazine Antiques* 4, no. 6 (December 1923): 275–76.

[18]Gail and Norbert Savage, "J. A. Davis," *Magazine Antiques* 104, no. 5 (November 1973): 872–75.

[19]Gail and Norbert Savage and Esther Sparks, *Three New England Watercolor Painters* (Chicago: Art Institute of Chicago, 1974), pp. 42–45.

[20]Louise Brownell Clark, *The Greenes of Rhode Island*, 2 vols. (New York: Knickerbocker Press, 1903), p. 545.

[21]According to vital records at the Warren Town Hall, George Sisson was a farmer, born in 1795. The rather sketchy account in Charles L. Anthony, *Genealogy of the Anthony Family in America, 1495 to 1904* (Sterling, Ill.: Privately printed, 1904), shows the marriage in 1824 of Rhoda Anthony (a second cousin of Giles Anthony, Jane Anthony's father) to Robert Sisson (Ibid., p. 100); in 1789 of Jonathan Anthony to Lydia Sisson; and in 1793 of Jonathan's brother, Elijah, to Lois, sister of Lydia Sisson. Jonathan and Elijah were first cousins of Jane Anthony's paternal grandfather Edward Anthony (Ibid., pp. 95, 97).

[22]Raymon Meyers Tingley, *The Tingley Family* (n.p., 1910), p. 44.

[23]*Catalogue of the Officers and Pupils of the Warren Ladies Seminary for the Year Ending December 1838* (Providence: Knowles, Vose and Company), pp. 2, 7.

[24]Tingley, *The Tingley Family*, p. 23.

[25]Massachusetts 1840 Census Index, p. 338.

[26]*Vital Records of Attleborough, Massachusetts, to the End of the Year 1849* (Salem, Mass.: 1934), p. 743.

[27]The date of Harriet's birth was found in New Hampshire vital statistics, which also indicated that she had lived in New Hampshire for eight years prior to her death there in 1918 at the age of seventy-six—confirming a birth year of 1842.

[28]Clarence Winthrop Bowen, *The History of Woodstock, Connecticut: Genealogies of Woodstock Families*, 8 vols. (Norwood, Mass.: Plimpton Press [vols. 1–6] and Worcester, Mass.: Printed for the [American Antiquarian] Society [New Haven, Conn.: Tuttle, Morehouse and Taylor Company], 1926–1943), 2:612.

[29]No birth or marriage record for a Jane Bowen could be found. However, Births, Marriages and Deaths for the Town of Thompson, vol. 3, 1847–1868 (Connecticut State Library, Hartford, Connecticut), lists the 1847 marriage of Aron Daniels to a Mary Jane Bowen, aged twenty-two; the latter was born in Thompson and, in all likelihood, was

Jane who, like her brother Jonathan, was referred to by her middle name.

[30]Sabra Ann Barber's death record at Westerly, Rhode Island, gives her birthplace as Norwich. She died from dysentery in 1889, aged sixty-five. This would make her twenty years of age when her portrait was painted in 1844.

[31]Edward Franklin Browning, *Genealogy of the Brownings in America from 1621 to 1908* (Newburgh, N.Y.: Privately printed, 1908), p. 148.

[32]Connecticut 1840 Census Index, p. 132.

[33]*Vital Records of Norwich, 1659–1848*, 2 vols. (Hartford, Conn.: Society of Colonial Wars in the State of Connecticut, 1913), 2:915.

[34]The 1850 Rhode Island census reports that Edward was employed as a bank cashier; according to Clark, *The Greenes*, p. 664, he was a cashier for twenty-five years at the Bank of America in Providence.

[35]Willard G. Bixby, *A Genealogy of the Descendants of Joseph Bixby, 1621–1701* (New York, 1919), p. 644.

[36]Clark, *The Greenes*, p. 545.

[37]Bowen, *History of Woodstock*, 2:222.

[38]Elisha S. Arnold, *The Arnold Memorial* (Rutland, Vt.: Tuttle Publishing Co., 1935), p. 242.

[39]Clark, *The Greenes*, pp. 445–46.

[40]Almon P. Hodges, *Genealogical Record of the Hodges Family of New England* (Boston: Frank H. Hodges, Publisher, 1896), p. 243.

[41]Arthur and Sybil Kern, "Was J. A. Davis Jane Anthony Davis? New Supporting Evidence," *Folk Art* (summer 1999): 27–31.

[42]Lillian May and Charles Morris Gardner, *Gardner History and Genealogy* (Privately printed, 1907), p. 137.

[43]Alden G. Beaman, comp., *Rhode Island Vital Records, New Series, Volume 3: Washington County, Rhode Island Births and Marriages from Gravestone Inscriptions, 1688–1850, Comprising the Towns of North Kingstown, South Kingstown, Exeter, Westerly, Charlestown, Richmond, Hopkinton* (Princeton, Mass.: Published by the compiler, 1977), p. 114.

[44]The confusion due to the similarity of the names *Wanton* and *Warren* is seen in another published genealogy of the Gardner/Gardiner family: Caroline E. Robinson, *The Gardiners of Narragansett* (Providence, R.I.: Daniel Goodwin, 1959), pp. 151, 194, 195. This work completely omits the generation of Joseph Wanton Gardner and records Joseph Warren as born in 1799 to Gould and Sarah (his father's parents and date of birth), as married to Mary Hendrick (actually his mother), and death in 1881 (the date of his father's death). As in the International Genealogical Index, his siblings are shown as his children.

[45]Frank O. Spinney, "Joseph H. Davis: New Hampshire Artist of the 1830's," *Magazine Antiques* 44, no. 4 (October 1943): pp. 177–80.

[46]Frank O. Spinney, *Primitive Painters in America: An Anthology by Jean Lipman and Alice Winchester* (New York: Books for Libraries Press, 1950), p. 97.

[47]Savage and Savage, *Three New England Watercolor Painters*, p. 22.

[48]Robert L. Taylor, *Early Families of Limington, Maine* (Limington: Privately printed, n.d.), pp. 94, 96.

[49]Walter G. Davis, *The Ancestry of Nicholas Davis, 1752–1832, of Limington, Maine* (Portland, Maine: Anthoensen Press, 1956), p. 1.

[50]New Hampshire Vital Statistics, State Archives, Concord, N.H.

[51]A birth record for this Joseph H. Davis has not been found. However, his death record gives the date of death as 28 May 1865, at fifty-three years, nine months, and eighteen days, calculating to a birth date of 10 August 1811.

[52]*New England Historical and Genealogical Register* 87 (1933): 126.

[53]Taylor, *Early Families of Limington*, p. 95.

[54]Lora A. W. Underhill, *Descendants of Edward Small of New England*, 3 vols. (Cambridge, Mass.: Riverside Press, 1910), 1:147.

[55]This list, in the collection of the Maine Historical Society, Portland, records "Joseph Davis and Wife / Emeline Davis, Joseph Davis 3d / Anna Davis John Nelson Davis / Richard Lewis Davis." Since Emeline was his older sister, and Anna, John Nelson, and Richard Lewis his younger siblings, "Joseph Davis 3d" must have been Joseph H. Davis.

[56]In the census he is listed as Joseph Davis Jr., undoubtedly a result of the census taker's assigning the "junior" designation to a son with the same given name as his father.

[57]George W. Chamberlain, *Vital Records of Lebanon, Maine, to the Year 1892*, 3 vols. (Augusta: Maine Historical Society, 1922–1923), 1:135 (birth of Sally Rogers, 6 December 1767); 2:180 (her marriage to Amos Chamberlin, 1 January 1788); 3:19 (her death in Lebanon in 1858).

[58]Charles T. Libby, *The Libby Family in America, 1602–1881* (Portland: B. Thurston and Co., 1882), p. 203. Ira Libby lived his entire life on his father's homestead in Berwick. According to the painting's inscription, it was done at "Beach Ridge." Localities called "Beach Ridge" are found in York (York Co.) and Sebago (Cumberland Co.), Maine, and "Beech Ridge" in Scarboro (Cumberland Co.), Sullivan (Hancock Co.), and the former town of Drew (Penobscot Co.), Maine (Stanley Bearce Attwood, *The Length and Breadth of Maine* [Augusta: Kennebec Journal Print Shop, 1946], pp. 104, 106).

[59]The obituary of Joseph Davis, father of the artist, reports that he died at eighty-nine years of age and that he "was the oldest member of the Free Church"; the *Maine Gazetteer*, p. 405, notes that John and Sarah Davis were members of Limington's Free Will Church (G. T. Ridlon Sr., *Saco Settlements and Families* [Portland: Privately printed, 1895], p. 234).

[60]Underhill, *Descendants of Edward Small*, 1:150.

[61]Ibid., 1:152.

[62]Libby, *Libby Family*, p. 122.

[63]Underhill, *Descendants of Edward Small*, 1:155.

[64]Ibid., 1:151.

[65]Ibid., 1:152.

[66]Rufus Emery, *Genealogical Records of Descendants of John and Anthony Emery of Newbury, Mass., 1590–1890* (Salem, Mass.: Emery Cleaves, 1890), p. 434.

[67]Taylor, *Early Families of Limington*, p. 119.

[68]The Maine 1840 census places an Oliver Fernald in North Berwick; Chamberlain, *Vital Records of Lebanon,* 3:40, records his death there on 30 March 1883.
[69]Elliott C. Cogswell, *History of Nottingham, Deerfield, and Northwood* (Manchester, N.H.: Printed by John Clark, 1878), p. 557.
[70]Everett S. Stackpole and Lucien Thompson, *History of the Town of Durham, New Hampshire* (Durham: Published by the Town, 1913), pp. 36, 37; *Vital Records of Dover, New Hampshire, 1686–1850* (Bowie, Md.: Heritage Books, 1977), p. 236.
[71]Katherine F. Richmond, *John Hayes of Dover, New Hampshire* (Tyngsboro, Mass., 1936), pp. 200, 201. Joseph Hayes was born 1 August 1783 in that part of Barrington, New Hampshire, now Strafford. His children were all born in Strafford, including the last two, born in 1832 and 1835.
[72]Ibid., p. 199.
[73]"Chamberlin, Capt. William B., d. 26 Mar[ch] 1842 at Brookfield, ae. 29 y[ears]."
[74]Records of the First Church of Biddeford, Maine, as cited in the notes of Sybil Noyes, a large body of which are held at the library of the Maine Historical Society, Portland, Maine.
[75]Kennebec County, Maine, Deeds, 95:351.
[76]Ibid., 95:351.
[77]A birth record for Elizabeth Ann Davis has not been found. However, the U.S. Census for Morristown, N.J., records her age as twelve years when taken on 20 December 1850, pointing to a birth year of 1838. According to the inscription on her tombstone, Elizabeth died 9 September 1863; if correct, this would indicate a birth in October 1839.
[78]York County, Maine, Deeds, 167:280.
[79]Kennebec County, Maine, Deeds, 119:457.
[80]Middlesex County, Mass., Deeds, 400:492.
[81]Ibid., 400:495.
[82]York County, Maine, Deeds, 183:207.
[83]Ibid., 187:20; 180:195; 190:79, 80, 269; 189:192; 192:159; 193:167; 185:65.
[84]Ibid., 197:288.
[85]Ibid., 198:445.
[86]Middlesex County, Mass., Deeds, 520:576.
[87]Edmund Drake Halsey, *History of Morris County, New Jersey* (New York: W. W. Munsell and Co., 1882), pp. 73, 74.
[88]This and his two subsequent patents are recorded in the files of the United States Patent Office.
[89]Morris County, N.J., Deeds, 65:268. This deed conveys two parcels of land from Joseph H. Davis and Elizabeth P., his wife, of the town of Morris, to Joseph Davis of the town of Woburn [Massachusetts].
[90]Middlesex County, Mass., Deeds, 468:717.
[91]Edward F. Johnson, *Woburn Records of Births, Deaths and Marriages,* 8 vols. (Woburn, Mass., 1890), 2:51. The same date of death is inscribed in a family Bible owned by a descendant.
[92]The notice of their wedding appeared in the 26 June 1822 issue of the *Providence Patriot* and the *Providence Gazette;* it is also recorded in *The Index of Marriages in the Massachusetts Centinel and Columbian Centinel, 1784–1840,* 8 vols. (Worcester, Mass., 1961), 3:764.
[93]This unsigned copy was later given to the John Carter Brown Library of Brown University, along with other material from the Brown family.
[94]Providence Town Papers, vol. 118, 1823–1824, no. 0043109, Rhode Island Historical Society.
[95]Ibid., vol. 121, #044058.
[96]Providence Town Council Meetings, January 1823–May 1824, vol. 170, p. 248, Rhode Island Historical Society.
[97]Beaman, *Rhode Island Vital Records,* p. 72.
[98]George Austin Morrison Jr., *The Clarke Families of Rhode Island* (New York, n.d.), pp. 48, 49, 74, 75.
[99]Records of the United States Marine Corps, National Archives and Records Administration, Washington, D.C.
[100]Record Group 127, Records of the United States Marine Corps, Registers of Discharge, vol. 1, entry 90 (National Archives).
[101]Nina Fletcher Little, in *Maine and Its Role in American Art,* ed. Gertrude Mellon and Elizabeth F. Wilder (New York: Viking Press, 1963), p. 42.
[102]Claude Weigers, a descendant of Royall's brother George, states in a personal communication: "In 1932 my mother visited her cousins in Bangor and vicinity. One of the cousins had had the original Smith family record by Royal [*sic*]. She made a copy of it and that is what I have. Those cousins are all gone now and I have lost contact with the Bangor ones." The whereabouts of the original record is still unknown.
[103]Davis, *The Ancestry of Nicholas Davis,* pp. 29–39.
[104]Alice C. Cousins and Olive W. Hannaford, *Recollections of Old Buxton, Maine* (Farmington, Maine: 1972), pp. 145, 146.
[105]This confusion between uncle and nephew was confounded by the fact that in both cases the first name was on some occasions spelled with one "l," on others with two.
[106]Town of Buxton Family Records, vol. 4, 1748–1891, p. 6. Town Clerk, Buxton, Maine.
[107]*The Records of the Church of Christ in Buxton, Me. During the Pastorate of Dr. Paul Coffin, D.D.* (Cambridge, Mass.: Printed for John Woodman, 1868), p. 74.
[108]Claude R. Weigers and Rosalie Trail Fuller, *Andrew M. and O. S. Smith, Sons of Maine and Nebraska Homesteaders* (Lincoln, Neb., 1979), pp. 9–11.
[109]York County, Maine, Probate Copy Books, vol. 20 (1819–1820), p. 138.
[110]Ibid., 20:139.
[111]Limington Town Papers. This information was obtained by Robert L. Taylor prior to the destruction of the town papers in a fire.
[112]York County, Maine, Probate Copy Books, vol. 30 (1821–1822), pp. 553, 554.
[113]Ibid., vol. 31 (1822–1823), p. 447.
[114]Limington Town Papers.
[115]Weigers and Fuller, *Sons of Maine,* pp. 16–19.
[116]Cumberland Co., Maine, Deeds, 157:567.
[117]Ibid., 162:254.
[118]Gorham, Maine, Town Records, January 1839.
[119]Emery, *Genealogical Records,* p. 412.
[120]Penobscot Co., Maine, Probate Copy Books, vol. 142 (1843), p. 441.

[121]Ibid., vol. 26 (1856), pp. 335, 336; vol. 31, p. 61.
[122]Philip Battell, "Benjamin Franklin Mason," *New England Historical and Genealogical Register* 26 (1872): 226–27.
[123]Emma Forbes Ware, *Ware Genealogy: Robert Ware of Dedham, Massachusetts, 1642–1699, and His Lineal Descendants* (Boston: Charles H. Pope, 1901), pp. 129, 130. Pomfret Town Records, Births, 1929, p. 70.
[124]Alfred Frankenstein and Arthur K. D. Healy, *Two Journeymen Painters* (Middlebury, Vt.: Sheldon Museum, 1950), p. 9.
[125]Arthur and Sybil Kern, "Thomas Ware: Vermont Portrait Painter," *Clarion* (winter 1983/1984): 36–45.
[126]Henry Swan Dana, *History of Woodstock, Vermont* (Boston and New York: Houghton, Mifflin and Company, 1889), pp. 470–75.
[127]George Chandler, *The Chandler Family: Descendants of William and Annis Chandler Who Settled at Roxbury, Mass. 1637* (Worcester, Mass.: Press of Charles Hamilton, 1883), pp. 380, 419–20.
[128]C. H. Vilas, *A Genealogy of the Descendants of Peter Vilas* (Madison, Wisc.: C. H. Vilas, 1875), p. 60.
[129]Groce and Wallace, *Dictionary of Artists in America*, p. 654.
[130]Jean Lipman and Alice Winchester, *Primitive Painters in America, 1750–1950* (New York: Dodd Mead and Company, 1950), p. 181.
[131]Woodstock Births (1773–1863) and Deaths (1822–1857), Book A, p. 28. Town Clerk, Woodstock, Vt.
[132]Dana, *History of Woodstock*, p. 130.
[133]Joshua Bailey Richmond, *The Richmond Family, 1594–1886, and Pre-American Ancestors, 1040–1594* (Boston: Privately printed, 1897), pp. 52, 120.
[134]Dana, *History of Woodstock*, pp. 83, 84.
[135]Richmond, *The Richmond Family*, p. 120.
[136]Charles Edney Marcy, *History and Genealogy of John Marcy, 1662–1724* (Woodstock, Conn.: Charles Edney Marcy, 1980), p. 135.
[137]Communication from Lauren Hewes, Assistant Curator, Shelburne Museum, Shelburne, Vt.
[138]Henry Hobart Vail, *Pomfret, Vermont*, 2 vols. (Boston: Cockayne, 1930), 2:582.
[139]Edward T. Fairbanks, *The Town of St. Johnsbury, Vt.* (St. Johnsbury: Cowles Press, 1907), pp. 21–27.
[140]Orline St. John Alexander, *The St. John Genealogy* (New York: Grafton Press, 1907), p. xiii. The usually interchangeable names *Pamelia, Parmelia, Permelia* arose as the name *Pamela* became popular in the middle eighteenth century; they reflect the early pronunciation of the name, with the accent on the second syllable.
[141]Richmond, *The Richmond Family*, p. 255.
[142]Ware, *Ware Genealogy*, p. 130; Vail, *Pomfret, Vermont*, 2:593.

SECTION VIII

Checklists

Selected Checklist of Manuscript, Watercolor, and Needlework Family Registers and Family Trees in New England, 1780–1846

Peter Benes

Design categories

Symmetrical decorations, progressions
Paired images
Architectural motifs
Chains/circles
Hearts
Adjacent hearts: Charlestown Academy
Tree genealogies
Tree genealogies: Mrs. Gill's Academy
Tree and paired-hearts (eastern Middlesex County)
Tree and paired-hearts (northern Middlesex County)
Tree and paired-hearts (Gloucester's fifth parish)
Tree and paired-hearts (New Hampshire)
Climbing roses and paired-hearts

Symmetrical decorations, progressions

1. Buckman/Pote. William Buckman (1706–1776) and Ann Pote (1716–1776); m. 2 February 1736; ch. 1737–1757. Falmouth, Maine. Watercolor, 13 × 8 in. NSDAR. Allen, *Family Record*, entry 2; John E. Frost, *Maine Probate Abstracts*, 2 vols. (Camden, Maine: Picton Press, 1991), index, s.v. "Buckman."

2. Walker/Snow. George Walker (b. 1731) and Elizabeth Snow (b. 1731); m. 15 September 1754; ch. 1755–1771. Kittery Point, Maine. Watercolor; 2 sheets, each 9 × 7 in. NMAH. Allen, *Family Record*, entries 13 and 14.

3. Knight/Knight. Samuel Knight (1729–1776) and Mary Knight (1729–1787); m. 22 November 1750; ch. 1753–1765. Falmouth, Maine, circa 1780s. Watercolor. WM. Charles S. Tibbetts, "The Knight Family, [Descendants of] John Knight of Newbury, Mass., and His Brother, Richard Knight," MS at NEHGS, 1941, part 1, p. 25. Illustrated in Peter Andrews, "Genealogy: The Search for a Personal Past," *American Heritage* 33, no. 5 (August/September 1982): 13.

4. Poor/Merlis. [ ]Noyes Poor (1758–1837) and Lydia Merlis (1777–1852); m. 5 July 1796; ch. 1796–1813. Attributed to Mary Little Poor. Ink and wash. NEHGS. Copy shown at *The Art of Family* meeting at NEHGS, 22 August 1996.

Paired images

5. Sargent/Currier. Stephen Sargent (1773–1858) and Betsey Currier (1774–1829); m. 25 January 1804; ch. 1804–1820. Warner, N.H.; "Tho. Hatckett." Watercolor, 12 × 10 in. NHHS. Allen, *Family Record*, entry 19.

6. Prescott/Jewell. Eliphalet Prescot (b.1772) and Mary Jewell (b.1775); 30 December 1792; ch. 1793–1822. Sandwich, N.H. Watercolor, 14 × 12 in. NHHS. *Decorative Arts of New Hampshire: A Sesquicentennial Exhibition* (Concord, N.H., New Hampshire Historical Society, 1973), entry 96.

7. Dudley/Glidden. Moses Dudley (1766–1843) and Nancy Glidden (1764–1843); m. 26 April 1788; ch. 1789–1811. Raymond, N.H., 1805; "George Melville." Watercolor, 9 × 15 in. NHHS. *Decorative Arts of New Hampshire*, entry 95; Allen, *Family Record*, entry 17.

8. Church/Humphrey. Asa Church (1766–1747) and Juliaette Humphrey (1772–1845); m. 29 October 1789; ch. 1790–1816. Jericho, Vt. Watercolor, 22 × 18 in. SM. Allen, *Family Record*, entry 22.

9. Richardson/Travis. Loa Richardson (1770–1826) and Salley Travis (b. 1773); m. 30 March 1797; ch. 1798–1813. New England[?], circa 1810. Paper cutwork. OSV. Illustrated in Andrews, "Genealogy," p. 14.

Architectural motifs

10. Stoughton/Prior. William Stoughton (1750–1831) and Eleanor Prior (1755–1840); m. 7 April 1788; ch. 1789–1796. East Windsor, Conn., 1796; "W S." Watercolor. NA. Allen, *Family Register,* entry 6.

11. Jones/[ ]. William Jones and Ann [ ]; m. 28 February 1785; ch. 1787–1801. Boston[?]; "Wrought by Harriet Jones 1802." Embroidery. Location unknown. Ethel S. Bolton and Eva J. Coe, *American Samplers* (1923; reprint, New York: Weathervane Books, 1973), plate 85.

12. Dodds/Morse. John Dodds (b. 1755) and Hannah Morse (b. 1758); m. 6 February 1777; ch. 1777–1806. "Done by John Dodds April 1806." Watercolor. Location unknown. Illustrated, *Kennedy Quarterly* 12, no. 1 (January 1973): entry 5.

13. Batten/Thorpe. John Batten (b. 1765) and Procinda Thorp (b. 1772); m. 6 February 1794; ch. 1795–1812. Salem, Mass.; "Nancy Batten Aged 14 1809." Embroidery. Private collection. Allen, *Family Record,* entry 13.

14. Harwood/Airmet. Peter Harwood (b. 1766) and Elizabeth Airmet (b. 1770); m. 22 January 1787; ch. 1789–1812. 1814; "Elizabeth A. Harwood." Embroidery. Location unknown. Bolton and Coe, *American Samplers,* plate 85.

15. Wheeler/Rice. Eliphalet Wheeler (1791–1854) and Clarissa Rice (1791–1873); m. 4 February 1813; ch. 1813–1822. "W. Nixon, Pinx. Framingham 1820." Watercolor. Private collection. Arthur B. Kern and Sybil B. Kern, *Magazine Antiques* (September 1983): p. 518.

16. Loring/Floyd; Loring/Blake; Loring/Bates. Mathew Loring (b. 1758) and Nancy Floyd (b. 1747); m. 15 January; ch. 1787–1797. Mathew Loring (b. 1758) and Sarah Blake (b. 1768); m. 17 January 1799; ch. 1800. Mathew Loring (b. 1758) and Mercy Bates (b. 1765); m. 6 June 1801; ch. 1802–1811. Boston; "Wrought by Hannah Loring aged 12 At Miss Perkins Academy Boston 1812. " Embroidery. MMA. Bolton and Coe, *American Samplers,* opp. p. 227; *Family Record,* entry 54.

17. Merriam/Wheeler. Joseph Merriam (b. 1767) and Lucy Wheeler (b. 1774); m. 12 December 1799; ch. 1800–1820. Concord, Mass.; "By J. Merriam, Jr 1826" (1805–1832). Watercolor. Location unknown. Photocopy in Merriam genealogy folder, Special Collections, Concord Free Public Library, Concord, Mass. *Concord, Massachusetts, Births, Marriages and Deaths, 1635–1850* (Concord: Printed by the Town, n.d. [1891]), p. 386.

18. Barrett/Nichols. Chester Barrett (1777) and Achsah Nichols (1779); m. 30 November 1801; ch. 1802–1815. Massachusetts (Franklin Co.), circa 1816; "J. Forbes scrip." Watercolor, 16 × 13 in. NHHS. Allen, *Family Record,* entry 10.

Chains/circles

19. Root/Cole. Ezekiel Root (1764–1802) and Cynthia Cole (b. 1767); m. 14 February 1788; ch. 1789–1800. Farmington, Conn. Watercolor, 9 × 11 in. NA. Allen, *Family Record,* entry 7.

20. Wells/Dwight. Moses Wells and Abigail Dwight; m. [ ]; ch. [ ]. Hatfield, Mass., 1807; Sally D. Wells (b. 1795). Embroidery. HD. Curator's report, Historic Deerfield.

21. Giles/Baldwin. John Giles (1762–1825) and Susan Baldwin (1764–1788); m. 1787. John Giles and Mary Adams; m. 6 April 1789; ch. 1790–1806. Groton, Mass.; "Family Record / Wrought by P. Giles / Groton Semy. Mass." Embroidery. Location unknown. Copy in possession of the author.

22. Newcomb/Pratt. John R. Newcomb (1769–1821) and Mary Pratt (1770–1837); m. 4 December 1790; ch. 1790–1812. Quincy, Mass.; "Done by Emeline Newcombe Quincy South School, March 9th. 1846." Watercolor. NSDAR. Allen, *Family Record,* entry 12.

23. Newcomb/[ ]. John Newcombe (1804–1848) and [ ]; m. [ ]; ch. [ ]. Quincy, Mass.; Emeline Newcombe Quincy South School, March 1846. Watercolor. NSDAR. Allen, *Family Record,* entry 12.

24. Burrell/Pratt. B. Burrell (b. 1787) and Mary Pratt (b. 1792); m. 1816: ch. 1818–1836. Massachusetts[?]. Location unknown. Copy in possession of the author.

25. Parker/Clark. Blake Parker (b. 1806) and Mary Clark (b. 1807); m. 30 September 1830; ch. 1831–1846. Medfield, Mass.; "Done at Medfield School March 15 1854 F. D. Parker." Frances D. Parker (b. 1839).Watercolor and gilt. NEHGS. Copy shown at *The Art of Family* meeting at NEHGS, 22 August 1996.

26. Howe/Richardson; Richardson/Howe. James Howe and Susan Richardson; John Richardson and Jane Howe. Boston, 1803; "John Howe...Inscripsit...." Pen and wash. Location unknown; ex collection Nina F. Little. Nina F. Little, *Country Arts in Early American Homes* (New York: E. P. Dutton, 1975), fig. 73.

Hearts

27. Camp/Camp. Joseph Camp (b. 1744) and Anna Camp (b. 1749); m. 1768; ch. 1772–1790. Newington, Conn.; "Made by Anna Camp in January AD 1787" (b. 1773).

Watercolor and ink, 13 × 14 in. Newington Historical Society and Trust. Newington [Conn.] Historical Society and Trust, Gift of the Camp Family, 79-12:55. See Peter Benes, *Two Towns: Concord and Wethersfield* (Concord, Mass.: Concord Antiquarian Museum, 1982), entry 294.

28. Dodge/Moody; Dodge/Dudley. Daniel Dodge (1745–1835) and Martha Moody (1735–1798); m. 18 November 1769; ch. 1770–1780. Daniel Dodge and Mary Kimball Dudley (1746–1813); m. 24 January 1799. Newbury, Mass., 1809; "Daniel Moody Lankester, Newbury East School, B. H. Cheever." Watercolor. NEHGS. Illustrated in *American Heritage* 33, no. 5 (August/September 1982): back cover.

29. Stanwood/Marchant; Stanwood/Dodge; Stanwood/Burnham. Joseph Stanwood and Eunice Marchant (1763–1784); m. [ ]; ch. 1763. Joseph Stanwood and Sarah Dodge (1772–1810); m. [ ]; ch. 1786–1804. Joseph Stanwood and Ruth Burnham (b. 1769). Newbury, Mass.; "Taken by Atkinson Stanwood Aet 13 Feby 25th 1814." Watercolor, 15 × 12 in. Historical Society of Old Newbury. "The Genealogy of Joseph Stanwood's Family," Historical Society of Old Newbury, Gift of Mary E. Couch in 1924. See Peter Benes, *Old Town and the Waterside* (Newburyport: Historical Society of Old Newbury, 1986), entry 45; Allen, *Family Record*, entry 9.

30. Stanwood/Marchant; Stanwood/Dodge; Stanwood/Burnham. Joseph Stanwood (1764–1833) and Eunice Marchant (1763–1784); m.[ ]; ch. 1763 Joseph Stanwood and Sarah Dodge (1772–1810); m. [ ]; ch. 1786–1804. Joseph Stanwood and Ruth Burnham (b. 1769). Newbury, Mass.; "Atkinson Stanwood, Newburyport, June 7, 1816." Watercolor, 10 × 8 in. SPNEA. Selina Little to the author, 29 and 31 March 1996.

Adjacent hearts: Charlestown Academy, Charlestown, Massachusetts

31. Hunt/T[uft]; Hunt/Snow. Reuben Hunt (b. 1783) and Eliza T[uft] (1786–1817); m. 27 October 1814; ch. 1815–1816. Reuben Hunt (b. 1783) and Sarah Snow (1785–1823); m. 10 March 1819; ch. 1820–1822. Charlestown, Mass.; "Wrought by Eliza Ann Hunt aged nine years 1821." Embroidery. Cooper-Hewitt Museum. Sandra Brant and Elissa Cullman, *Small Folk: A Celebration of Childhood in America* (New York: Dubbon, 1980), entry 82; Cynthia V. A. Schaffner and Susan Klein, *Folk Hearts: A Celebration of the Heart Motif in American Folk Art* (New York: Alfred A. Knopf, 1984), opp. p. 43.

32. Howe/Richardson. Jonathan Howe and Frances Richardson; m. 3 September 1807; ch. 1809–1824. "Wrought by Frances Howe / Charlestown Feb 12 1827 / Aged 10 years." Embroidery. Location unknown. Sotheby's 4590Y, Lot 680.

33. Williams/Corey. John Williams (b. 1773) and Abigail Corey (b. 1776); m. 28 December 1796; ch. 1798–1816. "Lucy Ann Williams Charlestown November 19 1830 Aged 14 years." Embroidery. Location unknown. Sotheby's 5156, Lot 511.

34. Wild/Healy. Elisha Wild and Caroline Healy (b. 1798); m. 26 February 1818; ch. 1818–1824. "Wrought by Rebecca J. Wild / Charlestown Jany 1831 / Aged 10 years." Embroidery. Mary Jane Edmonds. Schaffner and Klein, *Folk Hearts*, p. 43.

Tree genealogies

35. Russell and Shoemaker family. New Bedford, Mass.; "Drawn Sept 1838... by J S Russell." Watercolor, 17 × 10 in. New Bedford Whaling Museum. "Russell Family Tree, by Joseph S. Russell," New Bedford Whaling Museum, AR 80.48.

36. Emery/Emery. Moses Emery (1715–1789) and Lydia Emery (1717–1800); m. 24 March 1838; ch. 1739–1764; grandchildren, great-grandchildren. Newbury, ca. 1815. Ink and watercolor, 23 × 17 in. Gregory H. Laing. Rufus Emery, *Genealogical Records of John and Anthony Emery, Newbury, Mass.* (Salem: Cleaves, 1890), pp. 13, 18; Elizabeth K. Folsom, *Genealogy of the Folsom Family*, 2 vols. (Rutland, Vt.: Tuttle, 1938), 1:321–23.

37. Gilson/Barrett. Ephraim H. Gilson (b. 1787) and Lydia Barrett (b. 1790); m. ca. 1811; ch. 1812–1833. Townsend, Mass., ca. 1833. Watercolor. NHA. Federal Census 1820, 1850.

38. Butterfield/[ ]; Butterfield/Comins. Levi Butterfield (1762–1837) and Jarusha [ ]; m. 1781; ch. 1783–1785. Levi Butterfield (1762–1837) and Isabela Comins (1771–1838); m. 1787; ch. 1789–1816 Putney, Vt., or Jefferson County, N.Y. Watercolor, 14 × 9 in. NEHGS. Copy shown by Abbott L. Cummings at the *The Art of Family* meeting at NEHGS, 22 August 1996. Copy also owned by Shirley M. Barnes, Wayland, Mass.

Tree genealogies: Mrs. Gill's Academy, West Cambridge, Massachusetts

39. Reed/Wyman. Daniel Reed (1768?–1820) and Priscilla Wyman (1766–1840); m. 26 November 1789; ch. 1790–1803. Mrs. Gill's Academy, West Cambridge, Mass.; attributed to Abigail Reed (b. 1797). Watercolor. Private collection. Brian E. Hogg to the author, 15 February 1989; Benjamin Cutter and William Cutter, *History of the Town of Arlington* (Boston: Clapp, 1880), p. 288.

40. Tufts/Cutler. John Tufts (b. 1776) and Rebecah Cutler (b.1779); m. ca. 1798; ch. 1799–1812. On back: "Done by Rebecca Tufts Fessenden at Mrs. Gill's Academy, West Cambridge, Mass" (b. 1799). Watercolor. Arthur Liverant in 1988. *Kennedy Quarterly* 9 (December 1969): 215; Arlington Vital Records, p. 16; *Vital Records of Cambridge* (Boston, 1915), 2:103, 395; Cutter and Cutter, *History of the Town of Arlington*, p. 211; Glee F. Krueger to the author, 17 January 1988; Glee F. Krueger, *New England Samplers* (Sturbridge, Mass.: Old Sturbridge Village, 1978), p. 188.

41. Russell/Adams. Edward Russell (1764–1808) and Lydia Adams (b. 1767–1790); m. 11 May 1786; ch. 1786–1801. West Cambridge, Mass., ca. 1809. Embroidery, 24 × 19 in. NSDAR. Bolton and Coe, *American Samplers*, pp. 113, 218; Cutter and Cutter, *History of the Town of Arlington*, p. 296; *Maine Antique Digest*, May 1986, p. 11–B (hereafter cited as *MAD*); Allen, *Family Record*, no. 59, owned by NSDAR Museum in 1989.

42. Fessenden/Munroe. Ichabod Fessenden (1769–1830) and Rebecca Munroe (b. 1771); m. 1795; ch. 1796–1816. West Cambridge, Mass., 1821; "Sophronia Fessenden AE 14 Yrs" (b. 1807). Watercolor. Private collection. Cutter and Cutter, *History of the Town of Arlington*, p. 238; Charles Hudson, *History of the Town of Lexington, Middlesex County, Massachusetts* (Boston: Wiggin and Lunt, 1868), p. 158; Fessenden papers (private collection); *Cambridge Vital Records*, p. 129.

Tree and paired-hearts: The school-taught embroidered group in eastern Middlesex County

43. Townsend/Jenison. David Townsend (1795–1814) and Sarah Jenison (1748–1814); m. 23 November 1773; ch. 1775–1789. Watertown, Mass., ca. 1790; Embroidery. Concord Museum. *Vital Records of Waltham, Mass., to the Year 1850* (Boston: NEHGS, 1904), pp. 91, 91, 292; *Watertown, Massachusetts, Records*, 8 vols. (Watertown, Mass.: Historical Society, 1894–1939), 3:126, 158; Henry Bond, *Genealogies of the Families and Descendants of the Early Settlers of Watertown*, 2 vols. (Boston: Little, Brown, 1855), 1:605.

44. Davis/Stearns. Thaddeus Davis (b. 1754) and Sarah Stearns (1759–1807); m. 28 September 1779; ch. 1780–1795. Bedford, Mass., ca. 1800. Embroidery. Sandy Macfarlane. Billerica Vital Records, pp. 185, 320; Bedford Vital Records, pp. 18–20; Sheila Rideout to the author, 15 December 1986; Avis S. Van Wagenen, *Genealogy and Memoirs of Isaac Stearns* (Syracuse, N.Y.: Courier, 1901), p. 79; Bond, *Genealogies of the Families and Descendants*, 1:467–71.

45. Wellington/Ball. Benjamin Wellington (1743–1812) and Martha Ball (b. 1745); m. 8 December 1766; ch. 1769–1789. Lexington, Mass., ca. 1801. Patty Wellington[?] (1785–1846). Embroidery. Betty Ring. Elizabeth D. Garrett, "American Samplers," *Magazine Antiques* (April 1975): 688; Ring, "Collecting," p. 90; Ring communication; Hudson, *History of the Town of Lexington*, pp. 254–55; Bond, *Genealogies of the Families and Descendants*, 1:12, 632.

46. Wyman/Putnam. Abel Wyman (b. 1747) and Ruth Putnam (b. 1751); m. 20 October 1772; ch. 1773–1791. Burlington, Mass; "Lucy P. Wyman's work / 1807" (b. 1791). Embroidery. Private collection. Bolton and Coe, *American Samplers*, p. 230, plate 76; Garrett, "American Samplers," p. 688; Burlington Vital Records, pp. 48–50; Edward F. Johnson, *Woburn Records of Births, Deaths and Marriages*, 3 vols. (Boston, 1891), 1:291–92, 3:318; Rideout communication.

47. Meriam/Simonds. Rufus Meriam (1762–1847) and Martha Simonds (1766–1849); m. 23 August 1785; ch. 1787–1804. Lexington, Mass., ca. 1808; "Eliza Meriam's Work" (b. 1793). Embroidery. Private collection. Hudson, *History of the Town of Lexington*, pp. 140, 214.

48. Fisk/Hagar. Abraham Fisk (b. 1773) and Grace Hagar (b. 1774); m. 20 November 1794; ch. 1796–1811. Waltham, Mass., ca. 1811; "Lorenza Fisk Work" (b. 1796). Embroidery. LHS. Waltham Vital Records, pp. 36–39, 345, 161; Bond, *Genealogies of the Families and Descendants*, 1:211, 268; Susan B. Swan, *Plain and Fancy* (New York: Holt, Rinehart, Winston, 1977), p. 84.

49. Underwood/Munroe. Joseph Underwood (1749–1829) and Mary Munroe (b. 1749); m. 21 March 1771; ch. 1772–1790. Lexington, Mass., ca. 1813; "Mary M. Smith" (b. 1798). Embroidery. LHS. Hudson, *History of the Town of Lexington*, pp. 151, 255, 251, 642.

50. Parker/Simonds. Robert Parker (1771–1840) and Elizabeth Simonds (1772–1849); m. 25 October 1793; ch. 1794–1806. Lexington, Mass.; "Eliza E. Parker 1818" (b. 1804). Embroidery. Location unknown. Bolton and Coe, *American Samplers*, pp. 113, 204; Hudson, *History of the Town of Lexington*, p. 173; Theodore Parker, *John Parker of Lexington* (Worcester, Mass.: Hamilton, 1893), p. 157.

51. Bright/Bright. Francis Bright (1766–1828) and Susanna Bright (b. 1778); m. 27 December 1797; ch. 1798–1818. Watertown, Mass., ca. 1820; "Lucretia Bright" (1807–1828). Embroidery. NSDAR. Garrett, "American Samplers," p. 688; *Watertown, Massachusetts, Records*, 3:153; 161, 188; Bond, *Genealogies of the Families and Descendants*, 1:111, 214; Anne Sebba, *Samplers* (New York: Thames and Hudson, 1979), p. 106.

52. Locke/Foster. Loah Locke (1783–1865) and Mary Foster (1784–1851); m. 15 March 1805; ch. 1805–1819. Lexington, Mass.; "Lydia Locke, 1825" (b. 1813). Embroidery. Private collection. Hudson, *History of the Town of Lexington*, p. 125; Judith Lund to the author, 24 September and 3 October 1982; 30 December 1986; 10 January 1987.

53. Garfield/Hagar. Joseph Garfield (b. 1761) and Susanna Hagar (b. 1769); m. 4 April 1787; ch. 1788–1811. Waltham, Mass., ca. 1825; "Susan Garfield" (b. 1795). Embroidery. Private collection. *Waltham Vital Records*, pp. 41, 45, 155; Glee F. Krueger to the author, 29 July 1982; 14 January and 5 and 26 February 1987; Bond, *Genealogies of the Families and Descendants*, 1:235, 268.

54. Plympton/Holden. Thomas Ruggles Plympton (b. 1782) and Betsy Holden; m. 2 October 1805; ch. 1806–1822. Waltham[?], Mass., ca. 1825–1829; "Louisa H. Plympton" (b. 1816). Embroidery. Private collection. Levi B. Chase, *A Genealogy and Historical Notices of the Plimpton or Plympton Family in America* (1884); *Antiques and Arts Weekly,* 13 May 1983; Sotheby's 4938, Lot 625; *Waltham Vital Records,* pp. 74, 205.

55. Howland/Hastings. Benjamin Howland (b. 1770) and Hephsibah Hastings; m. 3 June 1794; ch. 1795–1811. Dover, Mass., ca. 1824; "Wrought by Hephsibah Howland" (b. 1809). Embroidery. Private collection. *Howland Quarterly* 32 (January–April 1968); Franklyn Howland, *A Brief Genealogical and Biographical History* (New Bedford, Mass.: privately printed, 1885), p. 350.

56. Mulliken/Whiting. John Mulliken (b. 1754) and Lydia Whiting (b. 1757); m. 13 June 1780; ch. 1781–1793. Lexington, Mass.; "Faustina Mulliken's Work" (b. 1793). Embroidery. Location unknown. Marc Matz and Heidi Pribell, *The Collections of Cornelia Van Rensselaer Hartman* (Cambridge, Mass.: auction catalogue, Sunday, 11 June 1989), pp. 255–56, back cover.

Tree and paired-hearts: Other examples in northwestern Middlesex County and lower New Hampshire

57. Whitney/Whitcomb. Oliver Whitney (1786–1855) and Mercy Whitcomb (1791–1865); m. 16 March 1809; ch. 1811–1823. Lunenberg, Mass., ca. 1825. Embroidery. Private collection. *Vital Records of Harvard, Massachusetts, to the Year 1850* (Boston, 1917), pp. 111–18; 232; *MAD,* June 1986, p. 16–A; Frederick C. Pierce, *The Descendants of John Whitney* (Chicago: privately printed, 1895), pp. 102, 199; Sheila Rideout to the author, 15 December 1986.

58. Sterns/Lane. John Sterns (Stearns) (1765–1836) and Mary Lane (1776–1815); m. 10 February 1800; ch. 1802–1818. Billerica, Mass., ca. 1815–1820. Watercolor. Location unknown. *MAD* 7:3 (April 1979); Van Wagenen, *Genealogy and Memoirs of Isaac Stearns,* pp. 185–87, where the record is cited as a "rude picture, representing a family-tree, with a heart-shaped apple to record each birth"; Bond, *Genealogies of the Families and Descendants,* 1:471.

59. Farwell/Carter. Asa Farwell (b. 1768) and Vashti Carter (1772–1853); m. 19 February 1796; ch. 1797–1814. Fitchburg, Mass., ca. 1807. Watercolor. Pam Boynton. *The Old Records of the Town of Fitchburg* (Fitchburg, Mass.: City Council, 1898–1913), 2:244; 313–14; 3:159.

60. Morse/Bigelow. Hezekiah Morse (b. 1768) and Sarah Bigelow (b. 1771); m. 1790; ch. 1791–1799. Leonard Morse (b. 1791) and Clarissa Bartell; m. 1822. Weston, Mass., ca. 1809; "Sally Morse Ae 10 year" (b. 1799). Embroidery. Location unknown. Sheila Rideout to the author, 15 December 1986; Betty Ring to the author, 9 January and 26 February 1986; *Vital Records of Sherborn, Massachusetts, to the Year 1850* (Boston, 1911), pp. 68, 214; *Town of Weston: Births, Deaths, and Marriages, 1707–1900* (Boston: Town, 1901), pp. 129, 164; Abner Morse, *Genealogical Register of the Inhabitants of Sherborn and Holliston* (Boston: Damrell and Moor, 1856), p. 180.

61. Rice/Hubbard. John Rice (b. 1768) and Lucy Hubbard (b. 1775); ch. 1793–1806. Ashby[?], Mass.; "Lucy Rice 1811"[?] (b. 1799). Embroidery. Location unknown. Bolton and Coe, *American Samplers,* pp. 113, 214; *Concord, Mass., Births, Marriages and Deaths,* p. 362.

62. Rice/Hubbard. John Rice (b. 1768) and Lucy Hubbard (b. 1775); ch. 1793–1806. Ashby[?], Mass., ca. 1818; "Elmira Rice"[?] (b. 1803). Embroidery. Location unknown. Bolton and Coe, *American Samplers,* p. 213; *Concord, Mass., Births, Marriages and Deaths,* p. 362.

63. Sawyer/Wyman. Josiah Sawyer (1772–1800) and Patty [Martha] Wyman (b. 1771); m. 1794[?]; ch. 1795–1800. Samuel Ryan (b. 1781) and Patty [Martha] Wyman (b. 1771); m. 1802; ch. 1803–1816. Sharon, N.H., ca. 1816. Watercolor. Location unknown. Garbisch Sale No. 73, p. 33; H. Thornton King Jr., *Sliptown: The History of Sharon, New Hampshire* (Tokyo: Tuttle, 1965), pp. 107–9, 124–31.

64. K[ ]/K[ ]. John K. (b. 1769) and Olive K. (b. 1776); m. 1795. Sharon[?], N.H., ca. 1816. Watercolor. Location unknown. Pam Boynton to the author, 30 October 1986.

Tree and paired-hearts: Sandy Bay Parish (Gloucester's fifth parish, now the town of Rockport)

65. Rowe/Dennison. William Rowe (b. 1764) and Betsy Dennison (1762–1843?); m. 28 July 1782; ch. 1782–1806. Gloucester, Mass., ca. 1790; "William Saville Glocester September 17 [ ]." Watercolor. SBHS. *Vital Records of Gloucester, Massachusetts,* 3 vols. (Topsfield, Mass.: Topsfield Historical Society), 2:174, 177; 3:266 (hereafter cited as *Gloucester Vital Records*).

66. Lane/Marchant. David Lane (b. 1750) and Hannah Marchent (b. 1754); m. 12 November 1772; ch. 1774–1793. Gloucester, Mass., ca. 1791; "William Saville [ ]." Watercolor. Howard and Catherine Feldman. Schaffner and Klein, *Folk Hearts,* p. 56; *Kennedy Quarterly* 2 (January 1973): 6; *Gloucester Vital Records,* 1:409, 469; 2:328; cited as P.R. 564.

67. Parsons/Lane; Parsons/Knights. James Parsons (b. 1745) and Deborah Lane (1745–1785); m. 17 December 1768; ch. 1769–1780. James Parsons (b. 1745) and Patience Knights (b. 1762); m. 4 July 1785; ch. 1786–1793. Gloucester, Mass., ca. 1793; "by William Saville." Watercolor. SPNEA, Beauport collection. William Blanford and Elizabeth Blanford, *Beauport Impressions* (Boston: SPNEA, 1965), p. 53; *Gloucester Vital Records,* 2:406.

68. Woodbury/Lane. John Woodbury (1739–1790) and Susanna Lane (1744–1823); m. 8 February 1762; ch. 1762–1878. "Gloucester April 30th 1795 / Drawn by William Saville." Watercolor. CAHA. *Gloucester Vital Records,* 1:420, 2:593; cited as P.R. 592.

69. Channel/Burnham; Channel/[ ]. Abraham Channel (b. 1759) and Abagail Burnham (1754–1794); m. 4 January 1779; ch. 1780–1792. Abraham Channel and Wealthy [ ] (b. 1782); m. 1 June 1814; ch. 1814–1820[?]. "Gloucester July 10th, 1795 / Drawn by William Saville." Watercolor. Ex collection Nina Fletcher Little. Nina F. Little, *Little by Little* (New York: E. P. Dutton, 1985), p. 143; *Vital Records of Ipswich, Massachusetts,* 3 vols. (Salem, Mass.: Essex Institute, 1910), 2:73, 91, 3:516.

70. Grover/Tarr. Ebenezer Grover (b. 1769) and Sally Tarr (b. 1773); m. 11 March 1792; ch. 1793–1800. Gloucester, Mass.; "Gloucester May 1st 1801 / Drawn by William Saville." Watercolor. SPNEA, Beauport collection. Blanford and Blanford, *Beauport Impressions,* pp. 52–53; *Gloucester Vital Records,* 1:308, 2:249; cited as P.R. 426.

71. Hicks/Parsons. Joseph Hicks (1778–1823) and Susanna Parsons (b. 1782); m. 21 November 1803; ch. 1804–1823. Gloucester, Mass.; "Gloucester April 4th / 1805[?] Drawn by Joshua P[ ]." Watercolor. Location unknown. *Kennedy Quarterly* 10 (December 1970): entry 240; *Gloucester Vital Records,* 1:358, 526, 2:284; 3:172.

72. Tarr/Somes. Jabez Tarr (1759–1844) and Peggy Somes (1765–1827); m. 2 December 1782; ch. 1784–1809. Gloucester, Mass., ca. 1809. Watercolor. SBHS. Marshall W. S. Swan, *Town on Sandy Bay: A History of Rockport, Massachusetts* (Rockport, Mass.: Town, 1980), pp. 82–83; *Vital Records of Rockport, Massachusetts* (Salem, Mass.: Essex Institute, 1924), p. 115; *Gloucester Vital Records,* 1:536, 2:510, 3:305; cited as P.R. 903.

73. Parsons/Goss; Davis/Goss. James Parsons (1788–1808) and Tammy Goss (b. 1790); m. 18 December 1806; ch. 1807. Timothy Riggs Davis (b. 1781) and Tammy Goss (b. 1790); m. 11 November 1809; ch. 1810–1832. Gloucester, Mass.; "Gloucester July 24th 1811 / Drawn by Joshua Pool Jr." Watercolor. Private collection. *Gloucester Vital Records,* 1:290, 2:236, 413.

74. Dennison/Griffin. James Dennison (b. 1770) and Thomasin Griffin (1777–1839); m. 14 November 1799; ch. 1800–1818. Gloucester, Mass.; "Gloucester April 10th, 1815 / Taken by William Saville." Watercolor. CAHA. *Gloucester Vital Records,* 1:178, 245, 3:118.

75. Bickford/Clark. Andrew Bickford (b. 1783) and Olive Clark (b. 1790); m. 1 December 1808; ch. 1810–1826. Gloucester, Mass., ca. 1820; "Done by J. Pool." Watercolor. Location unknown. Schaffner and Klein, *Folk Hearts,* p. 57; *Vital Records of Rockport,* p. 47; *Gloucester Vital Records,* 1:151, 2:84, 3:70; cited as P.R. 174.

76. Doyle/Clark. Felix Doyle (1794–1824) and Tamma Clark (1796–1839); m. 18 March 1816; ch. 1816–1826. Gloucester, Mass., ca. 1821. Watercolor. SBHS. *Gloucester Vital Records,* 2:187, 3:122; cited as P.R. 189.

77. Colbey/Tarr. Benjamin Colbey (b. 1792) and Lois Tarr (1797–1869); m. 25 December 1816; ch. 1817–1831. Gloucester, Mass., ca. 1824. Watercolor. SBHS. *Gloucester Vital Records,* 2:537.

78. Denen/Gott. Job Dennen (b. 1790) and Lucy Gott (b. 1796); m. 1 June 1817; ch. 1817–1838. Gloucester, Mass., ca. 1838; "By Wm. Richardson." Watercolor. Mr. and Mrs. Erving Wolf. Brant and Cullman, *Small Folk,* entry 76; *Gloucester Vital Records,* 1:211; 2:175; 3:115, cited as P.R. 282.

79. Rowe/Poole. John Rowe Jr. (1737?–1781?) and Sarah Poole (1740–1789); m. 11 January 1759; ch. 1759–1779. Gloucester, Mass. Watercolor[?]. Location unknown. *Gloucester Vital Records,* P.R. 34; 1:556, 603; 3:256, 266.

80. Clarke/Lane. Henry Clarke Jr. (b. 1774) and Sally Lane; m. 1 June 1798; ch. 1802–1825. Gloucester, Mass. Watercolor[?]. Location unknown. *Gloucester Vital Records,* P.R. 172; 1:152–54; 2:334.

81. Grimes/Priestly. Mary Grimes (1770–1836) and Tammy Priestly (1771–1847); m. 23 May 1792; ch. 1793–1809. Gloucester, Mass. Watercolor[?]. Location unknown. *Gloucester Vital Records,* P.R. 419; 1:306–7; 3:152.

82. Hale/Tarr. George Dennison Hale (b. 1797) and Betsy H. Tarr (b. 1800); m. 7 February 1822; ch. 1822–1837. Gloucester, Mass. Watercolor[?]. Location unknown. *Gloucester Vital Records,* P.R. 431; 1:314–16, 702; 2:254.

83. Knight/Brooks. Thomas Parsons Knights (1767–1847) and Elizabeth Brooks (1772–1820); m. 4 December 1792; ch. 1794–1815. Gloucester, Mass. Watercolor[?]. Location unknown. *Gloucester Vital Records,* P.R. 535; 1:117, 398–401; *Vital Records of Rockport,* p. 101.

84. Pool/Robbins. Ebenezer Pool (1753–1809) and Dorcas Robbins (b. 1760); m. 12 April 1778; ch. 1786–1787. Gloucester, Mass. Watercolor[?]. Location unknown. *Gloucester Vital Records,* P.R. 769; 1:548; 2:431; *Vital Records of Rockport,* p. 109.

85. Pool/Tarr. Moses Pool (1762–1810) and Hannah Tarr (1756–1849); m. 22 November 1785; ch. 1789–1800. Gloucester, Mass. Watercolor[?]. Location unknown. *Gloucester Vital Records,* P.R. 771; 1:554, 707; 2:434, 3:247; *Vital Records of Rockport,* p. 109.

86. Robbards/Brown. Solomon Robbards (1773–1823) and Polly Brown; m. 25 November 1802; ch. 1803–1815. Gloucester, Mass. Watercolor[?]. Location unknown. *Gloucester Vital Records,* P.R. 827; 1:586; 2:460.

87. Robbins/Thurston. Thomas Robbins (1732?–1818) and Dorcas Thurston (1739?–1825); ch. 1758–1776.

Gloucester, Mass. Watercolor[?]. Location unknown. *Gloucester Vital Records,* P.R. 824; 1:587; 3:259; *Vital Records of Rockport,* p. 111.

88. Saville/Harraden. Thomas Saville (1764–1845) and Betsey Harraden (1764–1830); m. 10 May 1787; ch. 1788–1810. Gloucester, Mass. Watercolor[?]. Location unknown. *Gloucester Vital Records,* P.R. 891; 1:323, 641–42; 2:492.

89. Tarr/Robbins. Andrew Tarr (1767–1829) and Annis Robbins (1773–1844); m. 27 December 1791; ch. 1792–1815. Gloucester, Mass. Watercolor[?]. Location unknown. *Gloucester Vital Records,* P.R. 942; 1:587, 700–716; 2:533; 3:303.

90. Tuttle/Whittredge. Simon Tuttle (1762–1849) and Phebe Wittredge (1760–1847); m. 1790; ch. 1790–1811. Gloucester, Mass. Watercolor[?]. Location unknown. *Gloucester Vital Records,* P.R. 981; 1:735–36; 1:555.

Tree and paired-hearts: Examples in central New Hampshire now tentatively attributed to Joseph Odiorne and others

91. Blake/Smith. Enoch Blake Jr. and Lydia Smith (b. 1797); m. 1818 [?]; ch. 1820–1823. Pittsfield, N.H., ca. 1820 or 1823. Watercolor. Don Randall. Don Randall to the author, 21 May 1989.

92. K[ ]/Blake. Asa K. and Sally Blake; m. 26 February 1817; no children listed. Pittsfield [?], N.H. Watercolor. Tillou collection. Reproduced in *Nineteenth-Century Folk Painting: Our Spirited National Heritage* (Storrs, Conn.: William Benton Museum of Art, 1973), no. 25.

93. [Copy of] Sleeper/Clough. Benjamin Sleeper (1779–1840) and Miriam Clough (1779–1861); m. March 1806; ch. 1816. Amanda A. Sleeper (b. 1816) and Samuel Gilman Kelley (b. 1809); m. 26 October 1836; ch. 1838–1843. Gilmanton, N.H., ca. 1863. Watercolor, 13 × 10 in. SPNEA, Beauport collection.

94. Seavy family record. Drake estate, Pittsfield[?], N.H. Watercolor. Location unknown. *MAD,* September 1987, 22–A. The accompanying caption reads: "The Drakes were founding fathers of Pittsfield."

Climbing roses and paired-hearts from the Nantucket area

95. Gardiner/Beard. Ebenezer Gardiner Jr. (1732–1788) and Ruth Beard (1733–1823); m. 21 November 1751; ch. 1752–1770. Nantucket, Mass., ca. 1778. Watercolor. NHA. *Vital Records of Nantucket, Massachusetts, to 1850,* 5 vols. (Boston: NEHGS, 1925–1928), 1:105, 2:27, 51, 78, 3:495; 5:296, 317 (hereafter cited as *Nantucket Vital Records*).

96. Coffin/Joy. Zaccheus Coffin (1751–1788) and Thankful Joy (1749–1810); m. 22 March 1770; ch. 1771–1780. Ca. 1788; "Nantucket / Drawn by Phebe Folger" (1771–1857). Watercolor. NHA. *Nantucket Vital Records,* 1:249, 343, 2:225, 249, 253, 3:323, 5:186, 190; Alexander Starbuck, *The History of Nantucket* (Boston: Goodspeed, 1924), p. 719.

97. Gardiner/Paddock; Cartwright/Bunker; Cartwright/ Paddock. Peter Gardiner (1754–1776) and Abigail Paddock (1759–1842); m. 12 May 1776; no ch. Benjamin Cartwright (1749–1812) and Elisabeth Bunker (1754–1787); m. 1772; ch. 1772–1785. Benjamin Cartwright (1749–1812) and Abigail Paddock (1759–1842); m. 24 April 1788; ch. 1789–1799. Nantucket, Mass.; "dron by Eunice Gardner 1796" (1776–1857). Watercolor. NHA. *Nantucket Vital Records,* 1:176–82; 2:64; 3:178; 522, 5:105–6; 314.

98. Hiller/Smith. Thomas Hiller (1771–1839) and Elizabeth Smith (1763–1837); m. 3 November 1784; ch. 1785–1805. Nantucket, Mass., ca. 1794–1796; "Edw.d D. Burke, Pinxit." Watercolor. NHA. *Nantucket Vital Records,* 2:137, 389, 475; 4:39, 5:351.

99. Marshall/Burnell. Obed Marshall (1744–1817) and Susanna Burnell (1747–1814); m. 12 February 1767; ch. 1767–1787. Nantucket, Mass., ca. 1790–1800; "Edw.d D. Burke Pinxt." Watercolor. Paul Madden Nantucket Probate Records, 6:104, Nantucket, Mass.; *Nantucket Vital Records,* 3:166.

100. Wood/Tupper. Obadiah Wood (1756–1825) and Martha Tupper (1762–1846); m. 20 January 1784; ch. 1785–1802. Nantucket, Mass., ca. 1796; "Edw.d D. B[ ]." Watercolor. Charles H. Carpenter Jr. *Nantucket Vital Records,* 2:597; 4:517.

101. Gardner/Chase. Crispus Gardner (1742–1805) and Margaret Chase (1743–1803); m. 8 December 1768; ch. 1769–1782. Nantucket, Mass., ca. 1810–1820; "Daniel Stanton Pinxit." Watercolor. Robert Cary Caldwell. *Nantucket Vital Records,* 1:205; 3:208, 494, 5:293, 310.

102. Folger/Starbuck. Walter Folger (1734–1826) and Elizabeth Starbuck (1738–1821); m. 13 January 1757; ch. 1758–1778. Nantucket, Mass., ca. 1780–1790. Watercolor. NHA. *Nantucket Vital Records,* 5:262, 281.

103. Copp/Brown. Samuel Copp (1743) and Dolley Brown (b. 1744); m. 10 December 1769; ch. 1770–1787. Stonington, Conn., ca. 1790; "John B. Copp Pinxit." Watercolor. SI. Richard A. Wheeler, *History of Stonington and Genealogies* (1900; reprint, Mystic, Conn., 1966), pp. 323–24; Malcolm C. Watkins, "Smithsonian Preview," *Magazine Antiques* 85 (January 1964); Allen, *Family Record,* entry 1.

104. Folger/Folger. Alexander Folger (1773–1846) and Rebecca Folger (1778–1823); m. 9 May 1800; ch. 1801–1813. Nantucket, Mass., ca. 1813. Watercolor. NHA. *Nantucket Vital Records,* 5:256, 275.

105. Pent/Ripley. Samuel Pent (1777–1841) and Deborah Ripley (b. 1780); m. 24 November 1805; ch. 1806–1823.

Martha's Vineyard, Mass., ca. 1825–1830. Watercolor. Pam Boynton. Charles E. Banks, *History of Martha's Vineyard,* 3 vols. (Edgartown: Duke's County Historical Society, 1925), p. 417; *Vital Records of Edgartown, Massachusetts, to the Year 1850* (Boston: NEGHS, 1906), pp. 166, 257.

106. Myrick/Mitchell. George Myrick Jr. (1790–1863) and Eliza Mitchell (1791–1864); m. 7 September 1815; ch. 1816–1829. Nantucket, Mass., ca. 1829. Watercolor. NHA. *Nantucket Vital Records,* 2:339; 4:202, 226; 5:458.

107. [copy of] Gardiner/Beard. Ebenezer Gardiner Jr. (1732–1778) and Ruth Beard (1733–1823); m. 21 November 1751; ch. 1752–1770. Nantucket, Mass., nineteenth century. Watercolor. NHA. Found over Gardiner/Beard, Nantucket Historical Association.

108. Starbuck/Barnard; Starbuck/Fullenton; Starbuck/Coffin. Nathaniel Starbuck (b. 1746) and Eunice Barnard (b. 1748–1774); m. 30 October 1765; ch. 1767–1774. Nathaniel Starbuck (b. 1746) and Salley Fullenton (b. 1754–1777); m. 2 January 1777; no ch. Nathaniel Starbuck (b. 1746) and Patience Coffin (b. 1749–1817); m. 20 September 1778; ch. 1777–1781. Nantucket, Mass., ca. 1781. Watercolor. Location unknown. Copy from Nantucket Historical Association.

109. Paddock/Starbuck. David Paddock (1778–1850) and Mary Starbuck (1779–1842); m. 28 July 1804; ch. 1807–1816. Nantucket, Mass., ca. 1834[?]. Watercolor. Location unknown. Copy from Nantucket Historical Association.

110. Hall/Dean; Hall/Fox. Obed Hall (b. 1787) and Abigail Dean (d. 1804). Obed Hall (b. 1787) and Eliza Fox (b. 1784); m. 16 June 1805; ch. 1806–1816. Raynham, Mass.; "JW" and "Ba[r]tlett [N.H.] 1817." Watercolor. Location unknown. Sotheby's 3572, lot 203; Georgia D. Merrill, ed., *History of Carrol County, N.H.* (Boston: Ferguson, 1889), pp. 917, 919.

Checklist of Printed Family Registers and Memorial Prints, 1790–1900

Georgia Brady Barnhill

Arranged by maker. Each entry in the checklist contains the following information: the artist, engraver, or lithographer of the print; the title on the print or a supplied title if it is in brackets; medium; the place of publication, publisher, and date; and location in public collections and a corresponding call number, when available. The genealogical information on various impressions is noted, and a general description of the imagery is provided. The abbreviation for American Antiquarian Society (MWA) follows library usage. Other abbreviations are (CHS) Connecticut Historical Society, (LC) Library of Congress, Prints and Photographs Division, (MCNY) Museum of the City of New York, (NEHGS) New England Historic Genealogical Society, and (OSV) Old Sturbridge Village.

1. Alden, Albert. Family Register [Relief print]. Barre, Massachusetts: [Albert Alden]; 1820; 36.5 × 28.5 cm. OSV. Attributed to Albert Alden because he was the only known printmaker in Barre, Massachusetts, at the time. Records family of William (born 2 January 1803) and Elmira Clark Cutting (born 15 July 1806); married 17 September 1828. Stylized leaves surround form.

2. Alden, Albert. In Memory of [Relief engraving]. [Barre, Massachusetts?]: [Albert Alden?]; 1830; 51.9 × 43.8 cm. OSV (2 impressions). Very large monument topped by urn overflowing with ivy, set at edge of stream; man and woman to right. One of the OSV impressions records family of Ezekiel Woodbury family. Biographical information is printed on a slip pasted on the memorial. Attributed to Alden on the basis of style; there was an Ezekiel Woodbury in Barre, Massachusetts, who died at the age of 87 in 1821.

3. Andrews, O. J. Marriage Certificate / [and] / Photographic / Family Record [Lithograph]. Bloom, Kansas: O. J. Andrews; 1888; 69.3 × 51.0 cm. LC PGA. Calligraphic ornamentation with birds, plants; scroll for data. Designed and Executed with a pen by O. J. Andrews.

4. Baillie, James. Family Register [Lithograph]. New York: J. Baillie, 118 Nassau St.; [1845–7]. MWA Cross Family Art Archive. Records family of Deborah P. Wilder (born Dublin, New Hampshire, 2 August 1818) and Joseph Cross (born Swanzey, New Hampshire, 11 August 1818); married Peterborough, New Hampshire, 6 May 1845. Four columns with domestic scenes at the top of each one.

5. Baillie, James. Family Register [Lithograph]. New York: J. Baillie, 118 Nassau St.; 1846; 22.8 × 31.4 cm. MWA; OSV; New-York Historical Society. OSV impression records family of John S. W. (16 February 1806–14 April 1879) and Delia Freeman May (4 April 1810–2 November 1869); married 4 April 1833, of Sturbridge. NYHS impression records family of Horatio N. Green (born 7 July 1821) and Sarah A. Dickens (born 1 December 1827); married at Highland Mills 18 November 1845. First child born in 1846. No plate number. On verso (NYHS only) is *Wreck of the Steamer Oregon* published by J. Baillie, 1846. MWA blank. Plate number 70. Rectangular frame of stylized leaves surrounds four columns with domestic scenes at the top of each one.

6. Baillie, James. In / Memory / of [Lithograph]. New York: J. Baillie, 118 Nassau St.; [1845–7]; 32.0 × 22.0 cm. MWA Lithf BailJ Inmev. Records deaths of Sally S. Derby on 11 May 1843, aged 52; Harriet Derby on 27 April 1844, aged 20; and Mary Fidelia Derby on 4 December 1838, aged 7. Monument on left derived from Cooke monument in St. Paul's Churchyard. Church in background. Girl, man, and woman to right, similar to groups in several N. Currier prints.

7. Baillie, James. In / Memory / of [Lithograph]. New York: J. Baillie, 87th St. near 3rd Avenue.; 1849; 30 × 21.5 cm. MWA Lithf BailJ Inme. Impression at MWA is blank. Monument at left; to right boy kneels; man and woman standing in front of church.

8. Baillie, James. The Mothers Grave [Lithograph]. New York: James Baillie, 118 Nassau St.; [1845–7]; 32.3 × 22.1 cm. OSV. Blank. Small dog, two girls by large monument with urn ornamented with wreaths on top. See Kellogg print (CHS 815) for same monument. In left background is church steeple. Printed on monument: "Sacred / To the Memory / of an Affectionate / Mother."

9. Baillie, James. The Mothers Grave [Lithograph]. New York: J. Baillie, 87th St. Near 3rd Avenue; 1848; 31.7 × 22.2 cm. MWA; OSV; LC A Size USZ62-60406. Generic memorial print. Dog, kneeling girl, and standing boy to left of gravestone with text, "Sacred to the memory / of an / Affectionate Mother." / Six lines of verse. Church steeple on left.

10. Baillie, James. Sacred to / the Memory of [Lithograph]. New York: James Baillie; [1845–7]; 32.4 × 21.8 cm. OSV. Records death of George W. M. Welch on 4 September 1847, at the age of 18, from yellow fever in New Orleans. Girl and kneeling father to left of monument with elaborate urns. Church in background to left. Plate number 7.

11. Baillie, James. Sacred to the / Memory of [Lithograph]. New York: J. Baillie; [1845–7]; 22 × 33 cm. MWA Lithf BailJ Sacr. MWA impression records death of Deborah F. Nickerson, who died in Boston, Massachusetts, 14 July 1847, aged 27 years. Woman holding handkerchief in right hand standing to left of monument surmounted by urn supported by putti. Church in background to right. Plate number 1.

12. Baillie, James. Sacred to the / Memory of [Lithograph]. New York: J. Baillie, 118 Nassau St.; [1845–7]; 32.5 × 21.7 cm. MWA; University of Vermont Bailey/Howe Library. MWA impression inscribed: Mary J. Sears, / died Dec. 7th 1846 / Aged 2 yrs. 24 days / 4 lines of verse. Plate number 6. University of Vermont impression inscribed: *Sarah Mead, died Sept. 12th 1848 / Sarah N. Mead, " " 23d, 1848 / Cyrus H. Mead, died June / 11th, 1863.* This impression lacks address for Baillie and is Plate no. 47. Monument with three urns to left of standing boy and kneeling woman holding handkerchief in two hands. Church in background to right.

13. Baillie, James. Sacred to the / Memory of [Lithograph]. New York: James Baillie, 87th St. near 3d Avenue; [1848–9]; 32.2 × 22.2 cm. LC A Size USZ62-60412. Woman with two children to left of monument with ornate sculpture on top; church in background at left. Plate no. 45.

14. Baillie, James. To the / Memory of [Lithograph]. New York: James Baillie, 118 Nassau St.; [1845–7]; 10 × 14 in. Shelburne Museum 27.6.12-70. Girl in profile kneeling on left of monument; boy and girl standing to right; river and church in background to left.

15. Baillie, James. To the / Memory of / [Lithograph]. New York and New Bedford, Mass.: J. Baillie, 118 Nassau St. and J. Soul; 1845; 22.5 × 33 cm. MWA Lithf BailJ Toth. Records names and dates of death of five children of Dunn family who died between 1819 and 1842. Small grave marker at right bears name of Baxter Derby who died 11 July 1842, at the age of two months. Woman holding handkerchief in right hand standing to left of monument surmounted by large urn; church in background to right.

16. Bales, C. R. Family / Record [Lithograph]. Eldora, Iowa: C.R. Bales; 1872. LC PGA C Size. Angels, vignettes of sunset over lake with infant in boat and moon over graveyard and mountain; Lord's Prayer; calligraphic ornamentation. Lithographed by Ferdinand Mayer & Sons, New York.

17. Barker, Enoch W. Family Record [Engraving]. Chicago: Barker & Brother; 1873; 60.8 × 45.2 cm. LC PGA. Wreaths surround spaces for data; also angels and putti. Printed by the Western Bank Note and Engraving Company of Chicago.

18. Batterson, James G. [Memorial Print] [Lithograph]. Hartford, New York, and Buffalo: Kelloggs & Comstock and D. Needham, 12 Exchange Place; 1848. CHS 689. Man stands to left of tall monument, decorated with Gothic detail. Filled in for Maria, 1812–1844. No printed inscription on monument. Artist's signature appears at foot of monument.

19. Batterson, James G. [Memorial print] [Lithograph]. Hartford, New York, and Buffalo: Kelloggs & Comstock, 150 Fulton St., N.Y. and 136 Main St., Hartford; D. Needham; 1848; 33.5 × 22 cm. CHS x1996.14.43. Woman stands with boy and girl to left of tall monument. No printed inscription on monument. Artist's signature appears at foot of monument. Plate number 338.

20. Bevan, Stacy. Family Register [Lithograph]. Cincinnati: Strobridge Lith. Co.; 1881; 66.8 × 54.5 cm. LC PGA. Calligraphic ornamentation with flowers, scrolls, and pages of open books for data. Designed by Stacy Bevan, Bloomingsport, Indiana. "Salesmen Wanted" noted on form. Deposited in 1881.

21. Bishop, Granville. The Garland Family Register [Lithograph]. Noblesville, Ind.: Bishop & Vaught; 1895; 49.2 × 63.4 cm. LC PGA. Floral ornamentation surrounds space for recording marriage data and names of children.

22. Bleichrode, A. M. Memory Table / for dear departed ones [Lithograph]. New York; 1874. LC PGA D Size. Text in Hebrew, German, and English; pages of open book provide space for data; in center is temple flanked by trees and plants.

23. Blythe, Benjamin. Keep Sacred the Memory of Your Ancestors [Line engraving]. ; 1805; 23 × 16.2 cm. MWA. Figures of Faith, Hope, Charity, and Peace, flowers, a cornucopia, and an eagle ornament the form. The initials "BB" and the date appear in an oval at the bottom. Impression at MWA is blank. Although a resident of Salem through 1782, it is not known where Blythe resided in 1805. He died in Zanesville, Ohio, in 1811.

24. Bowen, Abel. In Memory of / John Barnes, Who Died April 15, 1834 / Aged 49. [Relief print]. [Boston]; [1834]; 5½ × 6⅜ in. MWA. Woman with right arm raised and finger pointing upwards standing to left of monument with urn; river and church complex in background to right. Title is printed on monument. Bowen's signature is on broken tomb in foreground.

25. Brown, Mannevillette Elihu Dearing. [Memorial Print] [Lithograph]. Boston: W. & J. Pendleton; 1827; 24.8 × 31.7 cm. Boston Athenaeum; MWA Lithf Pend BrowM Memo (2 copies). Impression at Boston Athenaeum inscribed: "Sacred / To the Memory / of / Miss Lucy Newman / Died December 27th 1832 / Aged 25 Years / Blessed are the dead who die in the Lord." MWA copy 2 records deaths of four members of the Houghton family between 1826 and 1837. Woman dressed in classical costume stands to right of monument set in forested landscape. Monument resembles a tomb in the Père Lachaise Cemetery in Paris dedicated to the memory of Madame Dugazon, reproduced in F. G. T. de Johmont's *Les Mausolees Francais* (Paris: Firmin Didot, 1821).

26. Brunton, Richard. Keep sacred the memory of your ancesters [*sic*] / Register / [Line engraving]. ; 22.3 × 17.5cm. CHS 1972.16.0. Records family of Sarah Gleason (born 25 April 1753) and Stephen Heath (born 25 May 1750); married 23 September 1770. Figures of Faith, Hope, Charity, and Peace, birds, flowers, beehive, and Fame ornament the form.

27. Brunton, Richard. Keep sacred the memory of your ancestors / Register / [Line engraving]. ; 29.5 × 17.3 cm. CHS 1992.138.0; Shelburne Museum 27.6.12-7. CHS impression records family of Asahel (15 May 1765–9 September 1813) and Mary Loomis Nearing (March 1774–20 September 1825), married 21 October 1792. He died in Fort Meigs, Ohio. Shelburne Museum impression records family of Betsy Stoddard (1773–1872) and Jonas Clark, Jr. (1774–1854) of Rutland County, Vermont. Faith, Hope, Charity, and Peace, Eagle, Fame, flowers, pelican feeding young, beehive, birds, cornucopia, flowers ornament the form. At the bottom checkerboard design suggests a floor.

28. Brunton, Richard. Keep sacred the Memory of your Ancestors / Register [Line engraving]. ; 33.8 × 22.3 cm. CHS 1981.19.0 or 2274. Blank. Faith, Hope, Charity, Peace, Fame, eagle, flowers, cornucopia, beehive, pelican feeding her young, and birds ornament the form. Checkerboard pattern at bottom suggests a floor. Eunice Pinney (1770–1849) of Simsbury, Conn., made a close copy of this form in watercolor recording the family of Butler Pinney (born 1767 and married 1798). This is in the Karolik Collection, Museum of Fine Arts, Boston.

29. Brunton, Richard. Keep Sacred the Memory of Your Ancesters [*sic*] [Line engraving]. n.p.; 22 × 16 cm. (sight). OSV. Records family of "Vashtite" Stebbins (born October 1770) and Jesse Hitchcock (born 3 September 1766), married 19 January 1792. Faith, Hope, Charity, Peace, Fame, eagle, flowers, infant, beehive, and cornucopia ornament form. A watercolor at OSV recording the family of Prudence and Parker Willard copies this form very closely, including the spelling of the word "ancesters."

30. Brunton, Richard. Keep Sacred the Memory of Your Ancesters [*sic*] [Line engraving]. ; 22.4 × 17.7 cm. OSV; MWA. OSV impression records family of Sally Fiske (born 4 April 1782) and Zenas L. Leonard (born 16 January 1773); married 1 September 1799. MWA impression (handcolored) records family of Ezekiel Richardson (born 11 March 1769); married 20 December 1790. Faith, Hope, Charity, Peace, Fame, birds, pelican feeding her young, infant, beehive, and cornucopia ornament the form.

31. Brunton, Richard. Keep sacred the memory of your ancestors / Register / [Line engraving]. ; 1805; 22.6 × 16.0 cm. CHS 1985.3.0; OSV. CHS impression records family of Oliver (7 June 1782–22 February 1850) and Hannah (Tarbell) Shattuck (born 20 December 1789). Signed R. B. at lower left. OSV impression records family of Nathan and Sibbel (Shattuck) Blood. Figures of Faith, Hope, Charity, Peace, pelican feeding her young, bird's nest, cornucopia, and flowers ornament the form.

32. Brunton, Richard. Register [Line engraving]. ; [ca. 1790?]; 25.4 × 19.0 cm. CHS 1981.22.0. Records family of Jonathan (10 September 1752–22 April 1808) and Abigail (Babcock) Gardner (2 February 1767–7 July 1832). Handcolored. Faith, Hope, Charity, Peace, Fame, flowers, cornucopia, and birds ornament the form.

33. Brunton, Richard. Register [Line engraving]. ; 1800. Connecticut State Library, Special Genealogical Files. Records family of Joseph (born 29 April 1762) and Chloe (White) Foster (born 22 October 1767); married 15 March 1784. Space for data enclosed in oval; figures of Faith, Hope, Peace, and Charity, cornucopias, flowers ornament form.

34. Brunton, Richard. Register [Line engraving]. ; 1800. Connecticut State Library, Special Genealogical Files. Records family of Timothy Burns (b. Oct. 18, 1780); m. Sept. 12, 1802 (wife's name not given). Figures of Faith, Hope, Peace, Charity, flowers, birds, cornucopia, and beehive ornament the form.

35. Brunton, Richard. Register [Line engraving]. ; 1811; 27.3 × 22.4 cm. CHS 1979.65.0; Historic Deerfield 1999.19.2. CHS impression records family of James (1 July 1741–30 June 1828) and Hannah (Watt) Gibson (17 February 1746–2 August 1831); married 13 November 1766. Historic Deerfield impression uncolored; records family of Joseph A. Hall (born 7 March 1786) and married 16 May 1811. Wife's name not given. Signed and dated by Brunton at lower left. Faith, Hope, Charity, Peace, flowers, birds, beehive, cornucopia, and eagle ornament the form.

36. Brunton, Richard. Remember your Ancestor / Register / [Line engraving]. ; [ca. 1803?]; 22.2 × 17.6cm. CHS 1973.7A.3; Museum of Fine Arts, Boston, 60.863. CHS handcolored impression records family of Andrew C. (born 19 January 1780) and "Jerish" Bradford (born 6 May 1782). MFA impression records family of Elijah and Elizabeth (Winn) Marshall, married in 1803. Another impression, used for family of Moses and Susanna Coffin, married in 1803, is reproduced in *Art in America*, Spring 1953, p. 70. Imagery of the four seasons, flowers, birds, and pelican feeding her young ornament the form. Brunton's monogram in circle at bottom.

37. Brunton, Richard. Remember your Family / Register [Line engraving]. ; 1800; 9¾ × 7 in. MWA. Title on banner held by eagle; register surrounded by oval; at the four corners, human figures representing the four seasons; birds, flowers, agricultural ornaments, spider containing fire complete the imagery. Records family of Josiah (born 25 March 1770) and Anne Shattuck (born 9 September 1774); married Pepperell, Massachusetts 24 November 1794.

38. Bucholzer, Henry. In / Memory / of [Lithograph]. New York: J. Baillie, 87th St. near 3rd Avenue,; 1849; 32.5 × 22.1 cm. MWA; Metropolitan Museum of Art. Signed H. B. on stone. Plate number 53. MWA impression is inscribed: Kesiah Walker / who died / January 10th 1835 / Aged 10 years. Metropolitan Museum impression is inscribed: Payne Warren Higgins / who died Sept. 8. 1849 / Aged 2 years and 7 months. / 2 lines of poetry. Girl, woman, and man to left of monument surmounted by elaborate urn with child's face enfolded by wings sculpted on it. In left background is church steeple.

39. Caldwell & Co. The Soldier's Grave [Lithograph]. New York: Caldwell & Co.; 1862; 49.2 × 63.5 cm. MWA. Issued without color. Text on monument: Sacred / to / the memory of / [Daniel S. Malion, Co. C. 1st H.A.] who died in defence of his Country / [At Camp / Parole / Dec. 15th / 1864] / How sleep the brave / who sink to rest; / With all their Country's / wishes blest. Woman in graveyard leans against gravestone bearing the text, child wrapped in blankets asleep at her knees; older couple in background at gate to graveyard.

40. Calvert Lith. Co. Marriage Certificate and Family Record [Lithograph]. Detroit: A. W. Morrison; 35.7 × 45.4 cm. LC PGA. Spaces for photographs and names of children surround shield in center draped with flags.

41. Chicago Bank Note Company. In Memoriam [Lithotint]. Chicago: Freeman & Iverson; 1893; 47.0 × 35.3 cm. LC PGA C Size. Scene of woman holding onto cross in sea, graveyard, angel.

42. Colby & Welch. The Floral Record [Lithograph]. : Colby & Welch; 1870. LC PGA B Size. Twelve ovals containing cards of flowers surround central tablet for genealogical data flanked by angels; photographs of family members could be placed over the flowers.

43. Confederate Family Record [Photogravure]. ; 1900; 63.4 × 45.5 cm. LC PGA. Portraits of Thomas J. Jackson, Robert E. Lee, Jefferson Davis; scenes of General "Joe" Wheeler at San Juan and destruction of Cevera's fleet, 1898. Deposited 19 December 1904.

44. Conover, J. S. Family Record [Lithograph]. [Detroit?]: Merchants Lithography Co.; 1869; 59.0 × 46.5 cm. LC PGA. Form features calligraphic ornamentation with putti, flowers, branches. Executed with a steel pen by J. S. Conover, Coldwater, Mich.

45. Cooper, W. A. Cooper's / Illuminated / Album Star / Register [Lithograph]. Kingsville, Ohio: Cooper & Fox. LC PGA. Form includes fourteen spaces for names or photographs of family members and friends; ornamentation includes birds and stylized leaves.

46. Cory, C. P. Family / Record / of [Chromolithograph]. Chicago: Chapman Brothers Lithography; 1888; 50.3 × 39.2 cm. LC B Size USZ62-68681. Scenes of family life in corners surround tree in center of form; spaces for ten *carte-de-visite* photographs.

47. Cory, C. P. Family / Record / of [Lithotint]. Chicago: Chapman Brothers Lith.; 1888; 50.3 × 39.4 cm. LC USZ62-11472. Same format and scenes as in other Cory item except tree has been replaced with reproduction of J. A. Wilcox's engraving, *Life's Morning and Evening* (1873). Some of the ovals have waves in them. Text describes the fleeting nature of life.

48. Cowles, Maria B. Family Register. Marriages / and Births. [Lithograph]. Hartford: Kellogg & Comstock; 1850; 53.5 × 44.2 cm. MWA Lithff KellC Fami. Records family of Josephus Woodcock (born 14 March 1805) and Catherine S. Davis (born 23 July 1809); married 19 May 1829. Large branch of roses and leaves provides background for scroll for names and dates.

49. Crider & Brother. Our Family [Lithograph]. York, Penn.: Crider & Brother; 1871; 41.0 × 29.8 cm. LC PGA B Size. Spaces for eight photographs; angels and tree of life below title; family scene in center. Lithographed in Baltimore by A. Hoen & Co.

50. Crider & Brother. This Certifies / / were united in / Marriage. [Lithograph]. York, Pennsylvania: Crider & Brother; 1894; 18 × 14 in. Henry Ford Museum & Greenfield Village 94.7.1. Marriage certificate features arched spaces for photographs, vignette of couple in flower-draped sailboat, tree, and flowers. Records marriage of Mamie Ewing and Joseph H. Hale of Columbus, Ohio. Form has photographs of the African American couple who were married on 6 February 1899.

51. Crider, D. W. This Certifies / That . . . Were United / In / Holy Matrimony [Lithograph]. York, Pa.: Crider & Bros.; 1877; 40.2 × 29.4 cm. LC PGA. Certificate features vignette of couple in flower-draped sailboat; scene of wedding; open Bible at foot of certificate. Ovals for photographs of the bride and groom. Lithographed by A. Hoen & Co., Baltimore.

52. Crider, H. M. This Certifies / / were united in / Holy Matrimony. [Lithograph]. York, Pennsylvania: Crider & Brothers; 1868; 48.0 × 38.3 cm. Shelburne Museum; Vermont Historical Society. Certificate features ovals for photographs, vignette of couple in flower-draped sailboat, tree, and flowers. Lithographed by A. Hoen & Co., Baltimore. Shelburne form records marriage of Martha Adella Gay and Louis G. Wells in Charleston, Vermont, on 24 September 1874. Vermont H. S. form records marriage of Joseph N. Harris and Ella E. Day in Ludlow, Vermont, on 14 March 1877.

53. Crider, H. M. This Certifies / that . . . and / Were United in Holy Matrimony [Lithograph]. York, Penn.: Crider & Bro.; 1868; 40 × 29.5 cm. LC PGA. Printed in black with gold highlights. Vignettes of couple in boat, hands united, tree, Bible. Lithographed by A. Hoen & Co. of Baltimore. Coypright by H. M. Crider.

54. Crider, H. M. This Certifies / that . . . Holy Matrimony [Lithograph]. York, Pa.: H. M. Crider; 1880; 39.6 × 29.0 cm. LC PGA. Vignette of couple in sailboat; tree trunk anchored on Bible; space for two photographs. Lithographed by Thomas Hunter in Philadelphia.

55. Crider, H. M. This is to Certify / . . . Holy Matrimony [Lithograph]. York, Pa.: H. M. Crider; 1879; 39.5 × 29.0 cm. LC PGA. Spaces for three photographs; vignette of wedding above; cornucopias; fountain in center.

56. Currier & Ives. Family Register [Lithograph]. New York: Currier & Ives, 152 Nassau St.; 1853; 32.8 × 23 cm. MWA. Records family of Whiting B. Dudley (born 1823) and Rosanna Hotchkiss (born 1824); married 24 March 1844 [?]. Above spaces for the names of the bride and groom are portraits of a man and woman in wedding finery. Plate number 74.

57. Currier & Ives. Family Register [Lithograph]. New York: Currier & Ives, 152 Nassau St.; 1857; 23.5 × 32.2 cm. MWA Lithf Currl Fami; MCNY 56.300.1293. Four columns for family data with circles above containing scenes of a family, parents with infant and girl, wedding, and angel with infant. Roses surround the scenes and vines on columns. Both impressions are blank. Plate number 73. Gale 0.

58. Currier & Ives. Family Register [Lithograph]. New York: Currier & Ives, 152 Nassau St.; 1860; 23 × 32.8 cm. NEHGS Gen 1 M 152; MWA Lithf Currl Fami. NEHGS impression records family of Margaret A. Daley (born 4 August 1850) and John A. McCabe (born 27 May 1847), married by Rev. Father Murphy in Bangor, 9 November 1873. MWA impression is blank. Scenes of a family, parents with infant, marriage, and graveyard are above spaces for data separated by heavy columns with roses on them. Plate number 74. Gale 2008.

59. Currier & Ives. Family Register [Lithograph]. New York: Currier & Ives, 152 Nassau St.; 1864; 34. 5 × 41.7 cm. NEHGS G 1 E 70; LC PGA Currier & Ives 1864. NEHGS form records family of Catherine M. Jepson (born Pownal, Vermont 27 October 1826) and Leysander Edwards (born Shelburne, Mass. 8 November 1822), married North Adams, Mass., 4 October 1847. Scenes of family, parents with infant in cradle, wedding, and graveyard are above spaces for family data separated by columns of flowers. Floral decoration all around the form. Gale 2011.

60. Currier & Ives. Family Photograph Register [Lithograph]. New York: Currier & Ives, 125 Nassau Street; 1872; 23.5 × 32.3 cm. New-York Historical Society. Records family of G. Henry (23 July 1854–8 August 1924) and Frances M. Rafuse (b. 25 October 1854); married 1882. Oval spaces for photographs of two parents and eight children at the top of the form; four additional spaces at bottom. Gale 2001.

61. Currier & Ives. Marriage Certificate [Lithograph]. New York: Currier & Ives, 152 Nassau St.; 1869; 32.5 × 23.3 cm. MWA. Records marriage of Lewis B. Thurber and Mary E. Gordon of Patchogue, Long Island, on 31 January 1870, performed by S. H. Stansbury. Minister on left; bride and groom and two attendants.

62. Currier & Ives. Marriage Certificate. This certifies . . . [Lithograph]. New York: Currier & Ives, 115 Nassau St.; 1875; 22.9 × 34.5 cm. New-York Historical Society. Records marriage of Abel N. Moore of Moscow, Maine, and Isanah A. Baker of Moscow, Maine, on 16 October 1870. There are oval spaces for photographic portraits of the bride and groom. Gale 4347.

63. Currier & Ives. The Soldier's Grave [Lithograph]. New York: Currier & Ives, 152 Nassau St.; 1862; 32.6 × 21.6 cm. MWA Lithf Currl Sold; MCNY 56.300.1307. Clearly designed for families of Civil War casualties, a monument bears the inscription: *In Memory of . . . / of the . . . / who died at . . . / 186 . / A Brave and Gallant Soldier, and a True Patriot. /* [four lines of poetry]. Mourning woman kneels at left of monument; marching soldiers in background at right. Plate number 204. Gale 5997.

64. Currier & Ives. The Soldier's Memorial [Lithograph]. New York: Currier & Ives, 152 Nassau St.; 1863; 40.0 × 29.4 cm. LC B Size USZ62-35580. Clearly designed for families of Civil War casualties. Text on monument: *In Memory of . . . / of the . . . / who died at . . . / 186 / A Brave and Gallant Soldier, / and a True Patriot. /* [four lines of poetry]. Woman holding handkerchief to face standing to left of monument; marching soldiers in background; another monument at left. Gale 5999.

65. Currier & Ives. The Soldier's Grave [Lithograph]. New York: Currier & Ives; 1865; 12 × 8½ in. Old Print Gallery, Dec. 1998, p. 79. Woman leaning on right side of monument inscribed: *In Memory of / . . . of the . . . who died at . . . 18 . A brave and gallant soldier / and a true patriot. /* [four lines of poetry].

66. Currier & Ives. To / the Memory of [Lithograph]. New York: Currier & Ives, 152 Nassau St.; 1857; 33.3 × 21.8 cm. MCNY 56.300.1301. Girl places roses on ground at left; woman and boy kneel beside monument at right. Wrought iron fence circles the monument with elaborate cross on top. Reproduced in *A Time to Mourn*, p. 161, cat. 116. Plate number 78. Gale 6590.

67. Currier, Charles. Family Register. [Lithograph]. New York: C. Currier, 33 Spuce [*sic*] St.; 1830; 24 × 33.2 cm. MCNY 56.300.1294. Columns for data are separated by columns with Ionic capitals. Above are scenes of a family of four walking in a village, mother with infant on lap, couple being married, woman mourning at left of monument. Black and white proof. Plate number 65. Gale 2019.

68. Currier, Charles. To the / Memory of [Lithograph]. New York: C. Currier, 33 Spruce St.; 1830; 22 × 32.6 cm. MWA Lithf CurrC Toth. Woman mourns at right of monument in graveyard; church in background at right. Black and white proof.

69. Currier, Nathaniel. Family Register [Lithograph]. New York: N. Currier, 2 Spruce St.; 1835; 22.7 × 33 cm. NEHGS Gen. 1 M18. Records family of Polly Woodbury (born 7 December 1794) and Palmer Marble (born 24 September 1784), married in Sutton, Massachusetts 22 September 1814. Scenes of family walking outside, mother and child and infant in cradle, wedding, and mother and child beside monument. Spaces for data separated by columns with Ionic capitals.

70. Currier, Nathaniel. Family Register [Lithograph]. New York: N. Currier, 2 Spruce St.; 1835; 22.8 × 32.6 cm. MWA. Records family of Samuel A. Flagg of Worcester (born 3 May 1808) and Sarah A. (Baker) Flagg (born 1 April 1813); married 13 January 1836. Space for data is flanked by allegorical figures of Charity and Hope on pedestals; below title is pelican feeding her young in nest.

71. Currier, Nathaniel. Family Register [Lithograph]. New York: N. Currier, 2 Spruce St.; 1840; 23.3 × 32.4 cm. NEHGS Gen 1 L94; MWA Lithf CurrN Famivvv. NEHGS impression records family of Relief Sarvin (28 March 1800–13 February 1872) and Levi Leland (20 November 1789–14 January 1874). MWA has two impressions that record families of Viola Dunne and Philander Derby (1816–1902), married in Petersham, Massachusetts, 27 February 1837; and Mercy Nelson and Phineas Dodge. Space for data is flanked by allegorical figures of Charity and Hope on pedestals. Below title is pelican feeding her young in nest.

72. Currier, Nathaniel. Family Register [Lithograph]. New York: N. Currier, 2 Spruce St.; 1840; 24.6 × 35 cm. MWA Lithf CurrN Fami. MWA has two impressions of this form recording family of Mary T. Moffett (born Brimfield, Massachusetts, 23 June 1799) and Lyman Bugbee (born Cazenovia, New York, June 1, 1802), married Cazenovia, New York, 25 May 1825; and family of Susan Taylor (born Southborough, Massachusetts, 12 January 1800) and Samuel Banister (born Southborough 20 April 1803), married Southborough 20 April 1828. Scenes of family walking outside, mother with child in lap and infant in cradle, wedding, and woman and girl in graveyard. Columns, three with floral ornamentation, separate spaces for data.

73. Currier, Nathaniel. Family Register [Lithograph]. New York: N. Currier, 2 Spruce St.; 1840; 22.6 × 33.2 cm. MWA, Vermont Historical Society, Historic Deerfield. Vermont H. S. impression records family of Nathaniel W. Martin (b. Charlotte, Vermont 27 May 1805) and his two wives—Laura W. (18 October 1807–31 July 1843, Fort Anne Village, New York) and Adelia A. Marshall (born Poultney, Vermont 10 August 1805). First marriage was Middletown, Vermont, 1 October 1826; second, Poultney 7 March 1844. Historic Deerfield form records family of Ebenezer (14 November 1793–7 August 1857) and Rebecca Stebbins; married at Sunderland, Massachusetts, 20 February 1812. This form copied closely by E. B. & E. C. Kellogg (Plate number 45; impression in Vermont H.S.). Scenes of family walking outside, mother and boy with infant in cradle, wedding, woman and boy kneeling by monument in graveyard. Spaces for data separated by columns with Ionic capitals.

74. Currier, Nathaniel. Family Register [Lithograph]. New York: N. Currier, 2 Spruce St.; 1845; 23.5 × 31.7 cm. OSV; AAS Lithf CurrN Famiv; Shelburne Museum 27.6.12-51. OSV impression records family of Samuel and Sarah Freeman through 1888; AAS impression records family of Levi (17 March 1786–12 September 1873) and Sally (Stratton) Derby (17 August 1790–11 May 1842); married in Athol, Massachusetts, 14 January 1810. Shelburne impression records family of Horace Colburn (born 29 March 1805) and Amaranth Smith (born 18 December 1811) of Shrewsbury. Scenes of family walking outside, mother with infant in cradle, wedding, boy and mother by monument. Spaces for data separated by Gothic-style columns.

75. Currier, Nathaniel. Family Register [Lithograph]. New York: N. Currier, 152 Nassau St., Corner of Spruce; 1846; 22.8 × 33.8 cm. MCNY 56.300.1292; NEHGS Gen. 1 H 96; MWA Lithf CurrN Famivv. MCNY impression bears copyright statement for Sarony & Major, 1846; records family of Lydia Whitaker (Windsor, Vermont 25 December 1811–Montpelier, Vermont 21 June 1886) and Mulfred D. Bullard (Stockbridge, Massachusetts 6 June 1808–Lancaster, New Hampshire 30 May 1872); married 11 January 1828. NEHGS impression records family of Ann (born 10 December 1793) and Joseph (born 3 June 1789) Howard, married in New York 12 April 1812. MWA impression (plate no. 487) records family of Sallie McAfee (born 25 December 1789) and Samuel Emerson (born 1785), married in New Boston, New Hampshire, 28 December 1809. Gale 2005, except copyright by N. Currier. Title on banner above scenes of family by fireplace, parents with infant on sofa, wedding, and deathbed scene. Four small landscapes below spaces for data. Very ornate.

76. Currier, Nathaniel. Family Register [Lithograph]. New York: N. Currier; 1846; 22 × 33.8 cm. NEHGS Gen 1 R 59. Records family of Laura W. Wing (born 26 February 1813) of Wayne, Maine, and Alfred Raymond (born 5 June 1809) of Harpswell, Maine. Title on ribbon; scenes of family seated in parlor, parents with infant on sofa, wedding, mother and child kneeling by monument. Elaborate columns with floral ornamentation separate spaces for data. Flowers also surround the scenes. Plate number 73. Gale 2006.

77. Currier, Nathaniel. Family Register [Lithograph]. New York: N. Currier, 152 Nassau St.; 1855; 22 × 34 cm. OSV. Records family of Joseph (2 October 1810–1 January 1876) and Lucy (Munroe) Westgate (1810–14 December 1880) of Sturbridge, Massachusetts. Information for two generations. He was born in Morristown, N.J., she in Spencer, Mass. Their children were born in Sturbridge. Scenes of family walking outside, mother with infant in cradle, wedding, and boy and mother by monument are surrounded by stylized acanthus leaves. Slender columns separate the spaces for data.

78. Currier, Nathaniel. In / Memory / of [Lithograph]. New York: N. Currier, 2 Spruce St.; 35.6 × 24.8 cm. Greenfield Village and Henry Ford Museum. Inscription on tomb: *Harriet S. Daughter / of Noah and Betsy Torrey / who died January 21st 1849 / aged 24 years /* [four lines of poetry]. Composition based on J. R. Smith's St. Paul's Churchyard, with more of church steeple and sky showing than other forms. Reproduced in *A Time to Mourn,* p. 160, cat. 113.

79. Currier, Nathaniel. In / Memory / of [Lithograph]. New York: N. Currier, 2 Spruce St.; 33 × 22.5 cm. MCNY 56.300.1296. Inscribed "*Our Father & Mother / William David / Who went in to the spirit / world June 12, 1851 / and of his wife / Mary Fletcher who / joined him in the / far off land Oct. 25 / 1860.*" Gale 3337. Boy, man, and woman stand to right of monument derived from J. R. Smith's St. Paul's Churchyard. The figures are similar to those in MCNY57.100.77. Church in background.

80. Currier, Nathaniel. In / Memory / of [Lithograph]. New York: N. Currier, 2 Spruce St.; 33.1 × 22.0 cm. MCNY 56.300.1304. Impression blank. Plate number 280. Composition derived from J. R. Smith's St. Paul's Churchyard. Man and woman to right of monument.

81. Currier, Nathaniel. In / Memory / of [Lithograph]. New York: N. Currier, 2 Spruce St.; 33.5 × 27.5 cm. MCNY 56.300.1305. Impression is blank. Composition derived from J. R. Smith's St. Paul's Churchyard. Girl, man, and woman to right of monument.

82. Currier, Nathaniel. In / Memory / of Mrs. Phebe M. Burns, / wife of / Mr. David Burns [Lithograph]. New York: N. Currier, 2 Spruce St.; 14 × 10 in. Greenfield Village and Henry Ford Museum 00.8.1838. Mrs. Burns, born 18 October 1825, died 6 April 1845. Eight lines of verse on monument. Inscription printed by letterpress. Woman, man, and girl stand to left of monument derived from J. R. Smith's St. Paul's Churchyard; glimpse of church in background between trees.

83. Currier, Nathaniel. In / Memory / of [Lithograph]. New York: N. Currier, 2 Spruce St.; 21.8 × 31.7 cm. Shelburne Museum 27.6.12-5. Inscribed: *Charles Smith / who died in Boston March 21st / 1835 in the 24th year of his Age. / Samuel Smith, Jr. / Died Feby. 16th 1841 / Aged 28 Yrs., / Mary S. Pond (?) / Died Feby 5th 1846 Aged 32 Yrs.* Woman stands to right of monument, elbow resting on monument. Church in background to left.

84. Currier, Nathaniel. In / Memory / of [Lithograph]. New York: N. Currier, 2 Spruce St.; 14¼ × 10 in. Henry Ford Museum & Greenfield Village 38.309.1238. Composition derived from J. R. Smith's St. Paul's Churchyard. Girl, man, and woman to right of monument. Small flowers instead of grass surround base of monument.

85. Currier, Nathaniel. In / Memory / of [Lithograph]. New York: N.Currier, 2 Spruce St.; 1840; 32.9 × 27.7 cm. MWA Lithf CurrN Inmev; MCNY 57.100.77. MCNY impression has letterpress inscription: *Joseph Henry / Eldest Son of / Joseph M. and Maria P. Perkins, / who died / August 29th. A.D. 1842, / Aged 5 years, 4 Months, and 6 Days.* Composition derived from J. R. Smith's St. Paul's Churchyard; girl with roses, man, and woman to right of monument. Gale 3336.

86. Currier, Nathaniel. In / Memory / of [Lithograph]. New York: N. Currier, 2 Spruce St.; 1840; 32.8 × 27.7 cm. Metropolitan Museum of Art 54.90.797, The Edward W. C. Arnold Collection of New York Prints, Maps, & Pictures. Bequest of E. W. C. Arnold, 1954. Inscription on tomb: *Paul Revere / Patriot / Born 1735 January 14/ died 1818 Age 83.* Composition derived from J. R. Smith's St. Paul's Churchyard; girl, man, and woman to right of monument. Very similar to MCNY 57.100.77 except that imprint is just below border.

87. Currier, Nathaniel. In / Memory / of [Lithograph]. New York: N. Currier, 2 Spruce St.; 1845; 33 × 22.8 cm. OSV; MWA Lithf CurrN Inme. OSV impression records deaths of James Worcester (died 4 June 1843) and Mary Worcester (died 9 January 1838). MWA impression records deaths of four children of the Leland family who died between 1818 and 1845. Man with top hat at side and woman to left of monument derived from J. R. Smith's St. Paul's Churchyard. Church in background.

88. Currier, Nathaniel. In / Memory / of [Lithograph]. New York: N. Currier, 2 Spruce St.; 1845; 33 × 22.6 cm. OSV. Records death of Sarah (Peaslee) Sanborn on July 20, 1849, at the age of 25. Based on the composition of J. R. Smith's St. Paul's Churchyard, but reversed. Man, woman, and girl to left of monument. Church on left of composition instead of right.

89. Currier, Nathaniel. In / Memory / of [Lithograph]. New York: N. Currier, 2 Spruce St.; 1845; 33 × 22.3 cm. MCNY 56.300.1303 and 57.100.74. MCNY 57.300.1303 inscribed: *Edgar L. Curtis / Born / December 25th / 1843 / Died / February 25th / 1849.* Based on J. R. Smith's St. Paul's Churchyard, but church is on left. Man, woman, and girl to left of monument. Very similar to impression at OSV except lines in the masonry of church are white instead of black.

90. Currier, Nathaniel. In / Memory of [Lithograph]. New York: N. Currier, 2 Spruce St.; 1846; 33.9 × 22.3 cm. MCNY 57.100.75; Henry Ford Museum & Greenfield Village 89.0.332.134, Metropolitan Museum of Art 54.90.798, Edward W.C. Arnold Collection of New York Prints, Maps, & Pictures, Bequest of E. W. C. Arnold, 1954. Composition based on J. R. Smith's St. Paul's Churchyard. Boy, woman, and man to right of monument. Boy gestures. Monument varies from prototype. Plate no. 153. Gale 3331.

91. Currier, Nathaniel. In / Memory / of [Lithograph]. New York: N. Currier, 152 Nassau St.; 1847; 33.7 × 22 cm. MCNY 57.100.76. Inscribed: *Mary Ann Harvey / Born March 22d. 1802 / Died April 1st, 1828 / Silas A. Harvey /*

Born September 21st. 1825 / Died March 2nd. 1847 / Composition based on J. R. Smith's St. Paul's Churchyard. Monument differs from prototype; urn supported by two putti. Girl, woman, man to right. Plate number 72. Gale 3334.

92. Currier, Nathaniel. Sacred to the / Memory / of [Lithograph]. New York: N. Currier, 152 Nassau St. Cor. Spruce St.; 1846; 14 × 10¼ in. Henry Ford Museum & Green Village 38.309.1233. Impression is blank, but is inscribed on verso: *To the Memory of / James Decater / Charity R. Catten / Millissa Ann Decater / Nathaniel R. Catten.* Woman with girl and boy in her arms stands to left of monument surmounted with three urns; church in background.

93. Currier, Nathaniel. Sacred to the / Memory of [Lithograph]. New York: N. Currier; 1846; 12½ × 8½ in. Old Print Gallery, Dec. 1998, p. 79. Woman and boy kneel to left of monument with two urns and three statues on it; churchyard in background.

94. Currier, Nathaniel. Sacred to the / Memory of [Lithograph]. New York: N. Currier, 152 Nassau, Corner Spruce St.; 1847; 36.2 × 25.4 cm. Greenfield Village and Henry Ford Museum 00.3.1842. Inscribed: *Amanda R. Olds / who Died / Sept. 24th.* Reproduced in *A Time to Mourn*, p. 102, cat. 117. Man leans on gravestone on left; boy looks at monument bearing inscription. Church in left background.

95. Currier, Nathaniel. Sacred to the / Memory of [Lithograph]. New York: N. Currier, 152 Nassau St.; 1847; 33.3 × 22.1 cm. MCNY 56.300.1302; 46.256.1; University of Vermont Bailey/Howe Library. MCNY 46.256.1 records family of James Merritt Ives. Impression at the University of Vermont inscribed: *Mrs. Elmina Crandall / who died June 16, A.D. 1865, aged 45 years / Farewell—no more I tread your gr*[*ound?*]. Woman and girl to right of monument with three urns. Plate number 186. Gale 5733.

96. Currier, Nathaniel. Sacred to the / Memory / of [Lithograph]. New York: N. Currier, 152 Nassau St. Cor. of Spruce St.; 1849; 10 × 14 in. Henry Ford Museum & Greenfield Village 38.309.1234. Two women and girl stroll in churchyard; monument at right; gothic church in left background.

97. Currier, Nathaniel. To the / Memory of [Lithograph]. New York: N. Currier, 2 Spruce St.; 22 × 32.6 cm. MWA Lithf CurrN Toth; Henry Ford Museum & Greenfield Village 38.309.1237. Man to left of monument; elbow rests on it. Church in left background. Gale 6588.

98. Currier, Nathaniel. To the / Memory of [Lithograph]. New York: N. Currier, 2 Spruce St.; 30.5 × 38.1 cm. MCNY 56.300.1299; Greenfield Village and Henry Ford Museum 00.3.1866; Shelburne Museum 27.6.12-4. Greenfield Village impression inscribed: *Elias Rich / Who Died / June 9th 1836 / 82. Tho thou art gone / We think of thee as in Heaven.* Reproduced in *A Time to Mourn*, p. 161, cat. 115. Plate number 82. Shelburne Museum impression inscribed: *To the memory of Laura A. Smith, died Jany 21st 1848 aged 25 years. Caroline F. Smith died Nov. 4th 1848 aged 14 years; Elisa M. Smith died Oct. 7, 1849, aged 23 years.* Woman rests elbow on right side of monument; church in left background.

99. Currier, Nathaniel. To the / Memory of [Lithograph]. New York: N. Currier, 2 Spruce St.; 25.4 × 35.6 cm. MWA; MCNY 56.300.1298; Greenfield Village and Henry Ford Museum 38.309.1235. MCNY impression inscribed: *Nathaniel Morton / born March 17th, 1771 ; and who died Sept. 16th 1810 / Aged 39 yrs. & 5 mos. and 29 days.* Greenfield Village impression inscribed: *Eliphalet Rhodes / Who died Feby., 10th 1841 / Aged 51 years.* Reproduced in *A Time to Mourn*, p. 160, cat. 112. Woman leaning on left side of monument; church in right background. Gale 6589.

100. Currier, Nathaniel. To the / Memory of / Wm. H. Harrison / Born February 9th 1773, / Inaugurated President of the United States March 4th. 1841 / Died April 4th. 1841, AE. 68. [Lithograph]. New York: N. Currier, 2 Spruce St.; 24.0 × 33.0 cm. MCNY 56.300.1297; Huntington Library. MCNY impression with inscription and four lines verse printed on the monument. Woman mourns on right side of monument; church in background at left. Plate number 125. Impression at the Huntington lacks printed inscription about Harrison. Inscribed: *Mary E. Litchfield, / who died / April 9, 1842, / Aged / 15 Years,2 Months, / & 11 Days.*

101. Currier, Nathaniel. To the / Memory of [Lithograph]. New York: N. Currier, 2 Spruce St.; 22.8 × 32.8 cm. University of Vermont Bailey/Howe Library. Woman to right of monument rests her right elbow on it. Church in background to right. Inscribed: *Rhoda K. Williams / Who Died August 10th / 1838. Aged 1 Yr. 8 Months, / & / Martha L. Williams / Who Died Sept. 12th. 1847 / Aged 1 Yr 9 Months. & days.* / Plate no. 25. Very similar to form published by Charles Currier.

102. Currier, Nathaniel. To the / Memory of [Lithograph]. New York: N. Currier, 2 Spruce St.; 8⅝ × 12¾ in. Old Print Gallery, Dec.1998, p. 78. Two standing children to left of monument; girl kneeling to right. In background is river and building beyond.

103. Currier, Nathaniel. To the / Memory / of [Lithograph]. New York: N. Currier, 33 [?] Spruce St.; 1835; 28.6 × 33.1 cm. OSV; Henry Ford Museum and Greenfield Village 38.309.1239. OSV impression records death of Henry E. Peck, on 27 December 1836, at the age of 33. Woman at left rests elbow on monument in graveyard; church in background.

104. Currier, Nathaniel. To the / Memory of [Lithograph]. New York: N. Currier, 33 Spruce St.; 1835; 22.8 × 32.6 cm. OSV. Records death of Mary A. Blanchard on 1 April 1842, at the age of 7 years and 8 months. Boy and girl to left of elaborate monument in center; older girl kneels to right of it.

105. Currier, Nathaniel. To the / Memory of [Lithograph]. New York: Nathaniel Currier, 2 Spruce St.; 1845; 23.6 × 32.8 cm. NEHGS Gen 1 Li 140; Collection of Sherman

Adams, courtesy of Library of Congress. NEHGS impression trimmed above imprint. Woman rests elbow on right side of large monument in graveyard; at left is church. Records deaths of Mrs. Ruth Lincoln on 17 July 1829 aged 74; and her husband, Mr. Abner Lincoln, on 22 June 1840, aged 87. Also on monument: "*My children dear, / I pray draw near, / A father's grave you'll see / Not long ago I was with you and / soon you'll be with me.*" This form lacks its imprint. Very similar in composition to N. Currier form at Greenfield Village and Henry Ford Museum (*A Time to Mourn*, cat. 115).

106. Currier, Nathaniel. To the / Memory of [Lithograph]. New York: N. Currier, 2 Spruce St.; 1845; 22.5 × 32.8 cm. MCNY 56.300.1300. Uncolored proof. Woman to right of monument; church in background at right. Gale 6584 without plate number.

107. Currier, Nathaniel. To the / Memory of [Lithograph]. New York: Nathaniel Currier, 2 Spruce St.; 1845; 23.0 × 33.7 cm. LC USZ62-2879. Three children, two standing and one kneeling, to left of monument; river with church on far shore in background. Deposited in the Library of Congress, 16 September 1845.

108. Currier, Nathaniel. To the / Memory of [Lithograph]. New York: N. Currier, 2 Spruce St.; 1846; 23.3 × 33.3 cm. MWA; MCNY 57.100.78. MWA impression inscribed: *Harriett P. Alvard / who died May 23th 1849, Ae 19 /* [eight lines of poetry]. Woman to left of monument with three urns; gothic church in background. Plate number 71. Gale 6585.

109. Curtiss, George B. Family Record [Lithograph]. Chicago: George B. Curtiss; 55.0 × 43.5 cm. LC PGA. Angels, putti, flowers ornament form. Lithographed in Chicago by Jackson, Buehlow & Co. Designed and Executed with a Steel Pen by G. B. Curtiss.

110. Cutler, Jervis. Register [Line engraving]. ; 1805; 22.4 × 17.2 cm. MWA. Records family of Nathan Lombard (born 5 September 1777); married 14 March 1802; wife's name not given. Faith, Hope, Charity, and Peace, cornucopias, birds, and flowers ornament this form. The allegorical figures are reversed from form signed by Cutler. Attributed to Cutler on the basis of resemblance to signed example.

111. Cutler, Jervis. (1768–1846). Register [Line engraving]. ; 1805; 22.3 × 17.2 cm. MWA. Hope, Faith, Peace, and Charity, cornucopias, flowers ornament this form. Blank. Signed by Cutler at lower right.

112. Davis, J. F. Family Record [Lithograph]. Williamsport, Penn.: J. F. Davis; 1894; 49.5 × 38.0 cm. LC PGA Hoen & Co. Above title and space for births, marriages, and deaths are angels; four scenes relating to death below. Lithographed by A. Hoen & Co., Baltimore. Similar to form issued by A. Hoen and Company in 1870.

113. Dittmore, Henry. Family Record [Lithograph]. Allegheny City, Penn.; 51.0 × 68.2 cm. LC PGA. Spaces for photographs; patriotic and religious imagery. Printed note: "Photographs to be inserted here with slide behind."

114. Edgerton, Reverend D. [Family Register] [Lithograph]. n.p.; 1884; 66.8 × 52.0 cm. LC PGA. Portraits of Lincoln and Washington above one of the Garfield Family; also an acrostic on the name Garfield. Text of marriage ceremony below spaces for names, birth, marriage, and death dates; stylized floral border.

115. Enterprise Supply Co. Original Pen Work / Family Record [Letterpress]. Augusta, Maine: Enterprise Supply Co.; 1895; 54.0 × 38.0 cm. LC PGA. Calligraphic form printed in blue, pink, green, and gold; birds and religious imagery.

116. Estee, J. J. Family Record [Lithograph]. Poultney, Vt.: J. J. Estee, M.D.; 1852; 22½ × 18 in. (sheet). Shelburne Museum 27.6.12-64. Kneeling male and female figures with text of Lord's Prayer surround space for genealogical data.

117. Family History [Lithograph]. n.p.; 26.5 × 20.3 cm. LC PGA. Simple decorated border around large blank space.

118. Family Record [Letterpress]. ; 1886; 44.5 × 38.0 cm. LC PGA C Size. Birds in oval surrounding space for genealogical data; printed in four colors and black. Copyrighted 1886 by the Publishers. Similar to form issued by the Enterprise Supply Company.

119. Family Record / Births [Lithograph]. n.p.; n.d.; 38.0 × 44.5 cm. LC PGA. Simple black border with embellishments around divided blank space.

120. Family Record / In God we hope / [Line engraving]. n.p.; 1820; 40.6 × 32.3 cm. OSV 20.21.31. Records family of Abijah (born 1754) and Dorothy (Wheeler) Wood; married 9 December 1779. Possibly filled out between 1821 (at the time of Dorothy's death) and 24 September 1823, when Abijah married Lydia Rockwood. Imported from England? Two watercolors at Old Sturbridge Village are based on this form. One is by M. Holton recording the family of Samuel and Sarah (Cushman) Clark; the other is by Susannah Townsend, dated 12 October 1830. A sampler at the Shelburne Museum by Julia Maria Upham, made in Wethersfield, Vt., in 1817, is also based on this design. Figures of Charity and Hope on pedestals flank arch with two ovals for names of parents, and tablet for names and dates of birth and death for children. Beneath arch bearing title is pelican feeding young in nest.

121. Family Record / The Twelve Different Stages of / Human Life, / From the Cradle to the Grave. [Line engraving]. New York: E. Gaylord & Co.; 1816; 45.3 × 34.5 cm. MWA. Columns frame space for the list of births, marriages, deaths. Around that space from the lower left are vignettes portraying the twelve stages of life. Scene of the Last Judgment between arch connecting the two columns and the space for genealogical data.

122. Family Register [Lithograph]. n.p.; n.d.; 22.2 × 35 cm. NEHGS Gen 1 S 291. Records family of Mitty Williams (born 11 March 1784) and Hiram Sexton (born Grantham, New Hampshire, 2 May 1779), married Dec. 1804 in "Brimfield, Vermont." Ornamented with acanthus leaves and romanesque columns.

123. Family Register. [Lithograph]. n.p.; n.d.; 36.4 × 28.9 cm. MWA. Records family of Julia B. Raymond and Henry Gorham, married January 1831. Similar to family register published by D. W. Kellogg & Co. featuring figures of Charity and Hope flanking spaces for data.

124. Family Register [Lithograph]. n.p.; n.d.; 24.0 × 34.6 cm. Metropolitan Museum of Art 62.635.220, Gift of Harry G. Friedman, 1962. Records family of John W. Hasty (Limington [Maine?] 14 August 1804–17 March 1840) and Mary Ann Pease (born Parsonsfield [Maine?] 4 October 1811); married 11 May 1831. Mary Ann married George B. Hasty 2d on 23 December 1841. Scenes of family walking outside, mother with infant in cradle and boy seated on floor, wedding, boy and mother by tomb in cemetery.

125. Ferry, Hiram. Family Register [Engraving and printed form]. Northampton, Mass.: H. Ferry & Co.; 1830; 36.5 × 28 cm. OSV; MWA. OSV impression records family of Eleipha (6 February 1802–5 February 1859) and John C. March (9 July 1800–22 December 1870). MWA impression records family of Huldah Loveren (born 7 June 1792) and Daniel Simons (born 21 February 1793); married 8 June 1816. Features engravings of a man and woman at the top of the form. A watercolor by Julia Maria Abbe painted in 1840 copies the oval portraits. Reproduced in D. Brenton Simons, "New England Family Record Broadsides and 'The Letterpress Artist' of Connecticut," *The New England Historical and Genealogical Register* 153 (Oct. 1999).

126. Fine Art Publishing Company. Family Record [Lithograph]. Pittsfield, Mass.: Fine Art Publishing Company; 1884; 24½ × 21 in. Private collection (Scott Andrew Bartley). Records family of Charles A. (20 August 1843–6 April 1919) and Melina Filetta (Green) Bixby (9 November 1850–23 March 1924), married 12 November 1868. Family register includes spaces for grandparents as well as children. Family lived in Plymouth Notch, Vermont. Calligraphic feathers surround the space for recording names.

127. Forbes & Company. Family Record [Lithograph]. Boston: Forbes & Company; 1875; 35.4 × 44.2 cm. LC PGA B Size. Scene of family reading Bible between the words of the title; columns for genealogical information. Texts of Ten Commandments and the Lord's Prayer. Deposited in the Library of Congress in 1875.

128. Fox, Henry G. This certifies that / The Rite of / Holy Matrimony . . . [Engraving]. Brooklyn, N.Y.: Henry G. Fox; 1857; 21.6 × 25.0 cm. (trimmed). Metropolitan Museum of Art 61.663.230, Gift of Harry G. Friedman, 1961. Records marriage of Benjamin Reed and Jane Plough, both of Hurley, New York, on 1 January 1873. At top two allegorical figures in flower-strewn boat, clasped hands at bottom, floral decoration on sides.

129. Freeman, J. T. Family Record / Births / and Marriages / of Parents [Lithograph]. Boston: J. T. Freeman; 1879; 68.8 × 52.4 cm. LC PGA. Spaces for data in the shapes of memorial tablets and open books.

130. Fuller Brothers. Firemen's Register / Our Home Protectors [Photogravure]. Washington, D.C.: Fuller Bros.; n.d.; 56.4 × 45.8 cm. LC PGA. Scenes of fires and firefighting surround central space for data.

131. Fulton & Eastman. Family Record [Engraving]. New York: A. & J.McLees; 1848; 49.0 × 36.0 cm. LC PGA B Size. Two putti in center, several angels' heads worked into calligraphic design. Designed and executed by Fulton & Eastman; engraved by Archibald & James McLees, 70 Broadway.

132. Gast, A. Photograph Family Record [Lithograph]. St. Louis and New York: A. Gast & Co.; 1884; 49.3 × 66.0 cm. LC PGA. Spaces for ten photographs in Gothic framework; garland of flowers entwined in framework.

133. Gibson, John. Certificate / of / Marriage [Lithograph]. New York: John Gibson, 82 Beekman Street; 1876; 17 × 12 in. Private Collection (aGatherin' 1998). Records marriage of Seward France and Alice Vandervarken of Seward, N.Y., in 1878. Photographs of the bride and groom affixed to certificate, which includes oval vignette of ship sailing away from town into rising sun.

134. Gibson, John. Certificate of Marriage [Engraving]. New York: J. Gibson; 1884; 21 × 15 in. Shelburne Museum 27.17–99. Records marriage of Emma Field and Homer Holmes, in Chittenden County, Vermont, 1884. At the bottom is scene of swans on a lake, village, and locomotive. Photographs of the bride and groom.

135. Gies & Company. Allegorical Family Record [Lithograph]. Buffalo, New York: Moline Plow Company; 1881; 33.7 × 44.3 cm. LC B Size; USZ62-1065. Spaces for names of couple, birth and death dates, "removed from" and "settled at." Agricultural scenes provide the imagery.

136. Goodenough, E. This is to Certify / that . . . / Holy Matrimony [Engraving]. New York: E. Goodenough, 122 Nassau St.; 1866; 19.3 × 28.0 cm. Metropolitan Museum of Art, 1976.64.2. Records marriage of John Rudick and Susan Reed of Forestburgh, New York, on 2 April 1868.

137. Gould, James G. Family Register [Engraving]. Chicago: J. C. Fuller, 148 Madison St.; 1868; 55.2 × 38.5 cm. LC D Size. Spaces to record names of parents, births, marriages, and deaths ornamented with angels and floral garlands. Texts on banners: "Children shall be like Olive Plants round about thy Table" and "Whom God hath joined together let not Man put asunder." Designed and executed with a Pen by Professor James G. Gould; printed by the Chicago Lithography Company.

138. Great Western Supply House. God Bless / Our / Family / Family Record [Chromolithograph]. Chicago: Great Western Supply House; 1894; 39.0 × 53.5 cm. LC PGA. Ten ovals for photographs surrounded with floral ornamentation.

139. Hoen, A. and Company. Family Record [Lithograph]. Baltimore: A. Hoen and Company; 1870. LC PGA A Size. Above title and space for births, marriages, and deaths are angels; four scenes relating to death below. Text: "*One less to love on earth, one more to meet in heaven.*"

140. Holliday, Enoch J. Family Record [Lithograph]. St. Louis: Enoch J. Holliday; 1872; 24 × 20 in. Henry Ford Musem & Greenfield Village 00.347.3. Circular and oval spaces for photographs and/or inscriptions; tablets in shape of gravestones for inscriptions. Decorated with angels, cupids, and birds.

141. Home Art Picture Co. Family Record. Chicago: Home Art Picture Co.; 1894; 54.2 × 39.0 cm. LC PGA. Ten oval spaces for photographs; open book and scrolls for names; scene at bottom of family reading Bible.

142. Hovey, Fred A. [Family Record] [Lithograph]. St. Louis; 1881; 62.0 × 46.3 cm. LC PGA C Size. Fifteen ovals for photographs in ornate frames; vignettes of man hiking and man contemplating cross below; above two scenes of children. Lithographed by C. Hamilton & Co., St. Louis.

143. Hubbard, Edwin. Ancestral Tree [Lithograph]. Hartford: Kellogg & Hanmer; 1845; 35.1 × 24.5 cm. CHS. Tree with spaces on trunk and branches for names of family members in different generation. Form is blank. Priced at $.25.

144. Hubbard, Edwin. The Ancestral Register [Engraving]. Hartford: Kellogg & Hubbard; 1847; 38.2 × 50.7 cm. LC PGA C Size. Stylized family tree. Engraved by Jarvis Griggs Kellogg.

145. Hursen, S. Illustrated Family Register [Lithograph]. Lawton, Mich.: Hursen & McKinney; 1868; 61.3 × 50.3 cm. LC PGA. Elaborate floral border contains portraits of children, young adults, and older man and woman; above is a wedding scene, below is an aged couple. Lithographed by Hatch & Co., 111 Broadway, New York.

146. Hutson, Henry A. Family Record [Photomechanical print]. n.p.: Henry A. Hutson; 1908; 45.6 × 33.3 cm. LC PGA. Two angels hold wreath below all-seeing eye; eight blank ovals surround four scrolls for data. Designed and Executed with steel pen by Henry A. Hutson.

147. In Memory / of [Wood engraving]. ; 1830; 30.5 × 40.6 cm. (sheet). Yale University Art Gallery; Peabody Essex Museum. Monument with urn at center; woman to left; church on far shore of river. Reproduced in *American Allegorical Prints* (New Haven, 1996), p. 10, cat. no. 33. Filled in to commemorate the death of Emeline Jenness, who died in 1828, and her mother, Sally Jenness, who died in 1833. Impression at the Peabody Essex Museum commemorates Anna Marie McKenzie who died in 1836, aged less than one year. The composition resembles one by Kellogg (Clark Art Institute 1981.21) and one by William S. Pendleton in Boston, ca. 1835 (Smithsonian Institution), reproduced in Harry T. Peters, *American on Stone*, pl. 114.

148. In / Remembrance / of Our / Dear Departed [Lithograph]. ; 1894; 47.5 × 37.7 cm. LC PGA B Size. Elaborate composition with two angels seated on plinth before boat on river.

149. Johnson, L. H. Emblematic Family Register [Lithograph]. Terre Haute, Ind.: William B. Burford; 1880; 22 × 27 in. LC PGA D Size. Landscapes, scenes of courtship, marriage, parents and children, and graveyard surround the open pages of book with columns for names and dates of birth, marriage, and death. Reproduced in *Family Record*, p. 103.

150. Keach, A. Judson. Faith / Hope / Charity / In Memoriam [Lithograph]. n.p.; 1887; 66.5 × 43.8 cm. LC PGA. Large monument with mourning figure at top. Copyrighted 1887.

151. Kelloggs & Comstock. Family Register [Lithograph]. Hartford and New York: Kelloggs & Comstock; D. Needham; 1848; 23 × 33.2 cm. CHS 1987.79.0. Four scenes above: family walking in field, two women with children, wedding, woman and child in front of gravestone; four scenes of buildings below. Floral designs on sides. Title on banner separating scenes of domestic life from space for data. Records family of Catherine (born 18 September 1803) and John Parsons (born 27 July 1796); married at Cornville 23 May 1824.

152. Kelloggs & Comstock. "I know that my Redeemer Liveth" [Lithograph]. Hartford and Buffalo: Kelloggs & Comstock; Ensign, Thayer & Co., Buffalo; 1848; 32.5 × 21.2 cm. CHS x1996.14.40 and x1996.14.37; LC USZ62-60411. Entire image framed by Gothic columns; title on tablet below. Woman with child and dog kneels before monument. Gothic church behind her. Inscription on tablet: *In / Memory of* [1996.14.40 is blank; 1996.14.37 records death of A. W. Cowles].

153. Kelloggs & Bulkeley. Illustrated Household Record [Lithograph]. Hartford: George Champlin; 1867; 43.5 × 33.5 cm. LC PGA B Size. Scenes of infancy, courtship, death, childhood, wedding, finis (sunset) surround central space for recording genealogical data.

154. Kellogg & Hanmer. In / Memory / of [Lithograph]. Hartford: Kellogg & Hanmer, 1 Central Row; 1845; 32.8 × 23.9 cm. CHS 1972.66.4. Monument in graveyard; church and ship in background. Inscribed: *Josephine T. Keney / Who died Dec. 23, 1845 / Aged 3 Years and 5 Months.*

155. Kellogg & Comstock. In / Memory / of [Lithograph]. Hartford, New York, and Buffalo: Kellogg & Comstock, 150 Fulton Street & 136 Main Street, Hartford; Ensign & Thayer,

12 Exchange Street, Buffalo; 1848; 32 × 23.5 cm. CHS x1996.14.41. Monument set in churchyard, church in background. Plate number 65.

156. Kelloggs & Comstock. In / Memory / of [Lithograph]. Hartford and Buffalo: Kellogg & Comstock; D. Needham; 1848; 32.1 × 21.6 cm. CHS x1996.14.33; LC USZ62-60408. Based on J. R. Smith's St. Paul's Churchyard, but urn is neoclassical. CHS impression records death of Anna Norton. Printed on LC form: *Sarah Clements, / Who Died Nov. 9, 1844 Aged* [ ] / *Hale Clements, Who Died Sept. 20, 1843 Aged 29 /* [four lines poetry].

157. Kelloggs & Comstock. In / Memory / of [Lithograph]. Hartford and New York: Kelloggs & Comstock; Ensign & Thayer; 1848. OSV. Man and woman to left of tall monument. Records death of Levi Flagg in 1847, aged 77; and Ruth Flagg, on March 18, 1847, aged 79. Plate number 66.

158. Kelloggs & Comstock. In / Memory of [Lithograph]. Hartford, New York, and Buffalo: Kelloggs & Comstock, 150 Fulton St., N.Y. & 136 Main St., Hartford, Conn.; D. Needham, 12 Exchange St., Buffalo; 1848; 35.6 × 25.4 cm. Greenfield Village and Henry Ford Museum 00.27.102. Woman stands to left of monument set in churchyard. Church in background to right. Inscribed: *William Judd / Born March 1st A.D. 1812 / Died April 15th A.D. 1856 / Aged 44 Years one Month / and fifteen days.* Reproduced in *A Time to Mourn*, p. 161, cat. 114.

159. Kelloggs & Thayer. The Mother's Grave [Lithograph]. Hartford, New York, and Buffalo: Kelloggs & Thayer, 144 Fulton St., N.Y.; E. B. & E. C. Kellogg, 136 Main St., Hartford; D. Needham, 223 Main St., Buffalo; 1846; 33.7 × 21.5 cm. CHS x1996.14.44; LC A size USZ62-60606. Weeping girl seated on ground to left of monument. Text on monument: *Sacred / to / the memory of / an affectionate / Mother.*

160. Kelloggs & Thayer. To the / Memory / of [Lithograph]. Hartford, New York, and Buffalo: Kelloggs & Thayer, 144 Fulton St., N.Y.; E. B. & E. C. Kellogg, 136 Main St., Hartford; D. Needham, 223 Main St., Buffalo; 1847; 21.5 × 32.5 cm. CHS 1938.33.0. Young woman seated on ground to left of elaborate monument; girl and boy standing to right. River in background; church on far bank. Records deaths of Marcia Ingalls, missionary to Burma, in 1845, and her children.

161. Kellogg & Comstock. To the / Memory of [Lithograph]. Hartford, New York, and Buffalo: Kellogg & Comstock, 87 Fulton St., N.Y. & 136 Main St., Hartford; Ensign & Thayer, 12 Exchange St., Buffalo; 1848; 31.9 × 21.3 cm. CHS 1957.53.3; x1996.14.42. Woman and boy to left of monument; man and girl to right. Church spire in background to left. CHS 1957.53.3 records death of Avis Brown on 7 March 1854.

162. Kelloggs & Comstock. To the / Memory of [Lithograph]. Hartford and Buffalo: Kelloggs & Comstock, 150 Fulton St., N. Y. and 136 Main St., Hartford; D. Needham, 12 Exchange St., Buffalo; 1848; 33.8 × 22.6 cm. CHS x1996.14.32. Monument topped with column to left; boy, man, and girl to right. Plate number 337.

163. Kellogg, Daniel Wright. [Family Register] [Lithograph]. Hartford: D. W. Kellogg & Co.; 1830; 23.5 × 40.7 cm. CHS 67825. Records family of Hosea White (30 May 1804–Charlton, Massachusetts 21 May 1888) and two wives: Lucyna (Wardsboro, Vermont 24 September 1811–Southbridge, Massachusetts 3 September 1850); married Wardsboro 24 October 1835; and Elmira (born 20 March 1831); married Southbridge 25 May 1853. Scenes of family walking outside, woman and two children, wedding; allegorical figure of Hope has replaced mourning figures by gravestone. Three of five columns have floral decorations.

164. Kellogg, Daniel Wright. Family Register [Lithograph]. Hartford: D. W. Kellogg & Co.; 1830; 37.5 × 30 cm. MWA Lithf KellD Fami; CHS 49738a. Impression at CHS records family of Charles Chandler Button (1788–1877). Figures of Charity and Hope flank spaces for data. Three ovals for names of parents and marriage information.

165. Kellogg, Daniel Wright. In Memory of / [Lithograph]. Hartford: D. W. Kellogg & Co.; 1830; 28.7 × 31.5 cm. CHS 1978.103.5 (two impressions). Circular monument flanked by two willow trees set in landscape; church beyond river to the right.

166. Kellogg, Daniel Wright. In / Memory / of [Lithograph]. Hartford: D. W. Kellogg & Co.; 1830; 36 × 29.1 cm. MWA; Sterling and Francine Clark Art Institute 1981.19. Very similar to N. Currier's print of same title (Gale 3336), but trees are different. Based on St. Paul's Churchyard by J. R. Smith. MWA impression inscribed: *Mary Emily Sibley / Died Sept. 14, 1843 / Aged 13 Months, 16 days.* Impression is trimmed so imprint is lacking. Clark Art Institute impression has imprint.

167. Kellogg, Daniel Wright. To the / Memory / of [Lithograph]. Hartford: D. W. Kellogg & Co. and Willis Thrall; 1830; 32.3 × 41 cm. CHS 1960.101.2; Metropolitan Museum of Art. CHS impression records death of Asenath Townsley, killed at Southbridge Factory, 2 June 1829, aged 18 years. Woman standing on steps of large monument, right hand obscuring face. Church on left beyond river bank.

168. Kellogg, Daniel Wright. To the / Memory / of [Lithograph]. Hartford: D. W. Kellogg & Co.; 1830; 28.5 × 35.3 cm. CHS 997; Sterling and Francine Clark Art Institute 91.205. Man and two women stand to right of monument; river in background with house on opposite shore.

169. Kellogg, Daniel Wright. To the / Memory / of / [Lithograph]. Hartford: D. W. Kellogg & Co.; 1830; 32.8 × 41.5 cm. CHS x1996.14.30; LC USZ62-28016. CHS impression records death of David Lee in 1843. Woman standing on steps of large monument; church on far shore of river.

170. Kellogg, Daniel Wright. To the / Memory / of [Lithograph]. Hartford: D. W. Kellogg & Co.; 1830; 30.0 × 37.5 cm. MWA Lithf KellD Toth; CHS x1996.14.48. Two women and man stand to right of monument; church and village in right background.

171. Kellogg, Daniel Wright. To the / Memory / of [Lithograph]. Hartford: D. W. Kellogg & Co.; 1830; 38.5 × 29.8 cm. MWA Lithf KellD Tothv; CHS 1991.100.0; x1996.14.46. Impression at CHS (x1996.14.46) records death of Artemas Wood on 19 August 1836, in Fort Gibson, Arkansas. Monument in center; woman stands to right; church and village in background to right.

172. Kellogg, Daniel Wright. To the / Memory / of [Lithograph]. Hartford: D. W. Kellogg & Co.; 1830; 29.0 × 33.0 cm. MWA Lithf KellD Tothvv. Woman stands to left of monument in center set in graveyard. Church in background to the right. Her elbow rests on monument. Lydia Gay painted a close copy of this print in November 1842 in memory of her father, aged 45, who died on 28 September 1839. She was a student at the Hancock (New Hampshire) Literary and Scientific Institute. The watercolor is in the author's collection.

173. Kellogg, Daniel Wright. To the / Memory of [Lithograph]. Hartford: D. W. Kellogg; 1830; 31.8 × 39.2 cm. Sterling and Francine Clark Art Institute 1981.21. Records death of Cleaver D. McKean on 3 December 1848, aged 21 years. Woman stands on steps of monument in the center. Church is beyond river in the right background. Watercolor theorem featuring similar composition without female figure reproduced in *The Decorator* (Fall 1998), p. 6. This is a memorial to Elizabeth R. Daniels, died 15 October 1833, aged 24 years.

174. Kellogg, E. B. &. E. C. Family Register [Lithograph]. Hartford: E. B. & E. C. Kellogg; 1841 Aug; 22.7 × 33.2 cm. CHS 49738. Records family of John Green (born South Brimfield [now Wales], Massachusetts 27 September 1806) and Arminda (Jenks) Green (born Palmer, Massachusetts 5 September 1808); married at Palmer 29 December 1824. At top are scenes of mother with seated child and infant in cradle, wedding, woman kneeling by gravestone; below is scene of woman standing in field with man plowing behind her, family walking outside, and hay wagon being loaded. Flowers in elaborate vases at sides.

175. Kellogg, E. B. &. E. C. Family Register [Lithograph]. Hartford, New York, and Buffalo: E. B. & E. C. Kellogg, Kelloggs & Thayer, D. Needham; 1847; 30.3 × 37.5 cm. Vermont Historical Society. Form closely copied from one by Nathaniel Currier (impressions at MWA, Vermont Historical Society, Historic Deerfield). Scenes of family walking outside, child with mother with infant in cradle, wedding, boy and woman kneeling by gravestone. Columns for data separated by columns with Ionic capitals. Plate number 45.

176. Kellogg, E. B. &. E. C. Family Register [Lithograph]. Hartford and New York: E. B. & E. C. Kellogg & George Whiting, 87 Fulton St.; 1858; 22.2 × 32.8 cm. CHS 49738b. Records family of Richard Chase (b. 1840), married in Canaan, Conn. This form is surrounded by the same vignettes as CHS 49738, but they are set in far more elaborate frame. Plate number 251.

177. Kellogg, E. B. &. E. C. Family Register [Lithograph]. Hartford and New York: E. B. & E. C. Kellogg, 245 Main St., Hartford; Phelps & Watson, 18 Beekman St., N.Y., George F. Whiting, 87 Fulton St., N.Y.; 1858; 23.8 × 33.9 cm. OSV. Scenes of family walking outside, child seated next to mother with infant in cradle, wedding, and boy and woman kneeling by gravestone are separated by flowers. Columns with Egyptian-style capitals separate spaces for data. Plate number 45.

178. Kellogg, E. B. &. E. C. In / Memory / of [Lithograph]. Hartford, New York, and Buffalo: E. B. & E. C. Kellogg, 136 Main St., Hartford; Kelloggs & Thayer, 144 Fulton St., New York and D. Needham, 223 Main Street, Buffalo; 1847; 33.0 × 28.8 cm. CHS 815; x1996.14.31; LC PGA; Henry Ford Museum & Greenfield Village 00.3.3946. LC impression records death of Daniel S. Ackerman on 13 May 1851, aged 20. HFM impression records death of Warren Louis Russell, son of Leister and Phebe Russell, on 1 August 1847, aged 6, in Superior, Michigan. Man and woman to left of large vertical monument similar to one in Baillie's *The Mother's Grave*. Church in background to left. Plate no. 66.

179. Kellogg, E. B. &. E. C. In / Memory / of [Lithograph]. Hartford, New York, and Buffalo: Kelloggs & Thayer, 144 Fulton St., New York; E. B. & E. C. Kellogg, 136 Main St.; D. Needham, 223 Main St.; 1847; 32.9 × 23.8 cm. CHS 814. Monument set in churchyard. Plate number 65.

180. Kellogg, E. B. &. E. C. In / Memory / of [Lithograph]. Hartford, New York, and Buffalo: Kellogg & Thayer; E. B. & E. C. Kellogg; D. Needham; 1847; 32.2 × 23.5 cm. CHS x1996.14.38. Woman leaning on monument based on George Cooke's tomb in J. R. Smith's St. Paul's Churchyard; church in background to right.

181. Kellogg, E. B. &. E. C. In / Memory / of / [blank] / I have fought a good fight, I have finished /my course, I have kept the faith / [Lithograph]. Hartford and New York: E. B. & E. C. Kellogg; Phelps & Watson; E. P. Whiting; 1861; 33.2 × 22.8. CHS 1958.38.13. Soldier and woman to left of monument. Designed as memorial for Civil War soldiers.

182. Kellogg, E. B. &. E. C. To the / Memory / of / [blank] / 6 lines of Scripture [Lithograph]. Hartford, New York, and Buffalo: E.B. & E. C. Kellogg, 144 Fulton St., N.Y., and 136 Main St., Hartford; D. Needham, 223 Main St., Buffalo; 1841; 31.8 × 21.8 cm. CHS 1995.43.3; Smithsonian Institution, Harry T. Peters Collection. Two men flank obelisk set in graveyard. The Smithsonian impression is reproduced in *A Time to Mourn*, p. 162, cat. 118.

183. Kilburn, Samuel S. Family Record [Relief print]. Boston: F. Gleason; 1854; 23.7 × 33.2 cm. Boston Athenaeum;

MWA (in periodical). Scenes of family on porch of house, mother with infant in arms, wedding, and sick room surrounded by floral ornaments. Engraved by [Richard C.?] Major. Issued in *Gleason's Pictorial Drawing-Room Companion,* volume 4, no. 1 (Jan. 7, 1854), p. 12. Text on page 13 accompanies image noting how future generations will appreciate the information preserved on the form. Circulation of *Gleason's Pictorial Drawing-Room Companion* was 110,000 copies per week.

184. Kinsman & Flint. Family Record [Lithograph]. Vineland, N.J.: Kinsman & Flint; 1878; 57.5 × 45.0 cm. LC PGA C Size. Calligraphic design ornamented with animals, human heads, etc.; spaces for thirteen photographs and for inscriptions on scrolls and pages of open books.

185. Kinsman, S. Family Record [Photolithograph]. New York: Robert A. Weicke; 1879; 55.0 × 44.5 cm. LC PGA C Size. Spaces for photographs; scrolls and pages of open books for genealogical data; texts of Ten Commandments and Lord's Prayer below.

186. Kurz & Allison. Family Record [Lithograph]. Chicago: Kurz & Allison, 76 & 78 Wabash Ave.; 1890. LC D Size; USZ62-31499. Spaces for photographs of parents above circular space for marriage information and pages of open book for births and deaths; flanked by angels and surrounded by ten circular vignettes of scenes of family life.

187. Lilly, W. J. Family / Record [Lithograph]. n.p.; 1891; 70.0 × 50.8 cm. LC PGA. Floral ornamentation and putti; spaces for photographs and tablets for recording data. Drawn with a pen by W. J. Lilly.

188. Long, Rev Edwin M. Genealogical Tree. / To trace and preserve a family for five or more generations. [Lithograph]. Philadelphia: Daughaday & Becker; 1869; 22½ × 28½ in. Private collection; LC D Size USZ62-11473. This form was copyrighted by Long; George G. Heiss drew it on stone and lithographed it; Daughaday & Becker appear as publisher. There is a tree with limbs with spaces for names; elderly couple seated on bench at bottom; two monuments are labeled "Memory." Church in background.

189. Lyons, W. H. Family Record. n.p.; 1891; 58.0 × 46.3 cm. LC PGA. Calligraphic ornamentation with birds in border; executed with a pen and printed in pink, green, blue, gold inks; blank space in center for recording genealogical data.

190. [Marriage certificate] [Chromolithograph]. n.p.; 1874; 44.8 × 38.0 cm. LC PGA B Size. Couple blessed by angel; tree of virtue in center; scenes of childhood, family life, old age, and graveyard; spaces for seven photographs.

191. McClure, Jacob W. Family Register [Lithograph]. St. Louis: McClure & Newton; 1867; 42.3 × 32.7 cm. LC PGA B size. Bald eagle in nest with wing above scroll for names and dates; texts of Declaration of Independence, Fifth Commandment, Lord's Prayer, and Psalm 123.

192. Moline Plow Company. Allegorical Family Record [Chromolithograph]. Moline, Ind.: Moline Plow Company; 1881; 33.8 × 44.5 cm. LC PGA. Eight pastoral vignettes; no dedicated space for recording data. See form by Gies & Company for another form published by the Moline Plow Company.

193. Morgan, W. J. & Co. In Memoriam [Lithograph]. Cleveland: W. J. Morgan & Co.; 1870; 34.5 × 45.3 cm. LC USZ62-60405. Central monument with oval space for photograph flanked by two winged putti; title on banner above. Monument set in large cemetery with river and hills in background. Label affixed: "Memorial Chart Designed by John H. LaPierre and Lewis W. Gleason, Cleveland, Ohio."

194. Morgan, W. J. & Co. In Memoriam [Lithograph]. Cleveland: L. W. Gleason & J. W. LaPierre; 1877; 36.0 × 47.4 cm. LC PGA. Central monument with oval for photograph flanked by two winged putti; title on banner above. Monument set in large cemetery with river and hills in background.

195. Muhlbauer & Behrle. Family Record [Lithograph]. Chicago: Muhlbauer & Behrle; n.d.; 57.5 × 39.5 cm. LC PGA. Angels and cross above spaces for dates of marriages, births, and deaths; three vignettes depicting Roman Catholic sacraments.

196. Nevins, Mrs M. And Jesus Called / A Little Child [Lithograph]. n.p.; 1887; 40.2 × 31.8 cm. LC PGA B Size. Raphael's angels' heads at top of form; two crosses with printed inscriptions from scripture; center space for data about child.

197. Nutting, Benjamin F. To the Memory of [Lithograph]. Boston: Prentiss Whitney; 1837; 32.2 × 40.2 cm. MWA Lithf MoorT Nutt Toth. Woman dressed in classical costume leans on large monument based on that of Bosquillon in F. G. T. de Joliment's *Les Mausolees Francais* (Paris: Firmin Didot, 1821). The print was lithographed by the firm of Thomas Moore in Boston.

198. Ogan, James R. Home / Family Record [Lithograph]. Indianapolis: James R. Ogan & Son; 1883; 65.0 × 48.3 cm. LC PGA. Vignettes of beehive, ship (voyage of life), hourglass (end of time), sheaf of wheat, angels and all seeing eye with clasped hand; open books and tablet for data. Designed and wholly executed with a pen by James R. Ogan.

199. Oplinger, G. T. Gems and / Family Record [Lithograph]. Slatington, Penn.: G. T. Opinger; 1877; 69.2 × 53.2 cm. LC PGA. Spaces for twelve photographs surround space for marriage data; open book for other genealogical data; floral decoration. Printed by H. Bencke in New York.

200. Our Family [Chromolithograph]. n.p.; 1889; 55.8 × 71.6 cm. LC PGA. Same format as form published by C. D. Phelps. Framed flowers surround scroll and banners on which data could be recorded.

201. Our Friends [Lithograph]. n.p.; n.d. LC PGA. Ovals for photographs surround central space for data; monument below with inscription "O Grave where is thy Victory; O Death where is thy Sting" provides additional space. Ovals surrounded by floral garlands with lines to record age, stature, weight, complexion, eye color, hair color, habit, and education.

202. Pendleton's Lithography. Family Register [Lithograph]. Boston: Pendleton's Lithography.; 1826; 37.2 × 29.8 cm. OSV. Records families of James (14 November 1776–25 April 1806) and Sarah (Farnum) Harkness (7 April 1780–10 September 1853); married 31 March 1797; and Caleb (born 9 March 1765) and Sarah (F[arnum]) (Harkness) Wall, married 5 August 1807. Figures of Charity and Hope flank three ovals for names of parents and date of marriage and tablet for names of children. Moon rises above arch.

203. Pendleton, William S. To the / Memory / of [Lithograph]. Boston: Wm. S. Pendleton, 204 Washington St.; 1826. Smithsonian Institution, Harry T. Peters Collection. Records death of Susannah K. Palmer on 12 December 1811, aged 3 years and 6 months. Woman rests left elbow on monument; hand obscures face. To right is boat on river; church on far bank. Very similar to anonymous relief print at Yale University Art Gallery. Reproduced in *A Time to Mourn*, p. 160, cat. 111.

204. Phelps, C. D. Our Family [Chromolithograph]. Louisville, Kentucky: C. D. Phelps; 1890; 56.0 × 70.8 cm. LC PGA. Framed flowers surround scroll and banners on which data could be recorded. Photographs could be pasted over flowers; small spaces for names and text of Lord's Prayer. Deposited 1890.

205. Pittman & Co. In Memoriam. [Lithograph]. Cincinnati: Pittman & Co.; 1876. Smithsonian Institution, Harry T. Peters Collection. Records death of Mrs. Erastus Kilbourn on 14 August 1877, aged 74 years. Bird's eye view of rural cemetery with river. Reproduced in *A Time to Mourn*, p. 162, cat. 120. There is an oval space for a photograph or other memento such as a hair piece (as is affixed to this impression).

206. Porter, Rufus. Family Register [Relief print with letterpress text]. Boston: Printed by Henry Bowen; 1820. Records family of Sarah Jewell (born 17 August 1797) and Edward Jewell, Jr. (born 13 December 1794); married 24 September 1821. Printed form has pair of birds at top; spaces for names of parents, marriage date, children's births, names, and deaths. Reproduced in *Rufus Porter Rediscovered* by Jean Lipman (Yonkers: Hudson River Museum, 1980).

207. Rhodes, Julius D. Let the Dead [Lithograph]. Buffalo: J. D. & J. H. Rhodes; 1875; 54.0 × 43.8 cm. LC PGA D Size. Willow trees, crosses, floral ornamentation surround spaces for names of parents and other family members. Designed and executed with a Steel pen by Julius D. Rhodes. Heavily printed in black.

208. Ring, Stoughton &. Co. Family Record [Photolithograph]. Vineland, N.J.: Ring, Stoughton & Co.; 1878; 50.5 × 42.3 cm. LC PGA D Size. Calligraphic ornamentation. Photolithographed by T. Hunter of Philadelphia.

209. Robinson, Lewis (attrib). There / is Rest in / Heaven / Sacred to the Memory [Line engraving]. [Reading, Vt.]: [Lewis Robinson]; 1840 May; 15 × 19.5 cm. Vermont Historical Society. Records death of Irene Rice on 9 September 1842, aged 49 years. Man and woman weeping to left of monument; younger woman leans against it on the right; church in background to right. The monument and the two figures to the left of it are probably based on Thomas Clarke's *Sacred to the Memory of the Illustrious G. Washington* of 1801, although the man wears long pants rather than knee breeches.

210. Robinson, Lewis. Though we die yet we shall live again [Line engraving]. Reading, Vt.: Lewis Robinson; 1830; 25.5 × 31 cm. Vermont Historical Society; Bailey/Howe Library, University of Vermont. The impression at the University of Vermont records death of Francis Asbury Fay, son of Ariel and Mary Ann Fay, on 27 [?] September 1834, aged 1 year. Small monument on left; man and woman weep to right. This print is not described in an article by Marcus A. McCorison and George R. Dalphin, "Lewis Robinson—Entrepreneur," *Vermont History* 30 (October 1962).

211. Sarony & Major. Family Register [Lithograph]. New York: Sarony & Major, 117 Fulton Street; 1847; 64.0 × 40.5 cm. LC PGA Sarony & Major. Space for data surrounded by the text for the Lord's Prayer with head of Christ at the top and heads of two women at the right and left in the middle of the sheet. Deposited in the Library of Congress 23 September 1847. Designed and executed originally with a Pen by Ric [*sic*] Pratt.

212. Sarony & Major. Sacred / to / The Memory of [Lithograph]. New York: Sarony & Major, 136 Nassau St. cor Beekman St. LC A Size, USZ63-60409. Woman on left kneeling before monument surmounted by figures of three angels; church at right.

213. Sarony & Major. Sacred / to / The Memory of [Lithograph]. New York: Sarony & Major, 136 Nassau cor. Beekman; 1846; 31.2 × 21.7 cm. LC A Size USZ62-60410. Man and woman stand to left of monument; set in wooded glade with pool in foreground. Deposited in the Library of Congress 20 March 1846.

214. Sayer, R. Family Record / for the Family of [Lithograph]. Portland, Maine: George Stinson & Company; 1872; 47.5 × 38.0 cm. LC B Size USZ62-60609. Spaces for births, deaths, marriages; pictures of a man and a woman above title; birds and flowers form a decorative border. Lithographed in Boston by Armstrong & Company.

215. Sayer, R. Family Record, / For the Family of / [Engraving]. Portland, Maine: George Stinson & Co.; 1872; 22 × 18 in. Henry Ford Museum & Greenfield Village 33.338.44.

Spaces for births, deaths, and marriages; pictures of a man and a woman above title; birds and flowers form a decorative border. Engraved by J. C. Buttre.

216. Schory, Reverend Theodore. In Memory of / [Chromolithograph]. Indianapolis: William B. Burford; 1896; 52.0 × 40.0 cm. LC PGA C Size. Scene of graveyard and boat with cross in foreground; building in clouds above; two angels with wreath for monument.

217. Schubert, O. V. Family / God Bless Our Home / Angel / Record [Lithotint]. Cleveland: O. V. Schubert Lith. Co.; 1877; 58.0 × 48.3 cm. LC PGA. Space for thirteen photographs, floral ornamentation.

218. Schutz, J. In / Memory of [Lithograph]. New York: N. Currier, 152 Nassau St.; 1849; 32.7 × 22.0 cm. Metropolitan Museum of Art, 54.90.799 The Edward W.C. Arnold Collection of New York Prints, Maps, & Pictures,. Bequest of E. W. C. Arnold, 1954. Signed at lower left by Schutz. Composition based on J. R. Smith's St. Paul's Churchyard. Boy, woman, and map to right of monument. Boy gestures. Monument varies from prototype. Plate no. 153. Variant of Gale 3331.

219. Short, C. F. Family Record [Lithograph]. [San Francisco?]: C. F. Short; 1870; 47.8 × 37 cm. LC B Size USZ62-12745A; USZC4-1493. Imagery includes Tree of Virtues and four scenes of family life in corners. Incorporates ten spaces for photographs of family members. Reproduced in *Family Record*, p. 103.

220. Short, C. F. Family and Friends / of . . . and . . . [Chromolithograph]. San Francisco: C. F. Short; 1884; 55.6 × 43.7 cm. LC PGA. Central vignette of family in parlor; other vignettes of children playing and of parents and grandparents with children; five ovals with classical figures and three with advertisements for Short, "Publisher of Popular Subscription Pictures."

221. Short, E. F. Freedman"s National and Family Record [Lithograph]. Cincinnati: Strobridge & Co.; 1873; 43.3 × 51.8 cm. LC PGA. Three panels: center reserved for nine photographs; at left, three vignettes relating to slavery; at right vignettes showing former slaves as citizens. "Not Slaves, but American Citizens / In Liberty's light we now rejoice." Below, Lincoln reading Emancipation Proclamation to his Cabinet.

222. St. Joe Steam Printing Co. Our / Family [Lithotint]. St. Joseph, Mo.: St. Joe Steam Printing Co.; 42.2 × 55.8 cm. LC PGA C Size. Spaces for twelve photographs; two angels and two putti in center; floral ornamentation.

223. Staples, John R. Family Record / of [Lithograph]. n.p.; 1878; 41.0 × 30 cm. LC PGA. Plain form, limited calligraphic flourishes. Executed with a pen by John R. Staples.

224. Stirn, Henry. Photographic Family Record / of [Lithotint]. n.p.: Henry Stirn; 1872; 54.0 × 42.3 cm. LC PGA. Spaces for photographs of parents and ten children; vignette of family in center; columns for names of children, dates of birth, marriage, death.

225. Stokes, J. W. The Automatic / Family Record / and / Marriage Certificate [Lithograph]. Busnell, Ill.: J. W. Stokes; 1884; 53.2 × 68.8 cm. LC C Size USZ62-11474. Form provides spaces in the shape of gravestones to record genealogical data. Floral ornamentation. Deposited 17 November 1891.

226. Strobridge & Company. Family / Record / of [Lithograph]. St. Louis: C. F. Short. LC PGA Strobridge. Scenes of family life in corners surround Tree of Virtues; ten spaces for photographs of family members.

227. Strobridge & Company. In Memoriam [Lithograph]. Cincinnati: Pittman & Co.; 1876; 26.2 × 34.4 cm. Private Collection. Oval below title for photograph; to left is a bird's-eye view of a rural cemetery; to right of river being crossed by a boat is heaven with figures floating across tropical landscape and a heavenly city in background. Photograph of Amanda Bolton, born 6 February 1810, married 31 December 1829, died 23 July 1877. Twelve-line poem begins: "*It is not the tear at this moment shed.*" Photograph was taken in Burlington, N.Y., by S. A. Fisher & Co.

228. Strobridge & Company. Photograph / Family / Record [Chromolithograph]. Cincinnati: J. Hale Powers & Co.; 1873; 51.2 × 40.6 cm. LC C Size; USZ62-35582. Scenes of family life in the corners surround several generations of a family gathered around the piano in a parlor; oval spaces for ten photographs.

229. Strouse, Robert H. The / Commerce / is the Mother / of / Civilization / Art Enobles / a Nation. / Family Register [Engraving]. Indianapolis: Robert H. Strouse; 1896; 53.0 × 68.0 cm. LC PGA. Allegorical figures of Industry, Art, and Abundance with views of the pyramids of Egypt and Niagara Falls. Portraits of Washington, Columbus, and Lincoln at bottom. Vignettes of log cabin, modern home, agriculture, train, man herding cattle, industry surround the form.

230. This is to certify / That [Engraving]. n.p.; n.d.; 34.5 × 26.5 cm. LC USZ62-84373. Records marriage of Richard Butterworth of Burlington County to Mrs. Sarah S. Crammer, 10 March 1855; John S. Swain, minister. Rococo mantling surrounds text and scene of wedding reception in elegant space with high ceiling and large wall mirrors.

231. Thurston, Herline &. Co. This Certifies that . . . were united in the Bonds of Matrimony. [Lithograph]. Philadelphia: Thurston, Herline & Co.; 1866; 28.5 × 22.7 cm. MWA Lithf Thur This. Records marriage of two African Americans, Henry J. Maxwell (born 1836) and Martha Louisa Dibble, married in Camden, South Carolina, on 13 September 1870, by Jonathan Johnson. Two ovals for photographs above title are surrounded by floral ornamentation and separated by an angel.

232. To the / Memory of [Lithograph]. n.p.; 1835; 23.2 × 33.3 cm. MWA. MWA has two impressions that record deaths of John Wadsworth on 21 August 1831, and Rachel Wadsworth on 26 March 1839. Mourning woman stands to right of tomb with hands clasped; other graves and church on left. Composition similar to one of Nathaniel Currier's.

233. Towne, A. B. Family Record [Lithograph]. n.p.; 1892; 52.8 × 61.3 cm. LC PGA. Three central spaces for data surrounded by flowers and birds with nets, one containing small birds. Deposited 4 June 1892.

234. Trimmer, A. M. Family / Record / of [Lithograph]. Chambersburg, Pa.: Trimmer; 1875; 67.7 × 47.5 cm. LC PGA. Spaces for ten photographs surrounded by flowers, birds, butterfly; two angels with quills flank title. Lithographed by Breuker & Kessler of Philadelphia.

235. Trumbull, Rollin H. Family Record. [Lithograph]. Chicago: Trumbull and Carver; 1866; 24 × 19¾ in. NEHGS, MSS D1; Private Collection. NEHGS form records family of Dean (born Orleans, Massachusetts 17 November 1821) and Rosilla Snow Sparrow (born Eastham, Masschusetts, 17 December 1821); married at Eastham, 24 January 1841. The calligraphy on this form executed by J. N. Macomb & Son of South Dartmouth, Massachusetts, 1 January 1872. Other form filled in for the family of John L. Tracy (born Thomaston, Maine 28 March 1833) and Hannah C. Hart (born St. George, Dec. 25, 1838); married in Rockland, 9 February 1855. Two angels flank space for names of parents; scrolls, open books provide spaces for marriages, birth, and death dates.

236. Trumbull, Rollin H. Family Record [Lithograph]. Chicago: Chicago Lith. Company; 1866; 56.5 × 46.0 cm. LC PGA. Two angels flank spaces for marriages, birth, and death dates. Designed and wholly executed with a pen by R. H. Trumbull.

237. Trumbull, Rollin H. Family Record [Lithograph]. Chicago: Rollin H. Trumbull; 1872; 53.0 × 41.8 cm. LC PGA C Size. Pictures of couple and children; spaces for genealogical data; calligraphic ornamentation. Executed with a pen. Lithographed by Lithogr. Institute, Essroger, Ruehlow & Co.

238. Twitchell, Lonsville. Illustrated / Photographic Family Memorial [Lithograph]. n.p.: Giles; n.d. LC PGA. Space in center for genealogical data surrounded by spaces for photographs and scenes of family life. At bottom is text of the Lord's Prayer.

239. Vallendar & Co. Peace be with you / Family Record. Cleveland: Vallendar & Co.; 43.0 × 41.3 cm. LC PGA Vallendar C Size. Spaces for eleven photographs; angel above, floral ornamentation in Romanesque architectural frame.

240. Van Deventer, Judson W. Van Deventers Photograph / Family Register / Written in Heaven [Lithograph]. Defiance, Ohio: J. W. Van Deventer; 62.2 × 46.3 cm. LC PGA. Spaces for twelve photographs and data on scrolls and pages of open book; angels and putti decorate form. Designed and executed with a Pen by J. W. Van Deventer.

241. Vickroy, J. M. Family Record [Lithograph]. n.p.; n.d. LC D Size. Space in center for names of grandparents, parents, children, births, marriages, and those "called away" surrounded by scenes of family life including childhood days, courtship, wedding, district school, college, a model home, our last resting place (a "rural" cemetery), and over the ocean of life; the vignette at the top is "Our Pilgrim Parents 1620." Ovals for photographs.

242. Westcott, T. E. Family Memorial [Lithograph]. Mt. Vernon, Ill.: T. E. Westcott; 59.0 × 43.5 cm. LC PGA. Spaces for ten photographs; inscriptions on books and scrolls; calligraphic style.

243. Whitney, Simon. Register. / Married / Their Children [Lithograph]. Boston: Lithographed by E. W. Bouve; 1839; 68 × 41 cm. Boston Athenaeum, MWA Lithff Bouv Whit Regi. Boston Athenaeum impression records family of Nancy Houston and Bradford Holmes (born 1805); married 8 September 1839. A large cross bears the title and space for the family record.

244. Wickwire, Ira G. Family Record [Lithograph]. Buffalo: The Courier Lith. Co.; 1881; 65.1 × 49.0 cm. LC D Size—PGA Courier Lith. Title and four columns for Parents, Births, Marriages, Deaths surrounded by elaborate floral borders. Wickwire designed and copyrighted the form.

245. Williams, Henry. Family Register. [Line engraving]. Newark, N.J.: Peter Maverick; 1809; 22¾ × 18¼ in. New-York Historical Society; Private collection; MWA. Privately owned impression records family of Elizabeth Robbins and Windsor Smith of Hadley, Massachusetts. Reproduced in *Family Record*, p. 101, cat. 156. MWA impression records family of Daniel Lamb (21 January 1738–27 December 1819) of South Hadley, Massachusetts, and Content Pendleton (9 May 1742–September 1798); married 21 March 1758. Additional entry for second wife, Cynthia Lampheare (born 31 January 1761); married 22 September 1799. The design of the composition is credited on the plate to Ransom Hinman. An exhaustive search has failed to identify other works by such an artist. Another possibility is presented by entries in the New York City directories in 1829 and 1830 for Anson Hinman, painter. 1100 copies of this form were sold at the 1831 auction of Maverick's prints, suggesting that it was created near the end of his life. Betty Ring has identifed six embroidered or manuscript forms based on this engraving. Charity and Hope flank three ovals for names of parents and wedding date and tablet for names of children. Pelican feeding nestlings beneath arch over which sun rises.

246. Williams, Henry. Family Register [Line Engraving]. [Boston]: William B. Annin, engraver; 1823; 39.9 × 30.4 cm. OSV. Records family of Sarah Coggeshall (born 18 August 1774) and George Durfee (born 11 September 1772). Possibly filled out ca. 1831 or 1832. Charity and Hope flank two ovals for names of parents and tablet for names of children. Pelican feeding young below title. Sun rises over arch.

Subject Index

A History of the Type

The text of this book is set in Berthold Walbaum, a typeface based on the 1800 design by Justus Erich Walbaum of Weimar. In 1919 the Berthold Foundry of Berlin aquired Walbaum's original punches and matrices, and in 1976 it reissued a new version of the face designed by Günter Gerhard Lange.

Walbaum is a direct relative of Firmin Didot's and Giambattista Bodoni's roman type designs, as evidenced in the thin, unbracketed serifs; in the contrast of stroke weight, which makes for a visually vibrant page; and in the equalized height of the capitals and ascenders. Walbaum also demonstrates the condensed letterform and increased x-height introduced in the roman du roi type cut by Phillippe Grandjean for the Imprimerie Royale of Louis XIV in 1702. These types represent a significant break with the humanist calligraphic tradition in typography born from the types of Nicholas Jenson and Aldus Manutius in the fifteenth century. Henceforth, printing types began to be understood as stylistically independent from the written hand.